THE ULTIMATE DIRECTORY OF ENGLISH & SCOTTISH FOOTBALL LEAGUE GROUNDS

1888 ~ 2005

(Second Edition)

By Paul and Shirley Smith

Published by:
Yore Publications
12 The Furrows, Harefield,
Middx. UB9 6AT.

© Paul & Shirley Smith 2002

....

All rights reserved.
No part of this publication may be reproduced
or copied in any manner without the prior permission
in writing of the copyright holders.

British Library Cataloguing-in-Publication Data.
A catalogue record for this book
is available from the British Library.

ISBN 0954 783042

Printed and bound by
Cromwell Press
Trowbridge, Wilts.

This book is dedicated to
Rhoda Rowland

Terry Tighe scoring *Accrington Stanley's* goal in their 2-1 home defeat to *Queens Park Rangers* on September 12th. 1958 at **Peel Park** (See P.99). The attendance was 5,336 and in view is the new main stand purchased that year from the Aldershot Military Tattoo site for a bargain price of £1,450. Unfortunately the Directors had failed to take into account the expenses incurred in its' dismantling, transport and re-erection which pushed the true cost to nearer £16,000 and eventually propelled the club closer to the financial precipice!

Photograph Courtesy of Garth Dawson

1st EDITION
Published 2002
ISBN 1874427 348

Every effort has been made to trace the ownership of any copyright material, seek permission to use same, and acknowledge that this has been given, however, apologies are offered should copyright have been inadvertently infringed

ALL MAPS ARE REPRODUCED BY KIND PERMISSION OF THE SYNDICS OF CAMBRIDGE UNIVERSITY

PHOTOGRAPHS ON FRONT & BACK COVERS
Borough Briggs, Somerset Park, Cliftonhill Park and Strathclyde Homes Stadium; All courtesy of Paul Clements [*Redweb (www.stirlingalbionfc.com)*].
Cathkin Park, Volunteer Park, The Dell, Underhill & Athletic Ground *(Aberdare)*; All courtesy of Dave Twydell
Carrow Road, Upton Park and Arsenal Stadium [Paul Claydon], Feethams [Vince Taylor], Victoria Park [Jon Weaver] & Bramall Lane [Owen Pavey]; All courtesy of *Groundtastic Magazine*

THE ULTIMATE DIRECTORY OF
ENGLISH & SCOTTISH FOOTBALL LEAGUE GROUNDS
1888-2005

The primary aim of this publication is to catalogue all of the grounds used for League and Scottish League fixtures in England, Wales and Scotland and to present some historic and statistical information about each. To this end we have been able to include a map of each venue (some of which have had to be superimposed upon older versions), a short description of its development, the National Grid* reference (of particular use for those grounds that have departed under redevelopment) and individual club statistics thus giving a unique record of each of the grounds.

Research has revealed that up to the end of the 2004/5 season no less than 132 Football League clubs have played on 206 grounds and 82 Scottish League teams at 117 venues and we are indebted to the many club historians, acknowledged elsewhere and throughout the text, for their assistance in piecing this information together. This has been particularly helpful in Scotland where ground sharing, particularly for the odd game, has been almost endemic over the years, leading to a highly complex situation. Being of a wide scope we have also drawn heavily on those who have gone before, particularly Dave Twydell with his excellent *Rejected FCs Series* and *Grounds for a Change* and Simon Inglis' *The Football Grounds of Great Britain*, whilst *The Breedon Book of Football Records* proved to be invaluable.

One of the more surprising statistics is just how many grounds have disappeared in the wake of the tragic fire at *Valley Parade* and the *Hillsborough* disaster. The subsequent requirement for all-seat stadia revealed the weaknesses, as if they were not already known, of some of the older grounds and we have witnessed a plethora of new venues. This, allied to the promotion of clubs from the Football Conference, has meant that no less than 48 grounds were utilized in the two leagues for the first time between 1990 and 2003. An aspect of this, and a sign of the times in which we live, is the selling of the grounds name to sponsors who although they supply welcome finance provide us with some pretty unwieldy nomenclature as in Southampton FCs "The Friends Provident St Mary's Stadium". An off-shoot is that there is now a tendency for grounds to be re-named on a regular basis and, where appropriate, these have been listed under their original title.

Within this book, the grounds are listed more or less in alphabetical order, the "The" in some titles has been ignored as has sponsors names and some minor alphabetical adjustments have had to be made to conserve space. The **Club Index Section** lists the clubs in alphabetical order with the grounds that they have played on and **Appendix 1**, at the back of this volume, shows the sequence in which they first hosted League football. All the statistics are, as far as we are able to ascertain, correct up to the end of Season 2004/5 and **Appendix 2** lists all the new grounds on stream and those proposed

Finally, in compiling this, we have had contact with many people whom are passionate about their club, large or small, struggling or successful and in a world that seems to be populated solely by *Arsenal, Liverpool* and *Manchester United* hangers-on it has been an utterly refreshing experience. May we wish all those real soccer fans out there, Good Sport and thanks!

Paul & Shirley Smith, Kings Heath, Birmingham 2005.

---

* *The **National Grid**, a system of establishing the precise co-ordinates of any point within Great Britain, can be found on any map published by the Ordnance Survey since WWII. The country is divided into 48 62.14 mile [100km] squares, each one given a two-letter code, and then numerically into 6.214 mile [10km] squares. These are then divided into smaller and smaller units depending upon the accuracy of the co-ordinates required. In this publication we have used eight figure co-ordinates pinpointing the centre spot of each ground to within about 30ft*

CONTENTS

Alphabetical List of Clubs and Grounds	P 6 - 9
Grounds of the Football League	P 10 - 147
Grounds of the Scottish Football League	P 147 - 228
Appendix 1 - Venues Listed by Order of Opening	P 229 - 230
Appendix 2 - New Grounds	P 231 - 232

ACKNOWLEDGEMENTS & THANKS

A volume such as this is utterly dependent upon the assistance and knowledge of others. We have drawn this together and it is for the enthusiasm and time taken on our behalf that we wish to address our thanks to;

Libraries;
Tony Rawlings, Anne Taylor, Karen Amies, Andrew Alexander and Ian Walker at the Cambridge University Map Library. Peter Milne and Bill Todd at the National Library of Scotland, Edinburgh and Margaret Connolly at the Mitchell Library, Glasgow.

Members of Staff at the following Main Libraries;
Airdrie, Alloa, Beith, Birmingham, Blackburn, Blackpool, Bolton, Brighton, Burton, Coalville, Coatbridge, Crewe, Dartford, Dumbarton, Dumfries, Dundee, Dunfermline, Durham, East Renfrew, Elgin, Falkirk, Gillingham, Glasgow, Glossop, Greater Manchester County Record Office, Greenwich, Grimsby, Hamilton, High Wycombe, Inverness, Kilmarnock, Liverpool, Merthyr Tydfil, Middlesbrough, Milton Keynes, Nelson, Nottingham, Paisley, Perth, Reading, Rotherham, Sandbach, Sandwell, Scunthorpe, Sheffield, Southend on Sea, Stalybridge, Stepps, Stirling, Stockport, Stratford, Walsall, Walthamstow and West Lothian

Club Historians;
We would particularly wish to thank Tony Matthews for his considerable input and Brian Tabner and Tony Brown for their assistance in filling in many of the missing statistical gaps in the Football League section. To these, may we add indeed our thanks to the following club historians and contributors;

Jack Rollin *(Aldershot)*, Alf Marchetti *(Ashington)*, Arthur Bower *(Barnsley)*, Roger Harrison *(Blackpool)*, Simon Marland *(Bolton Wanderers)*, Peter Waller *(Bradford City)*, Dave Twydell *(Brentford)*, Tim Carder *(Brighton & Hove Albion)*, Keith Brookland *(Bristol Rovers FC)*, David Steele *(Carlisle United)*, Charles Sumner *(Chester City)*, Stuart Basson *(Chesterfield)*, Rev Nigel Sands *(Crystal Palace)*, Tony Bluff *(Doncaster Rovers)*, Gordon Wright *(Durham City)*, Graham Webster *(Essex CCC)*, The Late Tom Bone *(South Shields & Gateshead)*, Roger Triggs *(Gillingham)*, John Meynell *(Halifax Town)*, Ed Law *(Hartlepool United)*, Norman Leat *(Leyton FC)*, Paul Hiscock *(Leyton Orient)*, Donald Nannestad *(Lincoln City)*, Roger Wash *(Luton Town)*, David Watkins *(Merthyr Town)*, Frank Grande *(Northampton Town)*, Ken Smales *(Nottingham Forest)*, Peter Wynne-Thomas *(Notts County & Nottinghamshire CCC)*, Peter Orme *(Notts County)*, Matt Hill *(Peterborough United)*, Richard J. Owen, *(Hon Club Historian @ Portsmouth FC)*, David Downs *(Reading)*, Tom Nicholl *(Rochdale)*, Gerry Somerton *(Rotherham Town & United)*, John Staff *(Scunthorpe United)*, Richard Stocken *(Shrewsbury Town)*, Dave Goody *(Southend United)*, Geoff Wilde *(Southport)*, Colin Jones *(Swansea City)*, Dick Mattick *(Swindon Town)*, John Lovis *(Torquay United)*, Gil Upton *(Tranmere Rovers)*, Steve Durham *(Workington)*, Paul Third & Dave MacDermid *(Aberdeen)*, John Henderson *(Airdrieonians)*, Robin Marwick *(Albion Rovers)*, John Glencross *(Alloa Athletic)*, George Cant *(Arbroath)*, Duncan Carmichael *(Ayr, Ayr Parkhouse & Ayr United)*, Tommy Brandon *(Beith)*, Robin Murdie *(Berwick Rangers)*, Steve Mitchell *(Brechin City)*, Cyril George *(Celtic & Rangers)*, John Taylor *(Clyde)*, David Allan *(Cowdenbeath)*, Jim McAllister *(Dumbarton)*, Norrie Price *(Dundee)*, Peter Rundo *(Dundee United)*, Duncan Simpson *(Dunfermline Athletic)*, Jim Stewart *(East Fife)*, Drummond Calder *(East Stirlingshire)*, Robert Weir *(Elgin City)*, Michael White *(Falkirk)*, Christine & Barry Stevens *(Forfar Athletic)*, Eddie McDowell *(Greenock Morton)*, Scott A. Struthers *(Hamilton Academical)*, Douglas Dalgleish & David Steed *(Heart of Midlothian)*, Ricky Raginia *(Hibernian)*, Ian Broadfoot *(Inverness Caledonian Thistle)*, John Livingston *(Kilmarnock)*, Allan Grieve *(King's Park & Stirling Albion)*, Duncan Bennett *(Livingston)*, David Baxter *(Meadowbank Thistle)*, David Smith *(Montrose)*, John Swinburne *(Motherwell)*, Robert Reid *(Partick Thistle)*, Ian Black *(Queen of the South)*, Hector Cook *(Queen's Park)*, John Litster *(Raith Rovers)*, Alan Cameron *(Ross County)*, Alastair Blair *(St Johnstone)*, Jim Crawford *(St Mirren)*, Sandy Reid *(Stenhousemuir)* and Bert Bell *(Author of "Still Seeing Red" [1996], a comprehensive history of Third Lanark)*.

Others who have provided invaluable assistance include David Richards, John Conliffe of the Congleton Chronicle, John & Hazel Tomkinson, Albert Robinson of the Whitwick Local History Society, Garth Dawson, Ian Paterson John Robinson, John Russell, Stan Briggs, Gary Parle, Colin Timbrell, Chris Ashbridge, David Woods, Peter Poulding, SJ Fletcher, Peter Cogle, Bob MacPherson, Dominic McKenzie, Greger Lindberg, David Powter *(Winger Magazine)* and the late John Williams.

Finally, from a photographic viewpoint, we like to thank Paul Claydon at *Groundtastic* Magazine, and Paul Clements at RedWeb [www.stirlingalbionfc.com] for their very generous help in sourcing and donating pictures.

BIBLIOGRAPHY

The Football Grounds of Britain *by Simon Inglis* (Collins Willow, 1990) ISBN 0 00 218249 1
The Breedon Book of Football Records *by Gordon Smales* (Breedon Books, 2000) ISBN 1 85983 214 8
Football League Grounds for a Change *by Dave Twydell* (Dave Twydell, 1991) ISBN 0 9513321 4 7
Rejected FC Volume 1 *by Dave Twydell* (Yore Publications, 1992) ISBN 1 874427 00 3
Rejected FC Volume 2 *by Dave Twydell* (Yore Publications, 1995) ISBN 1 874427 21 6
Rejected FC Volume 3 *by Dave Twydell* (Yore Publications, 1995) ISBN 1 874427 26 7
Rejected FC of Scotland Volume 1 *by Dave Twydell* (Yore Publications, 1992) ISBN 0 9513321 9 8
Rejected FC of Scotland Volume 2 *by Dave Twydell* (Yore Publications, 1993) ISBN 1 874427 30 5
Rejected FC of Scotland Volume 3 *by Dave Twydell* (Yore Publications, 1993) ISBN 1 874427 17 8
Groundtastic Magazine

PREFACE TO THE SECOND EDITION [2005]

We are delighted to have had the opportunity to present an updated and corrected Second Edition and particularly pleased that a number of contributors have taken the trouble to contact us to point out inaccuracies. As far as the Football League is concerned our major *faux pas* was probably in missing out the fact that *Leeds United* was exiled for four fixtures following the closure of **Elland Road** in 1971 and we are indebted to John Robinson, who also informed us of a *Crystal Palace* home fixture that took place at **The Dell**, and Stan Briggs for reminding us! *Manchester United* also played a home game at **Anfield** and John Russell, one of several to point this out, also supplied us with an excellent critique on the grounds and some playing records of *Manchester United*.

Gary Parle, a *Lincoln City* supporter, has spent some time in researching *Gainsborough Trinity* and confirmed what we had thought inasmuch as the club was obliged to play more home games elsewhere than we had recorded when **Northolme** was required by the cricket club. He has traced two other "home" games both of which took place at **Sincil Bank**, and Colin Timbrell informed us of another match played by *Bristol Rovers* at **Ashton Gate**. Charles Sumner, official Historian of *Chester City*, put us straight as to the precise location of the **Deva Stadium** relative to the England/Wales border and we are also indebted to Chris Ashbridge, David Woods, Peter Poulding and SJ Fletcher for their general comments as well as input of data.

Having escaped relatively unscathed with our Football League entries we had hoped that the paucity of records regarding many of the clubs and grounds in the Scottish Football League would lead to a good response and, perhaps, the filling of a few "gaps". For some of these we are very thankful to Peter Cogle for his provision of details of a number of ground records as well as the confirmation of many others, but it is the clarification of a couple of sites that form the major alterations to this part of the book. Thanks to research by Bob MacPherson he has established that **Westmarch** was located on the west side of the railway line, some few hundred yards west of the site that we had indicated. We were always very wary of this one as much of the information available was "sketchy" but, by noting some additional entries drawn from the *St Mirren FC* Minute Book, he was able to pinpoint it to a Trotting Ground on the north side of Pattison Road and west of Greenhill Road. Similarly we were able to fully concur with a theory about **Old Ralston Park** by Dominic McKenzie in which he thought that redundant earthworks visible on the contemporary map to the east of **New Ralston Park** were very likely to be the remains of the embankments of the old ground and not as we had shown it, based on a 6in Scale 1909 County Series.

If it's Saturday it must be ....

And finally, in 2003, two intrepid football fans used the *Directory* as the basis for a sponsored charity challenge event when Gareth and Robin Griffiths, both *Burton Albion* supporters visited all the 206 grounds and sites that had been used by that time for Football League fixtures in just 9 days!

They travelled an incredible 3,200 miles, spent 127.5 hours on the road and, as well as checking the accuracy of our co-ordinates and providing us with valuable information as to current site usage, managed to raise £2,500 for the British Diabetic Association and MacMillan Cancer Relief Fund.

Robin and Gareth check in at *Swindon Town's* **County Ground** on September 18th, 2003, Day Six of their record-setting trip.

ALPHABETICAL LIST OF FOOTBALL LEAGUE & PREMIER LEAGUE CLUBS 1888-2004 AND **INDEX TO GROUNDS**

ABERDARE ATHLETIC (1921-1927)
Athletic Ground .... P. 17

ACCRINGTON (1888-1893)
Thorneyholme Road P.127

ACCRINGTON STANLEY (1921-1962)
Peel Park .... P. 99

ALDERSHOT (1932-1992)
Recreation Ground P.109

ARSENAL (1893-)
[ALSO PLAYED AS **WOOLWICH ARSENAL**]
Manor Ground .... P. 81
Lyttelton Ground (Leyton CC) .... P. 79
Priestfield Rd (New Brompton FC) P.106
Arsenal Stadium .... P. 15

ASHINGTON (1921-1929)
Portland Park P.103

ASTON VILLA (1888-)
Wellington Road P.143
Villa Park P.140

BARNET (1991- 2001, 2005-)
Underhill Stadium P.131

BARNSLEY (1898-)
Oakwell .... P. 94

BARROW (1921-1972)
Holker Street .... P. 68

BIRMINGHAM CITY (1892-)
[ALSO PLAYED AS **SMALL HEATH**]
Muntz Street .... P. 88
St Andrew's P.113

BLACKBURN ROVERS (1888-)
Leamington Street .... P. 75
Ewood Park .... P. 52

BLACKPOOL (1896-1899, 1900-)
The Athletic Grounds .... P. 18
Raikes Hall P.109
Bloomfield Road .... P. 23

BOLTON WANDERERS (1888-)
Pikes Lane P.101
Burnden Park .... P. 32
Reebok Stadium P.111

BOOTLE (1892-1893)
Hawthorne Road .... P. 63

BOSTON UNITED (2002-)
York Street P.147

AFC BOURNEMOUTH (1923-)
Dean Court / Fitness First Stadium . P. 41
Avenue Stadium (Dorchester Town) P. 18

BRADFORD CITY (1905-)
Valley Parade P.135
Leeds Road (Huddersfield Town FC) P. 76
Elland Road (Leeds United FC) .... P. 51
Odsal Stadium (Bradford N. RFL) . P. 94

BRADFORD PARK AVENUE (1908-1970)
Park Avenue .... P. 99

BRENTFORD (1920-)
Griffin Park .... P. 62

BRIGHTON & HOVE ALBION (1920-)
Goldstone Ground .... P. 60
Priestfield Stadium (Gillingham FC) P.106
Withdean Stadium P.147

BRISTOL CITY (1901-)
St John's Lane P.116
Ashton Gate .... P. 16

BRISTOL ROVERS (1920-)
Eastville Stadium .... P. 48
Ashton Gate (Bristol City FC) ..... P. 16
Twerton Park (Bath City FC) P.131
Memorial Ground (Bristol RUFC) .. P. 83

BURNLEY (1888-)
Turf Moor P.130

BURTON SWIFTS (1892-1901)
Peel Croft P.100

BURTON UNITED (1901-1907)
Peel Croft P.100

BURTON WANDERERS (1894-1897)
Derby Turn .... P. 45

BURY (1894-)
Gigg Lane .... P. 59

CAMBRIDGE UNITED (1970-2005)
Abbey Stadium .... P. 11

CARDIFF CITY (1920-)
Ninian Park .... P. 92

CARLISLE UNITED (1928-2004, 2005-)
Brunton Park .... P. 31

CHARLTON ATHLETIC (1921-)
The Valley P.134
The Mount .... P. 85
Selhurst Park (Crystal Palace FC) .. P.119
Upton Park (West Ham United FC) P.132

CHELSEA (1905-)
Stamford Bridge P.125

CHELTENHAM TOWN (1999-)
Whaddon Road P.145

CHESTER CITY (1931-2000, 2004-)
Sealand Road P.117
Moss Rose (Macclesfield Town FC) P. 87
Deva Stadium .... P. 45

CHESTERFIELD (1899-)
Recreation Ground P.110

COLCHESTER UNITED (1950-1990, 1992-)
Layer Road .... P. 74

COVENTRY CITY (1919-)
Highfield Road .... P. 66

CREWE ALEXANDRA (1892-1896, 1921-)
Alexandra Recreation Ground ...... P. 13
The Vicarage (Sandbach St Mary FC) P.136
Gresty Road [2nd] .... P. 62

CRYSTAL PALACE (1920-)
The Nest .... P. 89
The Dell (Southampton FC) .... P. 43
Selhurst Park P.119

DARLINGTON (1921-)
Feethams .... P. 53
New Stadium .... P. 91

DARWEN (1891-1899)
Barley Bank .... P. 20

DERBY COUNTY (1888-)
Racecourse Ground P.107
Baseball Ground .... P. 21
Pride Park P.107

DONCASTER ROVERS (1901-1903, 1923-1998, 2003-)
Intake Ground .... P. 70
Belle Vue .... P. 22

DURHAM CITY (1921-1928)
Kepier Haughs .... P. 72
Holiday Park .... P. 66

EVERTON (1888-)
Anfield .... P. 14
Goodison Park .... P. 61

EXETER CITY (1920-2003)
St James' Park P.114

FULHAM (1907-)
Craven Cottage .... P. 40
Loftus Road (QPR FC) .... P. 78

GAINSBOROUGH TRINITY (1896-1912)
Northolme .... P. 92
Bowling Green Ground .... P. 28
Sincil Bank (Lincoln City FC) P.121

GATESHEAD (1930-1960)
Redheugh Park P.110

GILLINGHAM (1920-1938, 1950-)
Priestfield Stadium P.106
Stonebridge Rd (Gravesend & N) . P.126

GLOSSOP (1898-1915)
North Road .... P. 93

GRIMSBY TOWN (1892-)
Abbey Park .... P. 11
Blundell Park .... P. 24

HALIFAX TOWN (1921-1993, 1998-2002)
The Shay P.120

HARTLEPOOL UNITED (1921-)
Victoria Park P.139

HEREFORD UNITED (1972-1998)
Edgar Street .... P. 48

HUDDERSFIELD TOWN (1910-)
Leeds Road .... P. 76
Elland Road (Leeds United FC) .... P. 50
Alfred McAlpine Stadium .... P. 13

HULL CITY (1905-)
The Circle (Hull CC) .... P. 36
Anlaby Road .... P. 36
Boulevard Ground (Hull RLFC) .... P. 27
Boothferry Park .... P. 25
Kingston Communications Stadium P. 73

IPSWICH TOWN (1938-)
Portman Road P.104

KIDDERMINSTER HARRIERS (2000-2005)
Aggborough .... P. 12

LEEDS CITY (1905-1919)
Elland Road .... P. 50

LEEDS UNITED (1920-)
Elland Road .... P. 50
Leeds Road (Huddersfield Town) .. P. 76
Hillsborough (Sheffield Wed) ..... P. 65
Boothferry Park (Hull City) .... P. 25

6

LEICESTER CITY (1894-)
Filbert Street .... P. 56
City Ground (Nottm Forest FC) . P. 37
The Walkers Stadium P.141

LEYTON ORIENT (1905-)
[ALSO PLAYED AS **CLAPTON ORIENT**]
Millfields Road .... P. 83
Lea Bridge Stadium .... P. 75
Wembley Stadium P.143
Brisbane Road .... P. 30

LINCOLN CITY (1896-1908, 1909-1911, 1912-1920, 1921-1987, 1988-)
John O'Gaunt's .... P. 71
Sincil Bank P121

LIVERPOOL (1893-)
Anfield .... P. 14

LOUGHBOROUGH (1895-1900)
Athletic Ground .... P. 17
Filbert St (Leicester City FC) ..... P. 56
The Vicarage P.137

LUTON TOWN (1897-1900, 1920-)
Dunstable Road .... P. 47
Kenilworth Road .... P. 72

MACCLESFIELD TOWN (1997-)
Moss Rose .... P. 87

MAIDSTONE UNITED (1989-1992)
Watling Street (Dartford FC) P.141

MANCHESTER CITY (1892-)
[ALSO PLAYED AS **ARDWICK**]
Hyde Road .... P. 69
Maine Road .... P. 80
City of Manchester Stadium .... P. 35

MANCHESTER UNITED (1892-)
[ALSO PLAYED AS **NEWTON HEATH**]
North Road .... P. 93
Bank Street .... P. 20
Old Trafford .... P. 96
Maine Road (Manchester City FC) P. 80
Victoria Ground (Stoke City FC) . P.138
Anfield (Liverpool FC) .... P. 14

MANSFIELD TOWN (1931-)
Field Mill .... P. 55

MERTHYR TOWN (1920-1930)
Penydarren Park P.101

MIDDLESBROUGH (1899-)
Linthorpe Road .... P. 77
Ayresome Park .... P. 19
Victoria Ground (Hartlepool FC) P.138
Riverside Stadium P.111

MIDDLESBROUGH IRONOPOLIS (1893/4)
The Paradise Ground .... P. 98

MILLWALL (1920-)
The Den .... P. 44
Fratton Park (Portsmouth FC) .... P. 57
Selhurst Park (Crystal Palace FC) P.119
The New Den .... P. 91

MILTON KEYNES DONS (1977-)
[ALSO PLAYED AS **WIMBLEDON**]
Plough Lane P.103
Selhurst Park (Crystal Palace FC) P.119
National Hockey Stadium .... P. 88

NELSON (1921-1931)
Seedhill P.118

NEW BRIGHTON (1923-1951)
Sandheys Park P.117
Tower Athletic Ground P.128

NEW BRIGHTON TOWER (1898-1901)
Tower Athletic Ground P.128

NEWCASTLE UNITED (1893-)
St James' Park P.115

NEWPORT COUNTY (1920-)
Somerton Park P.122

NORTHAMPTON TOWN (1920-)
The County Ground .... P. 39
Sixfields Stadium P.122

NORTHWICH VICTORIA (1892-1894)
The Drill Field .... P. 46

NORWICH CITY (1920-)
The Nest .... P. 90
Carrow Road .... P. 33

NOTTINGHAM FOREST (1892-)
Town Ground P.129
City Ground .... P. 37
Meadow Lane (Notts County FC) P. 82

NOTTS COUNTY (1888-)
Trent Bridge (Notts CCC) P.130
Meadow Lane .... P. 82
Castle Ground .... P. 34
Town Ground (Nottm Forest FC) P.129
City Ground (Nottm Forest FC) .. P. 37

OLDHAM ATHLETIC (1907-)
Boundary Park .... P. 27

OXFORD UNITED (1962-)
Manor Ground .... P. 81
Kassam Stadium .... P. 71

PETERBOROUGH UNITED (1960-)
London Road .... P. 77

PLYMOUTH ARGYLE (1920-)
Home Park .... P. 67
Plainmoor (Torquay United FC) P.102

PORTSMOUTH (1920-)
Fratton Park .... P. 57

PORT VALE (1892-1896, 1898-1907, 1919-)
Cobridge Athletic Grounds ...... P. 38
The Old Recreation Ground .... P. 97
Vale Park P.133

PRESTON NORTH END (1888-)
Deepdale .... P. 42

QUEENS PARK RANGERS (1920-)
Loftus Road .... P. 78
White City Stadium P.146
Arsenal Stadium .... P. 15

READING (1920-)
Elm Park .... P. 51
Madejski Stadium .... P. 79

ROCHDALE (1921-)
Spotland P.123

ROTHERHAM TOWN (1893-1896)
Clifton Grove .... P. 38

ROTHERHAM UNITED (1919-)
Millmoor .... P. 85

RUSHDEN & DIAMONDS (2001-)
Nene Park .... P. 89

SCARBOROUGH (1987-1999)
Seamer Road .... P. 118

SCUNTHORPE UNITED (1950-)
The Old Show Ground .... P. 95
Glanford Park .... P. 60

SHEFFIELD UNITED (1892-)
Bramall Lane .... P. 29

SHEFFIELD WEDNESDAY (1892-)
[ALSO PLAYED AS **THE WEDNESDAY**]
Olive Grove .... P. 97
Hillsborough .... P. 65

SHREWSBURY TOWN (1950-2003, 2004-)
Gay Meadow .... P. 58

SOUTHAMPTON (1920-)
The Dell .... P. 43
St Mary's Stadium P.116

SOUTHEND UNITED (1920-)
The Kursaal .... P. 74
Southend Stadium P.123
Roots Hall P.112

SOUTHPORT (1921-1978)
Haig Avenue .... P. 63

SOUTH SHIELDS (1919-1930)
Horsley Hill .... P. 68

STALYBRIDGE CELTIC (1921-1923)
Bower Fold .... P. 28

STOCKPORT COUNTY (1900-)
Green Lane .... P. 61
Edgeley Park .... P. 49
Old Trafford (Manchester Utd FC) P. 96

STOKE CITY (1888-1890, 1891-1908, 1919-)
Victoria Ground P.138
Vale Park (Port Vale FC) P.133
Britannia Stadium .... P. 31

SUNDERLAND (1890-)
Newcastle Road .... P. 90
Roker Park P.112
St James' Park (Newcastle Utd FC) P.109
Stadium of Light P.125

SWANSEA CITY (1920-)
Vetch Field P.136

SWINDON TOWN (1920-)
The County Ground .... P. 39

THAMES (1930-1932)
West Ham Stadium P.144

TORQUAY UNITED (1927-)
Plainmoor P.102

TOTTENHAM HOTSPUR (1908-)
White Hart Lane P.145

TRANMERE ROVERS (1921-)
Prenton Park P.105

WALSALL (1892-1895, 1896-1901, 1921-)
The Chuckery .... P. 35
The Oval (Wednesbury OA FC) . P. 98
West Bromwich Road P.144
Fellows Park .... P. 54
The Hawthorns (WB Albion FC) . P. 64
Bescot Stadium .... P. 22

WATFORD (1920-)
Cassio Road .... P. 34
Vicarage Road P.137

WEST BROMWICH ALBION (1888-)
Stoney Lane P.126
The Hawthorns .... P. 64

WEST HAM UNITED (1919-)
Upton Park P.132

WIGAN ATHLETIC (1978-)
Springfield Park P.124
JJB Stadium .... P. 70

WIGAN BOROUGH (1921-1931)
Springfield Park P.124

WOLVERHAMPTON WANDERERS (1888-)
Dudley Road .... P. 47
Molineux .... P. 86
The Hawthorns (WB Albion FC) .. P. 64

WORKINGTON (1951-1977)
Borough Park .... P. 26

WREXHAM (1921-)
Racecourse Ground P.108

WYCOMBE WANDERERS (1993-)
Adams Park .... P. 12

YEOVIL TOWN (2003-)
Huish Park .... P. 69

YORK CITY (1929-2004)
Fulfordgate .... P. 58
Bootham Crescent .... P. 24

LAST MATCH AT **HORSLEY HILL**

South Shields entertained *Accrington Stanley* in their last ever Football League match on May 3rd, 1930 at **Horsley Hill** (See Page 68) and this photograph shows the final League goal scored here, by John Jepson of *Accrington Stanley* [out of picture]. The dark blue shirted *South Shields* players are Carr, the goalkeeper, Sinclair and Turnbull. The game ended in a 2-2 draw and the club re-formed as *Gateshead FC* and moved to **Redheugh Park** (See Page 110) for the commencement of the 1930-31 season.
Photograph Courtesy of Dave Twydell

ALPHABETICAL LIST OF SCOTTISH FOOTBALL LEAGUE & SCOTTISH PREMIER LEAGUE CLUBS 1888-2004 AND **INDEX TO GROUNDS**

ABERCORN (1890-1915)
Underwood Park P.225
Old Ralston P.207
New Ralston P.207

ABERDEEN (1904-)
Pittodrie P.209

AIRDRIE UNITED (2002-)
Excelsior Stadium P.176

AIRDRIEONIANS (1894-2002)
Broomfield Park P.158
Broadwood Stadium (Clyde FC) .. P.157
Excelsior Stadium P.176

ALBION ROVERS (1903-1915, 1919-)
Meadow Park [Whifflet] P.196
Cliftonhill Park P.166
Somerset Park (Ayr United FC) P.219
Broomfield Park (Airdrie FC) P.158

ALLOA ATHLETIC (1921-)
Recreation Park P.212

ARBROATH (1921-)
Gayfield Park P.181
Greater Gayfield P.181

ARMADALE (1921-1932)
Volunteer Park P.226

ARTHURLIE (1901-1915, 1923-1929)
Dunterlie Park [1st] P.172
Dunterlie Park [2nd] P.172
Dunterlie Park [3rd] P.173
Bellsdale Park (Beith FC) P.154

AYR (1897-1910)
Somerset Park P.219

AYR PARKHOUSE (1903-1904, 1906-1910)
Beresford Park P.154

AYR UNITED (1910-)
Somerset Park P.219
Beresford Park P.154
Dens Park (Dundee FC) P.170

BATHGATE (1921-1929)
Mill Park P.199

BEITH (1923-1926)
Bellsdale Park P.154

BERWICK RANGERS (1955-)
Shielfield Park P.218
Tynecastle (Hearts FC) P.224
Meadowbank Stad. (M'bank Th) .. P.195
Cliftonhill Park (Albion Rovers FC) P.166
Recreation Park (Alloa Athletic FC) P.212
Bayview Park (East Fife FC) P.152
Ochilview Park (Stenhousemuir FC) P.205

BO'NESS (1921-1932)
Newtown Park P.200

BRECHIN CITY (1923-1926, 1929-1939, 1954-)
Glebe Park P.182

BROXBURN UNITED (1921-1926)
Sports Park P.220

CAMBUSLANG (1890-1892)
Whitefield Park P.228

CELTIC (1890-)
Celtic Park [1st] P.161
Celtic Park [2nd] P.162
Shawfield Park (Clyde FC) P.217
Firhill Park (Partick Thistle FC) ... P.178
Easter Road (Hibernian FC) P.175
Hampden Park [3rd] (Qn's Pk FC) P.185

CLACKMANNAN (1921-1922, 1923-1926)
Chapelhill Park P.164
Recreation Park (Alloa Athletic FC) P.212

CLYDE (1891-)
Barrowfield Park P.152
Shawfield Park P.217
Celtic Park [2nd] (Celtic FC) P.162
Ibrox Park [2nd] (Rangers FC) P.189
Firhill Park (Partick Thistle FC) P.178
Douglas Park (Hamilton Acad FC) P.171
Broadwood Stadium P.157

CLYDEBANK [1] (1914-1931)
Clydeholm P.168

CLYDEBANK [2] (1966-2002)
New Kilbowie Park P.201
Boghead Park (Dumbarton FC) ... P.155
Cappielow (Greenock Morton FC) P.159

COWDENBEATH (1905-)
North End Park P.205
Central Park P.163

COWLAIRS (1890-1891, 1893-1895)
Springvale Park P.221

DUMBARTON (1890-1897, 1906-1954, 1955-)
Boghead Park P.155
Cliftonhill Park (Albion Rovers FC) P.166
Strathclyde Homes Stadium P.223

DUMBARTON HARP (1923-1925)
Meadow Park P.196

DUNDEE (1893-)
West Craigie Park P.227
Carolina Port P.160
Dens Park P.170
Tannadice Park (Dundee Utd FC) . P.165

DUNDEE UNITED (1910-1922, 1923-)
[ALSO PLAYED AS **DUNDEE HIBERNIAN**]
Tannadice Park P.165

DUNDEE WANDERERS (1894-1895)
East Dock Street P.173
Clepington Park P.115

DUNFERMLINE ATHLETIC (1912-)
East End Park P.174
Central Park (Cowdenbeath FC) .. P.163

DYKEHEAD (1923-1926)
Parkside P.208

EAST FIFE (1921-)
Bayview Park P.153
Bayview Stadium P.152

EAST STIRLINGSHIRE (1900-1939,
1948-1949, 1955-1964, 1965-)
Merchiston Park P.198
Firs Park P.179
Brockville Park (Falkirk FC) P.157

EAST STIRLING CLYDEBANK (1964/65)
New Kilbowie Park P.201

EDINBURGH CITY (1931-1939)
New Powderhall P.204
Marine Gardens (Leith Athletic FC) P.193
City Park P.163

ELGIN CITY (2000-)
Borough Briggs P.156

FALKIRK (1902-)
Brockville Park P.157
Ochilview Park (Stenhousemuir FC) P.205
The Falkirk Stadium P.177

FORFAR ATHLETIC (1921-1939, 1949-)
Station Park P.222

GALSTON (1923-1926)
Portland Park P.210
Bellsdale Park (Beith FC) P.154

GREENOCK MORTON (1893-)
Cappielow Park P.159
Clune Park (Port Glasgow Ath FC) P.167
Boghead Park (Dumbarton FC) .. P.155
St Mirren Park (St Mirren FC) P.216

GRETNA (2002-)
Raydale Park P.215

HAMILTON ACADEMICAL (1897-)
Douglas Park P.171
Cliftonhill (Albion Rovers FC) P.166
Firhill (Partick Thistle FC) P.178
Fir Park (Motherwell FC) P.177
The Ballast Stadium P.150

HEART OF MIDLOTHIAN (1890-)
Tynecastle Park P.224
Easter Road (Hibernian FC) P.175

HELENSBURGH (1923-1926)
Ardencaple Park P.150

HIBERNIAN (1893-)
Easter Road P.175
Tynecastle Park (Hearts FC) P.224

INVERNESS CALEDONIAN THISTLE (1994-)
Telford Street P.223
Caledonian Stadium P.160
Pittodrie Park (Aberdeen FC) P.209

JOHNSTONE (1912-1926)
Newfield Park P.200

KILMARNOCK (1895-)
Rugby Park P.214
Cappielow (Greenock Morton FC) P.159
Somerset Park (Ayr United FC) ... P.219

KING'S PARK (1921-1939)
Forthbank Park P.180
Duckburn Park (Dunblane FC) ... P.169

LEITH ATHLETIC (1891-1915, 1924-1926,
1927-1939, 1947-1948)
Bank Park P.151
Hawkhill P.187
New Logie Green (St Bernards FC) P.202
Chancelot Park P.164
Old Logie Green P.203
New Powderhall P.204
Royal Gymnasium (St Bernards FC) P.213
Marine Gardens P.193
Meadowbank P.194
Old Meadowbank P.194

LINTHOUSE (1895-1900)
Langlands Park P.191

LIVINGSTON (1995-)
Meadowbank Stadium P.195
Almondvale Stadium P.149

LOCHGELLY UNITED (1914-1926)
Recreation Park P.211

MID-ANNANDALE (1923-1926)
Kintail Park P.191

MEADOWBANK THISTLE (1974-1995)
Meadowbank Stadium P.195
Bayview Park (East Fife FC) P.153
Firs Park (East Stirlingshire FC) ... P.179
Ochilview Park (Stenhousemuir FC) P.205
Tynecastle (Hearts FC) P.224

MONTROSE (1923-1926, 1929-1939, 1955-)
Links Park P.192

MOTHERWELL (1893-)
Dalziel Park P.169
Fir Park P.177

NITHSDALE WANDERERS (1923-1927)
Crawick Holm P.168

NORTHERN (1893-1894)
Hyde Park P.187

PARTICK THISTLE (1893-)
Meadowside P.197
Rugby Park (Kilmarnock FC) P.214
Ibrox Park [2nd] (Rangers FC) P.189
Shawfield Park (Clyde FC) P.217
Pittodrie (Aberdeen FC) P.209
Clune Park (Port Glasgow Ath FC) P.167
Douglas Park (Hamilton Acad FC) P.171
Celtic Park [2nd] (Celtic FC) P.162
Hampden Park [3rd] (Qn's Pk FC) P.185
Easter Road (Hibernian FC) P.175
Cappielow Park (Morton FC) P.159
Firhill Park P.178

PEEBLES ROVERS (1923-1926)
Whitestone Park P.228

PETERHEAD (2000-)
Balmoor Stadium P.151

PORT GLASGOW ATHLETIC (1893-1911)
Clune Park P.167

QUEEN OF THE SOUTH (1923-)
Palmerston Park P.208

QUEEN'S PARK (1900-)
Hampden Park [2nd] P.183
Cathkin Park (Third Lanark FC) .. P.161
Hampden Park [3rd] P.185
New Cathkin Park (Thd Lanark FC) P.183
Ibrox Park [2nd] (Rangers FC) P.189
Lesser Hampden P.184

RAITH ROVERS (1902-)
Stark's Park P.222
East End Park (Dunfermline Ath FC) P.174

RANGERS (1890-)
Ibrox Park [1st] P.188
Meadowside (Partick Thistle FC) .. P.197
Ibrox Park [2nd] P.189
Hampden Park [3rd] (Qn's Pk FC) P.186

RENTON (1890, 1891-1897)
Tontine Park P.225

ROSS COUNTY (1994-)
Victoria Park P.226

ROYAL ALBERT (1923-1926)
Raploch Park P.210

ST BERNARDS (1893-1939)
New Logie Green P.202
Ibrox Park [2nd] (Rangers FC) P.189
New Powderhall P.204
Royal Gymnasium P.213
Old Logie Green (Leith Ath FC) .. P.203
Tynecastle (Hearts FC) P.224

ST JOHNSTONE (1911-)
Recreation Ground P.211
Muirton Park P.199
McDiarmid Park P.192

ST MIRREN (1890-)
Westmarch P.227
St Mirren Park P.216
Somerset Park (Ayr United FC) ... P.219
Easter Road (Hibernian FC) P.175
Hampden Park [3rd] (Qn's Pk FC) P.185
Ibrox Park [2nd] (Rangers FC) P.189

SOLWAY STAR (1923-1926)
Kimmeter Park Green P.190

STENHOUSEMUIR (1921-)
Ochilview Park P.205

STIRLING ALBION (1947-)
Annfield Park P.149
Recreation Park (Alloa Ath FC) ... P.212
Ochilview Park (Stenhousemuir FC) P.205
Forthbank Stadium P.180

STRANRAER (1955-)
Stair Park P.221

THIRD LANARK (1890-1967)
Cathkin Park P.161
Ibrox Park [2nd] (Rangers FC) P.189
New Cathkin Park P.183
Hampden Park [3rd] (Qn's Pk FC) P.185

THISTLE (1893-1894)
Braehead Park P.156

VALE OF LEVEN (1890-1892, 1905-1926)
Millburn Park P.198

THE FOOTBALL LEAGUE

Following the establishment of the Football Association in 1863 and founding of the FA Challenge Cup Competition in 1872, the game moved away from its roots within the Public Schools and Universities to become a very popular winter pastime across all communities. With the British Empire at its zenith, the playing of Association Football quickly spread around the globe to ultimately became the undisputed world's number one sport.

In Britain, apart from the Cup competitions, teams played against each other on an *ad hoc* friendly basis, a very loose arrangement which meant that kick-off times were determined by the time that the visitors turned up, if they did at all. By the mid-1880s these games were attracting large gates and the players receiving wages, a situation that demanded that some sort of disciplined arrangement was required to ensure that matches were played on a pre-set date and time.

In order to counter these problems, William MacGregor, a committee member of *Aston Villa FC*, suggested establishing a league competition and, having contacted a number of the leading clubs, the FOOTBALL LEAGUE commenced in 1888. At this time, and for many years to come, the game was split between amateur, principally in the south of the country, and professional status and this divide can clearly be seen in the line up for the first season which commenced on September 8th, 1888. The founder members, and their grounds, were;

Accrington *(Thorneyholme Road)*, Aston Villa *(Wellington Road)*, Blackburn Rovers *(Leamington Street)*, Bolton Wanderers *(Pikes Lane)*, Burnley *(Turf Moor)*, Derby County *(Racecourse Ground)*, Everton *(Anfield)*, Notts County *(Trent Bridge)*, Preston North End *(Deepdale)*, Stoke *(Victoria Ground)*, West Bromwich Albion *(Stoney Lane)* and Wolverhampton Wanderers *(Dudley Road)*.

Initially these League games only formed a part of a club's season and they ran in parallel with the usual fixture list of friendly matches. From the outset 2 points were awarded for a win and 1 for a draw, teams on the same number of points were separated by goal average (the ratio of goals scored:goals against) and minimum admission charges were subsequently fixed.

The success of the Football League led to a rival Football Alliance being formed in 1889 and in 1892 teams from the latter were invited to form a Second Division of the Football League. The founder members and their grounds were;

Ardwick [Manchester City] *(Hyde Road)*, Bootle *(Hawthorne Road)*, Burslem Port Vale *(Cobridge Athletic Grounds)*, Burton Swifts *(Peel Croft)*, Crewe Alexandra *(Alexandra Recreation Ground)*, Darwen *(Barley Bank)*, Grimsby Town *(Abbey Park)*, Lincoln City *(John O'Gaunts)*, Northwich Victoria *(Drill Field)*, Sheffield United *(Bramall Lane)*, Small Heath [Birmingham City] *(Muntz Street)* and Walsall Town Swifts *(The Chuckery)*.

Promotion and relegation between the two divisions was decided by a series of Test Matches and it was not until 1898/99 that the issue was decided by automatic promotion and relegation.

To accommodate the rise of professionalism in the south of England, the Southern League had been formed in 1894 and in 1920 clubs in its 1st Division were invited *en bloc* to form a new Football League Division 3. One year later this became Division 3 (South) when 21 northern teams joined the new Division 3 (North) giving a Football League membership of 88 clubs. It remained as this until 1950 when four more clubs joined and in 1958 the regional arrangement was dispensed with upon the formation of Divisions 3 and 4.

Over the years the number of teams moving between divisions has varied and in 1987 play-off matches were introduced to ensure that more clubs were engaged in promotion issues and inject additional interest into the end of the season. Up until this year also, the bottom clubs in the Football League were obliged to offer themselves for re-election but from now on automatic promotion and relegation [notwithstanding the thorny issue of ground suitability] between the League and the Football Conference commenced.

In 1992 the Premier League was formed from Division One and as a result Divisions 2, 3 and 4 moved up one place and became 1, 2 and 3 respectively. This major change was no more than a cynical device to ensure that TV and Sponsorship money stayed within the top division rather than being shared more equally throughout the Football League. It has since been re-labelled as "The Premiership" but it is pleasing to note, however, that this has not impeded the process of movement of clubs between the Leagues, unlike in Scotland where ground criteria is rigidly taken into consideration or under the *aegis* of the Rugby Football Union where the Premier Division has all but cut itself off from the rest of the main body and regularly alters the rules of promotion and relegation to suit its members.

In 2003 the automatic promotion and relegation of two clubs from the Football Conference to the Football League commenced and in the following year, as the result of some mind-numbing commercial re-branding, Division 1 became known as "The Championship" with Divisions 2 and 3 moving up one place yet again to become Divisions 1 and 2!

NB. For the purposes of this book Premier League statistics are considered as to be those of the Football League and where a Division is quoted this is based on the pre-1992 arrangement unless it is of a later date in which case it is suffixed "[New]"

ABBEY PARK
HOME GROUND OF GRIMSBY TOWN

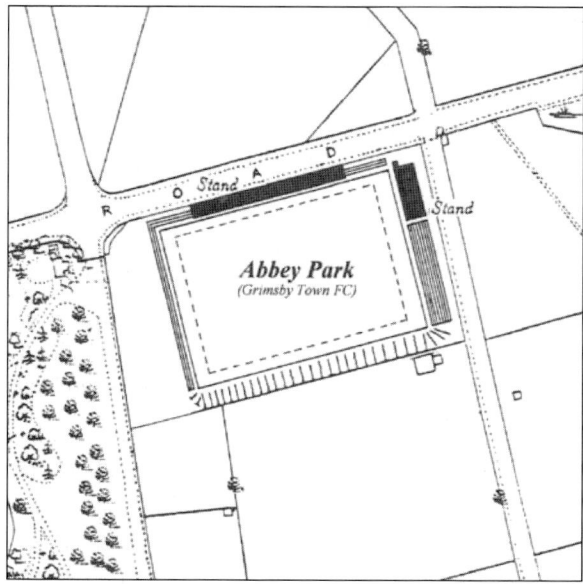

MAP EXTRACT; GROUND AS IN c1892 DRAWN FROM SKETCHES AND SUPERIMPOSED ON LINCOLNSHIRE 22.11 [1908]
SITE LOCATION; **TA27200855**

Although no map exists, from contemporary accounts an accurate diagram of the ground can be constructed. The main seated stand was on the north side of the 114 x 75 yards sized pitch with a smaller 300 seater stand, removed from the previous ground at *Clee Park*, on the east. Standing accommodation was supplied by an 800 capacity stand at the east end, a raised bank on the south side and duckboards dispersed around the perimeter. Dressing rooms were provided in the south east corner of the ground.

Abbey Park opened on August 30th, 1889 with a friendly match against *West Bromwich Albion*, which *Grimsby Town* won by 6-1, and was vacated in 1899. A housing development was later constructed on the site.

PLAYING RECORD OF GRIMSBY TOWN
LEAGUE PROGRAMME

First Match; 2-1 v. Northwich Victoria (5,000) (September 3rd, 1892)
Last Match & Highest Home Win; 9-2 v. Darwen (2,500) (April 15th, 1899)
Highest Gate; 10,000 v. Newcastle United (3-2) (December 26th, 1896) & v. Woolwich Arsenal (3-1) (April 8th, 1897)
Lowest Gate; 700 v. Loughborough (7-0) (December 4th, 1897)
Highest Home Defeat; 1-4 v. Woolwich Arsenal (4,000) (February 12th, 1898)

No. of Matches Played by Grimsby Town; 104

The club was a founder member of the Football League Division 2 in 1892 and moved to **Blundell Park** in 1899.

A TOTAL OF **38** TEAMS TOOK PART IN **104** LEAGUE FIXTURES AT THIS VENUE

ABBEY STADIUM
HOME GROUND OF CAMBRIDGE UNITED

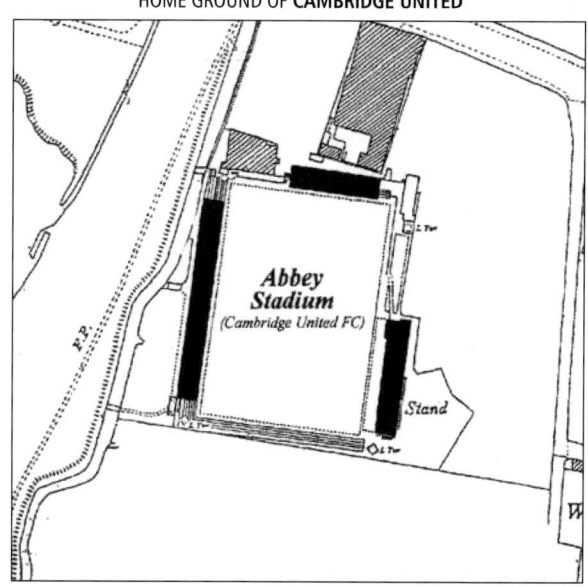

MAP EXTRACT; GROUND AS IN **1970** DRAWN FROM AERIAL PHOTOGRAPHS AND SUPERIMPOSED ON CAMBRIDGESHIRE 40.15 [1927]
SITE LOCATION; **TL47285929**

Located on the east side of the city, the ground opened in 1933 when *Cambridge United (as Abbey United)* moved here from *The Celery Trenches*. The land was donated to the club by its' President, Mr Henry Clement Francis, who also paid for a small seated stand and enclosure fencing.

The main stand on the east side was first built in 1969 and subsequently extended to the full length of the 110 x 74 yards pitch, whilst there was covered terracing on the north and west sides and a very narrow uncovered terrace at the south end. In 2001 the pitch was moved 16 yards to the south to accommodate the future construction of an enlarged north stand whilst a new 1,600 seat stand was constructed on the adjacent allotments at the south end in 2002.

The all time attendance record of 14,000 was established when *Chelsea FC* visited on May 1st, 1970 to inaugurate the floodlights and the capacity for the 2004/5 season was 9,617 with 4,784 seats.

PLAYING RECORD OF CAMBRIDGE UNITED
LEAGUE PROGRAMME

First Match; 1-1 v. Lincoln City (6,843) (August 15th, 1970)
Last Match; 0-0 v. Notts County (4,723) (May 7th, 2005)
Highest Gate; 9,766 v. Ipswich Town (1-1) (March 21st, 1992)
Lowest Gate; 1,235 v. Lincoln City (0-2) (April 30th, 1985)
Highest Home Win; 7-2 v. Mansfield Town (4,343) (March 20th, 1999). 6-0 v. Hartlepool United (2,273) (February 11th, 1989) & v. Darlington (4,561) (September 18th, 1971)
Highest Home Defeat; 1-5 v. Millwall (5,223) (April 17th, 2001)

PLAY OFF MATCHES

1-1 v. Maidstone United (7,264) (May 13th, 1990)
1-1 v. Leicester City (9,225) (May 10th, 1992)

No. of Matches Played by Cambridge United; 795
(League Programme; 723, Play Off Matches; 2)

The club was elected into the Football League Division 4 in 1970 and was later involved in a Football League Play Off Match at the neutral venue of *Wembley Stadium*. The club was relegated into the Football Conference in 2005.

A TOTAL OF **93** TEAMS TOOK PART IN **795** LEAGUE FIXTURES AT THIS VENUE

ADAMS PARK
HOME GROUND OF WYCOMBE WANDERERS

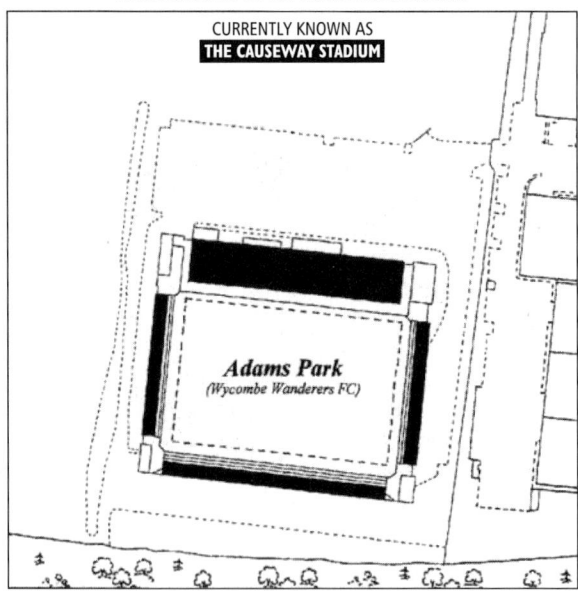

MAP EXTRACT; GROUND AS IN **1999** AND DRAWN FROM AERIAL PHOTOGRAPHS
SITE LOCATION; **TQ83139310**

Situated at the west end of an industrial estate, and to the west of the town centre, *Wycombe Wanderers FC* moved here from *Loakes Park* in 1990.

When opened it was a typical modern purpose-built stadium, with a cantilever style two-tier main stand on the south side and covered accommodation on the other three sides. In 2001 a new 2,000 seat stand was constructed at the east end and in 2003 the club arranged a sponsorship deal with Causeway Technologies and the name of the ground was changed to the *Causeway Stadium*. The capacity for the 2004/5 season was 10,000 with 8,250 seats and the pitch size 115 x 75 yards.

PLAYING RECORD OF WYCOMBE WANDERERS
LEAGUE PROGRAMME

First Match; 1-0 v. Chester City (5,607) (August 21st, 1993)
Highest Gate; 9,250 v. Reading (0-2) (February 26th, 2002)
Lowest Gate; 2,836 v. Rotherham United (1-1) (April 18th, 1996)
Highest Home Win; 5-0 v. Burnley (5,786) (April 15th, 1997)
Highest Home Defeat; 2-5 v. Colchester United (6,025) (September 18th, 1993) & v. Oldham Athletic (3,920) (September 20th, 2003). 0-4 v. Stoke City (4,345) (November 23rd, 1999) & v. Cardiff City (5,889) (April 8th, 2003)

PLAY OFF MATCHES
2-1 v. Carlisle United (6,265) (May 18th, 1994)

No. of Matches Played by Wycombe Wanderers; 275
(League Programme; 274, Play Off Matches; 1)

The club was promoted into the Football League Division 3 from the Football Conference in 1993. The club was also involved in a Football League Play Off Match at the neutral venue of **Wembley Stadium**.

AT THE END OF SEASON 2004/5, A TOTAL OF **68** TEAMS HAD TAKEN PART IN **275** LEAGUE FIXTURES AT THIS VENUE

AGGBOROUGH
HOME GROUND OF KIDDERMINSTER HARRIERS

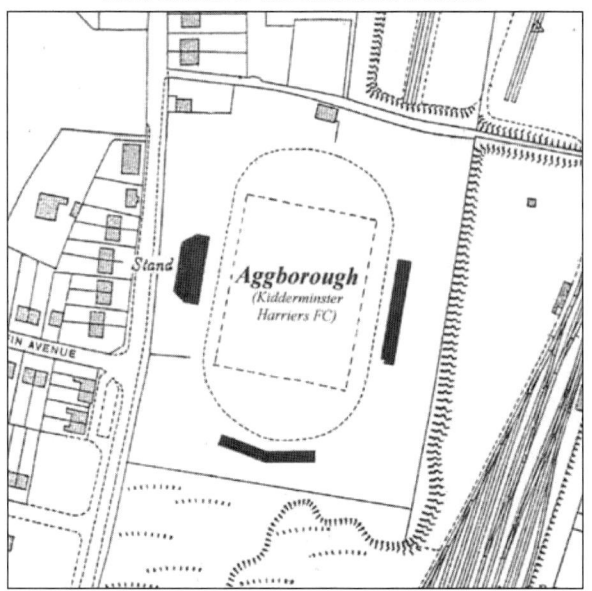

MAP EXTRACT; WORCESTERSHIRE 14.3 [**1938**]
SITE LOCATION; **SO83587585**

When the ground opened in May 1890 the facilities included a grandstand on the west side and the pitch was enclosed by an oval banked running track. A new 460 seat grandstand was built in 1935 and other pre-WWII improvements included the provision of cover at the south end and on the east side.

Following the war the running track was replaced by a cycle track and the record attendance of 9,155 was established at the FA Cup 1st Round Replay v. *Hereford United* (1-2) on November 27th, 1948. *Aggborough* also hosted the first ever FA Cup tie to be played under floodlights when *Kidderminster Harriers* met *Brierley Hill Alliance* in a Qualifying Round replay on September 14th, 1955.

A new stand was constructed on the east side in 1979 and, in the 1983, concrete terracing installed around the ground. The ground was rebuilt in the 1990s, the oval track removed, a new mainstand built in 1994 and covered terracing provided at each end. In 2003 a new 2,040 seat cantilever roofed stand was constructed on the east side and the capacity for the 2004/5 season was 6,293 with 3,150 seats. The pitch size was 112 x 72 yards.

PLAYING RECORD OF KIDDERMINSTER HARRIERS
LEAGUE PROGRAMME

First Match; 2-0 v. Torquay United (5,122) (August 12th, 2000)
Last Match; 1-4 v. Grimsby Town (2,340) (April 30th, 2005)
Highest Gate; 5,122 v. Torquay United (2-0) (August 12th, 2000)
Lowest Gate; 2,002 v. York City (4-1) (October 23rd, 2001)
Highest Home Win; 4-1 v. York City (2,002) (October 23rd, 2001), v. Rochdale (3,856) (December 26th, 2001) & v, York City (2,569) (March 6th, 2004)
Highest Home Defeat; 1-5 v. Swansea City (4,288) (December 26th, 2004)

No. of Matches Played by Kidderminster Harriers; 115

The club was promoted into the Football League Division 3 from the Football Conference in 2000 and relegated back into the Conference in 2005.

A TOTAL OF **42** TEAMS TOOK PART IN **115** LEAGUE FIXTURES AT THIS VENUE

ALEXANDRA RECREATION GROUND
HOME GROUND OF CREWE ALEXANDRA

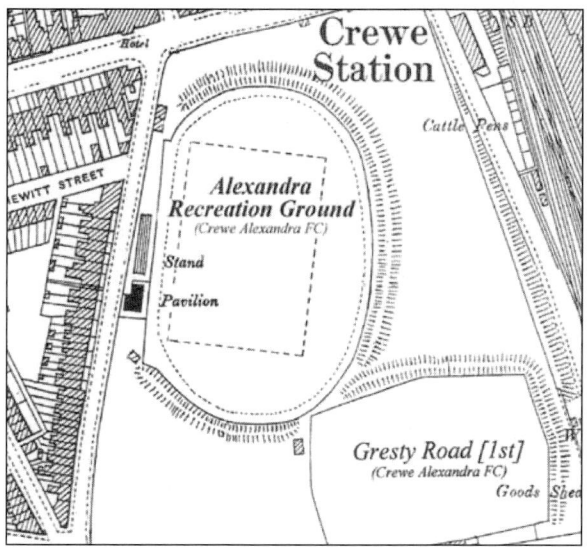

MAP EXTRACT; CHESHIRE 56.7 & 56.8 [1898]
SITE LOCATION; SJ70925466

Opened in 1877 the stadium was utilized for cricket, athletics and bicycle racing as well as for football. Generally oval in shape, the facilities, a 100ft long stand and pavilion were on the west side and raised banking surrounded the arena. The ground hosted the FA Cup Semi-Final between *Aston Villa* and *Glasgow Rangers* (3-1) on March 5th, 1887 (when the probable ground record attendance of 7,000 was established) and an *England* v. *Wales* match on February 4th, 1889. The club left in 1896 and the site is now occupied by Rail House, a car park and part of the *Gresty Road [2nd]* ground.

NB The "Football Ground" in the south east corner is the venue (Gresty Road [1st]) to which the club returned in 1897 and used until 1906 when avoiding lines were constructed on the west side of the station. The pitch was moved a few yards to the west to the site now known as *Gresty Road [2nd]*.

PLAYING RECORD OF CREWE ALEXANDRA
LEAGUE PROGRAMME

First Match; 1-0 v. Grimsby Town (2,000) (September 10th, 1892)
Last Match & Highest Home Defeat; 0-7 v. Liverpool (3,000) (March 28th, 1896)
Highest Gate; 4,000 v. Northwich Victoria (4-2) (September 17th, 1892)
Lowest Gate; 100 v. Notts County (0-3) (January 16th, 1895)
Highest Home Win; 5-0 v. Burslem Port Vale (2,000) (November 26th, 1892) & v. Middlesbrough Ironopolis (2,000) (September 30th, 1893)

No. of Matches Played by Crewe Alexandra; 54
Some Information Kindly Supplied by; Brian Tabner

The club was a founder member of the Football League Division 2 in 1892 and failed to gain re-election in 1896. Following the *Liverpool* match at the ground on March 28th, 1896 there was still one home game to be played to complete the season. This took place at *The Vicarage* at Sandbach and may have been played at a different venue either because the lease had expired or the *Alexandra Recreation Ground* had been required for another sport. The club played on several other grounds prior to moving to *Gresty Road [2nd]* and their election back into the Football League in 1921.

A TOTAL OF **21** TEAMS TOOK PART IN **54** LEAGUE FIXTURES AT THIS VENUE

THE ALFRED McALPINE STADIUM
HOME GROUND OF HUDDERSFIELD TOWN

CURRENTLY KNOWN AS
THE GALPHARM STADIUM

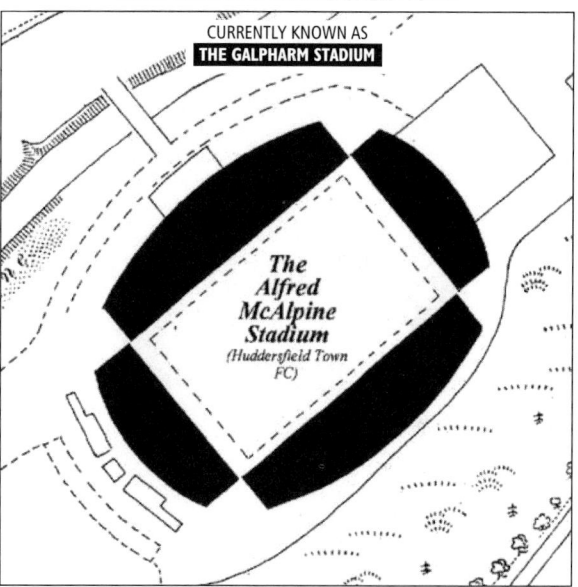

MAP EXTRACT; GROUND AS IN **2000** DRAWN FROM AERIAL PHOTOGRAPHS AND SUPERIMPOSED ON YORKSHIRE 246.11 [1932]
SITE LOCATION; **SE15451860**

Constructed on the site of industrial wasteland, Huddersfield Town moved across the River Colne from **Leeds Road** in 1994. Upon opening, the award-winning stadium (it received the RIBA Building of the Year Award in 1995) consisted of a two tier 8,281 seat stand on the west side and a 7,329 seat stand on the east. Within months of the first game a 4,053 seat stand was opened at the south end and in 1996 the stadium was completed with the construction of an all seater stand at the north end. The main feature of the design is the near-elliptical planform of the stadium with each roof supported by a banana shaped truss. The capacity for the 2004/5 season was 24,500 and the pitch size 116 x 75 yards.

PLAYING RECORD OF HUDDERSFIELD TOWN
LEAGUE PROGRAMME

First Match; 0-1 v. Wycombe Wanderers (13,334) (August 20th, 1994)
Highest Gate; 20,741 v. Sunderland (1-1) (October 21st, 1998)
Lowest Gate; 7,179 v. Colchester United (2-1) (January 22nd, 2002)
Highest Home Win; 7-1 v. Crystal Palace (10,656) (August 28th, 1999)
Highest Home Defeat; 0-4 v. Port Vale (15,610) (May 3rd, 1998)

PLAY OFF MATCHES
1-1 v. Brentford (14,160) (May 14th, 1995)
0-0 v. Brentford (16.523) (April 28th, 2002)
2-2 v. Lincoln City (19,467) (May 19th, 2004)

No. of Matches Played by Huddersfield Town; 256
(League Programme; 253, Play Off Matches; 3)

The club moved here from *Leeds Road* in 1994 and was also involved in Football League Play Off Matches at the neutral venues of *Wembley Stadium* and the *Millennium Stadium*.

AT THE END OF SEASON 2004/5, A TOTAL OF **81** TEAMS HAD TAKEN PART IN **256** LEAGUE FIXTURES AT THIS VENUE

ANFIELD

HOME GROUND OF **EVERTON** & **LIBERPOOL**
TEMPORARY HOME GROUND FOR **MANCHESTER UNITED**

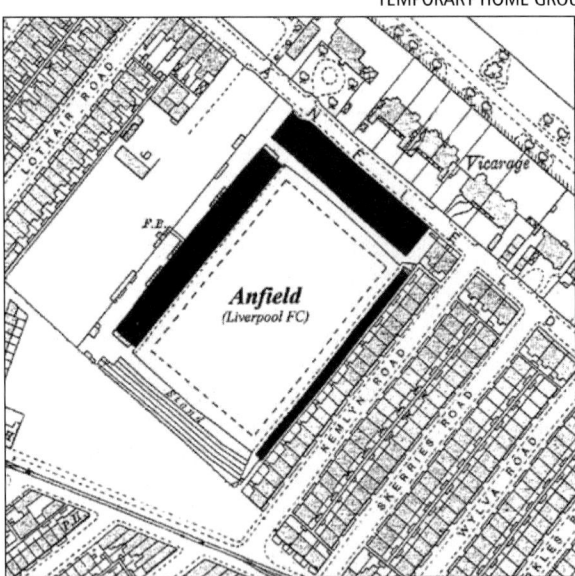

MAP EXTRACT; LANCASHIRE 106.7 [1908]
SITE LOCATION; **SJ36279311**

Everton FC moved here from the *Priory Road Ground* and played their first match, a 5-0 victory, against *Earlestown FC* on September 28th, 1884. Changing facilities were provided at the nearby Sandon Hotel, hoardings surrounded the field with the pitch enclosed by railings and an open seated stand sited on the Anfield Road side. Although within a few years considerable improvements had been made, with open stands at each end of the pitch and covered stands on each side, substantial regular rent increases led to *Everton FC* looking at alternative sites within the area. At the end of the 1891/92 season a move was made to *Goodison Park* on the other side of Stanley Park.

The landlord, John Houlding, quickly established a new football club to utilize his ground and within one year *Liverpool FC* was elected to the Football League. The ground then saw major developments; in 1895 a 3,000 seater stand was built on south east side, in 1903 a new stand was constructed on Anfield Road and in 1906 the first "Kop" was built. In 1928 the accommodation of the "Kop" was increased to 30,000 when it was extended and covered and the all time ground record of 61,905 was established after WWII at a 4th Round FA Cup tie against *Wolverhampton Wanderers* (2-1) on February 2nd, 1952.

In the 1990s the ground was totally rebuilt, the "Kop" end was demolished and replaced with a 12,000 seat stand whilst the construction of further new stands and refurbishments completed an all-seater stadium with a capacity of 45,362 for the 2004/5 season. The pitch size was 110 x 75 yards and in 2005 plans were in hand to move across the road into a new stadium, *New Anfield*, in Stanley Park.

PLAYING RECORD OF MANCHESTER UNITED
LEAGUE PROGRAMME
Match Played; 3-1 v. Arsenal (27,649) (August 20th, 1971)
No. of Matches Played by Manchester United; 1
Information Kindly Supplied by; John Robinson & John Russell
This match was played here when *Old Trafford* was closed following crowd trouble.

PROGRAMME COVER ON THE RIGHT
The cover for Season 1957/58 featured this crude illustration which nonetheless shows that the stands were installed with barrel roofs.
Programme Courtesy of Peter Miles

PLAYING RECORD OF EVERTON
LEAGUE PROGRAMME
First Match; 2-1 v. Accrington (9,000) (September 8th, 1888)
Last Match; 2-5 v. Bolton Wanderers (4,000) (April 18th, 1892)
Highest Gate & Highest Home Defeat; 1-5 v. Preston North End (18,000) (November 16th, 1889)
Lowest Gate; 2,079 v. West Bromwich Albion (0-1) (February 23rd, 1889)
Highest Home Win; 8-0 v. Stoke (7,500) (November 2nd, 1889)
No. of Matches Played by Everton; 46
Some Information Kindly Supplied by; Brian Tabner
The club was a founder member of the Football League in 1888 and moved to *Goodison Park* in 1892.

PLAYING RECORD OF LIVERPOOL
LEAGUE PROGRAMME
First Match; 4-0 v. Lincoln City (5,000) (September 9th, 1893)
Highest Gate; 58,757 v. Chelsea (2-2) (December 27th, 1949)
Lowest Gate; 1,000 v. Loughborough (1-0) (December 7th, 1895)
Highest Home Win; 10-1 v. Rotherham Town (2,000) (February 18th, 1896)
Highest Home Defeat; 0-6 v. Sunderland (30,000) (April 19th, 1930)
TEST MATCHES
4-0 v. Small Heath (20,000) (April 18th, 1896)
2-0 v. West Bromwich Albion (20,000) (April 25th, 1896)
No. of Matches Played by Liverpool; 2,019
(League Programme; 2,017, Test Matches; 2)
The club was elected into the Football League Division 2 in 1893 and was also involved in a Test Match at the neutral venue of *Ewood Park*.

AT THE END OF SEASON 2004/5, A TOTAL OF **80** TEAMS HAD TAKEN PART IN **2,066** LEAGUE FIXTURES AT THIS VENUE

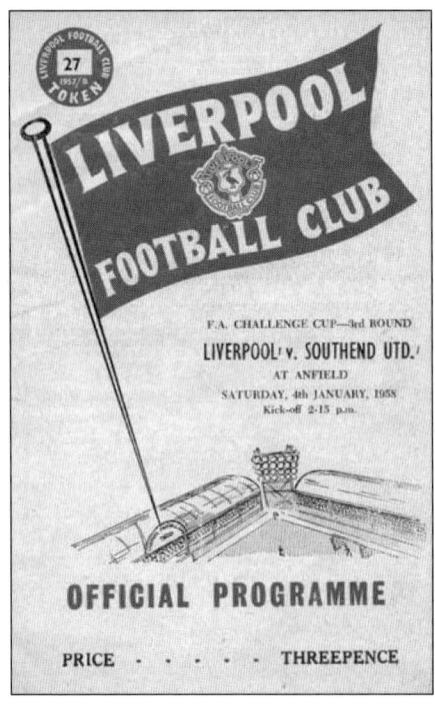

ARSENAL STADIUM

HOME GROUND OF **ARSENAL**
TEMPORARY HOME GROUND FOR **QUEENS PARK RANGERS**

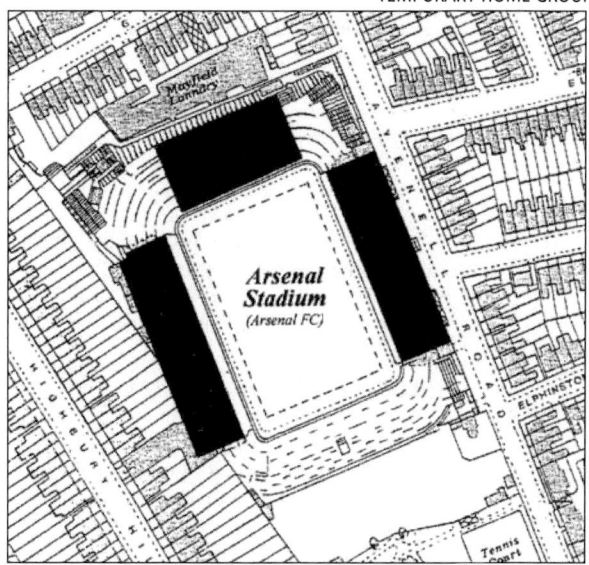

MAP EXTRACT; LONDON 11.14 [**1936**]
SITE LOCATION; **TQ31518601**

Woolwich Arsenal FC moved from the ***Manor Ground*** in Plumstead ready for the start of the 1913/14 season and, in view of their new location, changed the club name to *The Arsenal FC*. First known as *Highbury*, the ground, as built, consisted of a 9,000 seat multi-span roofed main stand on the east side with large banks of open terracing surrounding the remainder of the pitch.

The major redevelopment of the ground took place in the 1930s with the construction of the Ferrier-designed West Stand in 1932, a double decker construction with standing accommodation for 17,000 and 4,100 seats. The North Bank was roofed in 1935 and the original East Stand replaced with a similar structure to the West Stand in 1936. During this period the name of the stadium was officially changed from *Highbury* to *Arsenal Stadium*.

Wartime bombing put paid to the roof over the North Bank and, apart from its replacement in 1954, little in the way of improvements were made until the ground was substantially rebuilt in the 1990s as an all-seater stadium with the East and West Stands being thoroughly refurbished and new stands being constructed at each end. At the start of the 2004/5 season, the pitch size was 110 x 71 yards and with a capacity of only 38,548 plans were in hand to move to a new larger ground, ***Emirates Stadium***, on a brownfield site at nearby Ashburton Grove.

PLAYING RECORD OF QUEENS PARK RANGERS
LEAGUE PROGRAMME

Match Played; 3-1 v. Coventry City (25,000) (March 1st, 1930)
No. of Matches Played by Queens Park Rangers; 1
This match was played here due to crowd trouble at *Loftus Road*

PLAYING RECORD OF ARSENAL
LEAGUE PROGRAMME

First Match; 2-1 v. Leicester Fosse (20,000) (September 6th, 1913)
Highest Gate; 73,295 v. Sunderland (0-0) (March 9th, 1935)
Lowest Gate; 4,554 v. Leeds United (0-3) (May 5th, 1966)
Highest Home Win; 9-1 v. Grimsby Town (15,751)
(January 28th, 1931)
Highest Home Defeat; 2-6 v. Sheffield United (30,000)
(March 26th, 1921). 0-5 v. Huddersfield Town (25,000)
(February 14th, 1925)
No. of Matches Played by Arsenal; 1,672

Following its move here from the ***Manor Ground*** the club name was changed to *Arsenal FC* in 1914 and it was elected into Division 1 from Division 2 (despite finishing only fifth) in 1920. The first match to be broadcast on radio was the 1-1 draw between *Arsenal* and *Sheffield United* played here on January 22nd, 1927.

AT THE END OF SEASON 2004/5, A TOTAL OF **63** TEAMS HAD TAKEN PART IN **1,673** LEAGUE FIXTURES AT THIS VENUE

The east, main stand, of **Arsenal Stadium** in its final form with seating installed throughout the structure
Photograph by Paul Claydon. Courtesy of Groundtastic Magazine

ASHTON GATE

HOME GROUND OF **BRISTOL CITY**
TEMPORARY HOME GROUND FOR **BRISTOL ROVERS**

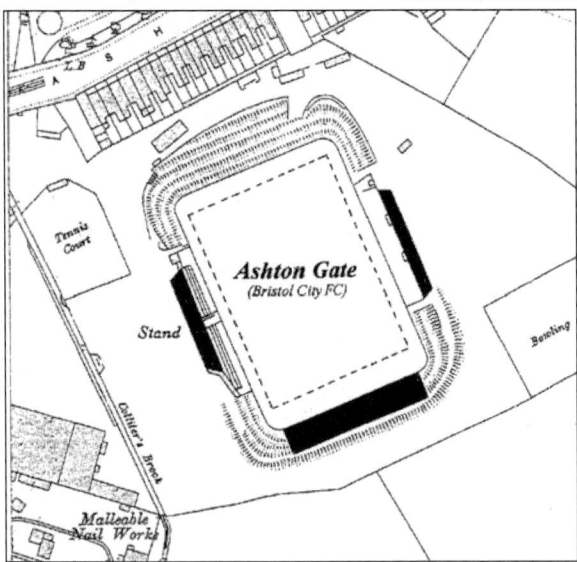

MAP EXTRACT; GLOUCESTERSHIRE 75.4 [**1912**]
SITE LOCATION; **ST56987142**

Opened in 1896, this was initially the home ground of *Bedminster FC*, who merged with *Bristol City* in 1900. However, it was not until 1904 that the amalgamated club finally moved from *St John's Lane* to the much larger *Ashton Gate*. In the early years there were two stands, Nos 1 and 2, on each side of the pitch and, in the 1920s, a covered terrace was installed at the Winterstoke Road end of the ground. No.1 Stand was destroyed during WWII and ultimately replaced by a new grandstand in the 1950s whilst on the opposite side, the Harry Dolman Stand, with the roof suspended from a cross girder, was completed in 1970. By the end of season 2001/2 a 21,497 capacity all-seater stadium had been created with the construction of a new grandstand, on the site of the old one, and new stands at each end of the ground surrounding the 120 x 75 yards sized pitch.

PLAYING RECORD OF BRISTOL CITY
LEAGUE PROGRAMME

First Match; 3-4 v. Bolton Wanderers (14,000) (September 3rd, 1904)
Highest Gate; 38,688 v. Liverpool (2-1) (May 16th, 1977)
Lowest Gate*; 3,169 v. Halifax Town (3-0) (February 15th, 1983)
Highest Home Win; 9-0 v. Aldershot (17,428) (December 28th, 1946)
Highest Home Defeat; 1-6 v. Burnley (7,416) (March 28th, 1932), v. Norwich City (10,432) (January 15th, 1949) & v. Wolverhampton Wanderers (15,432) (November 7th, 1998)

PLAY OFF MATCHES

1-0 v. Sheffield United (25,335) (May 15th, 1988)
1-3 v. Walsall (25,128) (May 25th, 1988)
1-2 v. Brentford (15,581) (May 11th, 1997)
0-0 v. Cardiff City (16,307) (May 13th, 2003)
2-1 v. Hartlepool United (18,434) (May 15th, 2004)

No. of Matches Played by Bristol City; 1,838
(League Programme; 1,833, Play Off Matches; 5)

The club moved here from *St John's Lane* in 1904 and was involved in a Football League Play Off Match at the neutral venue of the *Millennium Stadium*.

*NB. This is assumed to be the lowest recorded gate here.

PLAYING RECORD OF BRISTOL ROVERS
LEAGUE PROGRAMME
1ST PERIOD

Matches Played; 2-2 v. Grimsby Town (4,461)
(August 30th, 1980)
0-0 v. Oldham Athletic (3,808) (September 13th, 1980)
0-0 v. Newcastle United (5,171) (September 27th, 1980)

2ND PERIOD

Match Played; 3-4 v. Swindon Town (8,196) (April 11th, 1987)

No. of Matches Played by Bristol Rovers; 4

Information Kindly Supplied by; Keith Brookland & Colin Timbrell

On August 16th, 1980, the south stand at the *Eastville Stadium* burned down, forcing the club to move in with *Bristol City FC*. They played five games here in total before returning. To counteract any potential crowd trouble and allow for an extra large gate, the match v. *Swindon Town* was subsequently moved here from *Twerton Park*.

AT THE END OF SEASON 2004/5, A TOTAL OF **105** TEAMS HAD TAKEN PART IN **1,841** LEAGUE FIXTURES AT THIS VENUE

This 1969/70 season programme cover features a view of the ground looking south towards the covered end. The match featured ended in a 2-0 win for the hosts

ATHLETIC GROUND
HOME GROUND OF ABERDARE ATHLETIC

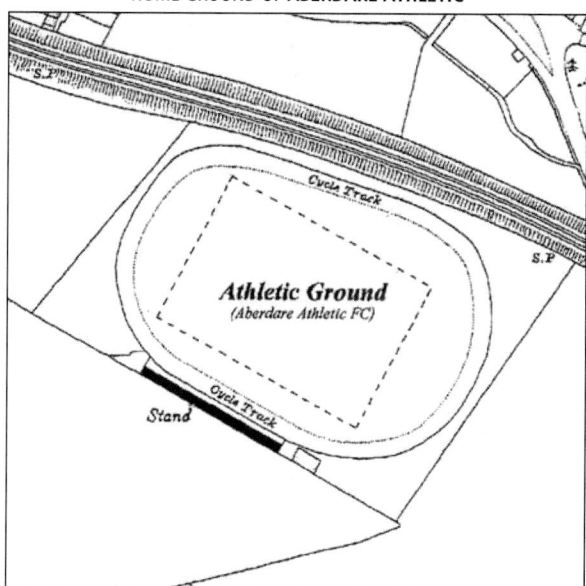

MAP EXTRACT; GLAMORGAN 11.15 [**1920**]
SITE LOCATION: **SO00790253**

Also known as the *Ynys Stadium*, the site was first used in 1893 by *Aberdare Town FC*, predecessor of *Aberdare Athletic*. Located to the east of the town, the ground initially possessed few facilities but by 1920 a narrow grandstand had been constructed on the south side and the pitch was circumvented by a cycle track. *Aberdare Athletic* was formed in 1920 and, with the hope of Football League membership, the grandstand was rebuilt, and subsequently extended, the cycle track dispensed with and embankments constructed behind both goals.

The club was elected to the League in 1921 and the all-time attendance record of 22,584 set at the *Wales v. Scotland Schoolboys* International on May 14th, 1921. *Aberdare Athletic* failed to gain re-election in 1927 and vacated the *Athletic Ground* in 1934. A new Sports Centre was subsequently established on the site.

PLAYING RECORD OF ABERDARE ATHLETIC
LEAGUE PROGRAMME

First Match; 0-0 v. Portsmouth (9,722) (August 27th, 1921)
Last Match; 2-2 v. Brighton & Hove Albion (1,242)
(May 7th, 1927)
Highest Gate; 16,350 v. Bristol City (0-1) (April 2nd, 1923)
Lowest Gate; 745 v. Crystal Palace (2-3) (February 26th, 1927)
Highest Home Win; 8-1 v. Watford (2,774) (January 2nd, 1926)
Highest Home Defeat; 0-7 v. Coventry City (3,797)
(April 18th, 1927)
No. of Matches Played by Aberdare Athletic; 126
Some Information Kindly Supplied by; Brian Tabner

The club was elected into the Football League Division 3 in 1921 and re-elected in 1923 before failing to gain re-election in 1927.

A TOTAL OF **26** TEAMS TOOK PART IN **126** LEAGUE FIXTURES AT THIS VENUE

ATHLETIC GROUND
HOME GROUND OF LOUGHBOROUGH

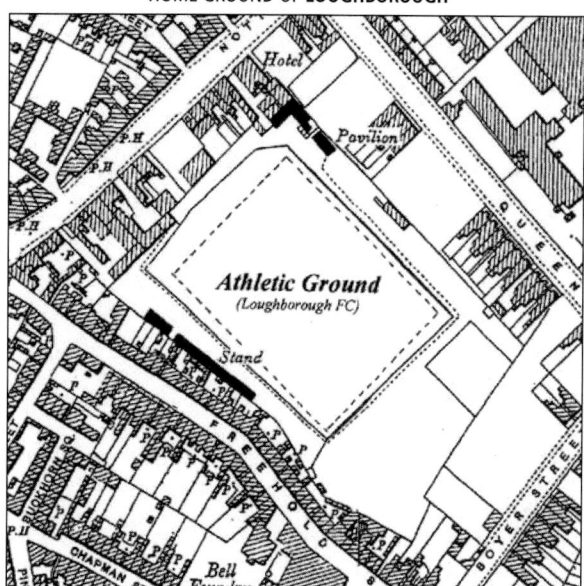

MAP EXTRACT; LEICESTERSHIRE 17.8 & 18.5 [**1903**]
SITE LOCATION: **SK54121993**

Located at the rear of the Greyhound Hotel, on the south side of Nottingham Road, it was principally utilized for cricket until *Loughborough FC* started using it in 1886. The dressing rooms were located at the rear of the Hotel, and the facilities included a pavilion on the north side and a small grandstand on the south. The record gate was probably the 10,000 who attended the Midland League match v. *Leicester Fosse* on October 7th, 1893. After *Loughborough* failed to gain re-election to the League in 1900 the ground was demolished in 1908 and the site subsequently covered by housing.

PLAYING RECORD OF LOUGHBOROUGH
LEAGUE PROGRAMME

First Match; 3-3 v. Newton Heath (2,000) (September 14th, 1895)
Last Match; 1-2 v. Gainsborough Trinity (100) (April 28th, 1900)
Highest Gate; 6,000 v. Leicester Fosse (0-2) (November 11th, 1899)
Lowest Gate; 100 v. Lincoln City (0-1) (April 23rd, 1900) & v.
Gainsborough Trinity (1-2) (April 28th, 1900)
Highest Home Win; 10-0 v. Darwen (1,500) (April 1st, 1899)
Highest Home Defeat; 0-5 v. Gainsborough Trinity (1,000) (February 5th, 1898)

No. of Matches Played by Loughborough; 74

The club was elected into the Football League Division 2 in 1895 and failed to gain re-election in 1900. The ground was closed in 1896/7 (after crowd trouble at the *Walsall* match on October 10th, 1896), between January 23rd and February 6th, 1899 (because of crowd trouble at a reserve fixture versus *Coalville FC* in January 1899) and for one month following crowd trouble at the *Woolwich Arsenal* fixture (2-3) on March 3rd, 1900. During these periods of closure, and to avoid fixture clashes with the cricket club, some matches were played at *Filbert Street* and *The Vicarage* at Whitwick.

A TOTAL OF **28** TEAMS TOOK PART IN **74** LEAGUE FIXTURES AT THIS VENUE

THE ATHLETIC GROUNDS
HOME GROUND OF BLACKPOOL

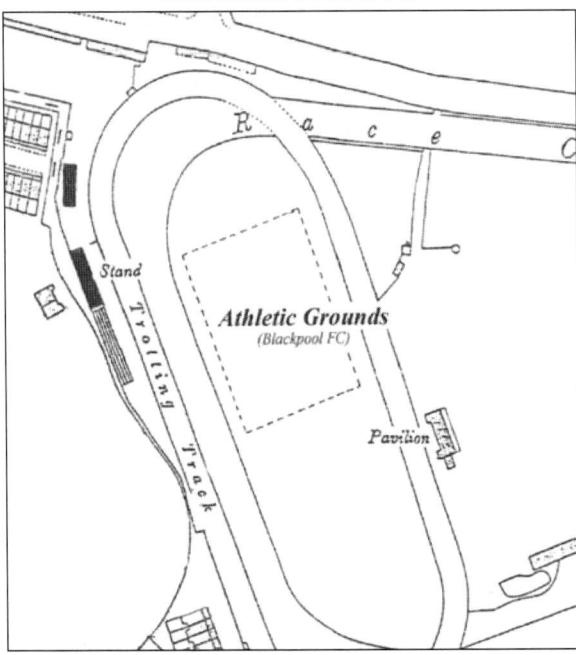

MAP EXTRACT; LANCASHIRE 51.9 [1912]
SITE LOCATION; **SD32363485**

Located within Stanley Park, the ground was further out, eastwards from the town than *Blackpool FCs* previous venue at *Raikes Hall*. The Park itself was a 24 acre enclosure around the perimeter of which ran a racecourse. A cricket pitch and pavilion were located in the centre and there was a cinder covered oval trotting and cycling track at the west end of the site. By the time that the club arrived here the trotting track had been out of use for some years and was rapidly decaying. From contemporary accounts it would appear that the pitch itself was located within the oval of this track, with the covered stand and a short length of uncovered seating previously installed on the west side being the only facilities. The whole site was subsequently incorporated into the Stanley Park Leisure Complex but by 2003 it had succumbed to housing.

PLAYING RECORD OF BLACKPOOL
LEAGUE PROGRAMME

First Match; 1-1 v. Burnley (4,000) (September 11th, 1897)
Last Match; 1-2 v. Glossop North End (-) (December 31st, 1898)
Highest Gate; 4,000 v. Darwen (1-0) (April 8th, 1898),
v. Burnley (1-1) (September 11th, 1897) & v. Newton Heath (0-4)
(January 15th, 1898)
Lowest Gate; 200 v. Luton Town (1-0) (April 30th, 1898)
Highest Home Win; 5-0 v. Gainsborough Trinity (-) (December 18th, 1897) & v. Lincoln City (1,000) (February 19th, 1898)
Highest Home Defeat; 0-4 v. Newton Heath (4,000) (January 15th, 1898) & v. Burslem Port Vale (1,000) (September 24th, 1898)

No. of Matches Played by Blackpool; 22
Information Kindly Supplied by; Roger Harrison

This venue, with the stands and spectator areas remote from the pitch, proved to be very unpopular with supporters and when it became apparent that the proposed re-development of *Raikes Hall* had been delayed the club were able to return there midway through the 1898/9 season.

A TOTAL OF **18** TEAMS TOOK PART IN **22** LEAGUE FIXTURES AT THIS VENUE

THE AVENUE STADIUM
TEMPORARY HOME GROUND FOR AFC BOURNEMOUTH

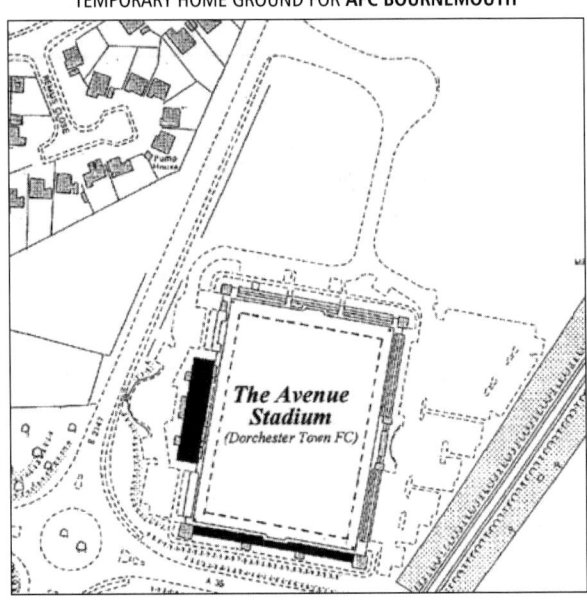

MAP EXTRACT; GROUND AS IN **1991** DRAWN FROM MAPS AND SUPERIMPOSED ON SY6889 [1953]
SITE LOCATION; **SY68638908**

Opened in August 1990, *The Avenue Stadium* is located to the south of the town, on the east side of Weymouth Road. The facilities include a 710 seat covered main stand on the west side, covered terracing on the east and south sides and uncovered terracing at the north end, giving a ground capacity of 5,009. *Dorchester Town FC's* record attendance is 4,159 v. *Weymouth* on December 1st, 1999. *AFC Bournemouth* moved in for a short period at the start of the 2001/2 season whilst **Dean Court** was being rebuilt.

PLAYING RECORD OF AFC BOURNEMOUTH
LEAGUE PROGRAMME

Matches Played; 0-1 v. Blackpool (3,709) (August 18th, 2001)
0-0 v. Swindon Town (3,370) (September 8th, 2001)
3-2 v. Bury (3,004) (September 15th, 2001)
1-0 v. Reading (3,691) (September 25th, 2001)
3-2 v. Oldham (3,312) (October 5th, 2001)
2-0 v. Wigan Athletic (2,908) (October 9th, 2001)
0-2 v. Brentford (3,934) (October 20th, 2001)
4-2 v. Notts County (3,209) (October 27th, 2001)

No. of Matches Played by AFC Bournemouth; 8

This ground was used for the first eight matches until **Dean Court** was ready to re-open as the *Fitness First Stadium* after the start of the 2001/2 season.

A TOTAL OF **9** TEAMS TOOK PART IN **8** LEAGUE FIXTURES AT THIS VENUE

AYRESOME PARK
HOME GROUND OF MIDDLESBROUGH

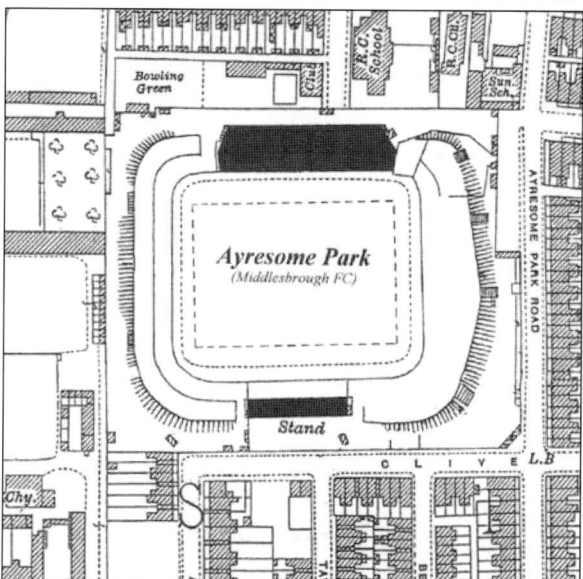

MAP EXTRACT; YORKSHIRE 6.14 [1915]
SITE LOCATION; NZ48771909

PLAYING RECORD OF MIDDLESBROUGH
LEAGUE PROGRAMME

First Match; 2-3 v. Sunderland (30,000) (September 12th, 1903)
Last Match; 2-1 v. Luton Town (23,903) (April 30th, 1995)
Highest Gate; 53,596 v. Newcastle United (1-0) (December 27th, 1949)
Lowest Gate; 3,364 v. Notts County (0-1) (February 9th, 1985)
Highest Home Win; 9-0 v. Brighton & Hove Albion (32,136) (August 23rd, 1958), 10-3 v. Sheffield United (6,461) (November 18th, 1933)
Highest Home Defeat; 3-7 v. Bradford City (25,000) (December 25th, 1909). 0-5 v. Bury (8,000) (February 12th, 1910) & v. Huddersfield Town (18,470) (August 25th, 1962)

PLAY OFF MATCHES
2-0 v. Bradford City (25,868) (May 18th, 1988),
2-0 v. Chelsea (25,381) (May 25th, 1988).
1-1 v. Notts County (22,343) (May 19th, 1991)

No. of Matches Played by Middlesbrough; 1,689
(League Programme; 1,686, Play Off Matches; 3)
Some Information Kindly Supplied by; Brian Tabner

The club moved here from *Linthorpe Road* in 1903. In 1986 the club was in severe financial difficulties and, as it was barred from playing at *Ayresome Park* at the start of the season, played the first match at *Victoria Park*. In 1995 the club moved to the *Riverside Stadium*.

A TOTAL OF 87 TEAMS TOOK PART IN 1,689 LEAGUE FIXTURES AT THIS VENUE

Located on the south side of Ayresome Street and partially sited on the north west corner of **The Paradise Ground**, the former home of *Middlesbrough Ironopolis FC*, Middlesbrough FC moved here from **Linthorpe Road** in 1903. It had a capacity of 40,000 and was well-appointed for the time, with a new full length stand constructed on the north side and the grandstand from **Linthorpe Road** re-erected on the south.

The ground was gradually improved, with replacement of the South Stand, construction of concrete terraces and covering of the west end bringing the capacity up to 54,000. It was subsequently refurbished to host some of the Group 4 World Cup matches in 1966 involving roofing of the east end and the installation of an additional 7,600 seats.

Middlesbrough FC moved out to the **Riverside Stadium** in 1995 and the ground was demolished.

The Archibald Leitch designed main stand and paddock on the north side of the ground. The seats shown are amongst those installed onto the terracing for the 1966 World Cup.
Photograph by Paul Claydon. Courtesy of Groundtastic Magazine

DIAGRAM SHOWING THE DISPOSITION OF THE PARADISE GROUND & AYRESOME PARK

Middlesbrough Ironopolis FC folded in 1894 and part of the site of their **Paradise Ground**, [See Page 98] as shown above, was utilized for *Ayresome Park* in 1903.

BANK STREET
HOME GROUND OF **MANCHESTER UNITED**

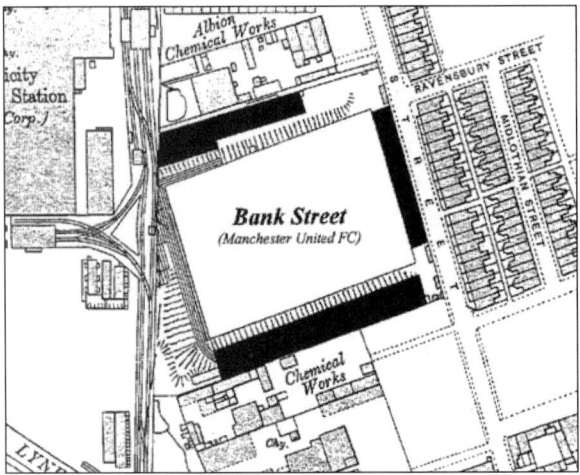

MAP EXTRACT; LANCASHIRE 104.8 [**1908**]
SITE LOCATION; **SJ87519875**

Sandwiched between two chemical works and abutting a railway line, *Newton Heath FC* opened their *Bank Street* ground in 1893. It was originally known as *Bank Lane* and had been utilized as an athletics stadium by the *Bradford & Clayton Athletic Co*. Initially it had little in the way of facilities but following the purchase of the lease of the ground in 1898 major improvements were made. The running track was removed, covered stands provided on the north and south sides and the Bank Street end, and extensive embankments constructed, some with concrete terracing. The facilities for the players included separate changing rooms and a pavilion that overlooked the ground from the top of the main stand. At the completion of these alterations, the ground had covered accommodation for 8,000 and a capacity of 50,000. *Bank Street* was vacated in 1910 when the club, now as *Manchester United*, moved to *Old Trafford* and sold it to Manchester Corporation for use as a coal storage depot for the adjacent Power Station. The site was subsequently cleared and redeveloped as a car park for the Velodrome used in the 2002 Commonwealth Games.

PLAYING RECORD OF MANCHESTER UNITED
[ALSO AS NEWTON HEATH]
LEAGUE PROGRAMME

First Match; 3-2 v. Burnley (10,000) (September 2nd, 1893)
Last Match; 5-0 v. Tottenham Hotspur (7,000) (January 22nd, 1910)
Highest Gate; 50,000 v. Newcastle United (1-1) (February 8th, 1908)
Lowest Gate; 500 v. Burton United (3-1) (April 21st, 1902)
Highest Home Win; 9-0 v. Walsall Town Swifts (6,000) (April 3rd, 1895) & v. Darwen (2,000) (December 24th, 1898)
Highest Home Defeat; 2-6 v. Derby County (7,000) (March 17th, 1894) & v. Nottingham Forest (12,000) (November 27th, 1909)

TEST MATCHES
2-0 v. Burnley (7,000) (April 21st, 1897)
1-1 v. Sunderland (18,000) (April 24th, 1897)

No. of Matches Played by Manchester United; 283
(League Programme; 281, Test Matches; 2)
Some Information Kindly Supplied by; Tony Matthews & John Russell

The club moved here from *North Road* in 1893 and changed the club name to *Manchester United* in 1902. The club was also involved in Test Matches at the neutral venues of *Ewood Park* and the *Cobridge Athletic Grounds* and moved to *Old Trafford* in 1910.

A TOTAL OF **51** TEAMS TOOK PART IN **283** LEAGUE FIXTURES AT THIS VENUE

BARLEY BANK
HOME GROUND OF **DARWEN**

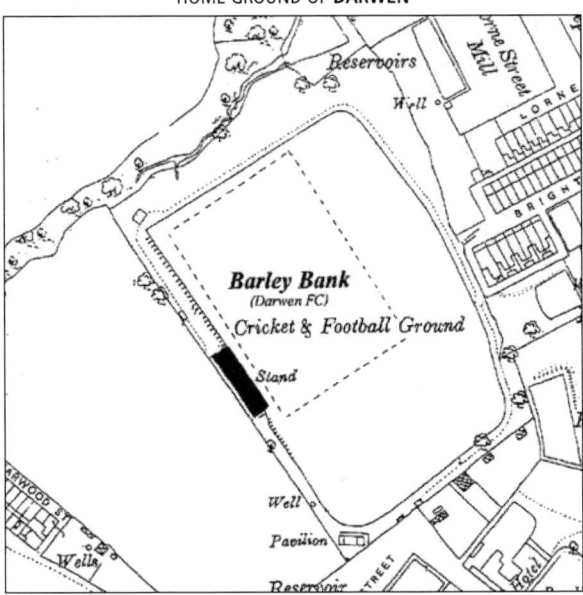

MAP EXTRACT; LANCASHIRE 60.12 [**1894**]
SITE LOCATION; **SD68522294**

The home ground of *Darwen CC*, the football pitch was laid out at the north west end and the sparse spectator facilities included a covered stand, seating 1,200, and raised banking on the west side. A temporary stand was erected on the east side, for use during the football season, and dressing tents installed at the south east end of the pitch.

The record attendance of 14,000 was set at a friendly match v. *Blackburn Rovers* on March 18th, 1882 and, following the end of their Football League career, in 1899, *Darwen FC* moved to the *Anchor Ground*, taking the main stand with them. *Barley Bank* was subsequently utilized for housing.

PLAYING RECORD OF DARWEN
LEAGUE PROGRAMME

First Match; 1-2 v. Bolton Wanderers (7,000) (September 5th, 1891)
Last Match; 1-1 v. Newton Heath (1,000) (April 22nd, 1899)
Highest Gate; 8,000 v. Preston North End (0-4) (January 1st, 1892)
Lowest Gate; 200 v. New Brighton Tower (2-4) (December 31st, 1898)*
Highest Home Win; 12-0 v. Walsall (2,000) (December 26th, 1896)
Highest Home Defeat; 1-7 v. Sunderland (4,000) (April 23rd, 1892)

No. of Matches Played by Darwen; 116
Some Information Kindly Supplied by; Brian Tabner

The club was elected into the Football League in 1891 and failed to gain re-election in 1899. The match v. *Loughborough* (1-1) on February 22nd, 1896 (300) was played on the cricket ground due to the football pitch being in an unplayable condition. The club was also involved in Test Matches at the neutral venues of *Hyde Road* and the *Victoria Ground*.

*NB. Some record books show an attendance of 800 for this fixture

A TOTAL OF **42** TEAMS TOOK PART IN **116** LEAGUE FIXTURES AT THIS VENUE

THE BASEBALL GROUND
HOME GROUND OF DERBY COUNTY

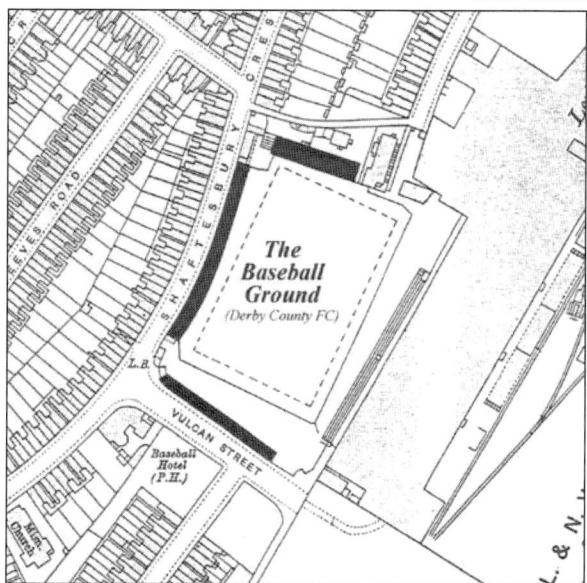

MAP EXTRACT; DERBYSHIRE 55.1 [1914]
SITE LOCATION; **SK35833426**

Mr Francis Ley, owner of the adjacent foundry, developed the site as a sports ground for his workforce in the 1880s and, following a trip to the USA in 1889, adapted the venue to accommodate baseball. *Derby County FC* first used the ground in 1892 and when they moved in from the *Racecourse Ground* on a permanent basis in 1895, the pitch was enlarged and a stand brought from their previous ground and re-erected, probably on the north side. Football and baseball shared the facilities (including dressing rooms in the north east corner and a terrace on the east side) for a few years and by 1914 stands had been constructed on the west side and at the south end. The club purchased the ground for £10,000 in 1924 and in the years leading up to WWII constructed a new 3,300 seat main stand on the west side, double deck seated stands at each end and a cover over the east side.

Post war improvements included the installation of seats in the main stand paddock and on the terraces at each end and the construction of an all-seat stand on stilts on the east side. The terracing on the east side was subsequently installed with seating giving an all seat capacity in 1996 of 17,451.

Derby County FC moved to **Pride Park** in 1997 and *The Baseball Ground* was used for youth team and occasional reserve fixtures until 2004 when the site was demolished and replaced with housing

PLAYING RECORD OF DERBY COUNTY
LEAGUE PROGRAMME

Matches Played Prior to Tenancy; 0-1 v. Sunderland (6,000) (March 19th, 1892)
1-0 v. Burnley (5,000) (November 12th, 1892)
First Match (of Tenancy); 2-0 v. Sunderland (10,000) (September 14th, 1895)
Last Match; 1-3 v. Arsenal (18,287) (May 11th, 1997)
Highest Gate; 41,826 v. Tottenham Hotspur (5-0) (September 20th, 1969)
Lowest Gate; 500 v. Grimsby Town (2-2) (April 22nd, 1903)
Highest Home Win; 9-0 v. The Wednesday (5,000) (January 21st, 1899)
Highest Home Defeat; 1-7 v. Manchester City (13,625) (January 29th, 1938), v. Middlesbrough (19,537) (August 29th, 1959) & v. Liverpool (20,531) (March 23rd, 1991)

PLAY OFF MATCHES
2-1 v. Blackburn Rovers (22,920) (May 13th, 1992)
2-0 v. Millwall (17,401) (May 15th, 1994)

No. of Matches Played by Derby County; 1,860
(League Programme; 1,858, Play Off Matches; 2)

The club moved here permanently from *The Racecourse Ground* in 1895. The match v. *Fulham* on April 21st, 1984 was abandoned after 88 minutes, but the 1-0 result was allowed to stand. The club was also involved in a Football League Play Off Match at the neutral venue of **Wembley Stadium**. *Derby County FC* moved to **Pride Park** for the start of the 1997/98 season.

A TOTAL OF **95** TEAMS TOOK PART IN **1,860** LEAGUE FIXTURES AT THIS VENUE

The *Baseball Ground* being demolished in 2003, with the stand at the north end still almost intact but just a bit of the back wall of the main stand remaining on the west side
Photograph by Phil Morris, Courtesy of Groundtastic Magazine

BELLE VUE
HOME GROUND OF DONCASTER ROVERS

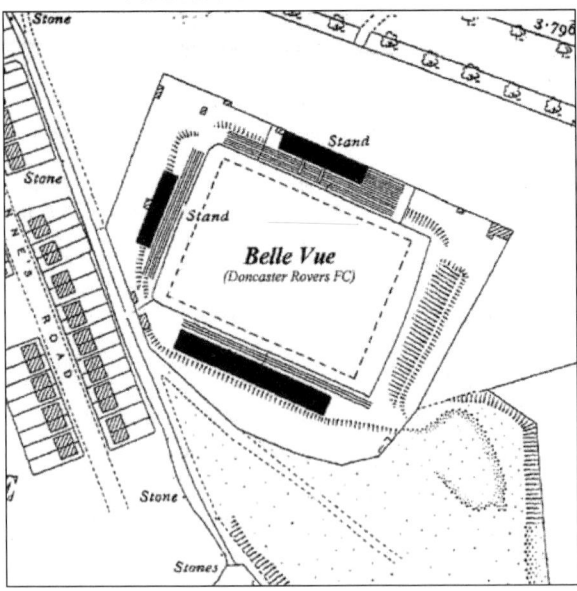

MAP EXTRACT; YORKSHIRE 285.2 [1930]
SITE LOCATION; SE59480262

Located at the south end of Doncaster Racecourse, *Belle Vue* opened in 1922 when *Doncaster Rovers FC* moved here from *Bennetthorpe*. The banking around the ground and foundation for the pitch were formed from ash which had been transported from local coal tips and the facilities included a new stand (later extended), along the north side, and the 700 seat stand removed from *Bennetthorpe* (and, previously, the *Intake Ground*) and re-erected at the west end. Subsequently, the Popular Side, opposite the main stand, was expanded and covered in 1938 but in the 1980s both this cover and the North Stand had to be demolished for safety reasons. A large section of the east end was also removed to accommodate a ball court and, following mining subsidence, the south or Popular side was re-modelled in 1989 and a replacement cover installed. The main stand was seriously damaged, although not destroyed, by an arson attack in 1995.

The main claim to fame of *Belle Vue* was that at 118 x 77 yards the pitch was the largest in the Football League, but this was latterly reduced in size. At the start of the 2004/5 season, the capacity was 9,706 with 1,259 seats.

PLAYING RECORD OF DONCASTER ROVERS
LEAGUE PROGRAMME

First Match; 0-0 v. Wigan Borough (10,923) (August 25th, 1923)
Highest Gate; 37,099 v. Hull City (0-0) (October 2nd, 1948)
Lowest Gate; 739 v. Barnet (0-2) (March 3rd, 1998)
Highest Home Win; 10-0 v. Darlington (6,150) (January 25th, 1964)
Highest Home Defeat; 1-6 v. Fulham (15,189) (March 15th, 1958)
No. of Matches Played by Doncaster Rovers; 1,547
(Including expunged matches v. Accrington Stanley on February 27th, 1962 & v. Aldershot on February 15th, 1992)
Information Kindly Supplied by; Tony Bluff

The club moved here from *Bennetthorpe* in 1922, was elected into the Football League Division 3 [N] in 1923, relegated to the Football Conference in 1998 and promoted back into Division 3 via the Play Offs in 2003.

AT THE END OF SEASON 2004/5, A TOTAL OF **111** TEAMS HAD TAKEN PART IN **1,547** LEAGUE FIXTURES AT THIS VENUE

BESCOT STADIUM
HOME GROUND OF WALSALL

MAP EXTRACT; GROUND AS IN **1999** DRAWN FROM AERIAL PHOTOGRAPHS AND SUPERIMPOSED ON SP0096 [1950]
SITE LOCATION; **SP00739636**

Constructed on the site of the Brockhurst Sewage Farm, *Walsall FC* moved to *Bescot Stadium* from *Fellows Park* in 1990. When originally built the ground had a continuous propped roof covering seated stands on each side of the pitch and terracing at each end. In 1992 the south end was converted to a seated stand and in 2002 it was subsequently rebuilt with two tiers of seats and a cantilever roof.

In 2002 a 2,300 seat second tier was added to the stand at the north end giving an all seater capacity of 11,300 by the commencement of the 2004/5 season. The pitch size was 110 x 73 yards.

PLAYING RECORD OF WALSALL
LEAGUE PROGRAMME

First Match; 2-2 v. Torquay United (5,219) (August 25th, 1990)
Highest Gate; 11,049 v. Rotherham United (3-2) (May 9th, 2004)
Lowest Gate; 2,399 v. Northampton Town (1-2) (January 28th, 1992)
Highest Home Win; 5-1 v. Fulham (3,378) (September 17th, 1994), v. Notts County (5,211) (September 30th, 2000), v. Swansea City (5,227) (January 20th, 2001) & v. Wycombe Wanderers (4,530) (March 24th, 2001)
Highest Home Defeat; 1-6 v. Coventry City (8,264) (January 17th, 2004)

PLAY OFF MATCHES
2-4 v. Crewe Alexandra (7,398) (May 19th, 1993)
4-2 v. Stoke City (8,993) (May 16th, 2001)
No. of Matches Played by Walsall; 340
(League Programme; 348 [Including one expunged match v. Aldershot on October 26th, 1991], Play Off Matches; 2)
Information Kindly Supplied by; Tony Matthews

The club moved here from *Fellows Park* in 1990 and was also involved in a Football League Play Off Match at the neutral venue of the *Millennium Stadium.*

AT THE END OF SEASON 2004/5, A TOTAL OF **84** TEAMS HAD TAKEN PART IN **340** LEAGUE FIXTURES AT THIS VENUE

BLOOMFIELD ROAD
HOME GROUND OF BLACKPOOL

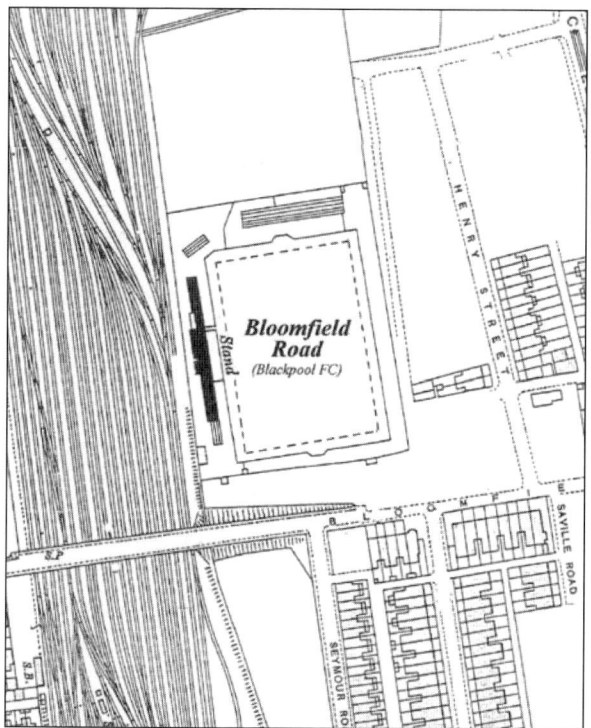

MAP EXTRACT; LANCASHIRE 50.16 [1912]
SITE LOCATION; SD30983476

PLAYING RECORD OF BLACKPOOL
LEAGUE PROGRAMME

First Match; 1-1 v. Gainsborough Trinity (2,000) (September 8th, 1900)
Highest Gate; 38,098 v. Wolverhampton Wanderers (2-1) (September 17th, 1955)
Lowest Gate; 1,634 v. Doncaster Rovers (1-1) (April 28th, 1986)
Highest Home Wins; 7-0 v. Reading (6,638) (November 7th, 1928) & v. Sunderland (33,172) (October 5th, 1957).
Highest Home Defeat; 0-6 v. Manchester United (23,966) (February 27th, 1960)

PLAY OFF MATCHES
2-1 v. Scunthorpe United (7,596) (May 22nd, 1991)
2-0 v. Barnet (7,588) (May 13th, 1992)
0-3 v. Bradford City (9,593) (May 15th, 1996)
2-0 v. Hartlepool United (5,720) (May 13th, 2001)

No. of Matches Played by Blackpool; 1,993
(League Programme; 1,989 [Including one expunged match v. Aldershot on March 10th, 1992], Play Off Matches; 4)
Information Kindly Supplied by; Roger Harrison

The club moved here from *Raikes Hall* in 1899 and it was elected back into the Football League Division 2 in 1900. The first Football League match to be televised live took place here on September 9th, 1960 when *Blackpool* drew 1-1 with *Bolton Wanderers*. The club was also involved in Football League Play Off Matches at the neutral venues of *Wembley Stadium* and the *Millennium Stadium*.

AT THE END OF SEASON 2004/5, A TOTAL OF **109** TEAMS HAD TAKEN PART IN **1,993** LEAGUE FIXTURES AT THIS VENUE

South Shore FC moved to *Bloomfield Road* from *Cow Gap Lane* in 1899 and the first game played at the new ground was against the *1st South Lancashire Regiment* on October 21st, 1899. At the time of the first match, the grandstand had not been built nor was there an enclosure to the pitch but a small stand was later removed from *Cow Gap Lane* and re-erected at the new venue in the north west corner. In the same year, *Blackpool FC* amalgamated with *South Shore FC* and moved here from *Raikes Hall*.

A stand was constructed along the west side in 1900 and, by 1912, an open stand was also in place behind the north end. In 1925, the South Stand and a small stand linking the south and west sides were completed and, by WWII, a large bank (which was roofed in the immediate post-war years) had been constructed at the north end and the east side covered.

In the 1970s the roof over the north end was deemed unsafe and demolished and eventually only half of this end was available for spectators. In 2001 the west and north sides were demolished and a new 7,700 seat stand with a continuous cantilever roof constructed as the first phase in the planned redevelopment of the ground as a 16,000 seat stadium. The remaining old stands were demolished in 2003 and a temporary 1,700 seat open stand constructed on the east side giving an all seat capacity of 11,295 at the start of the 2004/5 season. The pitch size was 112 x 74 yards.

PROGRAMME COVER ON THE RIGHT
From the days when small town clubs could still compete successfully in the top flight - this match ended in a 2-1 win for the hosts.
Programme Courtesy of John Litster

BLUNDELL PARK
HOME GROUND OF GRIMSBY TOWN

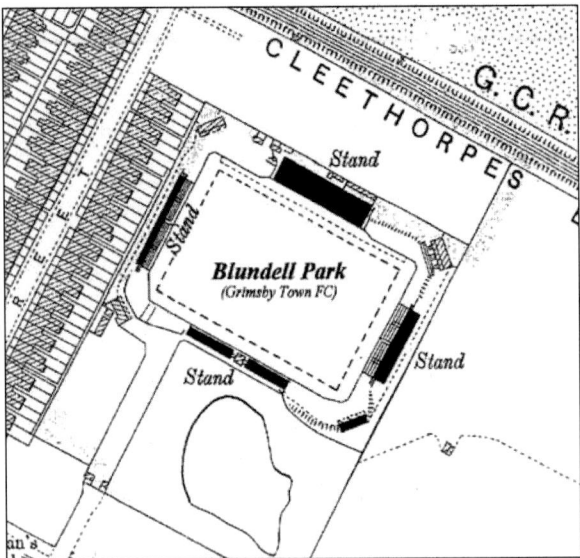

MAP EXTRACT; LINCOLNSHIRE 22.8 [1908]
SITE LOCATION; **TA29470995**

Located in Cleethorpes, the ground was opened at the start of the 1899/1900 season on September 2nd. *Grimsby Town FC* had moved here from *Abbey Park* and brought with them all the fixtures and fittings plus the two stands, one of which was re-sited at the east end of the pitch and the other on the south side. The facilities also included a cover which was installed at the west end but players had to change at the nearby Imperial Hotel. Subsequent improvements included a new main stand, erected on the north side in 1901 and extended to the east corner in the 1920s, replacement of the original stand on the south side with a new cover and wooden terracing and a replacement 700 seat stand at the east end. Prior to WWII a record attendance of 31,637 witnessed the 5th Round FA Cup match against *Wolverhampton Wanderers FC* (1-1) on February 20th, 1937.

In 1982 the south stand was replaced once again, this time with a two tier 2,400 seat structure stretching for about half of the pitch length and later modernization included the installation of seats throughout the stadium. At the start of the 2004/5 season the all-seated capacity was 10,033 with an 111 x 74 yards sized pitch.

PLAYING RECORD OF GRIMSBY TOWN
LEAGUE PROGRAMME

First Match; 3-3 v. Luton Town (4,000) (September 2nd, 1899)
Highest Gate; 26,288 v. Arsenal (2-2) (November 10th, 1934)
Lowest Gate; 1,833 v. Brentford (0-2) (May 3rd, 1969)
Highest Home Win; 8-0 v. Tranmere Rovers (7,109) (September 14th, 1925)
Highest Home Defeat; 4-7 v. Middlesbrough (10,288) (February 8th, 1927). 0-6 v. West Bromwich Albion (12,242) (January 7th, 1928)

PLAY OFF MATCHES
1-0 v. Fulham (8,689) (May 13th, 1998)

No. of Matches Played by Grimsby Town; 2,015
(League Programme; 2,014, Play Off Matches; 1)

The club moved here from *Abbey Park* in 1899, failed to gain re-election in 1910 and was elected into Division 2 in 1911. The club was also involved in a Football League Play Off Match at the neutral venue of *Wembley Stadium.*

AT THE END OF SEASON 2004/5, A TOTAL OF **122** TEAMS HAD TAKEN PART IN **2,015** LEAGUE FIXTURES AT THIS VENUE

BOOTHAM CRESCENT
HOME GROUND OF YORK CITY
LATER KNOWN AS KITKAT CRESCENT

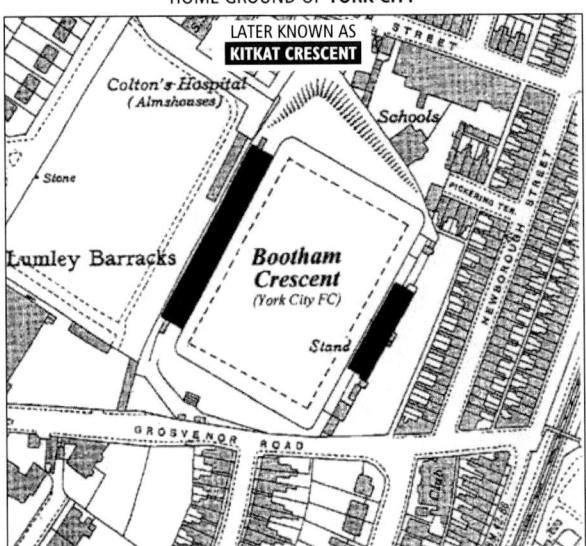

MAP EXTRACT; YORKSHIRE 174.6 [1937]
SITE LOCATION; **SE59915297**

The ground had been used by *Yorkshire CCC* for some years before *York City* moved here from *Fulfordgate* in 1932. By the time the first football match was played in August, a main stand had been constructed on the east side, terraces constructed and the west side covered with roofing removed from the former ground. The record attendance of 28,123 was subsequently established at the FA Cup Round 6th Round tie v. *Huddersfield Town* (0-0) on March 5th, 1938.

Post war improvements saw concreting of the terraces and an extension to the main stand before seating was installed on the west side in 1974. Further alterations in the 1990s, erection of a cover over the north end and further extensions to the main stand (including the provision of cover over the main stand paddock) by the end of the 2002/3 season gave the ground a capacity of 9,034 with 3,509 seats. The pitch size was 115 x 75 yards. The lease on the ground expired in 2003 but the club was allowed to remain at *Bootham Crescent* rent-free for 2003/4 season until the tenancy was secured. In 2005 the ground was re-named as *KitKat Crescent* in a 2-year sponsorship deal

PLAYING RECORD OF YORK CITY
LEAGUE PROGRAMME

First Match; 2-2 v. Stockport County (8,106) (August 31st, 1932)
Last Match; 1-2 v. Leyton Orient (3,462) (May 1st, 2004)
Highest Gate; 21,010 v. Hull City (1-3) (April 23rd, 1949)
Lowest Gate; 1,167 v. Northampton Town (1-2) (May 5th, 1981)
Highest Home Win; 9-1 v. Southport (8,801) (February 2nd, 1957)
Highest Home Defeat; 0-7 v. Rochdale (3,826) (January 14th, 1939)

PLAY OFF MATCHES
1-0 v. Bury (9,206) (May 19th, 1993)
0-0 v. Stockport County (8,744) (May 15th, 1994)

No. of Matches Played by York City; 1,471
(League Programme; 1,469 [Including expunged matches v. Accrington Stanley on November 18th, 1961 & v. Aldershot on November 23rd, 1991], Play Off Matches; 2)

The club moved here from *Fulfordgate* in 1932 and was also involved in a Football League Play Off Match at the neutral venue of *Wembley Stadium.* The club was relegated to the Football Conference at the end of the 2003/4 season.

A TOTAL OF **100** TEAMS TOOK PART IN **1,471** LEAGUE FIXTURES AT THIS VENUE

BOOTHFERRY PARK

HOME GROUND OF **HULL CITY**
TEMPORARY HOME GROUND FOR **LEEDS UNITED**

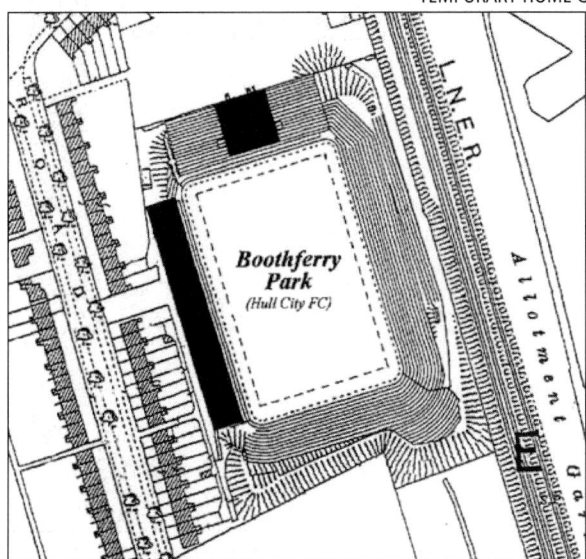

MAP EXTRACT; GROUND AS IN **1951** DRAWN FROM PLANS AND SUPERIMPOSED ON YORKSHIRE 240.1 [1928]
SITE LOCATION; **TA06302832**

Hull City FC bought the site, a former golf course, in 1930, but very little progress was made in constructing the ground before the outbreak of WWII when it was utilized by the Home Guard and for tank repairs. Post war shortages delayed the opening until August 1946 when the facilities were composed of a seated stand on the west side, terracing around the pitch and a temporary cover over the north end.

The record gate of 55,019 was established at the FA Cup 6th Round tie v. *Manchester United* (0-1) on February 26th, 1949 and the ground saw gradual improvement in the 1950s with the installation of a covered stand (with seats and standing accommodation) at the north end and a cover over the terraces on the east side, whilst Boothferry Park Halt, the ground's own railway station opened on January 6th, 1951. Further improvements followed in 1965 with the construction of a new seated stand at the south end.

Looking north from the south east corner with the covered terracing on the right and the supermarket and resultant very narrow terracing visible behind the north end. The entrance to the Railway Station was on the right
Photograph by Paul Claydon, Courtesy of Groundtastic Magazine

In 1982 the north end of the site was sold for the construction of a supermarket (involving the demolition of the north stand and reduction of the terracing to a few uncovered steps). The pitch size was 115 x 74 yards and capacity by the end of season 2001/2 was 15,160 with 5,262 seats. After the ground was vacated at the end of 2002 it remained standing until 2005 when the site was sold for redevelopment.

PLAYING RECORD OF HULL CITY
LEAGUE PROGRAMME

First Match; 0-0 v. Lincoln City (25,586) (August 31st, 1946)
Last Match; 0-1 v. Darlington (14,162) (December 14th, 2002)
Highest Gate; 50,103 v. Sheffield Wednesday (1-1) (February 4th, 1950)
Lowest Gate; 1,775 v. Torquay United (2-0) (November 20th, 1996)
Highest Home Win; 9-0 v. Oldham Athletic (11,007) (April 5th, 1958)
Highest Home Defeat; 0-5 v. Lincoln City (17,170) (October 10th, 1959)

PLAY OFF MATCHES
1-0 v. Leyton Orient (13,310) (May 13th, 2001)

No. of Matches Played by Hull City; 1,249
(League Programme; 1,248, Play Off Matches; 1)
Some Information Kindly Supplied by; Brian Tabner

The club moved here from *Anlaby Road* in 1946 and moved to **Kingston Communications Stadium** in 2002.

PLAYING RECORD OF LEEDS UNITED
LEAGUE PROGRAMME

Match Played; 1-1 v. Tottenham Hotspur (25,099) (August 25th, 1971)

No. of Matches Played by Leeds United; 1
Information Kindly Supplied by; Stan Briggs

This match took place here when *Leeds United* was ordered to play the first four fixtures of the 1971/2 season away from **Elland Road** following crowd disturbances during the game v. *West Bromwich Albion* (1-2) on April 17th, 1971.

A TOTAL OF **105** TEAMS TOOK PART IN **1,250** LEAGUE FIXTURES AT THIS VENUE

BOROUGH PARK
HOME GROUND OF WORKINGTON

MAP EXTRACT; GROUND AS IN **1961** DRAWN FROM PLANS AND SUPERIMPOSED ON CUMBERLAND 53.2 [1925]
SITE LOCATION; **NY00012928**

PLAYING RECORD OF WORKINGTON
LEAGUE PROGRAMME
First Match; 3-1 v. Chesterfield (11,000) (August 22nd, 1951)
Last Match; 0-1 v. Newport County (1,285) (May 14th, 1977)
Highest Gate; 18,628 v. Carlisle United (2-2) (December 26th, 1963)
Lowest Gate; 693 v. Exeter City (3-1) (December 15th, 1973)
Highest Home Win; 7-0 v. Swansea Town (4,206) (October 4th, 1965)
Highest Home Defeat; 1-7 v. Barnsley (1,057) (April 7th, 1976)
No. of Matches Played by Workington; 597
Information Kindly Supplied by; Steve Durham

The club was elected into the Football League Division 3 [N] in 1951 and failed to gain re-election in 1977

A TOTAL OF **62** TEAMS TOOK PART IN **597** LEAGUE FIXTURES AT THIS VENUE

The ground, built with assistance from the local council, opened in 1937 and the facilities included a 1,000 seat main stand on the west side and ash banking around the ground. *Workington FC* moved here from the adjacent *Lonsdale Park* and by the time that it entered the Football League in 1951 terracing had been installed and L-shaped covers erected in the north west and south west corners. The main stand was subsequently extended and, in 1956, a cover built on the east side.

The record attendance of 21,000 was established at the FA Cup 3rd Round tie v. *Manchester United* (1-3) on January 4th, 1958 and the venue, minus the original main stand which was closed and partially demolished in 1988, is still in use as the home ground for *Workington FC*.

The main stand in 1978. The roof was removed in 1988, by 1992 all the seats had been removed and just the rooms under the stand were still in use for *Workington FCs* home games in 2005
Photograph by Bob Lilliman. Courtesy of Groundtastic Magazine

The photograph on this programme cover features the *Reds* netting their goal, a John Ogilive effort at the south end of the ground, during the match v. *Rochdale* on December 26th, 1968. The game ended in a 2-1 win for the visitors and the *Workington* players in view are Brian Tinnion [10] and Tommy Spencer on the right. The cover installed over a section of the terracing on the east side can be seen as well as the unusually basic style of picket fence surrounding the perimeter. This match v. *Reading* finished in a 0-0 draw.

BOULEVARD GROUND
TEMPORARY HOME GROUND FOR **HULL CITY**

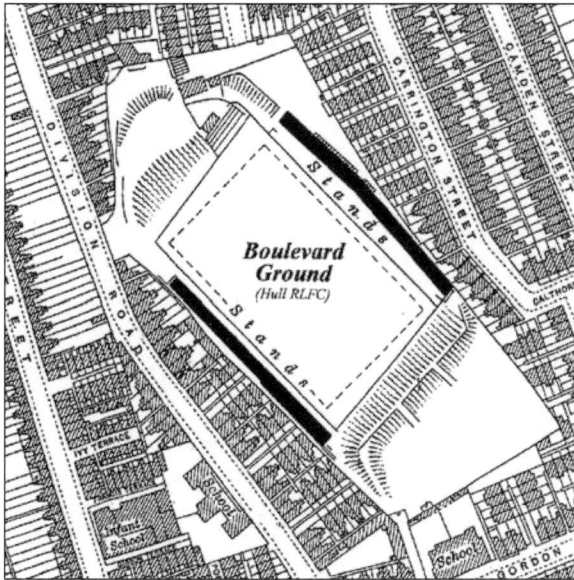

MAP EXTRACT; YORKSHIRE 240.2 [**1928**]
SITE LOCATION; **TA07662824**

Originally known as the *Hull Athletic Ground*, this Rugby League venue originally consisted of a covered grandstand on the north east side of an elongated oval arena. By the time that *Hull City FC* played their games here, a cycle track had been added, open seating installed at the north west end and alongside the grandstand and a covering built over the standing area on the south west side. The venue remained in use as the home ground for *Hull RLFC* until September 20th, 2002 when the final match, v. *Bradford Bulls*, was played here prior to the club moving to the **Kingston Communications Stadium** to groundshare with *Hull City FC*. The *Boulevard Ground* was retained by Kingston upon Hull City Council for junior and youth RFL matches and, during 2003 it was also proposed to stage greyhound racing here.

PLAYING RECORD OF HULL CITY
LEAGUE PROGRAMME

Matches Played; 0-1 v. Manchester United (10,000)
(October 28th, 1905)
3-1 v. Clapton Orient (3,000) (January 6th, 1906)
1-2 v. Glossop (7,000) (March 10th, 1906)
5-0 v. Glossop (7,000) (February 9th, 1907)
No. of Matches Played by Hull City; 4

Hull City FC had hoped to use the *Boulevard Ground* of *Hull RLFC* as their home ground when they joined the Football League in 1905 but at the last moment the Rugby League authorities ordered that no paid admission could be taken at the ground for Association Football games and they had to utilize **The Circle**. Within a few months the Rugby League relented and the club was able to use the *Boulevard Ground* for occasional games, the first one being switched in anticipation of a larger gate.

A TOTAL OF **4** TEAMS TOOK PART IN **4** LEAGUE FIXTURES AT THIS VENUE

BOUNDARY PARK
HOME GROUND OF **OLDHAM ATHLETIC**

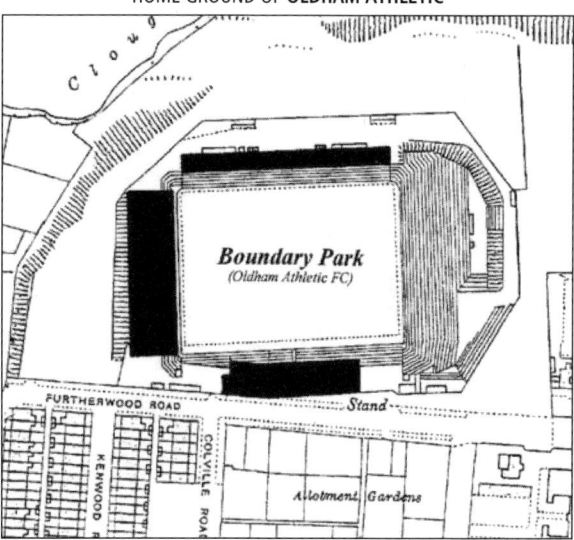

MAP EXTRACT; LANCASHIRE 97.1 [**1934**]
SITE LOCATION; **SD91590651**

Originally known as the *Athletic Ground* when opened in 1896 by *Oldham County FC* it was occupied by them until their demise in 1899. In the same year *Pine Villa FC* moved in from *Pine Mill*, changed the name of the club to *Oldham Athletic FC* but moved out to *Hudson Fold* after only a season. In the period before they returned to the ground in 1906 it was used by other clubs, principally *Werneth FC*.

By this time the ground possessed a main stand (replaced in 1913) on the south side and upon their election to the Football League one year later, another stand had been built on the north side of the pitch. Later improvements included the installation of a cover at the west end in 1928 and the record attendance of 47,671 was set at the FA Cup 4th Round tie v. *Sheffield Wednesday* (3-4) on January 25th, 1930.

Improvements in 1971 saw the replacement of the north stand with a covered seated stand fronted by an uncovered seated paddock, whilst in the 1990s the west end stand was refurbished and installed with seats and a new seated stand built at the east end giving an all-seated capacity of 13,624 at the start of season 2004/5. The pitch size was 110 x 74 yards.

PLAYING RECORD OF OLDHAM ATHLETIC
LEAGUE PROGRAMME

First Match; 2-1 v. West Bromwich Albion (17,000)
(September 14th, 1907)
Highest Gate; 45,120 v. Blackpool (1-2) (April 21st, 1930)
Lowest Gate; 2,264 v. Walsall (2-4) (April 12th, 1960)
Highest Home Win; 11-0 v. Southport (14,662)
(December 26th, 1962)
Highest Home Defeat; 1-7 v. Cardiff City (6,786)
(March 16th, 2002)
PLAY OFF MATCHES
2-1 v. Leeds United (19,216) (May 17th, 1987)
1-1 v. Queens Park Rangers (12,152) (May 10th, 2003)
No. of Matches Played by Oldham Athletic; 1,868
(League Programme; 1,867 [Including one expunged match v. Accrington Stanley on October 11th, 1961], Play Off Matches; 2)
The club was elected into the Football League Division 2 in 1907

AT THE END OF SEASON 2004/5, A TOTAL OF **108** TEAMS HAD TAKEN PART IN **1,868** LEAGUE FIXTURES AT THIS VENUE

BOWER FOLD
HOME GROUND OF STALYBRIDGE CELTIC

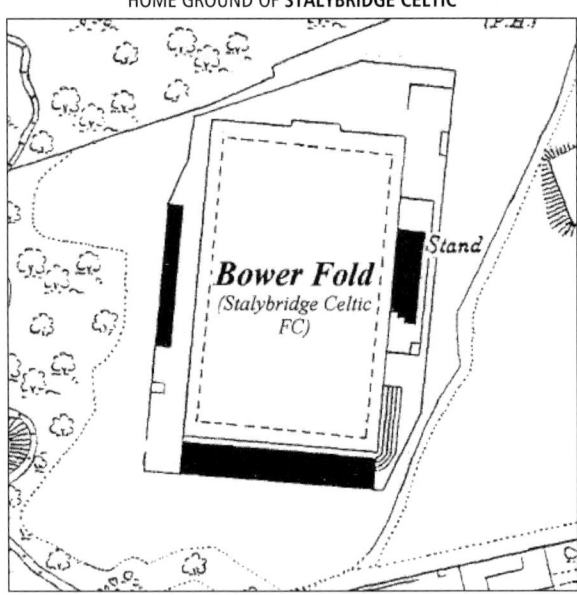

MAP EXTRACT; LANCASHIRE 105.12 [1933]
SITE LOCATION; **SJ97199763**

Located on the west side of Mottram Road, south east of the town centre, the ground was first used in 1906 with a 500 seat grandstand installed on the east side and banking constructed on the other three sides. Covered enclosures were subsequently constructed at the south end and on the west side.

Although the club record attendance is 9,753 for the FA Cup 1st Round Replay v. *West Bromwich Albion* (0-2) on January 17th, 1923 the actual ground record of 10,400 was set at the somewhat bizarre fixture of a charity match between the *Dick, Kerr's Ladies XI* and the *Rest of Lancashire* on February 8th, 1921! It is still in use as the home ground for *Stalybridge Celtic FC*.

PLAYING RECORD OF STALYBRIDGE CELTIC
LEAGUE PROGRAMME

First Match & Highest HomeWin; 6-0 v. Chesterfield (4,600)
(August 27th, 1921)
Last Match; 4-3 v. Halifax Town (3,000) (April 28th, 1923)
Highest Gate & Highest Home Defeat; 0-4 v. Stockport County
(7,475) (December 31st, 1921)
Lowest Gate; 2,000 v. Walsall (2-0) (April 14th, 1923)
No. of Matches Played by Stalybridge Celtic; 38

The club was a founder member of the Football League Division 3 [N] in 1921 and resigned in 1923.

A TOTAL OF 21 TEAMS TOOK PART IN 38 LEAGUE FIXTURES AT THIS VENUE

BOWLING GREEN GROUND
TEMPORARY HOME GROUND FOR GAINSBOROUGH TRINITY

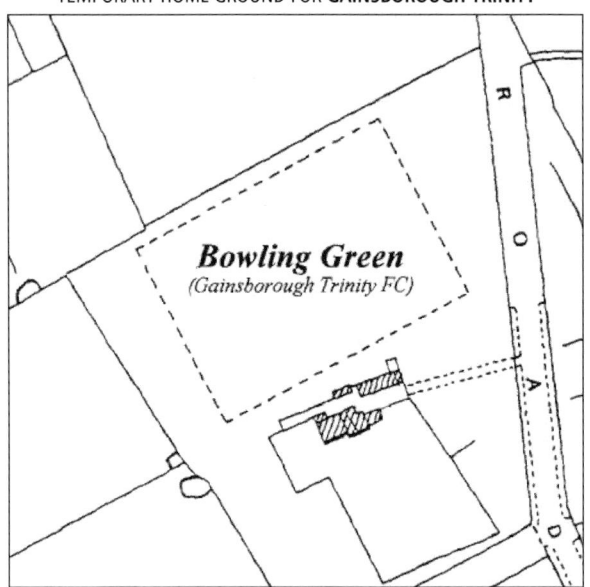

MAP EXTRACT; LINCOLNSHIRE 42.8 [1899]
SITE LOCATION; **SK80999036**

Located to the north west of the town centre and on the west side of Ropery Road, this temporary venue was probably sited on the north side of the Bowling Green. There was no enclosure and canvas sheeting, apparently borrowed from the local Agricultural Society, was erected around the ground with the teams presumably changing in the adjacent club house. Campbell Street and housing now occupy the site.

PLAYING RECORD OF GAINSBOROUGH TRINITY
LEAGUE PROGRAMME

Match Played; 3-0 v. Blackpool (-) (April 19th, 1902)
No. of Matches Played by Gainsborough Trinity; 1

This match was played here when *Northolme* was required for cricket. (NB. This may have happened on other occasions but these are not recorded)

A TOTAL OF 2 TEAMS TOOK PART IN 1 LEAGUE FIXTURE AT THIS VENUE

An aerial view of the original seated stand, dating from 1906, that remained at *Bower Field* until 1996.

Photograph Courtesy of Dave Twydell

BRAMALL LANE
HOME GROUND OF SHEFFIELD UNITED

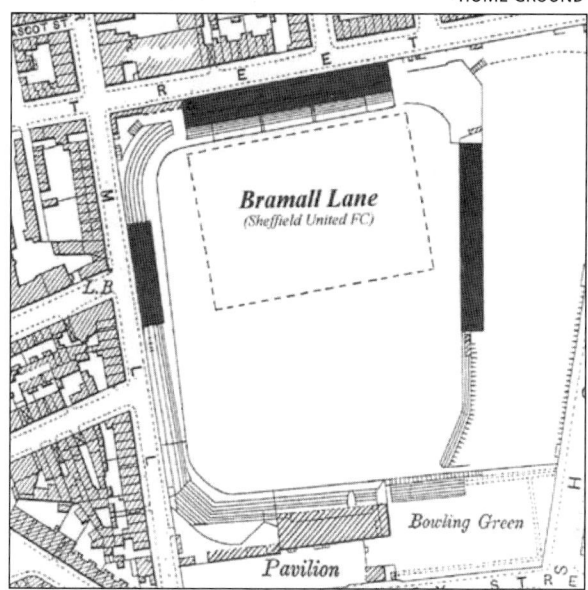

MAP EXTRACT; YORKSHIRE 294.12 [1905]
SITE LOCATION: **SK35308606**

The venue opened in 1854 initially as a cricket ground and became the headquarters for *Yorkshire CCC* in 1863. It rapidly became the focus of a number of sports in the area with cricket, bowls, lacrosse, tennis, cycling and athletics taking place as well as football which made its debut at the arena on December 29th, 1862 with a match between *Hallam* and *Sheffield FCs*.

The football-playing branch of *Wednesday CC* (one of the summer occupiers of the ground) used *Bramall Lane* on many occasions from 1868 and during the 1880s the facilities included a covered stand on the north side, terracing on the west side and a new pavilion on the south side. *Wednesday FC* moved to the **Olive Grove** in 1887 and with *Yorkshire CCC* moving their headquarters to *Headingley*, the Ground Committee quickly formed their own club, *Sheffield United FC*, to utilize the venue.

Two stands were constructed in the 1890s, a cover over the narrow terracing on the east side and a 2,000 seat replacement at the north end, the latter itself being replaced in 1902 by a 3,000 seat stand and paddock following a fire in 1900. Further developments in the early 1900s included the covering of the west end, linking up with the north stand, and, following the destruction of its roof in 1903, the enlargement and terracing of the east end. By this time all the covered accommodation was near the football pitch at the north end of the ground, whilst the southern end, which still accommodated standing spectators was uncovered and somewhat remote from the action.

Just prior to WWII the east end was roofed (only at the north end!) and the record attendance of 68,287 was set at the FA Cup 5th Round tie v. *Leeds United* (3-1) on February 15th, 1936. During hostilities the ground suffered bomb damage with the destruction of half of the north stand and the cover over the east end and, although the latter was re-roofed in 1948, it was not until 1954 that the north stand saw full restoration.

Although a new stand was constructed at the west end in 1966 it was in the 1970s that the greatest changes were undertaken when the cricket club was given notice to quit. The last County Championship match at *Bramall Lane* was played on August 7th, 1973 and within two years a new all seated south stand was constructed on the cricket square, finally enclosing the football pitch some 75 years after *Sheffield United* first took to the field.

Subsequent improvements include the installation of seats and re-roofing of the east end and a new 7,000 seat stand on the north side giving an all-seated capacity of 30,936 at the start of the 2004/5 season. The pitch size was 113 x 72 yards.

PLAYING RECORD OF SHEFFIELD UNITED
LEAGUE PROGRAMME

First Match; 4-2 v. Lincoln City (4,000) (September 3rd, 1892)
Highest Gate; 59,555 v. The Wednesday (2-0)
(January 15th, 1927)
Lowest Gate; 1,500 v. Bootle (8-3) (November 26th, 1892)
Highest Home Win; 11-2 v. Cardiff City (21,943) (January 1st, 1926.
10-0 v. Burnley (23,280) (January 19th, 1929)
Highest Home Defeat; 1-7 v. Huddersfield Town (22,163) (November 12th, 1927)

PLAY OFF MATCHES

1-1 v. Bristol City (19,066) (May 18th, 1988)
1-1 v. Ipswich Town (22,312) (May 10th, 1997)
2-1 v. Sunderland (23,800) (May 10th, 1998)
4-3 v. Nottingham Forest [aet] (30,212) (May 15th, 2003)

No. of Matches Played by Sheffield United; 2,094
(League Programme; 2,090, Play Off Matches; 4)

The club was a founder member of the Football League Division 2 in 1892. The club was also involved in a Test Match at the neutral venue of **The Castle Ground** and Football League Play Off Matches at the neutral venues of **Wembley Stadium** and the **Millennium Stadium**. The result was allowed to stand when the match v. *West Bromwich Albion* (0-3) on March 17th, 2002 was abandoned after 82 minutes due to the home side, with three sent off and others injured, not having enough players on the pitch.

AT THE END OF SEASON 2004/5, A TOTAL OF **98** TEAMS HAD TAKEN PART IN **2,094** LEAGUE FIXTURES AT THIS VENUE

Looking south from the north east corner of the ground after conversion to an all-seater stadium. The stand in view opened in 1975 and was constructed on the cricket square that hosted the 3rd Test Match of the 1902 Series between *England* and *Australia*. This was the only time that a Test Match was staged here and took place between July 3rd & 5th. The visitors won by 143 runs. [Sadly no changes there, then]
Photograph by Owen Pavey. Courtesy of Groundtastic Magazine

BRISBANE ROAD

HOME GROUND OF **LEYTON ORIENT**

MAP EXTRACT; LONDON 3.13 [**1914**]
SITE LOCATION; **TQ37858647**

Opened in 1905 by the local council as *Osborne Road*, the facilities included a 475 seat stand on the east side with embankments around the remainder of the pitch. *Leyton FC* became tenants in the same year and vacated the ground in 1914, following which it was used as the works ground for Bryant & May until their return in 1929. In 1937 the council declined to offer a new lease to *Leyton FC* and *Clapton Orient* moved in from **Lea Bridge Stadium** for the commencement of the 1937/8 season.

Following the end of WWII both the ground and the club were "re-branded" (*Brisbane Road* was now the home ground of *Leyton Orient FC*) and, in the next thirty years, improvements made to the stadium. The embankments were enlarged and concreted, the west side roofed and a new replacement stand, utilizing redundant steelwork from *Mitcham Greyhound Stadium*, constructed in two phases [in 1956 and 1962] on the east side. The record attendance of 34,345 was set at the FA Cup 4th Round tie v. *West Ham United* (1-1) on January 25th, 1964 and the west side was later re-terraced and installed with seats in 1977 whilst a new all seated stand was constructed at the south end in 2000.

In 2004 work commenced on the reconstruction of the stadium to include blocks of flats in each corner of the ground. The west stand and north terrace were totally demolished and the main stand on the east side truncated, temporarily reducing the ground's all-seat capacity to 4,800 at the commencement of the 2004/5 season. The pitch size was 115 x 80 yards.

PLAYING RECORD OF LEYTON ORIENT
LEAGUE PROGRAMME

First Match; 1-1 v. Cardiff City (14,598) (August 28th, 1937)
Highest Gate; 33,363 v. Birmingham City (0-1) (May 2nd, 1972)
Lowest Gate; 1,443 v. Halifax Town (1-0) (April 22nd, 1986)
Highest Home Win; 8-0 v. Crystal Palace (13,618) (November 12th, 1955), v. Rochdale (2,995) (October 20th, 1987),
v. Colchester United (3,412) (October 15th, 1988)
& v. Doncaster Rovers (4,437) (December 28th, 1997)
Highest Home Defeat; 2-7 v. Aldershot (8,797)
(February 25th, 1950)

PLAY OFF MATCHES

2-0 v. Scarborough (9,298) (May 21st, 1989)
2-1 v. Wrexham (13,355) (June 3rd, 1989)
0-0 v. Rotherham United (9,419) (May 16th, 1999)
2-0 v. Hull City (9,419) (May 16th, 2001)

No. of Matches Played by Leyton Orient; 1,353
(League Programme; 1,349, Play Off Matches; 4)
Information Kindly Supplied by; Paul Hiscock

The club moved here in 1937 and changed the name to *Leyton Orient* in 1946, to *Orient* in 1967 and back to *Leyton Orient* in 1987. The club was also involved in Football League Play Off Matches at the neutral venues of **Wembley Stadium** and the **Millennium Stadium.**

AT THE END OF SEASON 2004/5, A TOTAL OF **104** TEAMS HAD TAKEN PART IN **1,353** LEAGUE FIXTURES AT THIS VENUE

Brisbane Road under reconstruction in 2004. This view of the south east corner shows the south end of the main stand being demolished to make way for one of the four sets of flats.
Photograph by Vince Taylor. Courtesy of Groundtastic Magazine

BRITANNIA STADIUM
HOME GROUND OF **STOKE CITY**

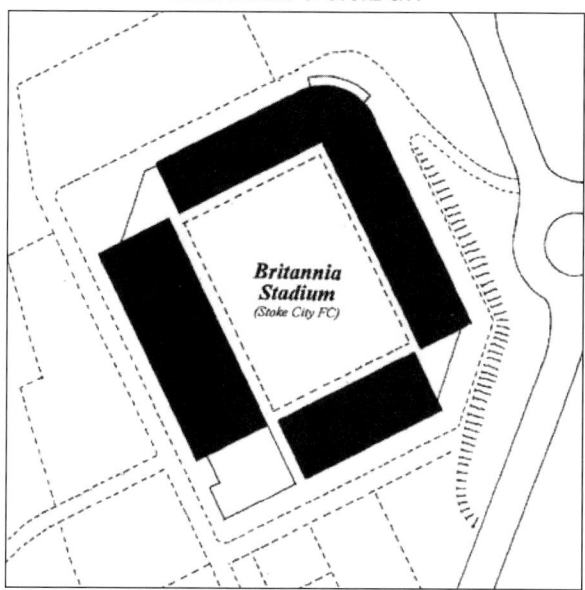

MAP EXTRACT; GROUND AS IN **1999** DRAWN FROM AERIAL PHOTOGRAPHS AND SUPERIMPOSED ON STAFFORDSHIRE 18.5 & 18.9 [1937]
SITE LOCATION; **SJ88334346**

Constructed on the site of Stafford Collieries and Ironworks, *Stoke City FC* moved to the *Britannia Stadium* from the *Victoria Ground* in 1997. The stadium consists of a cantilever roofed two-tier stand on the west side, a cantilever roofed stand at the south end and stands on the east side and north end with a continuous cantilevered roof giving an all-seat capacity of 28,383 at the start of the 2004/5 season. The pitch size was 115 x 75 yards.

PLAYING RECORD OF STOKE CITY
LEAGUE PROGRAMME

First Match; 1-2 v. Swindon Town (23,000) (August 30th, 1997)
Highest Gate; 28,000 v. Manchester City (2-5) (May 3rd, 1998)
Lowest Gate; 6,569 v. Wycombe Wanderers (2-2) (April 14th, 1999)
Highest Home Win; 5-0 v. Cambridge United (9,570) (February 6th, 2002)
Highest Home Defeat; 0-7 v. Birmingham City (14,940) (January 10th, 1998)

PLAY OFF MATCHES
3-2 v. Gillingham (22,124) (May 13th, 2000)
0-0 v. Walsall (23,689) (May 13th, 2001)
1-2 v. Cardiff City (21,245) (April 28th, 2002)

No. of Matches Played by Stoke City; 187
(League Programme; 184, Play Off Matches; 3)
Information Kindly Supplied by; Tony Matthews

The club moved here from *The Victoria Ground* in 1997 and it was also involved in a Football League Play Off Match at the neutral venue of the *Millennium Stadium*.

AT THE END OF SEASON 2004/5, A TOTAL OF **65** TEAMS HAD TAKEN PART IN **187** LEAGUE FIXTURES AT THIS VENUE

BRUNTON PARK
HOME GROUND OF **CARLISLE UNITED**

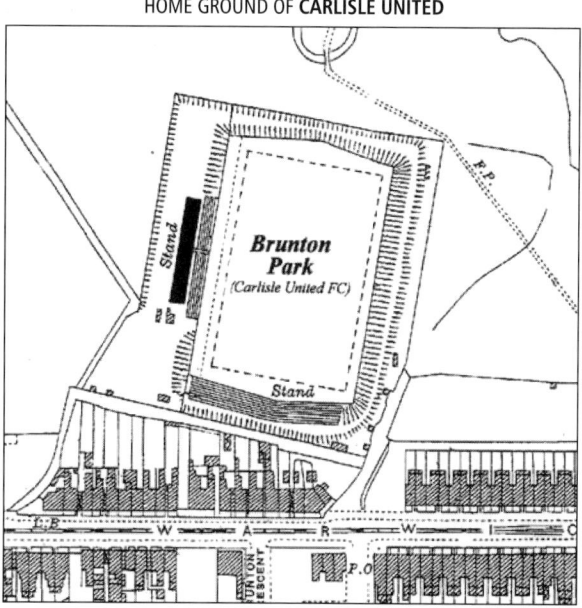

MAP EXTRACT; CUMBERLAND 23.4 [**1925**]
SITE LOCATION; **NY41505603**

Carlisle United FC, having moved from *Devonshire Park*, opened *Brunton Park* in September 1909. The facilities at that time consisting of a main stand and embankments, and by the early 1920s terracing had been constructed in front of the stand and at the south end. On their election to the Football League in 1928 the site was purchased for £2,000 and the ground further improved with an extension to the main stand and erection of a cover on the east side.

Following a fire in the previous year, a new main stand was built in 1954 (and extended in 1971) whilst further improvements included covering the south end in 1965 and the building of a new all seated stand on the east side in 1996. (Constructed so as to allow for the planned northwards expansion of the ground).

The record attendance of 27,603 was set at the FA Cup 5th Round tie v. *Middlesbrough* (1-2) on February 7th, 1970 and the capacity at the end of the 2003/4 season was 16,651 with 6,433 seats. The pitch size was 117 x 72 yards.

PLAYING RECORD OF CARLISLE UNITED
LEAGUE PROGRAMME

First Match; 2-2 v. Bradford City (11,771) (August 30th, 1928)
Highest Gate; 20,844 v. Liverpool (0-1) (October 5th, 1974)
Lowest Gate; 1,287 v. Chester City (0-2) (May 6th, 1987)
Highest Home Win; 8-0 v. Hartlepools United (7,346) (September 1st, 1928) & v. Scunthorpe & Lindsey United (9,518) (December 25th,1952)
Highest Home Defeat; 1-8 v. Rotherham United (14,639) (December 4th, 1948)

PLAY OFF MATCHES
0-2 v. Wycombe Wanderers (10,862) (May 15th, 1994)

No. of Matches Played by Carlisle United; 1,519
(League Programme; 1,518 [Including one expunged match v. Accrington Stanley on January 20th, 1962], Play Off Matches; 1)
Information Kindly Supplied by; David Steele

The club was elected into the Football League Division 3 [N] in 1928, relegated to the Football Conference in 2004 and promoted back via the Play Offs in 2005.

AT THE END OF SEASON 2004/5, A TOTAL OF **112** TEAMS HAD TAKEN PART IN **1,519** LEAGUE FIXTURES AT THIS VENUE

BURNDEN PARK
HOME GROUND OF BOLTON WANDERERS

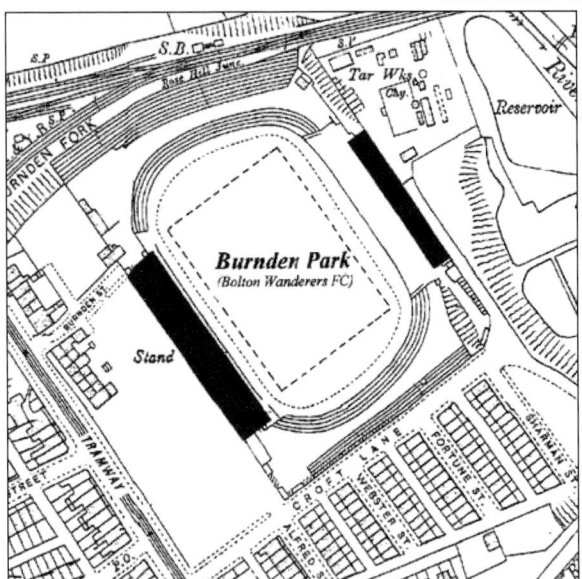

MAP EXTRACT; LANCASHIRE 87.13, 87.14, 95.1 & 95.2 [1908]
SITE LOCATION; **SD72510801**

Bolton Wanderers FC moved to *Burnden Park*, sited on industrial wasteland, from *Pikes Lane* in 1895 and opened it on August 15th with the town's 9th Annual Athletics Festival. The pitch was surrounded by an oval cycle track and the facilities included a 1,600 seat stand on the east side, a standing enclosure for 5,000 on the west and embankments around the remainder of the ground. Further improvements in 1905 included the removal of the cycle track and construction of a main stand on the west side whilst, one year later, the south end was terraced and covered.

The club bought the freehold to the ground in 1914, added an angled extension to the main stand in 1915 and replaced the stand on the east side with the 2,750 seat Burnden Stand in 1928. Following these alterations the record attendance of 69,912 was set at the FA Cup 5th Round tie v. *Manchester City* (2-4) on February 18th, 1933.

Immediately after the end of WWII a major disaster occurred at the ground during the FA Cup 6th Round, 2nd Leg with *Stoke City* (0-0) on March 9th, 1946 when hundreds broke into the packed ground at the north end, resulting in the death of 33 people and injuries to 400. Apart from modernizing the north end in the wake of this event, the only other alterations to the ground over the next forty years or so involved the installation of seats at the south end.

In 1986 part of the north end of the ground was sold to a food retail chain, resulting in the demolition of the west end of the terracing and construction of a supermarket, the back wall of which extended for over half of the pitch width. As an interim measure when *Bolton Wanderers FC* was promoted to the Premier League in 1995 a temporary 252 seat stand was squeezed in between the wall and the pitch.

The club moved to the *Reebok Stadium* in 1997 and the site is now totally occupied by the supermarket.

PLAYING RECORD OF BOLTON WANDERERS
LEAGUE PROGRAMME

First Match; 3-1 v. Everton (5,000) (September 14th, 1895)
Last Match; 4-1 v. Charlton Athletic (22,030) (April 25th, 1997)
Highest Gate; 55,477 v. Manchester United (1-0) (September 1st, 1951)
Lowest Gate; 2,902 v. Darlington (0-3) (November 5th, 1985)
Highest Home Win; 8-0 v. Barnsley (15,009) (October 6th, 1934)
Highest Home Defeat; 0-6 v. Manchester United (21,381) (February 25th, 1996)

PLAY OFF MATCHES

2-2 v. Aldershot [aet] (7,445) (May 17th, 1987)
1-1 v. Notts County (15,105) (May 13th, 1990)
1-0 v. Bury (19,198) (May 22nd, 1991).
2-0 v. Wolverhampton Wanderers (20,041) (May 17th, 1995)

No. of Matches Played by Bolton Wanderers; 1,878
(League Programme; 1,874, Play Off Matches; 4)
Information Kindly Supplied by; Simon Marland

The club moved here from *Pikes Lane* in 1895. A substitute player was used here in a Football League match for the first time ever when Keith Peacock of *Charlton Athletic* took the field in their 4-2 defeat against *Bolton Wanderers* on August 21st, 1965. The club was also involved in Football League Play Off Matches at the neutral venue of *Wembley Stadium.* The club moved to the *Reebok Stadium* in 1997.

A TOTAL OF **102** TEAMS TOOK PART IN **1,878** LEAGUE FIXTURES AT THIS VENUE

Looking north west with the main stand on the left and the incongruous supermarket at the north end. *Photograph Courtesy of Groundtastic*

CARROW ROAD
HOME GROUND OF NORWICH CITY

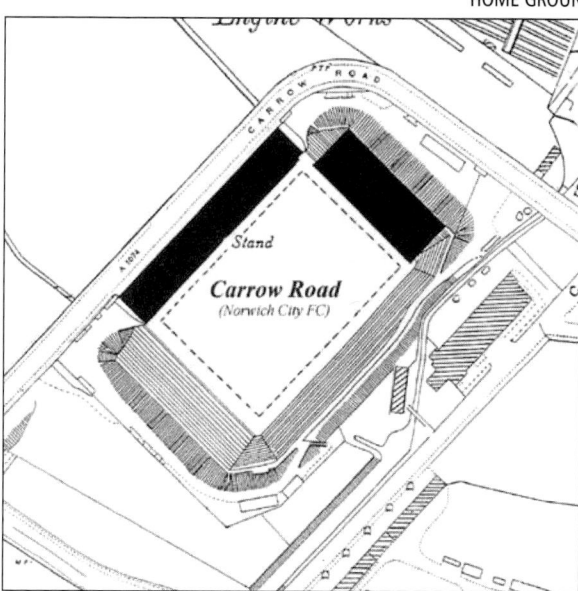

MAP EXTRACT; GROUND AS IN **1967** DRAWN FROM AERIAL PHOTOGRAPHS AND SUPERIMPOSED ON NORFOLK 63.15 [1928]
SITE LOCATION; **TG24080785**

The site was in use as a sports ground when *Norwich City* moved here from *The Nest* in 1935 and within less than three months *Carrow Road* had hosted its first Football League match and constructed a 3,500 seat main stand and paddock on the west side and embankments around the pitch. Further improvements carried out before the outbreak of WWII included the installation of a cover over the north end.

In 1959 a roof, which was subsequently linked to the one at the north end, was installed over the terraces on the east side. Confusingly called the South Stand (after Sir Arthur South rather than its disposition around the pitch) it was converted to an all-seater in 1975. The club purchased the freehold in 1971 and demolished the south end and replaced it with a new all seat stand in 1979.

A fire destroyed part of the main stand in 1984, necessitating the construction in 1985 of a replacement 3,100 seat stand, and further improvements in the 1990s included the installation of an all seat stand at the north end and corner extensions to the main stand. The record attendance of 43,984 was set at the FA Cup 6th Round tie v. *Leicester City* (0-2) on March 30th, 1963. At the end of the 2002/3 season the east side was demolished and an 8,000 seat structure constructed, whilst a 1,500 seat corner stand linking it to the one at the south end was installed in 2004/5. This gave an all seat capacity of 26,000 at the end of the 2004/5 season and the pitch size was 114 x 74 yards.

PLAYING RECORD OF NORWICH CITY
LEAGUE PROGRAMME
First Match; 4-3 v. West Ham United (29,779)
(August 31st, 1935)
Highest Gate; 37,863 v. Notts County (0-1) (April 28th, 1948)
Lowest Gate; 6,981 v. Walsall (3-2) (April 12th, 1956)
Highest Home Win; 8-0 v. Walsall (18,537)
(December 29th, 1951)
Highest Home Defeat; 1-6 v. Bournemouth & Boscombe Athletic
(23,404) (December 26th, 1946)
PLAY OFF MATCHES
3-1 v. Wolverhampton Wanderers (20,127) (April 28th, 2002)
No. of Matches Played by Norwich City; **1,351**
(League Programme; 1,350, Play Off Matches; 1)

The club moved here from *The Nest* in 1935 and it was also involved in a Football League Play Off Match at the neutral venue of the *Millennium Stadium.*

AT THE END OF SEASON 2004/5, A TOTAL OF **89** TEAMS HAD TAKEN PART IN **1,351** LEAGUE FIXTURES AT THIS VENUE

The newly-built stand on the east side in 2004.
Photograph by Paul Claydon. Courtesy of Groundtastic Magazine

CASSIO ROAD
HOME GROUND OF WATFORD

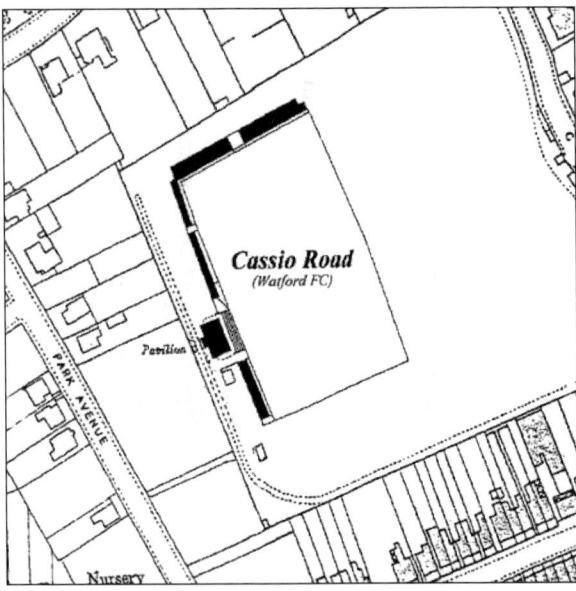

MAP EXTRACT; HERTFORDSHIRE 44.1 & 44.2 [**1914**]
SITE LOCATION; **TQ10429648**

Also known as the *West Herts. Sports Ground* the venue was utilized for cricket and athletics as well as accommodating a football pitch on the west side of the site. By the time that *Watford FC* joined the Football League in 1920 two sides had been well developed with a pavilion and covered standing areas on the west side and a covered enclosure at the north end with wooden duckboards being provided around the other two sides. *Watford FC* vacated the venue, which is still in use as a sports ground, in 1922 and moved to *Vicarage Road*.

PLAYING RECORD OF WATFORD
LEAGUE PROGRAMME

First Match; 0-2 v. Queens Park Rangers (10,466)
(September 4th, 1920)
Last Match; 1-0 v. Gillingham (5,000) (April 29th, 1922)
Highest Gate; 13,000 v. Luton Town (1-0) (March 25th, 1921)
Lowest Gate; 4,000 v. Swindon Town (2-2) (April 22nd, 1922)
Highest Home Win; 7-1 v. Northampton Town (7,000) (September 18th, 1920)
Highest Home Defeat; 0-3 v. Portsmouth (4,108)
(February 4th, 1922)
No. of Matches Played by Watford; 42

The club was a founder member of the Football League Division 3 in 1920 and moved to *Vicarage Road* in 1922.

A TOTAL OF **23** TEAMS TOOK PART IN **42** LEAGUE FIXTURES AT THIS VENUE

CASTLE GROUND
HOME GROUND OF NOTTS COUNTY

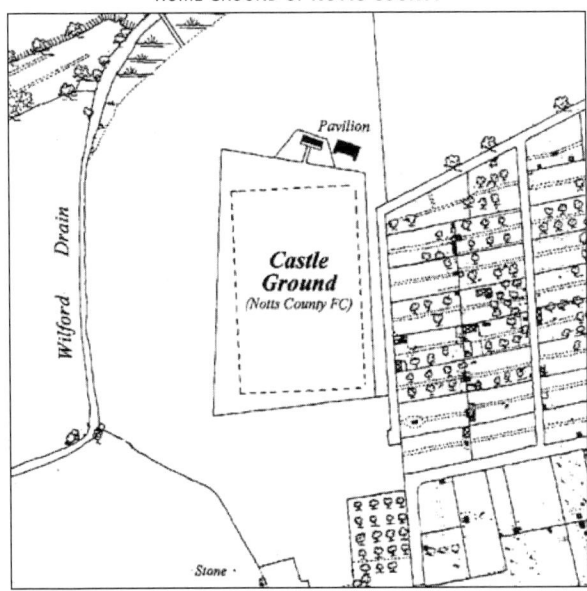

MAP EXTRACT; NOTTINGHAMSHIRE 42.6 [**1884**]
SITE LOCATION; **SK57333835**

Located to the south of the city centre and east of Queen's Drive, *Notts County FC* first played on the *Castle Ground* in 1880 but only used it intermittently for Football League matches after their move to *Trent Bridge*. The primary use of the venue was for cricket and had few facilities for players and spectators other than a pavilion at the north end of the ground.

In the 1890s, the area to the immediate west of the ground was acquired by the Great Central Railway for the line into Victoria Station and the site of Arkwright Street Engine Shed whilst the *Castle Ground* was utilized for housing.

PLAYING RECORD OF NOTTS COUNTY
LEAGUE PROGRAMME

Matches Played; 0-4 v. Bolton Wanderers (3,000)
(March 5th, 1889)
3-5 v. Derby County (5,000) (March 16th, 1889)
1-2 v. West Bromwich Albion (6,200) (September 21st, 1889)
3-1 v. Accrington (2,000) (March 13th, 1890)
0-1 v. Preston North End (7,500) (March 27th, 1890)
5-0 v. Accrington (4,000) (September 20th, 1890)
2-0 v. Preston North End (10,000) (September 5th, 1891)
1-0 v. Sunderland (10,000) (April 9th, 1892)
0-1 v. The Wednesday (10,000) (September 3rd, 1892)
1-1 v. Derby County (12,000) (September 17th, 1892)
3-0 v. Wolverhampton Wanderers (2,500) (April 8th, 1893)
3-2 v. Woolwich Arsenal (6,000) (September 9th, 1893)
2-1 v. Darwen (10,000) (September 15th, 1894)
No. of Matches Played by Notts County; 13
Information Kindly Supplied by; Peter Wynne-Thomas

These League matches were played here when *Nottinghamshire CCC* was using *Trent Bridge Cricket Ground*.

NEUTRAL TEST MATCHES
Sheffield United 1, Accrington 0 (6,000) (April 22nd, 1893)
No. of Matches Played; 1

A TOTAL OF **12** TEAMS TOOK PART IN **14** LEAGUE FIXTURES AT THIS VENUE

THE CHUCKERY
HOME GROUND OF **WALSALL**

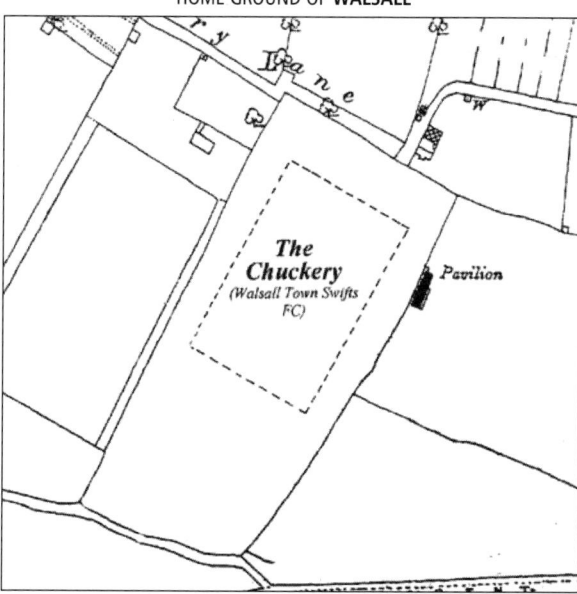

MAP EXTRACT; STAFFORDSHIRE 63.11 [**1887**]
SITE LOCATION; **SP02349813**

Located to the east of the town centre, The Chuckery consisted of a number of fields and both *Walsall Town FC* and *Walsall Swifts FC* had pitches here before they amalgamated as *Walsall Town Swifts* in 1888 and decided to use the "*Town*" pitch. This was undoubtedly because it was nearer the only facility available, the *Walsall Cricket Club* pavilion, located in an adjacent field, and available for use by the football club. The precise location of the pitch within the field is not known.

Walsall Town Swifts FC moved to **West Bromwich Road** in 1893 and *The Chuckery* was subsequently redeveloped for housing.

PLAYING RECORD OF WALSALL
[AS WALSALL TOWN SWIFTS]
LEAGUE PROGRAMME

Matches Played; 1-2 v. Darwen (4,000) (September 3rd, 1892)
1-3 v. Small Heath (2,500) (September 10th, 1892)
2-4 v. Ardwick (2,000) (September 17th, 1892)
2-1 v. Lincoln City (2,000) (October 8th, 1892)
3-1 v. Grimsby Town (2,500) (October 22nd, 1892)
4-4 v. Bootle (500) (December 24th, 1892)
3-3 v. Crewe Alexandra (1,000) (January 14th, 1893)
2-3 v. Northwich Victoria (500) (February 11th, 1893)
3-0 v. Burslem Port Vale (700) (February 18th, 1893)
3-2 v. Burton Swifts (1,000) (March 4th, 1893)
1-1 v. Sheffield United (2,000) (April 15th, 1893)

No. of Matches Played by Walsall; 11
Information Kindly Supplied by; Tony Matthews

The club was a founder member of the Football League Division 2 in 1892 as *Walsall Town Swifts FC*. The club moved to *West Bromwich Road* in 1893 but had to play two matches at *Wednesbury Old Athletic FC's The Oval* ground until it was ready.

A TOTAL OF **12** TEAMS TOOK PART IN **11** LEAGUE FIXTURES AT THIS VENUE

CITY OF MANCHESTER STADIUM
HOME GROUND OF **MANCHESTER CITY**

MAP EXTRACT; GROUND AS IN **2003** DRAWN FROM AERIAL PHOTOGRAPHS AND SUPERIMPOSED ON LANCASHIRE 104.8 & .9 [1934]
SITE LOCATION; **SJ86739850**

Constructed on a brownfield site formerly occupied by the Bradford Iron Works and Beswick Goods Station this venue originally opened for the Commonwealth Games on July 25th, 2002. It consisted of two tier stands on each side and a single tier stand at the south end with a continuous cantilevered roof. To accommodate the extra length of the athletics arena, three open seated temporary stands were installed at the north end giving an all-seat capacity of 38,000.

Following the completion of the event on August 4th, 2002, the running track was removed and the three stands at the north end demolished. The playing area was lowered by 16ft to accommodate a lower tier of seats throughout the stadium and the north end was reconstructed in similar fashion to the south. In its rebuilt form the stadium became a 48,000 seater with a continuous cantilevered roof and the first match to be played here was a friendly v. *Barcelona* (2-1) (36,518) on August 10th, 2003. The pitch size was 118 x 76 yards.

PLAYING RECORD OF MANCHESTER CITY
LEAGUE PROGRAMME

First Match; 1-1 v. Portsmouth (46,287) (August 23rd, 2003)
Highest Gate; 47,304 v. Chelsea (0-1) (February 28th, 2004)
Lowest Gate; 42,453 v. Birmingham City (3-0) (April 20th, 2005)
Highest Home Win; 6-2 v. Bolton Wanderers (47,101) (October 18th, 2003)
Highest Home Defeat; 0-3 v. Leicester City (46,966) (November 9th, 2003)

No. of Matches Played by Manchester City; 38

The club moved here from *Maine Road* at the commencement of the 2003/4 season and the first League goal at the stadium was scored by Yakubu Ayegbini of *Portsmouth FC* in the 24th minute of the first match.

AT THE END OF SEASON 2004/5, A TOTAL OF **23** TEAMS HAD TAKEN PART IN **38** LEAGUE FIXTURES AT THIS VENUE

THE CIRCLE & ANLABY ROAD

TEMPORARY HOME GROUND FOR **HULL CITY**   HOME GROUND OF **HULL CITY**

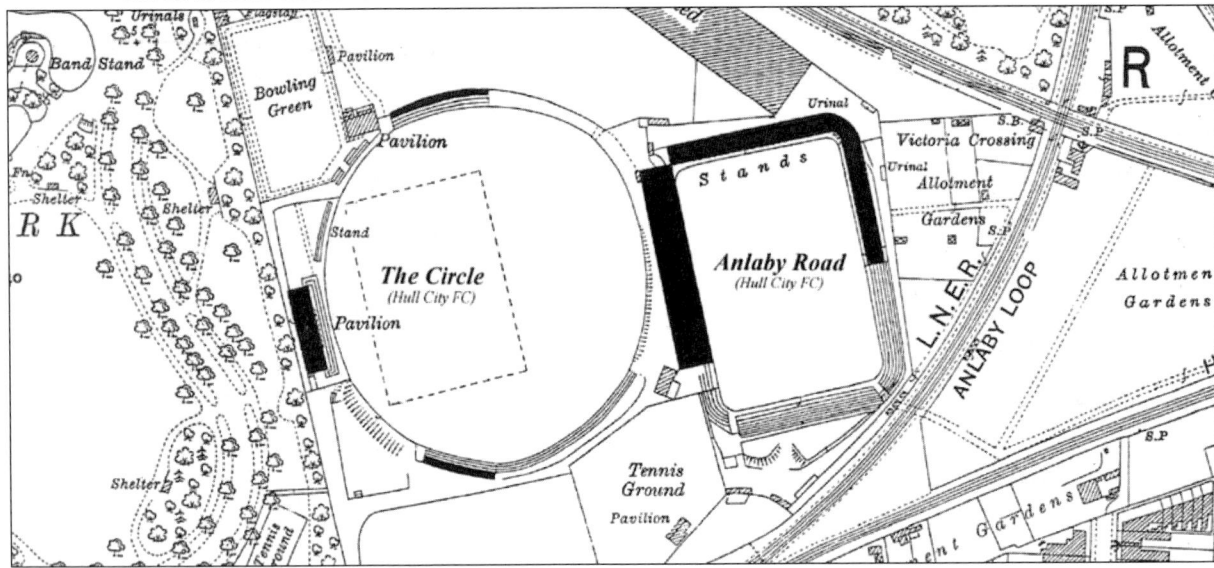

MAP EXTRACT; YORKSHIRE 240.2 [1928]

SITE LOCATION OF **THE CIRCLE**; TA07772894

The home ground of *Hull Cricket Club* the arena was, as the name implied, virtually circular with a main pavilion on the west side and another smaller pavilion on the north. *Hull City FC* was accommodated from 1905 and they installed a covered stand and a 1,000 capacity temporary stand. The orientation of the pitch, on the map, is assumed. The cricket ground was vacated in 1906 with *Hull City* moving to the *Anlaby Road* ground which had been constructed on the east side of the site.

The Circle remained in use as the home ground of the *Hull CC* until just prior to 2002 when this site and part of the *Anlaby Road* ground were taken over for the development of the **Kingston Communications Stadium** for the use of both *Hull City FC* and *Hull RLFC*.

PLAYING RECORD OF HULL CITY
LEAGUE PROGRAMME

Matches Played; 4-1 v. Barnsley (8,000) (September 2nd, 1905)
1-1 v. Burnley (6,000) (September 16th, 1905)
1-1 v. Burton United (6,000) (September 30th, 1905)
3-0 v. Chesterfield (3,000) (October 11th, 1905)
2-0 v. Gainsborough Trinity (3,500) (October 14th, 1905)
3-0 v. Stockport County (3,000) (November 11th, 1905)
5-2 v. Bradford City (5,000) (November 25th, 1905)
0-1 v. Grimsby Town (8,000) (December 16th, 1905)
0-0 v. Leeds City (10,000) (January 27th, 1906)
4-3 v. Chelsea (7,000) (February 10th, 1906)
0-3 v. Bristol City (8,000) (February 24th, 1906)

No. of Matches Played by Hull City; 11

The club was elected into the Football League Division 2 in 1905 and had hoped to use the **Boulevard Ground** of *Hull RLFC* but at the last moment the Rugby League authorities ordered that no paid admission could be taken at the ground for Association Football games. As a result, *Hull City FC* moved in with the *Hull CC* on a temporary basis until a new permanent ground could be built. Ironically, within a few months, the rugby authorities relaxed the constraints and occasional matches were played at the **Boulevard Ground**. In 1906 the club made the permanent move to **Anlaby Road**.

A TOTAL OF **12** TEAMS TOOK PART IN **11** LEAGUE FIXTURES AT THIS VENUE

SITE LOCATION OF **ANLABY ROAD**; TA07912894

Constructed along the east side of *The Circle*, the ground opened in 1906. A grandstand was built on the west side and covered standing accommodation provided on the north and part of the east sides. The original soil embankments were later improved with concrete terracing and the first grandstand, which only lasted until 1911 when it was destroyed by a fire, was replaced by a 4,000 seat covered structure.

The record attendance of 32,930 was set at the FA Cup 6th Round Replay v. *Newcastle United* (1-0) on March 6th, 1930. The ground suffered from considerable bomb damage during WWII and by the commencement of League Football in 1946 the first team had moved on to **Boothferry Park**. The junior teams continued to utilize the venue until 1965 when British Railways constructed a loop line across the ground.

PLAYING RECORD OF HULL CITY
LEAGUE PROGRAMME

First Match; 2-2 v. Blackpool (5,000) (March 24th, 1906)
Last Match; 2-2 v. Lincoln City (8,696) (August 26th, 1939)
Highest Gate; 24,110 v. Middlesbrough (3-3) (February 5th, 1927)
Lowest Gate; 1,900 v. Glossop (2-0) (April 24th, 1915)
Highest Home Win; 11-1 v. Carlisle United (5,298)
(January 14th, 1939)
Highest Home Defeat; 2-5 v. Bradford City (3,750)
(February 20th, 1936)

No. of Matches Played by Hull City; 595

In 1906 the club made the permanent move here from *The Circle* and one match was played at the *Boulevard Ground*. The club moved out at the commencement of WWII but was unable to return at its end and went to **Boothferry Park**.

A TOTAL OF **75** TEAMS TOOK PART IN **595** LEAGUE FIXTURES AT THIS VENUE

THE CITY GROUND

HOME GROUND OF **NOTTINGHAM FOREST**
TEMPORARY HOME GROUND FOR **LEICESTER CITY & NOTTS COUNTY**

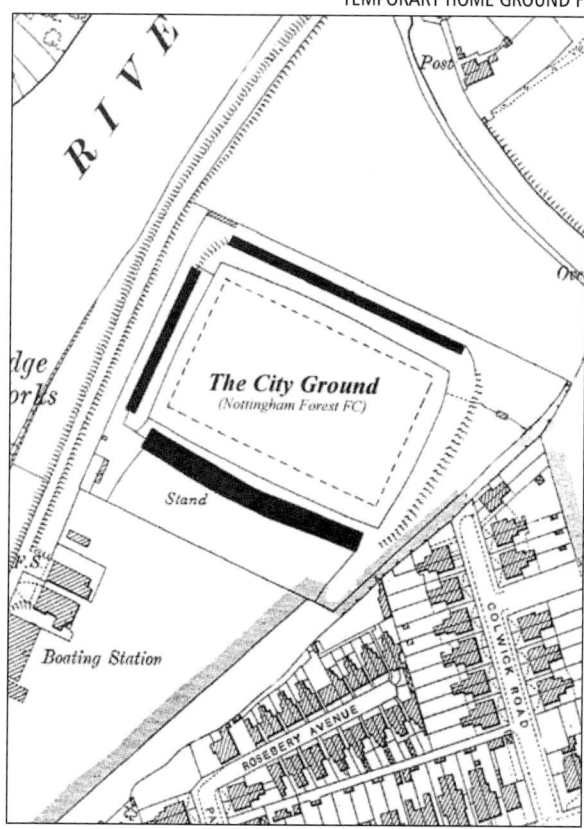

MAP EXTRACT; NOTTINGHAMSHIRE 42.6 [**1915**]
SITE LOCATION; **SK58373842**

PLAYING RECORD OF NOTTINGHAM FOREST
LEAGUE PROGRAMME
First Match; 0-1 v. Blackburn Rovers (15,000) (September 3rd, 1898)
Highest Gate; 49,946 v. Manchester United (3-1)
(October 28th, 1967)
Lowest Gate; 2,624 v. West Bromwich Albion (2-0)
(March 30th, 1904)
Highest Home Win; 12-0 v. Leicester Fosse (7,000) (April 21st, 1909)
Highest Home Defeat; 1-8 v. Manchester United (30,025) (February 6th, 1999)

PLAY OFF MATCHES
Match Played; 1-1 v. Sheffield United (29,064) (May 10th, 2003)
No. of Matches Played by **Nottingham Forest;** *1,970*

The club moved here from *The Town Ground* in 1898. The ground suffered from flooding in November 1946, forcing the club to play one home match at *Meadow Lane*. Flooding also occurred later in the season in March 1947 but on this occasion did not, as far as is known, entail the playing of home matches at any other venue. In 1968 the main stand burned down and five home games were also played at *Meadow Lane*.

PLAYING RECORD OF NOTTS COUNTY
LEAGUE PROGRAMME
Matches Played; 2-0 v. Stoke (5,000) (April 15th, 1899)
0-0 v. Newcastle United (10,000) (April 16th, 1900)
2-2 v. Everton (6,000) (April 21st, 1900)
2-2 v. Sunderland (12,000) (September 1st, 1900)
3-2 v. Everton (9,000) (April 9th, 1901)
2-2 v. Stoke (6,000) (April 13th, 1901)
2-0 v. Sunderland (10,000) (April 19th, 1902)
3-1 v. West Bromwich Albion (12,339) (September 6th, 1902)
1-2 v. Everton (12,000) (September 3rd, 1904)
2-2 v. Sunderland (3,000) (April 8th, 1905)
1-0 v. Newcastle United (16,000) (April 14th, 1906)
0-0 v. Bolton Wanderers (5,000) (September 1st, 1906)
1-0 v. Newcastle United (12,000) (April 6th, 1907)
2-2 v. Middlesbrough (6,000) (April 10th, 1907)
4-1 v. Woolwich Arsenal (3,000) (April 17th, 1907)
2-0 v. Liverpool (1,000) (April 20th, 1907)
0-2 v. Blackburn Rovers (12,000) (April 18th, 1908)
2-1 v. Woolwich Arsenal (15,000) (September 5th, 1908)
2-3 v. Leicester Fosse (16,000) (April 9th, 1909)
0-1 v. Manchester United (7,000) (April 13th, 1909)
2-3 v. Blackburn Rovers (6,000) (April 17th, 1909)
No. of Matches Played by **Notts County;** *21*
Information Kindly Supplied by; Peter Wynne-Thomas

These League matches were played here when *Nottinghamshire CCC* was using **Trent Bridge Cricket Ground**.

PLAYING RECORD OF LEICESTER CITY
PLAY OFF MATCHES
Match Played; 1-0 v. Portsmouth (24,538) (May 16th, 1993)
No. of Matches Played by **Leicester City;** *1*
Information Kindly Supplied by; Richard J. Owen
This match was played here due to rebuilding work at *Filbert Street*.

Nottingham Forest FC moved to *The City Ground* from the **The Town Ground** in 1898 and by WWI a covered main stand had been built on the south side, covering installed at the west end and on the north side and banking constructed at the east end.

The ground remained virtually unaltered until the 1950s when the west end terrace was extended and covered in 1954, a new 2,500 seat stand constructed on the east side and the terracing at the east end enlarged in 1957 giving a nominal capacity of 48,000 with 6,000 seats. During the 1960s the main stand was enlarged, refurbished and re-roofed and, after suffering fire damage in 1968 refurbished again.

A new cantilever roofed two tier all seat stand opened on the north side in 1980 and, in 1992, an all seat stand, was built at the east end and in the north east and south east corners. (To conform with planning requirements this stand is partially of two-tier design with the cantilever roof stepping down to a single tier at the south end). In 1994 a two-tier 6,706 seat stand was opened at the west end and the all seat capacity at the start of the 2004/5 season was 30,602. The pitch size was 112 x 78 yards.

AT THE END OF SEASON 2004/5, A TOTAL OF **89** TEAMS HAD TAKEN PART IN **1,992** LEAGUE FIXTURES AT THIS VENUE

CLIFTON GROVE
HOME GROUND OF **ROTHERHAM TOWN**

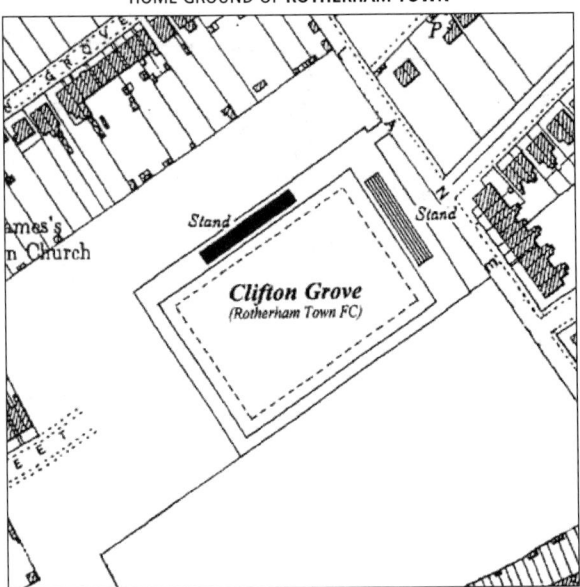

MAP EXTRACT; GROUND AS IN **c1894** DRAWN FROM PLANS AND SUPERIMPOSED ON YORKSHIRE 289.11[1903]
SITE LOCATION; SK44029283

Although no map exists, from contemporary accounts an accurate diagram of the ground can be constructed. The facilities included a covered seated stand, removed from *Rotherham Town FC's* previous ground at the *Clifton Lane Cricket Ground* and re-erected on the north side, and an open seated stand installed at the east end.

Located to the east of the town centre and occupying part of the south east corner of Clifton Grove and Middle Lane the ground opened with a Midland League match against *Grantham Rovers FC* on September 26th, 1891. Following the demise of the club in 1896 the site was redeveloped for housing.

PLAYING RECORD OF ROTHERHAM TOWN
LEAGUE PROGRAMME

First Match; 4-3 v. Grimsby Town (3,000) (September 9th, 1893)
Last Match & Lowest Gate; 2-2 v. Lincoln City (300) (March 16th, 1896)
Highest Gate; 3,000 v. Burton Wanderers (1-3) (September 1st, 1894) & v. Grimsby Town (4-3) (September 9th, 1893)
Highest Home Win; 6-1 v. Walsall (1,500) (November 17th, 1894)
Highest Home Defeat; 2-8 v. Lincoln City (1,000) (December 2nd, 1893)

No. of Matches Played by Rotherham Town; 44
Information Kindly Supplied by; Gerry Somerton

The club was elected into the Football League Division 2 in 1893 but failed to gain re-election in 1896.

A TOTAL OF **21** TEAMS TOOK PART IN **44** LEAGUE FIXTURES AT THIS VENUE

COBRIDGE ATHLETIC GROUND
HOME GROUND OF **PORT VALE**

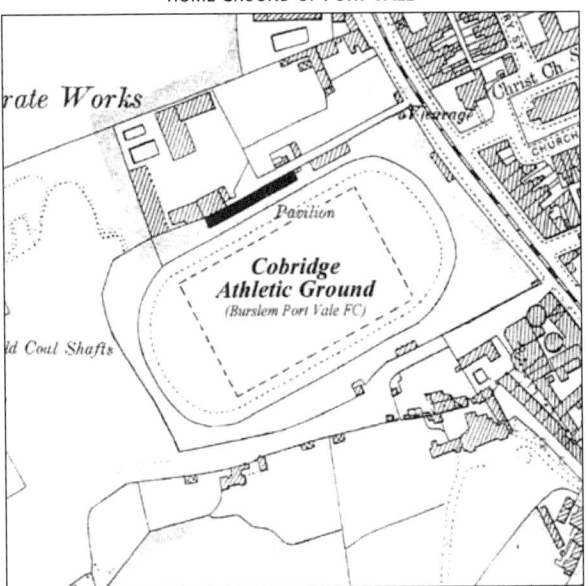

MAP EXTRACT; STAFFORDSHIRE 22.9 [**1900**]
SITE LOCATION; SJ87434861

Located to the south of Burslem and on the west side of Waterloo Road, the *Cobridge Athletic Ground* was built on waste ground and opened with an athletics meeting on September 4th, 1886. It had an oval cycle track, tennis courts, and a pavilion sited on the south side of the ground. *Burslem Port Vale* moved here from their *Moorland Road Ground* in the same year and played their first fixture, a friendly, against *Preston North End* on September 6th.

Within a few years and just prior to entering the Football League in 1892, new facilities, in the shape of a new main stand, pavilion and additional covered accommodation were installed on the north side. The ground was vacated by *Port Vale FC* in 1913 (having re-formed in 1908) and the venue was steadily improved as it continued in use, latterly for Greyhound Racing and American Football. Later known as *Cobridge Stadium* it was demolished and redeveloped, partially as housing and, by 2003, a Retirement Home.

PLAYING RECORD OF PORT VALE
[AS BURSLEM PORT VALE]
LEAGUE PROGRAMME

First Match; 4-1 v. Crewe Alexandra (1,500) (September 24th, 1892)
Last Match; 3-0 v. Blackpool (3,000) (April 27th, 1907)
Highest Gate; 12,000 v. Manchester City (1-1) (April 1st, 1899)
Lowest Gate; 100 v. Blackpool (0-1) (April 5th, 1902)
Highest Home Win; 7-1 v. Lincoln City (2,500) (March 16th, 1895)
Highest Home Defeat; 0-10 v. Sheffield United (1,000) (December 10th, 1892)

No. of Matches Played by Port Vale; 212
Information Kindly Supplied by; Tony Matthews

The club was a founder member of the Football League Division 2 in 1892 as *Burslem Port Vale*, failed to gain re-election in 1896, was elected to Division 2 in 1898 and failed to gain re-election in 1907.

NEUTRAL TEST MATCHES
Stoke 3, Newton Heath 0 (10,000) (April 27th, 1895)
No. of Matches Played; 1

A TOTAL OF **48** TEAMS TOOK PART IN **213** LEAGUE FIXTURES AT THIS VENUE

THE COUNTY GROUND
HOME GROUND OF **NORTHAMPTON TOWN**

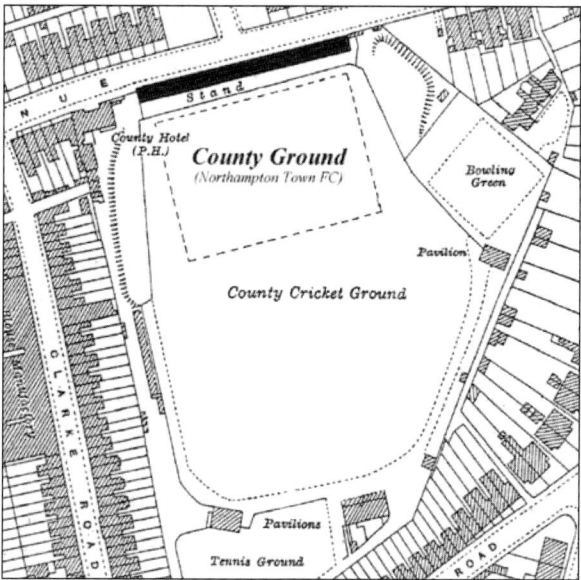

MAP EXTRACT; NORTHAMPTONSHIRE 45.6 [**1925**]
SITE LOCATION; **SP77156178**

The ground, on the east side of the town, was opened by the Northamptonshire County Cricket & Recreation Grounds Ltd in 1885 and was first used by *Northampton Town FC* in 1897. The football pitch was sited to the north of the cricket square and the club used the cricket pavilion, on the south side of the ground, until 1907 when a small stand and terrace were constructed on the north side. A replacement 2,000 seat main stand was constructed in 1924 (and rebuilt in 1930 following a fire) whilst small terraces, at each end of the pitch, were subsequently installed. Throughout the years duckboards provided a limited amount of standing accommodation on the south side of the pitch

Following WWII a cover was built over the west end, the east end was extended in 1965 and although the main stand was refurbished in 1980 it was condemned in 1985 and partially demolished leaving an uncovered paddock. At the same time part of the east end terracing was closed and the only alterations prior to *Northampton Town's* departure to *Sixfields Stadium* in 1994 were the provision of a temporary 400 seat stand in the paddock and installation of a new cover at the west end. The venue is still in use as the home ground of *Northamptonshire CCC*.

PLAYING RECORD OF NORTHAMPTON TOWN
LEAGUE PROGRAMME

First Match; 4-1 v. Grimsby Town (10,000) (September 4th, 1920)
Last Match; 0-1 v. Mansfield Town (4,993) (October 11th, 1994)
Highest Gate; 24,523 v. Fulham (2-4) (April 23rd, 1966)
Lowest Gate; 942 v. Chester City (0-2) (March 19th, 1985)
Highest Home Win; 10-0 v. Walsall (11,340) (November 5th, 1927)
Highest Home Defeat; 0-8 v. Walsall (5,757) (April 8th, 1947)
No. of Matches Played by Northampton Town; 1,488
(Including one expunged match v. Aldershot on February 4th, 1992)
Information Kindly Supplied by; Frank Grande

The club was a founder member of the Football League Division 3 in 1920 and moved to *Sixfields Stadium* in 1994.

A TOTAL OF **105** TEAMS TOOK PART IN **1,488** LEAGUE FIXTURES AT THIS VENUE

THE COUNTY GROUND
HOME GROUND OF **SWINDON TOWN**

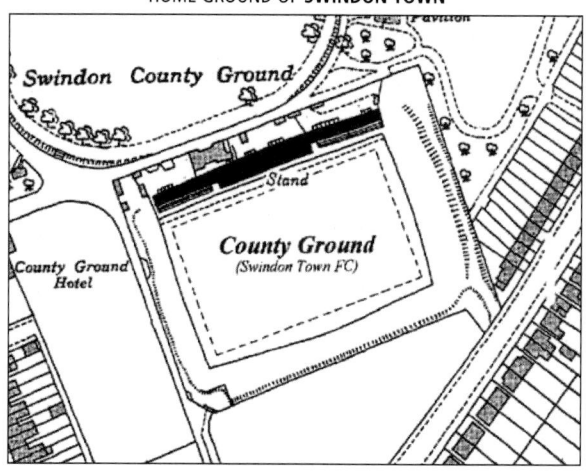

MAP EXTRACT; WILTSHIRE 15.4 [**1942**]
SITE LOCATION; **SU15978509**

When *Swindon Town FC* moved to *The County Ground* in 1895 they played on the cricket ground for one season before moving to a field adjacent to the south side of the venue. The facilities originally included a stand (extended in 1911) on the north side of the pitch whilst some terracing was constructed in 1908. The only major improvement prior to WWII was the installation of cover on the south side and at the west end in the 1930s.

In 1958 the cover on the south side was replaced when a grandstand was acquired from the Aldershot Military Tattoo (NB *Accrington Stanley* also purchased a stand from here at the same time for re-erection at their **Peel Park**) and a new 5,300 seat main stand constructed on the north side in 1971 before the record attendance of 32,000 was set at the FA Cup 3rd Round tie v. *Arsenal* (0-2) on January 15th, 1972. Further alterations were made during the 1990s, including the installation of additional seats at the front of the main stand, the replacement of the stand on the south side with a cantilever roofed 5,030 seat stand and the installation of seats at both ends. The all-seat capacity at the start of the 2004/5 season was 15,700 and the pitch size was 114 x 74 yards.

PLAYING RECORD OF SWINDON TOWN
LEAGUE PROGRAMME

First Match & Highest Home Win; 9-1 v. Luton Town (10,000)
(August 28th, 1920)
Highest Gate; 28,898 v. Watford (0-1) (March 29th, 1969)
Lowest Gate; 1,681 v. Darlington (1-0) (April 17th, 1984)
Highest Home Defeat; 0-6 v. Ipswich Town (10,337) (April 3rd, 1999)

PLAY OFF MATCHES

0-0 v. Wigan Athletic (12,485) (May 17th, 1987)
2-1 v. Gillingham [aet] (14,382) (May 25th, 1987)
1-0 v. Crystal Palace (16,656) (May 21st, 1989)
1-2 v. Blackburn Rovers (12,416) (May 16th, 1990)
3-1 v. Tranmere Rovers (14,230) (May 16th, 1993)
0-1 v. Brighton & Hove Albion (14,034) (May 16th, 2004)

No. of Matches Played by Swindon Town; 1,739
(League Programme; 1,733, Play Off Matches; 6)
Information Kindly Supplied by; Dick Mattick

The club was a founder member of the Football League Division 3 in 1920. The club was also involved in Football League Play Off Matches at the neutral venues of *Selhurst Park* and *Wembley Stadium*.

AT THE END OF SEASON 2004/5, A TOTAL OF **103** TEAMS HAD TAKEN PART IN **1,739** LEAGUE FIXTURES AT THIS VENUE

CRAVEN COTTAGE
HOME GROUND OF FULHAM

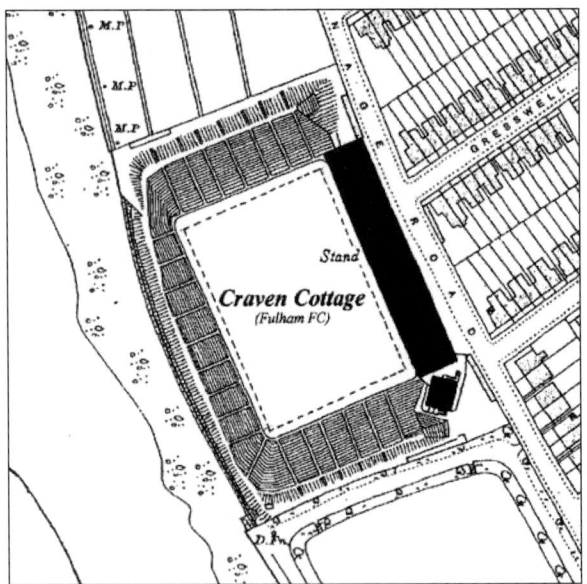

MAP EXTRACT; LONDON [1943]
SITE LOCATION; **TQ23587660**

Originally part of Anne Boleyn's hunting grounds, the site was an overgrown wilderness (devoid of the original cottage that had succumbed to a fire in 1888) when *Fulham FC* first leased it in 1894. It took them two years to construct a ground which, when opened in October 1896, was lacking all facilities except for embankments around the pitch.

Shortly after opening, an unusual 1,000 seat stand was constructed on the east side of the ground but this only lasted until 1905 when, under threat of closure by London County Council as a potential safety hazard (even in those days!), the decision was taken to make major alterations to the venue. A new main stand was built on the east side, terracing extended on the other three sides and a pavilion (known today as Craven Cottage) erected in the south east corner.

The ground remained virtually unchanged until the 1960s when the north end was extended and covered and a new 4,200 seat stand subsequently constructed on the west side. The capacity at the end of 2001/2 season, when the ground closed for planned redevelopment, was 18,623 with 7,023 seats and the pitch size was 110 x 75 yards.

It was hoped to rebuild *Craven Cottage* as a 30,000 seater stadium and re-open at the commencement of the 2003/4 season but legal protests from local residents and escalating costs led to the abandonment of the project. In 2004 seats were installed on the terraces as a temporary measure, and a roof was erected over the south end giving the ground a nominal all-seat capacity of 22,000, and allowing the club to return to the stadium for the 2004/5 season

PLAYING RECORD OF FULHAM
LEAGUE PROGRAMME

First Match; 0-1 v. Hull City (8,000) (September 3rd, 1907)
Last Match; 0-0 v. Leicester City (21,016) (April 27th, 2002)
FOLLOWING TEMPORARY REFURBISHMENT;
First Match; 2-0 v. Bolton Wanderers (17,541) (August 21st, 2004)

Highest Gate; 49,335 v. Millwall (2-1) (October 8th, 1938)
Lowest Gate; 1,000 v. Barnsley (2-0) (November 28th, 1914)
Highest Home Win; 10-1 v. Ipswich Town (19,374)
(December 26th, 1963)
Highest Home Defeat; 0-6 v. Port Vale (3,798) (March 28th, 1987)

PLAY OFF MATCHES
0-4 v. Bristol Rovers (10,188) (May 25th, 1989)
1-1 v. Grimsby Town (13,954) (May 9th, 1998)

No. of Matches Played by Fulham; 1,804
(League Programme; 1,802, Play Off Matches; 2)

The club was elected into the Football League Division 2 in 1907. In 2002 the club moved in to *Loftus Road* to groundshare with *Queens Park Rangers* in anticipation of the rebuilding of *Craven Cottage* but this did not materialize and *Fulham FC* returned in 2004 whilst the location for a new venue was being sought.

AT THE END OF SEASON 2004/5, A TOTAL OF **106** TEAMS HAD TAKEN PART IN **1,804** LEAGUE FIXTURES AT THIS VENUE

Looking north west across **Craven Cottage** in 2002, in its final form before the proposed major rebuild. In the event the reconstruction just consisted of the installation of seats on the terracing and a cover over the south end.

Photograph by Paul Claydon. Courtesy of Groundtastic Magazine

DEAN COURT & FITNESS FIRST STADIUM
HOME GROUND OF AFC BOURNEMOUTH

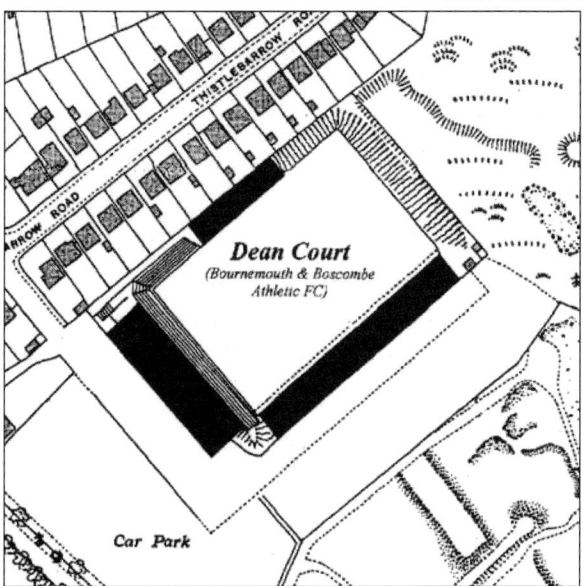

MAP EXTRACT; HAMPSHIRE 86.6 & 86.10 [**1941**]
SITE LOCATION; **SZ11509290**

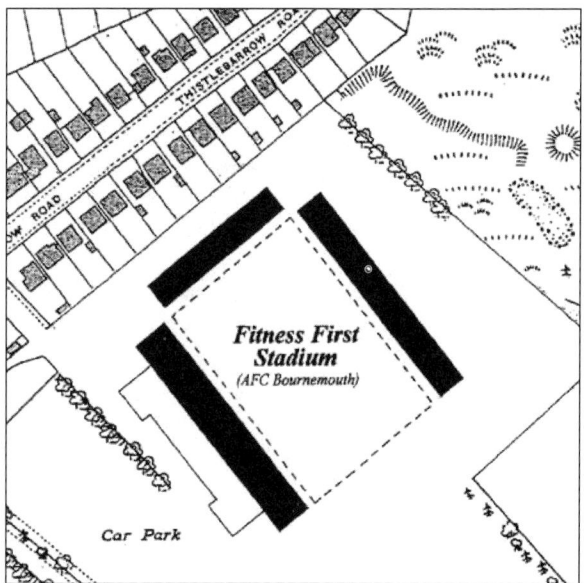

MAP EXTRACT; GROUND AS IN **2001** DRAWN FROM AERIAL PHOTOGRAPHS & SUPERIMPOSED ON HAMPSHIRE 86.6 & 86.10 [1941]

Constructed on the site of an old gravel pit, *Dean Court* was not immediately ready for occupation at the start of the 1910/11 season, so *Boscombe FC,* having moved from *Pokesdown*, played their matches at the adjacent *King's Park* until December. Even at this point the facilities, which eventually included a 300 seat stand, were not totally ready thus obliging the players to change at an adjacent hotel and access the ground through *King's Park*.

Some improvements were undertaken following the club's election to the Football League in 1923 when *Bournemouth & Boscombe Athletic FC,* as they had become known, purchased a batch of redundant material and fittings in 1927 from the Empire Exhibition at *Wembley* enabling them to build a new 3,700 seat main stand on the east side of the ground. The only other pre-WWII improvement was the construction of a covered terrace at the south end in 1936.

Following the FA Cup 6th Round tie on March 2nd, 1957 against *Manchester United* (1-2) at which the attendance record of 28,799 was set, a new cover was installed on the west side of the pitch. The club later purchased additional ground behind the north end with the intention of constructing a new stand and sports centre but having started it, ran out of money leaving just a skeletal construction. This scheme was aborted in 1984, leading to its demolition and replacement with housing and the only other improvements made up to the end of the 1990s was the refurbishment of the main stand.

In 2001 the ground was turned through 90° and re-opened as *The Fitness First Stadium* with all seated cantilever roofed stands around three sides of the ground (the south end remaining undeveloped) giving a capacity at the start of the 2004/5 season of 9,600. The pitch size is 112 x 74 yards.

PLAYING RECORD OF AFC BOURNEMOUTH
LEAGUE PROGRAMME

First Match; 0-0 v. Swindon Town (7,000) (September 1st, 1923)
Last Match; 2-0 v. Northampton Town (6,511) (April 28th, 2001)
FOLLOWING REBUILDING AS THE **FITNESS FIRST STADIUM;**
First Match; 3-0 v. Wrexham (5,031) (November 10th, 2001)
Highest Gate; 25,495 v. Queens Park Rangers (0-1) (April 14th, 1948)
Lowest Gate; 1,873 v. Lincoln City (2-2) (March 4th, 1986)
Highest Home Win; 10-0 v. Northampton Town (3,000) (September 2nd, 1939)
Highest Home Defeat; 3-7 v. Plymouth Argyle (7,352) (January 11th, 1975)

PLAY OFF MATCHES
3-1 v. Bury (7,945) (May 13th, 2003)
No. of Matches Played by AFC Bournemouth; 1,679
(League Programme; 1,678, Play Off Matches; 1)
Some Information Kindly Supplied by; Brian Tabner

The club was elected into the Football League Division 3 [S] in 1923 as *Bournemouth & Boscombe Athletic* and changed the name to *AFC Bournemouth* in 1971. In 2001, as the conversion of the ground to the *Fitness First Stadium* had not been completed, eight matches at the start of the season were played at *The Avenue Stadium* of *Dorchester Town FC.* The fastest ever League hat-trick was scored here in 2 mins 20 secs by James Hayter for *AFC Bournemouth* v. *Wrexham* (6-0) on February 24th, 2004. The club was also involved in a Football League Play Off Match at the neutral venue of the *Millennium Stadium.*

AT THE END OF SEASON 2004/5, A TOTAL OF **100** TEAMS HAD TAKEN PART IN **1,679** LEAGUE FIXTURES AT THIS VENUE

Looking west across the *Fitness First Stadium* to the new main stand.
Photograph by Adrian Brown. Courtesy of Groundtastic Magazine

DEEPDALE

HOME GROUND OF PRESTON NORTH END

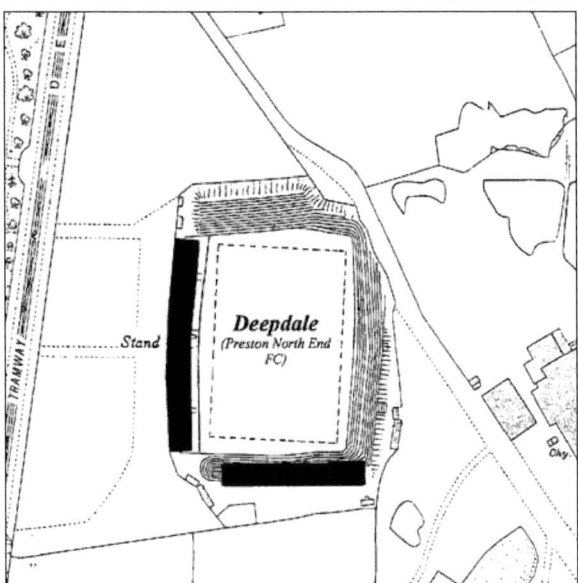

MAP EXTRACT; LANCASHIRE 56.6 [1912]
SITE LOCATION; **SD54723077**

PLAYING RECORD OF PRESTON NORTH END
LEAGUE PROGRAMME
First Match; 5-2 v. Burnley (6,000) (September 8th, 1888)
Highest Gate; 42,684 v. Arsenal (1-3) (April 23rd, 1938)
Lowest Gate; 300 v. Burnley (5-1) (September 21st, 1891)
& v. Notts County (6-0) (December 12th, 1891)
Highest Home Win; 10-0 v. Stoke (7,000) (September 14th, 1889)
Highest Home Defeat; 0-7 v. Blackpool (26,610) (May 1st, 1948)

PLAY OFF MATCHES
1-1 v. Port Vale (14,280) (May 22nd, 1989)
4-1 v. Torquay United [aet] (11,442) (May 18th, 1994)
0-1 v. Bury (13,297) (May 14th, 1995)
1-1 v. Gillingham (18,584) (May 16th, 1999)
2-1 v. Birmingham City [aet. 4-2 on penalties] (16,928) (May 17th, 2001)
2-0 v. Derby County (20,315) (May 15th, 2005)

No. of Matches Played by Preston North End; 2,166
(League Programme; 2,160, Play Off Matches; 6)
Some Information Kindly Supplied by; Brian Tabner

Preston North End CC moved a few hundred yards east to *Deepdale* from *Moor Park*, in 1875 and subsequently used the venue for athletics, football and rugby as well as cricket until 1881 when the club adopted football as its principal activity. Within a few years the facilities included two stands on the west side and uncovered stands on the east side and at the north end.

A 2,500 seat stand was built on the west side in 1906 and further additions included construction of a covered terrace at the south end and, in 1921, an extension to the terracing at the north end. In 1934 a pavilion was erected on the east side and joined at its south end by another pavilion in 1936 to create a stand occupying about two thirds of the pitch length.

In the 1990s work commenced on rebuilding the ground. The west stand was replaced with a 7,960 seat stand in 1996 and the north terraces subsequently removed and replaced with a 6,770 seat stand. In 2001 the south end was removed and a 6,100 seat stand installed giving an all-seat capacity of 22,225 at the start of the 2004/5 season. The pitch size was 110 x 75 yards.

The club was a founder member of the Football League in 1888. *Deepdale* has been in continuous use by Preston North End ever since then and, not surprisingly, currently holds the record for hosting the most number of Football League matches at 2,166. The first ever Football League goal was scored here by Jack Gordon of *Preston North End* in the match v. *Burnley* on September 8th and the 10-0 win v. *Stoke* on September 14th, 1889 was the first ever double-figure score in Football League history. The club was also involved in a Test Match at the neutral venue of the **Olive Grove** and Football League Play Off Matches at the neutral venues of **Wembley Stadium** and the **Millennium Stadium**.

AT THE END OF SEASON 2004/5, A TOTAL OF **103** TEAMS HAD TAKEN PART IN **2,166** LEAGUE FIXTURES AT THIS VENUE

The two "pavilions" on the east side of the ground, the last remaining pre-WWII stands after reconstruction of the west side and north and south ends. *Photograph Courtesy of Groundtastic Magazine*

PROGRAMME COVER ON THE RIGHT
The cover features a drawing of the ground as it was in the late 1960s, looking eastwards across the ground. The match featured, v. *Birmingham City*, ended in a 4-1 win for the home side.

THE DELL

HOME GROUND OF **SOUTHAMPTON**
TEMPORARY HOME GROUND FOR **CRYSTAL PALACE**

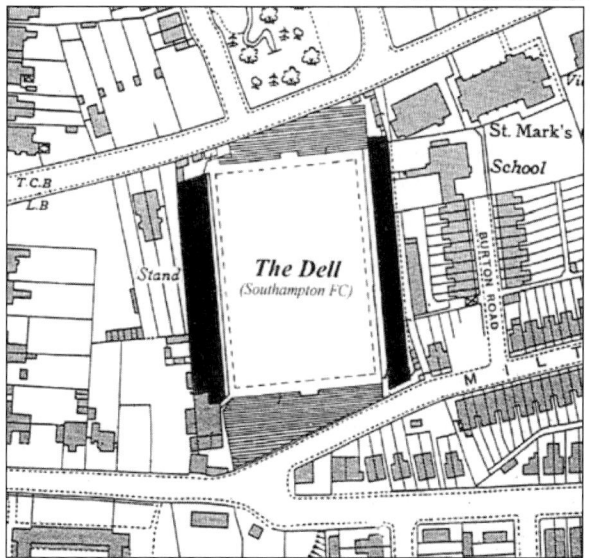

MAP EXTRACT; HAMPSHIRE 65.6 [1942]
SITE LOCATION; **SU41341296**

Occupying a near-trapezoidal and confined site, *The Dell* was first used by *Southampton FC* when they moved from the *County Ground* in 1898. The original facilities included a two tier stand and terracing on the east side, a stand on the west and steep terracing at each triangular shaped end.

Following the club's entry into the Football League in 1920, the stand on the east side was extended in 1922, the freehold purchased for £26,000 in 1926 and a new 4,500 seat two-tier stand constructed in 1927. With minor alterations to the terracing on the east side this now gave a nominal capacity of 33,000 but within two years the stand on the east side had burned down to be replaced in 1929 with a 2,500 seat two-tier structure.

Immediate post WWII improvements included the installation of three concrete platforms above the south end to increase the standing accommodation by 900 but these were demolished in 1981 to be replaced by a second tier of terracing whilst about the same time additional seating was installed on both sides of the pitch. During the 1990s the north end was rebuilt with 1,299 seats and a cantilevered roof, a new 2,897 seat stand constructed at the south end and seats installed throughout the ground giving it an all seat capacity of 15,250 with an 110 x 72 yards sized pitch.

Southampton moved to *St Mary's Stadium* in 2001 and the site was utilized for housing.

PLAYING RECORD OF SOUTHAMPTON
LEAGUE PROGRAMME

First Match; 4-0 v. Swindon Town (11,500) (August 30th, 1920)
Last Match; 3-2 v. Arsenal (15,252) (May 19th, 2001)
Highest Gate; 31,044 v. Manchester United (0-3) (October 8th, 1969)
Lowest Gate; 1,875 v. Port Vale (0-1) (March 30th, 1936)
Highest Home Win; 9-3 v. Wolverhampton Wanderers (23,266) (September 18th, 1965).
8-0 v. Northampton Town (10,000) (December 24th, 1921)
Highest Home Defeat; 0-6 v. Plymouth Argyle (12,723) (December 5th, 1931) & v. Brentford (7,765) (March 9th, 1959)
No. of Matches Played by Southampton; **1,341**

The club was a founder member of the Football League Division 3 in 1920 and moved to **St Mary's Stadium** in 2001

PLAYING RECORD OF CRYSTAL PALACE
LEAGUE PROGRAMME

Match Played; 2-1 v. Exeter City (12,000) (November 27th, 1920)
No. of Matches Played by Crystal Palace; **1**
Information Kindly Supplied by; John Robinson

This match was switched here following crowd trouble at the fixture v. *Southend United* (2-3) on November 3rd, 1920.

A TOTAL OF **91** TEAMS TOOK PART IN **1,342** LEAGUE FIXTURES AT THIS VENUE

Crowds swarm over the pitch after the last match at **The Dell**, a special friendly v. *Brighton & Hove Albion*, on May 26th, 2001.
Photograph by Pete Miles, Courtesy of Groundtastic Magazine

THE DEN

HOME GROUND OF **MILLWALL**

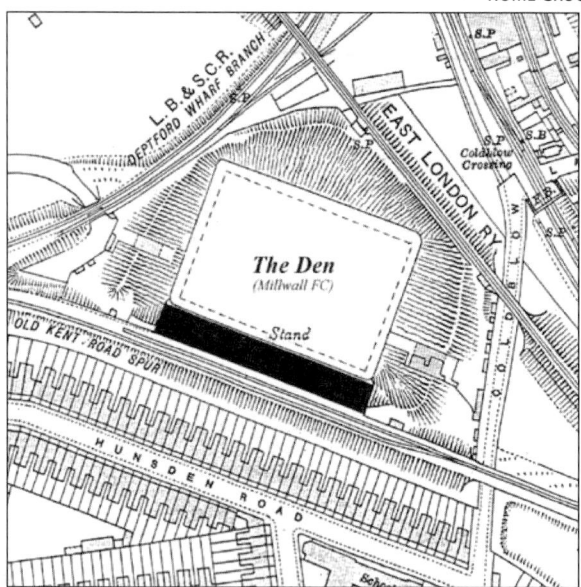

MAP EXTRACT; LONDON 9.4 [**1914**]
SITE LOCATION; **TQ35687757**

Sited on a vegetable plot and amidst a maze of railway lines, *Millwall FC* moved across the River Thames from the *North Greenwich Ground* to *The Den* in 1910. The original facilities included a main stand on the south side and embankments around the remainder of the ground.

A view of the north side, showing the terracing, cover and seats which were a later addition at the east end.
Photograph Courtesy of Groundtastic Magazine

No major improvements were made prior to the setting of the record attendance of 48,672 at the FA Cup 5th Round tie v. *Derby County* (2-1) on February 20th, 1937 but within a few years covers had been installed on all three sides of terracing. The ground suffered wholesale destruction during WWII resulting in the post war rebuilding of the terraces and construction of a new main stand roof and the only other improvements undertaken before *Millwall* moved to **The New Den** in 1993 consisted of an extension to the main stand, linking with the cover at the east end, and installation of seating in the main stand paddock and part of the north side. The site was subsequently utilized for housing.

PLAYING RECORD OF MILLWALL
LEAGUE PROGRAMME

First Match; 2-0 v. Bristol Rovers (25,000) (August 28th, 1920)
Last Match; 0-3 v. Bristol Rovers (15,821) (May 8th, 1993)
Highest Gate; 46,000 v. West Bromwich Albion (1-2) (October 19th, 1946)
Lowest Gate; 2,346 v. Bolton Wanderers (3-0) (May 5th, 1984)
Highest Home Win; 9-1 v. Torquay United (6,204) (August 29th, 1927) & v. Coventry City (10,000) (November 19th, 1927)
Highest Home Defeat; 1-7 v. Bury (9,167) (February 21st, 1948)

PLAY OFF MATCHES
1-2 v. Brighton & Hove Albion (17,370) (May 22nd, 1991)

No. of Matches Played by Millwall; 1,435
(League Programme; 1,434, Play Off Matches; 1)

The club was a founder member of the Football League Division 3 in 1920. *The Den* was closed by the FA in 1920, 1934, 1947, 1950 and 1978 following crowd trouble and two home games were played at alternative venues; **Selhurst Park** and **Fratton Park.** In 1993 the club moved to **The New Den.**

A TOTAL OF **99** TEAMS TOOK PART IN **1,435** LEAGUE FIXTURES AT THIS VENUE

DERBY TURN
HOME GROUND OF BURTON WANDERERS

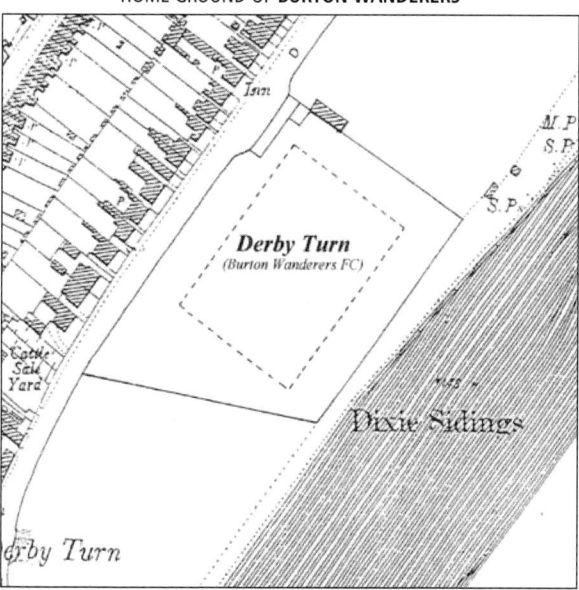

MAP EXTRACT; STAFFORDSHIRE 40.12 [1900]
SITE LOCATION; SK24802418

Although no map that shows the ground exists, it is known that the site was located at Derby Turn, north of the town centre, between Derby Road and the railway sidings and that it also hosted athletic meetings. As early maps of the area indicate only one suitably sized field it is assumed that this was the site of the ground. There was an adjacent clubhouse, probably one of the buildings shown, but details of any other facilities are not known.

The record attendance, for which temporary stands were installed, was 6,000 for the FA Cup 2nd Round match against *Notts County* (1-2) on February 10th, 1894. When *Burton Wanderers FC* vacated the ground upon amalgamation with *Burton Swifts FC* in 1901, the Midland Railway acquired most of the site to extend their Dixie Sidings.

PLAYING RECORD OF BURTON WANDERERS
LEAGUE PROGRAMME

First Match; 1-0 v. Newton Heath (2,500) (September 8th, 1894)
Last Match; 0-1 v. Loughborough (2,500) (April 19th, 1897)
Highest Gate; 5,000 v. Burton Swifts (1-0)(December 25th, 1896)
Lowest Gate; 800 v. Loughborough (4-0) (January 20th, 1896)
Highest Home Win; 9-0 v. Newcastle United (3,000) (April 15th, 1895)
Highest Home Defeat; 2-6 v. Small Heath (2,000) (February 13th, 1897)

No. of Matches Played by Burton Wanderers; 45
Some Information Kindly Supplied by; Brian Tabner

The club was elected into the Football League Division 2 in 1894 and failed to gain re-election in 1897, thus ending one of the more amazing chapters of Football League history when a town as small as Burton upon Trent actually had two clubs, let alone one, in membership between 1894 and 1897. The club amalgamated with *Burton Wanderers* in 1901 to become *Burton United*, and moved to *Peel Croft*.

A TOTAL OF 21 TEAMS TOOK PART IN 45 LEAGUE FIXTURES AT THIS VENUE

DEVA STADIUM
HOME GROUND OF CHESTER CITY

MAP EXTRACT; GROUND AS IN 1996 DRAWN FROM AERIAL
PHOTOGRAPHS AND SUPERIMPOSED ON CHESHIRE 38.10 [1911]
SITE LOCATION; SJ38386621

Having left **Sealand Road** in 1990 and taken up temporary residence at *Macclesfield Town FC's* **Moss Rose** ground, *Chester City* finally moved in to *Deva Stadium* in 1992. The unusual feature of this location is that the ground straddles the England-Wales border with part of the main office block being in England whilst the remainder of the ground is in Wales. All of the stands have cantilevered roofs and the capacity at the start of the 2004/5 season was 6,012 with 3,284 seats. The record attendance of 5,987 was set at the Football Conference Match v. *Scarborough* on April 17th, 2004 and the pitch size was 115 x 75 yards

PLAYING RECORD OF CHESTER CITY
LEAGUE PROGRAMME

First Match; 3-0 v. Burnley (4,981) (September 5th, 1992)
Highest Gate; 5,638 v. Preston North End (3-2) (April 2nd, 1994)
Lowest Gate; 1,191 v. Hull City (1-2) (March 28th, 1995)
Highest Home Win; 6-0 v. Doncaster Rovers (2,347) (February 8th, 1997)
Highest Home Defeat; 1-7 v. Brighton & Hove Albion (2,743) (February 26th, 2000)

PLAY OFF MATCHES
0-0 v. Swansea City (5,104) (May 11th, 1997)

No. of Matches Played by Chester City; 206
(League Programme; 205, Play Off Matches; 1)
Information Kindly Supplied by; Charles Sumner

The club moved here from *Moss Rose* in 1992, was relegated to the Football Conference in 2000 and won promotion back into the Football League in 2004.

AT THE END OF SEASON 2004/5, A TOTAL OF 62 TEAMS HAD TAKEN PART IN 206 LEAGUE FIXTURES AT THIS VENUE

DRILL FIELD

HOME GROUND OF NORTHWICH VICTORIA

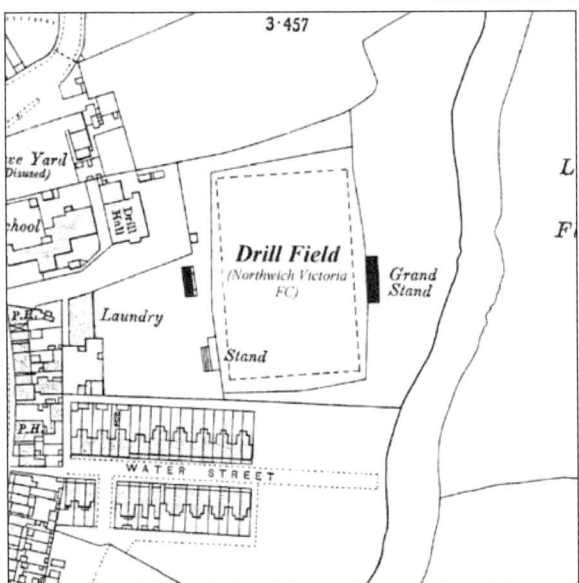

MAP EXTRACT; CHESHIRE 34.9 [1910]
SITE LOCATION; SJ66057357

Located to the south of the town centre, the site had been used by the 22nd Co. 3rd Battalion Cheshire Rifle Volunteers as a drilling ground when *Northwich Victoria FC* moved in in c1875. At that time it was not ideal for use as a football pitch with a thorn fence around part of the perimeter, a deep ditch so close to the playing area that it had to be covered with planks in order to accommodate corner kicks and a persistent risk of flooding from the adjacent River Dane, meandering around the east side. Another cause for concern, to the pitch at least, was that it was also used as an agricultural showground but despite these problems *Northwich Victoria* was able to play matches here.

The ground itself was naturally enclosed with the aforementioned river and thorn fence and the drill hall on the west side, with players changing in adjacent hotels and by the time that they joined the Football League in 1892 a proper enclosure had been formed, the ditch had been removed and a seated covered stand installed on the east side.

Subsequent improvements included the replacement of the stand with a covered enclosure, covered enclosures behind each goal and the construction of a new grandstand on the east side. The grandstand was later replaced and moved to the west side and the record attendance of 11,290 was set at a Cheshire League match v. *Witton Albion* on April 15th, 1949.

The main stand was replaced in 1968 with a 600 seat cantilever roofed structure and at the end of the 2001/2 season the ground was sold for housing redevelopment. The first team moved to groundshare with *Witton Albion* until their new ground at Wincham, *Victoria Stadium*, was ready. Planning difficulties ensued, however, and the reserves continued to play here until these were resolved in 2003 when the ground was demolished and the east side stand, still relatively new, dismantled for re-erection at the new venue.

PLAYING RECORD OF NORTHWICH VICTORIA
LEAGUE PROGRAMME

First Match; 0-3 v. Ardwick (3,000) (September 10th, 1892)
Last Match; 2-1 v. Middlesbrough Ironopolis (3,000)
(April 7th, 1894)
Highest Gate; 8,000 v. Crewe Alexandra (4-1) (October 22nd, 1892)
Lowest Gate; 300 v. Newcastle United (5-3) (November 18th, 1893)
Highest Home Win; 5-2 v. Walsall Town Swifts (1,500) (November 26th, 1892)
Highest Home Defeat; 0-7 v. Small Heath (500) (January 6th, 1894)
No. of Matches Played by Northwich Victoria; 25

The club was a founder member of the Football League Division 2 in 1892 and resigned in 1894.

A TOTAL OF **18** TEAMS TOOK PART IN **25** LEAGUE FIXTURES AT THIS VENUE

The 1968-vintage 600 seat main stand at *Drill Field*
Photograph by Paul Claydon. Courtesy of Groundtastic Magazine

DUDLEY ROAD
HOME GROUND OF **WOLVERHAMPTON WANDERERS**

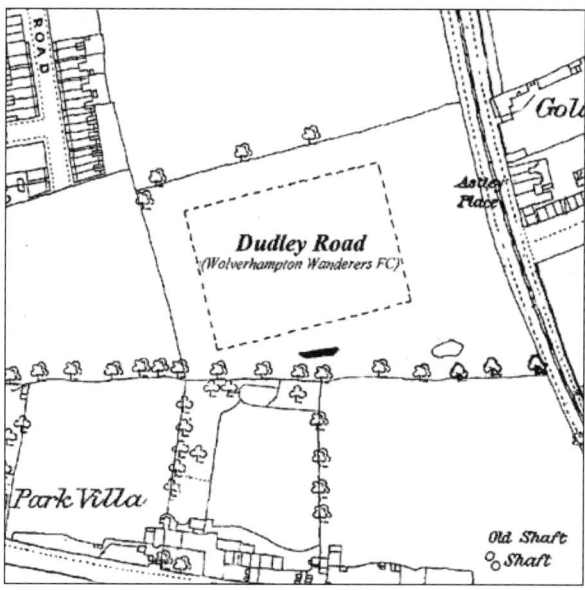

MAP EXTRACT; STAFFORDSHIRE 62.14 & 62.15 [**1889**]
SITE LOCATION; **SO91609674**

Located to the south of the city centre and on the west side of Dudley Road, the ground was first used by *St Lukes FC* in 1881. *St Lukes* amalgamated with *Goldthorn Hill FC* to form *Wolverhampton Wanderers FC* in 1884 and the venue was virtually devoid of any facilities, there was a small lean-to shelter on the south side and a small enclosure with wooden duckboards for standing spectators, when they became founder members of the Football League.

The record estimated attendance of 10,000 was established on March 2nd, 1889 for the visit of *Sheffield Wednesday* in the 3rd Round of the FA Cup (3-0) and this turned out to be the last fixture here before *Wolverhampton Wanderers* moved to *Molineux* for the start of the 1889/90 season. The site was later redeveloped with housing on both sides of Wanderers Avenue.

PLAYING RECORD OF WOLVERHAMPTON WANDERERS
LEAGUE PROGRAMME

Matches Played; 1-1 v. Aston Villa (2,500)
(September 8th, 1888)
0-4 v. Preston North End (5,000) (September 15th, 1888)
4-1 v. Burnley (4,000) (September 22nd, 1888)
2-2 v. Blackburn Rovers (5,000) (September 29th, 1888)
4-1 v. Derby County (6,000) (November 3rd, 1888)
3-2 v. Bolton Wanderers (5,000) (November 10th, 1888)
4-0 v. Accrington (3,000) (December 8th, 1888)
2-1 v. West Bromwich Albion (8,600) (December 15th, 1888)
4-1 v. Stoke (3,000) (December 22nd, 1888)
4-0 v. Everton (4,500) (January 26th, 1889)
2-1 v. Notts County (4,000) (February 23rd, 1889)

**No. of Matches Played by Wolverhampton Wanderers;
11**

Information Kindly Supplied by; Tony Matthews

The club was a founder member of the Football League in 1888 and the first ever League own goal was scored by George Cox of *Aston Villa* in the 1-1 draw on September 8th, 1888. The club moved to the **Molineux Ground** in 1889.

A TOTAL OF **12** TEAMS TOOK PART IN **11** LEAGUE FIXTURES AT THIS VENUE

DUNSTABLE ROAD
HOME GROUND OF **LUTON TOWN**

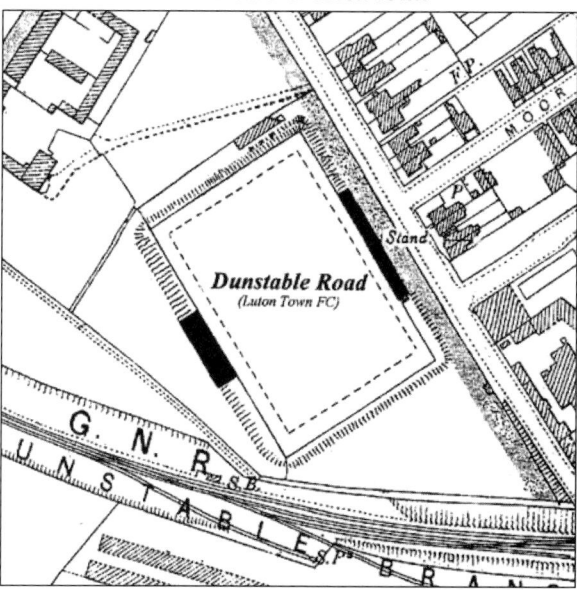

MAP EXTRACT; BEDFORDSHIRE 33.5 [**1901**]
SITE LOCATION; **TL08352174**

Located on the west side of Dunstable Road and adjacent to the north side of the Great Northern Railway line to Dunstable, *Luton Town* moved "across the tracks" from their *Dallow Lane* ground which had been on the south side of the line.

The ground, also known as *Bury Park*, was officially opened by the Duke of Norfolk on April 3rd, 1897 when *Loughborough FC* were played in a United Counties League match. The facilities included a covered seated stand which had been constructed on the east side, a covered standing enclosure on the west and raised embankments around the remainder of the pitch.

As the site was required for housing, *Luton Town* vacated the ground in 1905 and re-located at **Kenilworth Road**, a few hundred yards west along the railway line.

PLAYING RECORD OF LUTON TOWN
LEAGUE PROGRAMME

First Match; 4-0 v. Gainsborough Trinity (-) (September 11th, 1897)
Last Match; 1-2 v. Small Heath (1,000) (April 21st, 1900)
Highest Gate; 5,000 v. Grimsby Town (6-0) (December 27th, 1897)
Lowest Gate; 500 v. Grimsby Town (0-4) (December 30th, 1899)
& v. Burslem Port Vale (1-1) (February 10th, 1900)
Highest Home Win; 9-3 v. Lincoln City (3,000) (December 18th, 1897). 8-1 v. Darwen (-) (September 24th, 1898)
Highest Home Defeat; 1-6 v. Leicester Fosse (-) (January 14th, 1899)

No. of Matches Played by Luton Town; 49

Information Kindly Supplied by; Roger Wash & Brian Tabner

The club was elected into the Football League Division 2 in 1897 and did not seek re-election in 1900. In 1905 the club moved to *Ivy Road* (later re-named as **Kenilworth Road**)

A TOTAL OF **24** TEAMS TOOK PART IN **49** LEAGUE FIXTURES AT THIS VENUE

EASTVILLE STADIUM
HOME GROUND OF BRISTOL ROVERS

MAP EXTRACT; GLOUCESTERSHIRE 72.9 [1918]
SITE LOCATION; ST60907499

Located at Stapleton Hill the venue was in use by *Bristol Harlequins RUFC* before *Eastville Rovers FC* bought the site for £150 in 1897. The facilities initially included a covered 500 seat stand on the south side but the new owners, having changed their name to *Bristol Eastville Rovers FC*, quickly added a cover along the north side and additional banking around the ground.

Further alterations made following their election to the Football League (as *Bristol Rovers FC*) in 1920 included the construction of a new 2,000 seat south stand and, in 1931, the re-siting of the end terraces to accommodate a greyhound racing track. Having sold the ground to the greyhound company for £12,000 in 1940, post WWII improvements included the construction of a stand on the north side in 1958 and the installation of covering over the west end in 1961. During this period the record attendance of 38,742 was set at the FA Cup 4th Round tie v. *Preston North End* (3-3) on January 30th, 1960.

Speedway racing was tried out between 1977 and 1979 and, on August 16th, 1980, the south stand burned down, forcing the club to move in with *Bristol City* at *Ashton Gate*. *Bristol Rovers* returned after five games but finally moved out to *Twerton Park* in 1986. *Eastville Stadium* continued in use for greyhounds but by 2001 an IKEA store occupied the site.

PLAYING RECORD OF BRISTOL ROVERS
LEAGUE PROGRAMME

First Match; 3-2 v. Newport County (10,000) (September 1st, 1920)
Last Match; 1-1 v. Chesterfield (3,576) (April 26th, 1986)
Highest Gate; 34,612 v. Bristol City (2-0) (January 19th, 1952)
Lowest Gate; 1,500 v. Northampton Town (7-1) (January 16th, 1935)
Highest Home Win; 7-0 v. Brighton & Hove Albion (11,647) (November 29th, 1952), v. Swansea Town (28,731) (October 2nd, 1954) & v. Shrewsbury Town (8,902) (March 21st, 1964)
Highest Home Defeat; 0-7 v. Grimsby Town (14,577) (December 14th, 1957)

No. of Matches Played by Bristol Rovers; 1,277

The club was a founder member of the Football League Division 3 in 1920. In 1980, the club moved in with *Bristol City* at *Ashton Gate* for a short period and, in 1986 moved to Bath to groundshare **Twerton Park** with *Bath City FC*.

A TOTAL OF 97 TEAMS TOOK PART IN 1,277 LEAGUE FIXTURES AT THIS VENUE

EDGAR STREET
HOME GROUND OF HEREFORD UNITED

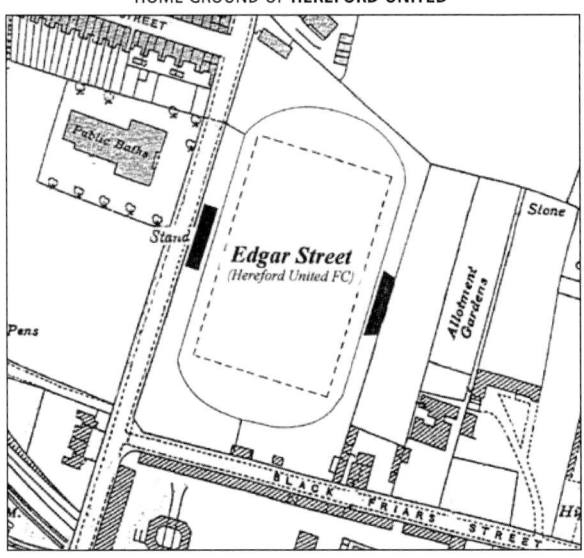

MAP EXTRACT; HEREFORDSHIRE 33.12 & 33.16 [1937]
SITE LOCATION; SO50904051

Opened in the late 19thC as an athletics ground, the football pitch was surrounded by an oval running track and by the 1930s stands were in place on both sides of the ground. *Hereford United FC* commenced playing at *Edgar Street* on their formation in 1924 and subsequent improvements included the construction of banking at both ends (removing part of the oval track), an additional stand on the west side and a new pitch length stand on the east side.

The record attendance of 18,114 was set at the FA Cup 3rd Round tie v. *Sheffield Wednesday* (0-3) on January 4th, 1958 and the main stand was removed and sold when a road widening scheme in 1968 forced the club to sell the strip of land on the west side of the site. A new 1,200 seat cantilever roofed main stand was subsequently built on the east side.

Following election to the Football League in 1972 a 1,200 seat cantilever roofed stand was constructed on stilts on the west side of the ground and, in 1989, a 600 seat extension was added to the main stand. *Edgar Street* is still in use as *Hereford United FCs* home ground.

PLAYING RECORD OF HEREFORD UNITED
LEAGUE PROGRAMME

First Match; 3-0 v. Reading (8,839) (August 19th, 1972)
Last Match; 1-1 v. Brighton & Hove Albion (8,532) (May 3rd, 1997)
Highest Gate; 14,849 v. Newport County (2-0) (April 7th, 1973)
Lowest Gate; 1,294 v. Stockport County (0-0) (March 2nd, 1983) & v. Northampton Town (1-2) (April 28th, 1992)
Highest Home Win; 6-1 v. Crewe Alexandra (3,493) (September 16th, 1978)
Highest Home Defeat; 1-6 v. Wolverhampton Wanderers (13,891) (October 2nd, 1976)

PLAY OFF MATCHES
1-2 v. Darlington (6,622) (May 12th, 1996)

No. of Matches Played by Hereford United; 567
(League Programme; 566 [Including one expunged match v. Aldershot on October 12th, 1991], Play Off Matches; 1)

Some Information Kindly Supplied by; Brian Tabner

The club was elected into the Football League Division 4 in 1972 and relegated to the Football Conference in 1997.

A TOTAL OF 76 TEAMS TOOK PART IN 567 LEAGUE FIXTURES AT THIS VENUE

EDGELEY PARK
HOME GROUND OF STOCKPORT COUNTY

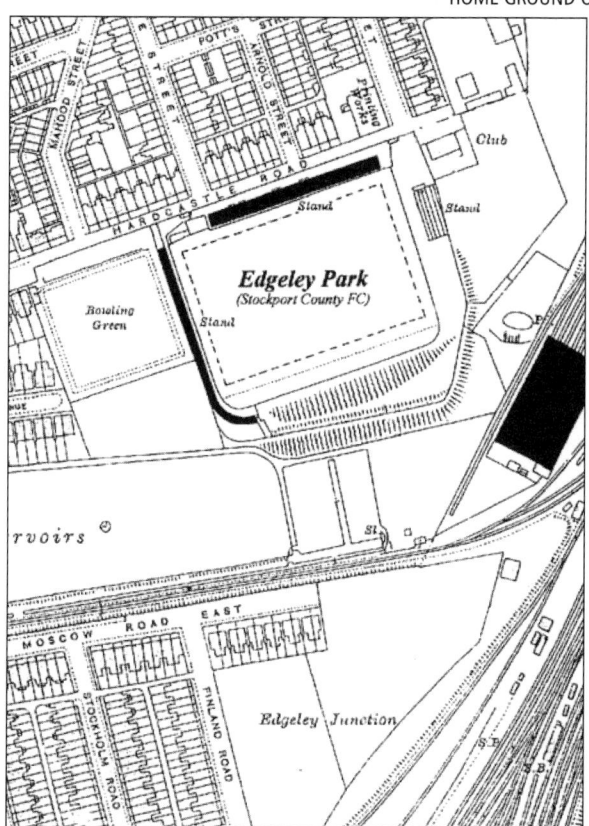

MAP EXTRACT; LANCASHIRE 111.16 [1922]
SITE LOCATION; **SJ89048932**

PLAYING RECORD OF STOCKPORT COUNTY
LEAGUE PROGRAMME
First Match; 1-1 v. Gainsborough Trinity (3,000)
(September 13th, 1902)
Highest Gate; 26,135 v. Lincoln City (2-0) (January 5th, 1937)
Lowest Gate; 1,039 v. Southend United (1-2) (February 15th, 1985)
Highest Home Win; 13-0 v. Halifax Town (7,807)
(January 6th, 1934)
Highest Home Defeat; 0-6 v. Peterborough United (7,004) (February 4th, 1961)

PLAY OFF MATCHES
0-2 v. Chesterfield (7,339) (May 14th, 1990)
1-0 v. Stoke City (7,537) (May 10th, 1992)
1-1 v. Port Vale (7,856) (May 16th, 1993)
1-0 v. York City (6,743) (May 18th, 1994)

No. of Matches Played by Stockport County; 1,993
(League Programme; 1,989 [Including one expunged match v. Accrington Stanley on September 29th, 1961], Play Off Matches; 4)

The club moved here from **Green Lane** in 1902 and failed to gain re-election in 1904 but was re-elected in 1905. The Football League match v. *Preston North End* on April 18th, 1903 was played at **Green Lane** due to the ground being required by the rugby club and the match v. *Leicester City* on May 7th, 1921 took place at **Old Trafford** after the ground was closed following crowd trouble. The club was also involved in Football League Play Off Matches at the neutral venue of **Wembley Stadium**.

AT THE END OF SEASON 2004/5, A TOTAL OF **113** TEAMS HAD TAKEN PART IN **1,993** LEAGUE FIXTURES AT THIS VENUE

The main stand and former paddock on the north side of the ground in 1997.

Photograph by Paul Claydon, Courtesy of Groundtastic Magazine

Opened in 1891, the ground was in use by *Stockport Rugby Club* when *Stockport County FC* moved in from **Green Lane** in 1902 but within a year the football club became sole tenants when the rugby club folded. A cover was installed on the south side in 1903, a new main stand constructed on the north side in 1913 and, by the 1920s a cover had been erected at the west end and an open seated stand built at the east. The final pre-WWII alteration occurred in 1935 when the main stand was destroyed by a fire and replaced in 1936 by a 2,000 seater.

The record attendance of 27,833 was set at the FA Cup 5th Round tie v. *Liverpool* (1-2) on February 11th, 1950 and early post war improvements included the extension of the cover on the south side. From 1978 safety measures resulted in drastic reductions in accommodation; the rear section of the south side terrace and the west stand were demolished, the east end terrace reduced in height and the paddock in front of the main stand closed, resulting in a nominal capacity of only 6,000 with 1,840 seats.

Major improvements took place in the 1990s with the installation of 2,411 seats and refurbishment of the south side stand and construction of a new 4,800 seat stand at the west end. 1,300 seats were subsequently installed on the terraces at the east end and at the start of the 2004/5 season the all-seat capacity was 11,541 and the pitch size 111 x 71 yards.

ELLAND ROAD

HOME GROUND OF **LEEDS CITY** & **LEEDS UNITED**
TEMPORARY HOME GROUND FOR **BRADFORD CITY** & **HUDDERSFIELD TOWN**

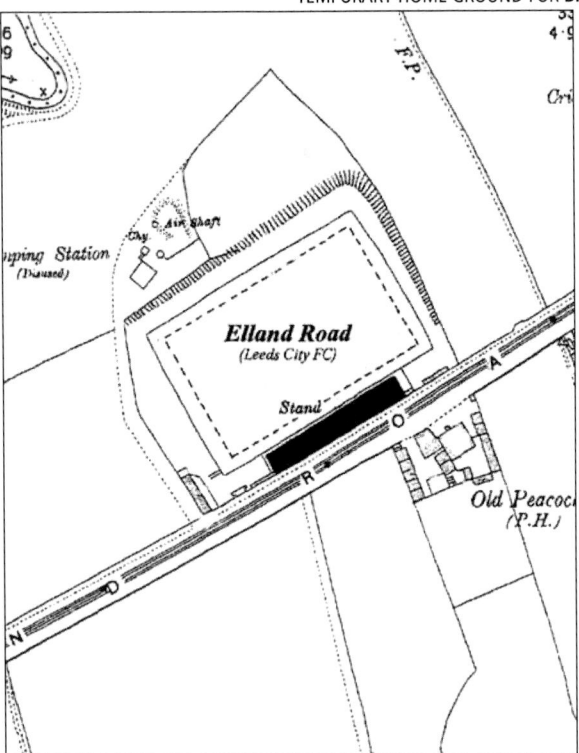

MAP EXTRACT; YORKSHIRE 218.9 [**1908**]
SITE LOCATION; SE28303134

This venue, originally known as *The Old Peacock Ground* and first used by *Holbeck RLFC* in 1896, was acquired by *Leeds City FC* in 1904. The facilities, at this point, consisted of stands on both sides of the pitch but within one year these had been demolished and a new 5,000 seat stand constructed on the south side with banking provided around the other three sides. The pitch was 115 x 73 yards and the potential capacity of the stadium was 22,000.

PLAYING RECORD OF LEEDS CITY
LEAGUE PROGRAMME

First Match; 0-2 v. West Bromwich Albion (6,802)
(September 9th, 1905)
Last Match; 1-1 v Wolverhampton Wanderers (12,000) (September 27th, 1919)
Highest Gate (West-East Pitch); 22,000 v. Bradford City (0-2) (December 30th, 1905)
(After rebuilding); 35,000 v. Bradford City (0-1) (February 1st, 1908)
Lowest Gate; 2,000 v. Chesterfield (3-0) (February 27th, 1906)
& v. Leicester Fosse (1-1) (April 30th, 1910)
Highest Home Win; 8-0 v. Nottingham Forest (14,000) (November 29th, 1913)
Highest Home Defeat; 0-7 v. Barnsley (8,000) (October 23rd, 1909)
No. of Matches Played by Leeds City; 194
(Including 4 expunged matches during the 1919/20 season)

The club was elected into the Football League Division 2 in 1905 and expelled from Division 2 on October 13th, 1919 for making illegal payments to players after playing four home games of the 1919/20 season. *Port Vale FC* was subsequently elected to take over their fixtures.

In 1906 an extra four acres of land at the north end of the site was purchased enabling the ground to be turned through 90°, the former main stand now occupied the south end, and a new main stand was built on the west side. The pitch measured 125 x 85 yards and additional banking raised the nominal capacity of the ground to 45,000. *Leeds City FC* folded in 1919 and the ground was taken over by *Northern Nomads FC*, an amateur club, for a short while until *Leeds United FC* was formed.

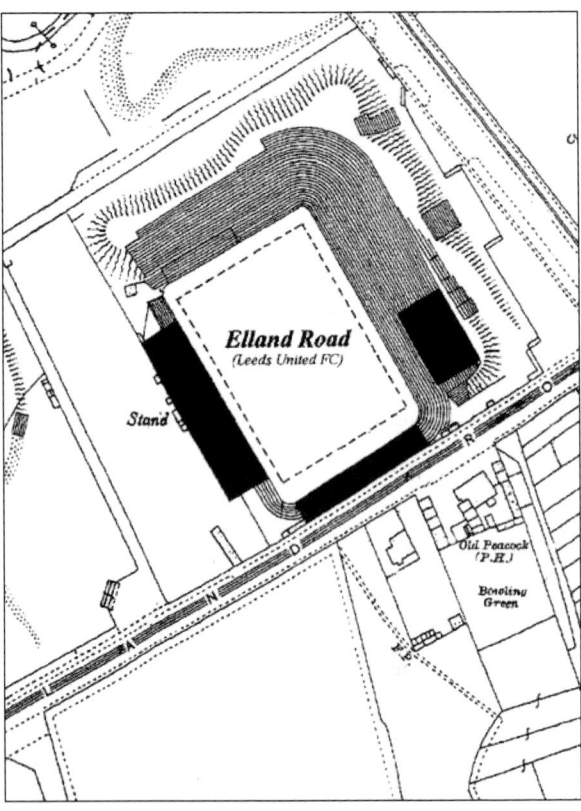

MAP EXTRACT; YORKSHIRE 218.9 [**1932**]

Considerable alterations were made up to WWII with the replacement of the stand at the south end, extension of the roof over the paddock on the west side, expansion of the north end and enlargement and covering of the east side

The main stand burned down in 1956 and was replaced with a 4,000 seat stand fronted by a paddock with standing accommodation for 6,000 but it was not until after the record attendance of 59,892 was set at the FA Cup 5th Round Replay v. *Sunderland* (1-1) on March 15th, 1967 that the major post war re-development of the ground took place. In 1968 the north end terrace was removed and a new propped cantilever stand built some 60 feet further north allowing for the later re-siting of the pitch to accommodate a new propped cantilever stand at the south end which was subsequently completed in 1974. During this period stands were also constructed in the north east, north west and south west corners but it was not until 1991 that the south east corner was similarly treated.

The final development came in the 1990s with the construction of a 17,000 seat stand on the east side and conversion of all standing areas to seating giving a capacity of 40,296 at the start of the 2004/5 season. The pitch size was 117 x 76 yards.

Cont ...

ELLAND ROAD [CONT...]

PLAYING RECORD OF LEEDS UNITED
LEAGUE PROGRAMME

First Match; 1-2 v. South Shields (16,958) (September 1st, 1920)
Highest Gate; 56,796 v. Arsenal (0-0) (December 27th, 1932)
Lowest Gate; 3,590 v. Sheffield Wednesday (3-0) (April 9th, 1930)
Highest Home Win; 8-0 v. Leicester City (11,871) (April 7th, 1934)
Highest Home Defeat; 0-5 v. Arsenal (20,855) (November 8th, 1980)

PLAY OFF MATCHES

1-0 v. Oldham Athletic (29,472) (May 14th, 1987)
1-0 v. Charlton Athletic (31,395) (May 25th, 1987)

No. of Matches Played by Leeds United; 1,625
(League Programme; 1,623, Play Off Matches; 2)

The club was elected into the Football League Division 2 in 1920. Due to crowd trouble at the League match v. *West Bromwich Albion* (1-2) on April 17th, 1971, *Leeds United* were ordered to play the first four home fixtures of the 1971/2 season away from *Elland Road* and these took place at *Leeds Road*, *Hillsborough* and *Boothferry Park*. It was also involved in a Football League Play Off Match at the neutral venue of *St Andrew's*.

PLAYING RECORD OF HUDDERSFIELD TOWN
LEAGUE PROGRAMME

Matches Played; 2-0 v. Derby County (30,167) (April 8th, 1950)
1-2 v. Newcastle United (37,765) (April 11th, 1950)

No. of Matches Played by Huddersfield Town; 2

Two matches were played here when *Leeds Road* was affected by a fire to the main stand.

PLAYING RECORD OF BRADFORD CITY
LEAGUE PROGRAMME

Matches Played; 3-1 v. Stoke City (6,999) (September 1st, 1985)
1-4 v. Sheffield United (7,448) (October 26th, 1985)
0-1 v. Grimsby Town (5,185) (March 1st, 1986)
1-0 v. Oldham Athletic (3,964) (March 4th, 1986)

No. of Matches Played by Bradford City; 4
Information Kindly Supplied by; Peter Waller

These matches were played here whilst *Valley Parade* was being rebuilt following the fire of May 11th, 1985.

AT THE END OF SEASON 2004/5, A TOTAL OF **82** TEAMS HAD TAKEN PART IN **1,825** LEAGUE FIXTURES AT THIS VENUE

ELM PARK
HOME GROUND OF READING

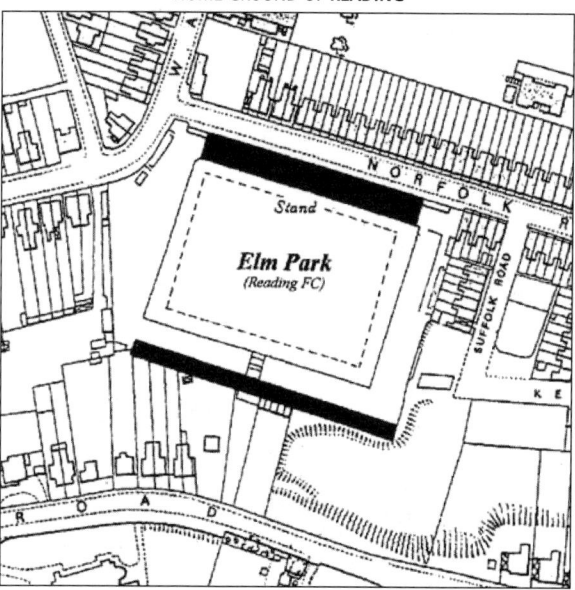

MAP EXTRACT; BERKSHIRE 37.2 [**1932**]
SITE LOCATION; SU69417318

Located to the west of the town centre, *Reading FC* moved here from the *Caversham Cricket Ground* in 1896. The facilities initially included some banking around the pitch and a stand on the north side of the ground. A later addition was an L-shaped cover over the terracing in the north west corner but this, along with the stand, was destroyed in a gale in 1925 resulting in the construction of a new main stand one year later.

The record attendance of 33,042 was set at the FA Cup 5th Round tie v. *Brentford* (1-0) on February 19th, 1927 and by 1932 a narrow cover, later extended to cover the whole side, had been installed on the south of the pitch. *Reading FC* moved out to *Madejski Stadium* in 1998 and the site was redeveloped with flats and houses.

PLAYING RECORD OF READING
LEAGUE PROGRAMME

First Match; 1-2 v. Gillingham (7,000) (September 1st, 1920)
Last Match; 0-1 v. Norwich City (14,817) (May 3rd, 1998)
Highest Gate; 29,092 v. Notts County (0-1) (September 24th, 1949)
Lowest Gate; 1,943 v. Preston North End (2-3) (October 2nd, 1982)
Highest Home Win; 10-2 v. Crystal Palace (8,241) (September 4th, 1946)
Highest Home Defeat; 2-7 v. Bristol City (17,529) (October 4th, 1947)

PLAY OFF MATCHES

0-0 v. Tranmere Rovers (13,245) (May 17th, 1994)

No. of Matches Played by Reading; 1,587
(League Programme; 1,586, Play Off Matches; 1)
Information Kindly Supplied by; David Downs

The club was a founder member of the Football League Division 3 in 1920. The club was also involved in a Football League Play Off Match at the neutral venue of *Wembley Stadium* and moved to the *Madejski Stadium* in 1998.

A TOTAL OF **97** TEAMS TOOK PART IN **1,587** LEAGUE FIXTURES AT THIS VENUE

EWOOD PARK
HOME GROUND OF BLACKBURN ROVERS

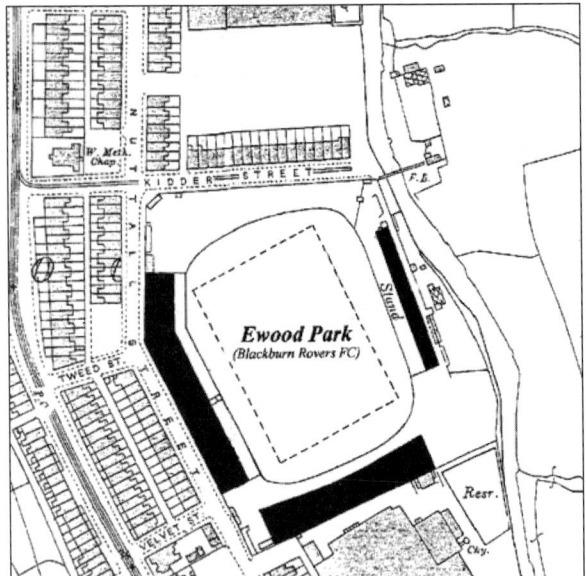

MAP EXTRACT; LANCASHIRE 70.3 & 70.4 [1911]
SITE LOCATION; **SD67822591**

Blackburn Rovers FC first played four games on this site, then known as *Ewood Bridge*, in 1881 whilst waiting to move into *Leamington Street* from *Alexandra Meadows*. By the time that the club made a permanent move here in 1890, it was known as *Ewood Park* and had been redeveloped as a sports ground. The football pitch was surrounded by an oval running track and the facilities included a main stand on the east side and two small stands on the west. Within a few years the ground earned a unique place in football history when the Football League match v. *West Bromwich Albion* on February 5th, 1898 became the first ever match recorded on movie film.

The ground saw considerable improvements in the period leading up to WWI, with the construction of concrete terracing and a cover at the south end, new seated stands on both sides of the pitch and it was probably at this time that the running track was dispensed with. The north end terracing was concreted in 1928 and the record attendance of 61,783 was set one year later at the FA Cup 6th Round tie v. *Bolton Wanderers* (1-1) on March 2nd.

The ground remained virtually unchanged until a cover was installed at the north end in 1960 and a new stand constructed on the east side in 1988. During the 1990s major alterations took place when the stadium was made an all-seater with the purchase of additional land around the site, construction of three new all-seater stands around the north, south and west sides and installation of seats in the east stand giving a capacity of 31,367 at the start of the 2004/5 season. The pitch size was 115 x 76 yards.

NEUTRAL TEST MATCHES
Newton Heath 0, Liverpool 2 (5,000) (April 28th, 1894)
Bury 1, Liverpool 0 (5,000) (April 27th, 1895)
No. of Matches Played; 2

PLAYING RECORD OF BLACKBURN ROVERS
LEAGUE PROGRAMME
First Match; 0-0 v. Accrington (10,000) (September 13th, 1890)
Highest Gate; 52,656 v. Preston North End (3-0) (December 26th, 1921)
Lowest Gate; 1,000 v. Newcastle United (4-3) (April 28th, 1898) (Test Match)
Highest Home Win; 9-0 v. Middlesbrough (29,189) (November 6th, 1954)
Highest Home Defeat; 1-7 v. Notts County (7,000) (March 14th, 1891) & v. Middlesbrough (26,506) (November 29th, 1947)

TEST MATCHES
1-3 v. Burnley (8,000) (April 21st, 1898)
4-3 v. Newcastle United (1,000) (April 28th, 1898)

PLAY OFF MATCHES
0-2 v. Chelsea (16,568) (May 15th, 1988)
0-0 v. Watford (14,008) (May 21st, 1989)
3-1 v. Crystal Palace (16,421) (May 31st, 1989)
1-2 v. Swindon Town (15,636) (May 13th, 1990)
4-2 v. Derby County (19,677) (May 10th, 1992)

No. of Matches Played by Blackburn Rovers; 2,097
(League Programme; 2,090, Test Matches; 2, Play Off Matches; 5)

Information Kindly Supplied by; Tony Matthews

The club moved here from *Leamington Street* in 1890 and it was also involved in a Football League Play Off Match at the neutral venue of *Wembley Stadium*.

AT THE END OF SEASON 2004/5, A TOTAL OF **95** TEAMS HAD TAKEN PART IN **2,097** LEAGUE FIXTURES AT THIS VENUE

This view of the Archibald Leitch designed main stand shows the brick built façade fronting onto Nuttall Street in the period immediately prior to demolition.

Photograph Courtesy of Groundtastic Magazine

FEETHAMS
HOME GROUND OF **DARLINGTON**

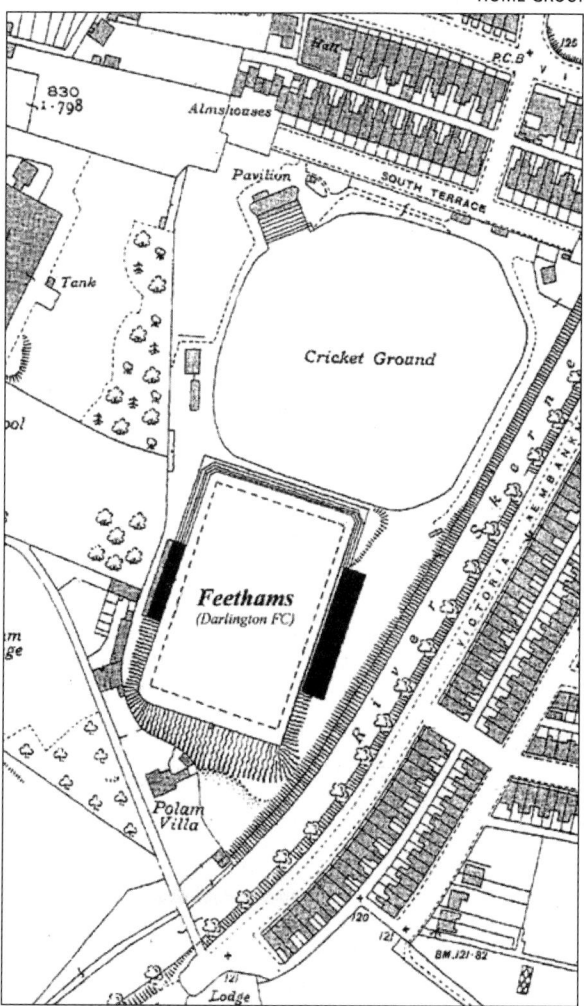

MAP EXTRACT; DURHAM 55.10 [**1939**]
SITE LOCATION; **NZ28851390**

PLAYING RECORD OF DARLINGTON
LEAGUE PROGRAMME
First Match; 2-0 v. Halifax Town (8,532) (August 27th, 1921)
Last Match; 2-2 v. Leyton Orient (5,723) (May 3rd, 2003)
Highest Gate; 17,978 v. Hull City (0-1) (March 12th, 1949)
Lowest Gate; 680 v. Tranmere Rovers (1-0) (February 25th, 1933)
Highest Home Win; 9-2 v. Lincoln City (8,365) (January 7th, 1928)
Highest Home Defeat; 0-7 v. Southport (1,088) (January 6th, 1973)

PLAY OFF MATCHES
2-1 v. Hereford United (6,584) (May 15th, 1996)
1-0 v. Hartlepool United (8,238) (May 17th, 2000)

No. of Matches Played by Darlington; 1,651
(League Programme; 1,626 [Including expunged matches v. Wigan Borough on September 19th, 1931 & v. Accrington Stanley on April 28th, 1962], Play Off Matches; 2)

Information Kindly Supplied by; Claire Dowron

The club was a founder member of the Football League Division 3 [N] in 1921, relegated to the Football Conference in 1988 and promoted into Division 4 in 1989. The match v. *Chesterfield* (2-1) on December 29th, 1923 (5,675) was played on the adjacent cricket ground due to the football pitch being frozen. The club was also involved in Football League Play Off Matches at the neutral venue of **Wembley Stadium**. *Darlington FC* moved to *The Reynolds Arena* at the end of the 2002/3 season. The club went into administration in 2004 and a return to *Feethams* to save money was considered but ultimately rejected.

A TOTAL OF **99** TEAMS TOOK PART IN **1,651** LEAGUE FIXTURES AT THIS VENUE

Despite only being built in 1961 the west stand had none of the attributes of contemporary architecture and was almost a replica of the outdated structure that it replaced!
Photograph by Vince Taylor. Courtesy of Groundtastic Magazine

The site was first used by *Darlington Cricket Club* in 1866 and, following their formation in 1883, *Darlington FC* played on the adjacent field. *Feethams* was gradually developed as two distinct arenas within the one ground (as compared to others, such as **Barley Bank** and **Bramall Lane** where the football and cricket pitches shared the same field). The cricket pavilion was constructed in 1906, a stand on the east side of the football pitch completed in 1919 and, following their admittance to the Football League in 1921, a stand built on the west side. Also by this time a narrow terrace had been constructed at the north end and embankments at the south.

The ground remained virtually unaltered until a cantilever roof was installed at the north end and the west stand destroyed by fire, just before the record attendance of 21,023 was set at the Football League Cup 3rd Round tie v. *Bolton Wanderers* (1-2) on November 14th, 1960. The west stand was subsequently replaced in 1961, a new east stand constructed in the 1990s, and the capacity at the end of the 2001/2 season was 8,379 with 3,958. The pitch size was 112 x 74 yards and it was planned that the ground would be retained for training and the staging of youth and reserve team fixtures after the club had moved to **The Reynolds Arena** at the end of the 2002/3 season. In the event it was not used and by 2005 was derelict.

FELLOWS PARK
HOME GROUND OF WALSALL

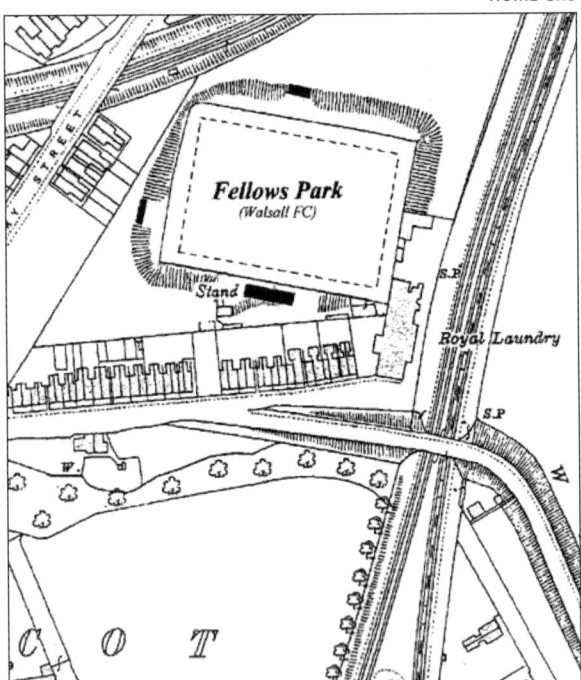

MAP EXTRACT; STAFFORDSHIRE 63.14 [1918]
SITE LOCATION; SP00269704

PLAYING RECORD OF WALSALL
LEAGUE PROGRAMME

First Match; 2-0 v. Burton Wanderers (2,500) (September 5th, 1896)
Last Match; 1-1 v. Rotherham United (5,697) (May 1st, 1990)
Highest Gate; 25,453 v. Newcastle United (1-0) (August 29th, 1961)
Lowest Gate; 1,047 v. Halifax Town (3-1) (January 25th, 1926)
Highest Home Win; 10-0 v. Darwen (2,000) (March 4th, 1899)
Highest Home Defeat; 0-7 v. Chelsea (6,860) (February 4th, 1989)

PLAY OFF MATCHES

1-1 v. Notts County (8,901) (May 18th, 1988)
0-2 v. Bristol City (13,941) (May 28th, 1988)
4-0 v. Bristol City (13,007) May 30th, 1988),

No. of Matches Played by Walsall; 1,452
(League Programme; 1,449 [Including one expunged match v. Wigan Borough on October 3rd, 1931], Play Off Matches; 3)
Information Kindly Supplied by; Tony Matthews

The club was re-elected to the Football League Division 2 in 1896 as *Walsall FC* and moved here from **West Bromwich Road**. In December 1900 the club was temporarily evicted and returned to **West Bromwich Road** to play the final six home games of the season. *Walsall FC* failed to gain re-election in 1901 and was elected as an original member of Division 3 [N] in 1921. In 1970 ten successive home games were postponed due to the waterlogged state of the pitch and, to relieve the backlog, the fixture v. *Brighton & Hove Albion* was played at *The Hawthorns*. In 1990 the club moved to **Bescot Stadium**.

A TOTAL OF **110** TEAMS TOOK PART IN **1,452** LEAGUE FIXTURES AT THIS VENUE

The ground was known as *Hillary Street* when *Walsall FC* moved here in 1896 and an unusual feature was that a laundry occupied the south east corner of the site and its perimeter wall, stretching beyond the goalmouth, was immediately adjacent to the east end of the pitch.

By WWI the facilities included a stand on the south side and, with the exception of the south east corner, embankments around the remainder of the ground. The name of the ground was altered to *Fellows Park* in the 1930s and, during this decade, a new main stand built on the south side and a roof erected over the north side.

Apart from the construction of terracing on the north and west sides the ground remained basically unaltered until the 1960s when further improvements were made. A roof was installed at the west end and, more significantly, the laundry site acquired, the ubiquitous wall demolished and replaced with a narrow bank of concrete terracing. The laundry itself was converted to the "Saddlers Club" whilst the terracing was only narrow as it was originally planned that it would form an enclosure in front of a new stand which in the event never materialized.

An extension to the main stand in 1975 was the last major alteration before the club moved out to *Bescot Stadium* in 1990. The site is now in use for a supermarket.

PROGRAMME COVER ON RIGHT
The aerial view, from the south, shows the ground almost in its final form with the narrow concrete terracing at the east end and cover over the north and west sides. The match ended in a 2-0 win for the hosts.

FIELD MILL GROUND
HOME GROUND OF MANSFIELD TOWN

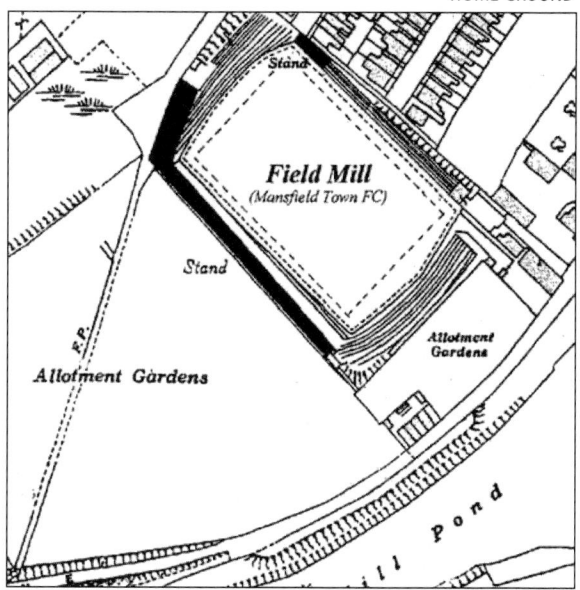

MAP EXTRACT; NOTTINGHAMSHIRE 27.4 [1939]
SITE LOCATION; **SK53566040**

Mansfield Town FC moved from *The Prairie* to the *Field Mill Ground* in 1919. The site had been used as a cricket ground as early as 1840 and was first used for football by *Greenhalgh FC* in 1861. A narrow 1,600 seat stand was constructed along the west side in 1922, and alterations in 1928 included the installation of a cover on the east side and the construction of an oval track for greyhound racing.

Following the club's election to the Football League in 1931, greyhound racing was dispensed with and a new stand built on the east side, utilizing seating from the west stand which reverted to standing accommodation.

After the club purchased the ground and adjacent allotments in 1947, the record attendance of 24,467 was set six years later at the FA Cup 3rd Round tie v. *Nottingham Forest* (0-1) on January 10th, 1953. A cover was installed at the north end in 1956 and a 2,400 seat grandstand, purchased from the *Hurst Park Racecourse* opened on the west side in 1966.

The ground was further improved in 2000/1 when 2,200 seat stands were constructed at each end of the ground and the main stand on the west side rebuilt giving an all-seater capacity of 9,990 at the start of the 2004/5 season. The pitch size was 115 x 72 yards.

PLAYING RECORD OF MANSFIELD TOWN
LEAGUE PROGRAMME
First Match; 3-2 v. Swindon Town (12,232) (August 29th, 1931)
Highest Gate; 19,496 v. Doncaster Rovers (1-2) (October 15th, 1949)
Lowest Gate; 800 v. Torquay United (4-0) (March 8th, 1939)
Highest Home Win; 9-2 v. Rotherham United (5,580) (December 27th, 1932)
Highest Home Defeat; 1-7 v. Reading (6,228) (March 12th, 1932), v. Peterborough United (3,545) (March 26th, 1966) & v. Queens Park Rangers (6,262) (September 24th, 1966)

PLAY OFF MATCHES
1-1 v. Chesterfield (6,582) (May 14th, 1995)
1-3 v. Northampton Town [aet. 5-4 on penalties] (9,243) (May 20th, 2004)

No. of Matches Played by Mansfield Town; 1,512
(League Programme; 1,510 [Including one expunged match v. Aldershot on January 11th, 1992], Play Off Matches; 2)

The club was elected into the Football League Division 3 [S] in 1931 and was involved in a Football League Play Off match at the *Millennium Stadium*.

AT THE END OF SEASON 2004/5, A TOTAL OF **99** TEAMS HAD TAKEN PART IN **1,512** LEAGUE FIXTURES AT THIS VENUE

The stand at the north end, one of a pair built at each end in 2001.
Photograph by Stephen Mumford. Courtesy of Groundtastic Magazine

FILBERT STREET

HOME GROUND OF **LEICESTER CITY**
TEMPORARY HOME GROUND FOR **LOUGHBOROUGH**

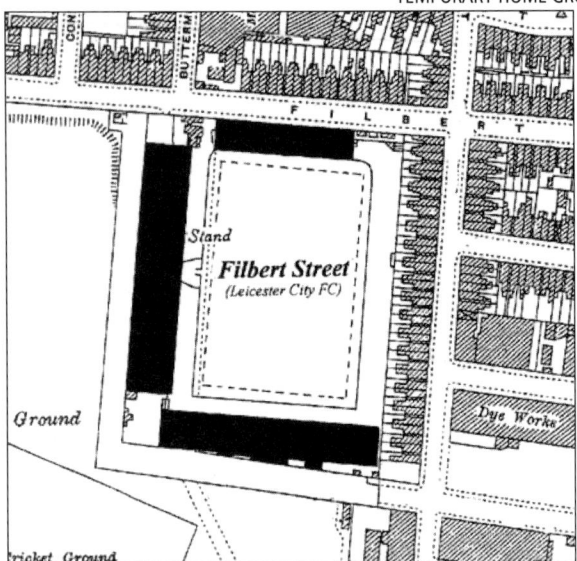

MAP EXTRACT; LEICESTERSHIRE 31.14 [**1930**]
SITE LOCATION; **SK58290323**

NEUTRAL TEST MATCHES
Derby County 2, Notts County 1 (8,000) (April 27th, 1895)
No. of Matches Played; 1

PLAYING RECORD OF LEICESTER CITY
LEAGUE PROGRAMME
First Match; 4-2 v. RotherhamTown (5,000) (September 8th, 1894)
Last Match; 2-1 v. Tottenham Hotspur (21,716) (May 11th, 2002)
Highest Gate; 42,486 v. Arsenal (3-3) (October 2nd, 1954)
Lowest Gate; 1,000 v. Gainsborough Trinity (0-0) (April 19th, 1897)
Highest Home Win; 10-0 v. Portsmouth (25,000) (October 20th, 1928)
Highest Home Defeat; 3-8 v. Aston Villa (25,000) (January 2nd, 1932). 0-6 v. Derby County (5,000) (December 28th, 1914) & v. West Ham United (6,000) (February 15th, 1923)

PLAY OFF MATCHES
5-0 v. Cambridge United (21,024) (May 13th, 1992)
2-1 v. Tranmere Rovers (22,593) (May 18th, 1994)
0-0 v. Stoke City (20,325) (May 12th, 1996)

No. of Matches Played by Leicester City; 1,972
(League Programme; 1,969, Play Off Matches; 3)

The venue was known as *Walnut Street* when *Leicester Fosse FC* moved here from their temporary home at *Aylestone Road Cricket Ground* in 1891. The facilities initially included a stand on the west side and a cover was subsequently installed at the south end.

Following the end of WWI, *Leicester City FC*, as they were now known, proceeded to redevelop the ground with the construction of a new main stand on the west side and, in 1927 replacement of the cover at the south end (removed and subsequently re-installed at the north end) with a new two tier stand. Within a year the record attendance of 47,298 was set at the FA Cup 5th Round tie v. *Tottenham Hotspur* on February 18th, 1928 and just before the outbreak of WWII a cover was constructed over the east side.

Although the main stand suffered some damage during WWII and this was rectified by 1949, there were only minor alterations to the ground in the 1970s, with the conversion of the stands on the north and east sides to all-seaters, before the main stand was replaced by a 9,300 seat structure in 1993.

At the end of the 2001/2 season, when the club moved to *The Walkers Stadium*, the all-seat capacity was only 21,500 with an 110 x 76 yards sized pitch. The site was sold for housing and although a proposal was made to remove the main stand to *Rotherham United FCs Millmoor Ground* all the buildings were demolished in May 2003 and the site cleared.

The club was elected into the Football League Division 2 in 1894 as *Leicester Fosse* and changed the name to *Leicester City* in 1919. The club was also involved in Football League Play Off Matches at *The City Ground* (switched due to rebuilding work at *Filbert Street*) and at the neutral venue of *Wembley Stadium*. The club moved to *The Walkers Stadium* in 2002.

A TOTAL OF **90** TEAMS TOOK PART IN **1,975** LEAGUE FIXTURES AT THIS VENUE

PLAYING RECORD OF LOUGHBOROUGH
LEAGUE PROGRAMME
Matches Played; 1-3 v. Blackpool (5,000) (February 4th, 1899)
2-3 v. Bolton Wanderers (4,000) (September 2nd, 1899)

No. of Matches Played by Loughborough; 2

The first match was played here when *The Athletic Ground* was closed between January 23rd and February 6th, 1899 because of crowd trouble at a reserve fixture versus *Coalville FC* in January 1899, whilst the second match was probably played here to accommodate a cricket match at *The Athletic Ground*.

This aerial view from the north shows the heavily confined nature of the site with any sort of expansion only possible on the west side. One of the effects of this restricted width was that the seats in the two-tier stand at the south end had to be set on a very steep angle
Photograph Courtesy of Groundtastic Magazine

FRATTON PARK

HOME GROUND OF **PORTSMOUTH**
TEMPORARY HOME GROUND FOR **MILLWALL**

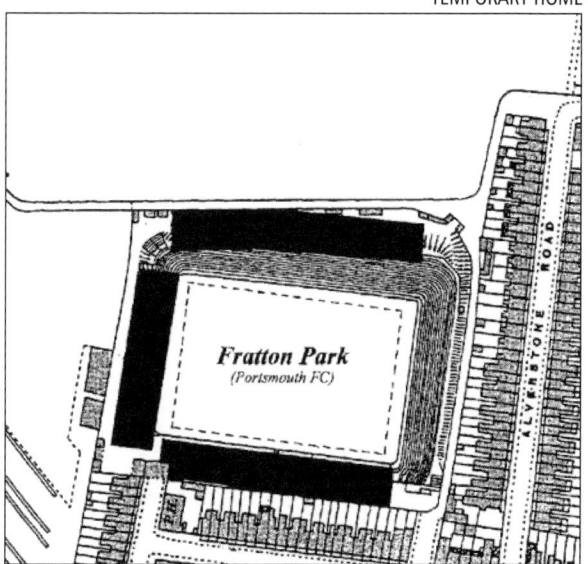

MAP EXTRACT; HAMPSHIRE 83.8 [**1939**]
SITE LOCATION; **SU66080004**

PLAYING RECORD OF PORTSMOUTH
LEAGUE PROGRAMME

First Match; 3-0 v. Swansea Town (20,232) (August 28th, 1920)
Highest Gate; 49,831 v. Wolverhampton Wanderers (1-1) (October 1st, 1949)
Lowest Gate; 4,688 v. Middlesbrough (0-0) (December 16th, 1972)
Highest Home Win; 9-1 v. Notts County (14,000) (April 9th, 1927)
Highest Home Defeat; 0-5 v. Birmingham City (28,952) (October 15th, 1955)

PLAY OFF MATCHES
2-2 v. Leicester City (25,438) (May 19th, 1993)

No. of Matches Played by Portsmouth; 1,732
(League Programme; 1,731, Play Off Matches; 1)
Information Kindly Supplied by; Richard J. Owen

The club was a founder member of the Football League Division 3 in 1920.

AT THE END OF SEASON 2004/5, A TOTAL OF **96** TEAMS HAD TAKEN PART IN **1,733** LEAGUE FIXTURES AT THIS VENUE

Portsmouth FC was formed in 1898 and purchased the site, in use as a market garden, for £4,950. The original facilities upon its opening in September 1899 included a seated stand on the south side and a cover on the north. A subsequent addition was a pavilion built on the south side, at the west end, in 1905. Major improvements were made upon joining the Football League in 1920 with the installation of a new 4,000 seat main stand on the south side and, in the years leading up to WWII a new stand was built on the north side and a cover erected at the west end.

Following the end of the war the record attendance of 51,385 was set at the FA Cup 6th Round tie v. *Derby County* (2-1) on February 26th, 1949 and *Fratton Park* hosted the first ever Football League match to be played under floodlights when *Newcastle United* visited for a Division One fixture (0-2) on February 22nd, 1956. The one major improvement undertaken in this period was the construction of a concrete two-tier stand at the west end but this only survived until 1988 when it was demolished due to the rapid deterioration of the material.

The stadium was refurbished and partially rebuilt during the 1990s with the installation of seats throughout the ground plus an extension to the roof on the north stand and the construction of a new 4,550 seat stand at the west end. The all-seater capacity at the start of season 2004/5 was 20,101 and the pitch size 114 x 72 yards. In 2005 plans were in hand to rotate the ground through 90° and rebuild it.

PLAYING RECORD OF MILLWALL
LEAGUE PROGRAMME

Match Played; 1-3 v. Bristol Rovers (3,392) (April 1st, 1978)

No. of Matches Played by Millwall; 1
Information Supplied by; Richard J. Owen

This match was played here after *The Den* was closed due to crowd trouble

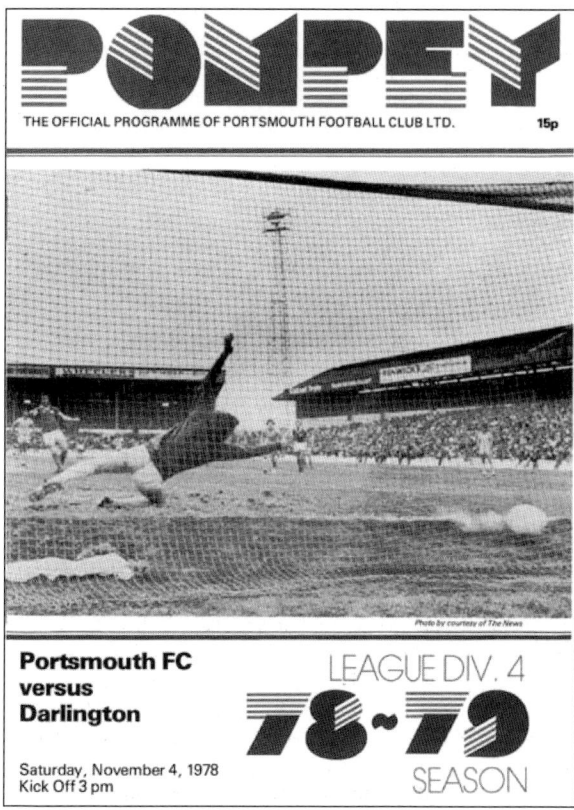

Colin Garwood scores a penalty for *Pompey* in their 3-1 win v. *Halifax Town* on October 21st, 1978. This view from behind the goal at the east end shows the pre-WWII north stand, on top of the terracing and the two-tier stand at the west end which had to be prematurely demolished. This match ended in a 3-0 home win.

FULFORDGATE
HOME GROUND OF YORK CITY

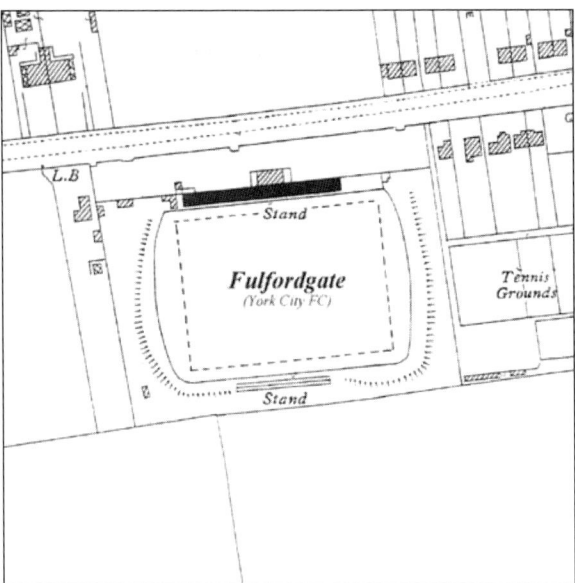

MAP EXTRACT; YORKSHIRE 174.15 [1931]
SITE LOCATION; SE61334944

The ground, located to the south of the city and on the south side of Heslington Lane, opened in 1922 on the formation of *York City FC*. A grandstand was constructed on the north side, an uncovered stand on the south and raised banking behind the goals. The ground subsequently saw some gradual improvements to the terracing and construction of a roof over the stand on the south side of the pitch. The record attendance of 12,583 was set on January 15th, 1930 when *Newcastle United FC* visited for an FA Cup 3rd Round Replay (1-2). *York City* moved to **Bootham Crescent** in 1932 and the site was redeveloped with housing.

PLAYING RECORD OF YORK CITY
LEAGUE PROGRAMME

First Match; 0-0 v. Wrexham (8,726) (September 4th, 1929)
Last Match; 7-2 v. Halifax Town (2,000) (April 28th, 1932)
Highest Gate; 10,120 v. Port Vale (0-2) (April 21st, 1930)
Lowest Gate; 1,735 v. New Brighton (4-1) (April 25th, 1931)
Highest Home Win; 7-2 v. Halifax Town (2,000) (April 28th, 1932).
6-0 v. Rochdale (4,720) (March 22nd, 1930)
Highest Home Defeat; 0-4 v. Southport (5,852)
(September 21st, 1929)

No. of Matches Played by York City; 62

The club was elected into the Football League Division 3 [N] in 1929 and moved to **Bootham Crescent** in 1932.

A TOTAL OF **25** TEAMS TOOK PART IN **62** LEAGUE FIXTURES AT THIS VENUE

GAY MEADOW
HOME GROUND OF SHREWSBURY TOWN

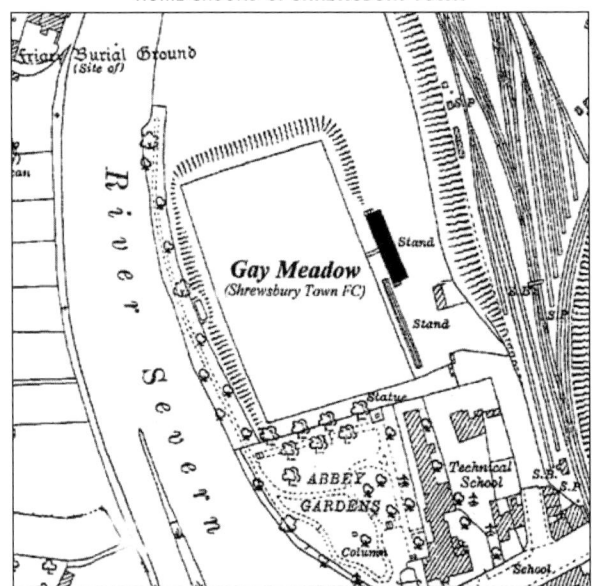

MAP EXTRACT; SHROPSHIRE 34.11 [c1930]
SITE LOCATION; SJ49581255

This site had been in regular use as a recreation ground when it was leased to *Shrewsbury Town FC* by the council in 1910 enabling them to move from *The Barracks*. When it opened with a Birmingham League game v. *Wolverhampton Wanderers Reserves* on September 10th, 1891 the only facilities were a small stand on the east side and a redundant railway carriage serving as dressing rooms and it was not until 1922 that these were replaced by a new stand, also on the east side.

The venue was steadily improved during the 1930s with the installation of concreted terracing around the ground, covers on the west side and at the north end and, just prior to WWII the construction of a second stand on the east side adjoining the original structure at its northern end.

Following their admission to the Football League in 1950 the club bought the freehold from the council and, in the 1960s the main stand was extended to the full length of the pitch and re-roofed.

The capacity at the start of the 2004/5 season was 8,000 with 2,500 seats and the pitch size was 114 x 74 yards.

PLAYING RECORD OF SHREWSBURY TOWN
LEAGUE PROGRAMME

First Match; 2-1 v. Wrexham (16,070) (August 21st, 1950)
Highest Gate; 18,917 v. Walsall (1-2) (April 26th, 1961)
Lowest Gate; 1,232 v. Charlton Athletic (3-3) (March 19th, 1974)
Highest Home Win; 7-0 v. Swindon Town (6,000) (May 6th, 1955)
Highest Home Defeat; 1-8 v. Norwich City (11,890)
(September 13th, 1952)

No. of Matches Played by Shrewsbury Town; 1,221
Information Kindly Supplied by; Richard Stocken

The club was elected into the Football League Division 3 [N] in 1950, relegated to the Football Conference in 2003 and promoted via the Play Offs in 2004.

AT THE END OF SEASON 2004/5, A TOTAL OF **102** TEAMS HAD TAKEN PART IN **1,221** LEAGUE FIXTURES AT THIS VENUE

GIGG LANE
HOME GROUND OF BURY

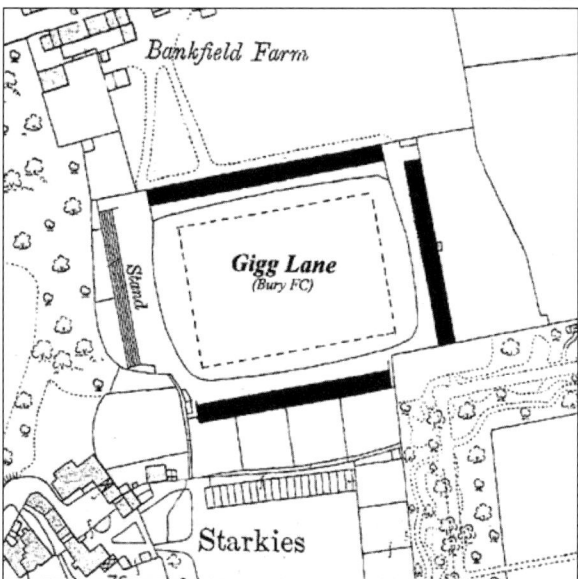

MAP EXTRACT; LANCASHIRE 88.13 [**1910**]
SITE LOCATION; **SD80550935**

PLAYING RECORD OF BURY
LEAGUE PROGRAMME
First Match; 4-2 v. Manchester City (7,070) (September 1st, 1894)
Highest Gate; 34,386 v. Blackpool (2-3) (January 1st, 1937)
Lowest Gate; 1,096 v. Northampton Town (1-2) (May 5th, 1984)
Highest Home Win; 8-0 v. Tranmere Rovers (4,492)
(January 10th, 1970)
Highest Home Defeat; 2-7 v. Newcastle United (13,809) (October 14th, 1961). 0-6 v. Stoke City (13,762) (March 13th, 1954)
& v. Huddersfield Town (4,145) (April 1st, 1989)

PLAY OFF MATCHES
0-0 v. Tranmere Rovers (7,019) (May 13th, 1990)
1-1 v. Bolton Wanderers (8,000) (May 19th, 1991)
0-0 v. York City (6,620) (May 16th, 1993)
1-0 v. Preston North End (9,094) (May 17th, 1995)
0-0 v. AFC Bournemouth (5,782) (May 10th, 2003)

No. of Matches Played by Bury; 2,110
(League Programme; 2,105, Play Off Matches; 5)
Some Information Kindly Supplied by; Brian Tabner

The club was elected into the Football League Division 2 in 1894. The club was also involved in a Test Match at the neutral venue of *Ewood Park* and a Football League Play Off Match at the neutral venue of *Wembley Stadium*.

AT THE END OF SEASON 2004/5, A TOTAL OF **115** TEAMS HAD TAKEN PART IN **2,110** LEAGUE FIXTURES AT THIS VENUE

Bury FC moved to *Gigg Lane* on their formation in 1885 and by 1890 the pitch was surrounded by an oval track and the facilities included included stands on both sides of the ground. Following their election to the Football League, and promotion to Division One in 1895, the ground was expanded to a nominal capacity of 20,000 with new stands being subsequently constructed at each end and a replacement structure installed on the south side.

Major alterations took place following the donation of the ground to the club from the landowners in 1922. In the 1920s the end terraces were rebuilt and expanded (eliminating the oval shape) a new main stand constructed on the north side and a 500 seat open stand (subsequently roofed) built on the south side alongside the existing stand which was installed with 2,000 seats. In the wake of these improvements the nominal capacity was set at 41,600 and just before the outbreak of WWII a new stand was opened at the west end.

Following the end of the war, the cover over the east end was destroyed in a gale but it was not until after the record attendance of 35,000 was attained at the FA Cup 3rd Round tie v. *Bolton Wanderers* (1-1) on January 9th, 1960 that the roof was replaced. Although, following safety measures in the 1980s, the capacity was reduced with the demolition of the small stand on the south side and near-closure of both the main and west stands, the ground was considerably improved during the 1990s with refurbishment of the aforementioned main and west stands and construction of new inter-connected stands on the east and south sides. The all-seater capacity at the start of season 2004/5 was 11,669 and the pitch size 112 x 72 yards.

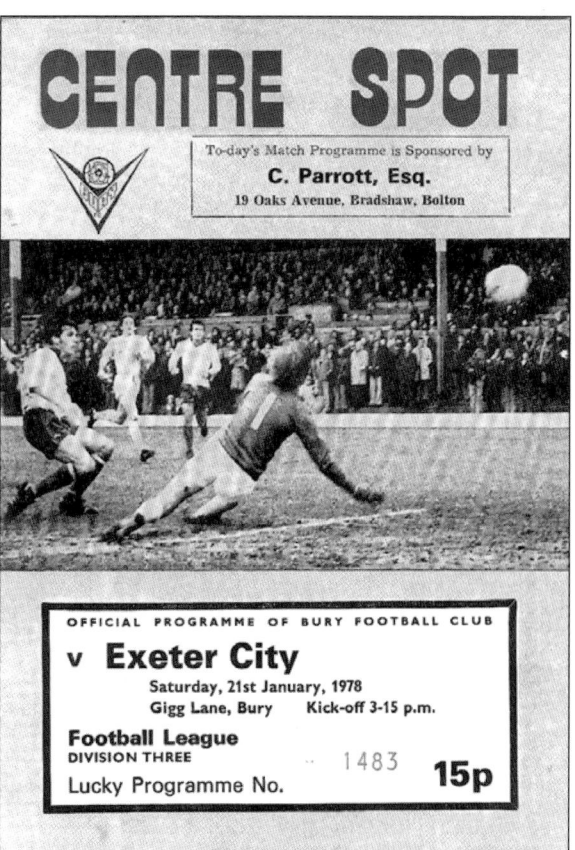

PROGRAMME COVER ON THE RIGHT
This cover features a view of the main stand at *Gigg Lane*. The match v. *Exeter City* finished in a 5-0 home win.

GLANFORD PARK
HOME GROUND OF **SCUNTHORPE UNITED**

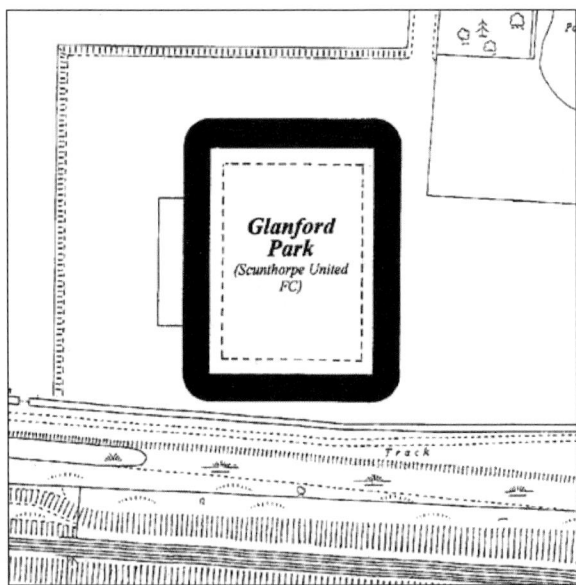

MAP EXTRACT; GROUND AS IN **1999** DRAWN FROM PLANS & AERIAL PHOTOGRAPHS AND SUPERIMPOSED ON SE8610/1 [1951]
SITE LOCATION; **SE86451089**

Constructed on a greenfield site, *Scunthorpe United FC* moved to *Glanford Park* from the **Old Show Ground** in 1988. The ground has a continuous part cantilever and propped roof which, when built, originally covered seated stands on each side of the pitch and terracing at each end. The south end was converted to a 1,678 seat stand in 1990 and the capacity at the start of the 2004/5 season was 9,200 with 6,400 seats. The pitch size was 111 x 73 yards.

PLAYING RECORD OF SCUNTHORPE UNITED
LEAGUE PROGRAMME
First Match; 3-1 v. Hereford United (3,663) (August 27th, 1988)
Highest Gate; 8,775 v. Rotherham United (0-0) (May 1st, 1989)
Lowest Gate; 1,524 v. Chester City (0-2) (February 18th, 1997)
Highest Home Win; 7-0 v. Northampton Town (2,814) (October 16th, 1993)
Highest Home Defeat; 0-5 v. Doncaster Rovers (4,366) (April 15th, 1995)

PLAY OFF MATCHES
0-2 v. Wrexham (5,516) (May 24th, 1989)
1-1 v. Blackpool (6,536) (May 19th, 1991)
2-0 v. Crewe Alexandra (7,938) (May 13th, 1992)
3-1 v. Swansea City (7,089) (May 18th, 1999)
0-1 v. Lincoln City (8,295) (May 14th, 2003)

No. of Matches Played by Scunthorpe United; 389
(League Programme; 384 [Including one expunged match v. Aldershot on February 29th, 1992], Play Off Matches; 5)
Information Kindly Supplied by; John Staff

The club moved here from **The Old Show Ground** in 1998 and was also involved in a Football League Play Off Match at the neutral venue of **Wembley Stadium**.

AT THE END OF SEASON 2004/5, A TOTAL OF **64** TEAMS HAD TAKEN PART IN **389** LEAGUE FIXTURES AT THIS VENUE

GOLDSTONE GROUND
HOME GROUND OF **BRIGHTON & HOVE ALBION**

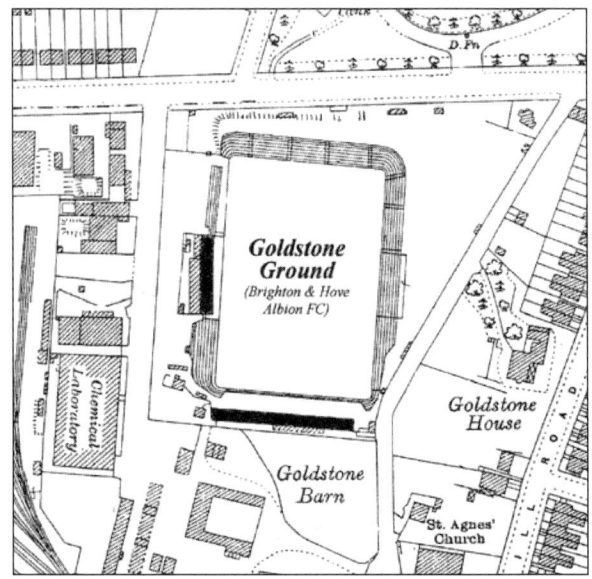

MAP EXTRACT; SUSSEX 65.8 [**1932**]
SITE LOCATION; **TQ28670586**

Goldstone Bottom, was first used as a sporting venue by *Brighton Hockey Club* in 1900 and when *Hove FC* took over a year later a stand was constructed at the south end. *Brighton & Hove Albion FC*, took over the lease when *Hove FC* moved out in 1904 and by 1910 the only addition to facilities had been the installation of a small stand on the west side, obtained from *Preston Park*.

The club bought the ground in 1926 and prior to WWII covers were constructed at each end but it was not until 1957 that a new main stand was built on the west side. (Later supplemented by a 974 seat temporary stand built alongside in 1979 and removed in 1985.) In 1980 the north stand roof was demolished and its replacement in 1985 was virtually the last alteration before the club vacated the *Goldstone Ground* in 1997. The site is now in use as a retail park.

PLAYING RECORD OF BRIGHTON & HOVE ALBION
LEAGUE PROGRAMME
First Match; 0-0 v. Merthyr Town (9,000) (September 1st, 1920)
Last Match; 1-0 v. Doncaster Rovers (11,341) (April 26th, 1997)
Highest Gate; 36,747 v. Fulham (3-0) (December 27th, 1958)
Lowest Gate; 1,933 v. Mansfield Town (1-1) (November 9th, 1996)
Highest Home Win; 9-1 v. Newport County (12,114) (April 18th, 1951) & v. Southend United (11,124) (November 27th, 1965)
Highest Home Defeat; 2-8 v. Bristol Rovers (10,762) (December 1st, 1973)

PLAY OFF MATCHES
4-1 v. Millwall (15,390) (May 19th, 1991)

No. of Matches Played by Brighton & Hove Albion; 1,537
(League Programme; 1,536, Play Off Matches; 1)
Information Kindly Supplied by; Tim Carder

The club was a founder member of the Football League Division 3 in 1920. The club was also involved in a Football League Play Off Match at the neutral venue of **Wembley Stadium**. By 1997 and due to financial circumstances, the club was forced to vacate the ground and move in with *Gillingham FC* at the **Priestfield Stadium** until a new temporary home back in Brighton, at the **Withdean Stadium**, became available in 1999.

A TOTAL OF **104** TEAMS TOOK PART IN **1,537** LEAGUE FIXTURES AT THIS VENUE

GOODISON PARK
HOME GROUND OF EVERTON

MAP EXTRACT; LANCASHIRE 106.2 [1908]
SITE LOCATION; SJ35919400

Everton FC vacated **Anfield** in 1892 and moved to a plot of land in nearby *Mere Green* that they had purchased for £8,090. When the ground (now known as *Goodison Park*) opened later that year it was considered to be one of the finest in Britain with two 4,000 seat open stands, a 3,000 seat covered stand and an open bank on the west side amongst the facilities. Within four years a cover had been installed at the rear of the west side and a new stand constructed on the east side.

The ground saw more major redevelopment during the early part of the 20thC with the opening of two-tier stands on the west side and at the north end prior to WWI and two-tier stands on the other two sides in the 1920s. *Goodison Park* then remained virtually unchanged until 1970 when the main stand, on the west side, was demolished and replaced with a three tier 10,045 seat structure. The ground was gradually made all-seater with the construction of a new stand at the south end and the introduction of seating throughout the refurbished and re-roofed east and north stands. The all-seat capacity at the start of the 2004/5 season was 40,170 and the pitch size 112 x 78 yards.

PLAYING RECORD OF EVERTON
LEAGUE PROGRAMME

First Match; 2-2 v. Nottingham Forest (14,000)
(September 3rd, 1892)
Highest Gate; 78,299 v. Liverpool (1-1) (September 18th, 1948)
Lowest Gate; 7,802 v. Sheffield Wednesday (2-2) (May 1st, 1935)
Highest Home Win; 9-1 v. Manchester City (16,000) (September 3rd, 1906) & v. Plymouth Argyle (37,018) (December 27th, 1930)
Highest Home Defeat; 3-7 v. Newcastle United (39,109) (December 26th, 1933). 0-6 v. Newcastle United (10,000) (October 26th, 1912)
No. of Matches Played by Everton; 2,032
The club moved here from *Anfield* in 1892.

AT THE END OF SEASON 2004/5, A TOTAL OF **69** TEAMS HAD TAKEN PART IN **2,032** LEAGUE FIXTURES AT THIS VENUE

GREEN LANE
HOME GROUND OF STOCKPORT COUNTY

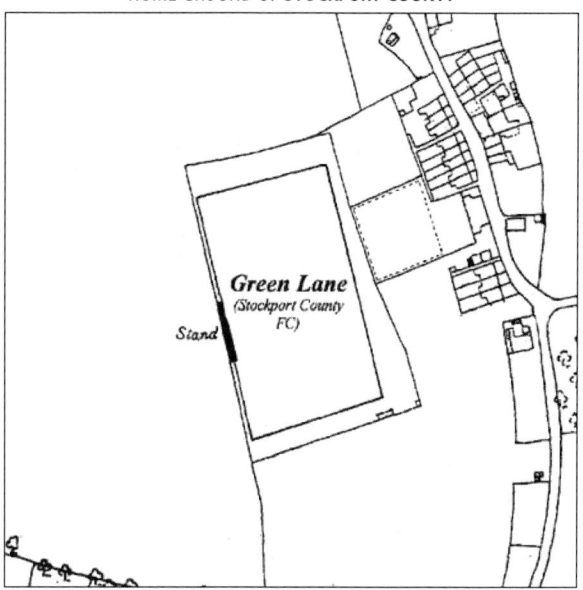

MAP EXTRACT; LANCASHIRE 111.12 [1895]
SITE LOCATION; SJ88459089

When *Heaton Norris FC* moved to the site from *Wilkes Field* in 1889 it was simply an open field but within a year the ground had been enclosed, a small covered stand installed on the west side, an open wooden stand built at the north end and a raised embankment constructed at the south. The ground was located at the rear of the Nursery Inn in Heaton Norris and the changing facilities were provided in a barn on Green Lane.

After the ground was vacated in 1902 *Green Lane* was used for a while for reserve team fixtures and the occasional first team game before being utilized for housing. The Nursery Inn is still extant and won the CAMRA Pub of the Year Award for 2002.

PLAYING RECORD OF STOCKPORT COUNTY
LEAGUE PROGRAMME

First Match, Highest Home Defeat & Highest Gate; 0-5 v. New Brighton Tower (5,000) (September 8th, 1900)
Last Match; 2-1 v. Gainsborough Trinity (3,000) (April 26th, 1902)
FOLLOWING THE MOVE TO **EDGELEY PARK**;
Match Played; 1-1 v. Preston North End (5,000) (April 18th, 1903)
Lowest Gate; 1,000 v. Bristol City (1-1) (January 11th, 1902)
Highest Home Win; 4-1 v. Walsall (2,000) (September 22nd, 1900)
No. of Matches Played by Stockport County; 35
Some Information Kindly Supplied by; Brian Tabner
The club was elected into the Football League Division 2 in 1900 and moved to *Edgeley Park* in 1902. The additional game was played here when *Edgeley Park* was required by the rugby club.

A TOTAL OF **24** TEAMS TOOK PART IN **35** LEAGUE FIXTURES AT THIS VENUE

GRESTY ROAD [2ND]
HOME GROUND OF CREWE ALEXANDRA

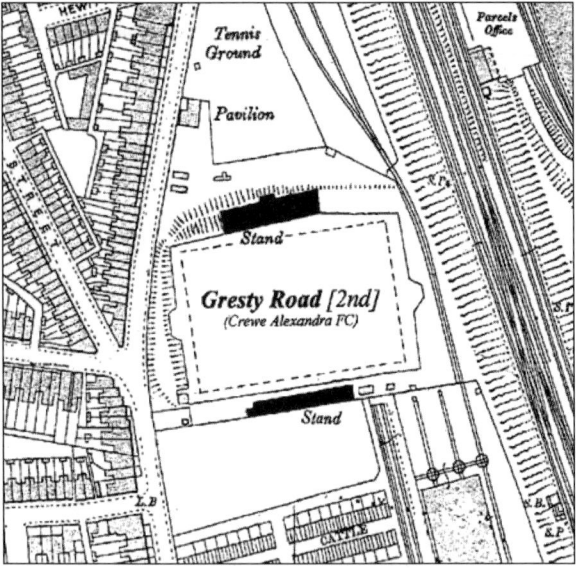

MAP EXTRACT; CHESHIRE 56.7 & 56.8 [1910]
SITE LOCATION; SJ70925455

Having occupied an adjacent ground *(Gresty Road [1st])* from 1897, *Crewe Alexandra FC* moved here in 1906. The facilities included a stand on each side of the pitch (at least one of which had been in use at the previous site) and some embankments and it was not until 1932 that a new main stand was constructed on the south side following a fire. The record attendance of 20,000 was set at the FA Cup 4th Round tie v. *Tottenham Hotspur* (2-2) on January 30th, 1960 and the venue was transformed in the 1990s with the construction of all-seat stands on all sides of the ground. At the start of the 2004/5 season the capacity was 10,100 and the pitch size was 112 x 74 yards.

PLAYING RECORD OF CREWE ALEXANDRA
LEAGUE PROGRAMME

First Match; 1-1 v. Tranmere Rovers (8,000) (September 3rd, 1921)
Highest Gate; 17,883 v. Port Vale (0-0) (September 28th, 1953)
Lowest Gate; 1,009 v. Northampton Town (0-1) (January 25th, 1986)
Highest Home Win; 8-0 v. Rotherham United (4,204) (October 1st, 1932)
Highest Home Defeat; 1-8 v. Rotherham United (2,116) (September 8th, 1973)

PLAY OFF MATCHES
2-2 v. Scunthorpe United (6,083) (May 10th, 1992)
5-1 v. Walsall (6,198) (May 16th, 1993)
1-1 v. Bristol Rovers (6,758) (May 17th, 1995)
2-2 v. Notts County (4,931) (May 12th, 1996)
2-1 v. Luton Town (5,467) (May 11th, 1997)

No. of Matches Played by Crewe Alexandra; 1,724
(League Programme; 1,719 [Including expunged matches v. Wigan Borough on September 12th, 1931, v. Accrington Stanley on March 2nd, 1962 & v. Aldershot on September 3rd, 1991], Play Off Matches; 5)
Some Information Kindly Supplied by; Brian Tabner

The club moved here from *Gresty Road [1st]* in 1906, and was elected as an original member of Football League Division 3 [N] in 1921. The club was also involved in Football League Play Off Matches at the neutral venue of *Wembley Stadium*.

AT THE END OF SEASON 2004/5, A TOTAL OF **101** TEAMS HAD TAKEN PART IN **1,724** LEAGUE FIXTURES AT THIS VENUE

GRIFFIN PARK
HOME GROUND OF BRENTFORD

MAP EXTRACT; MIDDLESEX 20.4 [1935]
SITE LOCATION; TQ17957792

The site had been in use as an orchard when *Brentford FC* moved here in 1904. The facilities included two stands that had been removed from the previous ground, one erected on the south side and used as the main stand and the other on the north side. Unfortunately, before a ball had been kicked the main stand was condemned as unsafe and players had to change in Clifden Road Public Baths. This stand was not replaced until 1927 but further improvements took place in the 1930s with the installation of new covers on the north side and west end and the addition of extra seating to the main stand. Following these alterations the record attendance of 38,678 was set at the FA Cup 6th Round tie v. *Leicester City* (0-2) on February 26th, 1949.

The main stand was partially rebuilt following a fire in 1983 and, in 1986, the west end was demolished, part of it sold off, and a new small two-tier constructed. Following the installation of seating on the north side the capacity, at the start of the 2004/5 season, was 13,870 with 8,905 seats and the pitch size 110 x 73 yards.

PLAYING RECORD OF BRENTFORD
LEAGUE PROGRAMME

First Match; 1-0 v. Millwall (12,000) (August 30th, 1920)
Highest Gate; 38,535 v. Arsenal (1-0) (September 8th, 1938)
Lowest Gate; 2,024 v. Walsall (3-2) (December 5th, 1927)
Highest Home Win; 9-0 v. Wrexham (10,500) (October 15th, 1963)
Highest Home Defeat; 2-6 v. Luton Town (9,000) (February 8th, 1964) & v. Bristol Rovers (5,434) (August 28th, 2000)

PLAY OFF MATCHES
2-2 v. Tranmere Rovers (9,330) (May 19th, 1991)
1-1 v. Huddersfield Town [3-4] (11,161) (May 17th, 1995)
2-1 v. Bristol City (9,496) (May 14th, 1997)
2-1 v. Huddersfield Town (11,191) (May 1st, 2002)
1-2 v. Sheffield Wednesday (10,823) (May 16th, 2005)

No. of Matches Played by Brentford; 1,723
(League Programme; 1,718, Play Off Matches; 5)
Information Kindly Supplied by; Dave Twydell

The club was a founder member of the Football League Division 3 in 1920. The club was also involved in Football League Play Off Matches at the neutral venues of *Wembley Stadium* and the *Millennium Stadium*.

AT THE END OF SEASON 2004/5, A TOTAL OF **104** TEAMS HAD TAKEN PART IN **1,723** LEAGUE FIXTURES AT THIS VENUE

HAIG AVENUE
HOME GROUND OF SOUTHPORT

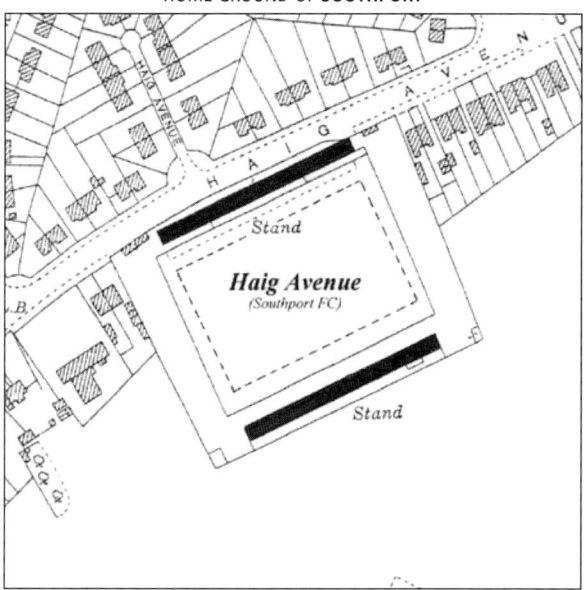

MAP EXTRACT; LANCASHIRE 75.14 [1928]
SITE LOCATION; **SD35371617**

When *Southport Central FC* moved from *Scarisbrook New Road* to *Ash Lane* in 1905 a timber seated stand was removed from the old ground and re-erected and extended on the north side of the new venue. The thoroughfare and ground were re-named as *Haig Avenue* in 1921, *Southport FC's* debut season in the Football League, and a new covered enclosure added on the south side of the pitch. Subsequent improvements included extending the covered enclosure around the west side and the installation of some concrete terracing giving a ground capacity of some 30,000. The record attendance of 20,111 was subsequently set at the FA Cup 4th Round Replay v. *Newcastle United* (1-1) on January 26th, 1932.

In 1966 the main stand burned down and a new 200 seat structure was subsequently erected in its place and although *Southport FC* dropped out of the League in 1978, the ground is still utilized for their home games.

PLAYING RECORD OF SOUTHPORT
LEAGUE PROGRAMME

First Match; 1-1 v. Durham City (7,000) (August 27th, 1921)
Last Match; 1-1 v. Huddersfield Town (1,465) (April 22nd, 1978)
Highest Gate; 14,766 v. Rochdale (3-2) (December 27th, 1949)
Lowest Gate; 773 v. Lincoln City (3-3) (April 2nd, 1935)
Highest Home Win; 8-1 v. Nelson (4,534) (January 1st, 1931)
Highest Home Defeat; 1-7 v Rochdale (4,699) (April 10th, 1926)
No. of Matches Played by Southport; 1,102
Information Kindly Supplied by; Geoff Wilde

The club was a founder member of the Football League Division 3 [N] in 1921 and failed to gain re-election in 1978.

A TOTAL OF **74** TEAMS TOOK PART IN **1,102** LEAGUE FIXTURES AT THIS VENUE

HAWTHORNE ROAD
HOME GROUND OF BOOTLE

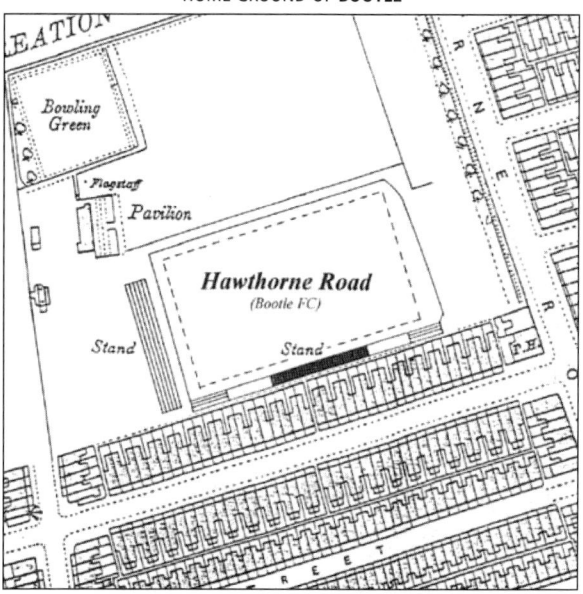

MAP EXTRACT; GROUND AS IN **1893** DRAWN FROM PLANS AND SUPERIMPOSED ON LANCASHIRE 106.2 [1908]
SITE LOCATION; **SJ34719457**

Located to the north of Liverpool city centre, *Bootle FC* moved to the cricket ground on *Hawthorne Road* in 1884. The pitch was on the south side of the ground and, at this time, the only facility was the cricket pavilion. There was a considerable improvement to spectator facilities in 1889 with the provision of an open seated stand behind the west end and covered and open stands on the south side.

The record attendance of 20,000 was set on December 26th, 1889 for the visit of *Everton* in a friendly match. *Bootle FC* folded after their one season in the Football League and *Bootle Athletic FC* took over for a while at *Hawthorne Road*. The cricket ground is still in existence but Wadham Road was later extended over the area that contained the football pitch.

PLAYING RECORD OF BOOTLE
LEAGUE PROGRAMME

Matches Played; 2-0 v. Sheffield United (4,000)
(September 10th, 1892)
1-1 v. Burslem Port Vale (3,000) (September 17th, 1892)
1-4 v. Small Heath (1,500) (November 5th, 1892)
2-5 v. Northwich Victoria (2,000) (December 3rd, 1892)
3-1 v. Grimsby Town (1,000) (December 17th, 1892)
5-1 v. Darwen (800) (December 31st, 1892)
5-3 v. Ardwick (800) (January 21st, 1893)
3-2 v. Burton Swifts (1,000) (February 25th, 1893)
7-1 v. Walsall Town Swifts (600) (March 18th, 1893)
2-1 v. Crewe Alexandra (1,000) (March 25th, 1893)
4-1 v. Lincoln City (2,000) (April 15th, 1893)
No. of Matches Played by Bootle; 11
Information Kindly Supplied by; Tony Matthews

The club was a founder member of the Football League Division 2 in 1892 but, due to financial problems, resigned at the end of the season.

A TOTAL OF **12** TEAMS TOOK PART IN **11** LEAGUE FIXTURES AT THIS VENUE

THE HAWTHORNS

HOME GROUND OF **WEST BROMWICH ALBION**
TEMPORARY HOME GROUND FOR **WALSALL** & **WOLVERHAMPTON WANDERERS**

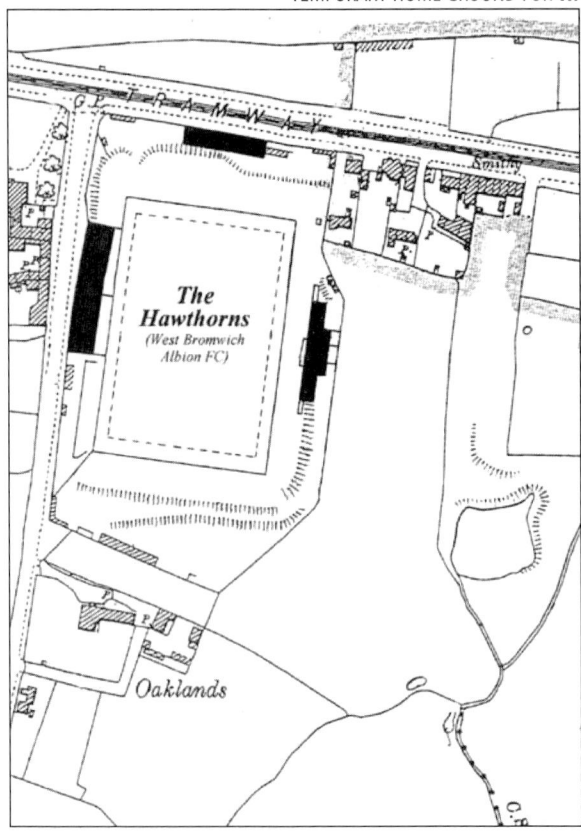

MAP EXTRACT; STAFFORDSHIRE 68.15 [**1902**]
SITE LOCATION; **SP02549014**

West Bromwich Albion FC moved to *The Hawthorns* from **Stoney Lane** in 1900 and re-erected the stand from their former ground on the east side whilst other facilities on opening included a new 5,000 seat main stand on the west side and embankments at each end. The freehold was purchased for £5,350 in 1913 and alterations that took place prior to WWI included the installation of a cover at the south end, the roofing and expansion of the banking on the east side (following the destruction of the stand by a fire in 1904) and refurbishment of the main stand.

Further improvements in the inter-war years included the installation of concrete terracing around the ground, an extension to the stand on the east side, the building of a 750 seat stand in the south west corner and the rebuilding of the main stand roof. The record attendance of 64,815 was set during this period at the FA Cup 6th Round tie v. *Arsenal* (3-1) on March 6th, 1937.

No further alterations took place until the 1950s when a stand was built in the north west corner and in 1964 the east side cover was removed to the north end and replaced by a 4,300 seat stand, the paddock of which was converted to all seats in 1976. A new 4,150 seat main stand was constructed on the west side in 1981 and, after re-roofing in 1985, the terrace at the south end demolished and replaced with a 5,755 seat stand in 1994. In the same year an 8,234 seat structure opened at the north end and, in 2001 the stand on the east side was demolished and replaced with a new 8,000 seat structure giving an all-seat capacity of 28,000 at the start of the 2004/5 season. The pitch size was 115 x 74 yards.

PLAYING RECORD OF WEST BROMWICH ALBION
LEAGUE PROGRAMME

First Match; 1-1 v. Derby County (20,104) (September 3rd, 1900)
Highest Gate; 60,945 v. Wolverhampton Wanderers (1-1) (March 4th, 1950)
Lowest Gate; 1,050 v. Sheffield United (0-2) (April 30th, 1901)
Highest Home Win; 9-2 v. Manchester City (26,222) (September 21st, 1957)
Highest Home Defeat; 0-6 v. Liverpool (27,128) (April 26th, 2003)

PLAY OFF MATCHES

2-0 v. Swansea City (26,045) (May 19th, 1993)
2-2 v. Bolton Wanderers (18,167) (May 13th, 2001)

No. of Matches Played by West Bromwich Albion; 2,064
(League Programme; 2,062, Play Off Matches; 2)
Information Kindly Supplied by; Tony Matthews

The club moved here from *Stoney Lane* in 1900 and was also involved in a Football League Play Off Match at the neutral venue of *Wembley Stadium*.

PLAYING RECORD OF WALSALL
LEAGUE PROGRAMME

Match Played; 0-3 v. Brighton & Hove Albion (7,535)
(February 25th, 1970)

No. of Matches Played by Walsall; 1
Information Kindly Supplied by; Tony Matthews

This match was played here due to the waterlogged state of the pitch at *Fellows Park*.

PLAYING RECORD OF WOLVERHAMPTON WANDERERS
LEAGUE PROGRAMME

Matches Played; 2-4 v. Barnsley (9,000) (November 29th, 1919)
2-2 v. Stockport County (6,000) (December 6th, 1919)

No. of Matches Played by Wolverhampton Wanderers; 2
Information Kindly Supplied by; Tony Matthews

Two home League matches were played here in 1919 when *Molineux* was closed following crowd trouble.

AT THE END OF SEASON 2004/5, A TOTAL OF **90** TEAMS HAD TAKEN PART IN **2,067** LEAGUE FIXTURES AT THIS VENUE

The 8,000 seat stand built on the east side in 2001. Higher than other stands in the ground, it was designed to accommodate an additional tier but there was no provision for linking to existing stands resulting in these huge in-fills of sheeting in the corners.

Photograph by Paul Claydon. Courtesy of Groundtastic Magazine

HILLSBOROUGH

HOME GROUND OF SHEFFIELD WEDNESDAY
TEMPORARY HOME GROUND FOR LEEDS UNITED

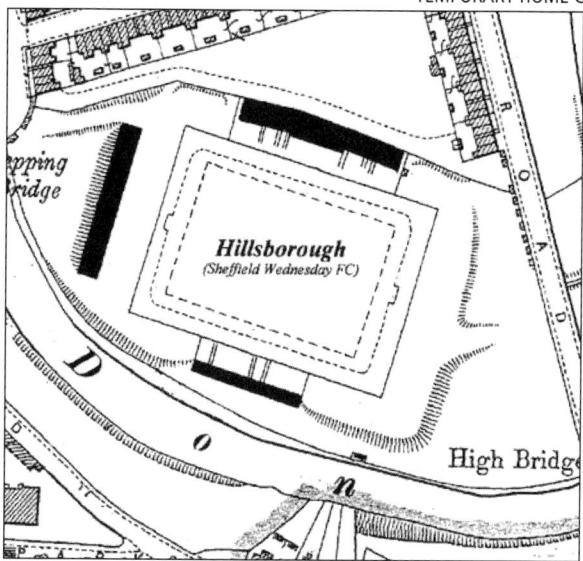

MAP EXTRACT; YORKSHIRE 288.15 [**1905**]
SITE LOCATION; **SK35299063**

Wednesday FC moved to *Owlerton* from the **Olive Grove** in 1899 and re-installed the stand from their former ground on the north side of the new enclosure. Another roof was added to the front of this building, to cover the paddock, and other facilities included shallow banking around the ground, a cover over part of the west end and by 1905 a small stand had been provided on the south side of the pitch.

Just prior to WWI the name of the ground changed to *Hillsborough* and the venue was considerable altered with the construction of a large embankment at the east end and the opening of a new 5,600 seat main stand on the south side giving a new nominal capacity of 50,000. Following further alterations in the 1920s, the expansion and covering of the west end and installation of a new stand in the north west corner, the capacity increased and the record attendance of 72,841 was set at the FA Cup 5th Round tie v. *Manchester City* (2-2) on February 17th, 1934.

The ground remained virtually unaltered until 1961 when the original stand on the north side was demolished and replaced by the largest cantilever stand built in Britain to that date with 9,882 seats. In the same decade, a new 4,465 seat two-tier stand was constructed at the west end and a new cover installed at the east end in 1986. *Hillsborough* was subsequently made an all-seater with the installation of seats on re-profiled terracing around the ground and the capacity, at the start of season 2004/5, was 39,859 with an 115 x 75 yards sized pitch.

PLAYING RECORD OF SHEFFIELD WEDNESDAY
LEAGUE PROGRAMME

First Match; 5-1 v. Chesterfield (12,000) (September 2nd, 1899)
Highest Gate; 65,384 v. Sheffield United (1-3) (January 5th, 1952)
Lowest Gate; 2,500 v. Everton (1-1) (April 5th, 1902)
Highest Home Win; 9-1 v. Birmingham (21,226) (December 13th, 1930)
Highest Home Defeat; 1-7 v. Nottingham Forest (30,060) (April 1st, 1995)

PLAY OFF MATCHES
1-0 v. Brentford (28,625) (May 12th, 2005)

No. of Matches Played by Sheffield Wednesday; 2,068
(League Programme; 2,067, Play Off Matches; 1)

The Wednesday moved here from the **Olive Grove** in 1899 and the club was re-named as *Sheffield Wednesday* in c1930. The club was also involved in a Football League Play Off Match at the neutral venue of the *Millennium Stadium*.

PLAYING RECORD OF LEEDS UNITED
LEAGUE PROGRAMME

Match Played; 5-1 v. Newcastle United (18,623) (September 1st, 1971)

No. of Matches Played by Leeds United; 1
Information Kindly Supplied by; Stan Briggs

This match took place here when *Leeds United* was ordered to play the first four fixtures of the 1971/2 season away from **Elland Road** following crowd disturbances during the game v. *West Bromwich Albion* (1-2) on April 17th, 1971.

AT THE END OF SEASON 2004/5, A TOTAL OF **99** TEAMS HAD TAKEN PART IN **2,069** LEAGUE FIXTURES AT THIS VENUE

Hillsborough in 2004 with the 1914-vintage main stand on the left and the cantilever structure on the right
Photograph by Stephen Mumford, Courtesy of Groundtastic Magazine

HIGHFIELD ROAD
HOME GROUND OF COVENTRY CITY

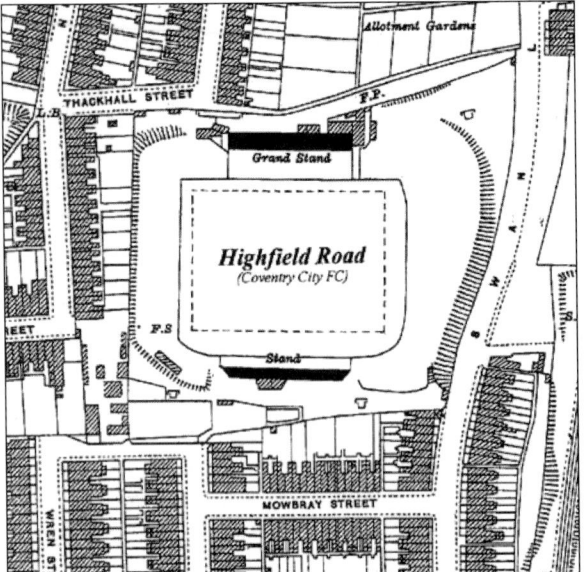

MAP EXTRACT; WARWICKSHIRE 21.12 [1925]
SITE LOCATION; SP34807945

The site was in use by the *Craven Cricket Club* when *Coventry City FC* moved here in 1899. The original facilities included a 2,000 seat stand on the south side and it was not until 1910 that a stand was constructed on the north side.

Following their entry into the Football League in 1919, embankments were constructed at the east end, and cover installed over the west end and further improvements were carried out prior to the outbreak of WWII with the building of a new main stand on the south side and the addition of extra terracing at the east end.

The ground saw major reconstruction work during the 1960s with the building of new stands on the north side (the roof of which was replaced twice within twenty years), at the west end and, following the destruction of the main stand by a fire, on the south side. In 1981 seating was installed throughout *Highfield Road* making it the first all-seated stadium in England (with a capacity of 20,616) but this proved unpopular with the fans and part of the ground eventually reverted to standing accommodation. During the 1990s a new all seat stand was constructed at the east end with a roof linking with a new cover (the third!) over the north stand, the main stand was re-roofed and much of the seating around the ground refurbished. At the end of the 2003/4 season the all-seat capacity was 23,627 and the pitch size was 110 x 75 yards. The club moved out in 2005 and the site was sold for housing.

PLAYING RECORD OF COVENTRY CITY
LEAGUE PROGRAMME

First Match; 0-5 v. Tottenham Hotspur (16,500) (August 30th, 1919)
Last Match; 6-2 v. Derby County (22,728) (April 30th, 2005)
Highest Gate; 51,455 v. Wolverhampton Wanderers (3-1)
(April 29th, 1967)
Lowest Gate; 2,059 v. Crystal Palace (2-2) (February 13th, 1928)
Highest Home Win; 9-0 v. Bristol City (7,035) (April 28th, 1934)
Highest Home Defeat; 1-6 v. Liverpool (23,204) (May 5th, 1990)

No. of Matches Played by Coventry City; 1,671

The club was elected into the Football League Division 2 in 1919 and moved to the *Ricoh Arena* at the end of the 2004/5 season.

A TOTAL OF **105** TEAMS TOOK PART IN **1,671** LEAGUE FIXTURES AT THIS VENUE

HOLIDAY PARK
HOME GROUND OF DURHAM CITY

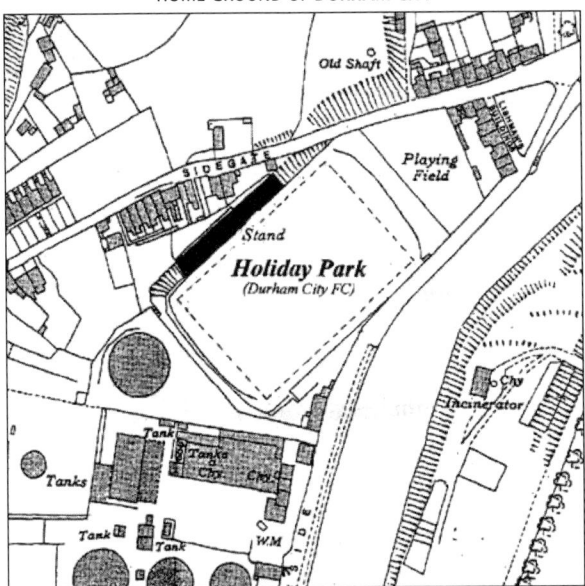

MAP EXTRACT; DURHAM 27.1 [1939]
SITE LOCATION; NZ27314295

Located in the "vee" of Sidegate and Framwellgate Waterside, *Durham City* moved here from *Kepier Haughs* in 1923. The small stand, removed from the old ground and re-erected here, was the only spectator accommodation provided during their stay in the Football League which ended in 1928. The record attendance of 7,182 was set at an FA Cup Qualifying Round tie v. *West Stanley* on September 17th, 1923.

A 2,000 seat stand was completed in 1932 and the stadium was also utilized for greyhound racing which reduced the size of the football pitch and eventually resulted in the demise of the club in 1939. In post war years it was enlarged and continued in use as a Greyhound Stadium but was subsequently demolished, the site being utilized by the Electricity Board.

PLAYING RECORD OF DURHAM CITY
LEAGUE PROGRAMME

First Match; 0-0 v. Rochdale (4,000) (September 1st, 1923)
Last Match; 5-1 v. Crewe Alexandra (1,000) (May 5th, 1928)
Highest Gate; 7,000 v. Wolverhampton Wanderers (2-3)
(January 1st, 1924)
Lowest Gate; 641 v. Wrexham (2-1) (April 28th, 1926)
Highest Home Win; 6-0 v. Barrow (2,000) (May 2nd, 1925)
Highest Home Defeat; 0-4 v. Lincoln City (1,305)
(April 21st, 1928)

No. of Matches Played by Durham City; 105
Some Information Kindly Supplied by; Brian Tabner

The club moved here from *Kepier Haughs* in 1923 and failed to gain re-election in 1928.

A TOTAL OF **27** TEAMS TOOK PART IN **105** LEAGUE FIXTURES AT THIS VENUE

HOME PARK

HOME GROUND OF PLYMOUTH ARGYLE

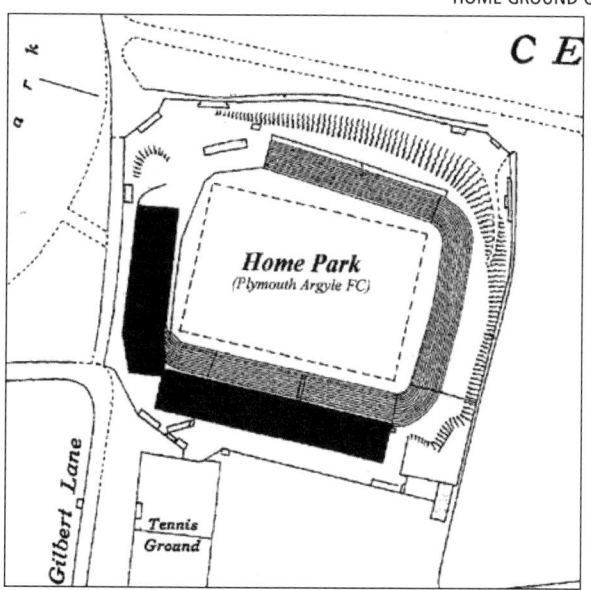

MAP EXTRACT; DEVON 123.4 [**1935**]
SITE LOCATION; **SX47205646**

Sited amidst farms and allotments, *Home Park* was first used from 1894 as a rugby ground by *Plymouth Albion* and *Devonport RUFCs*. The *Argyle Athletic Club* took over in 1901 and used the venue, at this point no more than a grassed area surrounded by an oval cinder track, for a diversity of sports including rugby, cricket, whippet racing, motorcycling, pony trotting and football.

To gauge public support a number of exhibition football matches involving Football League teams took place before the football branch, now known as *Plymouth Argyle FC*, played their first senior competitive game, a Southern League fixture v. *Northampton Town* on September 5th, 1903. By this time the facilities included stands at the west end and on the south side.

Following their admittance to the Football League in 1920, a new replacement main stand was constructed on the south side and a new cover (later extended) and concrete terracing installed at the west end. The record attendance of 44,526 was set a few years later at the FA Cup 3rd Round tie v. *Huddersfield Town* (1-1) on January 13th, 1934.

The ground was so devastated during WWII (both by the attentions of the Luftwaffe and general misuse by allied troops) that at the opening of the first post war season a double decker 'bus was initially parked alongside of the touchline to serve as dressing rooms on the lower deck and Director's and Press Boxes on the top. A pavilion, for director's use, was quickly built in the south east corner but despite these lack of facilities it was not until the 1950s that a new main stand was constructed on the south side and 1965 before a cover was installed on the north side. The roof over the west end was demolished in 1980 and replaced four years later and seats were installed on the north side in 1990.

In 2001 the two ends and the north side were demolished and replaced by a 12,600 seat horseshoe shaped stand with a continuous cantilever roof giving a capacity at the start of the 2004/5 season of 20,134 with 15,684 seats. The pitch size was 112 x 72 yards.

PLAYING RECORD OF PLYMOUTH ARGYLE
LEAGUE PROGRAMME

First Match; 1-1 v. Norwich City (17,356) (August 28th, 1920)
Highest Gate; 43,596 v. Aston Villa (2-2) (October 10th, 1936)
Lowest Gate; 2,525 v. AFC Bournemouth (2-0) (October 19th, 1982)
Highest Home Wins; 8-1 v. Millwall (15,799) (January 16th, 1932)
Highest Home Defeat; 0-6 v. Reading (12,098) (August 25th, 1956)

PLAY OFF MATCHES

1-3 v. Burnley (17,515) (May 18th, 1994)
3-1 v. Colchester United (14,525) (May 15th, 1996)

No. of Matches Played by Plymouth Argyle; 1,740
(League Programme; 1,738, Play Off Matches; 2)
Some Information Kindly Supplied by; Brian Tabner

The club was a founder member of the Football League Division 3 in 1920. The club was also involved in a Football League Play Off Match at the neutral venue of **Wembley Stadium** and the match v. *Ipswich Town* on March 18th, 1961 was played at **Plainmoor** following crowd trouble at *Home Park*.

AT THE END OF SEASON 2004/5, A TOTAL OF **104** TEAMS HAD TAKEN PART IN **1,740** LEAGUE FIXTURES AT THIS VENUE

The pavilion and main stand at *Home Park*
Photograph by Paul Claydon. Courtesy of Groundtastic Magazine

HOLKER STREET
HOME GROUND OF BARROW

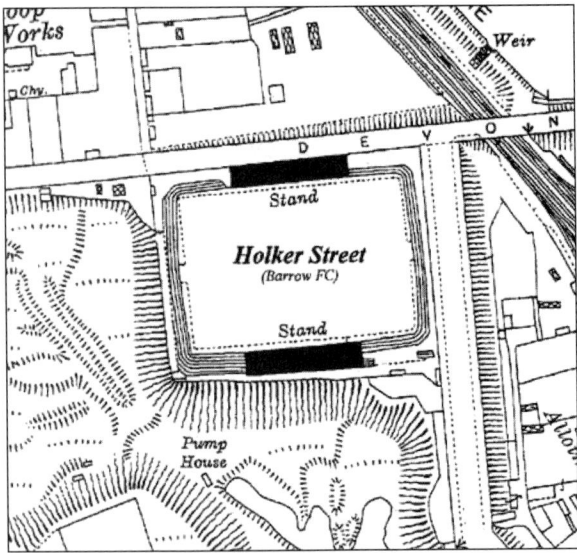

MAP EXTRACT; LANCASHIRE 21.7 [1933]
SITE LOCATION; SD19397042

Located to the north of the town centre, *Barrow FC* took over the *Holker Street* site, a former rubbish tip, in 1909. Considerable excavations were required to construct banking and make it safe for football prior to the installation of the fixtures and fittings from their previous ground at *Little Park*. A seated stand, subsequently extended, was built on the north side of the pitch in 1912 and concrete terracing and a covered enclosure, on the south side, installed after WWI.

Just prior to their entry into the Football League, the covering on the south side was removed and re-erected at the west end and replaced with a larger covered enclosure. These alterations resulted in a capacity of 20,000 and the record attendance of 16,874 was established at the FA Cup 3rd Round match against *Swansea Town* (2-2) on January 9th, 1954.

Some additional alterations were made, the installation of cover at the east end and renewal of the cover at the west, before *Barrow* failed to gain re-election in 1972. *Holker Street* is still in use as the home ground for *Barrow FC*.

PLAYING RECORD OF BARROW
LEAGUE PROGRAMME

First Match; 0-2 v. Stockport County (9,750) (August 27th, 1921)
Last Match; 0-3 v. Brentford (2,666) (April 24th, 1972)
Highest Gate; 11,644 v Wrexham (1-1) (March 26th, 1948)
Lowest Gate; 1,031 v. Cambridge United (1-1)
(November 27th, 1971)
Highest Home Win; 12-1 v. Gateshead (3,330) (May 5th, 1934)
Highest Home Defeat; 0-5 v. Wrexham (3,982) (December 4th, 1926) & v. Millwall (3,190) (February 6th, 1965)
No. of Matches Played by Barrow; 964
(Including one expunged match v. Accrington Stanley on September 18th, 1961)

The club was a founder member of the Football League Division 3 [N] in 1921 and was re-elected on no less than 10 occasions before finally failing in 1972. Bobby Knox of *Barrow* became the first ever substitute to score a goal in the Football League when he netted here in their 4-2 win v. *Wrexham* on August 21st, 1965.

A TOTAL OF **67** TEAMS TOOK PART IN **964** LEAGUE FIXTURES AT THIS VENUE

HORSLEY HILL
HOME GROUND OF SOUTH SHIELDS

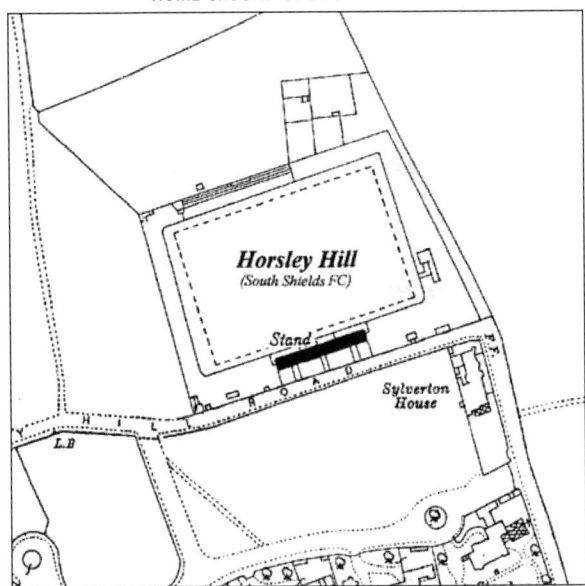

MAP EXTRACT; DURHAM 4.5 [1916]
SITE LOCATION; NZ37486629

Located on the north side of Horsley Hill Road in the Westoe district, it had been used by a Rugby Union Club when *South Shields FC* moved here from *Stanhope Road* in 1908. Originally the only facility was a pavilion at the east end but by 1916 an open seated stand had been installed on the north side and a covered main stand and paddock on the south.

South Shields FC entered the Football League in 1919 and the ground was further improved with the construction of terracing, installation of cover over the east end and north side and extension of the main stand. The record attendance of 24,348 was set at the FA Cup 5th Round tie v. *Swansea Town* (2-2) on February 19th, 1927 and the club moved out to *Redheugh Park* where it re-formed as *Gateshead FC*. The ground was subsequently used by a local football team and substantially improved for the greyhound racing that took place until post war years when it was demolished and replaced by a bowling alley. The site was later used for housing.

PLAYING RECORD OF SOUTH SHIELDS
LEAGUE PROGRAMME

First Match; 2-0 v. Fulham (18,000) (September 6th, 1919)
Last Match; 2-2 v. Accrington Stanley (1,752) (May 3rd, 1930)
Highest Gate; 21,000 v. Barnsley (3-2) (September 11th, 1920)
Lowest Gate; 1,239 v. Rotherham United (5-0) (February 1st, 1930)
Highest Home Win; 10-1 v. Rotherham United (3,134)
(March 16th, 1929)
Highest Home Defeat; 1-5 v. Leeds United (9,826) (August 27th, 1927) & v. Tranmere Rovers (5,452) (September 14th, 1929)
No. of Matches Played by South Shields; 231
Information Kindly Supplied by; Tom Bone & Brian Tabner

The club was elected into the Football League Division 2 in 1919, re-formed in 1930 as *Gateshead FC* and re-located to *Redheugh Park*.

A TOTAL OF **58** TEAMS TOOK PART IN **231** LEAGUE FIXTURES AT THIS VENUE

HUISH PARK
HOME GROUND OF YEOVIL TOWN

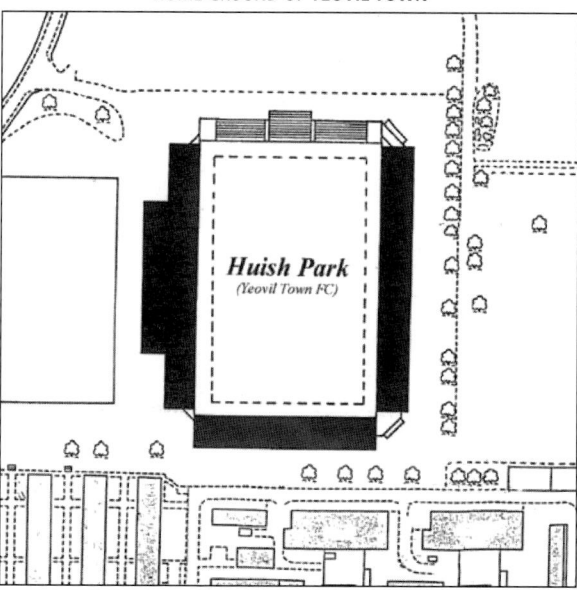

MAP EXTRACT; GROUND AS IN **2003** DRAWN FROM AERIAL PHOTOGRAPHS AND SUPERIMPOSED ON ST5216/7 [1951]
SITE LOCATION; **ST52741696**

Originally part of the site of Houndstone Camp, *Yeovil Town* moved here from *The Huish* in 1990. There are all-seater cantilever stands on the east and west sides of the ground and there was originally open terracing behind the goals, but in 2001 a cover was installed over the south end. The record attendance of 9,348 was set at the FA Cup 3rd Round tie v. *Liverpool* (0-2) on January 5th, 2004 and at the start of the 2004/5 season the capacity was 9,400 with 5,212 seats. The pitch size was 115 x 72 yards

PLAYING RECORD OF YEOVIL TOWN
LEAGUE PROGRAMME

First Match; 3-0 v. Carlisle United (6,347) (August 16th, 2003)
Highest Gate; 9,153 v. Bristol Rovers (4-2) (February 12th, 2005)
Lowest Gate; 4,639 v. Kidderminster Harriers (2-1) (December 7th, 2004)
Highest Home Win; 6-1 v. Oxford United (5,467) (September 18th, 2004)
Highest Home Defeat; 1-3 v. Notts County (7,221) (March 29th, 2005)

No. of Matches Played by Yeovil Town; 46

The club was promoted from the Football Conference in 2003 and Kevin Gall of *Yeovil Town FC* scored the first League goal here in the 4th minute of the first match.

AT THE END OF SEASON 2004/5, A TOTAL OF **30** TEAMS HAD TAKEN PART IN **46** LEAGUE FIXTURES AT THIS VENUE

HYDE ROAD
HOME GROUND OF MANCHESTER CITY

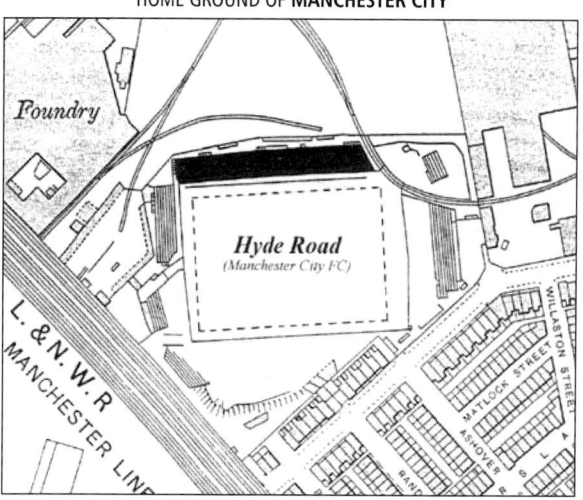

MAP EXTRACT; LANCASHIRE 104.11 [**1908**]
SITE LOCATION; **SJ86259697**

Originally a patch of industrial wasteland, located on the north side of Bennett Street, *Ardwick FC* moved here in 1887. The ground occupied an irregularly shaped site and players initially changed in a nearby public house. The main stand was constructed on the north side of the ground with embankments and terracing displaced at various points, and different angles, around the other three sides. The most bizarre feature could be found in the north east corner of the site. A railway line linking Galloway's Boiler Works to the Mineral Yard; passed between a corner stand and the playing area and clipped off the corner of the rectangular pitch area!

Over the years, although the spectator accommodation was "tidied up", with stands of varying lengths being built on each of the other sides, *Hyde Road* was still a rabbit warren of passages, arches and miscellaneous stands with a capacity of over 40,000. The main stand burned down in 1920 and although it was quickly replaced *Manchester City* moved out to *Maine Road* in 1923 and the site was subsequently used for an omnibus driver training school.

PLAYING RECORD OF MANCHESTER CITY
[ALSO AS ARDWICK]
LEAGUE PROGRAMME

First Match; 7-0 v. Bootle (4,000) (September 3rd, 1892)
Last Match; 0-0 v. Newcastle United (20,000) (April 28th, 1923)
Highest Gate; 42,000 v. Burnley (3-0) (March 26th, 1921)
Lowest Gate; 500 v. Walsall (5-0) (January 6th, 1897)
Highest Home Win; 11-3 v. Lincoln City (3,000) (March 23rd, 1895). 10-0 v. Darwen (8,000) (February 18th, 1899)
Highest Home Defeat; 2-6 v. Aston Villa (30,000) (September 16th, 1911)

TEST MATCHES

1-1 v. West Bromwich Albion (6,000) (April 18th, 1896)
3-0 v. Small Heath (9,500) (April 25th, 1896)

No. of Matches Played by Manchester City; 480
(League Programme; 478, Test Matches; 2)

The club was a founder member of the Football League Division 2 in 1892 as *Ardwick FC* and changed the name to *Manchester City* in 1894

NEUTRAL TEST MATCHES

Darwen 3, Notts County 2 (5,000) (April 22nd, 1893)
No. of Matches Played; 1

A TOTAL OF **59** TEAMS TOOK PART IN **481** LEAGUE FIXTURES AT THIS VENUE

INTAKE GROUND
HOME GROUND OF DONCASTER ROVERS

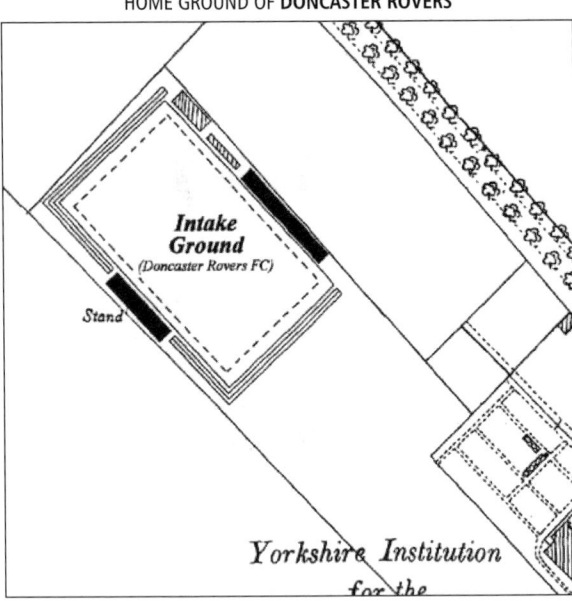

MAP EXTRACT; GROUND AS IN c1890 DRAWN FROM PLANS AND SUPERIMPOSED ON YORKSHIRE 285.2 [1903]
SITE LOCATION; SE58980306

The first match to be played at the *Intake Ground*, located at the rear of the Yorkshire Institution for the Deaf & Dumb and to the east of the town centre, was against *Elsecar FC* on April 26th, 1885. Although no map exists, from contemporary accounts an accurate diagram of the ground can be constructed and initially the facilities consisted of a small wooden stand which had to be rebuilt in 1891 following storm damage.

Some improvements to spectator accommodation were made over the years with the construction of a 1,000 seat main stand on the west side, a covered enclosure on the east and provision of wooden duckboards around the perimeter of the pitch.

The ground was requisitioned during WWI for use by the army and *Doncaster Rovers* moved out to *Bennetthorpe* in 1919, re-erecting their main stand there. The site is still in use as a sports field.

PLAYING RECORD OF DONCASTER ROVERS
LEAGUE PROGRAMME

First Match; 3-3 v. Burslem Port Vale (2,000) (September 7th, 1901)
Last Match; 0-2 v. Grimsby Town (3,000) (April 24th, 1905)
Highest Gate; 6,000 v. Middlesbrough (0-0) (March 28th, 1902)
Lowest Gate; 1,500 v. Bristol City (3-0) (October 5th, 1901) & v. Port Vale (2-2) (November 19th, 1904)
Highest Home Win; 4-0 v. Newton Heath (3,000) (February 22nd, 1902) & v. Preston North End (2,500) (April 19th, 1902)
Highest Home Defeat; 1-5 v. Gainsborough Trinity (-) (February 25th, 1905)

No. of Matches Played by Doncaster Rovers; 51
Information Kindly Supplied by; Tony Bluff

The club was elected into the Football League Division 2 in 1901, failed to gain re-election in 1903, elected to Division 2 in 1904 and failed to gain re-election in 1905. *Doncaster Rovers FC* moved to *Bennetthorpe* in 1919 and *Belle Vue* in 1922.

A TOTAL OF 24 TEAMS TOOK PART IN 51 LEAGUE FIXTURES AT THIS VENUE

JJB STADIUM
HOME GROUND OF WIGAN ATHLETIC

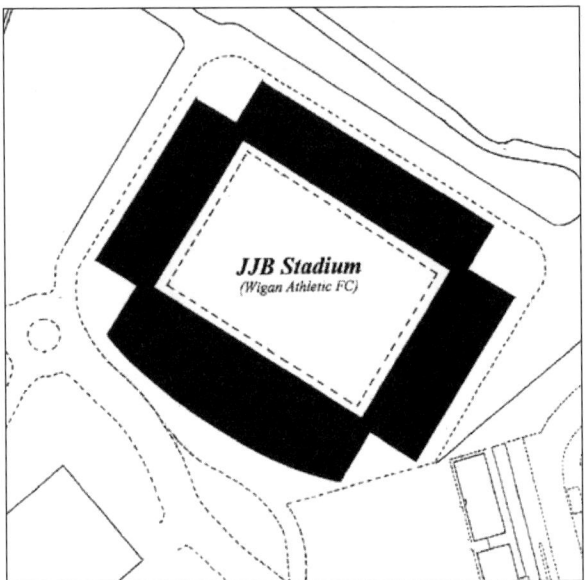

MAP EXTRACT; GROUND AS IN 1999 DRAWN FROM AERIAL PHOTOGRAPHS AND SUPERIMPOSED ON LANCASHIRE 93.7 [1939]
SITE LOCATION; SD56780589

Constructed on marshy wasteland adjacent to the west side of the Leeds & Liverpool Canal, *Wigan Athletic FC* moved to the *JJB Stadium* from *Springfield Park* in 1999. It is a typical modern purpose-built stadium consisting of four all-seater stands. At the start of the 2004/5 season it had a capacity of 25,000 with an 120 x 66 yards sized pitch.

PLAYING RECORD OF WIGAN ATHLETIC
LEAGUE PROGRAMME

First Match; 3-0 v. Scunthorpe United (7,481) (August 7th, 1999)
Highest Gate; 20,745 v. Sunderland (0-1) (April 5th, 2005)
Lowest Gate; 3,535 v. Cambridge United (4-1) (March 5th, 2002)
Highest Home Win; 6-1 v. Stoke City (7,047) (November 13th, 2001)
Highest Home Defeat; 1-3 v. Brentford (6,502) (April 7th, 2001)

PLAY OFF MATCHES
1-0 v. Millwall (10,642) (May 17th, 2000)
0-0 v. Reading (12,638) (May 13th, 2001)

No. of Matches Played by Wigan Athletic; 140
(League Programme; 138, Play Off Matches; 2)

The club moved here from *Springfield Park* in 1999 and was also involved in a Football League Play Off Match at the neutral venue of *Wembley Stadium*.

AT THE END OF SEASON 2004/5, A TOTAL OF 57 TEAMS HAD TAKEN PART IN 140 LEAGUE FIXTURES AT THIS VENUE

JOHN O'GAUNT'S
HOME GROUND OF LINCOLN CITY

MAP EXTRACT; LINCOLNSHIRE 70.11 [1889]
SITE LOCATION; SK97437038

Located to the south of the city centre, the ground was on the east side of the High Street, behind St Mary's Guildhall. *Lincoln City* was formed in 1884, playing their first match at *John O'Gaunt's* in the same year, and although it was an enclosed ground there were no facilities other than a dressing tent for the players. *Lincoln City* moved out to **Sincil Bank** in 1895 and the site was later utilized for the construction of Sibthorp Street and housing.

PLAYING RECORD OF LINCOLN CITY
LEAGUE PROGRAMME

First Match; 1-0 v. Sheffield United (2,000) (October 1st, 1892)
Last Match; 5-2 v. Crewe Alexandra (-) (April 13th, 1895)
Highest Gate; 7,500 v. Notts County (0-2) (March 23rd, 1894)
Lowest Gate; 1,500 v. Burslem Port Vale (3-4) (October 22nd, 1892), v. Newcastle United (2-1) (October 7th, 1893), v. Newton Heath (3-0) (December 29th, 1894), v. Walsall Town Swifts (1-0) (February 16th, 1895) & v. Burton Wanderers (0-2) (March 30th, 1895).
Highest Home Win; 6-0 v. Ardwick (2,000) (March 24th, 1894)
Highest Home Defeat; 1-5 v. Grimsby Town (2,000) (October 20th, 1894)

No. of Matches Played by Lincoln City; 40
Information Kindly Supplied by; Donald Nannestad

The club was a founder member of the Football League Division 2 in 1892 and moved to *Sincil Bank* in 1895.

A TOTAL OF 22 TEAMS TOOK PART IN 40 LEAGUE FIXTURES AT THIS VENUE

KASSAM STADIUM
HOME GROUND OF OXFORD UNITED

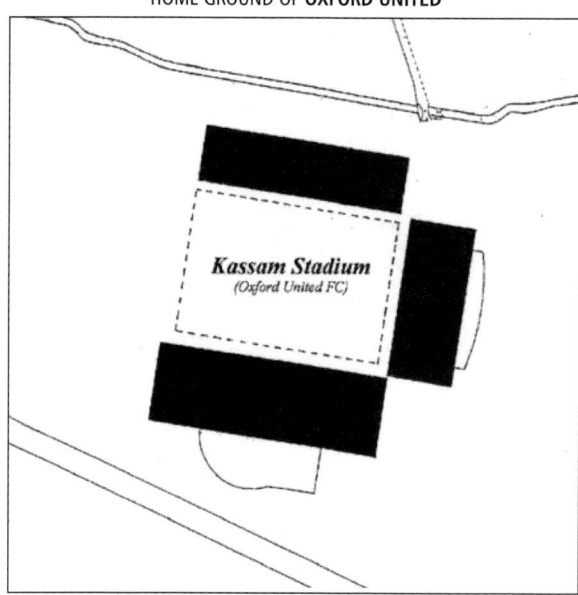

MAP EXTRACT; GROUND AS IN 2001 DRAWN FROM AERIAL PHOTOGRAPHS AND SUPERIMPOSED ON OXFORDSHIRE 39.12 [1937]
SITE LOCATION; SP54780231

Constructed on the site of a redundant sewage farm and opened in 2001, the *Kassam Stadium* consists of single tier all-seated cantilever roofed stands on the north and east sides and a twin-tier all-seated cantilever roofed main stand on the south. The west end was left undeveloped and at the start of the 2004/5 season it had an all-seat capacity of 12,500 with a pitch size of 112 x 78 yards. The record gate of 12,177 was established at the Worthington Cup 3rd Round match v. *Aston Villa* (0-3) on November 6th, 2002.

PLAYING RECORD OF OXFORD UNITED
LEAGUE PROGRAMME

First Match; 1-2 v. Rochdale (8,643) (August 11th, 2001)
Highest Gate; 11,121 v. Luton Town (1-2) (December 26th, 2001)
Lowest Gate; 4,089 v. Lincoln City (0-1) (October 16th, 2004)
Highest Home Win; 6-1 v. Halifax Town (6,046) (December 29th, 2001)
Highest Home Defeat; 0-2 v. Macclesfield Town (4,964) (September 18th, 2001), v. Leyton Orient (5,013) (March 4th, 2003) & v. Kidderminster Harriers (5,947) (December 28th, 2004)

No. of Matches Played by Oxford United; 92

The club moved here from the *Manor Ground* in 2001 and the first goal at the stadium was scored by Matt Doughty of *Rochdale FC* on August 11th, 2001.

AT THE END OF SEASON 2004/5, A TOTAL OF 37 TEAMS HAD TAKEN PART IN 92 LEAGUE FIXTURES AT THIS VENUE

KENILWORTH ROAD
HOME GROUND OF **LUTON TOWN**

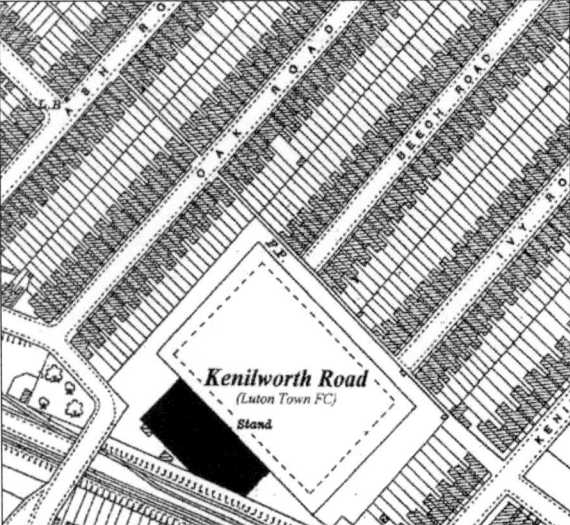

MAP EXTRACT; BEDFORDSHIRE 33.1 [**1924**]
SITE LOCATION: **TL08042179**

This constrained rhomboid shaped site, sandwiched between the railway line and housing, was originally called *Ivy Road* when *Luton Town FC* moved the short distance from **Dunstable Road** in 1905. The club brought the stand with them, re-installed it on the north side, constructed a main stand on the south side and built narrow banks at each end.

The main stand burned down in 1921 and a replacement, purchased from Kempton Racecourse, was installed on the same site. Further alterations carried out prior to WWII included the installation of a new cover and terracing on the north side, a new cover at the west end (later extended to link up with the main stand roof) and expansion of terracing at the east end. The club bought most of the houses at the west end and expanded the terracing into the back gardens and shortly after this the record attendance of 30,069 was set at the FA Cup 6th Round Replay v. *Blackpool* (1-0) on March 4th, 1959. The restricted nature of the site has allowed for only a few improvements with construction of new roofs at the east end of the south side, at the east end and installation of seats throughout the ground. At the start of the 2004/5 season the capacity was 9,970 and the pitch size 110 x 72 yards.

PLAYING RECORD OF LUTON TOWN
LEAGUE PROGRAMME

First Match; 2-2 v. Portsmouth (-) (August 30th, 1920)
Highest Gate; 27,911 v. Wolverhampton Wanderers (5-1) (November 5th, 1955)
Lowest Gate; 1,716 v. Clapton Orient (1-5) (January 11th, 1932)
Highest Home Win; 12-0 v. Bristol Rovers (14,296) (April 13th, 1936)
Highest Home Defeat; 2-7 v. Shrewsbury Town (4,914) (March 10th, 1965)

PLAY OFF MATCHES
2-2 v. Crewe Alexandra (8,168) (May 14th, 1997)

No. of Matches Played by Luton Town; 1,673
(League Programme; 1,672, Play Off Matches; 1)
Information Kindly Supplied by; Roger Wash

The highest-ever individual score was achieved here by Joe Payne when he netted ten goals in *Luton Town's* 12-0 win against *Bristol Rovers* on April 13th, 1936.

AT THE END OF SEASON 2004/5, A TOTAL OF **104** TEAMS HAD TAKEN PART IN **1,673** LEAGUE FIXTURES AT THIS VENUE

KEPIER HAUGHS
HOME GROUND OF **DURHAM CITY**

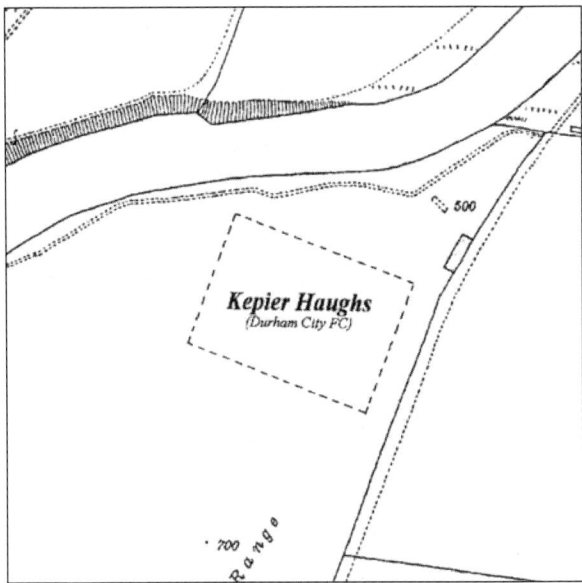

MAP EXTRACT; DURHAM 20.14 [**1920**]
SITE LOCATION; **NZ28324368**

Located to the north east of the city and on the east bank of the River Wear, the pitch was sited on a rifle range north of Kepier Hospital. *Durham City FC* moved here in 1920 and the only facility was a small wooden seated stand, but as no map or diagram exists it is not known precisely where this was located.

The record attendance of 7,886 was set at an FA Cup Qualifying Round tie v. *Darlington* on December 3rd, 1921. *Durham City* moved to **Holiday Park** in 1923 and the area is now in use as a school playing field.

PLAYING RECORD OF DURHAM CITY
LEAGUE PROGRAMME

First Match; 2-0 v. Southport (3,800) (September 3rd, 1921)
Last Match; 4-1 v. Barrow (1,000) (May 5th, 1923)
Lowest Gate; 1,000 v. Nelson (2-0) (April 14th, 1922)
& v. Barrow (4-1) (May 5th, 1923)
Highest Gate; 5,000 v. Ashington (1-0) (September 24th, 1921)
Highest Home Win; 7-1 v. Lincoln City (1,500) (February 17th, 1923)
Highest Home Defeat; 3-7 v. Darlington (3,000) (October 22nd, 1921)

No. of Matches Played by Durham City; 38
Information Kindly Supplied by; Gordon Wright & Brian Tabner.

The club was a founder member of the Football League Division 3 [N] in 1921. Sited some distance north east of the city centre, this ground turned out to be highly unpopular as it involved a long walk for spectators and there were no facilities when they got there! In 1923 the club was able to move to *Holiday Park*.

A TOTAL OF **21** TEAMS TOOK PART IN **38** LEAGUE FIXTURES AT THIS VENUE

KINGSTON COMMUNICATIONS STADIUM
HOME GROUND OF HULL CITY

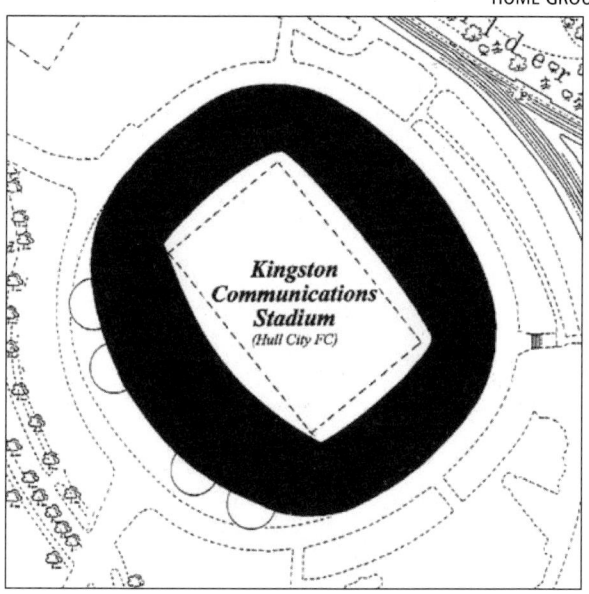

MAP EXTRACT; GROUND AS IN **2002** DRAWN FROM AERIAL PHOTOGRAPHS AND SUPERIMPOSED ON YORKSHIRE 240.2 [1928]
SITE LOCATION; **TA07772901**

PLAYING RECORD OF HULL CITY
LEAGUE PROGRAMME

First Match; 2-0 v. Hartlepool United (22,319) (December 26th, 2002)
Highest Gate; 24,277 v. Sheffield Wednesday (1-2) (April 30th, 2005)
Lowest Gate; 11,308 v. Bury (2-0) (December 6th, 2003)
Highest Home Win; 6-1 v. Kidderminster Harriers (13,683) (September 27th, 2003) & v. Tranmere Rovers (20,064) (December 16th, 2004)
Highest Home Defeat; 1-2 v. Wrexham (15,002) (April 5th, 2003) & v. Sheffield Wednesday (24,277) (April 30th, 2005)

No. of Matches Played by Hull City; 58

The club moved to this ground from **Boothferry Park** during December 2002 and Dean Keates of *Hull City FC* scored the first League goal here in the 21st minute of the first match.

AT THE END OF SEASON 2004/5, A TOTAL OF **46** TEAMS HAD TAKEN PART IN **58** LEAGUE FIXTURES AT THIS VENUE

Constructed on the site of *Hull City FCs* former grounds at **Anlaby Road** and **The Circle**, the 25,404 all seat capacity stadium is nominally oval in shape and consists of a single tier of 20,000 seats with an upper tier on the west side. The venue, used by both *Hull City FC* and *Hull RLFC*, has a continuous cantilever roof around three sides and a cantilever roof on the west side. It was originally known as *The Kingston upon Hull Community Super Stadium* and officially opened on December 18th, 2002 with a friendly match v. *Sunderland* (22,467). The record gate of 25,280 was established on February 17th, 2004 at the Under-21 Friendly International between *England* and *The Netherlands* (3-2). The pitch size was 114 x 74 yards

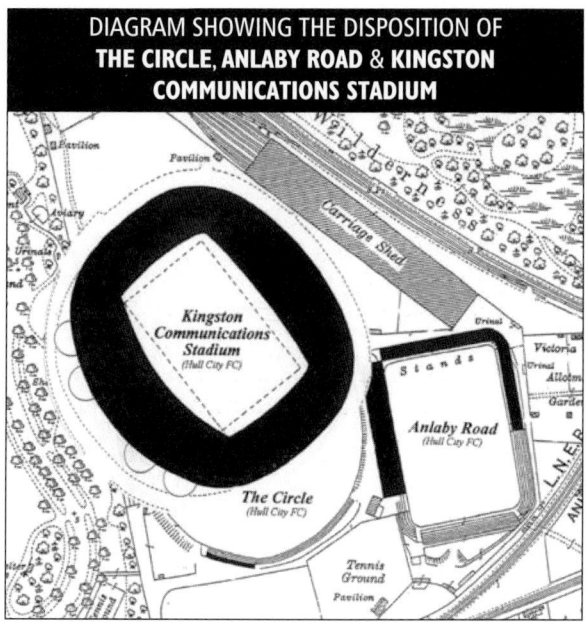

DIAGRAM SHOWING THE DISPOSITION OF **THE CIRCLE, ANLABY ROAD** & **KINGSTON COMMUNICATIONS STADIUM**

Taken at the *Lincoln City* fixture on February 8th, 2003, shortly after the ground opened, this view looks along the sweep of the curved roof from the south east corner towards the north end.
Photograph by Paul Claydon, Courtesy of Groundtastic Magazine

THE KURSAAL
HOME GROUND OF SOUTHEND UNITED

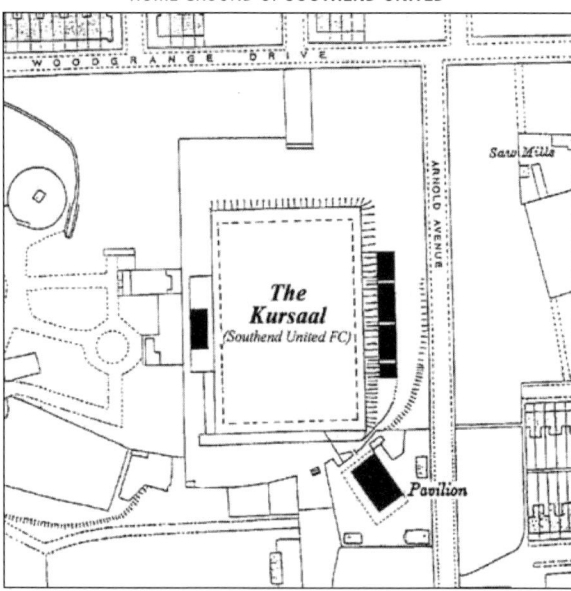

MAP EXTRACT; ESSEX N91.2 & N91.6 [1922]
SITE LOCATION; TQ89328523

Southend Athletic FC originally played here when the site was known as *The Marine Park*, but it was not until after WWI that the area was transformed into a large amusement park called *The Kursaal*. The football ground was on the east side of this park and more or less occupied the site of the former pitch. Initially the original pavilion, in the south east corner, was the only facility but a stand, on the east side, and concrete terracing along the other three sides were quickly constructed around the 115 x 75 yards sized pitch.

Southend United FC moved here from *Roots Hall*, played their first competitive match in 1919 and remained here until moving to **Southend Stadium** in 1934. Within two years the football ground was removed and, today, most of the whole amusement park has been redeveloped for housing.

PLAYING RECORD OF SOUTHEND UNITED
LEAGUE PROGRAMME

First Match; 2-0 v. Brighton & Hove Albion (8,000)
(August 28th, 1920)
Last Match; 0-0 v. Norwich City (4,700) (April 28th, 1934)
Highest Gate; 17,025 v. Brentford (1-0) (March 28th, 1932)
Lowest Gate; 1,500 v. Watford (1-4) (April 26th, 1922)
Highest Home Win; 7-0 v. Queens Park Rangers (8,126)
(April 7th, 1928)
Highest Home Defeat; 3-5 v. Newport County (2,580) (March 14th, 1934). 0-4 v. Watford (8,000) (September 13th, 1924) & v. Crystal Palace (10,285) (August 26th, 1933)

No. of Matches Played by Southend United; 294
Information Kindly Supplied by; Dave Goody

The club was a founder member of the Football League Division 3 in 1920 and moved to *Southend Stadium* in 1934.

A TOTAL OF **36** TEAMS TOOK PART IN **294** LEAGUE FIXTURES AT THIS VENUE

LAYER ROAD
HOME GROUND OF COLCHESTER UNITED

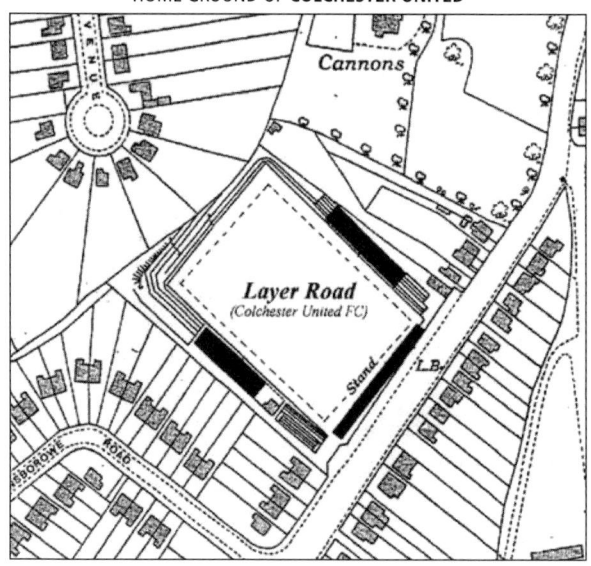

MAP EXTRACT; ESSEX N37.6 [1939]
SITE LOCATION; TL98522372

The site was first used in 1906 by the *4th Battalion King's Royal Rifle Corps*. Colchester Town FC took over when they vacated it in 1909 and bought it in 1919. No substantial improvements took place until the 1930s when a stand was built on the south side and covering installed on the north and east sides. During this period the club turned professional, as *Colchester United FC*, and the record attendance of 19,072 was set at the abandoned FA Cup 1st Round tie v. *Reading* on November 27th, 1948.

Some improvements were made following their election to the Football League in 1950 with the installation of covers over the terraces on each side of the main stand but it was not until the 1990s that a new roof was installed on the north side and the west end converted to seating and supplied with a roof. The capacity at the start of the 2004/5 season was 7,556 with 1,877 seats and the pitch size was 110 x 70 yards.

PLAYING RECORD OF COLCHESTER UNITED
LEAGUE PROGRAMME

First Match; 0-0 v. Bristol Rovers (15,000) (August 26th, 1950)
Highest Gate; 18,559 v. Ipswich Town (0-0) (February 16th, 1957)
Lowest Gate; 1,140 v. Swansea City (September 29th, 1987)
Highest Home Win; 9-1 v. Bradford City (4,415)
(December 30th, 1961)
Highest Home Defeat; 3-6 v. Southend United (8,915) August 27th, 1955). 0-5 v. Luton Town (3,967) (April 21st, 2003)

PLAY OFF MATCHES
0-2 v. Wolverhampton Wanderers (4,829) (May 14th, 1987)
1-0 v. Plymouth Argyle (6,511) (May 12th, 1996)
3-1 v. Barnet (5,863) (May 13th, 1998)

No. of Matches Played by Colchester United; 1,216
(League Programme; 1,213 [Including one expunged match v. Accrington Stanley on September 2nd, 1961] Play Off Matches; 3)

The club was elected into the Football League Division 3 [S] in 1950, relegated to the Football Conference in 1989 and promoted into Division 3 in 1992. The club was also involved in a Football League Play Off Match at the neutral venue of *Wembley Stadium*.

AT THE END OF SEASON 2004/5, A TOTAL OF **89** TEAMS HAD TAKEN PART IN **1,216** LEAGUE FIXTURES AT THIS VENUE

LEA BRIDGE STADIUM
HOME GROUND OF LEYTON ORIENT

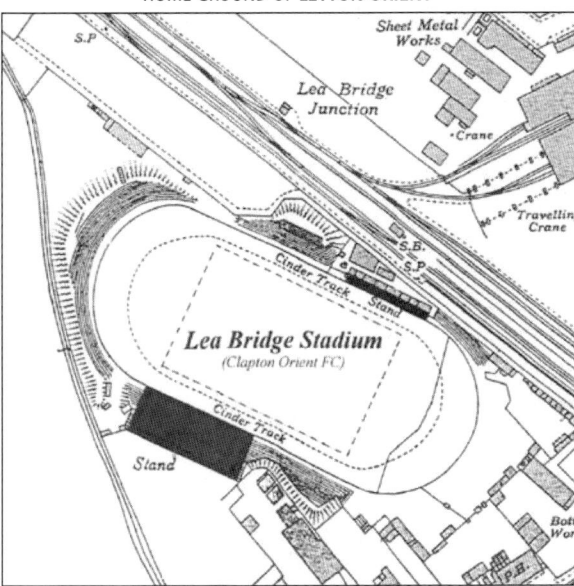

MAP EXTRACT; LONDON 2.12 [**1936**]
SITE LOCATION; **TQ36088713**

This venue was already well established as a speedway stadium and when *Clapton Orient FC* moved in from **Millfields Road** in 1930 there was a covered stand on the west side and shallow embankments around the remainder of the oval shaped arena.

Within a few weeks of moving in the Football League pointed out that the clearance between the edge of the pitch, which was already narrow, and the perimeter fence to the speedway track was too small and that remedial work needed to be carried out before any more matches could be sanctioned. Whilst this was being carried out *Clapton Orient* played a couple of games at **Wembley Stadium**. Subsequent improvements including the provision of a covered enclosure on the east side and concrete terracing around all the sides other than the south which remained as a flat standing area provided an overall capacity of about 20,000. The club moved to *Osborne Road* (later **Brisbane Road**) in 1937 and *Lea Bridge Stadium* continued in use for speedway into the post war era until it was closed and redeveloped as an industrial estate.

PLAYING RECORD OF LEYTON ORIENT
[AS CLAPTON ORIENT]
LEAGUE PROGRAMME

First Match; 3-1 v. Newport County (5,505) (September 3rd, 1930)
Last Match; 3-0 v. Southend United (2,541) (April 29th, 1937)
Highest Gate; 20,400 v. Millwall (1-0) (March 13th, 1937)
Lowest Gate; 1,747 v. Reading (2-2) (December 19th, 1931)
Highest Home Win; 9-2 v. Aldershot (9,832) (February 10th, 1934)
Highest Home Defeat; 1-5 v. Brentford (7,814)
(February 25th, 1933)

No. of Matches Played by Leyton Orient; 145

The club moved here from **Millfields Road** in 1930 but problems with the size of the pitch led them to play two games at **Wembley Stadium** whilst they were corrected. In 1937 they moved to **Brisbane Road** (or **Osborne Road** as it was known at this time).

A TOTAL OF **28** TEAMS TOOK PART IN **145** LEAGUE FIXTURES AT THIS VENUE

LEAMINGTON STREET
HOME GROUND OF BLACKBURN ROVERS

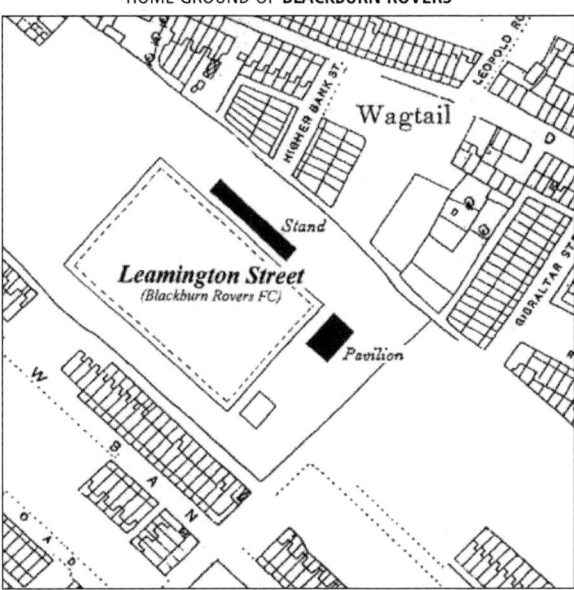

MAP EXTRACT; GROUND AS IN c**1890** DRAWN FROM PLANS AND SUPERIMPOSED ON LANCASHIRE 62.15 [**1900**]
SITE LOCATION; **SD66852870**

Although no map exists, from contemporary accounts an accurate diagram of the ground can be constructed. The facilities included a 600 seat covered seated stand on the north side, a pavilion at the east end and duckboards around the perimeter of the pitch. The ground was located to the north west of the town centre, at the north end of Leamington Street and *Blackburn Rovers FC* moved here from *Alexandra Meadows* in 1881. They joined the Football League as founder members in 1888 and moved to **Ewood Park** in 1890, the site of the ground quickly being redeveloped with housing.

PLAYING RECORD OF BLACKBURN ROVERS
LEAGUE PROGRAMME

First Match; 5-5 v. Accrington (5,000) (September 15th, 1888)
Last Match; 8-0 v. Stoke (4,000) (January 4th, 1890)
Highest Gate; 15,000 v. Preston North End (3-4)
(November 2nd, 1889)
Lowest Gate; 2,000 v. Burnley (4-2) (February 4th, 1889)
Highest Home Win; 9-1 v. Notts County (6,000)
(November 16th, 1889)
Highest Home Defeat; 2-4 v. Everton (12,000)
(December 28th, 1889)

No. of Matches Played by Blackburn Rovers; 22
Information Kindly Supplied by; Tony Matthews

The club was a founder member of the Football League in 1888. In 1890 the lease to the ground was probably acquired by building speculators, for the club was obliged to quickly seek a new location in that year and moved to **Ewood Park**.

A TOTAL OF **12** TEAMS TOOK PART IN **22** LEAGUE FIXTURES AT THIS VENUE

LEEDS ROAD

HOME GROUND OF **HUDDERSFIELD TOWN**
TEMPORARY HOME GROUND FOR **BRADFORD CITY** & **LEEDS UNITED**

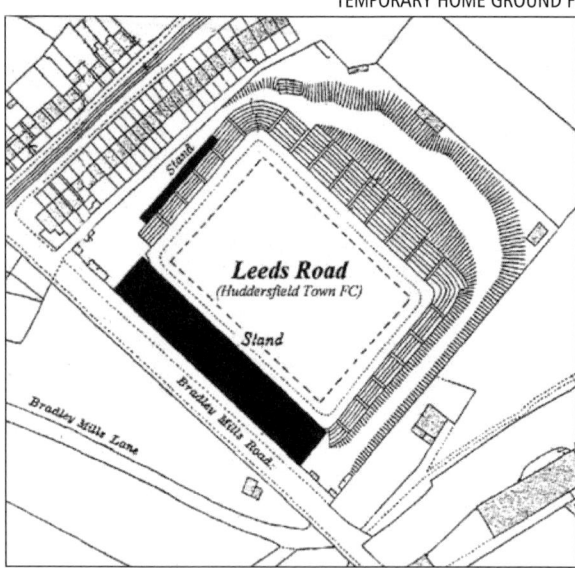

MAP EXTRACT; YORKSHIRE 246.11 & 246.12 [**1918**]
SITE LOCATION; SE15471792

PLAYING RECORD OF HUDDERSFIELD TOWN
LEAGUE PROGRAMME

First Match; 0-1 v. Burnley (7,371) (September 10th, 1910)
Last Match; 1-2 v. Blackpool (16,195) (April 30th, 1994)
Highest Gate; 52,479 v. Blackpool (2-1) (April 7th, 1951)
Lowest Gate; 1,624 v. Torquay United (1-1) (April 30th, 1979)
Highest Home Win; 10-1 v. Blackpool (11,932)
(December 13th, 1930)
Highest Home Defeat; 1-7 v. Wolverhampton Wanderers (32,496)
(September 29th, 1951)

PLAY OFF MATCHES
1-2 v. Peterborough United (16,167) (May 14th, 1992)
No. of Matches Played by Huddersfield Town; 1,556
(League Programme; 1,555, Play Off Matches; 1)

The club was elected into the Football League Division 2 in 1910 and had to play two matches at *Elland Road* following a fire in the main stand in 1950.

PLAYING RECORD OF LEEDS UNITED
LEAGUE PROGRAMME
Matches Played; 0-0 v. Wolverhampton Wanderers (20,686) (August 21st, 1971)
2-0 v. Crystal Palace (18,715) (September 4th, 1971)
No. of Matches Played by Leeds United; 2
Information Kindly Supplied by; Stan Briggs

These two matches took place here when *Leeds United* was ordered to play the first four fixtures of the 1971/2 season away from *Elland Road* following crowd disturbances during the game v. *West Bromwich Albion* on April 17th, 1971.

A TOTAL OF **100** TEAMS TOOK PART IN **1,564** LEAGUE FIXTURES AT THIS VENUE

In use as a recreation ground when purchased in 1907 by the Huddersfield Association Football Ground Co., *Huddersfield Town AFC* used the venue from their formation in 1908. Initially there were virtually no facilities as such with the pitch running north-south and parallel to Leeds Road but by the time of their admission into the Football League in 1910 the ground had been transformed. The pitch was turned through 90°, a new 4,000 seat main stand built on the south side, a cover installed at the west end and terracing constructed around the pitch giving a nominal capacity of 32,000.

In the 1920s a new roof was installed over the west end and, in the wake of extensive rebuilding and expansion of the terracing, the record attendance of 67,037 was set at the FA Cup 6th Round tie v. *Arsenal* (0-1) on February 27th, 1932. Following the end of WWII, the ground remained unaltered until the main stand was destroyed by a fire on April 3rd, 1950. The replacement opened for the following season and it was probably around this time, and due to the same fire, that the west end roof was also replaced.

The final improvement before *Huddersfield Town* moved to the new and adjacent *Alfred McAlpine Stadium* in 1994 was the installation of a cover over the north side in 1955. The site was subsequently sold and redeveloped as a retail park accommodating what was claimed to be the largest DIY superstore in Europe.

PLAYING RECORD OF BRADFORD CITY
LEAGUE PROGRAMME
Matches Played; 4-2 v. Hull City (4,930)
(September 14th, 1985)
2-0 v. Barnsley (5,707) (October 12th, 1985)
2-0 v. Sunderland (8,369) (January 1st, 1986)
3-2 v. Blackburn Rovers (5,263) (March 8th, 1986)
2-1 v. Middlesbrough (3,427) (April 23rd, 1986)
3-1 v. Shrewsbury Town (4,663) (April 26th, 1986)
No. of Matches Played by Bradford City; 6
Information Kindly Supplied by; Peter Waller

These matches were played here whilst *Valley Parade* was being rebuilt following the fire of May 11th, 1985.

A post-WWII general view of **Leeds Road** looking north west with the main stand on the left and the terracing, complete with 1955 vintage roof, on the right.

Photograph Courtesy of Groundtastic Magazine

LINTHORPE ROAD
HOME GROUND OF MIDDLESBROUGH

MAP EXTRACT; YORKSHIRE 16.2 [c1900]
SITE LOCATION; NZ49191956

Opened to football in 1880, *Linthorpe Road* occupied the northern half of an old cricket ground. The facilities consisted of a Grandstand, sited on the north side of the ground, narrow open seated areas around the other sides and a few outbuildings located on the east side which were utilized as dressing rooms and refreshment facilities.

Middlesbrough FC moved to *Ayresome Park* in 1903 and re-erected the Grandstand at their new ground. *Linthorpe Road* was subsequently redeveloped with St Aidan's Church and housing later occupying the site.

PLAYING RECORD OF MIDDLESBROUGH
LEAGUE PROGRAMME

First Match; 1-3 v. Small Heath (10,000) (September 9th, 1899)
Last Match; 1-1 v. Stoke (8,000) (April 25th, 1903)
Highest Gate; 17,000 v. Everton (1-0) (September 6th, 1902)
Lowest Gate; 3,000 v. Loughborough (3-0) (December 9th, 1899)
Highest Home Win; 9-2 v. Gainsborough Trinity (6,000)
(March 2nd, 1901)
Highest Home Defeat; 0-3 v. Bolton Wanderers (8,000)
(April 7th, 1900)
No. of Matches Played by Middlesbrough; 68
Information Kindly Supplied by; Tony Matthews

The club was elected into the Football League Division 2 in 1899 and moved to *Ayresome Park* in 1903.

A TOTAL OF **28** TEAMS TOOK PART IN **68** LEAGUE FIXTURES AT THIS VENUE

LONDON ROAD
HOME GROUND OF PETERBOROUGH UNITED

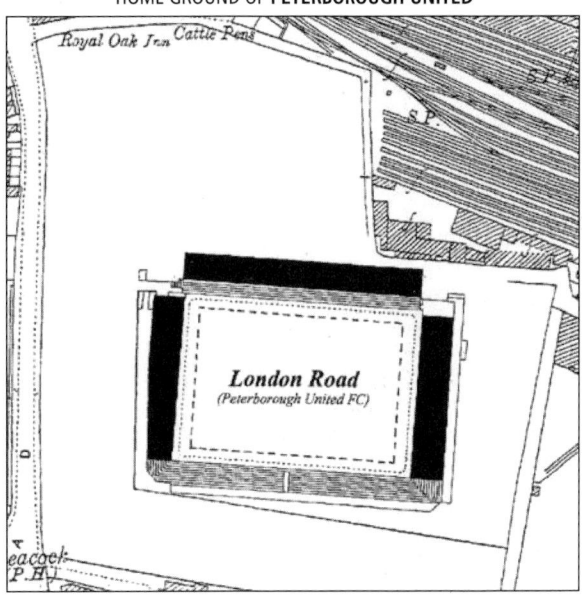

MAP EXTRACT; GROUND AS IN **1969** DRAWN FROM PLANS AND
SUPERIMPOSED ON NORTHAMPTONSHIRE 8.15 & 8.16 [1902]
SITE LOCATION; TL19379777

The site had been in use for football for many years before *Peterborough United FC* moved in on their formation in 1934 with the facilities at this time including a 400 seat stand on the north side. The ground was not improved until the 1950s when a short cover was installed at each end, the south side terraced and a new main stand built on the north side.

Following these alterations *London Road* remained virtually unchanged, apart from extensions to the covering at each end, until the 1990s when the main stand paddock was installed with seats and a new all-seat stand built on the south side.

The record attendance of 30,096 was set at the FA Cup 5th Round tie v. *Swansea Town* (0-0) on February 20th, 1965 and the capacity, at the start of the 2004/5 season, was 15,314 with 7,669 seats. The pitch size was 112 x 71 yards.

PLAYING RECORD OF PETERBOROUGH UNITED
LEAGUE PROGRAMME

First Match; 3-0 v. Wrexham (17,294) (August 20th, 1960)
Highest Gate; 26,307 v. Coventry City (2-0) (April 20th, 1964)
Lowest Gate; 1,464 v. Exeter City (0-0) (May 4th, 1985)
Highest Home Win; 8-1 v. Oldham Athletic (4,796)
(November 26th, 1969)
Highest Home Defeat; 0-5 v. Northampton Town (3,866) (October 12th, 1985) & v. Rotherham United (10,796) (December 26th, 1999)

PLAY OFF MATCHES
2-2 v. Huddersfield Town (11,751) (May 11th, 1992)
3-0 v. Barnet (10,515) (May 17th, 2000)
No. of Matches Played by Peterborough United; 1,037
(League Programme; 1,035, Play Off Matches; 2)
Information Kindly Supplied by; Matt Hill

The club was elected into the Football League Division 4 in 1960. The club was also involved in Football League Play Off Matches at the neutral venue of *Wembley Stadium*

AT THE END OF SEASON 2004/5, A TOTAL OF **92** TEAMS HAD TAKEN PART
IN **1,037** LEAGUE FIXTURES AT THIS VENUE

LOFTUS ROAD

HOME GROUND OF **QUEENS PARK RANGERS**
TEMPORARY HOME GROUND FOR **FULHAM**

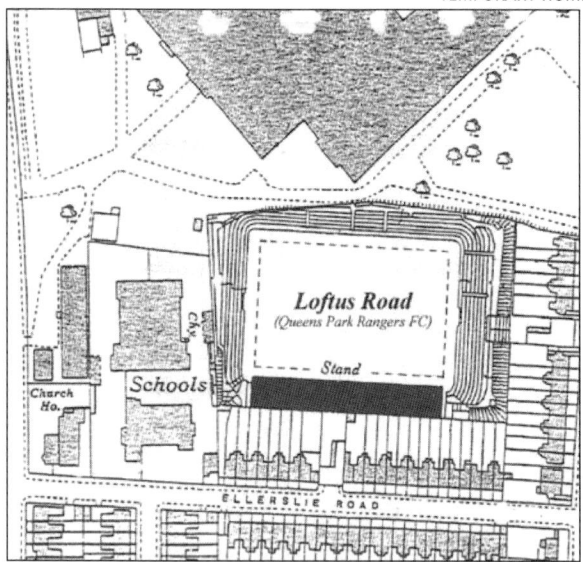

MAP EXTRACT; LONDON 4.10 [**1938**]
SITE LOCATION; **TQ22798040**

PLAYING RECORD OF FULHAM
LEAGUE PROGRAMME

First Match; 4-1 v. Bolton Wanderers (16,338) (August 17th, 2002)
Last Match; 0-1 v. Arsenal (18,102) (May 9th, 2004)
Highest Gate; 18,800 v. Arsenal (0-1) (November 3rd, 2002)
Lowest Gate; 14,017 v. Blackburn Rovers (0-4) (April 7th, 2003)
Highest Home Win; 4-1 v. Bolton Wanderers (16,338) (August 17th, 2002)
Highest Home Defeat; 0-4 v. Blackburn Rovers (14,017) (April 7th, 2003)

No. of Matches Played by Fulham; 38

The club moved here temporarily at the start of the 2002/3 season to accommodate the planned rebuilding of **Craven Cottage**. Due to planning difficulties and financial restraints the redevelopment was not carried out but seats were installed on the terraces and the club returned for the commencement of the 2003/4 season.

AT THE END OF SEASON 2004/5, A TOTAL OF **99** TEAMS HAD TAKEN PART IN **1,657** LEAGUE FIXTURES AT THIS VENUE

This confined site was in use as a rubbish dump when *Shepherd's Bush FC* moved in in 1904 and the only facility *in situ* when *Queens Park Rangers FC* took over in 1917 was a pavilion on the south side. The new tenants moved their stand from *Park Royal* and re-erected it on the south side whilst standing accommodation was provided by uncovered banks around the remainder of the pitch and the only alteration to the ground prior to WWII was the installation of a cover at the east end.

In 1948 the terraces were concreted and the club purchased the freehold to the ground and also some of the surrounding houses but it was not until after the 1960s that *Loftus Road* was finally developed. A two-tier stand was constructed on the north side in 1968, a replacement 5,000 seat stand built on the south side in 1972, and by 1981 a two-tier stand had been installed at each end. During the 1990s the standing accommodation was converted to seating and the capacity at the start of the 2004/5 season was 19,148. The pitch size was 112 x 72 yards.

PLAYING RECORD OF QUEENS PARK RANGERS
LEAGUE PROGRAMME

First Match; 1-2 v. Watford (20,000) (August 28th, 1920)
Highest Gate; 33,353 v. Leeds United (0-1) (April 27th, 1974)
Lowest Gate; 3,000 v. Cardiff City (5-1) (December 7th, 1935)
Highest Home Win; 9-2 v Tranmere Rovers (4,921) (December 3rd, 1960). 8-0 v. Merthyr Town (12,000) (March 9th, 1929)
Highest Home Defeat; 0-5 v. Barnsley (16,795) (January 21st, 1950)

PLAY OFF MATCHES
1-0 v. Oldham Athletic (17,201) (May 14th, 2003)

No. of Matches Played by Queens Park Rangers; 1,619
(League Programme; 1,618, Play Off Matches; 1)
Information Kindly Supplied by; Tony Matthews

The club was a founder member of the Football League Division 3 in 1920 and moved to the **White City Stadium**, with its superior facilities, for two periods in the 1930s and 1960s. The match v. *Coventry City* on March 1st, 1930 was played at **Highbury Stadium** due to crowd trouble. The club was also involved in a Football League Play Off Match at the neutral venue of the **Millennium Stadium**.

The problems of the restricted nature of this site are well illustrated in this view. To maximize seating accommodation the two narrow two tier stands have had to be butted together at right angles and built around one of the floodlight pylons.

Photograph by Owen Pavey. Courtesy of Groundtastic Magazine

THE LYTTELTON GROUND
TEMPORARY HOME GROUND FOR **WOOLWICH ARSENAL**

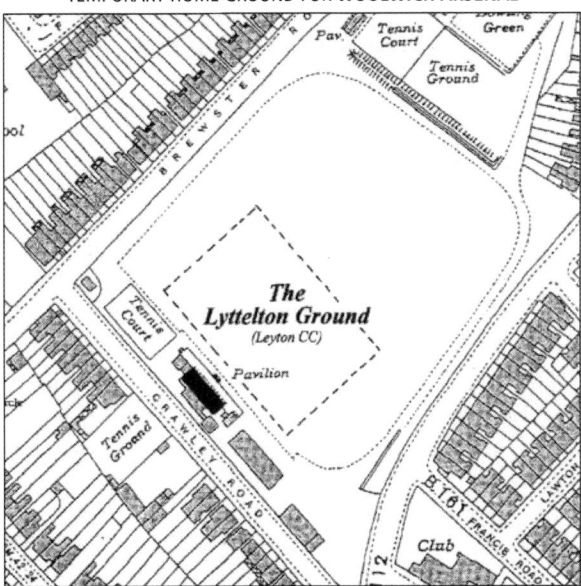

MAP EXTRACT; ESSEX 78.9 [**1939**]
SITE LOCATION; **TQ37948726**

Named after Lord Lyttelton from whom the land was purchased in 1886, the ground was located on the north east side of Crawley Road and just to the south of Leyton Midland Road Station. Prior to 1900, at least, it was the best equipped venue in the area and used for important football matches. The football pitch was at the west end of the ground and the facilities included a pavilion. After *Essex CCC* started to use it for County Cricket Championship matches the venue became known as *The County Ground* and it is now in use as a sports centre.

PLAYING RECORD OF ARSENAL
[AS WOOLWICH ARSENAL]
LEAGUE PROGRAMME

Match Played; 3-3 v. Leicester Fosse (4,000) (March 9th, 1895)
No. of Matches Played by Arsenal; 1
Information Kindly Supplied by; Norman Leat & Graham Webster
The match was played here due to the **Manor Ground** being closed for five weeks following a crowd disturbance at the *Burton Wanderers* fixture on January 26th, 1895.

A TOTAL OF **2** TEAMS TOOK PART IN **1** LEAGUE FIXTURE AT THIS VENUE

MADEJSKI STADIUM
HOME GROUND OF **READING**

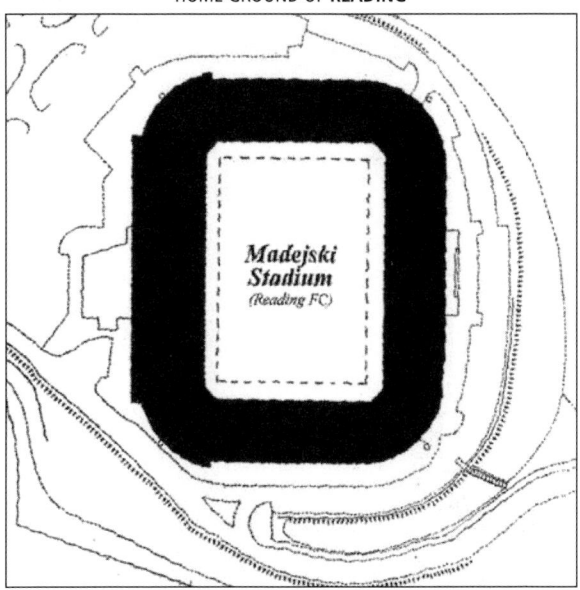

MAP EXTRACT; GROUND AS IN **1999** DRAWN FROM AERIAL PHOTOGRAPHS AND SUPERIMPOSED ON BERKSHIRE 37.11 [**1938**]
SITE LOCATION; **SU70836975**

Constructed on a greenfield site, *Reading FC* moved *to Madejski Stadium* from *Elm Park* in 1998. It is a typical modern purpose-built all-seater stadium with a two-tier stand on the west side and a continuous cantilevered roof. At the start of the 2004/5 season the capacity was 24,200 with a 114 x 76 yards sized pitch.

PLAYING RECORD OF READING
LEAGUE PROGRAMME

First Match; 3-0 v. Luton Town (18,108) (August 22nd, 1998)
Highest Gate; 24,060 v. Wolverhampton Wanderers (0-1) (May 14th, 2003) (Play Off Match)
Lowest Gate; 5,393 v. Bury (2-0) (October 20th, 1999)
Highest Home Win; 5-0 v. Oldham Athletic (7,768) (September 12th, 2000)
Highest Home Defeat; 0-6 v. Bristol Rovers (13,285) (January 16th, 1999)

PLAY OFF MATCHES
2-1 v. Wigan Athletic (22,034) (May 16th, 2001)
0-1 v. Wolverhampton Wanderers (24,060) (May 14th, 2003)
No. of Matches Played by Reading; 163
(League Programme; 161, Play Off Matches; 2)
Information Kindly Supplied by; David Downs
The club moved here from *Elm Park* in 1998 and was also involved in a Football League Play Off Match at the neutral venue of the *Millennium Stadium*.

AT THE END OF SEASON 2004/5, A TOTAL OF **61** TEAMS HAD TAKEN PART IN **163** LEAGUE FIXTURES AT THIS VENUE

MAINE ROAD

HOME GROUND OF **MANCHESTER CITY**
TEMPORARY HOME GROUND FOR **MANCHESTER UNITED**

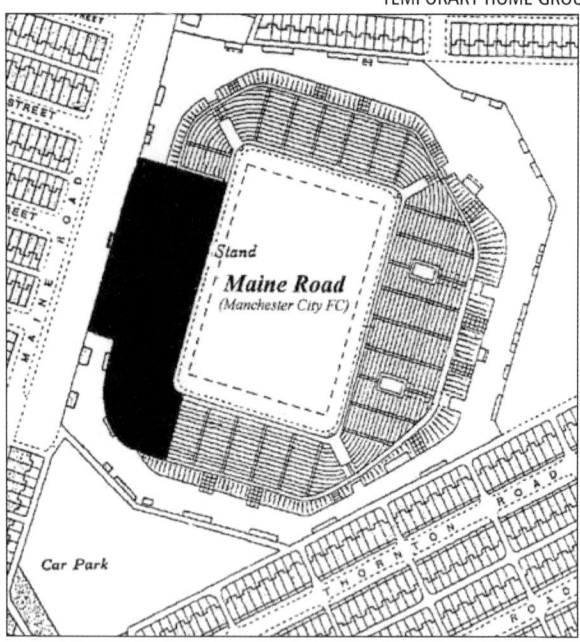

MAP EXTRACT; LANCASHIRE 111.2 & 111.3 [**1934**]
SITE LOCATION; **SJ84489497**

PLAYING RECORD OF MANCHESTER CITY
LEAGUE PROGRAMME

First Match; 2-1 v. Sheffield United (60,000) (August 25th, 1923)
Last Match; 0-1 v. Southampton (34,957) (May 11th, 2003)
Highest Gate; 78,000 v. Manchester United (0-0) (October 20th, 1947)
Lowest Gate; 3,000 v. Nottingham Forest (1-3) (February 13th, 1924)
Highest Home Win; 10-1 v. Huddersfield Town (19,583) (November 7th, 1987)
Highest Home Defeat; 2-7 v. West Bromwich Albion (20,996) (January 1st, 1934)

PLAY OFF MATCHES
1-0 v. Wigan Athletic (31,305) (May 19th, 1999)

No. of Matches Played by Manchester City; 1,539
(League Programme; 1,538, Play Off Matches; 1)

The club moved here from **Hyde Road** in 1923 and was also involved in a Football League Play Off Match at the neutral venue of **Wembley Stadium**. The club moved to **The City of Manchester Stadium** at the end of the 2002/3 season.

A TOTAL OF **86** TEAMS TOOK PART IN **1,602** LEAGUE FIXTURES AT THIS VENUE

The cavernous main stand on the west side of **Maine Road**, complete with the 1982 re-roofing.
Photograph by Patrick Snowsell. Courtesy of Groundtastic Magazine.

Manchester City FC moved from **Hyde Road** on completion of the *Maine Road* ground in 1923. Sited on a former clay pit, it consisted of a 10,000 seat main stand on the east side and with the embankments around the remainder of the stadium had a nominal capacity of about 90,000. Terraces had been constructed during the period prior to the establishment of the record attendance of 84,569 at the FA Cup 6th Round tie v. *Stoke City* (1-0) on March 3rd, 1934 and just before WWII the main stand roof was extended around the corner and along the south side.

Further improvements were undertaken after the 1940s with the installation of seating at the south end and a roof on the east side. In 1971 a new 8,100 seat stand was opened at the north end and eleven years later the main stand was re-roofed. The 1990s saw the construction of two new stands, a 5,000 seater at the south end and an 11,010 seat three-tier structure on the east side. At the end of the 2001/2 season the all-seat capacity was 34,996 and the pitch size was 117 x 76 yards. In 2003 *Manchester City* vacated the stadium and it was demolished in 2004 and replaced by housing.

PLAYING RECORD OF MANCHESTER UNITED
LEAGUE PROGRAMME

First Match; 2-1 v. Grimsby Town (41,025) (August 31st, 1946)
Last Match; 3-2 v. Portsmouth (49,808) (May 7th, 1949)
Highest Gate; 81,962 v. Arsenal (1-1) (January 17th, 1948)*
Lowest Gate; 8,456 v. Stoke City (1-1) (February 5th, 1947)
Highest Home Win; 6-2 v. Sheffield United (34,059) (May 26th, 1947) & v. Charlton Athletic (52,659) (August 30th, 1947)
Highest Home Defeat; 3-4 v. Grimsby Town (40,035) (October 11th, 1947) & v. Blackpool (51,187) (September 1st, 1948)

No. of Matches Played by Manchester United; 63
Information Kindly Supplied by; Tony Matthews

These matches were played here whilst **Old Trafford** was being rebuilt following severe bomb damage sustained in WWII.
*This attendance is also shown as 82,950 or 83,260 in some records and, as such, would be the highest for a Football League fixture

MANOR GROUND
HOME GROUND OF ARSENAL

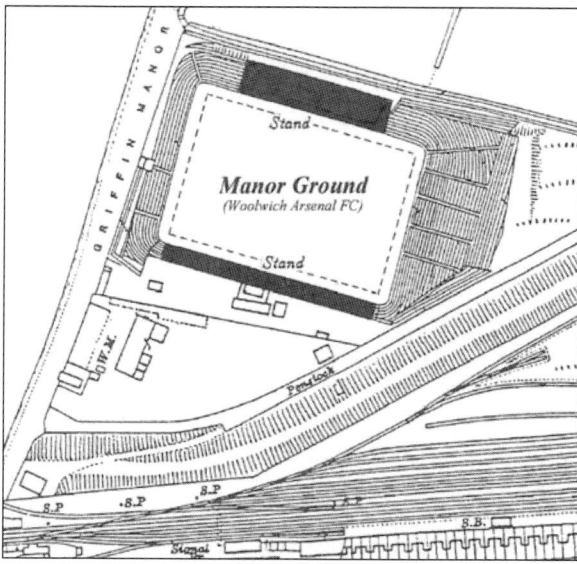

MAP EXTRACT; LONDON 10.4 [1914]
SITE LOCATION; TQ45047898

Royal Arsenal FC first used the site, north of Plumstead, in 1888 when it was known as the *Manor Field*. There were no facilities as such, wagons were borrowed from the nearby barracks to act as stands when the size of the crowd warranted it and players changed at the nearby Railway Tavern. It was after they had moved to the *Invicta Ground* in 1890 and returned three years later, as *Woolwich Arsenal FC*, that the venue was substantially improved and became known as the *Manor Ground*.

Initially a new 2,000 seat main stand was built on the north side with raised embankments on the south and wagons again in occasional use to provide additional standing accommodation. The Southern Outfall Sewer, running past the south east corner of the ground, provided a free view for spectators and, to counter this a full length seated stand was built along the south side and high concrete terracing constructed at the east end, effectively eliminating this problem.

During the remainder of the club's occupancy, the north stand was rebuilt and concrete terracing installed at the west end before they moved to *Highbury* (later *Arsenal Stadium*) in 1913. The site of the ground is now occupied by an industrial estate.

PLAYING RECORD OF ARSENAL
[AS WOOLWICH ARSENAL]
LEAGUE PROGRAMME

First Match; 2-2 v. Newcastle United (10,000) (September 2nd, 1893)
Last Match; 1-1 v. Middlesbrough (3,000) (April 26th, 1913)
Highest Gate; 32,850 v. Aston Villa (1-0) (October 8th, 1894)
Highest Home Win & Lowest Gate; 12-0 v. Loughborough (600) (March 12th, 1900)
Highest Home Defeat; 0-5 v. Liverpool (9,000) (October 28th, 1893)

No. of Matches Played by Arsenal; 343

The club was elected into the Football League Division 2 in 1893 as *Woolwich Arsenal FC*. The ground was closed for five weeks following a crowd disturbance at the *Burton Wanderers* fixture on January 26th, 1895 and home games were played at *Priestfield Road* and *The Lyttelton Ground*. In 1913 the decision was taken to re-locate to Islington, some ten miles away, and establish *Highbury Stadium*.

A TOTAL OF **51** TEAMS TOOK PART IN **343** LEAGUE FIXTURES AT THIS VENUE

MANOR GROUND
HOME GROUND OF OXFORD UNITED

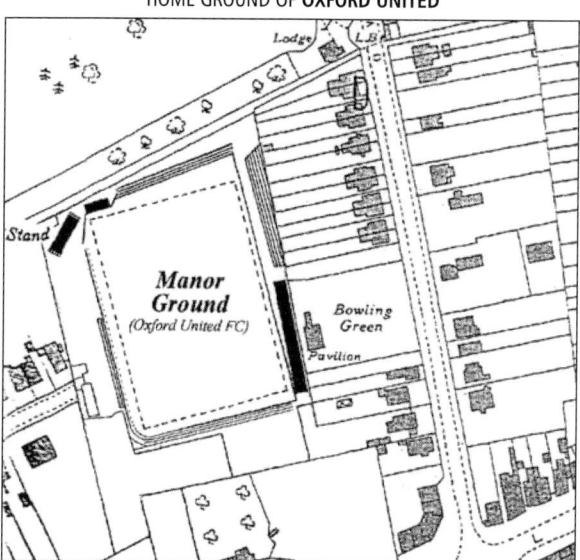

MAP EXTRACT; GROUND AS IN **1956** DRAWN FROM PLANS AND SUPERIMPOSED ON OXFORDSHIRE 33.16 [1947]
SITE LOCATION; SP54240716

This constrained site had been developed by the Headington Sports Ground Co. for cricket, bowls and tennis as well as football when *Headington United FC* moved here from *The Paddock* in 1925. The original facilities included a pavilion on the west side and a small narrow shelter on the east and this was how it remained until after WWII. Improvements to the football facilities, including the construction of a stand in the north west corner, led to the cricket club vacating the ground in 1949. The *Manor Ground* was bought for £10,000 in 1959 and by the time that the club, having changed its name to *Oxford United FC*, was elected to the Football League in 1960 the facilities included a main stand on the west side, an open terrace and two small stands at the north end, narrow terracing and a cover on the east side and an open terrace at the south end.

Further alterations, including minor expansion of the terrace at the north end and installation of a roof at the south end, were carried out before the record attendance of 22,750 was set at the FA Cup 6th Round tie v. *Preston North End* (1-2) on February 29th, 1964. During the 1980s improvements were made to the east side with the construction of two small seated stands and renewal of the existing cover and by 2001 the capacity was 9,650 with 6,769 seats and a 112 x 78 yards sized pitch.

The club moved to the *Kassam Stadium* in 2001 and the site was utilized for a hospital and housing development.

PLAYING RECORD OF OXFORD UNITED
LEAGUE PROGRAMME

First Match; 2-1 v. Lincoln City (10,368) (August 22nd, 1962)
Last Match; 1-1 v. Port Vale (7,094) (May 1st, 2001)
Highest Gate; 17,939 v. Derby County (0-2) (March 22nd, 1969)
Lowest Gate; 2,526 v. Chester (0-1) (November 10th, 1980)
Highest Home Win; 7-0 v. Barrow (5,201) (December 19th, 1964)
Highest Home Defeat; 1-7 v. Birmingham City (7,189) (December 12th, 1998)

No. of Matches Played by Oxford United; 872

The club was elected into the Football League Division 4 in 1962 and moved to the *Kassam Stadium* in 2001.

A TOTAL OF **97** TEAMS TOOK PART IN **872** LEAGUE FIXTURES AT THIS VENUE

MEADOW LANE

HOME GROUND OF **NOTTS COUNTY**
TEMPORARY HOME GROUND FOR **NOTTINGHAM FOREST**

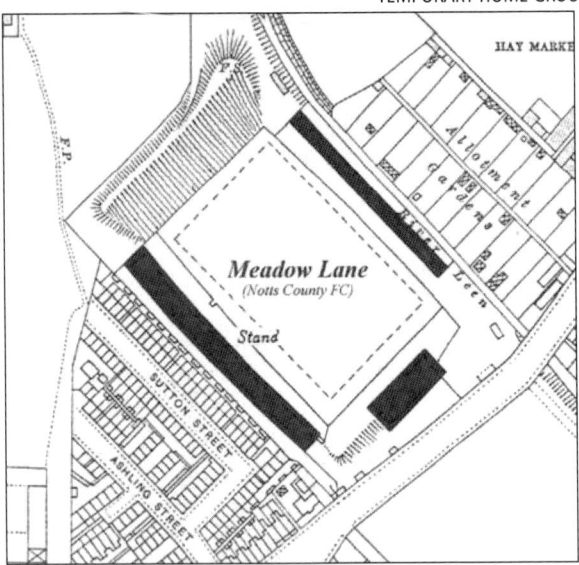

MAP EXTRACT; NOTTINGHAMSHIRE 42.6 [1914]
SITE LOCATION; SK58083872

Notts County FC moved from **Trent Bridge** to *Meadow Lane*, sandwiched between the River Leen and Sutton Street, in 1910. The facilities included a main stand on the south side, a cover on the north, embankments at the west end and a stand which had been removed from **Trent Bridge** and re-erected at the east end. The final major improvement prior to WWII occurred after the river was culverted, allowing for the construction of a new and larger stand on the north side.

The record attendance of 47,310 was set at the FA Cup 6th Round tie v. *York City* (0-1) on March 12th, 1955 and the only alteration prior to the 1990s was the demolition of the stand at the east end in 1978. In 1992 new all seat stands were constructed at each end and on the north side and, in 1994, a new main stand built giving an all seat capacity of 19,600 by the start of the 2004/5 season. The pitch size was 117 x 76 yards.

PLAYING RECORD OF NOTTS COUNTY
LEAGUE PROGRAMME
First Match; 1-1 v. Nottingham Forest (27,000) (September 3rd, 1910)
Highest Gate; 45,992 v. Nottingham Forest (2-0) (April 22nd, 1950)
Lowest Gate; 1,927 v. Chesterfield (2-0) (April 2nd, 1966)
Highest Home Win; 11-1 v. Newport County (26,843)
(January 15th, 1949)
Highest Home Defeat; 0-6 v. Ipswich Town (8,475)
(September 25th, 1982)
PLAY OFF MATCHES
1-3 v. Walsall (11,522) (May 15th, 1988)
2-0 v. Bolton Wanderers (15,197) (May 16th, 1990)
1-0 v. Middlesbrough (18,249) (May 22nd, 1991)
1-0 v. Crewe Alexandra (9,640) (May 15th, 1996)
No. of Matches Played by Notts County; 1,827
(League Programme; 1,823, Play Off Matches; 4)
Information Kindly Supplied by; Peter Wynne-Thomas & Peter Orme

The club moved here from **Trent Bridge** in 1910 and was also involved in Football League Play Off Matches at the neutral venue of *Wembley Stadium*

PLAYING RECORD OF NOTTINGHAM FOREST
LEAGUE PROGRAMME
1ST PERIOD
Match Played; 0-1 v. Manchester City (32,194)
(November 23rd, 1946)
2ND PERIOD
Matches Played; 0-0 v. Coventry City (22,260)
(September 14th, 1968)
3-3 v. Stoke City (21,519) (October 5th, 1968)
2-4 v. Newcastle United (17,651) (October 8th, 1968)
1-2 v. Ipswich Town (21,148) (October 19th, 1968)
0-0 v. Wolverhampton Wanderers (19,490) (November 2nd, 1968)
No. of Matches Played by Nottingham Forest; 6
Information Kindly Supplied by; Ken Smales

The match in the first period occurred when **The City Ground** was flooded during November 1946 and during the second period League matches were played here after fire destroyed the main stand at **The City Ground** during the League Match with *Leeds United* on August 24th, 1968.

AT THE END OF SEASON 2004/5, A TOTAL OF **111** TEAMS HAD TAKEN PART IN **1,833** LEAGUE FIXTURES AT THIS VENUE

The rebuilt *Meadow Lane*, looking west with the main stand on the left.
Photograph by Stephen Mumford. Courtesy of Groundtastic Magazine

MEMORIAL GROUND
HOME GROUND OF **BRISTOL ROVERS**

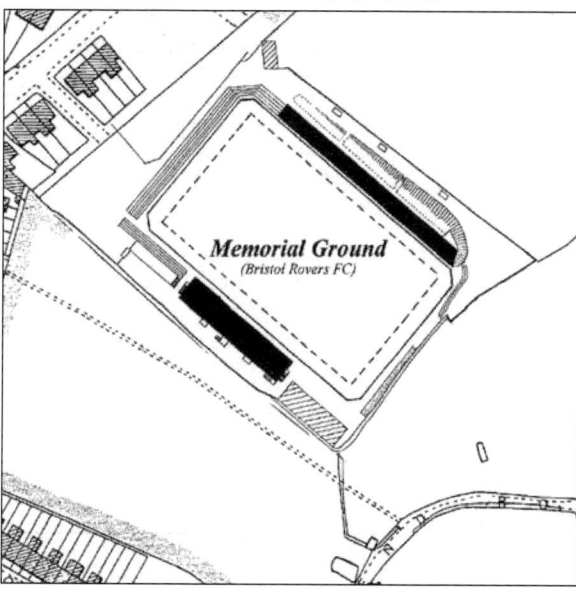

MAP EXTRACT; GROUND AS IN **1953** DRAWN FROM PLANS AND SUPERIMPOSED ON GLOUCESTERSHIRE 72.5 [1903]
SITE LOCATION; ST59607653

When *Bristol Rovers* moved in at the start of the 1996/7 season to share the ground with *Bristol RUFC* the only facilities were a main stand on the east side and uncovered terracing at the north end. A seated stand was subsequently built on the west side and in May 1998 they became joint owners when the ground was purchased by The Memorial Stadium Co. with each club holding a 50% stake. Just two months later the rugby club called in the receivers and the *Rovers* were able to assume total ownership as, under the terms of the contract any party not being able to meet the running costs could be bought out for £10,000.

The north end was subsequently covered whilst a canvas roofed temporary stand was installed at the south end giving a capacity of 11,917 with 4,000 seats at the start of the 2004/5 season. The pitch size was 110 x 74 yards.

PLAYING RECORD OF BRISTOL ROVERS
LEAGUE PROGRAMME
First Match; 1-1 v. Stockport County (6,380) (August 31st, 1996)
Highest Gate; 11,109 v. Wigan Athletic (1-1) (March 4th, 2000)
Lowest Gate; 4,123 v. Burnley (1-2) (November 19th, 1996)
Highest Home Win; 5-0 v. Wigan Athletic (6,038) (April 10th, 1998)
Highest Home Defeat; 0-4 v. Grimsby Town (4,801)
(December 12th, 1997)
PLAY OFF MATCHES
3-1 v. Northampton Town (9,173) (May 10th, 1998)
No. of Matches Played by Bristol Rovers; 207
(League Programme; 206, Play Off Matches; 1)
Information Kindly Supplied by; Keith Brookland

Bristol Rovers moved in from **Twerton Park** just after the start of the 1996/7 season (the ground was not quite ready for the first fixture v. *Peterborough United FC* on August 17th, 1996) to share the venue with *Bristol RUFC*.

AT THE END OF SEASON 2004/5, A TOTAL OF **61** TEAMS HAD TAKEN PART IN **207** LEAGUE FIXTURES AT THIS VENUE

MILLFIELDS ROAD
HOME GROUND OF **LEYTON ORIENT**

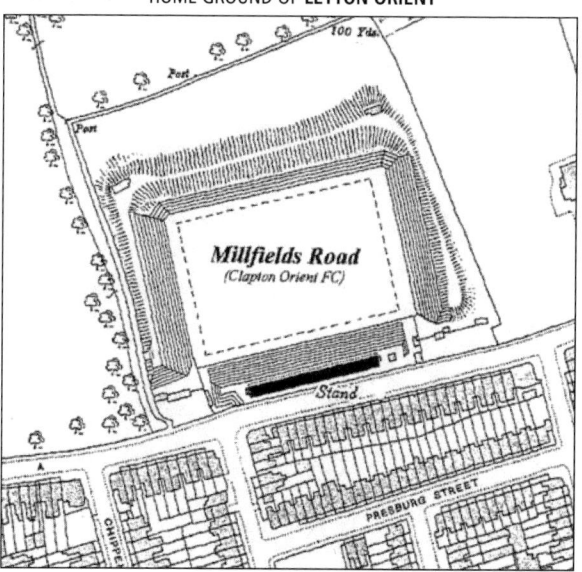

MAP EXTRACT; LONDON 2.16 [**1915**]
SITE LOCATION; TQ35738618

Originally known as the *Whittles Athletic Ground* and principally used for whippet racing, *Clapton Orient FC* moved here from *Pond Lane Bridge* in 1896. Slag, waste from the adjacent power station, was used to create large embankments around the ground and for a number of years there were no facilities and even by the time that they gained Football League membership in 1905 a rudimentary press box was the only covered accommodation on the ground!

A 2,000 seat grandstand, was finally built on the south side in 1906 and some concrete terracing later constructed around the ground. The grandstand was sold to *Wimbledon FC*, in 1923 for re-erection at **Plough Lane**, and replaced with a 3,000 seat stand, but it was not until the Clapton Stadium Syndicate became joint tenants and introduced greyhound racing in 1927 that major alterations took place. The stadium was rebuilt with an oval track, substantial concrete terracing installed around the three sides opposite to the main stand and new covering provided around the ground. Despite all these improvements, the poor financial state of *Clapton Orient* forced them to hand the ground over to their joint tenants and move out to **Lea Bridge Stadium** in 1930. It continued in use for greyhound racing, as *Clapton Stadium*, until the 1970s when it was replaced by housing.

PLAYING RECORD OF LEYTON ORIENT
[AS CLAPTON ORIENT]
LEAGUE PROGRAMME
First Match; 1-0 v. Hull City (3,000) (September 9th, 1905)
Last Match; 4-1 v. Brighton & Hove Albion (8,763) (May 3rd, 1930)
Highest Gate; 37,615 v. Tottenham Hotspur (2-3) (March 16th, 1929)
Lowest Gate; 2,362 v. Newport County (3-1) (March 31st, 1930)
Highest Home Win; 6-1 v. Luton Town (6,228) (April 19th, 1930)
Highest Home Defeat; 2-5 v. Blackpool (11,401) (January 21st, 1928). 0-4 v. Darlington (11,807) (November 6th, 1926) & v. Tottenham Hotspur (32,644) (October 18th, 1919)
No. of Matches Played by Leyton Orient; 421
Information Kindly Supplied by; Paul Hiscock

The club was elected into the Football League Division 2 in 1905 as *Clapton Orient*.

A TOTAL OF **69** TEAMS TOOK PART IN **421** LEAGUE FIXTURES AT THIS VENUE

MILLENNIUM STADIUM
VENUE FOR PLAY OFF FINALS

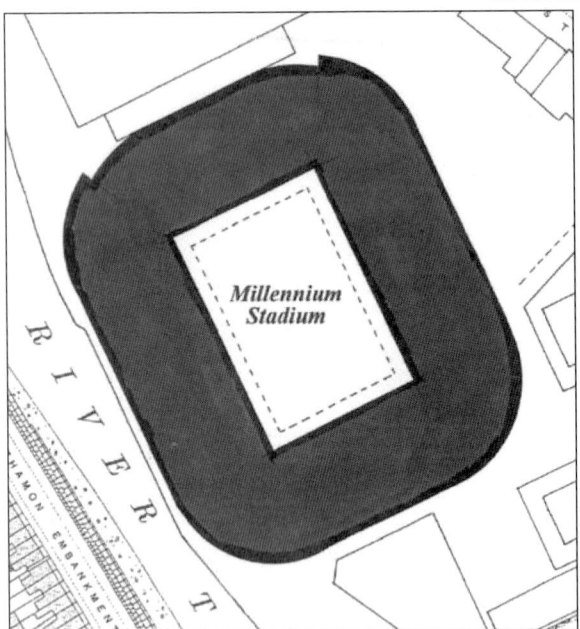

MAP EXTRACT; GROUND AS IN **2000** DRAWN FROM AERIAL PHOTOGRAPHS AND SUPERIMPOSED ON GLAMORGAN 43.15 [1920]
SITE LOCATION; **ST18007618**

Constructed on the site of *Cardiff Arms Park*, the *Millennium Stadium* opened in 2000. The 72,500 seats are dispersed around the ground within three tiers, 23.300 on the lower, 16,000 on the middle and 31,200 on the upper. The all-over roof, part of which acts as a retractable cover over the 130 x 86 yards playing area, is supported by cables off two 3.3ft diameter beams slung between four 250ft high masts. The football pitch size for the 2004/5 season was 110 x 74 yards.

Darren Carter of *Birmingham City* slots home the decisive penalty in the Play Off Final v. *Norwich City* at the **Millennium Stadium** on May 12th, 2002.
The retractable roof was closed for this game to eliminate the large shadow thrown across the pitch which has a detrimental effect on TV picture quality. This match was the first, and still the only, occasion of a Football League match being played totally under cover.
Photograph Courtesy of Blues Magazine

PLAY OFF FINALS
SEASON 2000/1
Division 2; *Blackpool 4, Leyton Orient 2 (23,600) (May 26th, 2001)*
Division 1; *Reading 2, Walsall 3 [aet] (50,496) (May 27th, 2001)*
Premier League; *Bolton Wanderers 3, Preston North End 0 (54,328) (May 28th, 2001)*
SEASON 2001/2
Division 2; *Cheltenham Town 3, Rushden & Diamonds 1 (24,368) (May 6th, 2002)*
Division 1; *Brentford 0, Stoke City 2 (42,523) (May 11th, 2002)*
Premier League; *Birmingham City 1, Norwich City 1 [aet. 4-2 on pens] (71,597) (May 12th, 2002)**
SEASON 2002/3
Division 2; *AFC Bournemouth 5, Lincoln City 2 (32,148) (May 24th, 2003)*
Division 1; *Cardiff City 1, Queens Park Rangers 0 [aet] (66,096) (May 25th, 2003)*
Premier League; *Sheffield United 0, Wolverhampton Wanderers 3 (69,473) (May 26th, 2003)*
SEASON 2003/4
Premier League; *Crystal Palace 1, West Ham United 0 (72,523) (May 29th, 2004)*
Division 1; *Bristol City 0, Brighton & Hove Albion 1 (65,167) (May 30th, 2004)*
Division 2; *Huddersfield Town 0, Mansfield Town 0 [aet. 4-1 on pens] (37,298) (May 31st, 2004)*
SEASON 2004/5
Division 2; *Lincoln City 0, Southend United 2 [aet] (19,653) (May 28th, 2005)*
Division 1; *Hartlepool United 2, Sheffield Wednesday 4 [aet] (59,808) (May 29th, 2005)*
Premier League; *West Ham United 1, Preston North End 0 (70,275) (May 30th, 2005)*

No. of Matches Played; 15

Play Off Finals were staged here as a temporary measure whilst **Wembley Stadium** was closed for rebuilding.
*NB. This match was the first Football League fixture to be played totally under cover.

AT THE END OF SEASON 2004/5, A TOTAL OF **27** TEAMS HAD TAKEN PART IN **15** LEAGUE FIXTURES AT THIS VENUE

MILLMOOR

HOME GROUND OF ROTHERHAM UNITED

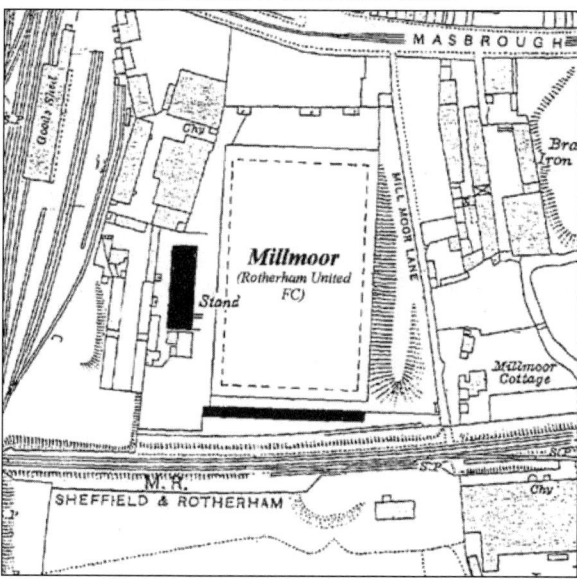

MAP EXTRACT; YORKSHIRE 289.10 [1923]
SITE LOCATION; SK41929257

This constrained site was an area of waste grassland when *Rotherham County FC* moved to *Millmoor* in 1905. The original facilities included an embankment along the east side and two small stands whilst a cover was later installed at the south end. A main stand was built on the west side in 1920, a cover installed at the east side in 1928 and a track was laid for the greyhound racing which took place during the 1930s.

Post WWII improvements were made following the purchase of the ground from British Railways in 1949. The terracing was concreted, the north end expanded (and subsequently roofed), the main stand roof extended over the paddock and the south end enlarged and re-roofed before the end of the 1960s, whilst the 1970s saw the installation of seating under the cover on the east side. Further alterations were the installation of an additional cover and seating on the east side and seating in the main stand paddock giving a capacity, at the start of the 2004/5 season, of 11,486 with 6,949 seats. The pitch size was 115 x 70 yards.

PLAYING RECORD OF ROTHERHAM UNITED
LEAGUE PROGRAMME

First Match; 2-0 v. Nottingham Forest (10,000) (August 30th, 1919)
Highest Gate; 25,170 v. Sheffield United (2-2) (December 13th, 1952)
Lowest Gate; 1,324 v. Mansfield Town (1-2) (May 5th, 1934)
Highest Home Win; 8-0 v. Oldham Athletic (10,398)
(May 26th, 1947)
Highest Home Defeat; 2-7 v. AFC Bournemouth (5,110) (October 10th, 1973)

PLAY OFF MATCHES

1-1 v. Swansea City (5,568) (May 18th, 1988)
0-0 v. Leyton Orient [2-4] (9,529) (May 19th, 1999)

No. of Matches Played by Rotherham United; 1,733
(League Programme; 1,731 [Including one expunged match v. Aldershot on February 1st, 1992], Play Off Matches; 2)
Information Kindly Supplied by; Gerry Somerton

The club was elected into the Football League Division 2 in 1919 as *Rotherham County* and changed the name to *Rotherham United* in 1925.

AT THE END OF SEASON 2004/5, A TOTAL OF **109** TEAMS HAD TAKEN PART IN **1,733** LEAGUE FIXTURES AT THIS VENUE

THE MOUNT

HOME GROUND OF CHARLTON ATHLETIC

MAP EXTRACT; LONDON 10.3 [1916]
SITE LOCATION; TQ38287379

The Mount was the home ground of *Catford Southend FC* when *Charlton Athletic* moved here from **The Valley** in 1923. It was sited in the south west corner of Mountsfield Park and the only facility was a small stand on the east side of the pitch. Although the new club hoped to effect considerable improvements these only amounted to the construction of an embankment on one side of the pitch and a temporary stand on the other.

After *Charlton Athletic* moved back to **The Valley** in 1924, *Catford Southend FC* folded just three years later and the football ground was removed, the site being re-incorporated into Mountsfield Park.

PLAYING RECORD OF CHARLTON ATHLETIC
LEAGUE PROGRAMME

Matches Played; 0-0 v. Northampton Town (8,000)
(December 22nd, 1923)
3-0 v. Queens Park Rangers (10,000) (December 26th, 1923)
0-0 v. Gillingham (8,000) (January 5th, 1924)
3-1 v. Brentford (3,000) (February 16th, 1924)
1-3 v. Bristol Rovers (4,000) (March 1st, 1924)
1-1 v. Portsmouth (3,000) (March 10th, 1924)
0-2 v. Brighton & Hove Albion (3,000) (March 22nd, 1924)
1-1 v. Luton Town (2,000) (April 5th, 1924)
1-0 v. Exeter City (4,000) (April 7th, 1924)
0-0 v. Reading (6,000) (April 19th, 1924)
0-1 v. Plymouth Argyle (5,000) (April 21st, 1924)
1-2 v. Bournemouth & Boscombe Athletic (1,000)
(May 3rd, 1924)

No. of Matches Played by Charlton Athletic; 12
Information Kindly Supplied by; Tony Matthews

Charlton Athletic FC moved here to groundshare with *Catford FC* and squandered £17,000 in a forlorn attempt to bring the ground up to a decent standard for Football League football. The fans refused to accept the venue as their home ground and with the pitch liable to subsidence, the club returned to **The Valley** after less than six months.

A TOTAL OF **13** TEAMS TOOK PART IN **12** LEAGUE FIXTURES AT THIS VENUE

MOLINEUX

HOME GROUND OF WOLVERHAMPTON WANDERERS

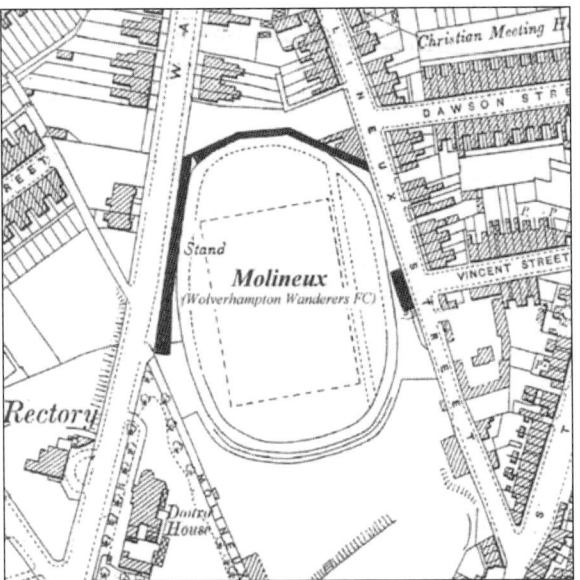

MAP EXTRACT; STAFFORDSHIRE 62.6 [1889]
SITE LOCATION; **SO91229916**

Wolverhampton Wanderers FC first played at *Molineux* in a Walsall County FA Cup Semi-Final v. *Walsall Town FC* in March 1886. At this time the venue, in an area on the north side of the Molineux Hotel, was primarily in use as a pleasure ground with a boating lake and skating rink and an oval sports field used for athletics, cycling and cricket as well as football.

The club moved in permanently from **Dudley Road** in 1889 and reconstructed the ground; all the gardens and the lake between the hotel (utilized as dressing rooms until c1905) and the oval were cleared away, a cover added to the existing 300 seat grandstand on the west side and narrow covers installed at the north end. The only alteration prior to WWI was an improvement to the terracing and installation of some new cover at the north end.

The ground was purchased in 1924 and, one year later, part of the west side cover was repositioned on the east (surviving only eight months before succumbing to a gale!) and a new main stand built on the west. Further major improvements took place with the removal of the oval and construction of new covered terracing at each end and the installation of a 3,450 seat stand on the east side prior to the record attendance of 61,315 being set at the FA Cup 5th Round tie v. *Liverpool* (4-1) on February 11th, 1939.

Molineux remained unaltered until 1979 when houses along the opposite side of Molineux Street were purchased and demolished enabling the pitch to be moved eastwards and a new 9,230 seat stand constructed on their site. Over the next 14 years new all-seat stands were constructed on each side of the ground and the capacity at the start of the 2004/5 season was 29,400. The pitch size was 116 x 74 yards.

PLAYING RECORD OF WOLVERHAMPTON WANDERERS
LEAGUE PROGRAMME

First Match; 2-0 v. Notts County (4,000) (September 7th, 1889)
Highest Gate; 56,661 v. West Bromwich Albion (1-1) (October 15th, 1949)
Lowest Gate; 900 v. Notts County (2-1) (October 17th, 1891) & v. Blackburn Rovers (6-1) (November 28th, 1891)
Highest Home Win; 10-1 v. Leicester City (25,540) (April 15th, 1938)
Highest Home Defeat; 0-8 v. West Bromwich Albion (8,000) (December 27th, 1893)

PLAY OFF MATCHES

0-0 v. Colchester United (16,330) (May 17th, 1987)
0-1 v. Aldershot (19,962) (May 25th, 1987)
2-1 v. Bolton Wanderers (26,153) (May 14th, 1995)
2-1 v. Crystal Palace (26,403) (May 14th, 1997)
1-0 v. Norwich City (27,418) (May 1st, 2002)
2-1 v. Reading (27,678) (May 10th, 2003)

No. of Matches Played by Wolverhampton Wanderers; 2,134

(League Programme; 2,128, Play Off Matches; 6)

Information Kindly Supplied by; *Tony Matthews*

The club moved here from **Dudley Road** in 1889. The first ever League penalty kick was awarded here to *Wolverhampton Wanderers* on September 14th, 1891 v. *Accrington* (5-0) and scored by John Heath. In 1919 the ground was closed following crowd trouble and two home League matches were played at **The Hawthorns**. The club was also involved in a Football League Play Off Match at the neutral venue of the *Millennium Stadium*.

AT THE END OF SEASON 2004/5, A TOTAL OF **108** TEAMS HAD TAKEN PART IN **2,134** LEAGUE FIXTURES AT THIS VENUE

A view of **Molineux** taken from the top of the terracing at the south end and showing the stadium in its final post-WWII state prior to the extensive rebuilding of the 1980s and 1990s

Photograph from Stephane Renauld Collection, Courtesy of Groundtastic Magazine

MOSS ROSE

TEMPORARY HOME GROUND FOR **CHESTER CITY**
HOME GROUND OF **MACCLESFIELD TOWN**

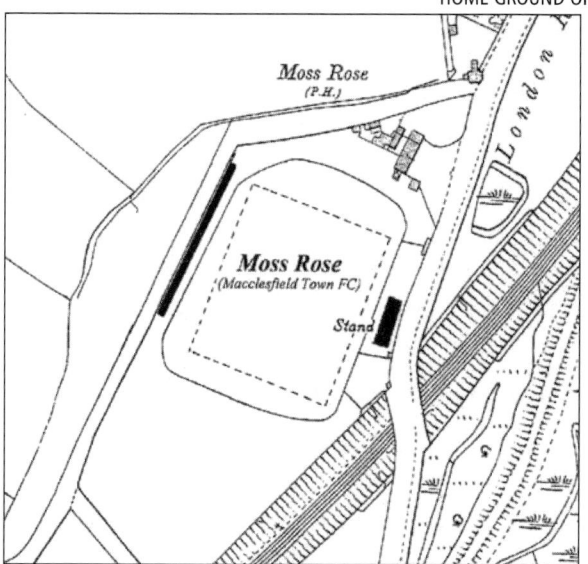

MAP EXTRACT; CHESHIRE 36.12 [**1909**]
SITE LOCATION; **SJ91617176**

PLAYING RECORD OF CHESTER CITY
LEAGUE PROGRAMME

First Match; 1-2 v. Exeter City (1,337) (September 1st, 1990)
Last Match; 1-0 v. Leyton Orient (2,008) (May 2nd, 1992)
Highest Gate; 4,895 v. Birmingham City (0-1) (April 11th, 1992)
Lowest Gate; 631 v. Reading (1-0) (March 5th, 1991)
Highest Home Win; 5-2 v. Exeter City (871) (February 11th, 1992)
Highest Home Defeat; 2-5 v. Darlington (1,020) (January 4th, 1992)

No. of Matches Played by Chester City; 46
Information Kindly Supplied by; Charles Sumner

Chester City FC, with no home ground, was obliged to play at *Moss Rose* for two seasons until Morrisons, the company that purchased the *Sealand Road* site for use as a supermarket, had constructed a new venue, the *Deva Stadium*, for the club's use in Chester.

PLAYING RECORD OF MACCLESFIELD TOWN
LEAGUE PROGRAMME

First Match; 2-1 v. Torquay United (3,379) (August 9th, 1997)
Highest Gate; 6,381 v. Manchester City (0-1) (September 12th, 1998)
Lowest Gate; 1,349 v. Lincoln City (2-0) (September 12th, 2000)
Highest Home Win; 5-2 v. Mansfield Town (1,541) (November 2nd, 1999). 4-0 v. Huddersfield Town (3,059) (December 13th, 2003)
Highest Home Defeat; 2-5 v. Cardiff City (2,376) (January 27th, 2001)

PLAY OFF MATCHES
1-1 v. Lincoln City (5,223) (May 21st, 2005)

No. of Matches Played by Macclesfield Town; 185
(League Programme; 184, Play Off Matches; 1)

The club was promoted into the Football League Division 3 from the Football Conference in 1997.

AT THE END OF SEASON 2004/5, A TOTAL OF **65** TEAMS HAD TAKEN PART IN **231** LEAGUE FIXTURES AT THIS VENUE

Hallifield FC moved here in 1897 and changed its name to *Macclesfield* in 1904. In 1906 a covered seated main stand was constructed on the east side and, about this time, a long narrow roof erected on the west side. The club record attendance of 9,003 was established at the Cheshire Senior Cup 1st Round tie v. *Winsford Athletic* (2-1) on February 4th, 1948.

The main stand was replaced in 1960 by a short cantilever roofed 650 seat structure and by the time that *Chester City* first used the ground for Football League fixtures in 1990 there was uncovered terracing at each end and a short cover, subsequently extended, over the terracing on the west side.

Further improvements saw the construction of an all-seat stand at the south end and a temporary all-seat stand with a canvas roof was provided on the west side of the ground following *Macclesfield Town FC's* entry into the Football League and subsequent promotion to the Second Division in 1998. This temporary structure was removed in 2000 and a new 1,743 seat stand built in its place. The capacity at the start of the 2004/5 season was 6,307 with 2,561 seats and the pitch size 109 x 72 yards.

The diminutive cantilever-roofed main stand on the east side of the ground
Photograph by Peter Miles. Courtesy of Groundtastic Magazine

MUNTZ STREET
HOME GROUND OF BIRMINGHAM CITY

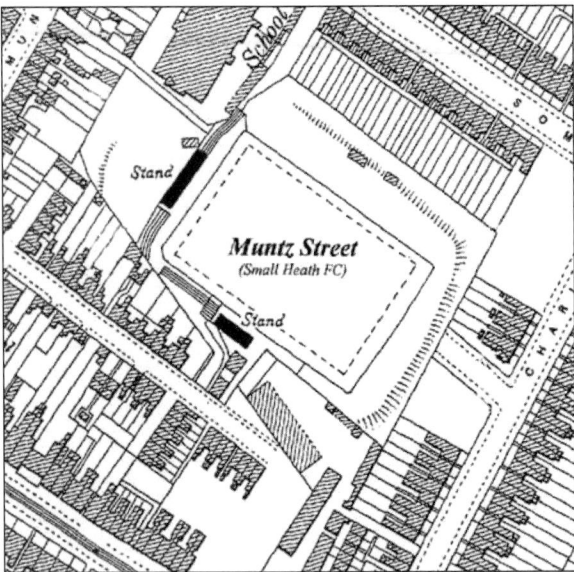

MAP EXTRACT; WARWICKSHIRE 14.10 [**1904**]
SITE LOCATION; **SP09988579**

Small Heath Alliance FC moved to *Muntz Street*, south east of the city centre, from *Ladypool Road* in 1877. The facilities initially only consisted of a small wooden stand on the south side of the pitch but subsequent improvements included the addition of concrete terracing to the west of this stand, embankments on the other three sides and the installation of an ornate grandstand at the west end. This grandstand was purchased from *Aston Villa* and removed from their *Wellington Road* ground after they vacated it in 1897. The club, by now called *Birmingham FC*, moved to *St Andrew's* mid-way through the 1905/6 season and the site was eventually used for Swanage Road and housing.

PLAYING RECORD OF BIRMINGHAM CITY
[AS SMALL HEATH AND BIRMINGHAM]
LEAGUE PROGRAMME
First Match; 5-1 v. Burslem Port Vale (2,500) (September 3rd, 1892)
Last Match; 3-1 v. Bury (10,000) (December 22nd, 1906)
Highest Gate; 30,000 v. Aston Villa (2-0) (September 16th, 1905)
Lowest Gate; 500 v. Crewe Alexandra (6-1) (December 6th, 1893)
Highest Home Win; 12-0 v. Walsall Town Swifts (2,000) (December 17th, 1892) & v. Doncaster Rovers (8,000) (April 1st, 1903)
Highest Home Defeat; 2-5 v. Bolton Wanderers (10,000) (March 25th, 1906)
TEST MATCHES
0-0 v. Liverpool (5,000) (April 20th, 1896)
8-0 v. Manchester City (2,000) (April 27th, 1896)
No. of Matches Played by Birmingham City; 235
(League Programme; 233, Test Matches; 2)
Information Kindly Supplied by; Tony Matthews

The club was a founder member of the Football League Division 2 in 1892 as *Small Heath FC*. The ground was notorious for its bumpy and muddy pitch and on more than one occasion FA Cup opponents offered the club financial inducements to switch venues. *Muntz Street* eventually became too small and the club (re-named as *Birmingham FC* in 1905) moved to *St Andrew's*. During this period the club was also involved in Test Matches at the neutral venues of the *Olive Grove* and the *Victoria Ground*.

A TOTAL OF **48** TEAMS TOOK PART IN **235** LEAGUE FIXTURES AT THIS VENUE

NATIONAL HOCKEY STADIUM
TEMPORARY HOME GROUND FOR MILTON KEYNES DONS

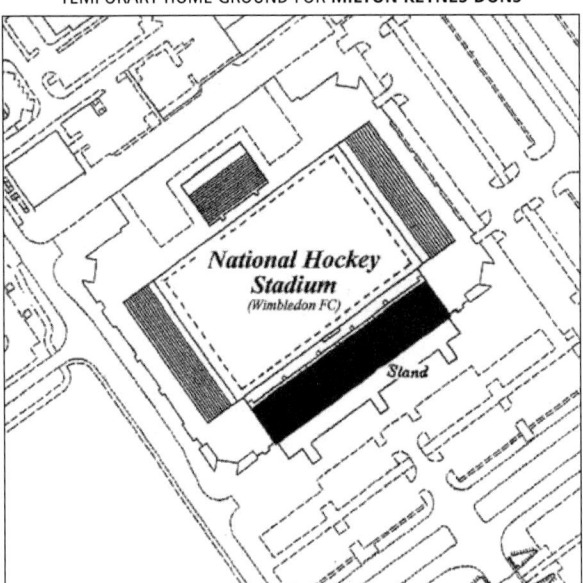

MAP EXTRACT; GROUND AS IN **2002** DRAWN FROM AERIAL PHOTOGRAPHS
SITE LOCATION; **SP84103848**

Located on a greenfield site on the east side of the main railway line the *National Hockey Stadium* was completed in 1995. It was originally conceived as a 20,000 all-seater venue but by 2002 only a cantilever roofed main stand on the south east side and an open stand on the north west had been built giving an all-seated capacity of 4,048.

To accommodate League Football the plastic pitch was ripped up and replaced by an enlarged turfed playing area and temporary open seated stands were installed at each end. During 2004 a roof was erected over the east end and the all-seat capacity was 9,000 at the start of the 2004/5 season. The pitch size was 110 x 74 yards

PLAYING RECORD OF MILTON KEYNES DONS
[ALSO AS WIMBLEDON]
LEAGUE PROGRAMME
First Match; 2-2 v. Burnley (5,639) (September 27th, 2003)
Highest Gate; 8,118 v. West Ham United (1-1) (November 25th, 2003)
Lowest Gate; 2,866 v. Preston North End (3-3) (April 10th, 2004)
Highest Home Win; 4-2 v. Hartlepool United (3,685) (September 25th, 2004). 3-0 v. Wrexham (3,601) (December 11th, 2004)
Highest Home Defeat; 1-4 v. Luton Town (7,620) (November 20th, 2004)
No. of Matches Played by Milton Keynes Dons; 42

Following approval by the FA *Wimbledon FC* planned to relocate here from *Selhurst Park* at the start of the 2003/4 season whilst awaiting completion of the *Denbigh North Stadium* but during June 2003 it went into administration and this move was delayed until September. The first League goal at the stadium was scored by Robbie Blake of *Burnley FC* in the 21st minute of the first match. At the end of the 2003/4 season the name of the club was changed to *Milton Keynes Dons*.

AT THE END OF SEASON 2004/5, A TOTAL OF **41** TEAMS HAD TAKEN PART IN **42** LEAGUE FIXTURES AT THIS VENUE

NENE PARK
HOME GROUND OF **RUSHDEN & DIAMONDS**

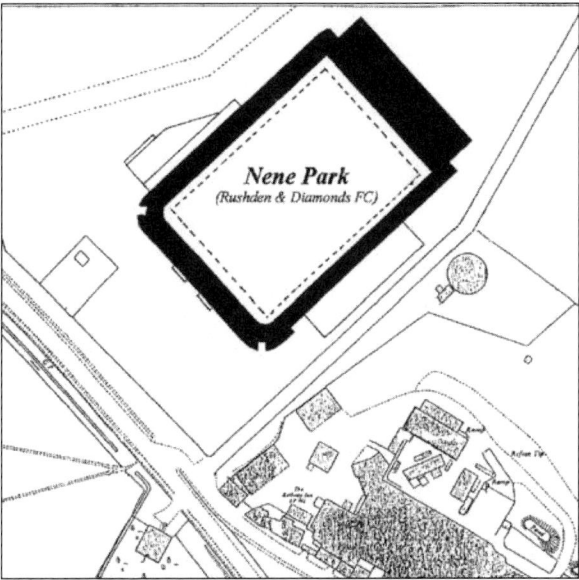

MAP EXTRACT; GROUND AS IN **2000** DRAWN FROM AERIAL PHOTOGRAPHS AND SUPERIMPOSED ON SP9570 [1950]
SITE LOCATION; **SP95507090**

Irthlingborough Diamonds FC moved to Nene Park in 1969 and constructed a covered terrace on the north side and a 350 seat stand on the south. In 1992 *Rushden Town FC* moved here from their *Hayden Road* ground and amalgamated with *Irthlingborough Diamonds* to form *Rushden & Diamonds FC*. In 1993 the stand and covering were demolished and 1,000 seat cantilever roofed stands subsequently built on each side of the pitch. A covered terrace, with its cantilevered roof linked to the stands with curved corners, opened in 1995 at the west end and a 2,000 seat stand (uncovered until 1998 when a curved cantilevered roof was installed) was built at the east end in 1996. The capacity at the start of the 2004/5 season was 6,441 with 4,641 seats and the pitch size was 111 x 75 yards.

PLAYING RECORD OF RUSHDEN & DIAMONDS
LEAGUE PROGRAMME
First Match; 0-0 v. Lincoln City (5,018) (August 16th, 2001)
Highest Gate; 6,291 v. Hartlepool United (1-1) (May 3rd, 2003)
Lowest Gate; 1,803 v. Bury (3-0) (February 22nd, 2005)
Highest Home Win; 5-1 v. Shrewsbury Town (4,144) (January 1st, 2003) & v. Notts County (3,504) (October 30th, 2004)
Highest Home Defeat; 1-4 v. Southend United (2,804) (September 4th, 2004) & v. Lincoln City (4,213) (March 25th, 2005)
PLAY OFF MATCHES
2-2 v. Rochdale (6,015) (April 27th, 2002)
No. of Matches Played by Rushden & Diamonds; 93
(League Programme; 92, Play Off Matches; 1)

The club was promoted into the Football League Division 3 from the Football Conference in 2001 and was also involved in a Football League Play Off Match at the neutral venue of the *Millennium Stadium.*

AT THE END OF SEASON 2003/4, A TOTAL OF **50** TEAMS HAD TAKEN PART IN **93** LEAGUE FIXTURES AT THIS VENUE

THE NEST
HOME GROUND OF **CRYSTAL PALACE**

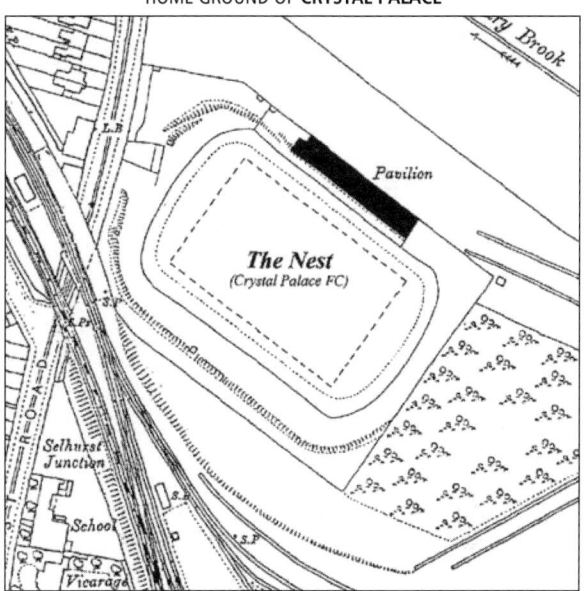

MAP EXTRACT; SURREY 14.6 [**1911**]
SITE LOCATION; **TQ33226756**

The Nest, or *Croydon Common Athletic Ground,* prior to WWI had been the home ground of *Croydon Common FC* but was vacant by the time that *Crystal Palace* took up the lease from the London Brighton & South Coast Railway in 1919. The facilities, which were not improved during their occupancy, consisted of a covered seated stand on the north side and banking around the other three sides.

After *Crystal Palace FC* moved to *Selhurst Park* in 1924 it was briefly occupied by the *Tramway FC* before the site of the ground was utilized in 1928 for construction of an electrical multiple unit inspection shed and expansion of the adjacent rolling stock maintenance depot. The site is still in use for Selhurst Depot.

PLAYING RECORD OF CRYSTAL PALACE
LEAGUE PROGRAMME
First Match; 0-0 v. Plymouth Argyle (9,500) (September 1st, 1920)
Last Match; 3-1 v. Barnsley (8,000) (May 3rd, 1924)
Highest Gate; 22,000 v. Brighton & Hove Albion (3-2) (December 27th, 1920)
Lowest Gate; 6,000 v. Grimsby Town (2-0) (February 9th, 1921), v. Manchester United (1-1) (April 19th, 1924) & v. Clapton Orient (2-1) (April 22nd, 1924)
Highest Home Win; 5-1 v. Northampton Town (20,000) (April 23rd, 1921) & v. Stoke (15,000) (November 24th, 1923)
Highest Home Defeat; 1-5 v. West Ham United (10,000) (March 31st, 1923)

No. of Matches Played by Crystal Palace; 83
Some Information Kindly Supplied by; Rev Nigel Sands

The club was a founder member of the Football League Division 3 in 1920. The match v. *Exeter City* on November 27th, 1920 was switched to *The Dell.* following crowd trouble at the fixture v. *Southend United* (2-3) on November 3rd, 1920. The facilities proved inadequate for the crowds that the club attracted in the League and moved to *Selhurst Park* in 1924.

A TOTAL OF **48** TEAMS TOOK PART IN **83** LEAGUE FIXTURES AT THIS VENUE

THE NEST
HOME GROUND OF NORWICH CITY

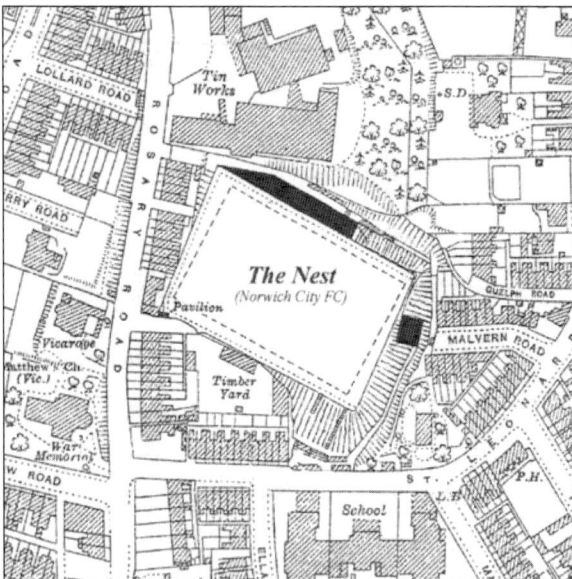

MAP EXTRACT; NORFOLK 63.11 [1928]
SITE LOCATION; TG24100871

Located on the east side of Rosary Road, *The Nest* occupied a cramped and awkwardly shaped site on a former chalk pit known as Rump's Hole. Initial construction involved the removal of lime kilns and filling of large holes but the most bizarre feature was a near-vertical cliff face at the east end of the pitch along which a series of walkways and platforms provided limited viewing.

When *Norwich City* moved here from *Newmarket Road* in 1908, the facilities included two stands removed from the former ground and re-erected along the sides of the pitch, a pavilion in the south west corner and a cover installed over a flat area at the east end. The cramped nature of the site ensured that standing accommodation around the touchline was severely restricted with most spectators dispersed on the cliff faces at the east end.

Although only limited improvements were made in preparation for their debut in the Football League in 1920, large gates were accommodated (sometimes not without mishap), culminating in the attendance at the FA Cup 5th Round tie against *Sheffield Wednesday* on February 16th, 1935 (0-1) when 25,007 spectators were squeezed in. *Norwich City* moved to *Carrow Road* at the end of this season and the site was later utilized for a small industrial estate.

PLAYING RECORD OF NORWICH CITY
LEAGUE PROGRAMME

First Match; 0-0 v. Plymouth Argyle (12,000)
(September 4th, 1920)
Last Match; 2-2 v. Swansea Town (7,415) (May 4th, 1935)
Highest Gate; 22,363 v. Newport County (2-1) (April 2nd, 1934)
Lowest Gate; 2,962 v. Exeter City (2-0) (February 14th, 1924)
Highest Home Win; 10-2 v. Coventry City (8,230)
(March 15th, 1932)
Highest Home Defeat; 1-5 v. Swindon Town (7,591)
(April 26th, 1930)
No. of Matches Played by Norwich City; 315

The club was a founder member of the Football League Division 3 in 1920 and moved to *Carrow Road* in 1935.

A TOTAL OF **49** TEAMS TOOK PART IN **315** LEAGUE FIXTURES AT THIS VENUE

NEWCASTLE ROAD
HOME GROUND OF SUNDERLAND

MAP EXTRACT; DURHAM 8.10 [1897]
SITE LOCATION; NZ39455845

The ground was on the west side of Newcastle Road, north of Crozier Street, and *Sunderland FC* moved here in 1886. A 1,000 seat grandstand was built on the north side of the pitch and terracing eventually installed around the other three sides. There were no other major improvements made before the club moved to *Roker Park* in 1898, the site being subsequently used for Netherburn Road and housing.

PLAYING RECORD OF SUNDERLAND
LEAGUE PROGRAMME

First Match; 2-3 v. Burnley (4,000) (September 13th, 1890)
Last Match; 4-0 v. Nottingham Forest (11,000) (April 23rd, 1898)
Highest Gate; 22,000 v. Aston Villa (0-0) (October 23rd, 1897)
Lowest Gate; 2,500 v. Stoke (4-0) (December 4th, 1897)
Highest Home Win; 8-0 v. Derby County (8,000)
(September 1st, 1894)
Highest Home Defeat; 0-3 v. Wolverhampton Wanderers (7,000)
(October 3rd, 1896)
TEST MATCHES
0-0 v. Notts County (7,000) (April 17th, 1897)
2-0 v. Newton Heath (8,000) (April 26th, 1897)
No. of Matches Played by Sunderland; 116
(League Programme; 114, Test Matches; 2)

The club was elected into the Football League in 1890 and moved to *Roker Park* in 1898

A TOTAL OF **21** TEAMS TOOK PART IN **116** LEAGUE FIXTURES AT THIS VENUE

THE NEW DEN
HOME GROUND OF MILLWALL

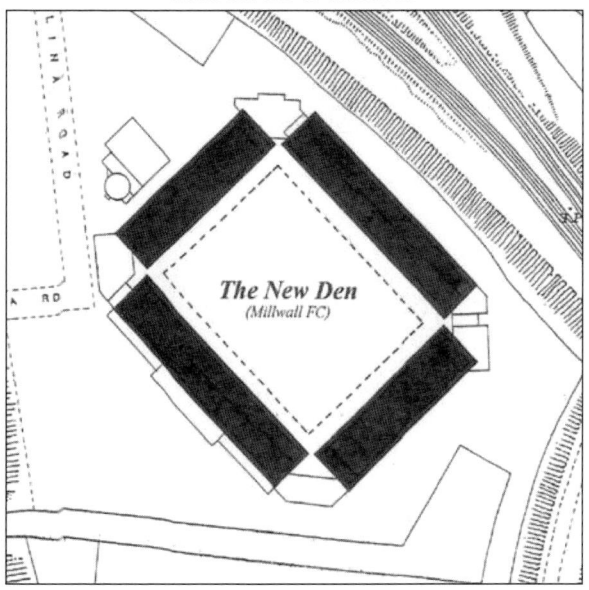

MAP EXTRACT; GROUND AS IN **1996** DRAWN FROM AERIAL PHOTOGRAPHS AND SUPERIMPOSED ON LONDON 9.4 [1914]
SITE LOCATION; **TQ35407818**

Constructed on the site of pre-WWI housing, *Millwall FC* moved to **The New Den** in 1994. It is a typical modern purpose-built stadium consisting of four two-tier all-seater cantilevered roof stands giving a capacity, at the start of the 2004/5 season, of 20,150. The pitch size was 112 x 74 yards.

PLAYING RECORD OF MILLWALL
LEAGUE PROGRAMME

First Match; 1-4 v. Southend United (10,273) (August 22nd, 1993)
Highest Gate; 18,510 v. Oldham Athletic (5-0) (May 5th, 2001)
Lowest Gate; 4,647 v. Walsall (0-1) (December 3rd, 1997)
Highest Home Win; 6-1 v. Colchester United (11,156) (December 26th, 2000)
Highest Home Defeat; 0-6 v. Rotherham United (7,177) (August 10th, 2002)

PLAY OFF MATCHES
1-3 v. Derby County (16,470) (May 18th, 1994)
0-0 v. Wigan Athletic (14,091) (May 13th, 2000)
0-1 v. Birmingham City (16,391) (May 2nd, 2002)

No. of Matches Played by Millwall; 279
(League Programme; 276, Play Off Matches; 3)

The club moved here from **The Den** in 1993.

AT THE END OF SEASON 2004/5, A TOTAL OF **70** TEAMS HAD TAKEN PART IN **279** LEAGUE FIXTURES AT THIS VENUE

NEW STADIUM
HOME GROUND OF DARLINGTON

PREVIOUSLY KNOWN AS **THE REYNOLDS ARENA** & CURRENTLY KNOWN AS **WILLIAMSON MOTORS STADIUM**

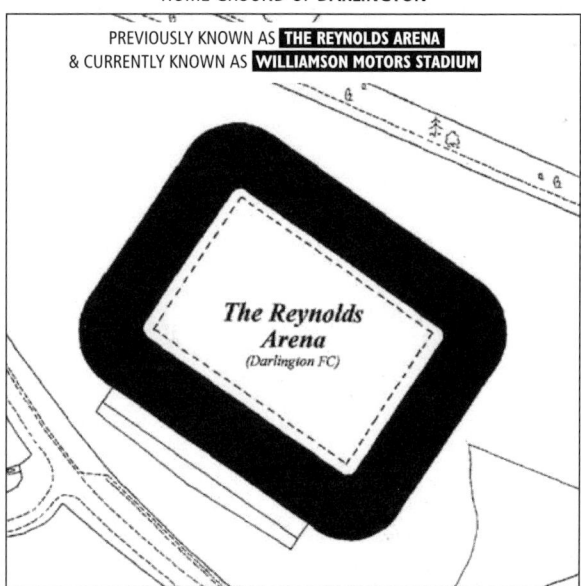

MAP EXTRACT; GROUND AS IN **2002** DRAWN FROM AERIAL PHOTOGRAPHS AND SUPERIMPOSED ON DURHAM 55.14 [1947]
SITE LOCATION; **NZ30151267**

Constructed on a greenfield site the 25,000 seat capacity stadium is composed of a continuous single tier of seats with a continuous cantilevered roof. When opened in 2003 it was known as *The Reynolds Arena*, named after the club chairman who was instrumental in having it built, but in 2004 the club went into administration and the ground reverted to the *New Stadium*. Later in the same year it was re-named as the *Williamson Motors Stadium* and probably holds a unique record in having been identified by three different names within less than one year. The pitch size was 110 x 74 yards.

PLAYING RECORD OF DARLINGTON
LEAGUE PROGRAMME

First Match; 0-2 v. Kidderminster Harriers (11,600) (August 16th, 2003)
Highest Gate; 11,600 v. Kidderminster Harriers (0-2) (August 16th, 2003)
Lowest Gate; 2,709 v. Swansea City (2-1) (February 22nd, 2005)
Highest Home Win; 4-0 v. Southend United (3,901) (October 2nd, 2004)
Highest Home Defeat; 0-4 v. Bristol Rovers (4,268) (October 11th, 2003)

No. of Matches Played by Darlington; 46

The club moved here from *Feethams* at the end of the 2002/3 season and the first League goal at the stadium was scored by Danny Williams of *Kidderminster Harriers FC* in the 50th minute of the first match.

AT THE END OF SEASON 2004/5, A TOTAL OF **30** TEAMS HAD TAKEN PART IN **46** LEAGUE FIXTURES AT THIS VENUE

NINIAN PARK
HOME GROUND OF CARDIFF CITY

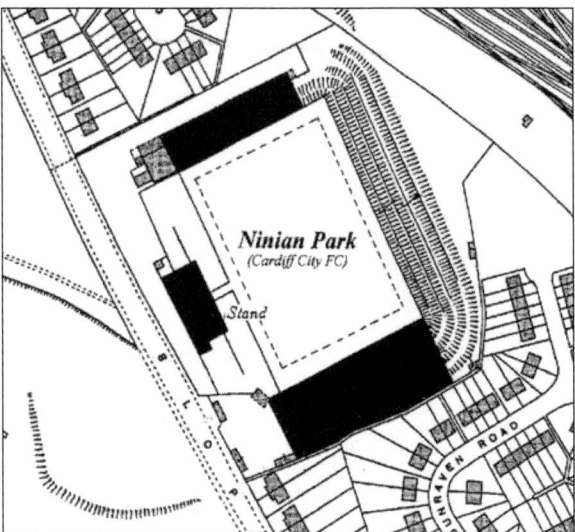

MAP EXTRACT; GLAMORGAN 43.14 [1940]
SITE LOCATION; **ST16767576**

The site had been in use as a rubbish tip when *Cardiff City FC* turned professional and moved here in 1910. The facilities, which included a canvas roofed 200 seat stand on the west side and embankments around the remainder of the ground, remained fairly basic until the 1920s when covers were installed at each end. The final alteration prior to WWII took place in 1937 when the main stand, on the west side, was replaced following a fire on January 18th.

Post war improvements, including the extension of the paddock in front of the main stand and the enlargement and covering of the east side, were carried out prior to the record attendance of 61,566 being set at the International match between *Wales* and *England* on October 14th, 1961. During the 1970s the main stand was extended to seat 6,000 and the roof removed from the south end for safety reasons whilst the 1990s saw the addition of seating on the east side, in the main stand paddock and at the north end. In 2001 a cover was supplied over the south end and seats installed on the west side to give a capacity at the start of the 2004/5 season of 22,000 with 12,647 seats. The pitch size was 110 x 70 yards.

PLAYING RECORD OF CARDIFF CITY
LEAGUE PROGRAMME

First Match; 0-0 v. Clapton Orient (25,000) (August 30th, 1920)
Highest Gate; 57,893 v. Arsenal (0-0) (April 22nd, 1953)
Lowest Gate; 1,510 v. Hartlepool United (4-0) (May 7th, 1987)
Highest Home Win; 9-2 v. Thames (6,000) (February 6th, 1932)
Highest Home Defeat; 1-9 v. Wolverhampton Wanderers (45,000)
(September 3rd, 1955)

PLAY OFF MATCHES

0-1 v. Northampton Town (11,369) (May 11th, 1997)
0-2 v. Stoke City [aet] (19,367) (May 1st, 2002)
1-0 v. Bristol City (19,146) (May 10th, 2003)

No. of Matches Played by Cardiff City; 1,660
(League Programme; 1,657 [Including one expunged match v. Aldershot on March 20th, 1992], Play Off Matches; 3)

The club was elected into the Football League Division 2 in 1920 and was involved in a Football League Play Off Match at the neutral venue of the **Millennium Stadium.**

AT THE END OF SEASON 2004/5, A TOTAL OF **102** TEAMS HAD TAKEN PART IN **1,660** LEAGUE FIXTURES AT THIS VENUE

NORTHOLME
HOME GROUND OF GAINSBOROUGH TRINITY

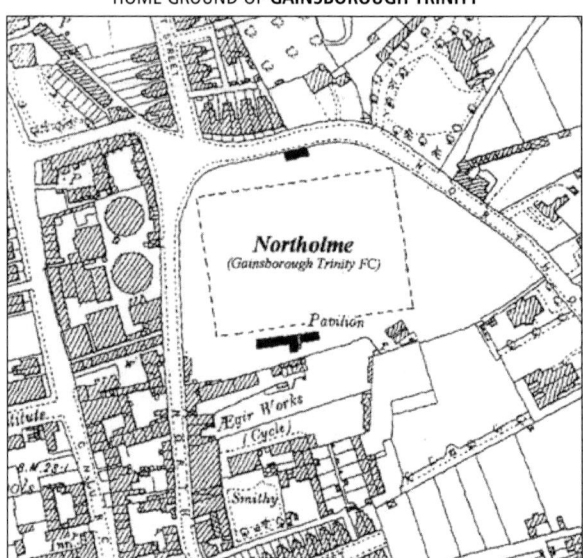

MAP EXTRACT; LINCOLNSHIRE 42.8 [1899]
SITE LOCATION; **SK81589033**

Northolme, as a cricketing venue, dates back to the 1850s and was first used by *Gainsborough Trinity FC* in 1884. Located to the north of the town centre, the only covered accommodation at this time was a small shelter in the south west corner of the ground. For many years the players changed in the nearby Sun Inn where an extension was built for the exclusive use of the football club.

Later improvements included the building of a 200 seat grandstand (replaced in 1910) on the south side, a new enclosure fence and a covered standing enclosure on the north side. No further changes were made to the facilities during their existence as a Football League club but, following the destruction by fire of the stand and the covering over the enclosure in the 1940s a new grandstand was built on the north side and other improvements made. The venue is still in use as the home ground for *Gainsborough Trinity FC*.

PLAYING RECORD OF GAINSBOROUGH TRINITY
LEAGUE PROGRAMME

First Match; 1-1 v. Manchester City (2,500)
(September 12th, 1896)
Last Match; 0-0 v. Stockport County (2,000) (April 27th, 1912)
Highest Gate; 5,600 v. Chelsea (3-1) (April 29th, 1911)
Lowest Gate; 500 v. Blackpool (3-0) (April 19th, 1902)
Highest Home Win; 7-0 v. Lincoln City (-) (March 27th, 1897) & v.
Blackpool (-) (December 17th, 1898)
Highest Home Defeat; 1-5 v. Bradford City (4,000)
(February 15th, 1908)

No. of Matches Played by Gainsborough Trinity; 279
(NB. This assumes that only three matches were played elsewhere when the venue was required for cricket)

Some Information Kindly Supplied by; Brian Tabner & Gary Parle

The club was elected into the Football League Division 2 in 1896 and failed to gain re-election in 1912. At least one game was played at the **Bowling Green Ground** and two played at **Sincil Bank** when *Northolme* was required for cricket. The match v. *Stockport County* on January 10th, 1903 was stopped after 86 minutes (at 1-1), due to bad light. The Football League ordered a replay, and this took place on February 7th, 1903 (Result: 0-0)

A TOTAL OF **45** TEAMS TOOK PART IN **279** LEAGUE FIXTURES AT THIS VENUE

NORTH ROAD
HOME GROUND OF GLOSSOP

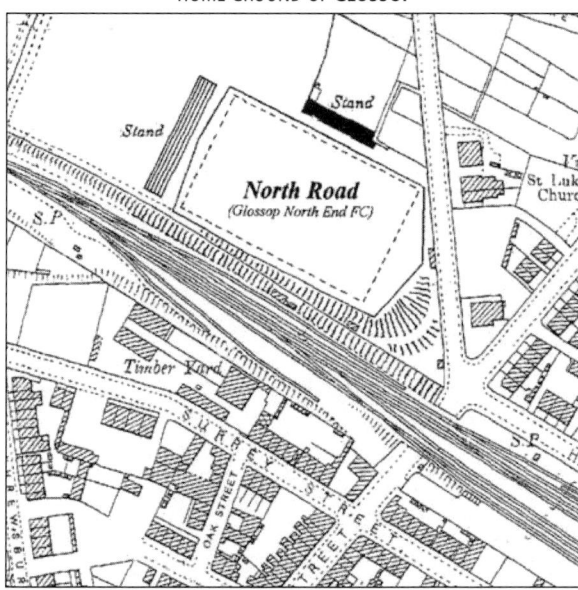

MAP EXTRACT; DERBYSHIRE 2.12 [1898]
SITE LOCATION; **SK03209450**

Glossop North End FC moved here from *The New Pyegrove* in time to coincide with their debut season in the Football League in 1898. The *North Road* venue was already an established cricket ground and the football pitch was tucked into the south east corner. A seated stand and dressing rooms were built on the north side of the pitch and embankments constructed along the south side and at the east end. A temporary wooden seated stand, removed during the cricket season, was installed at the west end.

The record attendance of 10,736 was set at the FA Cup 2nd Round tie v. *Preston North End* (0-1) on January 31st, 1914. Following the demise of *Glossop FC*, the football pitch continued in use and the venue is still in use as a sports ground.

PLAYING RECORD OF GLOSSOP
LEAGUE PROGRAMME

First Match; 4-1 v. Blackpool (4,000) (September 3rd, 1898)
Last Match; 1-1 v. Stockport County (500) (April 17th, 1915)
Highest Estimated Gate; 7,000 v. Sunderland (0-2) (October 7th, 1899)
Lowest Estimated Gate; 450 v. Derby County (1-1) (September 5th, 1914)
Highest Home Win; 7-0 v. Barnsley (-) (February 13th, 1904)
Highest Home Defeat; 0-5 v. Manchester United (3,000) (September 19th, 1903)

No. of Matches Played by Glossop; 309
Some Information Kindly Supplied by; Brian Tabner

The club was elected into the Football League Division 2 in 1898 as *Glossop North End* and re-named as *Glossop* in 1899 when they were promoted and became the smallest town ever with a club in Division 1. Financial difficulties caused *Glossop FC* to resign from the Football League after WWI.

A TOTAL OF **51** TEAMS TOOK PART IN **309** LEAGUE FIXTURES AT THIS VENUE

NORTH ROAD
HOME GROUND OF MANCHESTER UNITED

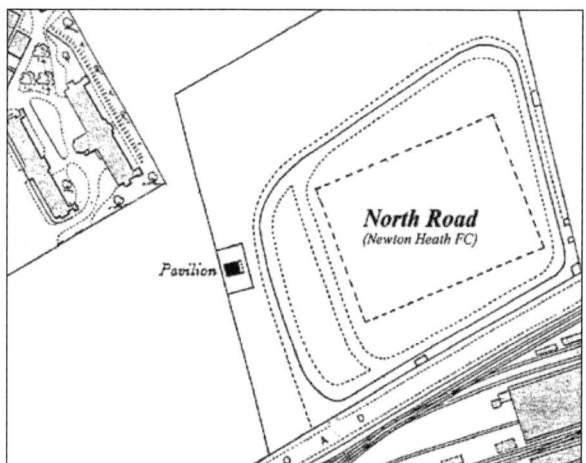

MAP EXTRACT; GROUND AS IN **1893** DRAWN FROM PLANS AND SUPERIMPOSED ON LANCASHIRE 104.3 [1908]
SITE LOCATION; **SD86800077**

Newton Heath L&YR FC was formed by workers at the Carriage & Wagon Works in 1878 and they used an unenclosed area of waste land, on the opposite side of North Road to their place of employment, for the football pitch. Some improvements had been made by the time that they joined the Football League, as *Newton Heath FC*, in 1892. The ground had been enclosed, a 1,000 seat stand installed and a pavilion constructed at the west end of the site but there were no facilities for standing spectators. The actual orientation of the pitch, shown in the map above, has been assumed but is the probable location, given the disposition of the footpaths. The club moved to *Bank Street* [then known as *Bank Lane*] in 1893 and the venue continued in use as a sports ground. In 2003 the site was taken over for use as a business park.

PLAYING RECORD OF MANCHESTER UNITED
[AS NEWTON HEATH]
LEAGUE PROGRAMME

Matches Played; 1-1 v. Burnley (10,000) (September 10th, 1892)
2-4 v. West Bromwich Albion (9,000) (October 8th, 1892)
10-1 v. Wolverhampton Wanderers (4,000) (October 15th, 1892)
3-4 v. Everton (4,000) (October 19th, 1892)
4-4 v. Blackburn Rovers (12,000) (November 5th, 1892)
1-3 v. Notts County (8,000) (November 12th, 1892)
2-0 v. Aston Villa (7,000) (November 19th, 1892)
1-0 v. Bolton Wanderers (4,000) (December 10th, 1892)
1-5 v. The Wednesday (4,000) (December 24th, 1892)
7-1 v. Derby County (3,000) (December 31st, 1892)
1-3 v. Nottingham Forest (8,000) (January 14th, 1893)
0-5 v. Sunderland (15,000) (March 4th, 1893)
1-0 v. Stoke (10,000) (March 31st, 1893)
2-1 v. Preston North End (9,000) (April 1st, 1893)
3-3 v. Accrington (3,000) (April 8th, 1893)

No. of Matches Played by Manchester United; 15
Information Kindly Supplied by; Tony Matthews

The club was elected into the Football League Division 1 in 1892 as *Newton Heath* and was also involved in Test Matches at the neutral venues of the *Olive Grove* and the *Victoria Ground*. *Newton Heath FC* moved to *Bank Street* in 1893.

A TOTAL OF **16** TEAMS TOOK PART IN **15** LEAGUE FIXTURES AT THIS VENUE

OAKWELL
HOME GROUND OF BARNSLEY

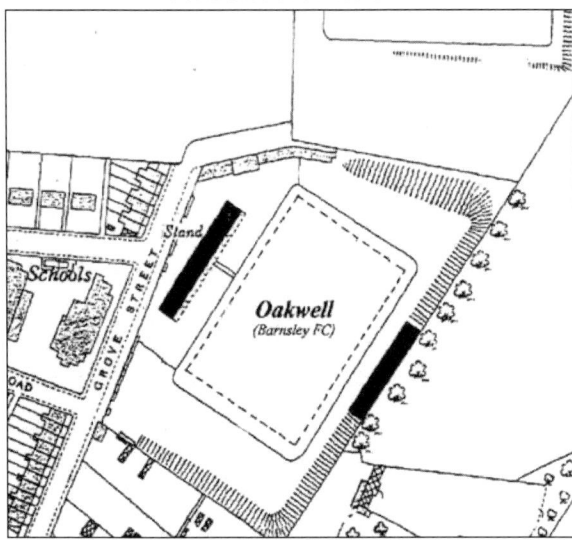

MAP EXTRACT; YORKSHIRE 274.8 [1931]
SITE LOCATION; SE35370642

Barnsley St Peter's FC moved from an adjacent field to *Oakwell* in 1888 but it was not until 1895 that the facilities included a stand. This stand quickly succumbed to a gale and, following their election to the Football League in 1898 (as *Barnsley FC*) and considerable ground re-levelling, the central section of the 1,200 seat main stand (later extended) was constructed in 1904. The only other alteration prior to the setting of the record attendance of 40,255 on February 15th, 1936 at the FA Cup 5th Round tie v. *Stoke City* (2-0) was the installation of a cover on the east side.

Post WWII improvements included the installation of a cover at the south end and extension of the terraces on the east side before the ground was extensively redeveloped during the 1990s. In 1993 additional land was purchased on the east side of the ground to facilitate the construction of a new 7,200 seat two-tier stand, whilst at the same time, and as a temporary measure, seating was installed at the north end. Later a new 4,508 seat stand was opened at the south end and seats provided in the main stand paddock before, in 2000, a 6,000 seat stand was completed at the north end. At the start of the 2004/5 season the all seat capacity was 23,186 and the pitch size was 110 x 75 yards.

PLAYING RECORD OF BARNSLEY
LEAGUE PROGRAMME
First Match; 2-1 v. Luton Town (-) (September 10th, 1898)
Highest Gate; 35,308 v. Sheffield Wednesday (4-0)
(October 9th, 1948)
Lowest Gate; 500 v. Woolwich Arsenal (3-2) (April 23rd, 1900)
Highest Home Win; 9-0 v. Loughborough (2,000) (January 28th, 1899)
Highest Home Defeat; 2-7 v. Middlesbrough (2,000)
(February 22nd, 1902)
PLAY OFF MATCHES
1-2 v. Birmingham City (19,050) (May 18th, 2000)
No. of Matches Played by Barnsley; 2,049
(League Programme; 2,048, Play Off Matches; 1)
Information Kindly Supplied by; Arthur Bower

The club was elected into the Football League Division 2 in 1898. The club was also involved in a Football League Play Off Match at the neutral venue of **Wembley Stadium.**

AT THE END OF SEASON 2004/5, A TOTAL OF **112** TEAMS HAD TAKEN PART IN **2,049** LEAGUE FIXTURES AT THIS VENUE

ODSAL STADIUM
TEMPORARY HOME GROUND FOR BRADFORD CITY

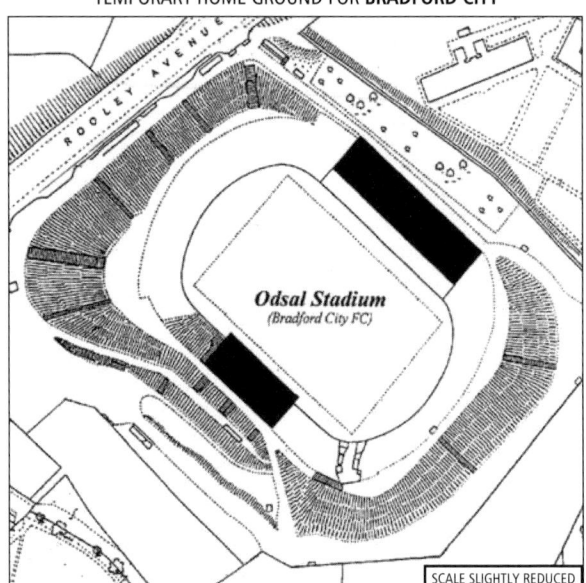

SCALE SLIGHTLY REDUCED

MAP EXTRACT; GROUND AS IN **1957** DRAWN FROM PLANS AND SUPERIMPOSED ON YORKSHIRE 216.16 [1934]
SITE LOCATION; SE16112985

Construction of the ground commenced in the 1920s with the embankments composed of dumped refuse forming an oval bowl with a limited amount of cover on both sides but a nominal capacity of 150,000. When the *Odsal Stadium* opened in 1934, *Bradford Northern RLFC* moved in and as well as rugby the venue was used for speedway, stock-car racing, pony trotting and show jumping.

The stadium saw very little development before the record attendance of 102,569 was set at the Rugby League Challenge Cup Final Replay between *Halifax* and *Warrington* in May 1954. In 2002 it was refurbished as the home ground for *Bradford Bulls RLFC*.

PLAYING RECORD OF BRADFORD CITY
LEAGUE PROGRAMME
First Match; 1-0 v. Crystal Palace (5,604) (November 2nd, 1985)
Last Match; 1-3 v. West Bromwich Albion (4,580)
(December 12th, 1986)
Highest Gate; 13,831 v. Leeds United (2-0) (September 20th, 1986)
Lowest Gate; 3,826 v. Millwall (0-2) (April 30th, 1986)
Highest Home Win; 3-0 v. Huddersfield Town (9,058) (March 22nd, 1986) & v. Reading (5,783) (November 1st, 1986)
Highest Home Defeat; 1-4 v. Stoke City (6,191)
(November 29th, 1986)

No. of Matches Played by Bradford City; 21
Information Kindly Supplied by; Peter Waller

These matches were played here whilst **Valley Parade** was being rebuilt following the fire of May 11th, 1985

A TOTAL OF **18** TEAMS TOOK PART IN **21** LEAGUE FIXTURES AT THIS VENUE

OLD SHOW GROUND

HOME GROUND OF **SCUNTHORPE UNITED**

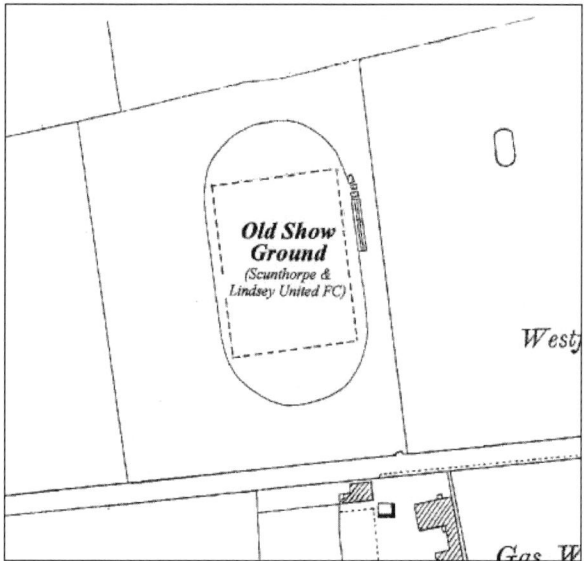

MAP EXTRACT; LINCOLNSHIRE [1907]
SITE LOCATION; **SE88791140**

Utilized as a venue for popular events in the town, when it was first used for football by *Brumby Hall FC* in 1899 the pitch was surrounded by an oval track and the only facility was an open seated stand on the east side. The club merged with others in 1899 and *Lindsey United FC* in 1910 (to form *Scunthorpe & Lindsey United FC*) whilst a new main stand was constructed on the west side in 1914.

MAP EXTRACT; GROUND AS IN **1964** DRAWN FROM PLANS AND SUPERIMPOSED ON SE8811 [1950]

In 1924 the ground was purchased for £2,700 and, following the destruction of the main stand by a fire, a new structure was completed in 1925. A cover was installed at the north end in 1938 and it was probably in this pre-WWII period that a cover was also erected on the east side.

The club was elected to the Football League in 1950 and the record attendance of 23,935 was set at the FA Cup 4th Round tie v. *Portsmouth* (1-1) on January 30th, 1954. Following this milestone the *Old Show Ground* saw considerable improvements with the installation of a cover at the south end, a 2,200 seat cantilever roofed stand on the east side in 1958 (the first of such design built in Britain and replacing a cover which had burned down) and the replacement of the roof at the north end in 1959.

Scunthorpe United FC moved to **Glanford Park** in 1988 and the site was utilized for a supermarket.

PLAYING RECORD OF SCUNTHORPE UNITED
LEAGUE PROGRAMME

First Match; 0-0 v. Shrewsbury Town (11,847) (August 19th, 1950)
Last Match; 1-1 v. Torquay United (6,483) (May 18th, 1988)
Highest Gate; 19,067 v. Grimsby Town (0-1) (April 2nd, 1956)
Lowest Gate; 1,106 v. Bury (2-2) (May 4th, 1982)
Highest Home Win; 8-1 v. Luton Town (2,755) (April 24th, 1965)
Highest Home Defeat; 2-7 v. Wigan Athletic (2,511) (March 12th, 1982)

PLAY OFF MATCHES

1-1 v. Torquay United (6,483) (May 18th, 1988)

No. of Matches Played by Scunthorpe United; 862
(League Programme; 861 [The scheduled home game v. Exeter City on April 2nd, 1974 was not played], Play Off Matches; 1)

Information Kindly Supplied by; John Staff

The club was elected into the Football League Division 3 [N] in 1950 as *Scunthorpe & Lindsey United* and re-named as *Scunthorpe United* in 1958. The club was also involved in a Football League Play Off Match at the neutral venue of **Wembley Stadium** and moved to **Glanford Park** in 1988.

A TOTAL OF **89** TEAMS TOOK PART IN **862** LEAGUE FIXTURES AT THIS VENUE

The pioneering cantilever 2,200 seat stand on the east side of the ground. Built in 1958 and devoid of roof supporting props this was very much the precursor of such a design of structure which can now be found in stadia throughout the country.

Photograph Courtesy of Dave Twydell

OLD TRAFFORD

HOME GROUND OF **MANCHESTER UNITED**
TEMPORARY HOME GROUND FOR **STOCKPORT COUNTY**

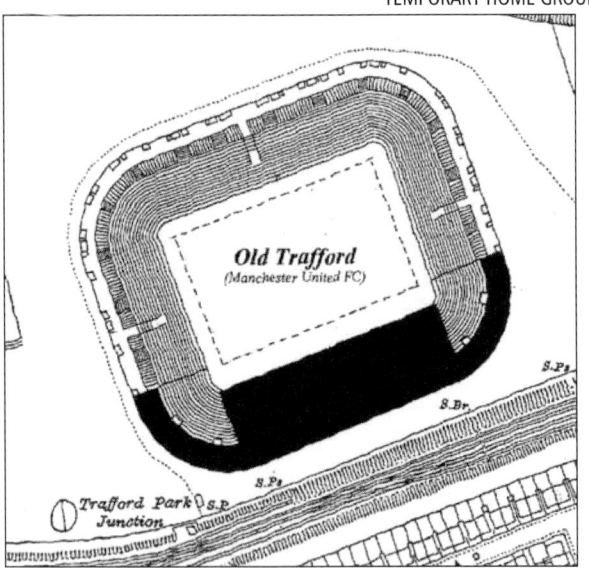

MAP EXTRACT; LANCASHIRE 104.13 [**1922**]
SITE LOCATION; SJ80759630

PLAYING RECORD OF MANCHESTER UNITED
LEAGUE PROGRAMME

First Match; 3-4 v. Liverpool (45,000) (February 19th, 1910)
Highest Gate; 70,504 v. Aston Villa (1-3) (December 27th, 1920)
Lowest Gate; 3,507 v. Southampton (2-3) (September 2nd, 1931)
Highest Home Win; 9-0 v. Ipswich Town (43,804) (March 4th, 1995)
Highest Home Defeat; 1-7 v. Newcastle United (50,217) (September 10th, 1927)

No. of Matches Played by Manchester United; 1,671

The club moved here from **Bank Street** in 1910. Following bomb damage sustained in WWII they played home matches at **Maine Road** between 1946 & 1949. The match v. *Arsenal* on August 20th, 1971 was played at **Anfield** and the fixture v. *West Bromwich Albion* on August 23rd, 1971 at the **Victoria Ground** following crowd trouble at *Old Trafford*.

* The gate of 67,989 v. *Portsmouth* (2-1) on February 26th, 2005 was the record attendance for a Premier League fixture up to the end of the 2004/5 season.

AT THE END OF SEASON 2004/5, A TOTAL OF **69** TEAMS HAD TAKEN PART IN **1,672** LEAGUE FIXTURES AT THIS VENUE

Manchester United FC moved here from **Bank Street** in 1910. The ground was well developed with terracing on all sides and around the curved corners, whilst a stand was sited on the south side giving a nominal capacity of 80,000. Although the only other improvements prior to WWII were extensions to the cover on the south side and installation of a roof over part of the north side, the record attendance of 76,962 was set at the *Wolverhampton Wanderers* v. *Grimsby Town* (5-0) FA Cup Semi-Final on March 25th, 1939.

Badly damaged during the war, the club was not able to use the partially reconstructed ground until 1949 (the main stand was still unroofed at this stage) following which the installation of the missing roof and continuation of cover around the west side were the main alterations up to 1960. Although, during the next thirty four years, *Old Trafford* was gradually converted to a 44,594 capacity all-seater stadium with a continuous cantilever roof it proved to be too small and a new rebuilding programme was undertaken.

The first replacement stand, a three-tier 25,500 seat structure, was built in 1996 following purchase of additional land on the north side and second tiers were added at the east end in 2000 and west end in 2001 to give a seating accommodation of 68,174*. In 2005 stands were installed in the north west and north east corners to increase the capacity to 75,600 and, as such, became the first League ground to have an all-seat capacity that exceeded that established when it had a mix of standing and seating accommodation. The pitch size was 116 x 76 yards.

PLAYING RECORD OF STOCKPORT COUNTY
LEAGUE PROGRAMME

Match Played; 0-0 v. Leicester City (13) (May 7th, 1921)
No. of Matches Played by Stockport County; 1

This match was played here after **Edgeley Park** was closed following crowd trouble and took place shortly after the *Manchester United* v. *Derby County* afternoon fixture had finished. As *Stockport County* had already been relegated the fans boycotted this game in protest and although this situation led to the record for the lowest ever Football League attendance being established when only 13 paid at the gate, it was also witnessed by a couple of thousand spectators who had stayed on following the previous match.

The programme cover in Season 1967/8 featured a view of the then-new cantilever stand on the north side, the first completed phase of the 1960s redevelopment of the ground. This match, v. *Burnley* finished in a 2-2 draw.

OLD RECREATION GROUND
HOME GROUND OF **PORT VALE**

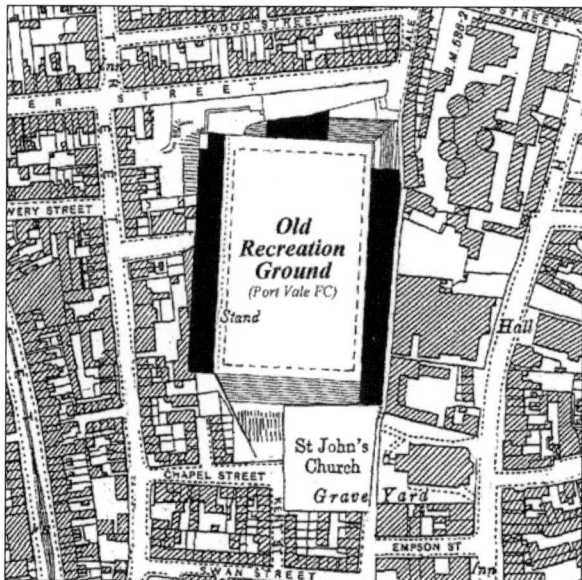

MAP EXTRACT; GROUND AS IN **1952** DRAWN FROM PLANS AND SUPERIMPOSED ON STAFFORDSHIRE 12.13 [c1900]
SITE LOCATION; SJ88284796

Port Vale FC moved to the *Old Recreation Ground*, north of Hanley town centre, from **Cobridge Athletic Ground** in 1913. Initially the facilities at this slightly irregularly shaped ground were fairly basic with players having to change at nearby stables but a grandstand was eventually erected along the west side of the pitch. Further improvements included the construction of concrete terracing around the ground and installation of covering on the east side and at the north end.

The club bought the ground from the local Corporation in 1927 and sold it back to them in 1943 before moving to *Vale Park* in 1950. The site is now in use for a multi-storey car park.

PLAYING RECORD OF PORT VALE
LEAGUE PROGRAMME

First Match; 0-1 v. Tottenham Hotspur (16,000) (October 27th, 1919)
Last Match; 0-1 v. Aldershot (9,645) (April 22nd, 1950)
Highest Gate; 22,697 v. Stoke (0-3) (March 6th, 1920)
Lowest Gate; 2,669 v. Hull City (4-0) (March 2nd, 1936)
Highest Home Win; 9-1 v. Chesterfield (9,950) (September 24th, 1932)
Highest Home Defeat; 1-7 v. Wolverhampton Wanderers (11,133) (December 12th, 1931)

No. of Matches Played by Port Vale; 501
Information Kindly Supplied by; Tony Matthews

After the club moved here it was elected into the Football League Division 2 in 1919 as *Port Vale* to take over *Leeds City FC's* fixtures. The club moved to *Vale Park* in 1950.

A TOTAL OF **84** TEAMS TOOK PART IN **501** LEAGUE FIXTURES AT THIS VENUE

OLIVE GROVE
HOME GROUND OF **SHEFFIELD WEDNESDAY**

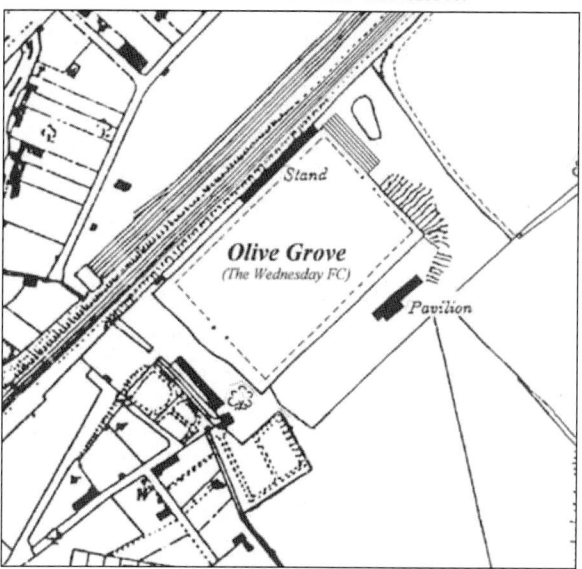

MAP EXTRACT; YORKSHIRE 294.12 [1894]
SITE LOCATION; SK35698565

The *Olive Grove*, south of the city centre and adjacent to the south east side of the Midland Railway main line, was little more than a 3.5 acre swamp when *The Wednesday FC* moved here from *Endcliffe* in 1887. By the time that they played their first match, against *Blackburn Rovers* on September 12th, 1887, the land had been drained, a stream diverted, a full length open 1,000 seat stand installed on the narrow north west side and flat cinder surfaces for standing spectators provided around the other three sides. At this time players changed in a local pub but later improvements included the provision of a pavilion, installation of covering over part of the main stand, an uncovered seating stand behind the north goal and a covered enclosure at the south west end.

The record attendance of 28,000 was set at the FA Cup 3rd Round match v. *Everton* (2-0) on March 2nd, 1895 and four years later the club moved to *Owlerton (Later Hillsborough)*. The site is now in use as a corporation yard.

PLAYING RECORD OF SHEFFIELD WEDNESDAY
[AS THE WEDNESDAY]
LEAGUE PROGRAMME

First Match; 5-2 v. Accrington (15,000) (September 10th, 1892)
Last Match; 1-3 v. Newcastle United (4,000) (April 15th, 1899)
Highest Gate; 20,000 v. Sunderland (3-2) (October 29th, 1892)
Lowest Gate; 1,000 v. Notts County (3-2) (April 3rd, 1893)
Highest Home Win; 6-0 v. West Bromwich Albion (15,000) (January 2nd, 1893) & v. Blackburn Rovers (10,000) (December 28th, 1896)
Highest Home Defeat; 0-5 v. Preston North End (5,000) (January 14th, 1893)

No. of Matches Played by Sheffield Wednesday; 107
Some Information Kindly Supplied by; Brian Tabner

The club was elected into the Football League Division 1 as *The Wednesday* in 1892.

NEUTRAL TEST MATCHES
Newton Heath 5, Small Heath 2 (Replay) (6,000) (April 27th, 1893)
Preston North End 4, Notts County 0 (8,000) (April 28th, 1894)
No. of Matches Played; 2

A TOTAL OF **22** TEAMS TOOK PART IN **109** LEAGUE FIXTURES AT THIS VENUE

THE OVAL
TEMPORARY HOME GROUND FOR WALSALL

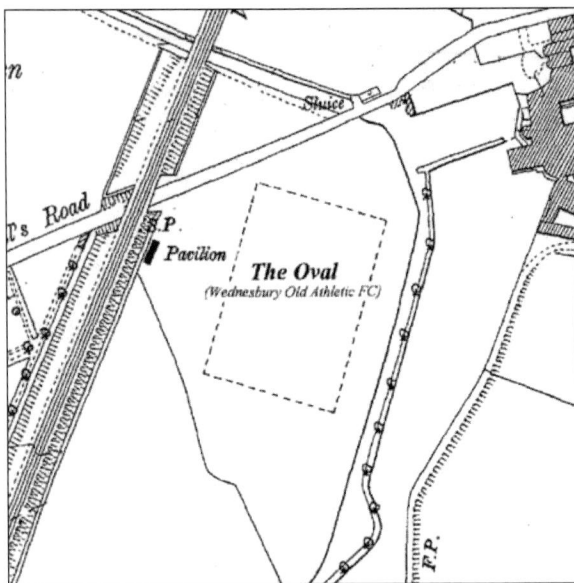

MAP EXTRACT; STAFFORDSHIRE 63.14 [1903]
SITE LOCATION; **SP00059608**

Located to the south of the town, *The Oval* was the home ground of *Wednesbury Old Athletic FC*. It is known that the facilities included a pavilion on the west side but the pitch orientation is assumed on the map. The site was not redeveloped and is now open land.

PLAYING RECORD OF WALSALL
[AS WALSALL TOWN SWIFTS]
LEAGUE PROGRAMME

Matches Played; 1-3 v. Small Heath (5,000)
(September 2nd, 1893)
0-5 v. Burslem Port Vale (3,000) (September 9th, 1893)

No. of Matches Played by Walsall; 2

Information Kindly Supplied by; Tony Matthews

The club played two matches here until **West Bromwich Road** was ready.

A TOTAL OF **3** TEAMS TOOK PART IN **2** LEAGUE FIXTURES AT THIS VENUE

The northern perimeter wall along St Paul's Road was all that remained of **The Oval** when photographed in 1990. Still visible then were bricked up holes in the wall which probably housed windows from which tickets were issued. *Photograph Courtesy of Dave Twydell*

PARADISE GROUND
HOME GROUND OF MIDDLESBROUGH IRONOPOLIS

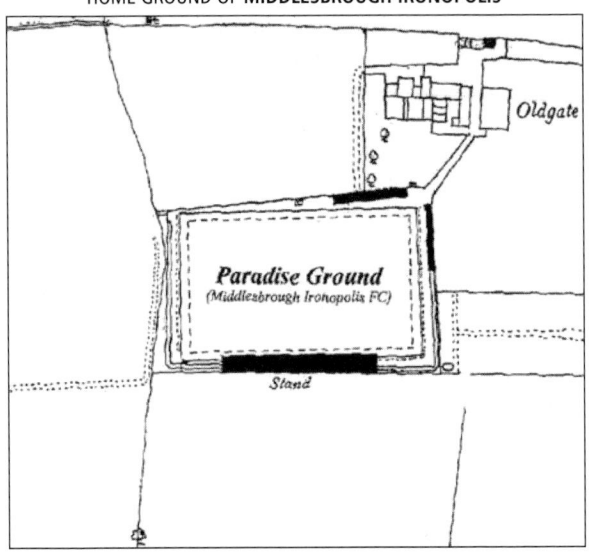

MAP EXTRACT; YORKSHIRE 6.14 & 16.2 [1894]
SITE LOCATION; **NZ48881902**

Located to the south west of the town centre, *The Paradise Ground* occupied a field on the east side of the Middlesbrough Union Workhouse, at the rear of Oldgate Farm. When it was first used in 1889 no covered accommodation was provided but improvements were gradually made until small covered stands had been built on three sides of the ground and some uncovered seating installed. Changing facilities were provided at the County Hotel, some distance away, which necessitated the provision of transport for players and officials.

The record attendance of 14,000 was established on February 18th, 1893 when *Preston North End FC* visited for an FA Cup 3rd Round match (2-2). *Middlesbrough Ironopolis FC* folded in 1894 and the north west corner of *The Paradise Ground* was used for part of the site of *Middlesbrough FC's* **Ayresome Park** which opened in 1903. The remainder of the site was later occupied by houses on the north side of Clive Road.

PLAYING RECORD OF MIDDLESBROUGH IRONOPOLIS
LEAGUE PROGRAMME

Matches Played; 0-2 v. Liverpool (2,000)
(September 2nd, 1893)
2-0 v. Ardwick (800) (September 23rd, 1893)
2-1 v. Burton Swifts (400) (October 28th, 1893)
2-6 v. Grimsby Town (3,000) (November 11th, 1893)
3-0 v. Small Heath (200) (November 25th, 1893)
6-1 v. Rotherham Town (600) (December 9th, 1893)
0-0 v. Notts County (500) (December 16th, 1893)
1-1 v. Newcastle United (2,000) (December 25th, 1893)
1-1 v. Walsall Town Swifts (1,500) (December 30th, 1893)
3-1 v. Burslem Port Vale (2,000) (January 1st, 1894)
2-0 v. Crewe Alexandra (400) (January 6th, 1894)
0-0 v. Lincoln City (500) (January 13th, 1894)
3-6 v. Woolwich Arsenal (500) (February 24th, 1894)
2-1 v. Northwich Victoria (2,000) (March 3rd, 1894)

No. of Matches Played by Middlesbrough Ironopolis; 14

Information Kindly Supplied by; Tony Matthews

The club was elected into the Football League Division 2 in 1893 and resigned in 1894.

A TOTAL OF **15** TEAMS TOOK PART IN **14** LEAGUE FIXTURES AT THIS VENUE

PARK AVENUE
HOME GROUND OF BRADFORD PARK AVENUE

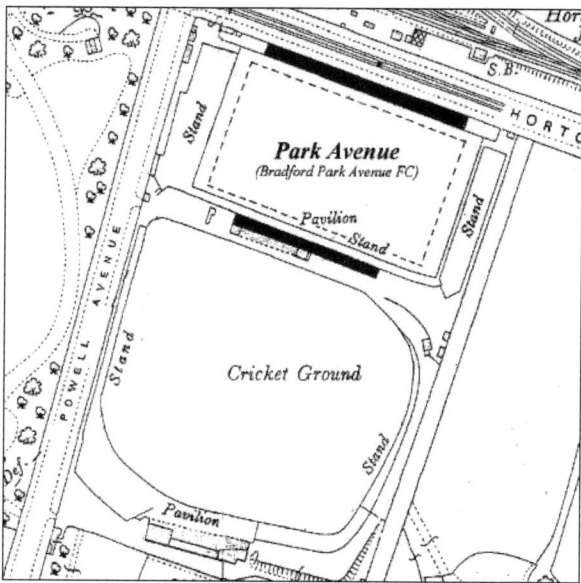

MAP EXTRACT; YORKSHIRE 216.7 & 216.8 [1908]
SITE LOCATION; SE15303194

The *Park Avenue* ground had been used for both rugby and cricket before the formation of *Bradford Park Avenue AFC* in 1907. The facilities, which originally included a covered seated stand on the south side (backing on to the cricket ground at a higher level) and standing areas around the ground, were improved with the construction of a new main stand (incorporating a covered seated area overlooking the cricket pitch) and a pavilion on the south side and the installation of a cover on the north side.

Later improvements included the provision of some concrete terracing and the installation of a cover at the west end. The record attendance of 34,810 was, unusually, set at a Wartime Cup match v. *Blackpool* on April 18th, 1944. The club failed to gain re-election to the Football League in 1970 and moved out to *Valley Parade* for their final season of existence in 1973. The club subsequently re-formed and the partially demolished site of *Park Avenue* remained derelict until it was utilized as the site of a Fitness First Gym in 2003.

PLAYING RECORD OF BRADFORD PARK AVENUE
LEAGUE PROGRAMME

First Match; 1-0 v. Hull City (12,000) (September 1st, 1908)
Last Match; 0-5 v. Scunthorpe United (2,563) (April 4th, 1970)
Highest Gate; 34,429 v. Leeds United (3-0) (December 25th, 1931)
Lowest Gate; 1,572 v. Port Vale (0-1) (May 5th, 1969)
Highest Home Win; 8-0 v. Walsall (7,680) (September 14th, 1925)
Highest Home Defeat; 1-6 v. Oldham Athletic (9,000) (March 8th, 1910)

No. of Matches Played by Bradford Park Avenue; 1,096
Information Kindly Supplied by; Tony Matthews

The club was elected into the Football League Division 2 in 1908, but having gained re-election at the end of three successive seasons from 1967 failed on the fourth occasion and dropped out of the League in 1970.

A TOTAL OF **103** TEAMS TOOK PART IN **1,096** LEAGUE FIXTURES AT THIS VENUE

PEEL PARK
HOME GROUND OF ACCRINGTON STANLEY

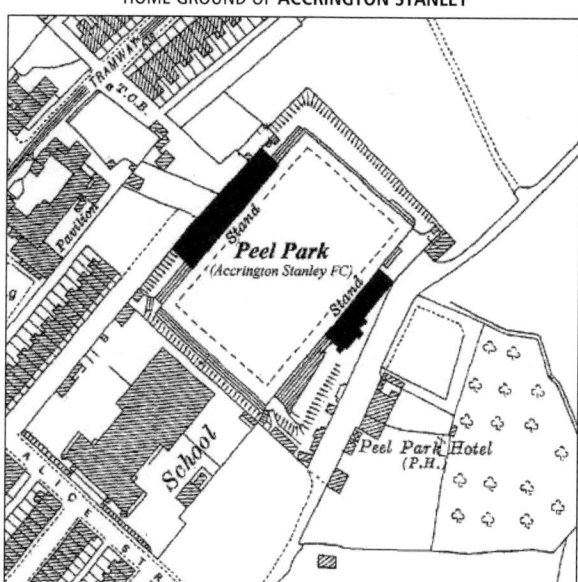

MAP EXTRACT; LANCASHIRE 63.11 [1931]
SITE LOCATION; SD76712928

Purchased in 1919 for £2,500, the site, part of the former grounds of the adjacent Peel Park Hotel, was located on the south side of the Burnley Road, north east of the town centre. By the time that *Accrington Stanley* joined the Football League, two years later as founder members of Division 3 [N], a covered seated stand had been erected on the south east side and banking constructed at the north east end. General improvements over the years included the concreting of the terraces all around the ground and installation of a covered enclosure at the south west end. The record attendance of 17,634 was established on November 15th, 1954 at a friendly game v. *Blackburn Rovers* to inaugurate the floodlights.

In April 1958 the Aldershot Military Tattoo Grandstand (See Photo on Page "2") was acquired and re-erected on the north west side of the ground. This provided cover for 4,700 seated and standing spectators and brought the capacity of the ground up to 24,600. Following their resignation from the Football League in 1962, *Accrington Stanley* continued to use the ground until the club folded in 1965. It was initially sold to a scrap dealer but part of the site is now in use as a school playing field.

PLAYING RECORD OF ACCRINGTON STANLEY
LEAGUE PROGRAMME

First Match; 4-0 v. Rochdale (11,500) (September 2nd, 1921)
Last Match; 0-2 v. Rochdale (2,690) (February 24th, 1962) [Result Expunged]
Highest Gate; 15,598 v. York City (2-2) (April 11th, 1955)
Lowest Gate; 925 v. York City (4-0) (March 30th, 1960)
Highest Home Win; 8-0 v. New Brighton (1,429) (March 17th, 1934)
Highest Home Defeat; 0-9 v. Barnsley (2,814) (February 3rd, 1934)

No. of Matches Played by Accrington Stanley; 694
(Including 18 expunged fixtures in 1961/62)

The club was a founder member of the Football League Division 3 [N] in 1921 and resigned from Division 4 in March 1962. Although the club immediately attempted to rescind their decision the League was adamant that it was obliged to accept their resignation and the playing record for 1961/62 was subsequently expunged from the records.

A TOTAL OF **62** TEAMS TOOK PART IN **694** LEAGUE FIXTURES AT THIS VENUE

PEEL CROFT

HOME GROUND OF BURTON SWIFTS & BURTON UNITED

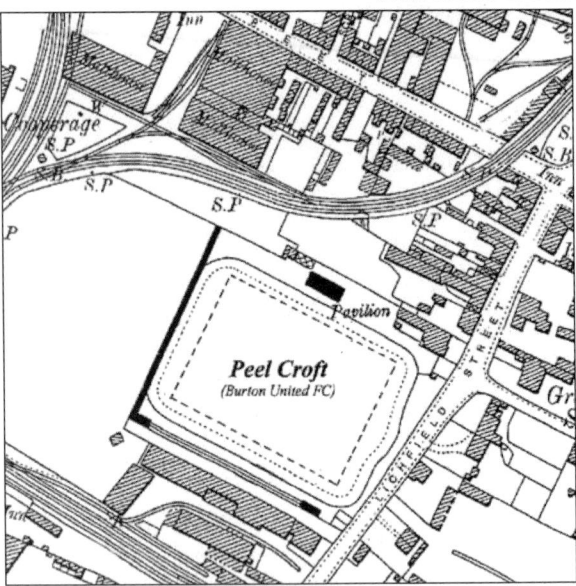

MAP EXTRACT; STAFFORDSHIRE 41.16 [1901]
SITE LOCATION; **SK24682244**

Previously in use as the home ground for *Burton RUFC*, *Peel Croft* was purchased by *Burton Swifts FC* in 1890. Improvements were immediately made with the construction of a pavilion/grandstand on the north side of the pitch and the installation of perimeter enclosure fencing. The ground was formally opened with a friendly fixture against *Derby County* on September 2nd, 1891.

Subsequent improvements included the construction of a narrow covered enclosure at the west end, terracing along the south side and an embankment at the east end. The record gate was probably the 5,500 who attended the FA Cup Qualifying Round match between *Burton Swifts* and *Burton Wanderers* on December 10th, 1892. *Burton Swifts* and *Burton Wanderers* amalgamated in 1901 as *Burton United FC* and the new club continued to utilize *Peel Croft*.

The grandstand was destroyed by a fire March 29th, 1907 but was quickly replaced with a 600 seat edifice which re-opened on September 21st, 1907. *Burton United*, having failed to gain re-election to the Football League at the end of the 1906/7 season, was disbanded in 1910 and the ground taken over by the previous tenants - *Burton RUFC* - who continued to use it. Although the rugby club members voted in 2004 to seek a new ground they were still here in 2005.

PLAYING RECORD OF BURTON SWIFTS
LEAGUE PROGRAMME

First Match; 7-1 v. Crewe Alexandra (-) (September 3rd, 1892)
Last Match; 1-0 v. Gainsborough Trinity (-) (April 20th, 1901)
Highest Gate*; 5,000 v. Newton Heath (1-2) (October 20th, 1894)
Lowest Gate*; 300 v. Luton Town (3-1) (February 3rd, 1900)
Highest Home Win; 7-0 v. Middlesbrough Ironopolis (-)
(March 17th, 1894)
Highest Home Defeat; 0-7 v. Liverpool (3,000)
(February 29th, 1896)
No. of Matches Played by Burton Swifts; 136
Information Kindly Supplied by; Brian Tabner

The club was a founder member of the Football League Division 2 in 1892 and, after finishing bottom of the table in 1901, amalgamated with *Burton Wanderers* to become *Burton United*.
*NB. Not all attendances are known and these are the highest and lowest gate figures of those that were recorded.

PLAYING RECORD OF BURTON UNITED
LEAGUE PROGRAMME

First Match & Highest Gate*; 1-1 v. Blackpool (4,000) (September 14th, 1901)
Last Match; 2-0 v. West Bromwich Albion (3,580) (April 27th, 1907)
Lowest Gate*; 1,000 v. Gainsborough Trinity (1-3) (April 24th, 1905)
Highest Home Win; 7-0 v. Stockport County (3,000)
(October 10th, 1903)
Highest Home Defeat; 0-6 v. Lincoln City (-) (November 23rd, 1901)

No. of Matches Played by Burton United; 106
Some Information Kindly Supplied by; Brian Tabner

Burton Swifts (having finished bottom and so requiring re-election) amalgamated with *Burton Wanderers* in 1901 to become *Burton United* and the new club was elected into the Football League Division 2. The club failed to gain re-election in 1907.
*NB. Not all attendances are known and these are the highest and lowest gate figures of those that were recorded.

A TOTAL OF **47** TEAMS TOOK PART IN **242** LEAGUE FIXTURES AT THIS VENUE

The replacement 600-seat main stand, which just missed out on *Burton United FCs* League career was still extant in 2005 and this view shows it in the 1980s
Photograph Courtesy of Dave Twydell

The terracing on the narrow south side of **Peel Croft** which was subsequently partially roofed.
Photograph by Paul Claydon. Courtesy of Groundtastic Magazine

PENYDARREN PARK
HOME GROUND OF MERTHYR TOWN

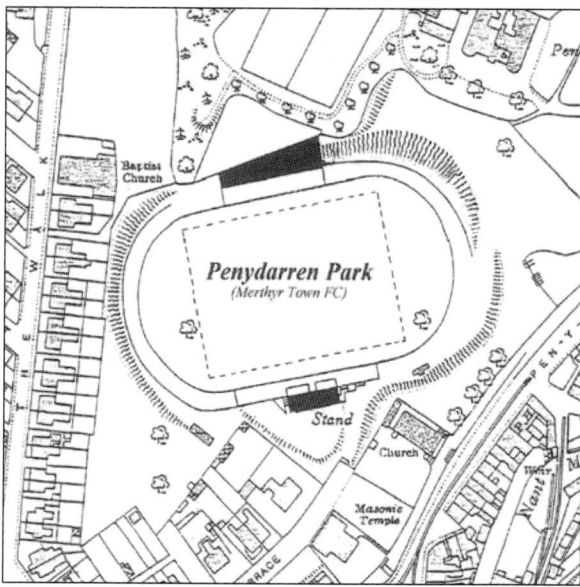

MAP EXTRACT; GLAMORGAN 12.1 [**1919**]
SITE LOCATION; **SO05000674**

Sited within Penydarren Park, the venue opened in 1904 for cycling and athletics and it was not until the formation of *Merthyr Town FC* in 1908 that it was revamped with a football pitch surrounded by an oval running track. The facilities originally included a small timber seated grandstand on the south side with embankments around the remainder of the arena and later improvements included the installation of a paddock in front of the grandstand and the construction of a covered enclosure on the opposite side. *Merthyr Town* folded in 1934 and the ground was used for greyhound racing for a while but in 1945 a re-formed *Merthyr Tydfil FC* took up residence and it is still their home ground today. It has regularly been used as the venue for Under-21 Internationals and as recently as September 9th, 2003 hosted the match between *Wales* and *Finland* (0-0) before a crowd of 1,311.

PLAYING RECORD OF MERTHYR TOWN
LEAGUE PROGRAMME

First Match; 2-1 v. Crystal Palace (10,000) (August 28th, 1920)
Last Match; 5-1 v. Newport County (1,189) (May 3rd, 1930)
Highest Gate; 21,686 v. Millwall (0-1) (December 27th, 1920)
Lowest Gate; 683 v. Coventry City (2-2) (April 14th, 1930)
Highest Home Win; 8-2 v. Swindon Town (5,418)
(October 8th, 1927)
Highest Home Defeat; 2-8 v. Brighton & Hove Albion (1,984)
(February 1st, 1930)
No. of Matches Played by Merthyr Town; 210
Information Kindly Supplied by; Mr David Watkins

The club was a founder member of the Football League Division 3 in 1920 and failed to gain re-election in 1930.

A TOTAL OF **31** TEAMS TOOK PART IN **210** LEAGUE FIXTURES AT THIS VENUE

PIKES LANE
HOME GROUND OF BOLTON WANDERERS

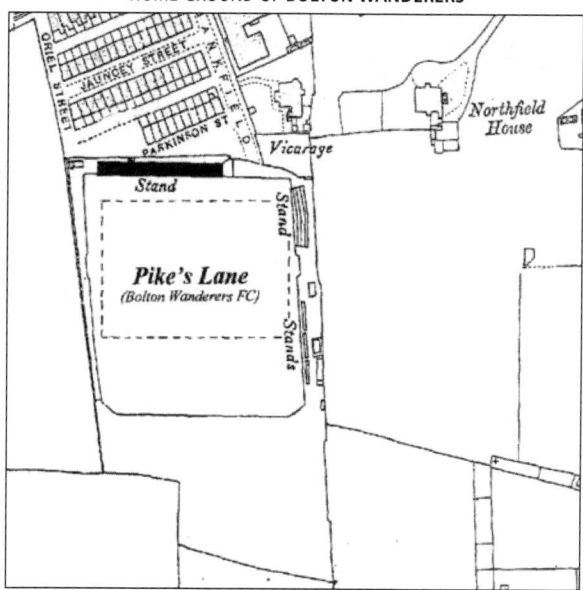

MAP EXTRACT; LANCASHIRE 87.13 [**1890**]
SITE LOCATION; **SD70300829**

Located on the south side of Deane Road, west of the town centre, *Bolton Wanderers FC* moved in to the 4.5 acre enclosure in 1880, the first match being played against *Great Lever FC* on September 10th. The arena was almost square in shape with shallow embankments on each side and later improvements included the installation of a covered grandstand on the north side, two wooden terraces at the east end and the construction of dressing rooms.

The record attendance of 20,000 was set at the FA Cup 3rd Round tie v. *Liverpool* (3-0) on February 24th, 1894. The club moved to **Burnden Park** in 1895, but poor pitch conditions at the new ground forced the reserves to continue playing here for a spell until it was rectified. The site was later redeveloped with housing and the continuation of Bankfield Street.

PLAYING RECORD OF BOLTON WANDERERS
LEAGUE PROGRAMME

First Match; 3-6 v. Derby County (5,000) (September 8th, 1888)
Last Match; 5-0 v. West Bromwich Albion (10,200) (April 13th, 1895)
Highest Gate; 14,000 v. Blackburn Rovers (2-0) (March 28th, 1891)
Lowest Gate; 1,500 v. Burnley (2-0) (January 6th, 1894)
Highest Home Win; 7-0 v. West Bromwich Albion (3,500) (December 7th, 1889)
Highest Home Defeat; 2-6 v. Preston North End (10,000) (October 12th, 1889). 0-5 v. Everton (12,000) (September 20th, 1890)
No. of Matches Played by Bolton Wanderers; 91
Information Kindly Supplied by; Brian Tabner

The club was a founder member of the Football League in 1888 and despite the ground being unpopular for both players (the pitch was inevitably a mud heap) and spectators (for whom the facilities were all but non-existent) it was another seven years before they were able to move to **Burnden Park**. The first ever League hat trick was scored here by Walter Tait of *Burnley* in their 4-3 win against *Bolton Wanderers* on September 15th, 1888.

A TOTAL OF **20** TEAMS TOOK PART IN **91** LEAGUE FIXTURES AT THIS VENUE

PLAINMOOR

HOME GROUND OF **TORQUAY UNITED**
TEMPORARY HOME GROUND FOR **PLYMOUTH ARGYLE**

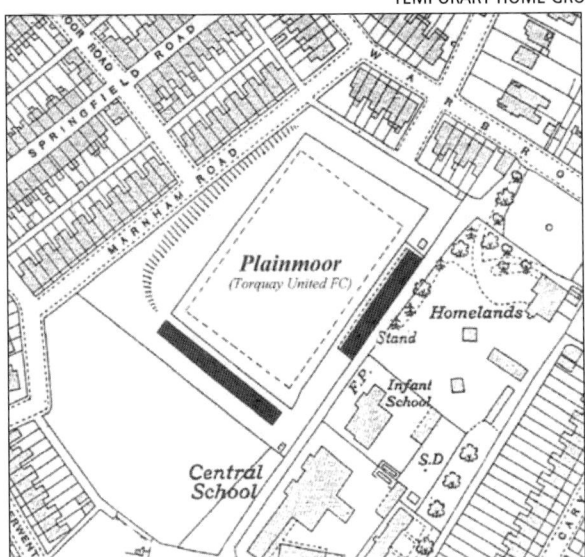

MAP EXTRACT; DEVON 116.10 [**1933**]
SITE LOCATION; **SX91976518**

Torquay Athletic RUFC established the venue at *Plainmoor* but moved out in 1905 to be replaced by *Ellacombe FC*. *Torquay United FC* moved in and merged with *Ellacombe* to form *Torquay Town FC* in 1910 and in 1921 merged with *Babbacombe FC* to form *Torquay United FC* and joined the Football League six years later.

The facilities at this time included banking on the west side, a main stand, purchased from *Buckfastleigh Racecourse*, on the east side and by 1933 a cover had been built at the south end. The only other alterations prior to the construction of a cover on the west side in the early 1950s was the installation of terracing around the ground.

Following the establishment of the record attendance of 21,908 at the FA Cup 4th Round tie v. *Huddersfield Town* (0-1) on January 29th, 1955 the main stand (later rebuilt following a partial fire in 1985) was extended and a cantilever roof subsequently built over part of the south end. The south end was rebuilt in the 1990s with a 1,275 seat stand, a new cover installed on the west side and the capacity at the start of the 2004/5 season was 6,283 with 2,446 seats. The pitch size was 112 x 74 yards.

PLAYING RECORD OF PLYMOUTH ARGYLE
LEAGUE PROGRAMME

Match Played; 1-2 v. Ipswich Town (9,626) (March 18th, 1961)
No. of Matches Played by Plymouth Argyle; 1
Information Kindly Supplied by; John Lovis

This match was played here following crowd trouble at **Home Park**.

PLAYING RECORD OF TORQUAY UNITED
LEAGUE PROGRAMME

First Match; 1-1 v. Exeter City (10,749) (August 27th, 1927)
Highest Gate; 16,454 v. Plymouth Argyle (1-3) (October 7th, 1950)
Lowest Gate; 967 v. Chester City (1-0) (May 2nd, 1984)
Highest Home Win; 9-0 v. Swindon Town (7,023) (March 8th, 1952)
Highest Home Defeat; 1-8 v. Scunthorpe United (2,137) (October 28th, 1995)

PLAY OFF MATCHES

2-1 v. Scunthorpe United (4,602) (May 15th, 1988)
3-3 v. Swansea City (5,000) (May 28th, 1988)
2-0 v. Burnley (5,600) (May 19th, 1991)
2-0 v. Preston North End (4,440) (May 15th, 1994)
4-1 v. Scarborough (5,386) (May 13th, 1998)

No. of Matches Played by Torquay United; 1,626
(League Programme; 1,621, Play Off Matches; 5)
Information Kindly Supplied by; John Lovis

The club was elected into the Football League Division 3 [S] in 1927 and was also involved in Football League Play Off Matches at the neutral venue of **Wembley Stadium**.

AT THE END OF SEASON 2004/5, A TOTAL OF **96** TEAMS HAD TAKEN PART IN **1,627** LEAGUE FIXTURES AT THIS VENUE

The main stand, complete with post-WWII extension, at **Plainmoor**
Photograph by Owen Pavey. Courtesy of Groundtastic Magazine

PLOUGH LANE
HOME GROUND OF WIMBLEDON

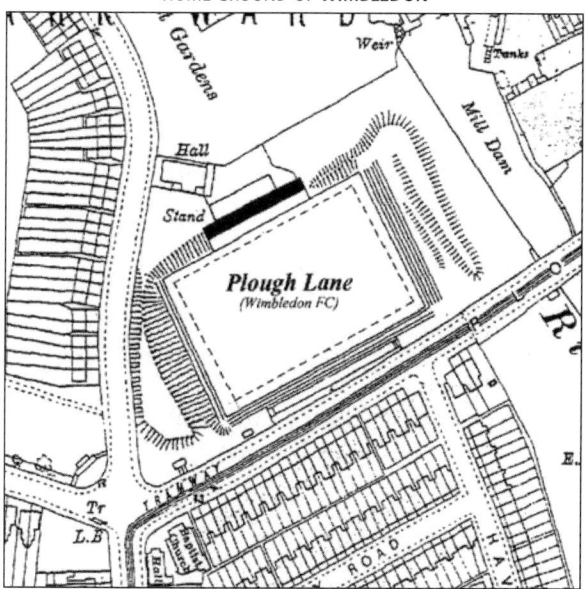

MAP EXTRACT; SURREY 7.2 [**1935**]
SITE LOCATION; **TQ25957153**

The site had been in use as a refuse tip when *Wimbledon FC* moved to *Plough Lane* in 1912. Details of the original facilities are not known but by the time that the record attendance of 18,080 had been set at the FA Amateur Cup tie v. *HMS Victory* on March 2nd, 1935 there were stands on each side of the ground (the stand on the south side having been purchased from *Clapton Orient FC* in 1925 and removed from **Millfields Road**), banking at the west end and terracing at the east.

Apart from patching up the south stand following war time bomb damage, *Plough Lane* remained unaltered until it was purchased from the council in 1959 for £8,250. The main stand was enlarged in the same year and, in 1960, a cover installed at the west end and concrete terracing constructed around the ground.

Wimbledon FC moved to **Selhurst Park** in 1991 to ground share with *Crystal Palace FC*, whilst *Plough Lane* was retained for reserve and youth teams fixtures. The ground remained extant in a derelict condition until 2002 when it was demolished for redevelopment with Merton Council proposing to establish a sports centre on the site.

PLAYING RECORD OF WIMBLEDON
LEAGUE PROGRAMME

First Match; 3-3 v. Halifax Town (4,616) (August 20th, 1977)
Last Match; 0-3 v. Crystal Palace (10,002) (May 4th, 1991)
Highest Gate; 15,978 v. Liverpool (1-3) (October 4th, 1986)
Lowest Gate & Highest Home Win; 6-0 v. Newport County (2,007) (September 3rd, 1983)
Highest Home Defeat; 3-6 v. Grimsby Town (2,485) (March 29th, 1980). 1-5 v. Arsenal (15,710) (August 27th, 1988)

No. of Matches Played by Wimbledon; 322

The club was elected into the Football League Division 4 in 1977. As the club rose in status the ground proved to be inadequate and after fruitlessly trying to find a site for a new venue within the area the club moved to **Selhurst Park** in 1991 to groundshare with *Crystal Palace*.

A TOTAL OF **89** TEAMS TOOK PART IN **322** LEAGUE FIXTURES AT THIS VENUE

PORTLAND PARK
HOME GROUND OF ASHINGTON

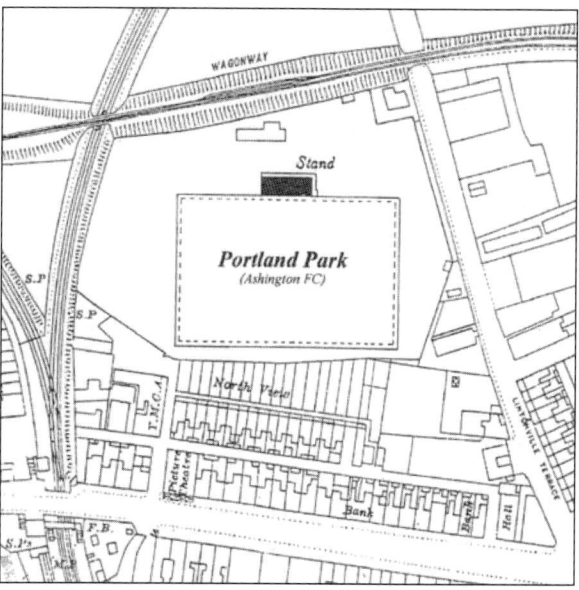

MAP EXTRACT; GROUND AS IN **1921** DRAWN FROM PLANS AND SUPERIMPOSED ON NORTHUMBERLAND 70.1 [**1917**]
SITE LOCATION; **NZ27378790**

When *Ashington FC* moved here in 1909 it was known as the *Station Road Ground* and was not re-named until 1914. Initially there were virtually no facilities but by 1921 a 1,000 seat grandstand had been built on the north side which, following their entry into the Football League that year, was refurbished. At the same time concrete terracing was introduced around the other three sides but no covered accommodation was provided for standing spectators.

The club failed to gain re-election in 1929 and the ground remained unchanged until the 1940s when it was substantially altered to facilitate greyhound racing, and subsequently speedway and stock car racing as well as football. The record attendance for a football match, of 13,199 was set at the FA Cup 2nd Round tie v. *Rochdale* (1-2) on December 9th, 1950 and *Portland Park* is still the home ground for *Ashington FC*.

PLAYING RECORD OF ASHINGTON
LEAGUE PROGRAMME

First Match & Highest Gate; 1-0 v. Grimsby Town (9,000) (August 27th, 1921)
Last Match & Lowest Gate; 0-3 v. Halifax Town (706) (April 27th, 1929)
Highest Home Win; 7-3 v. Rochdale (3,000) (February 18th, 1922). 6-0 v. Rotherham United (1,484) (April 28th, 1928)
Highest Home Defeat; 2-8 v. Bradford City (2,592) (October 13th, 1928)

No. of Matches Played by Ashington; 143
Information Kindly Supplied by; Alf Marchetti,

The club was a founder member of the Football League Division 3 [N] in 1921 but, being a mining town, succumbed to the depression of the 1920s and failed to gain re-election in 1929.

A TOTAL OF **29** TEAMS TOOK PART IN **143** LEAGUE FIXTURES AT THIS VENUE

PORTMAN ROAD
HOME GROUND OF IPSWICH TOWN

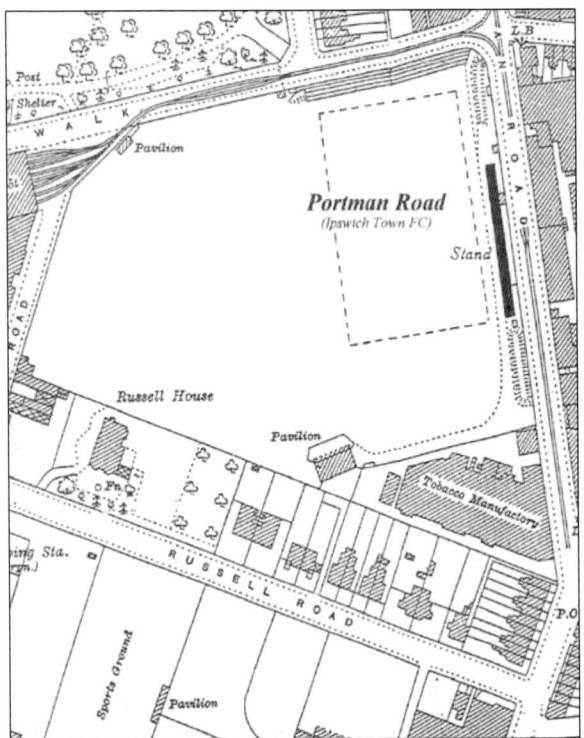

MAP EXTRACT; SUFFOLK 75.11 [1927]
SITE LOCATION; TM15734429

PLAYING RECORD OF IPSWICH TOWN
LEAGUE PROGRAMME

First Match; 4-2 v. Southend United (19,242) (August 27th, 1938)
Highest Gate; 35,109 v. Liverpool (1-0) (December 4th, 1976)
Lowest Gate; 3,116 v. Leyton Orient (0-1) (March 25th, 1953)
Highest Home Wins; 7-0 v. Portsmouth (12,354) (November 7th, 1964), v. Southampton (20,046) (February 2nd, 1974) & v. West Bromwich Albion (25,373) (November 6th, 1976).
Highest Home Defeat; 2-7 v. Manchester United (28,113) (September 3rd, 1963) & 0-6 v. Liverpool (25,608) (February 9th, 2002)

PLAY OFF MATCHES

0-0 v. Charlton Athletic (18,465) (May 14th, 1987)
2-2 v. Sheffield United (21,476) (May 14th, 1997)
0-1 v. Charlton Athletic (21,681) (May 10th, 1998)
4-3 v. Bolton Wanderers (21,755) (May 19th, 1999)
5-3 v. Bolton Wanderers [aet] (21,543) (May 17th, 2000)
1-0 v. West Ham United (28,435) (May 15th, 2004)
0-2 v. West Ham United (30,010) (May 18th, 2005)

No. of Matches Played by Ipswich Town; 1,300
(League Programme; 1,293, Play Off Matches; 7)

The club was elected into the Football League Division 3 [S] in 1938 and was involved in a Football League Play Off Match at the neutral venue of **Wembley Stadium.**

AT THE END OF SEASON 2004/5, A TOTAL OF **82** TEAMS HAD TAKEN PART IN **1,300** LEAGUE FIXTURES AT THIS VENUE

A view of **Portman Road** as an all-seater stadium. Taken in 2002 it shows the then-recently completed stand at the north end, the construction of which had been delayed by legal action.
Photograph by Owen Pavey. Courtesy of Groundtastic Magazine

Regarded as the premier sporting location in the town for some years, *East Suffolk CC* and *Ipswich RFC* were in residence at *Portman Road* when *Ipswich AFC* arrived from *Brook's Hall* in 1888. The two football codes amalgamated as *Ipswich Town* and played on the same area as the cricket pitch with a pavilion and wooden duckboards for standing spectators as the only facilities available for a number of years.

The rugby section moved out in 1893 and the Ipswich Cricket & Athletic Ground Company was formed in 1905 to provide the football club with their own pitch on waste land adjacent to the east side of the cricket ground. The facilities included a stand on the east side and, built one year later, a pavilion in the south west corner. After the stand roof blew off in 1911, the ground was commandeered by the army during WWI and by the time that they vacated in 1920 the pitch was totally ruined.

Whippet racing was experimented with in 1922 and no alterations to the ground were made until the 1930s when terraces and covering were built at each end and the stand (subsequently extended) installed with 650 second hand seats acquired from the redundant East Stand at **Arsenal Stadium.**

Post WWII improvements saw the installation of concrete terracing on the west side and at the north end and, in 1957, the construction of a seated stand on the west side. Major alterations commenced in 1971 with the opening of a new two-tier stand on the east side and this was extended just prior to the setting of the record attendance of 38,010 at the FA Cup 6th Round tie v. *Leeds United* (0-0) on March 8th, 1975. In 1984 the stand on the west side was enlarged with a third tier and supplied with a cantilever roof whilst, over the years, seats were gradually installed in all the standing areas eventually giving an all seater capacity of 22,438 by 1992.

A 7,130 seat stand was constructed at the south end in 2001 and, in 2002 a new 7,035 seat stand opened at the north end giving a capacity of 30,326 at the end of the 2004/5 season.

PRENTON PARK
HOME GROUND OF TRANMERE ROVERS

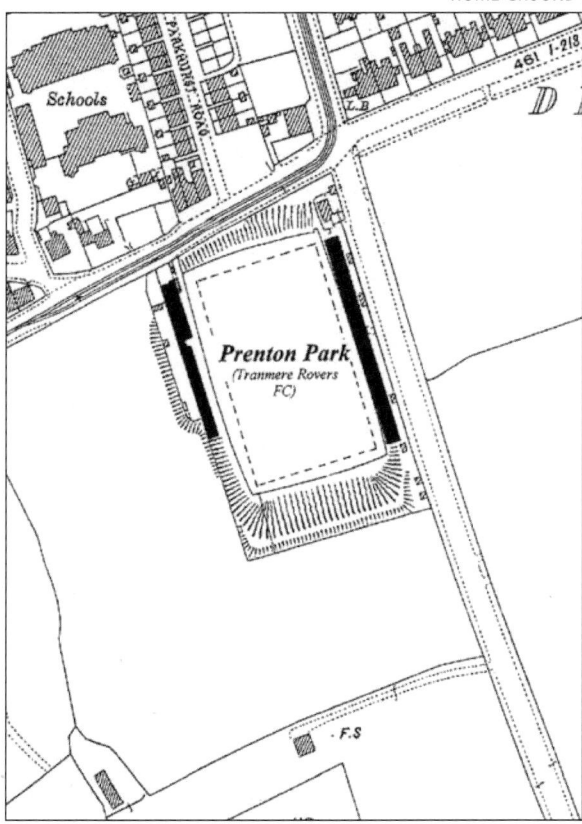

MAP EXTRACT; CHESHIRE 13.7 & 13.11 [1927]
SITE LOCATION; SJ31418682

PLAYING RECORD OF TRANMERE ROVERS
LEAGUE PROGRAMME

First Match; 4-1 v. Crewe Alexandra (7,011) (August 27th, 1921)
Highest Gate; 19,615 v. Wrexham (2-1) (April 30th, 1958)
Lowest Gate*; 984 v. Exeter City (2-2) (March 16th, 1979)
Highest Home Win; 13-4 v. Oldham Athletic (11,456) (December 26th, 1935)
Highest Home Defeat; 3-9 v. Manchester City (13,378) (December 26th, 1938)

PLAY OFF MATCHES
2-0 v. Bury (10,343) (May 16th, 1990)
1-0 v. Brentford (11,438) (May 22nd, 1991)
3-2 v. Swindon Town (16,083) (May 19th, 1993)
0-0 v. Leicester City (14,962) (May 15th, 1994)
1-3 v. Reading (12,207) (May 14th, 1995)
2-0 v. Hartlepool United [aet. 5-6 on penalties] (13,356) (May 17th, 2005)

No. of Matches Played by Tranmere Rovers; 1,729
(League Programme; 1,723 [Including one expunged match v. Accrington Stanley on August 19th, 1961], Play Off Matches; 6)

Information Kindly Supplied by; Gil Upton

The club was a founder member of the Football League Division 3 [N] in 1921. Robert Bell of *Tranmere Rovers* scored the first ever Football League treble hat-trick here (and missed a penalty!) in the 13-4 win against *Oldham Athletic* on December 26th, 1935. The club was also involved in Football League Play Off Matches at the neutral venue of **Wembley Stadium**.

*NB. A gate of only 843 was recorded for the fixture v. *Hartlepool United* (0-0) on December 19th, 1986, but this was abandoned after 27 minutes due to a floodlighting failure.

AT THE END OF SEASON 2004/5, A TOTAL OF **103** TEAMS HAD TAKEN PART IN **1,729** LEAGUE FIXTURES AT THIS VENUE

The large all-seater stand constructed at the south end in the 1990s.
Courtesy of Groundtastic Magazine

Tranmere Rovers FC, along with *Northern Nomads FC*, moved across Borough Road from the "old" *Prenton Park* in Devonshire Park to the "new" and current venue in 1912. The facilities included an 800 seat stand removed from the former ground and re-erected on the east side and another 800 seat stand on the west. Further improvements, including the construction of banking at the south end and the purchase of a second hand stand from *The Oval*, a local sports ground, and re-installation on the west side took place prior to WWI.

In the early 1920s *Northern Nomads* left *Prenton Park*, the ground was purchased for £7,500 and a full length cover (destroyed by bombing during WWII) installed on the east side whilst, in the 1930s, a roof was constructed at the north end and the south end extended. Following the end of the war the club arranged with the council to swap six feet of land on the east side (needed for a road scheme) for redundant tank traps that had been placed in Borough Road and these were craned on to the south end to form a foundation for extra banking and, apart from replacing the roof on the east side, this was the only alteration until the 1960s.

The stands on the west side were demolished in 1968 and a 4,000 seat structure built on the site, whilst four years later the record attendance of 24,424 was set at the FA Cup 4th Round tie v. *Stoke City* (2-2) on February 5th, 1972. In 1973 the cover over the north end was replaced following its destruction in a gale and this proved to be the final improvement until the ground was substantially rebuilt in 1994/5. In these two years it was converted to an all seat stadium with the construction of a new stand at the south end and general re-roofing and refurbishment around the remaining sides giving a capacity of 16,587 at the start of the 2004/5 season. The pitch size was 110 x 70 yards.

PRIESTFIELD STADIUM

HOME GROUND OF GILLINGHAM
TEMPORARY HOME GROUND FOR WOOLWICH ARSENAL & BRIGHTON & HOVE ALBION

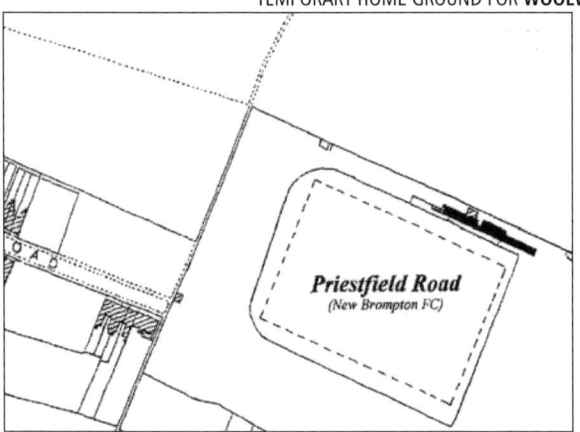

MAP EXTRACT; KENT 19.8 [**1896**]
SITE LOCATION; **TQ78296813**

New Brompton FC was founded in 1893 and a suitable plot of land in the east of the town purchased for £600. On opening it was known as the *New Brompton Football & Athletic Ground* and the facilities included a pavilion and a 400 seat covered stand on the north side. Although the venue hosted its first Football League match two years later when *Woolwich Arsenal* was banned from using its' **Manor Ground** and played one game here, *Priestfield Road*, as it was now known, had to be used for sheep grazing and a variety of events in order to make ends meet.

PLAYING RECORD OF ARSENAL
[AS WOOLWICH ARSENAL]
LEAGUE PROGRAMME
Match Played; 3-0 v. Burton Swifts (5,000) (February 23rd, 1895)
No. of Matches Played by Arsenal; 1

The match was played here due to the **Manor Ground** being closed for five weeks following a crowd disturbance at the *Burton Wanderers* fixture (1-1) on January 26th, 1895.

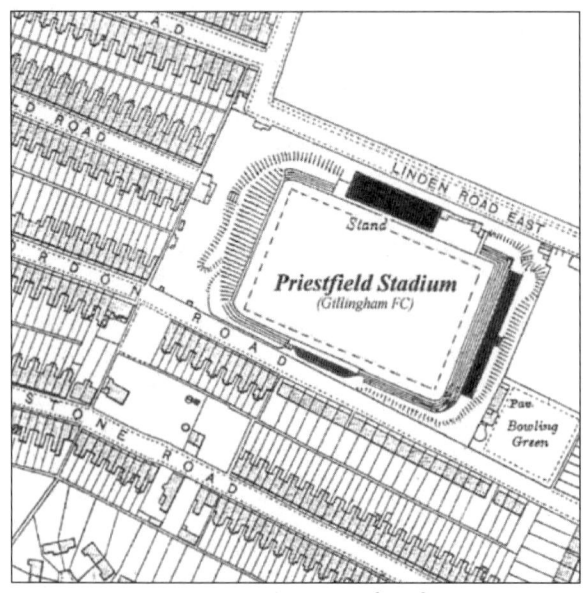

MAP EXTRACT; KENT 19.8 [**1932**]

A stand was constructed on the south side in 1899 and, upon their change of name to *Gillingham FC* in 1913, a new main stand (badly damaged within one month by a gale!) opened on the north side. Following their entry into the Football League in 1920 the terracing was expanded and improved and when, in 1927, a cover was built over the east end this was the last major improvement made prior to the record attendance of 23,002 being set at the FA Cup 3rd Round tie v. *Queens Park Rangers* (1-1) on January 10th, 1948.

In post-war years the name of the ground was altered again, this time to *Priestfield Stadium*. New terracing was constructed in 1955, the main stand refurbished in 1965 and seats installed in the main stand paddock in 1975 before the venue was radically altered during the 1990s when new stands were built on the south side and at the east end.

In 2001, a new two-tier main stand was opened on the north side and the west end was demolished and replaced with a temporary open seated stand giving an all-seater capacity of 10,952 at the start of the 2004/5 season. The pitch size was 114 x 75 yards.

PLAYING RECORD OF GILLINGHAM
LEAGUE PROGRAMME
First Match; 1-1 v. Southampton (11,500) (August 28th, 1920)
Highest Gate; 20,128 v. Millwall (4-3) (September 2nd, 1950)
Lowest Gate; 1,029 v. Exeter City (3-2) (November 13th, 1926)
Highest Home Win; 10-0 v. Chesterfield (4,099)
(September 5th, 1987)
Highest Home Defeat; 3-7 v. Coventry City (5,169)
(December 30th, 1933)
PLAY OFF MATCHES
3-2 v. Sunderland (13,804) (May 14th, 1987)
1-0 v. Swindon Town (16,775) (May 22nd, 1987)
1-0 v. Preston North End (10,505) (May 19th, 1999)
3-0 v. Stoke City [aet](10,386) (May 17th, 2000)
No. of Matches Played by Gillingham; 1,639
(League Programme; 1,635 [Including expunged matches v. Accrington Stanley on December 2nd, 1961 & v. Aldershot on November 30th, 1991], Play Off Matches; 4)
Information Kindly Supplied by; Roger Triggs

The club was a founder member of the Football League Division 3 in 1920, failed to gain re-election in 1938 and was elected to Division 3 [S] in 1950. The ground was closed for one match following crowd trouble at the *Oldham Athletic* game on January 14th, 1961 (2-3) and this was played at the **Stonebridge Road** ground of *Gravesend & Northfleet FC*. The club was also involved in Football League Play Off Matches at the neutral venues of **Selhurst Park** and **Wembley Stadium**.

PLAYING RECORD OF BRIGHTON & HOVE ALBION
LEAGUE PROGRAMME
First Match; 1-1 v. Macclesfield Town (2,336) (August 16th, 1997)
Last Match; 1-1 v. Rochdale (4,646) (May 8th, 1999)
Highest Gate; 6,339 v. Doncaster Rovers (0-0) (February 14th, 1998)
Lowest Gate; 1,025 v. Barnet (0-3) (November 5th, 1997)
Highest Home Win; 4-1 v. Rotherham United (2,870) (December 12th, 1998)
Highest Home Defeat; 0-4 v. Darlington (3,053) (March 13th, 1999)
No. of Matches Played by Brighton & Hove Albion; 46
Information Kindly Supplied by; Tim Carder,

As a temporary measure the club moved here from the **Goldstone Ground** and in 1999 moved to **Withdean Stadium**.

AT THE END OF SEASON 2004/5, A TOTAL OF **101** TEAMS HAD TAKEN PART IN **1,686** LEAGUE FIXTURES AT THIS VENUE

PRIDE PARK
HOME GROUND OF DERBY COUNTY

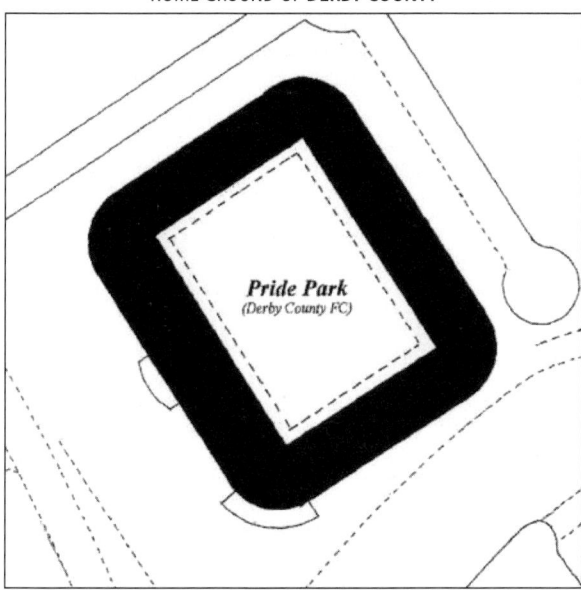

MAP EXTRACT; GROUND AS IN **2000** DRAWN FROM AERIAL PHOTOGRAPHS AND SUPERIMPOSED ON DERBYSHIRE 50.14 [1914]
SITE LOCATION; **SK37283532**

Constructed on a brownfield site partially occupied by a gas works, the stadium originally consisted of a horseshoe shaped stand with a continuous cantilever roof on the north, east and south sides and a cantilever roofed main stand on the west. At a later stage stands were constructed in the northwest and southwest corners giving an all-seat capacity of 33,597 at the start of the 2004/5 season. The pitch size was 115 x 75 yards.

PLAYING RECORD OF DERBY COUNTY
LEAGUE PROGRAMME

First Match; 1-0 v. Barnsley (27,232) (August 30th, 1997)
Highest Gate; 33,297 v. Everton (3-4) (March 23rd, 2002)
Lowest Gate; 18,459 v. Watford (3-2) (September 17th, 2003)
Highest Home Win; 5-1 v. Preston North End (24,162) (April 17th, 2004)
Highest Home Defeat; 0-5 v. Leeds United (30,217) (March 15th, 1998) & v. Sunderland (28,264) (September 18th, 1999)

PLAY OFF MATCHES
0-0 v. Preston North End (31,310) (May 19th, 2005)

No. of Matches Played by Derby County; 165
(League Programme; 164, Play Off Matches; 1)
Information Kindly Supplied by; Tony Matthews

Derby County FC moved here from **The Baseball Ground** at the start of the 1997/98 season.

AT THE END OF SEASON 2004/5, A TOTAL OF **49** TEAMS HAD TAKEN PART IN **165** LEAGUE FIXTURES AT THIS VENUE

RACECOURSE GROUND
HOME GROUND OF DERBY COUNTY

MAP EXTRACT; DERBYSHIRE 50.9 [**1913**]
SITE LOCATION; **SK36143679**

Although no map exists, from contemporary accounts the pitch, which *Derby County FC* used from their formation in 1884, was sited at the west end of the County Cricket Ground which occupied the southern half of Derby Racecourse. This arrangement was far from ideal as all the main facilities, which included a large grandstand and three areas of covered and open seating, were some 300 yards away on the east side of the Racecourse, whilst around the pitch there was no banking or covered accommodation.

Despite these drawbacks it was utilized for an FA Cup Final replay and Semi-Finals with a record crowd of over 15,000 present for the FA Cup Semi-Final between *Blackburn Rovers* and *Swifts* (2-1) on March 13th, 1886.

Derby County moved to **The Baseball Ground** in 1894 and the *County Cricket Ground* is still in use by *Derbyshire CCC*.

PLAYING RECORD OF DERBY COUNTY
LEAGUE PROGRAMME

First Match; 1-2 v. West Bromwich Albion (3,000) (September 15th, 1888)
Last Match; 0-0 v. Blackburn Rovers (1,500) (April 6th, 1895)
Highest Gate; 10,000 v. Preston North End (1-2) (September 10th, 1892)
Lowest Gate; 750 v. Darwen (2-1) (November 11th, 1894)
Highest Home Win; 9-0 v. Wolverhampton Wanderers (3,000) (January 10th, 1891)
Highest Home Defeat; 1-6 v. Everton (5,000) (November 5th, 1892)

No. of Matches Played by Derby County; 89
Information Kindly Supplied by; Tony Matthews

The club was a founder member of the Football League in 1888. Although it occupied a large area, the facilities for spectators were very poor and it became obvious that a new venue would be required. In 1892 *Derby County FC* played two matches at **The Baseball Ground** when race meetings took precedence at the ground and moved there permanently in 1895. The club was also involved in a Test Match at the neutral venue of **Filbert Street**.

A TOTAL OF **20** TEAMS TOOK PART IN **89** LEAGUE FIXTURES AT THIS VENUE

RACECOURSE GROUND
HOME GROUND OF WREXHAM

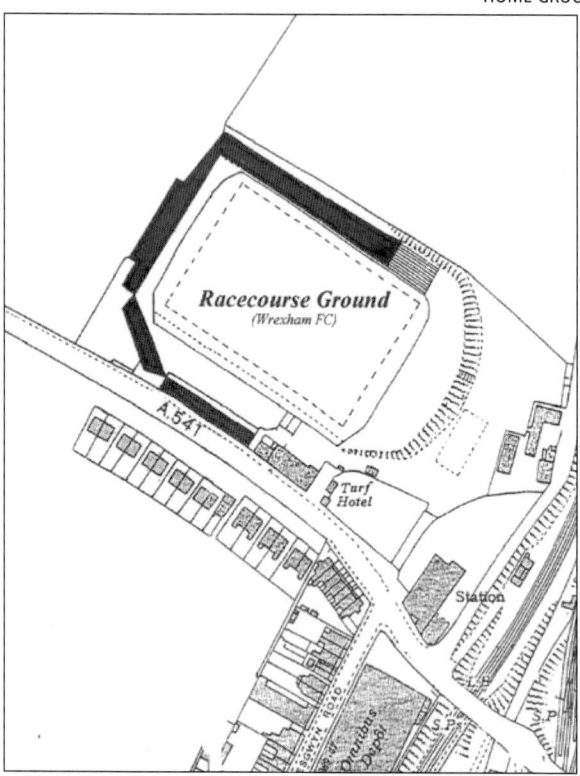

MAP EXTRACT; DENBIGH 28.7 & 28.8 [**1939**]
SITE LOCATION; **SJ32815098**

PLAYING RECORD OF WREXHAM
LEAGUE PROGRAMME
First Match; 0-2 v. Hartlepools United (10,000) (August 27th, 1921)
Highest Gate; 29,261 v. Chester (1-2) (December 26th, 1930)
Lowest Gate; 935 v. Southend United (1-3) (April 30th, 1987)
Highest Home Win; 10-1 v. Hartlepools United (6,546)
(March 3rd, 1962)
Highest Home Defeat; 2-6 v. Stoke City (6,525) (February 26th, 1927), v. York City (11,683) (August 21st, 1954)
& v. Burnley (3,181) (October 12th, 1991)

PLAY OFF MATCHES
3-1 v. Scunthorpe United (5,449) (May 21st, 1989)
0-0 v. Leyton Orient (7,913) (May 30th, 1989)

No. of Matches Played by Wrexham; 1,715
(League Programme; 1,713 [Including expunged matches v. Wigan Borough on October 24th, 1931 and v. Aldershot on September 17th, 1991], Play Off Matches; 2)

The club was a founder member of the Football League Division 3 [N] in 1921.

AT THE END OF SEASON 2004/5, A TOTAL OF **103** TEAMS HAD TAKEN PART IN **1,715** LEAGUE FIXTURES AT THIS VENUE

One of the more unusual post-WWII stands, the former balcony from the Majestic Cinema was purchased for £4,000 and re-erected at the east end. Nicknamed the "Pigeon Loft" it was installed in 1962 and removed in 1978.

Photograph Courtesy of Groundtastic Magazine

This large venue had been in use for horse racing since 1807 and cricket took place for many years prior to the formation of a football team in 1872. Initially the cricketing area was used for football, the *Wales* v. *Scotland* International match being played here in 1877, and it was not until 1902 that the area now known as the *Racecourse Ground* was established.

The pitch was surrounded by an oval cycle track and the facilities included a stand on the south side and banking around the remainder of the ground whilst the players changed in the adjacent Turf Hotel. *Wrexham FC* joined the Football League in 1921 and subsequent improvements made during this decade included the erection of a cover over the west end whilst, prior to WWII, the north side was covered and a stand constructed in the south west corner.

Modest post-war improvements included the installation of concrete terracing at the east end before the record attendance of 34,445 was set at the FA Cup 4th Round tie v. *Manchester United* (0-5) on January 26th, 1957. In 1962 a bizarre 700 seat stand, consisting of a redundant balcony and associated steelwork from the local Majestic Cinema was erected at the east end but only lasted for sixteen years before suffering demolition.

The 1970s saw considerable alterations with the building of a 2,750 seat two-tier stand on the north side, a similar 2,250 seat construction at the west end and, in 1980, roofing over the east end. Seats were subsequently installed on the remaining terracing on the north side and at the west end before a new all seat stand was opened on the south side in 2000, giving a capacity of 15,500 with 11,500 seats by the start of the 2004/5 season. The pitch size was 111 x 74 yards.

RAIKES HALL
HOME GROUND OF **BLACKPOOL**

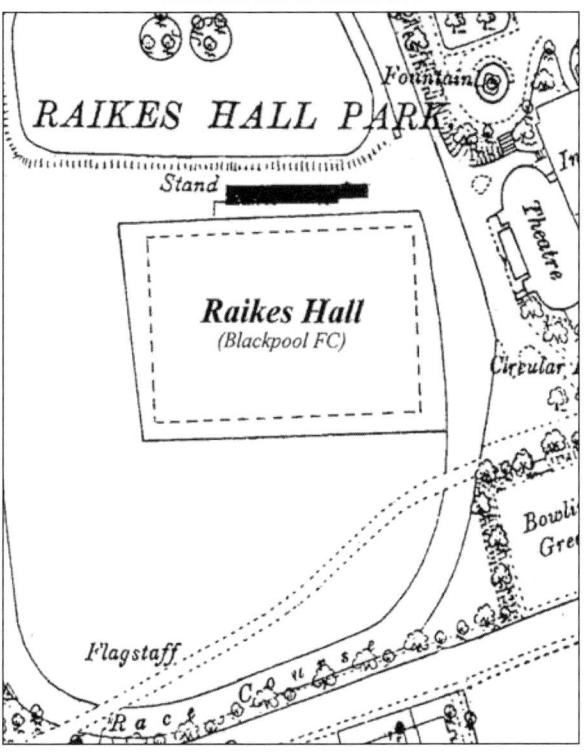

MAP EXTRACT; LANCASHIRE 50.12 [**1893**]
SITE LOCATION; **SD31503609**

Set within Raikes Hall Park, a pleasure grounds complex, the venue was first used by *Blackpool FC* in 1888. There was a covered seated grandstand on the north side of the pitch, backing on to the lake, but the other three sides, in order to accommodate cricket in the summer, were not banked or covered.

The club finally moved out to **Bloomfield Road** in 1899 and the whole park was redeveloped with housing with Leicester and Longton Roads being sited on the original pitch.

PLAYING RECORD OF BLACKPOOL
LEAGUE PROGRAMME

First Match; 5-0 v. Burton Wanderers (3,000)
(September 19th, 1896)
Last Match; 4-0 v. Gainsborough Trinity (-) (April 15th, 1899)
Highest Gate; 5,000 v. Newton Heath (4-2) (October 17th, 1896), v. Grimsby Town (1-0) (January 1st, 1897) &
v. Darwen (1-0) (April 16th, 1897)
Lowest Gate; 600 v. Barnsley (3-1) (March 15th, 1899)
Highest Home Win; 6-0 v. Darwen (-) (March 31st, 1899)
Highest Home Defeat; 3-6 v. Grimsby Town (4,000)
(February 18th, 1899)

No. of Matches Played by Blackpool; 25
Information Kindly Supplied by; Roger Harrison

The club was elected into the Football League Division 2 in 1896 and whilst in their debut season it became apparent that *Raikes Hall* was due for redevelopment they moved to **The Athletic Grounds** for the start of the 1897/98 season. They returned here midway through the 1898/99 fixtures but failed to gain re-election at the end of that season. The club moved to **Bloomfield Road** at the end of 1899.

A TOTAL OF **18** TEAMS TOOK PART IN **25** LEAGUE FIXTURES AT THIS VENUE

RECREATION GROUND
HOME GROUND OF **ALDERSHOT**

MAP EXTRACT; HAMPSHIRE 21.9 [**1937**]
SITE LOCATION; **SU87005061**

Aldershot FC leased the ground from the local council following the club's formation in 1926 and a unique feature (for Football League grounds) was that it was sited within a public park necessitating its' closure on match days to allow for the collection of gate money at the park entrances.

Within three years a seated stand was built on the south side, a stand installed on the north side (following their election to the Football League in 1932) and the east end covered after the end of WWII. The record attendance of 19,138 was set at the FA Cup 4th Round replay v. *Carlisle United* (1-4) on January 28th, 1970 and in 1980 the north stand was modernized and improved with the installation of additional seating giving a nominal capacity of 16,000 with 1,885 seats.

The venue is still in use as the home ground for *Aldershot Town FC* (reformed from *Aldershot FC*)

PLAYING RECORD OF ALDERSHOT
LEAGUE PROGRAMME

First Match; 1-2 v. Southend United (8,022) (August 27th, 1932)
Last Match; 0-3 v. Lincoln City (1,473) (March 14th, 1992)
Highest Gate; 15,611 v. Reading (1-1) (October 22nd, 1938)
Lowest Gate; 1,027 v. Port Vale (0-0) (September 17th, 1985)
Highest Home Win; 8-1 v. Gateshead (4,849) (September 13th, 1958)
Highest Home Defeat; 0-6 v. Reading (10,080) (March 12th, 1949)

PLAY OFF MATCHES
1-0 v. Bolton Wanderers (4,164) (May 14th, 1987)
2-0 v. Wolverhampton Wanderers (5,000) (May 22nd, 1987)

No. of Matches Played by Aldershot; 1,195
(League Programme; 1,193 [Including one expunged match v. Accrington Stanley on February 9th, 1962 and 17 expunged games during Season 1991/2], Play Off Matches; 2)
Information Kindly Supplied by; Jack Rollin

The club was elected into Division 3 [S] in 1932 and, following financial problems, wound up on March 20th, 1992. *Aldershot FC* withdrew from Division 4 on March 26th and the records for 1991/92 were expunged.

A TOTAL OF **84** TEAMS TOOK PART IN **1,195** LEAGUE FIXTURES AT THIS VENUE

RECREATION GROUND
HOME GROUND OF CHESTERFIELD

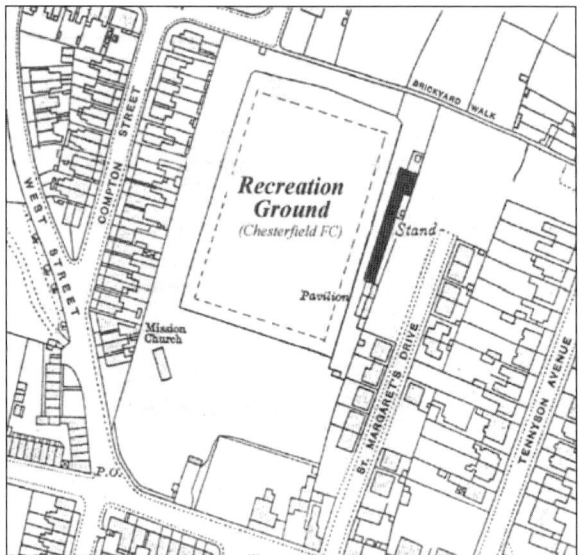

MAP EXTRACT; DERBYSHIRE 25.2 & 25.6 [1918]
SITE LOCATION: **SK37787153**

This ground at Saltergate was probably first used for football in the 1860s but it was not until 1887 that *Chesterfield FC* adopted the venue on a permanent basis. Details of the original facilities are not known but by c1900 (during their first period in the Football League) at least a small stand had been constructed on the east side and this had been supplemented by a pavilion by 1914.

The club re-joined the Football League in 1921 but it was not until 1932 that a replacement 2,200 seat main stand opened on the east side and the 1950s before the terracing was concreted and covers installed on the west side and at the south end. By 2000 parts of the ground had become dilapidated and the terracing on the west side was closed for safety reasons. This terracing was replaced by a new 1,200 seat stand in 2002 and both of the ends were re-terraced giving a capacity of 8,300 with 2,674 seats at the start of the 2004/5 season. The pitch size was 112 x 73 yards.

PLAYING RECORD OF CHESTERFIELD
LEAGUE PROGRAMME

First Match; 2-2 v. Lincoln City (5,000) (September 9th, 1899)
Highest Gate; 28,268 v. Newcastle United (2-0) (April 7th, 1939)
Lowest Gate; 1,435 v. Darlington (1-0) (May 4th, 1985)
Highest Home Win; 10-0 v. Glossop (3,000) (January 17th, 1903)
Highest Home Defeat; 3-7 v. Stockport County (9,408) (December 2nd, 1954). 0-6 v. Wrexham (3,325) (September 11th, 1976)

PLAY OFF MATCHES
4-0 v. Stockport County (8,277) (May 13th, 1989)
5-2 v. Mansfield Town (8,156) (May 18th, 1995)

No. of Matches Played by Chesterfield; 1,894
(League Programme; 1,892 [Including one expunged match v. Aldershot on September 28th, 1991], Play Off Matches; 2)

Information Kindly Supplied by; Stuart Basson

The club was elected into the Football League Division 2 in 1899, failed to gain re-election in 1909 and was elected as an original member of Division 3 [N] in 1921. The club was also involved in Football League Play Off Matches at the neutral venue of **Wembley Stadium**.

AT THE END OF SEASON 2004/5, A TOTAL OF **118** TEAMS HAD TAKEN PART IN **1,894** LEAGUE FIXTURES AT THIS VENUE

REDHEUGH PARK
HOME GROUND OF GATESHEAD

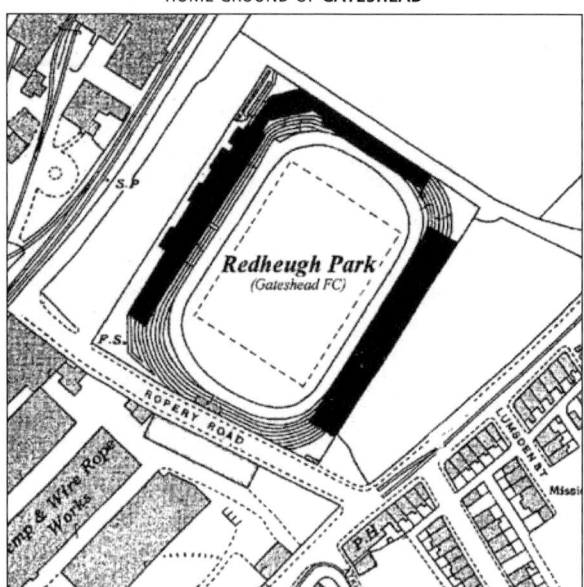

MAP EXTRACT; DURHAM 6.4 [1947]
SITE LOCATION; **NZ23786202**

Located in the Low Team area, south west of the town centre, *Redheugh Park* was constructed on the site of a clay pit by the Borough Council and opened in 1930. By the time that the ground was sub-let to the Redheugh Park Greyhound Racing Co. Ltd in 1937 there were stands and covered accommodation on all four sides of the oval shaped arena. Some improvements were made to facilitate greyhound racing but the stand at the south end was removed to make way for a totalisator board.

The racing ceased in 1948 and, following their failure to gain re-election in 1960, *Gateshead FC* continued to use the stadium until 1973 when they moved to the *Gateshead International Stadium*. *Redheugh Park* was subsequently demolished and part of the site utilized for a sports centre.

PLAYING RECORD OF GATESHEAD
LEAGUE PROGRAMME

First Match; 2-1 v. Doncaster Rovers (15,545) (August 30th, 1930)
Last Match; 3-0 v. Walsall (2,366) (April 25th, 1960)
Highest Gate; 20,752 v. Lincoln City (1-1) (September 25th, 1937)
Lowest Gate; 484 v. Accrington Stanley (0-1) (March 26th, 1952)
Highest Home Win; 7-0 v. Hartlepools United (6,329) (December 25th, 1947) & v. Accrington Stanley (9,623) (August 19th, 1950)
Highest Home Defeat; 0-5 v. Lincoln City (1,224) (April 7th, 1937), v. Crewe Alexandra (2,905) (December 24th, 1938) & v. Barrow (2,365) (April 26th, 1947)

No. of Matches Played by Gateshead; 504
Information Kindly Supplied by; Tom Bone

Gateshead FC was re-formed from *South Shields* in 1930 when the club relocated from **Horsley Hill** to **Redheugh Park**. The 484 gate for the *Accrington Stanley* match is the lowest post-WWII Football League attendance. The club failed to gain re-election in 1960.

A TOTAL OF **46** TEAMS TOOK PART IN **504** LEAGUE FIXTURES AT THIS VENUE

REEBOK STADIUM
HOME GROUND OF BOLTON WANDERERS

MAP EXTRACT; GROUND AS IN **2000**, DRAWN FROM AERIAL PHOTOGRAPHS
SITE LOCATION; **SD64630940**

Constructed on a greenfield site, the stadium is elliptical in shape with two-tier stands around the ground and a continuous roof supported off cables strung between pylons located in each corner. The all-seat capacity at the start of the 2004/5 season was 27,723 and the pitch size was 115 x 74 yards.

PLAYING RECORD OF BOLTON WANDERERS
LEAGUE PROGRAMME

First Match; 0-0 v. Everton (23,131) (September 1st, 1997)
Highest Gate; 28,353 v. Leicester City (2-2) (December 28th, 2003)
Lowest Gate; 10,180 v. Queens Park Rangers (3-1) (October 31st, 2000)
Highest Home Win; 5-2 v. Crystal Palace (24,449) (May 2nd, 1998)
Highest Home Defeat; 1-5 v. Coventry City (24,990) (January 31st, 1998)

PLAY OFF MATCHES

1-0 v. Ipswich Town (18,295) (May 16th, 1999)
2-2 v. Ipswich Town (18,814) (May 14th, 2000)
3-0 v. West Bromwich Albion (23,515) (May 17th, 2001)

No. of Matches Played by Bolton Wanderers; 167
(League Programme; 164, Play Off Matches; 3)
Information Kindly Supplied by; Simon Marland

The club moved here from ***Burnden Park*** in 1997 and it was also involved in Football League Play Off Matches at the neutral venues of ***Wembley Stadium*** and the ***Millennium Stadium***.

AT THE END OF SEASON 2004/5, A TOTAL OF **50** TEAMS HAD TAKEN PART IN **167** LEAGUE FIXTURES AT THIS VENUE

RIVERSIDE STADIUM
HOME GROUND OF MIDDLESBROUGH

MAP EXTRACT; GROUND AS IN **2000** DRAWN FROM AERIAL PHOTOGRAPHS AND SUPERIMPOSED ON NZ5020 [1951]
SITE LOCATION; **NZ50722060**

Constructed on the site of the Yorkshire Tube Works as part of an urban regeneration scheme, *Middlesbrough FC* moved to the *BT Cellnet Riverside Stadium* from ***Ayresome Park*** in 1995. The ground, as built, had a continuous cantilever roof covering three single-tier stands and a two-tier cantilever roofed stand on the west side giving an all seat capacity of 29,977. Stands were subsequently constructed in the north west and south west corners (enclosing the stadium) and by the start of the 2004/5 season the capacity was set at 35,100 and the pitch size was 115 x 75 yards. The record attendance of 35,000 was set at the Euro 2004 Group 7 *England* v. *Slovakia* (2-1) International Qualifying Match on June 11th, 2003.

PLAYING RECORD OF MIDDLESBROUGH
LEAGUE PROGRAMME

First Match; 2-0 v. Chelsea (28,286) (August 26th, 1995)
Highest Gate; 34,836 v. Norwich City (2-0) (December 28th, 2004)
Lowest Gate; 22,414 v. Charlton Athletic (2-1) (August 9th, 1997)
Highest Home Win; 6-0 v. Swindon Town (29,581) (March 11th, 1998)
Highest Home Defeat; 1-6 v. Arsenal (34,630) (April 24th, 1999)

No. of Matches Played by Middlesbrough; 194

The club moved here from ***Ayresome Park*** in 1995.

AT THE END OF SEASON 2004/5, A TOTAL OF **45** TEAMS HAD TAKEN PART IN **194** LEAGUE FIXTURES AT THIS VENUE

ROKER PARK
HOME GROUND OF SUNDERLAND

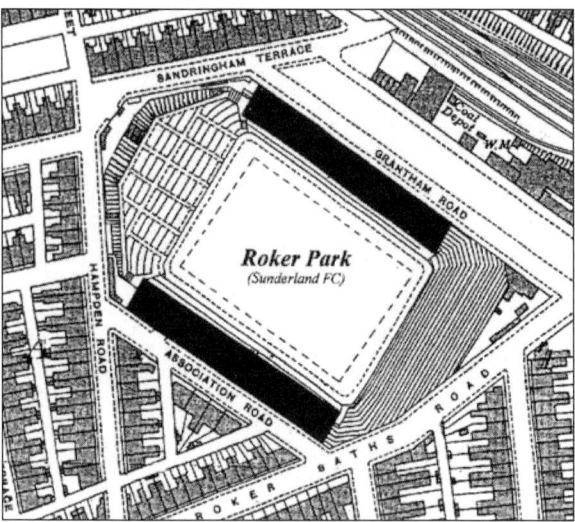

MAP EXTRACT; DURHAM 8.10 [1947]
SITE LOCATION; NZ40125868

The site had been in use as farmland when *Sunderland FC* moved here from *Newcastle Road* in 1898 and the original facilities included a 3,000 seat main stand on the east side, a cover over wooden terracing on the west side and banking at each end. After the south end was rebuilt with concrete terracing in 1911 it had a nominal capacity of 50,000.

The ground saw substantial improvements during the 1920s with the enlargement of the north end banking and construction of a new 5,875 main stand on the east side taking place before the setting of the record attendance of 75,118 at the FA Cup 6th Round replay v. *Derby County* (0-1) on March 8th, 1933. The final alteration prior to WWII was the installation of a new stand for 15,500 standing spectators on the west side. Apart from the addition of seating in the main stand paddock, the stadium remained unaltered until it was refurbished for the World Cup in 1966 with the installation of seats at the rear of the west stand, temporary seats in the paddocks and a roof and seats at the north end. The club moved to the *Stadium of Light* in 1997 and the ground was demolished and the site used for housing.

PLAYING RECORD OF SUNDERLAND
LEAGUE PROGRAMME

First Match; 1-0 v. Liverpool (30,000) (September 10th, 1898)
Last Match; 3-0 v. Everton (22,108) (May 3rd, 1997)
Highest Gate; 68,004 v. Newcastle United (2-2) (March 4th, 1950)
Lowest Gate; 4,832 v. Portsmouth (4-1) (April 29th, 1935)
Highest Home Win; 8-1 v. Charlton Athletic (36,510) (September 1st, 1956)
Highest Home Defeat; 1-6 v. Newcastle United (55,723) (December 26th, 1955) & v. Birmingham City (34,184) (April 5th, 1958)

PLAY OFF MATCHES
4-3 v. Gillingham [aet] (25,470) (May 17th, 1987)
0-0 v. Newcastle United (26,641) (May 13th, 1990)

No. of Matches Played by Sunderland; 1,815
(League Programme; 1,813, Play Off Matches; 2)

Following an attack on *The Wednesday* players in 1903 the match v. *Middlesbrough* in 1903/4 was played at *St James' Park*. The club was also involved in a Football League Play Off Match at the neutral venue of *Wembley Stadium*.

A TOTAL OF 82 TEAMS TOOK PART IN 1,815 LEAGUE FIXTURES AT THIS VENUE

ROOTS HALL
HOME GROUND OF SOUTHEND UNITED

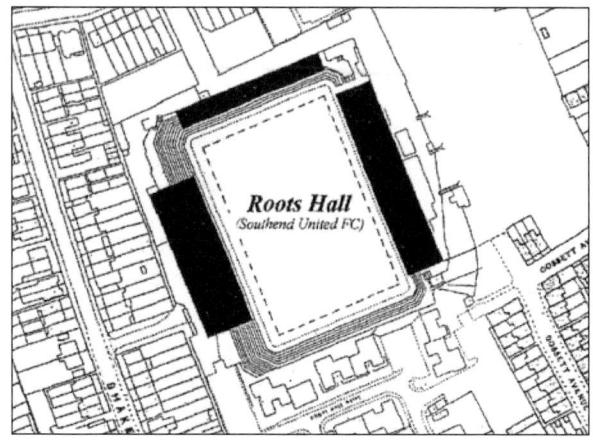

MAP EXTRACT; ESSEX N83.13 [1922]
SITE LOCATION; TQ87418691

Located in Prittlewell, some one mile north of Southend town centre, *Southend United FC* originally moved in in 1906. The basic facilities included a seated grandstand and flat standing areas around the pitch. The club moved out to *The Kursaal* in 1915 and the site was exploited for its deposits of sand and gravel resulting in a ground level drop of some 50ft by the time that the club returned here in 1953.

When *Roots Hall* opened in 1955 a main stand had been constructed on the east side, covers erected on the west side and at the north end and some concrete terracing installed around the ground. The south end was extended with additional concrete terracing in 1960 and, following the extension of the main stand in 1967, the record attendance of 31,090 was set at the FA Cup 3rd Round tie v. *Liverpool* (0-0) on January 10th, 1979.

After part of the south end was sold for redevelopment in 1988, further alterations included the installation of seating at the north end, roof extensions and seating on the west side and construction of a new 2,083 seat two-tier stand at the south end. The all-seat capacity at the start of the 2004/5 season was 12,392 and the pitch size was 110 x 74 yards.

PLAYING RECORD OF SOUTHEND UNITED
LEAGUE PROGRAMME

First Match; 3-1 v. Norwich City (17,700) (August 20th, 1955)
Highest Gate; 21,000 v. Leyton Orient (0-0) (September 3rd, 1955)
Lowest Gate; 1,006 v. Halifax Town (2-1) (March 5th, 1986)
Highest Home Win; 7-0 v. Workington (13,871) (March 29th, 1968)
Highest Home Defeat; 2-5 v. Chesterfield (9,895) (January 17th, 1959), v. Notts County (5,094) (January 24th, 1970), & v. Colchester United (2,190) (January 29th, 1985). 0-4 v. Bury (12,973) (August 29th, 1959), v. Bristol City (8,780) (September 14th, 1964), v. Newport County (4,913) (September 4th, 1981), v. Northampton Town (2,527) (December 6th, 1985), v. Northampton Town (8,387) (December 26th, 1986) & v. Watford (4,914) (February 4th, 1995)

PLAY OFF MATCHES
1-0 v. Northampton Town (9,152) (May 21st, 2005)

No. of Matches Played by Southend United; 1,151
(League Programme; 1,150, Play Off Matches; 1)
Information Kindly Supplied by; Dave Goody

The club moved here from *Southend Stadium* in 1955 and was involved in a Football League Play Off match at the neutral venue of the *Millennium Stadium*.

AT THE END OF SEASON 2004/5, A TOTAL OF 99 TEAMS HAD TAKEN PART IN 1,151 LEAGUE FIXTURES AT THIS VENUE

ST ANDREW'S
HOME GROUND OF BIRMINGHAM CITY

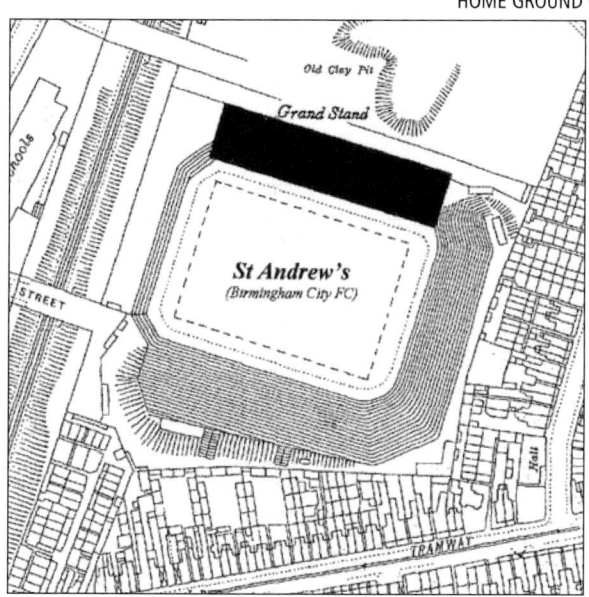

MAP EXTRACT; WARWICKSHIRE 14.6 [1912]
SITE LOCATION; **SP09058644**

The site had been in use as a brickworks before *Birmingham FC* moved here from **Muntz Street** in 1906 and the facilities upon opening included a 6,000 seat main stand on the north side and terracing around the remainder of the ground. In the 1930s covers were erected over part of the south side and at the west end before the record attendance of 67,341 was set at the FA Cup 5th Round tie v. *Everton* (2-2) on February 11th, 1939.

During WWII the city of Birmingham suffered from more bombing raids than any other outside of London and it was no surprise that the ground experienced considerable bomb damage (the demise of the main stand being assisted in 1942 by the inadvertent use of petrol, rather than water, to put out a small fire). Attempts were made to purchase the grandstand from the **Royal Gymnasium Ground** in Edinburgh but this was sold to *Leith Athletic FC* for £2,000 in 1947 and re-erected at **Old Meadowbank**. The south side was re-roofed in 1947 and, in the 1950s, a new main stand constructed on the north side and cover erected at the east end. A new stand was opened at the west end in 1964 and, apart from the installation of seats in the paddocks in front of the stands no further alterations took place until the 1990s.

In 1994 the terracing on the south side and at the east end was removed and replaced with two continuous cantilever roofed all seat stands and, in 2000, a two-tier all-seat stand was opened at the west end giving an all-seat capacity of 29,796 by the start of the 2004/5 season. The pitch size was 115 x 75 yards.

NEUTRAL PLAY OFF MATCHES
Division 1 Final Replay; Charlton Athletic 2, Leeds United 1 [aet] (15,841) (May 29th, 1987)
No. of Matches Played; 1

PROGRAMME COVER ON THE RIGHT
During the early 1960s *Birmingham City* featured this aerial view of the ground (including erroneous pitch markings!) on its programme covers. The picture shows the main stand on the left, the large covered terrace to the right and the narrower covered terrace between the railway line and the pitch at the bottom.

PLAYING RECORD OF BIRMINGHAM CITY
LEAGUE PROGRAMME
First Match; 0-0 v. Middlesbrough (32,000) (December 26th, 1906)
Highest Gate; 60,250 v. Aston Villa (2-2) (November 23rd, 1935)
Lowest Gate; 1,000 v. Blackpool (1-2) (November 27th, 1909)
& v. Burnley (2-1) (February 28th, 1910)
Highest Home Win; 11-1 v. Glossop (8,000) (January 6th, 1915)
Highest Home Defeat; 1-7 v. Burnley (20,000) (April 10th, 1926) &
v. West Bromwich Albion (28,865) (April 18th, 1960)

PLAY OFF MATCHES
1-0 v. Watford [aet. 6-7 on penalties] (29,100) (May 20th, 1999)
0-4 v. Barnsley (26,492) (May 13th, 2000)
1-0 v. Preston North End (29,072) (May 13th, 2001)
1-1 v. Millwall (28,282) (April 28th, 2002)

No. of Matches Played by Birmingham City; 1,849
(League Programme; 1,845, Play Off Matches; 4)
Information Kindly Supplied by; Tony Matthews

Birmingham FC moved here from *Muntz Street* in 1906 and changed the club name to *Birmingham City FC* in 1946. The first ever Football League hat-trick by a substitute was scored here by Geoff Vowden in the *Birmingham City* v. *Huddersfield Town* match (5-1) on September 7th, 1968. The club was also involved in a Football League Play Off Match at the neutral venue of the **Millennium Stadium**.

AT THE END OF SEASON 2004/5, A TOTAL OF **92** TEAMS HAD TAKEN PART IN **1,850** LEAGUE FIXTURES AT THIS VENUE

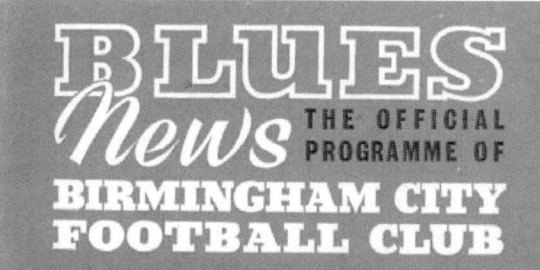

ST JAMES' PARK
HOME GROUND OF EXETER CITY

MAP EXTRACT; DEVON 80.6 [1932]
SITE LOCATION; SX92739345

Originally known as St James' Field, it was in use for rugby when *Exeter United FC* moved in in 1894 and, following their 1904 merging with *St Sidewell's FC* to form *Exeter City FC*, a stand was opened on the west side in 1908. The facilities also included banking on the east side but the site was so restricted that the pitch length was below the statutory FA minimum limit of 100 yards. In 1911 this was overcome when additional land was acquired, allowing the pitch to be lengthened, an embankment to be constructed at the north end and a narrow strip of standing accommodation to be installed at the south

Following their admission to the Football League in 1921, the ground was purchased for £5,000, a cover erected on the east side and a new main stand (replacing the original which burned down in 1925) built on the west side. The record attendance of 20,984 was set at the FA Cup 6th Round replay v. *Sunderland* (2-4) on March 4th, 1931, and the subsequent extension of the cover on the east side proved to be the last alteration to the ground before the 1980s.

In 1985 the east side was refurbished with the installation of a new cover and concrete terracing but this was all demolished in 2000 and replaced with a 2,200 seat stand whilst a new cover and terracing were installed at the north end giving a capacity at the end of the 2001/2 season of 9,036 with 3,865 seats. The pitch size was 113 x 71 yards.

PLAYING RECORD OF EXETER CITY
LEAGUE PROGRAMME

First Match; 3-0 v. Brentford (6,000) (August 28th, 1920)
Last Match; 1-0 v. Southend United (9,036) (May 3rd, 2003)
Highest Gate; 19,884 v. Plymouth Argyle (3-2) (February 3rd, 1951)
Lowest Gate; 1,515 v. Darlington (4-1) (April 30th, 1988)
Highest Home Win; 8-1 v. Coventry City (6,000) (December 4th, 1926) & v. Aldershot (2,000) (May 4th, 1935)
Highest Home Defeat; 1-7 v. Leyton Orient (8,874) (November 6th, 1954) & v. Brentford (2,759) (April 23rd, 1983)
No. of Matches Played by Exeter City; 1,701
(Including one expunged match v. Accrington Stanley on October 21st, 1961)

The club was a founder member of the Football League Division 3 in 1920 and was relegated to the Football Conference in 2003.

A TOTAL OF **94** TEAMS TOOK PART IN **1,701** LEAGUE FIXTURES AT THIS VENUE

The main stand, on the west side of the ground. This view clearly shows the difference in width of the structure, the northern end tapering to accommodate the proximity of the adjacent railway cutting.
Photograph by Paul Claydon. Courtesy of Groundtastic Magazine

ST JAMES' PARK

HOME GROUND OF NEWCASTLE UNITED

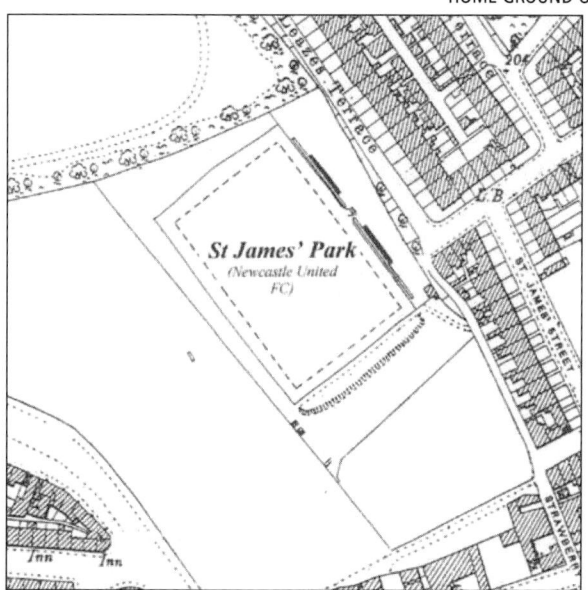

MAP EXTRACT; TYNESIDE 2 [1898]
SITE LOCATION; **NZ24326462**

PLAYING RECORD OF NEWCASTLE UNITED
LEAGUE PROGRAMME

First Match; 6-0 v. Woolwich Arsenal (2,000) (September 30th, 1893)
Highest Gate; 68,386 v. Chelsea (1-0) (September 3rd, 1930)
Lowest Gate; 1,000 v. Walsall Town Swifts (2-0) (March 10th, 1894)
Highest Home Win; 13-0 v. Newport County (52,137)
(October 5th, 1946)*
Highest Home Defeat; 1-9 v. Sunderland (56,000)
(December 5th, 1908)

TEST MATCHES
2-1 v. Stoke (17,000) (April 20th, 1898)
4-0 v. Blackburn Rovers (13,324) (April 30th, 1898)

PLAY OFF MATCHES
0-2 v. Sunderland (32,199) (May 16th, 1990)

No. of Matches Played by Newcastle United; 2,031
(League Programme; 2,028, Test Matches; 2, Play Off Matches; 1)
The club was elected into the Football League Division 2 in 1893
*This score is the record Football League home victory

PLAYING RECORD OF SUNDERLAND
LEAGUE PROGRAMME

Match Played; 2-1 v. Middlesbrough (25,000) (April 18th, 1903)
No. of Matches Played by Sunderland; 1
This match was played here following an attack on *The Wednesday* players at *Roker Park* in 1903.

AT THE END OF SEASON 2004/5, A TOTAL OF **87** TEAMS HAD TAKEN PART IN **2,032** LEAGUE FIXTURES AT THIS VENUE

Located at the south end of Town Moor, the field was first used by *Newcastle Rangers FC* in 1880 and subsequently by *West End FC* and *East End FC* who changed their name to *Newcastle United* in 1892. The club tried to remove a stand from their old ground at *Chillingham Road* and re-erect it at *St James' Park* but this was vetoed by the landlords (the Corporation and the Freemen) so the original facilities remained very basic with some shallow banking at each end and duckboards for standing spectators. The home team changed at the adjacent Lord Hill Inn but visiting teams (no doubt after having made a long and tiring journey) were obliged to find their own changing accommodation and transport to the ground!

Following election to the Football League in 1893 and promotion in 1898, additional land on the west side was leased enabling the pitch to be moved and additional terracing installed on the north and east sides and a main stand on the west side giving a nominal capacity of 30,000. The final alteration prior to WWI was carried out in 1905 when a new 4,680 seat stand and paddock opened on the west side and the only inter-war improvement was the installation of a cover at the north end in 1930.

This lack of change over a long period was not due to shortage of ambition by the club but to the refusal of the landlords to countenance any alterations and it was not until 1972 that a 3,400 seat stand was finally constructed on the east side followed by the removal of the roof over the north end in 1978 and construction of a new 6,607 seat stand on the west side in 1987.

From 1993 *St James' Park* was substantially rebuilt with the construction of new all-seat stands at each end and in each corner and, in 1999/2000, the installation of additional tiers on the west and north sides and in the north west corner giving the ground a distinctive lop-sided look. The all-seat capacity at the start of the 2004/5 season was 52,193 and the pitch size 110 x 73 yards.

The 1905-vintage main stand at **St James' Park** which survived until it was replaced with a 6,607 seat structure in 1985.
Photograph Courtesy of Groundtastic Magazine

ST JOHN'S LANE
HOME GROUND OF BRISTOL CITY

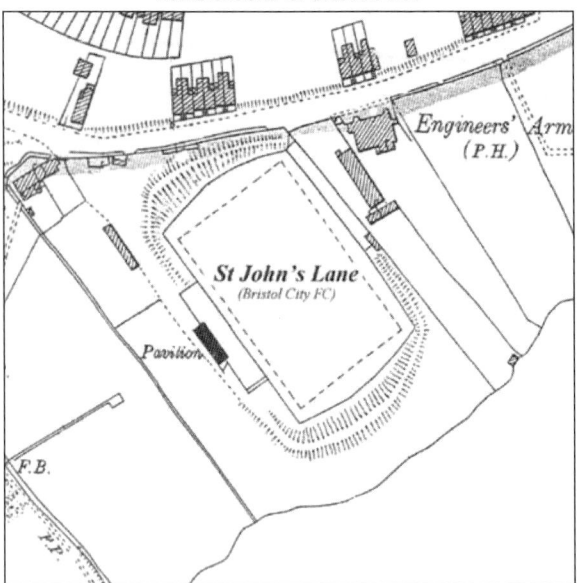

MAP EXTRACT; GLOUCESTERSHIRE 75.8 [1904]
SITE LOCATION; ST58717085

Located in the Bedminster district of the city, *Bristol South End FC* moved in in 1894. Being overlooked by a hill one of the first priorities was to erect screening to prevent a free view of the matches and this was done by employing a system of tall posts and pulleys to raise and lower large sheets of canvas as and when required. The facilities included a 500 seat stand on the west side of the pitch and embankments, which were subsequently raised, at each end of the pitch.

The record attendance of 17,909 was set at the FA Cup 1st Round tie v. *Sheffield United* (1-3) on February 6th, 1904. The club, having merged with *Bedminster FC* in 1901 and now called *Bristol City FC*, moved to **Ashton Gate**, the former home ground of *Bedminster*, in 1904. *St John's Lane*, albeit somewhat altered, was still used as a sports ground until 2003 when it was redeveloped as a housing estate.

PLAYING RECORD OF BRISTOL CITY
LEAGUE PROGRAMME

First Match; 3-0 v. Stockport County (7,000) (September 14th, 1901)
Last Match; 2-1 v. Burslem Port Vale (4,000) (April 23rd, 1904)
Highest Gate & Highest Home Defeat; 14,000 v Woolwich Arsenal (0-4) (September 26th, 1903)
Lowest Gate; 1,700 v. Stockport County (6-0) (February 13th, 1904)
Highest Home Win; 7-1 v. Stockport County (3,000) (January 24th, 1903)

No. of Matches Played by Bristol City; 51

The club was elected into the Football League Division 2 in 1901 but by 1904 it was apparent that the ground was too small and the club moved to **Ashton Gate**.

A TOTAL OF 23 TEAMS TOOK PART IN 51 LEAGUE FIXTURES AT THIS VENUE

ST MARY'S STADIUM
HOME GROUND OF SOUTHAMPTON

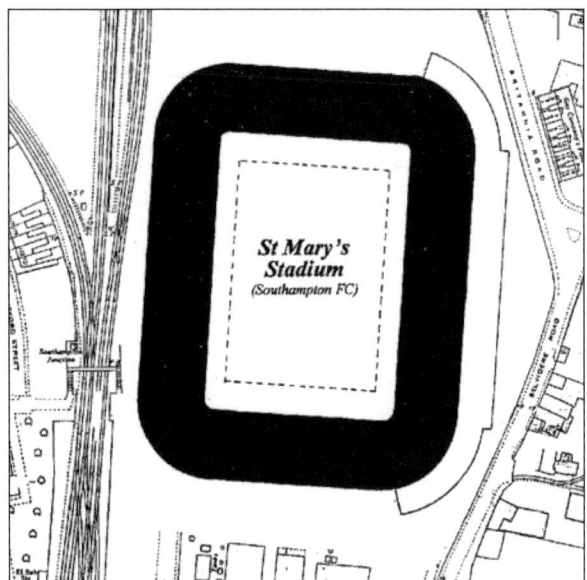

MAP EXTRACT; GROUND AS IN 2001 DRAWN FROM AERIAL PHOTOGRAPHS AND SUPERIMPOSED ON SU4210/11 [1951]
SITE LOCATION; SU42901200

Constructed in 2001 on the site of a former gas works the 32,251 seat capacity *Friends Provident St Mary's Stadium* (to give it its full title in 2002) is composed of a continuous single tier of seats with a continuous cantilevered roof. An attendance of 32,095 was recorded at the *England* v. *Macedonia* European Championship Group Match (2-2) on October 16th, 2002. The pitch size was 112 x 74 yards.

PLAYING RECORD OF SOUTHAMPTON
LEAGUE PROGRAMME

First Match; 0-2 v. Chelsea (31,107) (August 25th, 2001)
Highest Gate; 32,151 v. Arsenal (0-1) (December 29th, 2003)
Lowest Gate; 25,714 v. Charlton Athletic (0-0) (September 21st, 2002)
Highest Home Win; 4-2 v. Fulham (26,188) (October 27th, 2002). 3-0 v. Portsmouth (31,697) (December 21st, 2003)
Highest Home Defeat; 1-3 v. Aston Villa (26,794) (September 24th, 2001), v. Manchester United (31,858) (January 13th, 2002) & v. Chelsea (April 2nd, 2005)

No. of Matches Played by Southampton; 76

The club moved here from **The Dell** in 2001 and the first goal at the stadium was scored by Jimmy Hasselbaink of *Chelsea FC* on August 25th, 2001.

AT THE END OF SEASON 2004/5, A TOTAL OF 27 TEAMS HAD TAKEN PART IN 76 LEAGUE FIXTURES AT THIS VENUE

SANDHEYS PARK
HOME GROUND OF NEW BRIGHTON

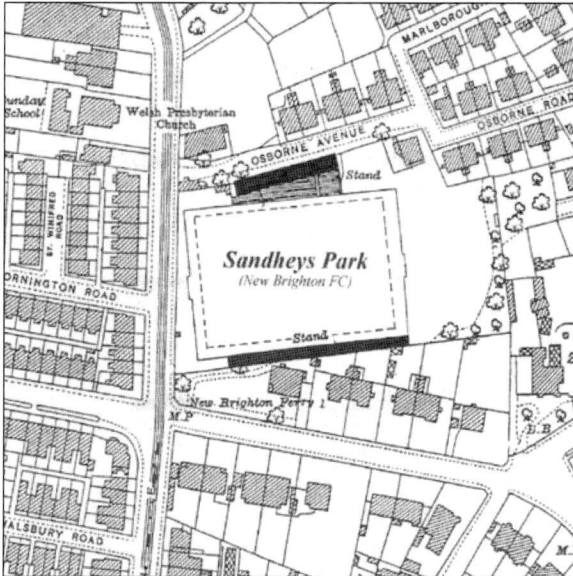

MAP EXTRACT; CHESHIRE 7.11 [1926]
SITE LOCATION; SJ30959299

The 3.5 acre site, located on the east side of Seabank Road, south of the town centre and previously in use as a school's football pitch, was purchased by *New Brighton FC* in 1921. Upon the opening of the ground in the same year, a 1,000 seat covered stand with a concrete terraced paddock had been provided on the north side and one of the two buildings which already existed on the site, Sandheys Lodge, was in use as dressing rooms. Later improvements, giving a nominal capacity of 20,000, included the installation of a covered standing enclosure on the south side.

The ground was badly damaged by bombing during 1942 and, following the end of WWII, the site requisitioned for temporary housing by Wallasey Corporation. *New Brighton* moved to **The Tower Athletic Ground** for the commencement of post war football and *Sandheys Park* was later redeveloped with permanent housing.

PLAYING RECORD OF NEW BRIGHTON
LEAGUE PROGRAMME

First Match; 0-0 v. Chesterfield (3,000) (August 29th, 1923)
Last Match; 4-2 v. Doncaster Rovers (3,441) (September 2nd, 1939)
Highest Gate; 15,173 v. Tranmere Rovers (1-0) (December 26th, 1924)
Lowest Gate; 1,081 v. Gateshead (4-1) (February 19th, 1938)
Highest Home Win; 7-1 v. Darlington (3,032) (April 8th, 1933)
Highest Home Defeat; 0-5 v. Lincoln City (6,000) (January 1st, 1936), 3-6 v. Doncaster Rovers (2,925) (March 11th, 1939)
No. of Matches Played by New Brighton; 335

The club was elected into the Football League Division 3 [N] in 1923 and moved to the **Tower Athletic Ground** in 1946.

A TOTAL OF 36 TEAMS TOOK PART IN 335 LEAGUE FIXTURES AT THIS VENUE

SEALAND ROAD
HOME GROUND OF CHESTER CITY

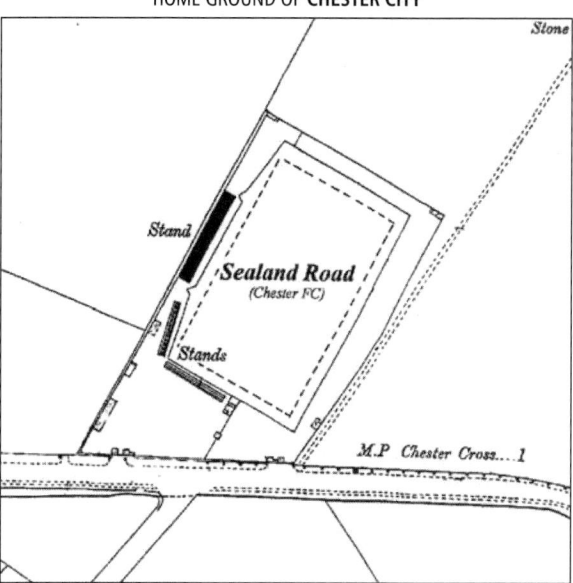

MAP EXTRACT; CHESHIRE 38.11 [1911]
SITE LOCATION; SJ39236697

Sited on the west side of the city, *Chester FC* moved to *Sealand Road* from *Whipcord Lane* in 1906 and by 1911 covered and open stands had been constructed on the west side and a short open stand installed at the south end.

A full length cover was subsequently built at the south end and, just before the club joined the Football League in 1931, a new main stand opened on the west side. At this time the ground was re-named as *The Stadium* and, apart from the installation of a roof on the east side which was extended in 1968, no further alterations took place until a new main stand was constructed in 1979.

The record attendance of 20,500 was set at the FA Cup 3rd Round replay v. *Chelsea* (2-3) on January 16th, 1952 and the club left to groundshare with *Macclesfield Town FC* at *Moss Rose* in 1990. The main stand roof was sold to *Port Vale* in 1992 for installation at *Vale Park* and the site subsequently used for a retail park.

PLAYING RECORD OF CHESTER CITY
LEAGUE PROGRAMME

First Match; 4-0 v. Wigan Borough (12,770) (August 29th, 1931) [Result Expunged].
3-1 v. Halifax Town (6,824) (September 12th, 1931)
Last Match; 2-0 v. Rotherham United (3,827) (April 28th, 1990)
Highest Gate; 16,835 v. Wrexham (0-3) (February 4th, 1933)
Lowest Gate; 880 v. Swindon Town (0-3) (February 8th, 1984)
Highest Home Win; 12-0 v. York City (3,775) (February 1st, 1936)
Highest Home Defeat; 0-5 v. Northampton Town (3,458) (August 15th, 1987)
No. of Matches Played by Chester City; 1,175
(Including expunged matches v. Wigan Borough on August 29th, 1931 and v. Accrington Stanley on December 23rd, 1961)
Information Kindly Supplied by; Charles Sumner

The club was elected into the Football League Division 3 [N] in 1931 as *Chester* and changed their name to *Chester City* in 1983. In 1990 the club was forced to sell the ground to pay off debts and, with no new venue then available, moved to the **Moss Rose** ground of *Macclesfield Town* (at that time a member of the Football Conference).

A TOTAL OF 80 TEAMS TOOK PART IN 1,175 LEAGUE FIXTURES AT THIS VENUE

SEAMER ROAD
HOME GROUND OF SCARBOROUGH

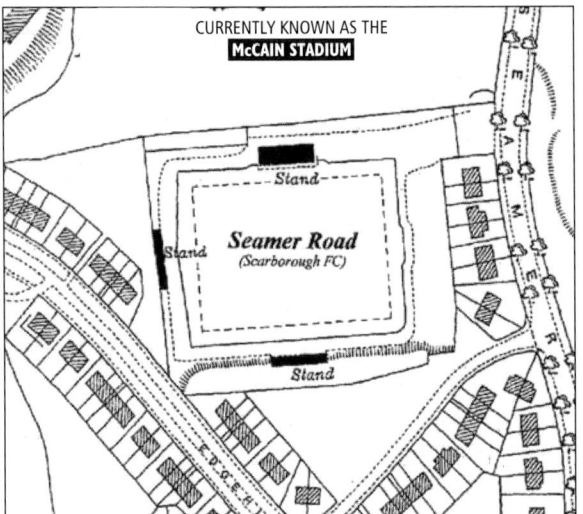

CURRENTLY KNOWN AS THE **McCAIN STADIUM**

MAP EXTRACT; YORKSHIRE 93.4 [**1928**]
SITE LOCATION; **TA03128669**

The ground opened in 1898 and when *Scarborough FC* moved in the pitch was surrounded by a running track and the facilities at *Seamer Road*, as it became known, included a 250 seat stand on the north side. By the 1920s small covered areas had been provided on banking on the south side and at the west end whilst, in 1922, a new 700 seat stand was built on the north side but this lasted only five years before succumbing to a fire.

The record attendance of 11,130 was set at the FA Cup 3rd Round tie v. *Luton Town* (1-1) on January 6th, 1938 and a larger cover was installed on the south side in 1953. The ground was purchased in 1960 and by 1969 the facilities also included terracing around the ground and a cover over part of the west end. The main stand was replaced by an 850 seat cantilever roofed structure in 1979 and in 1995, seven years after the ground was re-named as the *McCain Stadium*, a 1,350 seat cantilever roofed stand was constructed at the east end whilst, in 1996, a seated cantilever roofed stand opened at the west end giving a nominal capacity of 4,980 with 3,500 seats. The venue was still in use in 2005 as the home ground for *Scarborough*.

PLAYING RECORD OF SCARBOROUGH
LEAGUE PROGRAMME

First Match & Highest Gate; 2-2 v. Wolverhampton Wanderers (7,314) (August 15th, 1987)
Last Match; 1-1 v. Peterborough United (4,769) (March 8th, 1999)
Lowest Gate; 625 v. Wrexham (4-2) (December 7th, 1990)
Highest Home Win; 5-2 v. Torquay United (1,986) (September 24th, 1988)
Highest Home Defeat; 1-5 v. Cambridge United (1,650) (February 6th, 1999)

PLAY OFF MATCHES

1-0 v.. Leyton Orient (4,377) (May 24th, 1989)
1-3 v. Torquay United (5,246) (May 10th, 1998)

No. of Matches Played by Scarborough; 271
(League Programme; 269 [Including one expunged match v. Aldershot on September 14th, 1991], Play Off Matches; 2)

In 1986 the club was the first one to be promoted into the Football League Division 4 from the Football Conference and was relegated back into the Football Conference in 1999.

A TOTAL OF **50** TEAMS TOOK PART IN **271** LEAGUE FIXTURES AT THIS VENUE

SEEDHILL
HOME GROUND OF NELSON

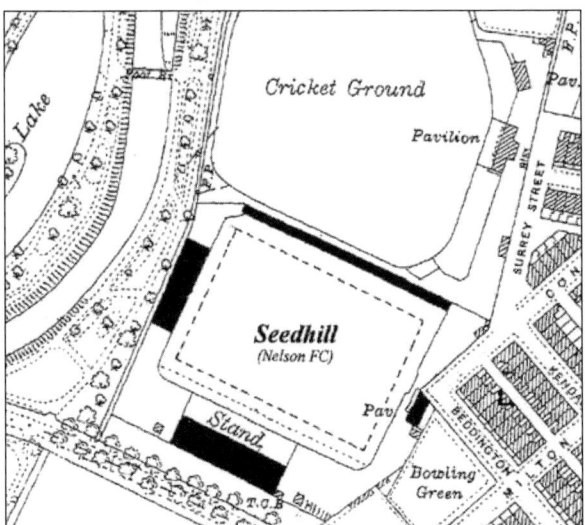

MAP EXTRACT; LANCASHIRE 56.7 [**1932**]
SITE LOCATION; **SD85453820**

Nelson FC moved to *The New Park Ground*, or *The Seedhill Cricket Ground* as it was later known, in 1889, the football pitch being accommodated on part of, and to the south of, the cricket square and some distance from the pavilion. This state of affairs continued until 1905 when part of the recreation ground, on the south side, was taken over. This enabled the pitch to be moved further south and a separate football ground was created utilizing the southern edge of the cricket ground and the northern part of the recreation ground. At the same time a small seated stand was erected on the south side of the pitch.

On their entry into the Football League in 1921 a new covered terrace was installed on the north side of the pitch and further improvements included the removal of the original stand, installation of a new 1,500 seat stand and additional covered accommodation (giving a capacity of 25,000) as well as enlarging the pitch to 110 x 75 yards.

Following their failure to gain re-election in 1931, *Nelson FC* continued to use the venue until moving to *Victoria Park* in 1970. It then hosted stock car racing until the site was acquired for the construction of the M65 in the late 1970s, the northbound carriageway passing over the east end of the pitch with odd bits of perimeter wall at the west end of the ground still extant in 1990.

PLAYING RECORD OF NELSON
LEAGUE PROGRAMME

First Match; 1-2 v. Wigan Borough (9,000) (August 27th, 1921)
Last Match; 1-4 v. Southport (1,323) (April 18th, 1931)
Highest Gate; 15,000 v. Bradford Park Avenue (2-2) (April 10th, 1926)
Lowest Gate; 850 v. Rochdale (1-0) (January 14th, 1930)
Highest Home Win; 7-0 v. Crewe Alexandra (6,000) (April 13th, 1925), v. Tranmere Rovers (4,354) (December 19th, 1925) & v. Wigan Borough (6,000) (December 25th, 1925)
Highest Home Defeat; 0-5 v. Bury (8,500) (February 16th, 1924) & v. Chesterfield (1,827) (April 4th, 1931)

No. of Matches Played by Nelson; 206
Some Information Kindly Supplied by; Brian Tabner

The club was a founder member of the Football League Division 3 [N] in 1921 and failed to gain re-election in 1931.

A TOTAL OF **47** TEAMS TOOK PART IN **206** LEAGUE FIXTURES AT THIS VENUE

SELHURST PARK

HOME GROUND OF **CRYSTAL PALACE**
TEMPORARY HOME GROUND FOR **CHARLTON ATHLETIC, WIMBLEDON & MILLWALL**

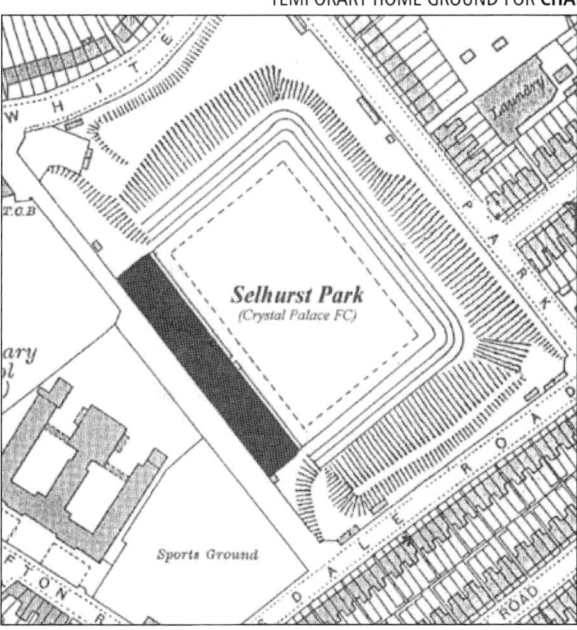

MAP EXTRACT; SURREY 14.2 [**1940**]
SITE LOCATION; **TQ33296832**

Crystal Palace FC bought the site, a former brick field, in 1922 for £2,570 and moved to *Selhurst Park* from *The Nest* in 1924. The facilities, which included a main stand on the west side and terracing and embankments around the pitch, remained virtually unaltered until a 5,000 seat stand was opened on the east side in 1969 and seats installed in the main stand paddock in 1979.

In 1981 land at the rear of the north end was sold for housing and a supermarket resulting in the construction of a new truncated terrace (subsequently roofed and installed with 2,500 seats in 1993) whilst the paddock on the east side was provided with 5,080 seats in 1990 and a double deck 8,147 seat stand with a curved cantilevered roof was opened at the south end in 1995. The all-seat capacity at the start of season 2004/5 was 26,400 and the pitch size 110 x 74 yards.

PLAYING RECORD OF CRYSTAL PALACE
LEAGUE PROGRAMME

First Match; 0-1 v. The Wednesday (25,000) (August 30th, 1924)
Highest Gate; 51,482 v. Burnley (2-0) (May 11th, 1979)*
Lowest Gate; 3,744 v. Carlisle United (1-1) (February 1st, 1986)
Highest Home Win; 9-0 v. Barrow (9,566) (October 10th, 1959)
Highest Home Defeat; 1-6 v. Millwall (12,896) (May 7th, 1927), v. Nottingham Forest (17,179) (January 27th, 1951) & v. Liverpool (18,084) (August 20th, 1994)

PLAY OFF MATCHES

2-0 v. Swindon Town (23,677) (May 24th, 1989)
3-0 v. Blackburn Rovers (30,000) (June 3rd, 1989)
1-0 v. Charlton Athletic (22,880) (May 15th, 1996)
3-1 v. Wolverhampton Wanderers (21,053) (May 10th, 1997)
3-2 v. Sunderland (25,287) (May 14th, 2004)

No. of Matches Played by Crystal Palace; 1,607
(League Programme; 1,602, Play Off Matches; 5)
Information Kindly Supplied by; Rev Nigel Sands

The club moved here from *The Nest* in 1924 and it was also involved in Football League Play Off Matches at the neutral venues of *Wembley Stadium* and the *Millennium Stadium*.

*NB. This highest gate is also shown as 51,801 in some records.

PLAYING RECORD OF WIMBLEDON
LEAGUE PROGRAMME

First Match; 2-0 v. West Ham United (10,081) (August 24th, 1991)
Last Match; 2-4 v. Wigan Athletic (1,054) (September 13th, 2003)
Highest Gate; 30,115 v. Manchester United (1-2) (May 9th, 1993)
Lowest Gate; 849 v. Rotherham United (2-1) (October 29th, 2002)*
Highest Home Win; 5-0 v. Watford (14,021) (December 4th, 1999) & v. Queens Park Rangers (9,446) (February 24th, 2001)
Highest Home Defeat; 2-6 v. Tottenham Hotspur (25,972) (May 2nd, 1998)

No. of Matches Played by Wimbledon; 252

The club moved here from *Plough Lane* in 1991 to groundshare with *Crystal Palace*. In 2002 the club obtained permission from the FA to relocate to Milton Keynes where it was planned to build a new stadium at *West Denbigh*. In the interim it arranged to play fixtures at the *National Hockey Stadium* but this was turned down by the Football League as unsuitable and planning permission was sought to instal temporary stands at the *Milton Keynes Bowl*. Problems were subsequently encountered and the club was finally given permission to use the *National Hockey Stadium* as a temporary venue in January 2003. It was proposed to move in at the start of the 2003/4 season but was delayed until September 27th following the club's slide into receivership.

*NB. Previous lowest attendances include 3,039 v. *Everton* on January 26th, 1993, the record lowest gate for a Premiership fixture and 3,121 v. *Sheffield Wednesday* on October 2nd, 1991, a post WWII record lowest gate for a Division 1 *[Highest Division]* fixture. Following the club's decision to relocate to Milton Keynes most of the fans boycotted the club and set up an alternative *AFC Wimbledon* resulting in poor attendances averaging only 2,786, and culminated in this gate which is the lowest for a Division 1 *[New]* match.

The main stand at **Selhurst Park**, on the west side of the ground
Photograph by Jon Weaver. Courtesy of Groundtastic Magazine

Cont ....

SELHURST PARK [CONT ...]

.... Cont

PLAYING RECORD OF CHARLTON ATHLETIC
LEAGUE PROGRAMME

First Match; 2-1 v. Sunderland (5,552) (October 5th, 1985)
Last Match; 1-1 v. West Ham United (16,086) (May 4th, 1991)
Highest Gate; 28,095 v. Liverpool (0-2) (January 23rd, 1988)
Lowest Gate; 3,059 v. Carlisle United (3-0) (November 30th, 1985)
Highest Home Win; 5-0 v. Manchester City (7,697)
(December 28th, 1986)
Highest Home Defeat; 0-4 v. Liverpool (13,982) (April 11th, 1990)

PLAY OFF MATCHES
2-1 v. Ipswich Town (11,234) (May 17th, 1987)
1-0 v. Leeds United (16,680) (May 23rd, 1987)

No. of Matches Played by Charlton Athletic; 119

Having been forced out of *The Valley*, *Charlton Athletic* moved here to groundshare. In 1991 the opportunity arose to return to their home ground but by the start of the 1991/92 season it was not ready and the club moved again, this time to groundshare at *Upton Park*. During this period the club was also involved in a Football League Play Off Match at the neutral venue of *St Andrew's*.

PLAYING RECORD OF MILLWALL
LEAGUE PROGRAMME

Match Played; 2-1 v. Newcastle United (33,362)
(December 13th, 1947)

No. of Matches Played by Millwall; 1

This match was played here after *The Den* was closed due to crowd trouble

NEUTRAL PLAY OFF MATCHES
Division 2/3 Play Off Final; Swindon Town 2, Gillingham 0 (18,491)
(May 29th, 1987)

No. of Matches Played; 1

AT THE END OF SEASON 2004/5, A TOTAL OF **101** TEAMS HAD TAKEN PART IN **1,980** LEAGUE FIXTURES AT THIS VENUE

A Programme from the early 1950s.   *Courtesy of Peter Miles*

THE SHAY
HOME GROUND OF HALIFAX TOWN

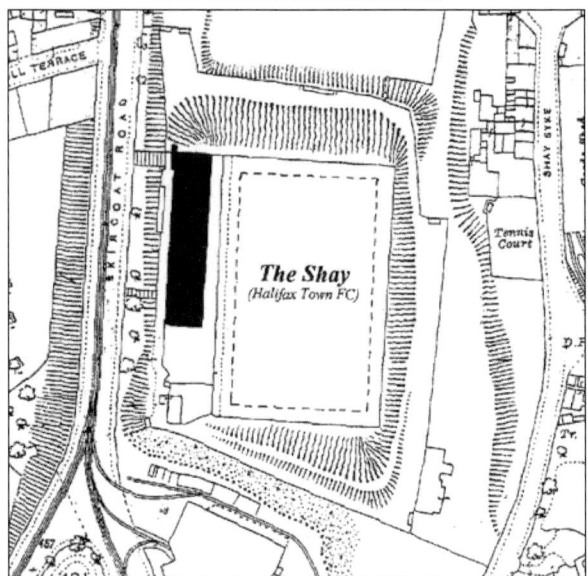

MAP EXTRACT; YORKSHIRE 231.9 [**1933**]
SITE LOCATION; SE09402441

On joining the Football League in 1921, *Halifax Town FC* moved to *The Shay* from *Exley* and purchased the main stand from *Manchester City FC's* **Hyde Road** ground for re-erection on the west side. The only other facilities at this time were embankments around the other three sides and at some stage a cover was installed on the east side. Following the end of WWII, speedway took place between 1948 and 1951 (and later between 1965 and 1985) and the record attendance of 36,885 was set at the FA Cup 5th Round tie v. *Tottenham Hotspur* (0-3) on February 14th, 1953. By 1965 only minor improvements had been made with the installation of seats under the cover on the east side and construction of a small amount of terracing on the west side and at the north end.

In conjunction with their joint tenants, *Halifax Blue Sox RLFC* and the site owners, Calderdale MBC, the 1990s saw the commencement of the rebuilding of *The Shay* with the removal of the speedway track and construction of covered terraces at both ends and installation of seats on the west side. Construction of a new main stand commenced on the east side in 2000 but a lack of finance led to it still not being completed by the end of the 2001/2 season when the capacity was 9,927 with 1,830 seats and the pitch size was 110 x 76 yards.

PLAYING RECORD OF HALIFAX TOWN
LEAGUE PROGRAMME

First Match; 5-1 v. Darlington (10,143) (August 27th, 1921)
Last Match; 2-4 v. Rushden & Diamonds (2,699) (April 20th, 2002)
Highest Gate; 19,935 v. Bradford City (2-1) (September 10th, 1927)
Lowest Gate; 856 v. Colchester United (1-1) (April 26th, 1976)
Highest Home Wins; 6-0 v. Bradford Park Avenue (8,421) (December 3rd, 1955) & v. Doncaster Rovers (2,350) (November 2nd, 1976)
Highest Home Defeat; 0-8 v. Fulham (5,809)
(September 16th, 1969)

No. of Matches Played by Halifax Town; 1,536
Information Kindly Supplied by; John Meynell

The club was a founder member of the Football League Division 3 [N] in 1921, relegated to the Football Conference in 1993, promoted into Division 3 in 1998 and relegated back into the Conference in 2002.

A TOTAL OF **95** TEAMS TOOK PART IN **1,536** LEAGUE FIXTURES AT THIS VENUE

SINCIL BANK

HOME GROUND OF **LINCOLN CITY**
TEMPORARY HOME GROUND FOR **GAINSBOROUGH TRINITY**

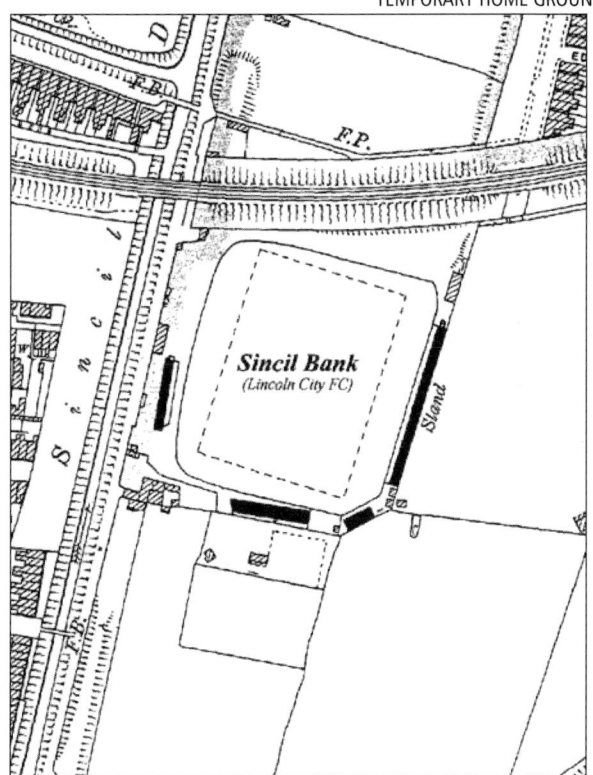

MAP EXTRACT; LINCOLNSHIRE 70.11 [**1907**]
SITE LOCATION; **SK97537002**

PLAYING RECORD OF LINCOLN CITY
LEAGUE PROGRAMME

First Match; 1-1 v. Woolwich Arsenal (1,200) (September 14th, 1895)
Highest Gate; 23,146 v. Grimsby Town (2-3) (March 5th, 1949)
Lowest Gate; 1,186 v. Torquay United (1-1) (March 17th, 1987)
Highest Home Win; 11-1 v. Crewe Alexandra (11,269) (September 29th, 1951)
Highest Home Defeat; 0-6 v. Barnet (3,067) (September 4th, 1991)

PLAY OFF MATCHES

Match Played; 5-2 v. Scunthorpe United (8,902) (May 10th, 2003)
1-2 v. Huddersfield Town (9,202) (May 15th, 2004)
1-0 v. Macclesfield Town (7,032) (May 14th, 2005)

No. of Matches Played by Lincoln City; 2,017
(League Programme; 2,014 [Including expunged matches v. Wigan Borough on September 14th, 1931 and v. Aldershot on November 2nd, 1991], Play Off Matches; 3)

Information Kindly Supplied by; Donald Nannestad

Lincoln City FC failed to gain re-election in 1908, was elected into Division 2 in 1909, failed to gain re-election in 1911, elected into Division 2 in 1912, failed to gain re-election in 1920, and elected as an original member of Division 3 [N] in 1921. It was the first club to be automatically relegated to the Football Conference in 1986 and was promoted back into Division 4 in 1987. The club was also involved in Football League Play Off Matches at the neutral venue of the *Millennium Stadium*.

AT THE END OF SEASON 2004/5, A TOTAL OF **125** TEAMS HAD TAKEN PART IN **2,019** LEAGUE FIXTURES AT THIS VENUE

Lincoln City FC moved here from **John O'Gaunt's** in 1895 and by 1900 the facilities included a main stand on the east side and covers on the west side and at the south end. The venue also hosted cricket, athletics and cycle races and in 1902 a cinder track was installed and some stands re-sited one of which, the main stand, blew down in 1908. Later improvements included the construction of a new main stand, the replacement of the south stand in 1929, following a fire, and the installation of a cover at the north end. In 1956 the latter was extended around the north east corner and the record attendance of 23,196 was subsequently set at the Football League Cup Round 4th Round Replay v. *Derby County* (0-3) on November 15th, 1967.

Sincil Bank saw major changes in the 1980s and 90s with the construction of new all seat stands on each side of the ground and at the start of the 2004/5 season it had an all-seat capacity of 11,100. The pitch size was 110 x 73 yards.

PLAYING RECORD OF GAINSBOROUGH TRINITY
LEAGUE PROGRAMME

Matches Played; 5-1 v. Grimsby Town (4,000) (April 22nd, 1899)
2-0 v. Walsall (1,000) (April 30th, 1900)

No. of Matches Played by Gainsborough Trinity; 2
Information Kindly Supplied by; Gary Parle

These matches were played here when *Northolme* was required for cricket.

The main stand on the east side of the ground in the 1990s. Built just after WWI, the original structure was condemned as a fire hazard in 1985 and summarily demolished the following year. This basically designed 1,600 seat stand was subsequently constructed on the site
Photograph by Jon Weaver. Courtesy of Groundtastic Magazine

SIXFIELDS STADIUM
HOME GROUND OF **NORTHAMPTON TOWN**

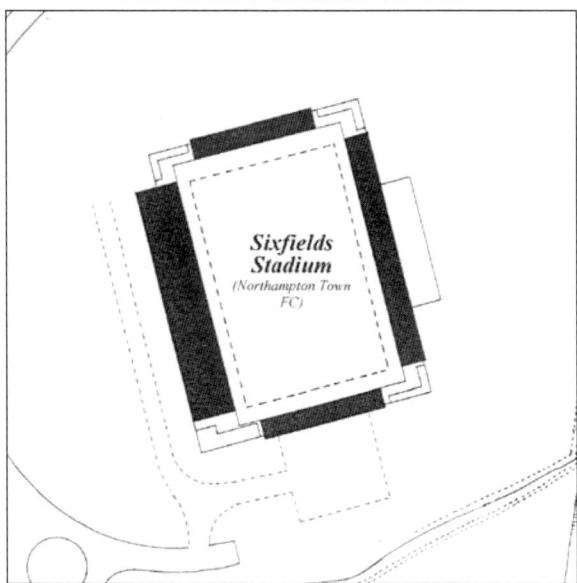

MAP EXTRACT; GROUND AS IN **1999** DRAWN FROM AERIAL PHOTOGRAPHS & SUPERIMPOSED ON NORTHAMPTONSHIRE 44.12 [**1937**]
SITE LOCATION; **SP72926020**

Constructed on the site of a tip, *Northampton Town FC* moved to *Sixfields Stadium* from **The County Ground** in 1994. It is a typical modern purpose-built stadium consisting of four all-seater cantilever roofed stands and had a capacity of 7,653 at the start of the 2004/5 season. The pitch size was 116 x 72 yards.

PLAYING RECORD OF NORTHAMPTON TOWN
LEAGUE PROGRAMME

First Match; 1-1 v. Barnet (7,461) (October 15th, 1994)
Highest Gate; 7,557 v. Manchester City (2-2)
(September 26th, 1998)
Lowest Gate; 3,090 v. Rochdale (2-1) (February 19th, 1996)
Highest Home Win; 5-1 v. Chester City (4,434) (January 18th, 1997)
& v. Rochdale (5,342) (October 23rd, 2004)
Highest Home Defeat; 0-5 v. Bury (4,208) (March 4th, 1995)
& v. Wycombe Wanderers (4,679) (January 4th, 2003)

PLAY OFF MATCHES

3-2 v. Cardiff City (7,302) (May 14th, 1997)
3-0 v. Bristol Rovers (7,501) (May 13th, 1998)
0-2 v. Mansfield Town (6,960) (May 16th, 2004)
0-0 v. Southend United (6,601) (May 15th, 2005)

No. of Matches Played by Northampton Town; 250
(League Programme; 246, Play Off Matches; 4)
Information Kindly Supplied by; Frank Grande

The club moved here from **The County Ground** in 1994 and was also involved in Football League Play Off Matches at the neutral venue of **Wembley Stadium**.

AT THE END OF SEASON 2004/5, A TOTAL OF **66** TEAMS HAD TAKEN PART IN **250** LEAGUE FIXTURES AT THIS VENUE

SOMERTON PARK
HOME GROUND OF **NEWPORT COUNTY**

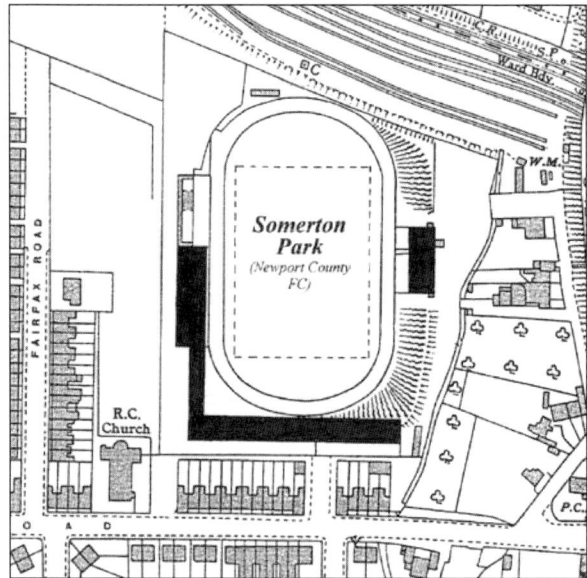

MAP EXTRACT; MONMOUTHSHIRE 34.1 [**1937**]
SITE LOCATION; **ST33228768**

Newport County FC first used *Somerton Park* on their formation in 1912. Details of the facilities at this time are not known but, by the time that it was taken over by the Cardiff Arms Park Greyhound Racing Company in 1931 a main stand had been built on the west side and cover erected over the south end.

Major alterations subsequently took place with the installation of a greyhound racing track, a new main stand on the east side and alterations to the banking. At the same time, the original stand was converted into a glass fronted social club overlooking the pitch.

In the 1960s the racing track was utilized for speedway and within twenty years the ground had been sold to the council, bought by the club and re-sold to the council before *Newport County FC* were relegated to the Football Conference in 1988. The club subsequently folded and although it re-formed some years later the ground was demolished in 1993 and the site used for housing.

PLAYING RECORD OF NEWPORT COUNTY
LEAGUE PROGRAMME

First Match; 0-1 v. Reading (12,000) (August 28th, 1920)
Last Match; 0-1 v. Rochdale (2,560) (May 7th, 1988)
Highest Gate; 24,268 v. Cardiff City (1-1) (October 16th, 1937)
Lowest Gate; 988 v. Peterborough United (0-4) (April 9th, 1988)
Highest Home Win; 10-0 v. Merthyr Town (1,997) (April 10th, 1930)
Highest Home Defeat; 2-7 v. West Bromwich Albion (20,521)
(September 28th, 1946)

No. of Matches Played by Newport County; 1,338

The club was a founder member of the Football League Division 3 in 1920, failed to gain re-election in 1931 and was elected to Division 3 [S] in 1932. *Newport County* was relegated to the Football Conference in 1988.

A TOTAL OF **91** TEAMS TOOK PART IN **1,338** LEAGUE FIXTURES AT THIS VENUE

SOUTHEND STADIUM
HOME GROUND OF SOUTHEND UNITED

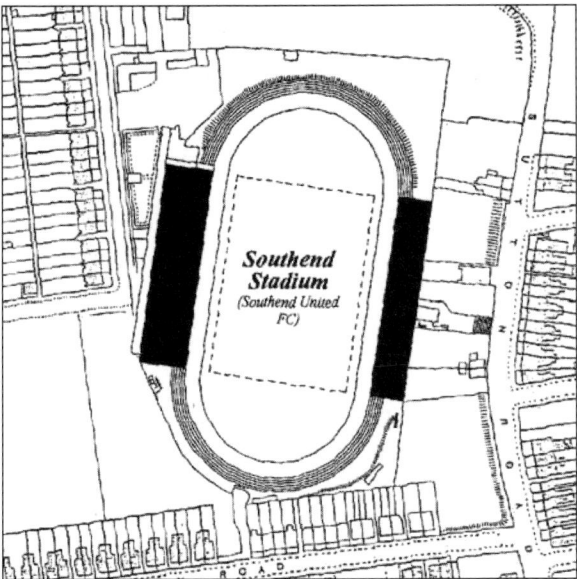

MAP EXTRACT; ESSEX N91.2 [1922]
SITE LOCATION; **TQ88478641**

Located to the north of the town, *Southend Stadium* was built on the site of a former brickworks and opened on May 19th, 1933. It was developed as a dual purpose venue with an oval track for greyhound racing disposed around a 112 x 72 yards sized football pitch. On opening, the facilities included a 2,000 seat covered stand on the west side with a large concreted terrace on the east side and narrow terracing at each end. Within a year a cover had been erected over the east side and the all-time record attendance of 22,862 was set at the FA Cup 3rd Round replay with *Tottenham Hotspur* (1-2) on January 15th, 1936. *Southend United FC* moved to **Roots Hall** in 1955 and the venue continued in use as a Greyhound Stadium until it was demolished in 1985. The site is now occupied by a Currys Superstore on Greyhound Way.

PLAYING RECORD OF SOUTHEND UNITED
LEAGUE PROGRAMME

First Match; 2-1 v. Aldershot (7,456) (August 29th, 1934)
Last Match; 3-2 v. Brentford (8,000) (April 30th, 1955)
Highest Gate; 21,000 v. Colchester United (4-2)
(October 14th, 1950)
Lowest Gate; 2,270 v. Notts County (1-0) (April 25th, 1939)
Highest Home Win; 9-2 v. Newport County (7,346)
(September 5th, 1936)
Highest Home Defeat; 0-4 v. Bristol City (7,500) (April 29th, 1953)
No. of Matches Played by Southend United; 305
Information Kindly Supplied by; Dave Goody

The club moved here from **The Kursaal** in 1934 and moved to **Roots Hall** in 1955

A TOTAL OF **35** TEAMS TOOK PART IN **305** LEAGUE FIXTURES AT THIS VENUE

SPOTLAND
HOME GROUND OF ROCHDALE

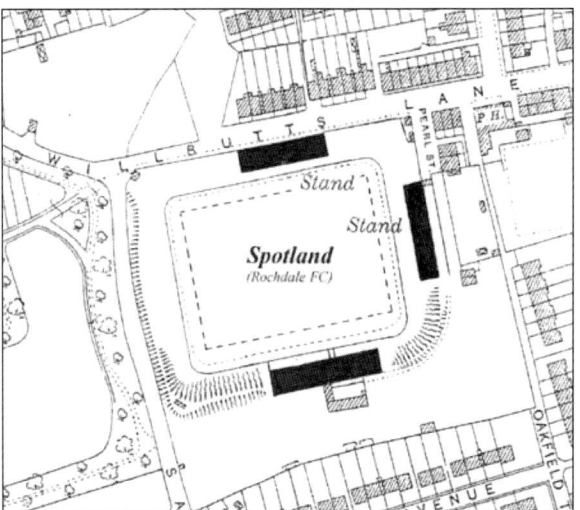

MAP EXTRACT; LANCASHIRE 88.4 [1930]
SITE LOCATION; **SD88191382**

When *Rochdale AFC* was formed in 1907 they commenced playing here and bought the freehold for £1,700 in 1914. The pitch was sited on the north side of the cricket square and the facilities included a stand on the north side. Alterations had been made by the time that the club joined the Football League in 1921, the cricketing area had been dispensed with and a main stand, which suffered damage on three subsequent occasions, built on the south side. The installation of covers on the north side and at the east end in the 1920s was the last improvement made in pre-WWII years. Some ground levelling took place in 1948 with the spoil forming additional banking in the south east corner. The record attendance of 24,231 was subsequently set at the FA Cup 2nd Round tie v. *Notts County* (1-2) on December 10th, 1949. Apart from the installation of a cover at the west end in 1961 and construction of terracing at the east end and some re-roofing around the ground in the 1980s the ground remained unchanged until a new 1,852 seat main stand was constructed on the south side in 1992.

Further improvements subsequently carried out included the construction of all seater stands on the north side and at the east end giving a capacity at the start of the 2004/5 season of 10,262 with 8,342 seats. The pitch size was 114 x 76 yards.

PLAYING RECORD OF ROCHDALE
LEAGUE PROGRAMME

First Match; 6-3 v. Accrington Stanley (7,000) (August 27th, 1921)
Highest Gate; 20,945 v. Bradford City (1-3) (April 30th, 1929)
Lowest Gate; 588 v. Cambridge United (0-2) (February 5th, 1974)
Highest Home Win; 8-1 v. Chesterfield (5,768)
(December 18th, 1926)
Highest Home Defeat; 1-7 v. Shrewsbury Town (2,647) (February 24th, 2001)
PLAY OFF MATCHES
1-2 v. Rushden & Diamonds (8,547) (April 30th, 2002)
No. of Matches Played by Rochdale; 1,737
(League Programme; 1,736 [Including one expunged match v. Accrington Stanley on October 7th, 1961], Play Off Matches; 1)
Information Kindly Supplied by; Tom Nicholl

The club was a founder member of the Football League Division 3 [N] in 1921.

AT THE END OF SEASON 2004/5, A TOTAL OF **97** TEAMS HAD TAKEN PART IN **1,737** LEAGUE FIXTURES AT THIS VENUE

SPRINGFIELD PARK
HOME GROUND OF WIGAN BOROUGH & WIGAN ATHLETIC

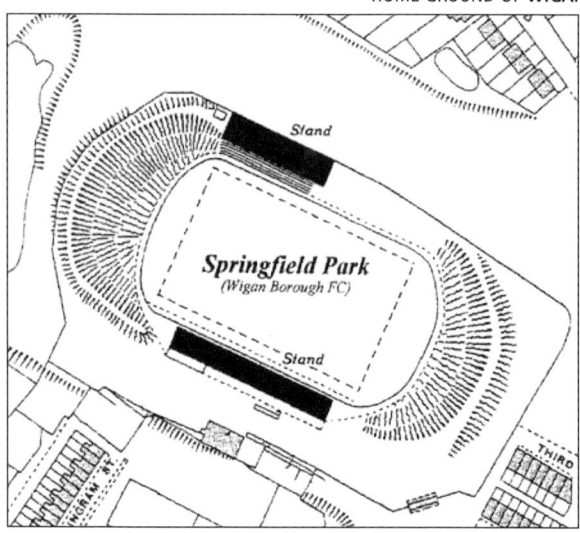

MAP EXTRACT; LANCASHIRE 93.3 [1938]
SITE LOCATION; **SD57000669**

The ground was opened by the Wigan Trotting & Athletic Grounds Co. on August 18th, 1897 with an athletics meeting. The football pitch was surrounded by trotting and cycle tracks and standing accommodation was provided by grass and cinder embankments at each end. A variety of football clubs (and *Wigan RLFC* for one season) used the venue before *Wigan Borough FC* moved in on their formation in 1920.

In the 1920s a 2,000 seat main stand was built on the south side and covers installed on the north side and at the west end before the record attendance of 30,611 was set at the *Wigan Borough* v. *Sheffield Wednesday* FA Cup 3rd Round tie (1-3) on January 12th, 1929. *Wigan Borough FC* folded in 1931 to be replaced in the following year by *Wigan Athletic FC* who bought the ground for £2,850.

No further alterations took place until a new main stand was built in 1954 (following a fire in 1953) and a cover erected at the west end in 1972 but removed four years later as it restricted the number of spectators who could occupy the terracing. The club moved to the *JJB Stadium* in 1999 and the ground was demolished and the site utilized for housing.

PLAYING RECORD OF WIGAN BOROUGH
LEAGUE PROGRAMME

First Match; 1-4 v. Nelson (9,000) (September 3rd, 1921)
Last Match; 3-2 v. Carlisle United (2,000) (October 17th, 1931)
Highest Gate; 15,500 v. Stockport County (4-0) (April 1st, 1929)
Lowest Gate; 600 v. Gateshead (3-3) (January 31st, 1931)
Highest Home Win; 9-1 v. Lincoln City (-) (March 3rd, 1923)
Highest Home Defeat; 1-5 v. Chesterfield (6,500) (December 6th, 1930)

No. of Matches Played by Wigan Borough; 211
(Including 5 expunged games in the 1931/2 season)

The club was a founder member of the Football League Division 3 [N] in 1921 and resigned from the Football League on October 26th, 1931

PLAYING RECORD OF WIGAN ATHLETIC
LEAGUE PROGRAMME

First Match; 0-3 v. Grimsby Town (9,227) (August 23rd, 1978)
Last Match; 1-1 v. Manchester City (6,762) (May 15th, 1999) (Play Off Match)
Highest Gate; 10,045 v. Bolton Wanderers (0-1) (December 26th, 1983)
Lowest Gate; 1,231 v. Chesterfield (2-3) (August 30th, 1994)
Highest Home Win; 7-1 v. Scarborough (3,094) (March 11th, 1997)
Highest Home Defeat; 2-6 v. Mansfield Town (2,084) (October 7th, 1995). 0-5 v. Bristol Rovers (3,288) (February 26th, 1983)

PLAY OFF MATCHES
2-3 v. Swindon Town (6,718) (May 14th, 1987)
1-1 v. Manchester City (6,762) ((May 15th, 1999)

No. of Matches Played by Wigan Athletic; 481
(League Programme; 479, Play Off Matches; 2)

The club was elected into the Football League Division 4 in 1978 and moved to the *JJB Stadium* in 1999.

A TOTAL OF **88** TEAMS TOOK PART IN **692** LEAGUE FIXTURES AT THIS VENUE

The rear of the main stand at *Springfield Park*, already looking derelict with hardly a window pane intact just two weeks after the final game.

Photograph by Tony Cunningham. Courtesy of Groundtastic Magazine

STADIUM OF LIGHT
HOME GROUND OF SUNDERLAND

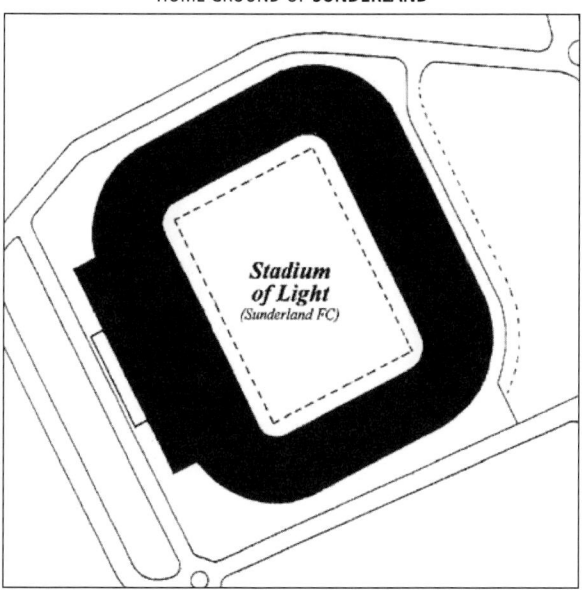

MAP EXTRACT; GROUND AS IN **1999** DRAWN FROM AERIAL PHOTOGRAPHS AND SUPERIMPOSED ON DURHAM 8.10 & 8.14 [**1895**]
SITE LOCATION; **NZ39325796**

Constructed on the site of Monkwearmouth Colliery the stadium opened in 1997 and originally consisted of three two-tier stands with a continuous cantilevered roof on the north, east and south sides linking to a three-tier cantilever roofed main stand on the west. In 2001 the north stand and north west corner were extended to three tiers giving an all-seat capacity of 48,353 at the start of the 2004/5 season. The pitch size was 115 x 75 yards.

PLAYING RECORD OF SUNDERLAND
LEAGUE PROGRAMME
First Match; 3-1 v. Manchester City (38,894) (August 15th, 1997)
Highest Gate; 48,335 v. Liverpool (0-1) (April 13th, 2002)
Lowest Gate; 22,107 v. Wigan Athletic (1-1) (December 2nd, 2003)
Highest Home Win; 7-0 v. Oxford United (34,567)
(September 19th, 1998)
Highest Home Defeat; 0-4 v. Arsenal (40,180) (May 11th, 2003)
PLAY OFF MATCHES
2-0 v. Sheffield United (40,092) (May 13th, 1998)
2-1 v. Crystal Palace [aet. 4-5 on penalties] (34,536) (May 17th, 2004)
No. of Matches Played by Sunderland; 170
(League Programme; 168, Play Off Matches; 2)

The club moved here from **Roker Park** in 1997 and was also involved in a Football League Play Off Match at the neutral venue of **Wembley Stadium**.

AT THE END OF SEASON 2004/5, A TOTAL OF **58** TEAMS HAD TAKEN PART IN **170** LEAGUE FIXTURES AT THIS VENUE

STAMFORD BRIDGE
HOME GROUND OF CHELSEA

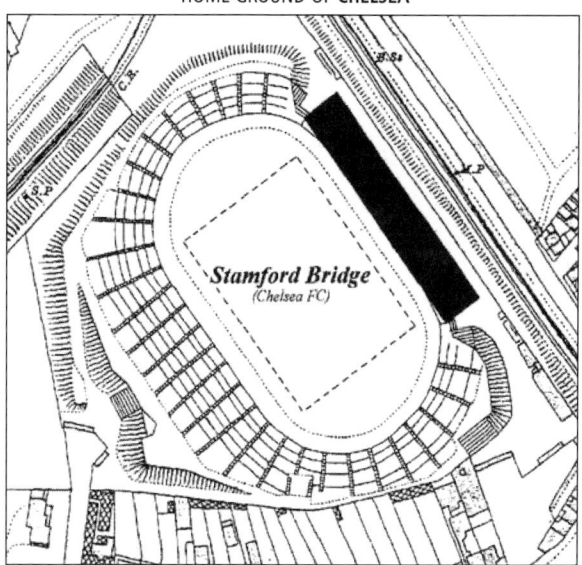

MAP EXTRACT; LONDON [**1934**]
SITE LOCATION; **TQ25727740**

Opened on April 28th, 1877 as the running track for the *London Athletic Club* the ground was sold in 1904 to Mr Gus Mears, who constructed a sports stadium to host cycling and athletics as well as football. A 5,000 seat stand was installed on the east side and a large oval shaped embankment built around the remainder of the ground. *Chelsea FC* was formed to occupy the ground and following election to the Football League the banking was expanded to raise the nominal capacity to 80,000. Although it was used for a variety of sports the only alterations in this period were the installation of a cover at the south end and a bizarre 2,500 seat stand on stilts in the north east corner.

In 1945 a gate of 74,496 was recorded for the friendly fixture against *Moscow Dynamo* but this was undoubtedly the largest attendance at the ground as 100,000 were estimated to have gained access, legally or otherwise. The first post war improvement was the construction of a seated stand on the west side in 1965. The stand on the east side was demolished in 1972 with a new three-tier all seat stand opening on the site in 1974 and, in the 1990s, new all seat stands, with suspended roofs were built at each end, corner stands installed and in 2001 the stand on the west side was rebuilt as a two-tier structure giving an all-seat capacity of 42,449 at the start of the 2004/5 season. The pitch size was 113 x 74 yards.

PLAYING RECORD OF CHELSEA
LEAGUE PROGRAMME
First Match; 5-1 v. Hull City (6,000) (September 11th, 1905)
Highest Gate; 82,905 v. Arsenal (1-1) (October 12th, 1935)
Lowest Gate; 3,000 v. Lincoln City (4-2) (February 17th, 1906)
Highest Home Win; 9-2 v. Glossop (12,000) (September 1st, 1906)
Highest Home Defeat; 0-6 v. Notts County (15,000)
(February 9th, 1924)
PLAY OFF MATCHES
4-1 v. Blackburn Rovers (22,757) (May 18th, 1988)
0-1 v. Middlesbrough (40,550) (May 28th, 1988)
No. of Matches Played by Chelsea; 1,830
(League Programme; 1,828, Play off Matches; 2)

The club was elected into the Football League Division 2 in 1905.

AT THE END OF SEASON 2004/5, A TOTAL OF **81** TEAMS HAD TAKEN PART IN **1,830** LEAGUE FIXTURES AT THIS VENUE

STONEBRIDGE ROAD
TEMPORARY HOME GROUND FOR GILLINGHAM

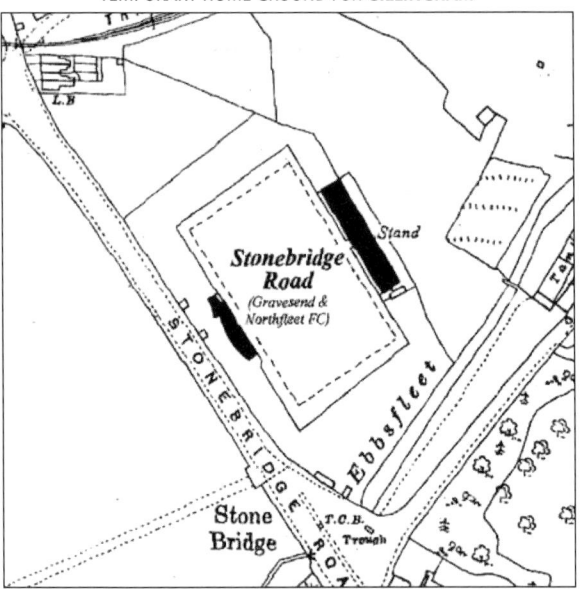

MAP EXTRACT; KENT 10.1 [**1933**]
SITE LOCATION; **TQ61457485**

The ground was first used in 1905 by *Northfleet United FC* and by 1908 the facilities included a small stand on the west side. A main stand was built on the east side in 1914 and by the time that *Gillingham FC* played here, a cover had been erected at the south end and the west side had been terraced and a new cover installed.

The venue was still in use in 2005 as the home ground for *Gravesend & Northfleet FC*.

PLAYING RECORD OF GILLINGHAM
LEAGUE PROGRAMME
Match Played; 0-3 v. Wrexham (3,934) (March 25th, 1961)
No. of Matches Played by Gillingham; 1
Information Kindly Supplied by; Roger Triggs

This match was played here when **Priestfield Stadium** was closed for one match following crowd trouble at the *Oldham Athletic* game (2-3) earlier in the season on January 14th, 1961.

A TOTAL OF **2** TEAMS TOOK PART IN **1** LEAGUE FIXTURE AT THIS VENUE

The main stand, on the east side of the pitch, at **Stonebridge Road**
Photograph by Paul Claydon. Courtesy of Groundtastic Magazine

STONEY LANE
HOME GROUND OF WEST BROMWICH ALBION

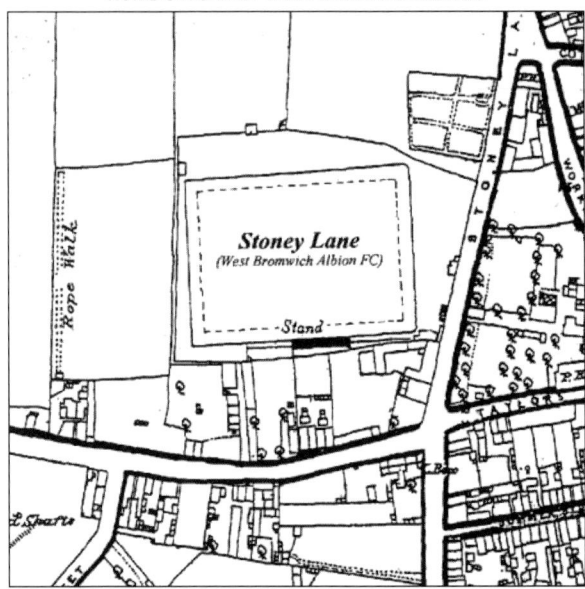

MAP EXTRACT; STAFFORDSHIRE 68.10 [**1904**]
SITE LOCATION; **SP00769176**

Located on the west side of Stoney Lane, north of the town centre, *West Bromwich Albion FC* moved here from the nearby *Four Acres* in 1885. The facilities included dressing rooms and a 600 seat covered wooden grandstand (subsequently removed to *The Hawthorns*) flanked by two open wooden stands on the south side. Standing areas, including banking on the north side were laid with ash footings.

No further improvements were made before the club moved to *The Hawthorns* in 1900 and although it was used as a training ground for a while, the site remained unused until the 1980s when it succumbed to housing.

PLAYING RECORD OF WEST BROMWICH ALBION
LEAGUE PROGRAMME
First Match; 4-3 v. Burnley (2,100) (September 29th, 1888)
Last Match; 8-0 v. Nottingham Forest (5,187) (April 16th, 1900)
Highest Gate; 19,700 v. Preston North End (4-5) (January 5th, 1895)
Lowest Gate; 405 v. Derby County (3-4) (November 29th, 1890)
Highest Home Win; 12-0 v. Darwen (1,109) (April 4th, 1892)
Highest Home Defeat; 0-5 v. Preston North End (5,150) (December 26th, 1888) & 3-6 v. Aston Villa (14,000) (October 21st, 1893)
TEST MATCHES
6-1 v. Manchester City (8,000) (April 20th, 1896)
2-0 v. Liverpool (15,000) (April 27th, 1896)
No. of Matches Played by West Bromwich Albion; 172
(League Programme; 170, Test Matches; 2)
Information Kindly Supplied by; Tony Matthews

The club was a founder member of the Football League in 1888 and moved to *The Hawthorns* in 1900.

A TOTAL OF **24** TEAMS TOOK PART IN **172** LEAGUE FIXTURES AT THIS VENUE

THORNEYHOLME ROAD
HOME GROUND OF ACCRINGTON

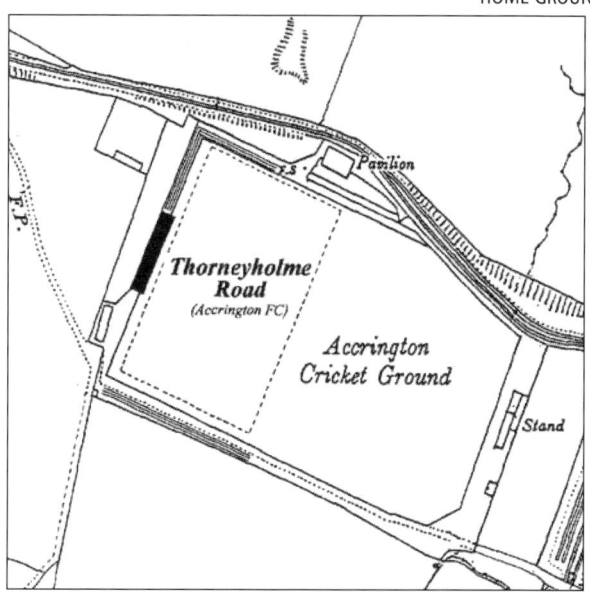

MAP EXTRACT; LANCASHIRE 63.11 [c**1900**]
SITE LOCATION; **SD76502986**

PLAYING RECORD OF ACCRINGTON
LEAGUE PROGRAMME
First Match; 4-4 v. Wolverhampton Wanderers (4,000)
(October 6th, 1888)
Last Match; 0-1 v. Aston Villa (2,000) (April 15th, 1893)
Highest Gate; 10,000 v. Blackburn Rovers (1-1) (January 2nd, 1893)
Lowest Gate; 900 v. Notts County (2-0) (November 21st, 1891)
Highest Home Win; 6-1 v. Derby County (3,000)
(November 16th, 1889)
Highest Home Defeat; 1-8 v. Notts County (2,000)
(October 12th, 1889)
No. of Matches Played by Accrington; 61
Information Kindly Supplied by; Tony Matthews

The club was a founder member of the Football League in 1888 and finished bottom in 1893, the first year of promotion and relegation between Divisions 1 and 2. *Accrington FC* lost the Play Off match 0-1 v. *Sheffield United* at the **Castle Ground**, Nottingham on April 22nd, 1893 and rather than drop down resigned from the League.

A TOTAL OF **17** TEAMS TOOK PART IN **61** LEAGUE FIXTURES AT THIS VENUE

Located to the north of the town centre, the ground was first used by *Accrington CC* when they moved here in 1878. *Accrington FC* was formed in the same year and from the outset shared the venue with the cricket club, the football pitch being sited at the west end of the ground. In addition to the cricket pavilion the facilities for spectators included uncovered seating at both ends of the pitch and some uncovered seating and a covered seated stand on the west side. Following their resignation from the Football League in 1893, *Accrington FC* continued to play here until their demise three years later. The ground was still in use for cricket in 2005 although the general area of the football pitch, earlier covered with tennis courts, had been partially landscaped.

The ground in 2002, looking west across the cricket ground towards seating and a prefabricated building on the site of the football pitch. The pavilion is a later replacement of the one employed during *Accrington's* Football League career.

Photograph Courtesy of Garth Dawson

TOWER ATHLETIC GROUND

HOME GROUND OF **NEW BRIGHTON TOWER & NEW BRIGHTON**

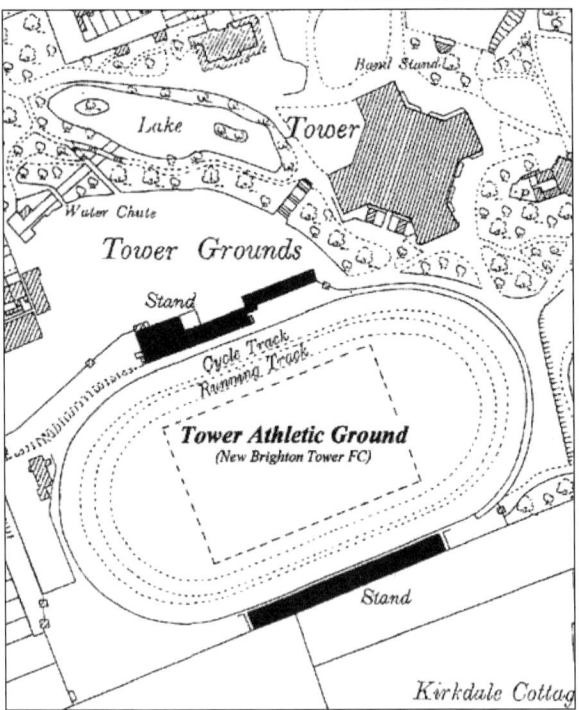

MAP EXTRACT; CHESHIRE 7.3 & 7.7 [1899]
SITE LOCATION; SJ31169374

PLAYING RECORD OF NEW BRIGHTON TOWER
LEAGUE PROGRAMME

First Match; 3-2 v. Gainsborough Trinity (2,000)
(September 10th, 1898)
Last Match; 1-0 v. Woolwich Arsenal (2,000) (April 27th, 1901)
Highest Gate; 10,000 v. Manchester City (0-1) (January 14th, 1899)
Lowest Gate; 1,000 v. Barnsley (6-2) (April 25th, 1900)
Highest Home Win; 7-0 v. Darwen (3,000) (December 22nd, 1898)
Highest Home Defeat; 1-4 v. Newton Heath (8,000)
(February 24th, 1900)

No. of Matches Played by New Brighton Tower; 51

The club was elected into the Football League Division 2 in 1898 and resigned in 1901.

PLAYING RECORD OF NEW BRIGHTON
LEAGUE PROGRAMME

First Match; 0-0 v. Bradford City (7,500) (September 4th, 1946)
Last Match; 1-0 v. Chester (2,421) (May 2nd, 1951)
Highest Gate; 14,291 v. Tranmere Rovers (2-1)
(September 21st, 1946)
Lowest Gate; 1,922 v. Barrow (1-2) (March 17th, 1951)
Highest Home Win; 4-0 v. Accrington Stanley (6,450) (October 12th, 1946), v. Oldham Athletic (6,898) (December 26th, 1946) & v. Crewe Alexandra (4,581) (March 22nd, 1947)
Highest Home Defeat; 0-6 v. Bradford City (3,590)
(February 3rd, 1951)

No. of Matches Played by New Brighton; 107

The club moved here from *Sandheys Park* in 1946 but failed to gain re-election in 1951

A TOTAL OF **48** TEAMS TOOK PART IN **158** LEAGUE FIXTURES AT THIS VENUE

A drawing of the proposed alterations to the *Tower Athletic Ground*, published prior to *New Brighton* moving in in 1946. The caption reads; "A sketch by Councillor K Kinna, architect, giving an impression of how New Brighton Football Club's ground at the Tower will look if the Board's plan to buy the ground and erect stands and covered accommodation are successful. The concrete cycle track will broken up [sic] at the Molyneux Drive end and "stepped" to give a "Spion Kop" effect. Spectators will be brought within twelve or fifteen feet of the playing pitch, creating more atmosphere than exists at present"

Courtesy of Dave Twydell

The New Brighton Tower Company constructed this large ground, under the shadow of the tower, as part of an entertainment complex built during the latter part of the 19thC. The pitch was surrounded by oval running and cycle tracks and the facilties included covered seated stands on both sides of the stadium and dressing rooms on the north side with standing areas at each end.

New Brighton Tower FC was formed by the Tower Company and played games here between 1897 and 1901 when they were wound up and resigned from the Football League. In subsequent years, although *Harrowby AFC* used the football pitch and a variety of motor sports and cycling events took place around the perimeter, the ground fell into decay. (This only mirrored the demise of the 567ft high tower which, for military reasons, was closed to visitors during WWI and consequently suffered from lack of maintenance. This lead to its dismantling in the 1920s leaving the derelict monolithic base to overlook the remains of the stadium).

To compound the problem, the advent of WWII saw the arena used as a depot and by the time that *New Brighton FC* moved here from *Sandheys Park* in 1946 the pitch was a morass of mud and bricks, the stands had fallen apart and weeds had taken over the terraces. The new club immediately made improvements, the pitch was re-turfed, a new stand installed on the south side, the west terrace partially renewed and later alterations included a couple of covered enclosures.

New Brighton failed to gain re-election to the Football League in 1951 and was forced to vacate the ground in 1954. A year later, along with *Wallasey Borough FC*, they were granted joint tenancy of the *Tower Athletic Ground* and the record attendance of 16,000 was set at the FA Cup 3rd Round tie v. *Torquay United* (2-1) on January 5th, 1957. The club bought the ground outright in 1958 and sold it to Wallasey Corporation for housing in 1977.

THE TOWN GROUND

HOME GROUND OF **NOTTINGHAM FOREST**
TEMPORARY HOME GROUND FOR **NOTTS COUNTY**

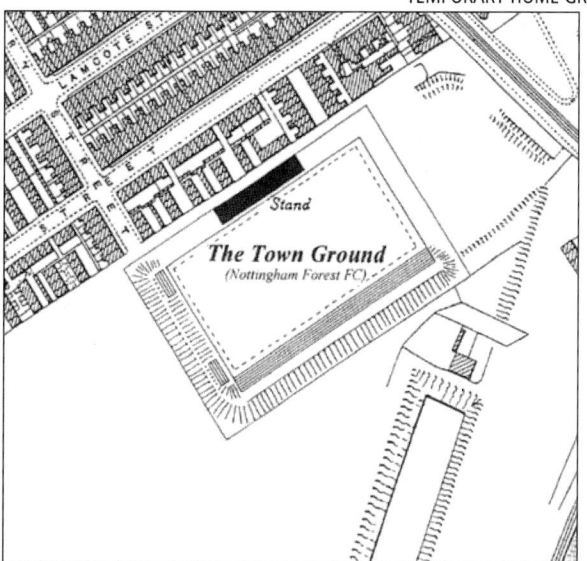

MAP EXTRACT; GROUND AS IN c1892 DRAWN FROM SKETCHES AND SUPERIMPOSED ON NOTTINGHAMSHIRE 42.6 [1901]
SITE LOCATION; SK57873823

PLAYING RECORD OF NOTTINGHAM FOREST
LEAGUE PROGRAMME

First Match; 3-4 v. Stoke (9,000) (September 10th, 1892)
Last Match; 3-1 v. Bury (6,000) (April 9th, 1898)
Highest Gate; 15,000 v. Notts County (1-1) (September 4th, 1897)
Lowest Gate; 1,500 v. Sheffield United (1-1) (November 18th, 1893)
& v. Darwen (4-1) (March 15th, 1894)
Highest Home Win; 7-1 v. Wolverhampton Wanderers (12,000)
(September 2nd, 1893)
Highest Home Defeat; 0-5 v. Sunderland (10,000)
(December 3rd, 1892)
No. of Matches Played by Nottingham Forest; 90

The club was elected into the Football League Division 1 in 1892 and moved to *The City Ground* in 1898.

PLAYING RECORD OF NOTTS COUNTY
LEAGUE PROGRAMME

Matches Played; 2-3 v. Liverpool (7,000) (September 7th, 1895)
3-1 v. Loughborough (1,000) (September 5th, 1896)
3-1 v. Newcastle United (6,000) (September 19th, 1896)

TEST MATCHES PLAYED

1-1 v. Burnley (15,000) (April 24th, 1897)
No. of Matches Played by Notts County; 4
(League Programme; 3, Test Matches; 1)
Information Kindly Supplied by; Peter Wynne-Thomas

These League matches were played here when *Nottinghamshire CCC* was using **Trent Bridge**.

A TOTAL OF 23 TEAMS TOOK PART IN 94 LEAGUE FIXTURES AT THIS VENUE

Although no map exists, some idea of the ground may be gleaned from contemporary accounts. On the north side was a 150ft long covered stand with press facilities and seats for 1,000 spectators with a standing area in front. Opposite to this was a 360ft banked area stretching the length of the pitch, with six tiers and a flat area on the top of the bank for additional viewing, whilst there was another section of banking at the west end with a few rows of open seating. The map, above, is based on this information with the location of the site being approximately fixed from photographs taken during the 1890s, including the one below.

The ground has a place in the history of Association Football, hosting the first match to utilize cross bars and goal nets during a representative game between the *North* and the *South* in 1891. *Nottingham Forest* vacated in 1898 and the whole area was subsequently used for housing.

This view, taken in c1895, of a match in progress at **The Town Ground** looks north across the ground and shows the covered stand and some of the housing in the adjacent Bathley Street.

TRENT BRIDGE
HOME GROUND OF NOTTS COUNTY

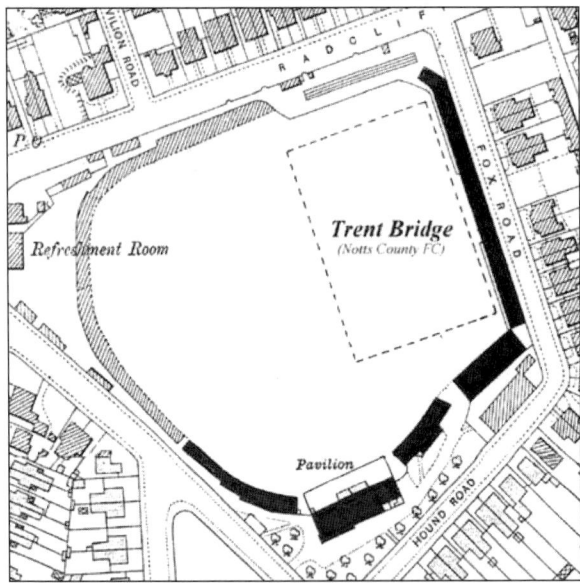

MAP EXTRACT; NOTTINGHAMSHIRE 42.6 & 42.10 [1901]
SITE LOCATION: **SK58473811**

Nottingham Forest FC first used *Nottinghamshire CCC's Trent Bridge* Cricket Ground in 1880 but only remained here for two years, moving to *Park Side* in Lenton, whilst *Notts County FC* took up residence at *Trent Bridge* in 1883.

The pitch was sited on the east side of the cricket square and the facilities, which were steadily improved, included covered terracing and seats on the east side, a stand and shallow banking at the south end and the provision of wooden duckboards and a temporary removable seated stand on the west side.

Notts County FC was not offered a renewal of the lease at *Trent Bridge* and moved out to *Meadow Lane* in 1910, taking the south stand with them and leaving the cricket club as sole occupants.

PLAYING RECORD OF NOTTS COUNTY
LEAGUE PROGRAMME

First Match; 3-3 v. Blackburn Rovers (4,000) (October 6th, 1888)
Last Match; 2-3 v. Aston Villa (13,000) (April 16th, 1910)
Highest Gate; 25,000 v. Everton (0-0) (December 26th, 1908)
Lowest Gate; 300 v. Crewe Alexandra (9-1) (February 17th, 1894)
Highest Home Win; 10-0 v. Burslem Port Vale (1,500) (February 26th, 1895)
Highest Home Defeat; 0-7 v. Preston North End (7,000) (November 3rd, 1888)

TEST MATCHES
1-0 v. Sunderland (7,000) (April 17th, 1897)

No. of Matches Played by Notts County; 313
(League Programme; 312, Test Matches; 1)
Information Kindly Supplied by; Peter Wynne-Thomas and Peter Orme

The club was a founder member of the Football League in 1888. The overlapping of the football and cricket seasons necessitated the playing of some home matches at **The Castle Ground, Town Ground** and **City Ground** and *Notts County* was also involved in Test Matches at the neutral venues of **Hyde Road**, the **Olive Grove** and **Filbert Street**. In 1910 the club moved to **Meadow Lane**.

A TOTAL OF **44** TEAMS TOOK PART IN **313** LEAGUE FIXTURES AT THIS VENUE

TURF MOOR
HOME GROUND OF BURNLEY

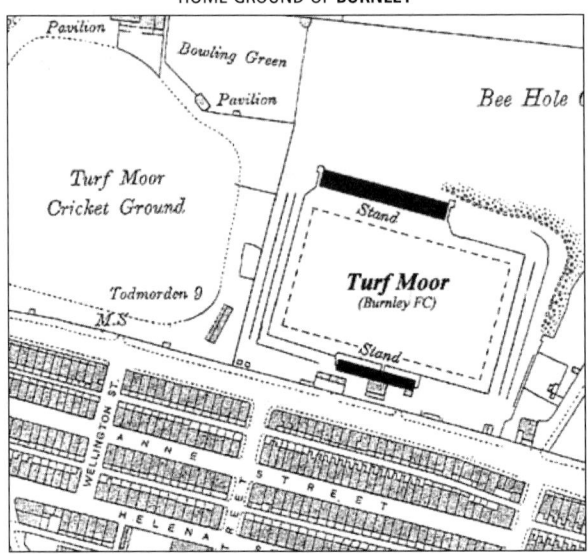

MAP EXTRACT; LANCASHIRE 64.3 [1912]
SITE LOCATION: **SD84933253**

Burnley FC moved to *Turf Moor* from *Calder Vale* in 1883 and within two years the facilities included an 800 seat stand on the south side, an embankment on the north and standing areas with duckboards at each end. Prior to WWI covers had been erected on the north side and at the west end whilst the record attendance of 54,775 was set at the FA Cup 3rd Round tie v. *Huddersfield Town* (1-0) on February 23rd, 1924.

Alterations prior to WWII included the commencement of terracing of the north side and this was duly completed and roofed by 1954. In 1969 a 4,500 seat stand was opened at the west end, a new all seat main stand constructed on the south side in 1974 and, in the 1990s, cantilever roofed two tier all-seated stands built on the north side and at the east end. By the start of the 2004/5 season the all-seat ground capacity was 22,546 and the pitch size 112 x 70 yards.

PLAYING RECORD OF BURNLEY
LEAGUE PROGRAMME

First Match; 4-1 v. Bolton Wanderers (3,000) (October 6th, 1888)
Highest Gate; 52,869 v. Blackpool (1-0) (October 11th, 1947)
Lowest Gate; 1,000 v. Bradford City (3-2) (November 28th, 1903)
Highest Home Win; 9-0 v. Darwen (5,000) (January 9th, 1892)
Highest Home Defeat; 1-7 v. Blackburn Rovers (3,000) (November 3rd, 1888)

TEST MATCHES
2-0 v. Newton Heath (10,000) (April 19th, 1897)
0-1 v. Notts County (11,000) (April 26th, 1897)
2-0 v. Blackburn Rovers (12,000) (April 23rd, 1898)
0-2 v. Stoke (9,000) (April 26th, 1898)

PLAY OFF MATCHES
1-0 v. Torquay United (13,620) (May 22nd, 1991)
0-0 v. Plymouth Argyle (18,794) (May 15th, 1994)

No. of Matches Played by Burnley; 2,158
(League Programme; 2,152 [Including one expunged match v. Aldershot on August 24th, 1991], Test Matches; 4, Play Off Matches; 2)

The club was a founder member of the Football League in 1888 and was also involved in a Football League Play Off Match at the neutral venue of **Wembley Stadium**.

AT THE END OF SEASON 2004/5, A TOTAL OF **107** TEAMS HAD TAKEN PART IN **2,158** LEAGUE FIXTURES AT THIS VENUE

TWERTON PARK
TEMPORARY HOME GROUND FOR BRISTOL ROVERS

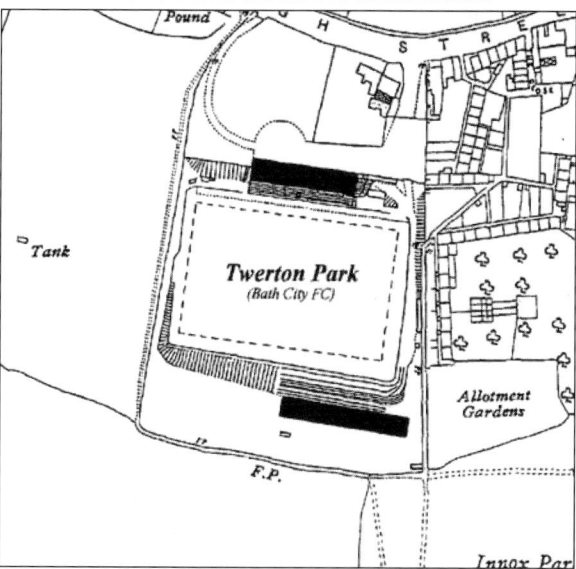

MAP EXTRACT; GROUND AS IN **1952** DRAWN FROM PLANS AND SUPERIMPOSED ON SOMERSET 13.8 [c1900]
SITE LOCATION; **ST72606450**

Bristol Rovers FC moved from *Eastville Stadium* in 1986 to ground-share with *Bath City FC* at *Twerton Park*. Occupying a constrained site, the facilities included a main stand on the north side (burned down in 1990 and subsequently rebuilt) narrow open terraces at each end and a partially covered narrow terrace on the south side.

The record attendance of 18,020 was set at the FA Cup 3rd Round tie between *Bath City* and *Brighton & Hove Albion* (0-1) on January 9th, 1960. *Bristol Rovers* moved to *The Memorial Ground* in Bristol in 1996 whilst *Bath City* continues to use it as their home ground.

PLAYING RECORD OF BRISTOL ROVERS
LEAGUE PROGRAMME

First Match; 1-0 v. Bolton Wanderers (4,092) (August 30th, 1986)
Last Match; 1-0 v. Peterborough United (6,232) (August 17th, 1996)
Highest Gate; 9,813 v. Bristol City (3-0) (May 2nd, 1990)
Lowest Gate; 2,282 v. Walsall (0-3) (March 11th, 1987)
Highest Home Win; 6-1 v. Wigan Athletic (5,169) (March 3rd, 1990)
Highest Home Defeat; 1-5 v. Barnsley (5,019)
(November 3rd, 1992)

PLAY OFF MATCHES
1-0 v. Fulham (9,029) (May 21st, 1989)
1-1 v. Port Vale (9,042) (May 31st, 1989)
0-0 v. Crewe Alexandra (8,538) (May 14th, 1995)

No. of Matches Played by Bristol Rovers; 233
(League Programme; 230, Play Off Matches; 3)

Information Kindly Supplied by; Keith Brookland & Colin Timbrell
Bristol Rovers FC was forced to move out permanently from *Eastville Stadium* and stayed here until they moved back to Bristol to ground-share with *Bristol RUFC* at *The Memorial Ground*. Due to potential crowd problems the fixture v. *Swindon Town* on April 11th, 1987 was moved to *Ashton Gate*. The new ground was not ready for the start of the 1996/7 season and the first home game of that season was played here v. *Peterborough United*. During this period the club was also involved in a Football League Play Off Match at the neutral venue of *Wembley Stadium*.

A TOTAL OF **70** TEAMS TOOK PART IN **233** LEAGUE FIXTURES AT THIS VENUE

UNDERHILL
HOME GROUND OF BARNET

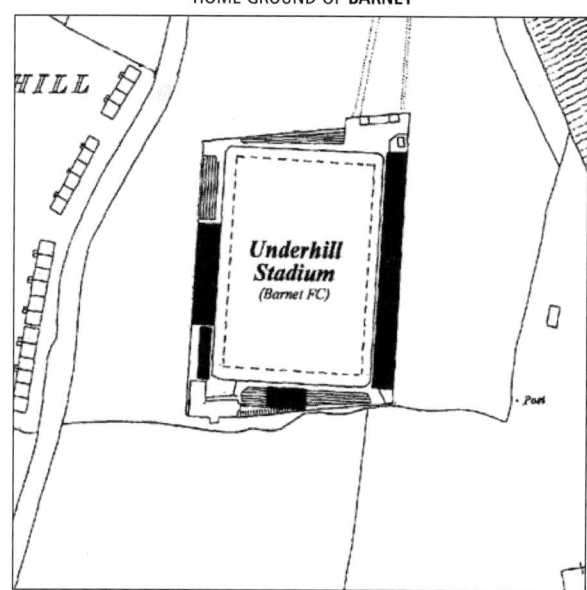

MAP EXTRACT; GROUND AS IN **1968** DRAWN FROM PLANS AND SUPERIMPOSED ON MIDDLESEX 6.8 [1914]
SITE LOCATION; **TQ25209569**

Barnet Alston FC moved to *Underhill* in 1907 and, apart from the construction of a stand in 1926, it remained more or less unchanged for nearly forty years. The record attendance of 11,026 was set at the FA Amateur Cup tie v. *Wycombe* on February 23rd, 1952 and it was not until the 1960s that a new main stand was constructed on the west side and covering installed on the east side and at the south end.

Barnet FC was promoted to the Football League in 1991 and improvements included the installation of additional seating on the west side and at the south end giving it a nominal capacity in 2004 of 5,500 with 1,000 seats and an 113 x 72 yards sized pitch.

PLAYING RECORD OF BARNET
LEAGUE PROGRAMME

First Match; 4-7 v. Crewe Alexandra (5,090) (August 17th, 1991)
Last Match; 2-3 v. Torquay United (5,523) (May 5th, 2001)
Highest Gate*; 5,629 v. Blackpool (1-0) (May 10th, 1992) (Play Off Match)
Lowest Gate; 1,194 v. Lincoln City (1-0) (February 25th, 1997)
Highest Home Win; 7-0 v. Blackpool (2,520) (November 11th, 2000)
Highest Home Defeat; 1-9 v. Peterborough United (2,330)
(September 5th, 1998)

PLAY OFF MATCHES
1-0 v. Blackpool (5,629) (May 10th, 1992)
1-0 v. Colchester United (3,858) (May 10th, 1998)
1-2 v. Peterborough United (4,536) (May 13th, 2000)

No. of Matches Played by Barnet; 227
(League Programme; 224 [Including one expunged match v. Aldershot on March 3rd, 1992], Play Off Matches; 3)

The club was promoted to Football League Division 4 from the Football Conference in 1991, relegated back to the Conference in 2001 and promoted back into the League again in 2005.
*NB. Although this is officially recorded as the highest gate at least one other attendance is thought to have exceeded this figure.

AT THE END OF SEASON 2004/5, A TOTAL OF **54** TEAMS HAD TAKEN PART IN **227** LEAGUE FIXTURES AT THIS VENUE

UPTON PARK

HOME GROUND OF **WEST HAM UNITED**
TEMPORARY HOME GROUND FOR **CHARLTON ATHLETIC**

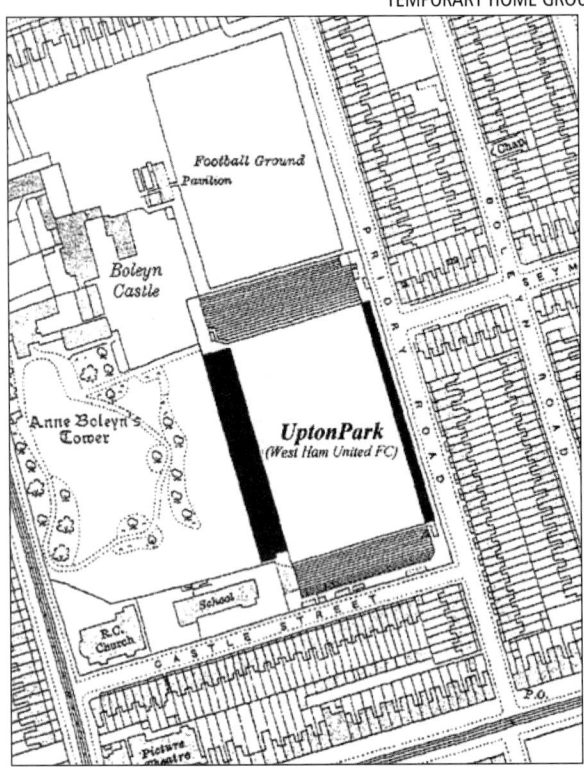

MAP EXTRACT; ESSEX N86.6 [**1919**]
SITE LOCATION; **TQ41458341**

PLAYING RECORD OF CHARLTON ATHLETIC
LEAGUE PROGRAMME

First Match; 2-1 v. Newcastle United (9,320) (August 18th, 1991)
Last Match; 1-3 v. Newcastle United (12,945) (November 14th, 1992)
Highest Gate; 15,357 v. Leicester City (2-0) (April 25th, 1992)
Lowest Gate; 3,654 v. Grimsby Town (1-3) (March 3rd, 1992)
Highest Home Win; 4-1 v. Bristol Rovers (4,721) (August 25th, 1992)
Highest Home Defeat; 1-4 v. Sunderland (5,842) (September 17th, 1991)

No. of Matches Played by Charlton Athletic; 33

Charlton Athletic moved here from **Selhurst Park** as a temporary measure whilst awaiting completion of **The Valley**.

PLAYING RECORD OF WEST HAM UNITED
LEAGUE PROGRAMME

First Match; 1-1 v. Lincoln City (27,000) (August 30th, 1919)
Highest Gate*; 42,322 v. Tottenham Hotspur (2-2) (October 17th, 1970)
Lowest Gate; 4,500 v. Doncaster Rovers (0-1) (February 24th, 1955)
Highest Home Win; 8-0 v. Rotherham United (25,040) (March 8th, 1958) & v. Sunderland (24,718) (October 19th, 1968)
Highest Home Defeat; 2-8 v. Blackburn Rovers (20,500) (December 26th, 1963)

PLAY OFF MATCHES

2-0 v. Ipswich Town (34,002) (May 18th, 2004)
2-2 v. Ipswich Town (33,723) (May 14th, 2005)

No. of Matches Played by West Ham United; 1,654
(League Programme; 1,652, Play Off Matches; 2)

The club was elected into the Football League Division 2 in 1919 and was involved in Football League Play Off Matches at the neutral venue of the *Millennium Stadium*.
NB. *A slightly higher gate of 43,528 may have been achieved against *Charlton Athletic* on April 18th, 1936, but this can not be verified as all the club records were destroyed during WWII.

AT THE END OF SEASON 2004/5, A TOTAL OF **81** TEAMS HAD TAKEN PART IN **1,687** LEAGUE FIXTURES AT THIS VENUE

The double-decked main stand, built on the west side in 1925 and replaced by a 15,000 seat cantilever roofed structure in 2001.
Photograph by Paul Claydon. Courtesy of Groundtastic Magazine

Known also (and more correctly) as *The Boleyn Ground*, the site was a cabbage patch when *West Ham United FC* moved here from *The Memorial Ground* in 1904. On opening the facilities included a main stand on the west side, a pavilion in the south west corner and embankments around the remainder of the pitch. Further improvements were made just prior to WWI with the building of a new main stand on the west side, installation of a cover on the east side and construction of terracing at each end.

The main stand was replaced yet again in 1925, this time with a double-deck structure, whilst the roof of the original stand was reinstalled at the south end. No further changes took place until the 1960s when a roof was installed at the north end, the stand on the west side extended and a new 3,490 two-tier cantilever roofed stand built on the east side.

In 1981 seats were installed in the west side paddock and during the 1990s the club purchased land behind the west side and the ground was made all-seater with the installation of seats on the east side and the construction of two-tier stands at each end. The west stand was demolished in 2001 and a new 15,000 seat stand constructed further back on the additional land on that side giving the opportunity to widen the pitch. In 2002 the pitch was raised by 4in and the first six rows of seats removed from the stand at the south end giving a capacity at the start of the 2004/5 season of 35,647. The pitch size was 112 x 72 yards.

VALE PARK

HOME GROUND OF **PORT VALE**
TEMPORARY HOME GROUND FOR **STOKE CITY**

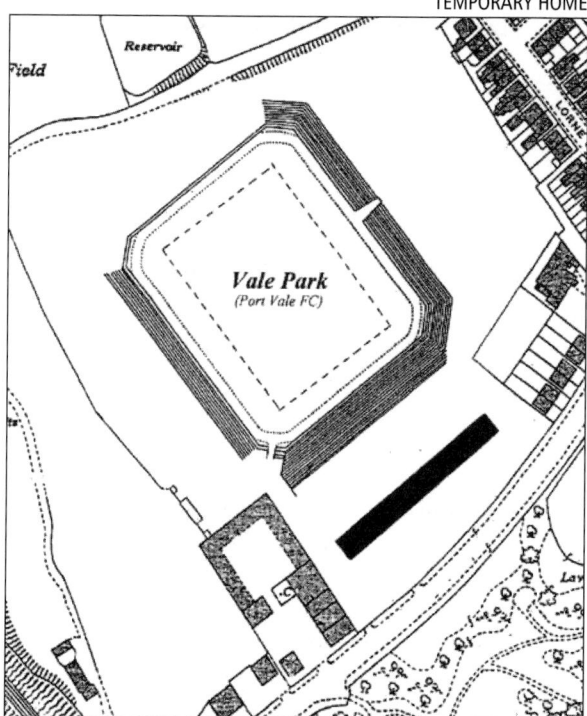

MAP EXTRACT; GROUND AS IN **1950** DRAWN FROM MAPS AND SUPERIMPOSED ON STAFFORDSHIRE 12.5 [1941]
SITE LOCATION; **SJ87185033**

PLAYING RECORD OF PORT VALE
LEAGUE PROGRAMME
First Match; 1-0 v. Newport County (30,196) (August 24th, 1950)
Highest Gate; 41,674 v. Stoke City (0-1) (April 25th, 1955)
Lowest Gate; 1,924 v. York City (0-0) (May 1st, 1982)
Highest Home Win; 8-0 v. Gateshead (16,899) (December 26th, 1958)
Highest Home Defeat; 1-7 v. Nottingham Forest (18,185) (February 2nd, 1957)

PLAY OFF MATCHES
3-1 v. Preston North End (13,416) (May 25th, 1989)
1-0 v. Bristol Rovers (17,353) (June 3rd, 1989)
1-0 v. Stockport County (12,689) (May 19th, 1993)

No. of Matches Played by Port Vale; 1,239
(League Programme; 1,236, Play Off Matches; 3)
Information Kindly Supplied by; Tony Matthews

The club moved here from **The Old Recreation Ground** in 1950. Port Vale FC was expelled from the Football League in 1968 for financial irregularities but was elected back into Division 4 for the following season. The club was also involved in a Football League Play Off Match at the neutral venue of **Wembley Stadium.**

AT THE END OF SEASON 2004/5, A TOTAL OF **97** TEAMS HAD TAKEN PART IN **1,240** LEAGUE FIXTURES AT THIS VENUE

Port Vale FC purchased the site, a former marl pit, in 1944 but post war shortages of building materials delayed the opening until 1950. Although it was terraced on three sides there was no cover whatsoever with temporary changing facilities being provided on the east side and some uncovered seating at the north end. Within a few months of opening a second hand roof was installed at the north end and around the north west corner, whilst in 1954 a 4,500 seat stand opened on the west side.

In 1959 the north end was terraced and the record attendance of 50,000 was set in the following year at the FA Cup 5th Round tie v. *Aston Villa* (1-2) on February 20th. The ground remained unaltered for over thirty years with the planned main stand on the east side (only the paddock and tunnel being built) not finally materializing until the ground saw wholesale improvements in the 1990s.

In 1991 the west side was fully installed with seats and in 1992 the roof from *Chester City FC's* main stand at **Sealand Road** was purchased and re-erected at the south end. Subsequently a new cover and seating were installed at the north end, a seated corner stand constructed in the north west corner and the south end fitted with 4,550 seats. Finally the long-awaited 5,000 seat main stand was partially constructed on the east side in 2001 which gave an all-seat capacity of 22,356 by the start of the 2004/5 season. The pitch size was 114 x 77 yards.

Looking north at **Vale Park** with the "main stand" visible to the right. The buildings in view just accommodated the dressing rooms and club offices with an uncovered paddock as the only spectator facility on that side of the ground. Although the construction of a main stand finally commenced after some fifty years, the lack of finance precluded its completion and it still remained unfinished in 2005 with only the northern end of the structure available for use.

Photograph by Paul Claydon. Courtesy of Groundtastic Magazine

PLAYING RECORD OF STOKE CITY
LEAGUE PROGRAMME
Match Played; 1-0 v. Middlesbrough (21,009) (January 17th, 1976)
No. of Matches Played by Stoke City; 1
Information Kindly Supplied by; Tony Matthews

This match was played here after the roof of the main stand at **The Victoria Ground** was blown off in a gale.

THE VALLEY
HOME GROUND OF CHARLTON ATHLETIC

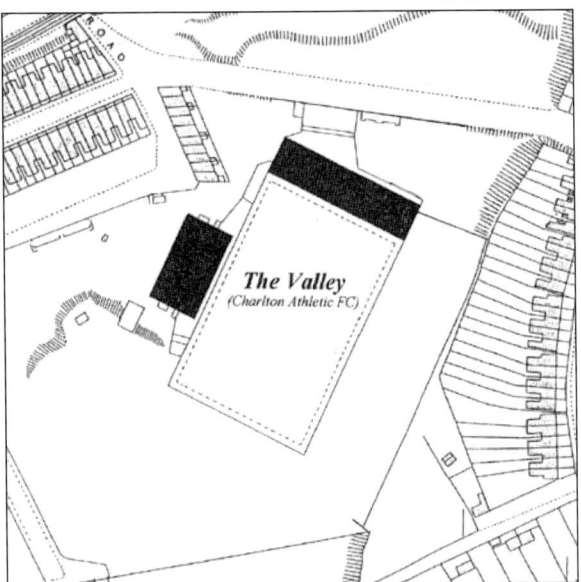

MAP EXTRACT; LONDON 12.15 [**1937**]
SITE LOCATION: **TQ41507834**

The site was a disused sand and chalk pit when *Charlton Athletic FC* moved here from the *Angerstein Athletic Ground* in 1919 and bought it for £3,000. Apart from embankments at each end and a large embankment on the east side there were no facilities and players had to change in a house in Ransom Road until a 2,500 seat stand was opened on the west side in 1922, one year after joining the Football League.

A cover was installed at the north end in 1934 and although the record attendance of 75,031 was set at the FA Cup 5th Round tie v. *Aston Villa* (1-1) on February 12th, 1938 no alterations were made to the ground until the 1970s when the main stand was re-roofed, seats installed at the north end and a new all seat stand constructed at the south end. *Charlton Athletic FC* moved out in 1985, to groundshare with *Crystal Palace* at **Selhurst Park**, and the ground fell into disuse and decay.

The main stand, on the west side of the ground.
Photograph by Owen Pavey. Courtesy of Groundtastic Magazine

The club returned in 1992 and the ground was substantially redeveloped with a refurbished all seat stand at the north end and new all seat stands constructed on the other sides giving a capacity of 20,043. In 2001 the north stand was rebuilt as a two tier structure with corner stands linking it to the east and west sides bringing the ground capacity up to 26,875 at the start of the 2004/5 season. The pitch size was 112 x 73 yards.

PLAYING RECORD OF CHARLTON ATHLETIC
LEAGUE PROGRAMME
1ST PERIOD;
First Match; 1-0 v. Exeter City (13,000) (August 27th, 1921)
Last Match; 1-3 v. Swansea Town (5,000) (December 8th, 1923)
No. of Matches Played; 51
2ND PERIOD;
First Match; 0-0 v. Northampton Town (5,000) (September 1st, 1924)
Last Match; 2-0 v. Stoke City (8,858) (September 21st, 1985)
No. of Matches Played; 1,147
3RD PERIOD [CURRENT];
First Match; 1-0 v. Portsmouth (8,337) (December 5th, 1992)
Highest Gate; 68,160 v. Arsenal (0-2) (October 17th, 1936)
Lowest Gate; 1,000 v. Southend United (0-0) (December 27th, 1924)
Highest Home Win; 8-1 v. Middlesbrough (23,790) (September 12th, 1953)
Highest Home Defeat; 0-7 v. Everton (16,859) (February 7th, 1931)

PLAY OFF MATCHES
1-2 v. Crystal Palace (14,618) (May 12th, 1996)
1-0 v. Ipswich Town (15,585) (May 13th, 1998)

Total No. of Matches Played by Charlton Athletic; 1,465
(League Programme; 1,463, Play Off Matches; 2)

The club was elected into Football League Division 3 [S] in 1921 but initially only stayed until midway through the 1923/24 season when the directors moved the club to **The Mount** at Catford in the hope of attracting additional support. They quickly returned to *The Valley* and remained here until 1985 when the club was forced out and spent the period between 1985 and 1992 at **Selhurst Park** and **Upton Park**. In 1992 *Charlton Athletic FC* was able to return once more. The club was also involved in a Football League Play Off Match at the neutral venue of **Wembley Stadium**.

AT THE END OF SEASON 2004/5, A TOTAL OF **93** TEAMS HAD TAKEN PART IN **1,465** LEAGUE FIXTURES AT THIS VENUE

VALLEY PARADE
HOME GROUND OF BRADFORD CITY

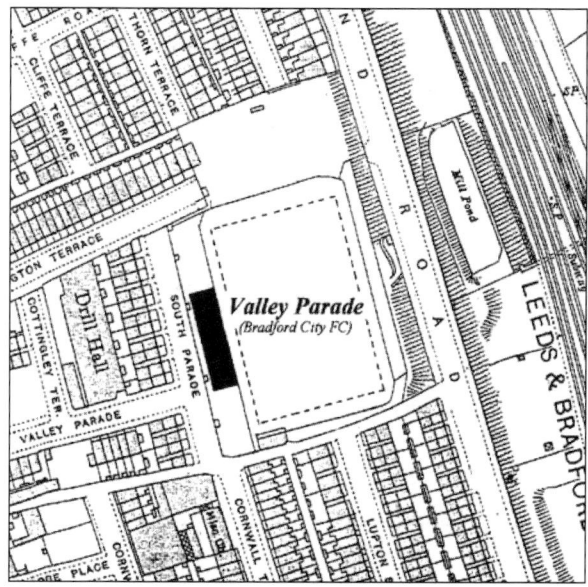

MAP EXTRACT; YORKSHIRE 216.4 [1908]
SITE LOCATION; SE15963423

PLAYING RECORD OF BRADFORD CITY
LEAGUE PROGRAMME
First Match; 1-3 v. Gainsborough Trinity (11,000)
(September 5th, 1903)
Last Match; 0-0 v. Lincoln City (11,000) (May 11th, 1985)
[Abandoned due to fire]
FOLLOWING REBUILDING;
First Match; 0-1 v. Derby County (14,502) (December 26th, 1986)
Highest Gate; 40,000 v. Manchester United (0-1)
(December 26th, 1911)
Lowest Gate; 1,249 v. Hereford United (0-1) (May 15th, 1981)
Highest Home Win; 11-1 v. Rotherham United (12,356)
(August 25th, 1928)
Highest Home Defeat; 1-7 v. Stockport County (3,308) (September 18th, 1965)
PLAY OFF MATCHES
2-1 v. Middlesbrough (16,017) (May 15th, 1988)
0-2 v. Blackpool (14,273) (May 12th, 1996)
No. of Matches Played by Bradford City; 1,952
(League Programme; 1,950 [Including one expunged match v. Accrington Stanley on September 16th, 1961], Play Off Matches; 2)
Information Kindly Supplied by; Peter Waller

The ground was first used by *Manningham Rugby Club* in 1886 who brought the main stand from their previous ground and re-erected it on the west side. A cinder track was laid around the pitch and apart from rugby it became the regular venue for athletics and archery.

In 1903 the club switched codes and emerged as *Bradford City FC* but the facilities remained basic with the teams having to change at premises outside the ground until *Valley Parade* was re-developed following promotion to Division 1 in 1908. A new 3,500 seat main stand was built on the west side, the north end terracing doubled in size and a cover and terracing constructed on the east side just before the record attendance of 39,146 was set at the FA Cup 4th Round tie v. *Burnley* (1-0) on March 11th, 1911.

The ground remained unchanged until 1951 when the structure on the east side was dismantled (the steelwork being sold to *Berwick Rangers* for their main stand at **Shielfield Park**), replaced in 1954 and dismantled again in 1960 after being declared unsafe due to problems with the foundations. In the same year a cover was installed at the south end and, in 1966, the pitch was moved slightly to the west to allow for some standing spectators on the now unoccupied east side. Four years later a new cover was installed on the east side and seats installed in the main stand paddock.

On May 11th, 1985 the main stand burned down killing no less than 56 spectators, seriously injuring 200 more and sending repercussions through football grounds in Britain with wholesale closures of unsafe stands and the compulsory expedition of remedial action following the amendment to the Safety of Sports Grounds Act (1975) in 1985 to include smaller football and rugby grounds.

In the wake of this tragedy the ground was rebuilt, a new 4,390 seat main stand opened in 1986 and all seat stands were eventually constructed on each side. The new all-seater stand at the north end was completed in 1999 and this was linked by a new corner stand to an enlarged, but at that time incomplete, main stand on the west side in 2001. At the start of the 2004/5 season the all-seat capacity was 25,136 and the pitch size 113 x 75 yards.

The club was elected into the Football League Division 2 in 1903. The ground was closed for two weeks in 1906 following an assault on a referee and a *Manchester United* player. The match v. *Lincoln City* on May 11th, 1985 was abandoned when the main stand was destroyed by a disastrous fire and after this the club played matches at **Leeds Road**, **Elland Road** and the **Odsal Stadium**. The club was also involved in a Football League Play Off Match at the neutral venue of **Wembley Stadium**.

AT THE END OF SEASON 2004/5, A TOTAL OF **110** TEAMS HAD TAKEN PART IN **1,952** LEAGUE FIXTURES AT THIS VENUE

After the fire! The site of the old wooden main stand, on the banking to the right, in the process of being cleared in 1985 prior to the building of a new 4,300 seater and eventual wholesale reconstruction of the ground

Photograph Courtesy of Groundtastic Magazine

VETCH FIELD
HOME GROUND OF SWANSEA CITY

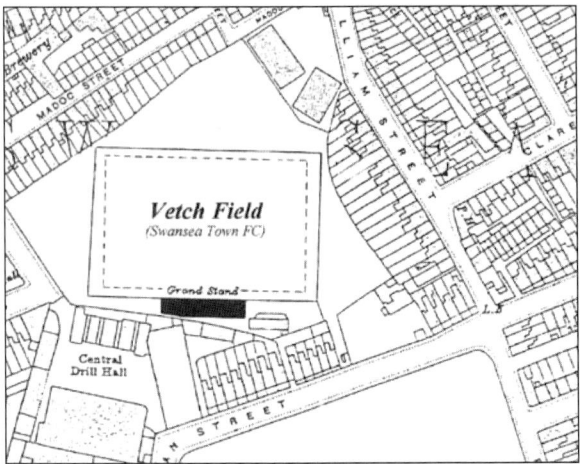

MAP EXTRACT; GLAMORGAN 24.5 [c1914]
SITE LOCATION; SS65099265

Known as the Old Town Ditch Field, *Swansea Town* moved here in 1912 and built a 1,100 seat main stand on the south side in 1913. In the 1920s a stand was built in the south west corner, the terracing enlarged on the north side and a two-tier 2,120 seat stand constructed at the west end.

Further alterations were carried out in 1959 when a cover was installed on the north side and the record attendance of 32,796 was set at the FA Cup 4th Round tie v. *Arsenal* (0-1) on February 17th, 1968. Following the club's elevation to Division One in 1981, a two-tier 1,841 seat stand was squeezed in at the east end and in the 1990s, for safety reasons, the upper tier was removed from the stand at the west end. At the start of the 2004/5 season the capacity was 11,477 with 3,414 seats and the pitch size was 112 x 74 yards.

PLAYING RECORD OF SWANSEA CITY
LEAGUE PROGRAMME
First Match; 2-1 v. Watford (12,000) (September 2nd, 1920)
Last Match; 1-0 v. Shrewsbury Town (11,469) (April 30th, 2005)
Highest Gate; 29,477 v. Leeds United (1-1) (October 1st, 1955)
Lowest Gate; 1,301 v. Northampton Town (1-1)
(September 18th, 1973)
Highest Home Win; 8-0 v. Hartlepool United (6,961) (April 1st, 1978)
Highest Home Defeats; 1-6 v. Bradford Park Avenue (16,217) (September 14th, 1946), v. Workington (8,285) (September 14th, 1965), v. Reading (3,511) (September 23rd, 1989) & v. Wigan Athletic (2,869) (April 6th, 1991)
PLAY OFF MATCHES
1-0 v. Rotherham United (9,148) (May 15th, 1988)
2-1 v. Torquay United (10,825) (May 25th, 1988)
2-1 v. West Bromwich Albion (13,917) (May 16th, 1993)
3-0 v. Chester City (10,027) (May 14th, 1997)
1-0 v. Scunthorpe United (7,828) (May 16th, 1999)
No. of Matches Played by Swansea City; 1,714
(League Programme; 1,709, Play Off Matches; 5)
Information Kindly Supplied by; Colin Jones

Swansea Town was a founder member of the Football League Division 3 in 1920 and changed the name to *Swansea City* in 1970. The club was also involved in a Football League Play Off Match at the neutral venue of *Wembley Stadium*. The club moved to the *New Stadium* at the end of the 2004/5 season.

A TOTAL OF **107** TEAMS TOOK PART IN **1,714** LEAGUE FIXTURES AT THIS VENUE

THE VICARAGE
TEMPORARY HOME GROUND FOR CREWE ALEXANDRA

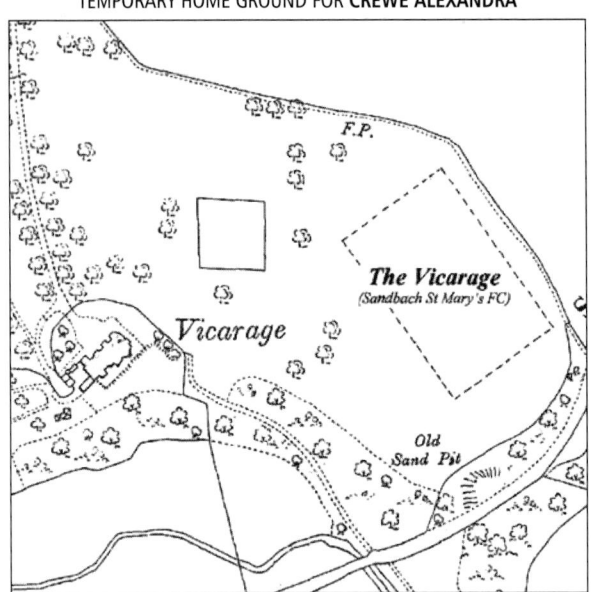

MAP EXTRACT; CHESHIRE 50.10 [1909]
SITE LOCATION; SJ77035960

Located about 1 mile south east of Sandbach (south off the A533), the pitch was sited in a field on the east side of the Vicarage and had a considerable drop of at least 50ft behind the goal at the south end down to Stannerhouse Lane. There were no facilities, spectators stood on the east side of the pitch alongside of a footpath and hedge and it is assumed that one of the outhouses at the Vicarage was utilized for changing rooms.

The ground was used by *Sandbach St Mary FC* amongst others for many years, up to WWII at least, before the pitch returned to agricultural use and the Vicarage is now a private house; Tall Chimneys.

PLAYING RECORD OF CREWE ALEXANDRA
LEAGUE PROGRAMME
Match Played; 1-2 v. Loughborough (-) (April 3rd, 1896)
No. of Matches Played by Crewe Alexandra; 1
Information Kindly Supplied by; David Richards, John Conliffe and John & Hazel Tomkinson

This match was played here due to non-availability of the *Alexandra Recreation Ground*.

A TOTAL OF **2** TEAMS TOOK PART IN **1** LEAGUE FIXTURE AT THIS VENUE

THE VICARAGE
TEMPORARY HOME GROUND FOR LOUGHBOROUGH

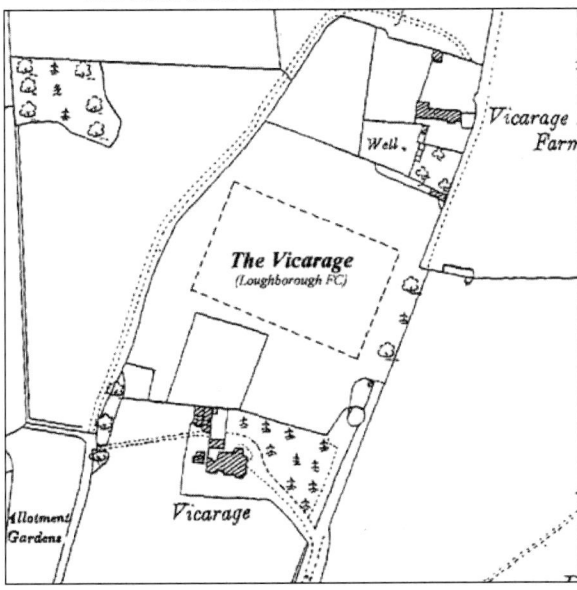

MAP EXTRACT; LEICESTERSHIRE 16.16 [c1900]
SITE LOCATION; **SK44111617**

Located to the east of Whitwick, on the north side of the Leicester Road, the football pitch was sited in a field at the rear of the Vicarage and the only facility was a small pavilion at the west end of the ground.

PLAYING RECORD OF LOUGHBOROUGH
LEAGUE PROGRAMME

Match Played; 1-2 v. Burslem Port Vale (500) (March 31st, 1900)
***No. of Matches Played by Loughborough;* 1**
Information Kindly Supplied by; Albert Robinson

This match was played here after ***The Athletic Ground*** was closed for one month following crowd trouble at the ***Woolwich Arsenal*** fixture (2-3) on March 3rd, 1900.

A TOTAL OF **2** TEAMS TOOK PART IN **1** LEAGUE FIXTURE AT THIS VENUE

VICARAGE ROAD
HOME GROUND OF WATFORD

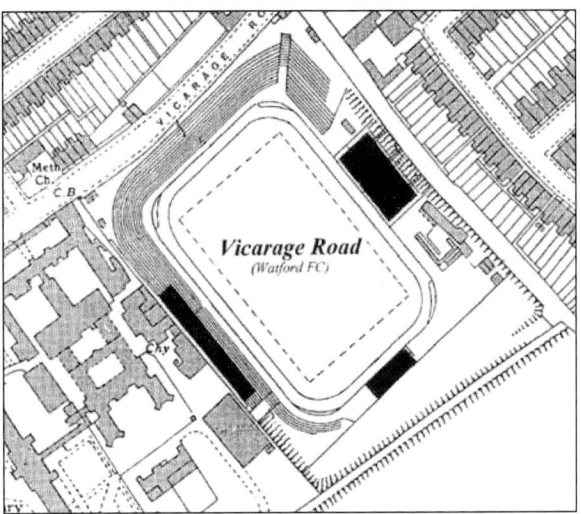

MAP EXTRACT; HERTFORDSHIRE 44.5 & 44.6 [c1930]
SITE LOCATION; **TQ10689577**

The site, a former gravel pit, had been in use as a recreation ground for a number of years before *Watford FC* moved here in 1922 from *Cassio Road*. The facilities included a new 3,500 seat main stand on the east side, stands on the west side and at the south end which had been brought from the previous ground and re-erected and a large embankment at the north end.

Within six years the venue was hosting greyhound racing and prior to WWII some of the terracing was concreted. In 1959 a new roof was installed at the south end and following the setting of the record attendance of 34,099 at the FA Cup 4th Round replay v. *Manchester United* (0-2) on February 3rd, 1969 the stand on the east side was extended with an additional 1,700 seats. In 1979 greyhound racing was finally dispensed with (it had ceased temporarily between 1970 and 1975) and in 1986 a new cantilever roofed all seat two tier stand was constructed on the west side.

Further improvements took place in the 1990s with the construction of new stands at each end and at the start of the 2004/5 season the all-seat capacity was 20,250 and the pitch size 115 x 75 yards.

PLAYING RECORD OF WATFORD
LEAGUE PROGRAMME

First Match; 0-0 v. Millwall (8,000) (August 30th, 1922)
Highest Gate; 27,968 v. Queens Park Rangers (0-1)
(August 20th, 1969)
Lowest Gate; 1,309 v. Clapton Orient (6-0) (December 20th, 1933)
Highest Home Win; 8-0 v. Sunderland (16,816)
(September 25th, 1982)
Highest Home Defeat; 1-7 v. Swindon Town (9,808)
(September 6th, 1951)

PLAY OFF MATCHES

1-1 v. Blackburn Rovers (13,852) (May 24th, 1989)
1-0 v. Birmingham City (18,535) (May 16th, 1999)
***No. of Matches Played by Watford;* 1,702**
(League Programme; 1,700, Play Off Matches; 2)
Some Information Kindly Supplied by; Brian Tabner

The club moved here from ***Cassio Road*** in 1922 and was also involved in a Football League Play Off Match at the neutral venue of ***Wembley Stadium***.

AT THE END OF SEASON 2004/5, A TOTAL OF **101** TEAMS HAD TAKEN PART IN **1,702** LEAGUE FIXTURES AT THIS VENUE

VICTORIA GROUND

HOME GROUND OF **STOKE CITY**
TEMPORARY HOME GROUND FOR **MANCHESTER UNITED**

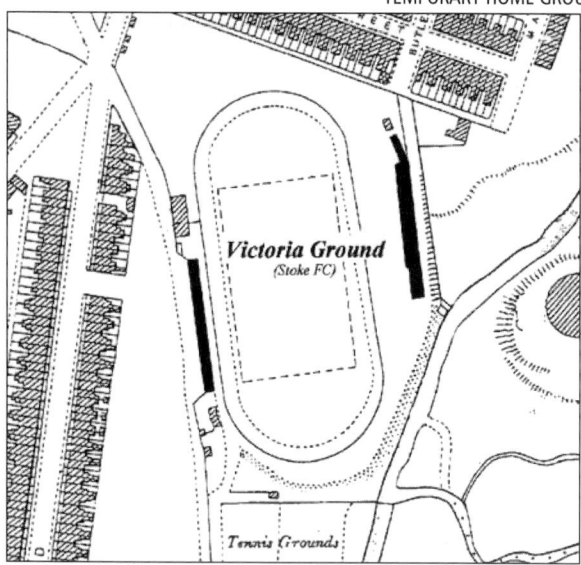

MAP EXTRACT; STAFFORDSHIRE 18.5 [1898]
SITE LOCATION; SJ87854468

Stoke FC moved to the *Victoria Ground*, in a field owned by the local church, from the *Athletic Ground* in 1883. The pitch was sited within a long oval running track and the facilities included a 1,000 seat stand on the west side and banking around the remainder of the ground. Improvements carried out prior to WWI included the building of a pavilion on the west side and a cover for standing spectators on the east side.

Following the end of WWI a new 2,000 seat main stand was constructed on the west side and, in 1930, the running track was dispensed with to allow for the extension of banking at the south end. This was subsequently covered and a 5,000 seat stand (with curved corners) completed on the east side in 1936. At the same time the terracing was improved with the installation of concrete slabs and the pitch was moved further south allowing for the expansion of terracing at the north end.

In 1963 a new main stand was opened on the west side, a new roof installed on the east side following a gale in 1976 and the last major alteration before *Stoke City* vacated the ground and moved to the **Britannia Stadium** in 1997 was the building of a two-tier stand at the north end. The stands were subsequently demolished and the site was still unused in 2005.

PLAYING RECORD OF MANCHESTER UNITED
LEAGUE PROGRAMME

Match Played; 3-1 v. West Bromwich Albion (23,146)
(August 23rd, 1971)

No. of Matches Played by Manchester United; 1

This match was played here when **Old Trafford** was closed following crowd trouble.

NEUTRAL TEST MATCHES

Newton Heath 1, Small Heath 1 (4,000) (April 22nd, 1893)
Darwen 1, Small Heath 3 (3,000) (April 28th, 1894)
No. of Matches Played; 2

PROGRAMME COVER ON RIGHT
The cover features views of the *Brighton & Hove Albion* match (1-0) and ground in 1977. This game finished in a 3-1 win for the visitors.

PLAYING RECORD OF STOKE CITY
LEAGUE PROGRAMME

First Match; 0-2 v. West Bromwich Albion (4,524)
(September 8th, 1888)
Last Match; 2-1 v. West Bromwich Albion (22,500)
(May 4th, 1997)
Highest Gate; 51,373 v. Arsenal (0-0) (March 29th, 1937)
Lowest Gate; 1,000 v. Newton Heath (7-1) (January 7th, 1893)
Highest Home Win; 10-3 v. West Bromwich Albion (8,224) (February 4th, 1937). 9-0 v. Plymouth Argyle (6,479) (December 17th, 1960)
Highest Home Defeat; 1-6 v. Tottenham Hotspur (27,156)
(September 15th, 1951)

TEST MATCHES
1-0 v. Newcastle United (14,000) (April 23rd, 1898)
0-0 v. Burnley (15,000) (April 30th, 1898)

PLAY OFF MATCHES
1-1 v. Stockport County (18,170) (May 13th, 1992)
0-1 v. Leicester City (21,037) (May 15th, 1996)

No. of Matches Played by Stoke City; 1,797
(League Programme; 1,793, Test Matches; 2, Play Off Matches; 2)
Information Kindly Supplied by; Tony Matthews

Stoke FC was a founder member of the Football League in 1888, failed to gain re-election in 1890, was elected in 1891 and resigned in 1908. It was elected into Division 2 in 1919 and the name was changed to *Stoke City* in 1925. The club was also involved in a Test Match at the neutral venue of **The Cobridge Athletic Grounds.** In 1976 the roof of the main stand blew off and the fixture v. *Middlesbrough* on January 17th, 1976 was played at *Vale Park*. The club moved to **The Britannia Stadium** in 1997.

A TOTAL OF **107** TEAMS TOOK PART IN **1,800** LEAGUE FIXTURES AT THIS VENUE

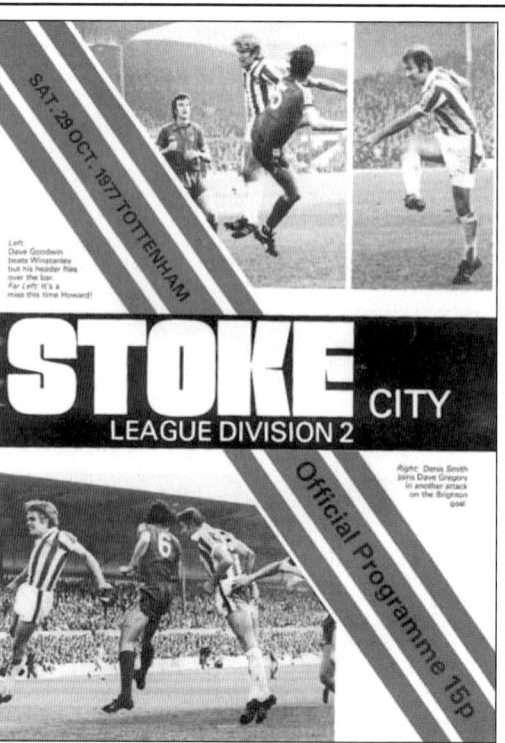

VICTORIA PARK

HOME GROUND OF **HARTLEPOOL UNITED**
TEMPORARY HOME GROUND FOR **MIDDLESBROUGH**

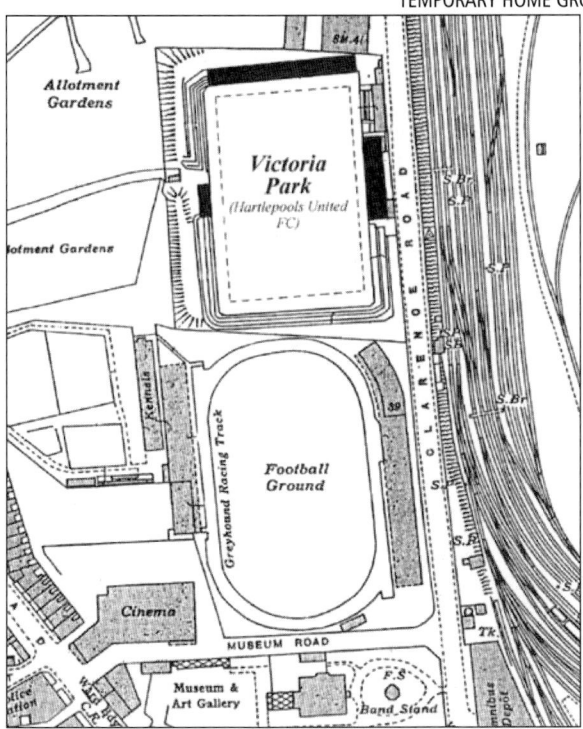

MAP EXTRACT; DURHAM 37.11 [**1947**]
SITE LOCATION; **NZ50863296**

PLAYING RECORD OF HARTLEPOOL UNITED
LEAGUE PROGRAMME

First Match; 0-1 v. Wrexham (10,000) (September 3rd, 1921)
Highest Gate; 17,118 v. Hull City (0-2) (October 9th, 1948)
Lowest Gate; 790 v. Stockport County (1-2) (May 5th, 1984)
Highest Home Win; 10-1 v. Barrow (3,870) (April 4th, 1959)
Highest Home Defeat; 1-8 v. Plymouth Argyle (2,389)
(May 7th, 1994)

PLAY OFF MATCHES

0-2 v. Darlington (6,995) (May 13th, 2000)
1-3 v. Blackpool (5,836) (May 16th, 2001)
1-1 v. Cheltenham Town (7,135) (April 27th, 2002)
1-1 v. Bristol City (7,211) (May 15th, 2004)
2-0 v. Tranmere Rovers (6,604) (May 13th, 2005)

No. of Matches Played by Hartlepool United; 1,726
(League Programme; 1,721, Play Off Matches; 5)
Information Kindly Supplied by; Ed Law

The club was a founder member of the Football League Division 3 [N] in 1921 as *Hartlepools United*. The name was changed to *Hartlepool* in 1968 and to *Hartlepool United* in 1977. The club was also involved in a Football League Play Off Match at the neutral venue of the **Millennium Stadium**. The League game v. *New Brighton* (3-0) on March 15th, 1947 featured the appearance of the oldest player to take part in a competitive match in England when *New Brighton's* manager Neil McBain, at the age of 52 years and 4 months, had to play as an emergency goalkeeper.

AT THE END OF SEASON 2004/5, A TOTAL OF **95** TEAMS HAD TAKEN PART IN **1,727** LEAGUE FIXTURES AT THIS VENUE

The site, part of a disused quarry and rubbish tip, was first used as a sporting venue by *West Hartlepool Rugby Club* in 1886. Following the demise of the rugby club *Hartlepools United FC* took the *Victoria Ground* over in 1908 and split the site into two parts, the northern portion as a football ground and the southern for rugby and, subsequently, greyhound racing.

Full details of the early facilities are not known but there was a main stand on the east side which was famously destroyed by bombs during a Zeppelin raid in 1916. As the council had plans to improve the road behind the stand only a temporary 620 seat replacement structure was installed in time for the club's entry into the Football League in 1921. Over the years leading up to 1947, terraces were installed around the ground and a cover constructed at the north end.

The record attendance of 17,426 was set at the FA Cup 3rd Round tie v. *Manchester United* (3-4) on January 5th, 1957 and a new cantilever roofed stand was constructed on the west side in 1968. The "temporary stand" having survived for 66 years was finally demolished as a safety measure in 1985, as were the covers at both ends in the following year.

The ground was improved during the 1990s with the construction of new covers at each end and a new cantilever roofed 1,650 seat main stand on the east side. The venue was re-named as *Victoria Park* and by the start of the 2004/5 season the capacity was 7,629 with 3,966 seats and the pitch size was 113 x 77 yards.

The east, "main stand" side of the ground in 1990 with a sundry assortment of temporary buildings housing dressing rooms and other club facilities. This situation prevailed for a number of years following the demolition of the "temporary" stand in 1985.
Photograph by Jon Weaver. Courtesy of Groundtastic Magazine

PLAYING RECORD OF MIDDLESBROUGH
LEAGUE PROGRAMME

Match Played; 2-2 v. Port Vale (3,690) (August 23rd, 1986)
No. of Matches Played by Middlesbrough; 1

This match was played here as *Middlesbrough FC* was barred from using **Ayresome Park**.

VILLA PARK
HOME GROUND OF ASTON VILLA

MAP EXTRACT; WARWICKSHIRE 8.13 [1917]
SITE LOCATION; **SP07919014**

PLAYING RECORD OF ASTON VILLA
LEAGUE PROGRAMME

First Match; 3-0 v. Blackburn Rovers (15,000) (April 17th, 1897)
Highest Gate; 69,492 v. Wolverhampton Wanderers (1-4) (December 27th, 1949)
Lowest Gate; 2,900 v. Bradford City (0-0) (February 13th, 1915)
Highest Home Win; 11-1 v. Charlton Athletic (21,997) (November 24th, 1959)
Highest Home Defeat; 0-7 v. West Bromwich Albion (38,037) (October 19th, 1935)

No. of Matches Played by Aston Villa; 1,966
Information Kindly Supplied by; Tony Matthews

The club moved here from **Wellington Road** in 1897. One of the individual League scoring records was set here when Ted Drake of *Arsenal* netted all seven of their goals in the 7-1 win against *Aston Villa* on December 14th, 1935.

AT THE END OF SEASON 2004/5, A TOTAL OF **81** TEAMS HAD TAKEN PART IN **1,966** LEAGUE FIXTURES AT THIS VENUE

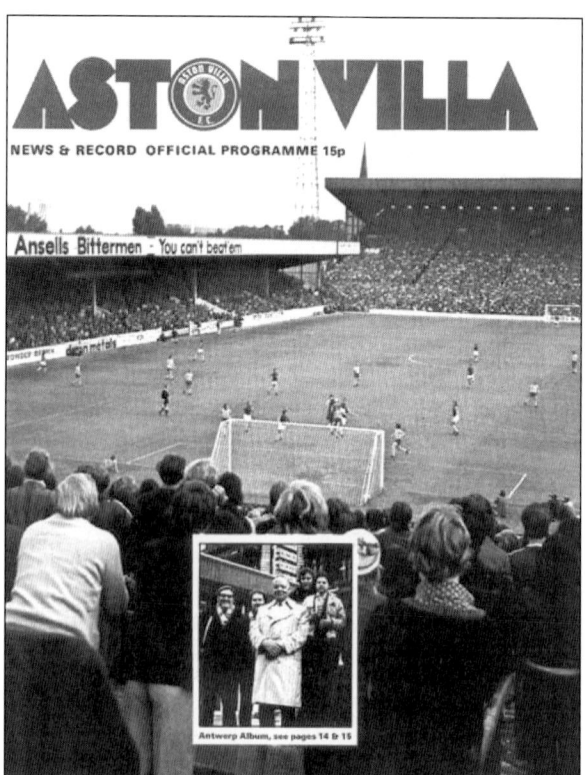

Viewed from the north end in 1975 this programme cover shows the east side and south end of *Villa Park* in 1975.

The *Aston Lower Grounds* were opened in the 1870s as a pleasure garden and a number of its buildings were retained when *Aston Villa FC* moved from **Wellington Road** in 1897 and laid out *Villa Park* on the site of the formal gardens and ornamental lake. The pitch was surrounded by a cycle track and the facilities included a 5,500 seat main stand on the east side, a pavilion and cover on the west side and embankments around the ends. Following the purchase of the ground for £8,250 in 1911 the facilities were improved with the removal of the cycle track, expansion of the end terraces to the pitch edge and installation of terracing in front of the stand on the east side whilst a new stand was subsequently completed on the west side.

The south end terrace was extended in 1940 (and subsequently roofed in 1962) and the record attendance of 76,588 was set at the FA Cup 6th Round tie v. *Derby County* (3-4) on March 2nd, 1946. A new roof was installed on the east stand in 1964 and seats installed in the paddock in 1966 as part of the preparations for the World Cup. In the 1970s seats were installed in the west stand paddock and a new two-tier 4,000 seat stand constructed at the north end.

In 1990 the terracing at the south end was refurbished and the roof extended but, as the result of poor planning, the whole end was demolished just four years later and replaced with a 13,462 seat two-tier stand. Also in 1990 the stand on the west side was refurbished whilst in 1993 the east stand was extended to the rear (necessitating a realignment to the road) and rebuilt as a two-tier structure giving an all-seat capacity in 2000 of 39,217.

In 2001 the main stand on the west side was expanded over the adjacent road and totally rebuilt and at the start of the 2004/5 season the ground capacity had increased to 42,584. The pitch size was 115 x 75 yards.

THE WALKERS STADIUM
HOME GROUND OF LEICESTER CITY

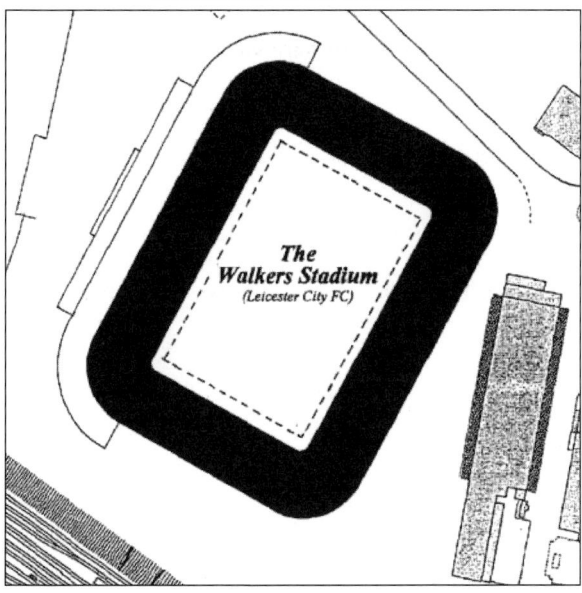

MAP EXTRACT; GROUND AS IN **2002** DRAWN FROM AERIAL PHOTOGRAPHS AND SUPERIMPOSED ON LEICESTERSHIRE 31.14 [1930]
SITE LOCATION; **SK58170285**

Constructed on the site of Freemen's Meadow Power Station, just south of the old *Filbert Street* ground the 32,500 seat capacity stadium is composed of a continuous single tier of seats with a continuous cantilevered roof. The pitch size is 110 x 72 yards.
NB. The ground was originally named *The Walkers Bowl* but following pressure from supporters was rapidly changed.

PLAYING RECORD OF LEICESTER CITY
LEAGUE PROGRAMME

First Match; 2-0 v. Watford (31,022) (August 10th, 2002)
Highest Gate; 32,148 v. Newcastle United (1-1) (December 26th, 2003)
Lowest Gate; 21,249 v. Preston North End (1-1) (October 2nd, 2004)
Highest Home Win; 4-0 v. Bradford City (24,651) (September 17th, 2002), v. Wimbledon (31,438) (February 22nd, 2003) & v. Leeds United (30,460) (September 15th, 2003)
Highest Home Defeat; 0-5 v. Aston Villa (31,056) (January 31st, 2004)

No. of Matches Played by Leicester City; 65

The club moved here from *Filbert Street* at the start of the 2002/3 season and Brian Deane of *Leicester City FC* scored the first League goal here in the 47th minute of the first match.

AT THE END OF SEASON 2004/5, A TOTAL OF **48** TEAMS HAD TAKEN PART IN **65** LEAGUE FIXTURES AT THIS VENUE

WATLING STREET
TEMPORARY HOME GROUND FOR MAIDSTONE UNITED

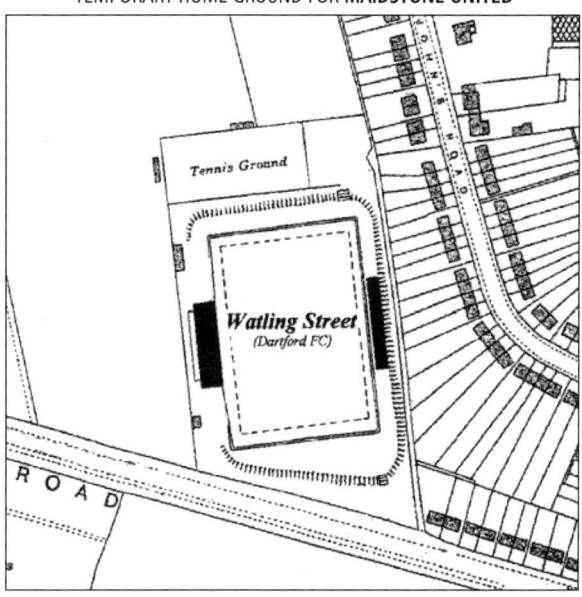

MAP EXTRACT; KENT 9.7 [**1938**]
SITE LOCATION; **TQ56237365**

The site was purchased by *Dartford FC* in 1921 and the facilites included a seated grandstand on the west side and banking around the ground. The stand burned down in 1926 and was replaced by a 1,000 seat edifice whilst, in 1930, a covered enclosure was constructed on the east side.
Additional terracing was installed at the south end and in front of the main stand before *Maidstone United FC* moved here from *The Athletic Ground* in 1988 to groundshare with *Dartford FC*. The financial demise of *Maidstone United* in 1992 also brought their hosts down with them and *Dartford FC* were forced to move out in the same year. The *Watling Street* ground was immediately demolished and replaced with housing.

PLAYING RECORD OF MAIDSTONE UNITED
LEAGUE PROGRAMME

First Match; 4-1 v. Scarborough (3,372) (August 26th, 1989)
Last Match; 0-0 v. Mansfield Town (1,602) (April 25th, 1992)
Highest Gate; 5,538 v. Cambridge United (0-2) (May 16th, 1990) (Play Off Match)
Lowest Gate; 846 v. Hereford United (3-2) (November 2nd, 1991)
Highest Home Win; 6-1 v. Scunthorpe United (1,778) (September 15th, 1990)
Highest Home Defeat; 1-4 v. Hartlepool United (1,704) (March 23rd, 1991)

PLAY OFF MATCHES

0-2 v. Cambridge United (5,538) (May 16th, 1990)

No. of Matches Played by Maidstone United; 69

(League Programme; 68 [Including one expunged match v. Aldershot on December 28th, 1991], Play Off Matches; 1)
The club was promoted into the Football League Division 4 from the Football Conference in 1988 and folded in 1992.

A TOTAL OF **33** TEAMS TOOK PART IN **69** LEAGUE FIXTURES AT THIS VENUE

WEMBLEY STADIUM

TEMPORARY HOME GROUND FOR **CLAPTON ORIENT**
VENUE FOR PLAY OFF FINALS

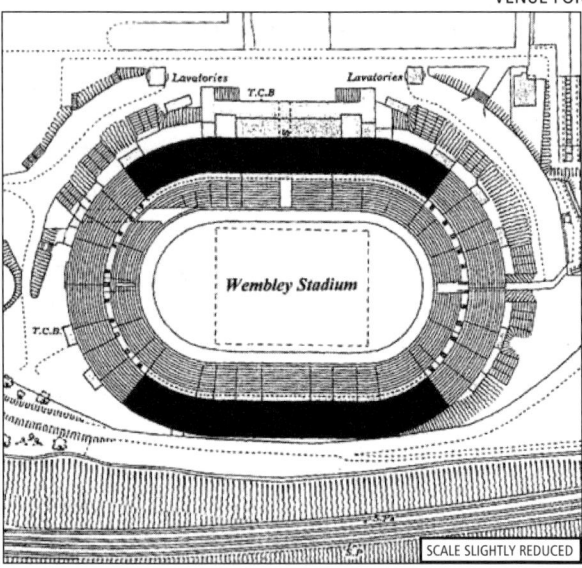

MAP EXTRACT; MIDDLESEX [1937]
SITE LOCATION; **TQ19368546**

Sited in parkland, the area was selected in 1921 for the British Empire Exhibition. The stadium opened in 1923 with the FA Cup Final between *West Ham United* and *Bolton Wanderers* on April 28th when the nominal 126,500 capacity was famously exceeded with an estimated 200,000 gaining access. The venue was oval in shape with the football pitch surrounded by a running track, covered seated stands were located on the north and south sides and the remainder of the ground was open terracing.

In 1960 the covering was extended around the stadium and it was made an all-seater in 1990 with a capacity of 80,000. *Wembley Stadium* closed in 2000 and with its poor infrastructure and location within a residential area there was very popular support for the new national stadium to be located at a more easily accessible site. Although the Government invited other locations to bid for the new venue this proved to be no more than a public relations exercise as the Football Association had already signed a deal with the stadium owners committing itself to the Wembley site for the next 25 years and despite considerable obstacles, not least of all the price of some £700m, the project to rebuild it was given the go ahead in 2002. The "new" *Wembley Stadium* is due to open in 2006.

PLAYING RECORD OF LEYTON ORIENT
[AS CLAPTON ORIENT]
LEAGUE PROGRAMME
Matches Played; 3-0 v. Brentford (10,300)
(November 22nd, 1930)
3-1 v. Southend United (2,500) (December 6th, 1930)
No. of Matches Played by Leyton Orient; 2

Two home games were played here in 1930 due to the pitch at *Lea Bridge Stadium* being found to be too narrow.

PLAY-OFF FINALS
SEASON 1989/90
Division 3; Cambridge United 1, Chesterfield 0 (26,404)
(May 26th, 1990)
Division 2; Notts County 2, Tranmere Rovers 0 (29,252)
(May 27th, 1990)
Division 1; Sunderland 0, Swindon Town 1 (72,873)
(May 28th, 1990)
SEASON 1990/91
Division 3; Blackpool 2, Torquay United 2 [aet. 4-5 on penalties]
(21,615) (May 31st, 1991)
Division 2; Bolton Wanderers 0, Tranmere Rovers 0 (30,217)
(June 1st, 1991)
Division 1; Brighton & Hove Albion 1, Notts County 3 (59,940)
(June 2nd, 1991)
SEASON 1991/92
Division 2; Blackpool 1, Scunthorpe United 1 [aet. 4-3 on penalties]
(22,741) (May 23rd, 1992)
Division 1; Peterborough United 2, Stockport County 1 (35,087)
(May 24th, 1992)
Premier League; Blackburn Rovers 1, Leicester City 0 (68,147)
(May 25th, 1992)
SEASON 1992/93
Division 2; Crewe Alexandra 1, York City 1 [aet. 3-5 on penalties]
(22,416) (May 29th, 1993)
Division 1; Port Vale 0, West Bromwich Albion 3 (53,471)
(May 30th, 1993)
Premier League; Leicester City 3, Swindon Town 4 (73,802)
(May 31st, 1993)
SEASON 1993/94
Division 2; Preston North End 2, Wycombe Wanderers 4 (40,109)
(May 28th, 1994)
Division 1; Burnley 2, Stockport County 1 (44,806)
(May 29th, 1994)
Premier League; Derby County 1, Leicester City 2 (73,671)
(May 30th, 1994)
SEASON 1994/95
Division 2; Bury 0, Chesterfield 2 (22,815) (May 27th, 1995)
Division 1; Bristol Rovers 1, Huddersfield Town 2 (59,175)
(May 28th, 1995)
Premier League; Bolton Wanderers 4, Reading 3 (64,107)
(May 29th, 1995)
SEASON 1995/96
Division 2; Darlington 0, Plymouth Argyle 1 (43,431)
(May 25th, 1996)
Division 1; Bradford City 2, Notts County 0 (39,972)
(May 26th, 1996)
Premier League; Crystal Palace 1, Leicester City 2 (73,573)
(May 27th, 1996)
SEASON 1996/97
Division 2; Northampton Town 1, Swansea City 0 (46,804)
(May 10th, 1997)
Division 1; Brentford 0, Crewe Alexandra 1 (34,149)
(May 25th, 1997)
Premier League; Crystal Palace 1, Sheffield United 0 (64,383)
(May 26th, 1997)

Cont ...

WEMBLEY STADIUM [CONT ...]

.... continued from previous Page

SEASON 1997/98
Division 2; Colchester United 1, Torquay United 0 (19,486) (May 22nd, 1998)
Division 1; Grimsby Town 1, Northampton Town 0 (62,988) (May 23rd, 1998)
Premier League; Charlton Athletic 4, Sunderland 4 [aet. 7-6 on penalties] (77,739) (May 23rd, 1998)

SEASON 1998/99
Division 2; Leyton Orient 0, Scunthorpe United 1 (36,985) (May 29th, 1999)
Division 1; Gillingham 2, Manchester City 2 [aet. 1-3 on penalties] (76,935) (May 30th, 1999)
Premier League; Bolton Wanderers 0, Watford 2 (70,343) (May 31st, 1999)

SEASON 1999/2000
Division 2; Peterborough United 1, Darlington 0 (33,383) (May 26th, 2000)
Division 1; Wigan Athletic 2, Gillingham 3 [aet] (53,764) (May 28th, 2000)
Premier League; Barnsley 2, Ipswich Town 4 (73,427) (May 29th, 2000)

Total No. of Play Off Matches Played; 33

Following the closure of *Wembley Stadium* in 2000, Play off Finals were re-located to the **Millennium Stadium** in Cardiff until the new stadium had been completed.

A TOTAL OF **46** TEAMS TOOK PART IN **35** LEAGUE FIXTURES AT THIS VENUE

Programme Courtesy of John Litster

WELLINGTON ROAD
HOME GROUND OF **ASTON VILLA**

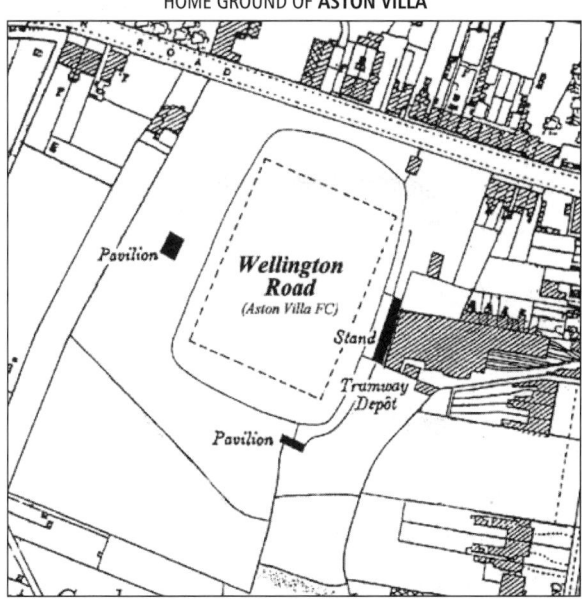

MAP EXTRACT; STAFFORDSHIRE 69.9 [**1904**]
SITE LOCATION; **SP06629078**

There were few facilities available when *Aston Villa* moved here from the *Lower Aston Grounds* and *Aston Park* in 1876. Located in Perry Barr, there was no accommodation for spectators, a hayrick had to be moved from the middle of the ground before matches could commence and players had to change in a blacksmith's shed.

Improvements made during the next few years included the installation of a grandstand which backed on to Birchfield Road Tram Depot on the east side, and two pavilions, but standing spectators had to make do with large flat areas around the pitch. A massive pitch invasion, the first ever serious crowd disorder at a football match, ensued when the ground record of 26,849 was set on January 7th, 1888 for the visit of *Preston North End* for a 5th Round FA Cup tie (1-3)

Aston Villa moved to **Villa Park** in 1897 and sold the grandstand to *Small Heath FC* for use at their **Muntz Street** ground. The site is now occupied by housing on Leslie and Wilmore Roads, a car park, public house and recreation ground.

PLAYING RECORD OF ASTON VILLA
LEAGUE PROGRAMME

First Match; 5-1 v. Stoke (2,000) (September 15th, 1888)
Last Match; 6-2 v. Bolton Wanderers (8,000) (March 22nd, 1897)
Highest Gate; 20,000 v. Sunderland (2-1) (October 5th, 1895) & v. Everton (1-2) (September 26th, 1896)
Lowest Gate; 600 v. Accrington (4-3) (October 27th, 1888)
Highest Home Win; 12-2 v. Accrington (8,000) (March 12th, 1892)
Highest Home Defeat; 1-6 v. Sunderland (16,000) (September 17th, 1892)

No. of Matches Played by Aston Villa; 119
Information Kindly Supplied by; Tony Matthews

The club was a founder member of the Football League in 1888 and, as its popularity increased, found that the ground with its poor spectator facilities and an uneven pitch was rapidly becoming unsuitable and moved to **Villa Park** in 1897.

A TOTAL OF **21** TEAMS TOOK PART IN **119** LEAGUE FIXTURES AT THIS VENUE

WEST BROMWICH ROAD
HOME GROUND OF WALSALL

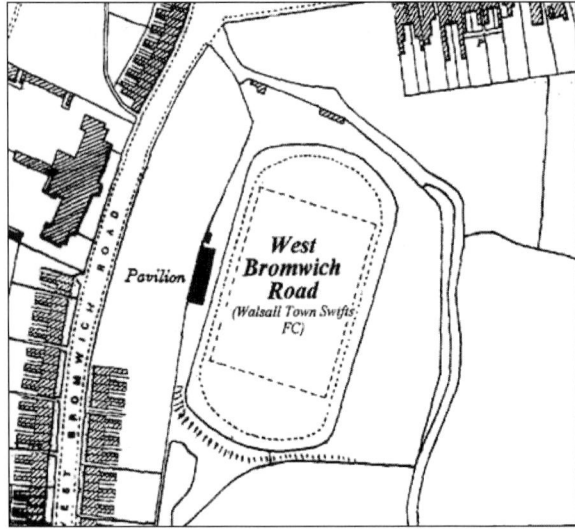

MAP EXTRACT; STAFFORDSHIRE 63.10 & 63.14 [1903]
SITE LOCATION; **SP01619711**

Located to the south of the town centre and on the east side of West Bromwich Road, *Walsall Town Swifts FC* moved into the ground in 1893. The pitch was surrounded by an oval running track and the facilities included a stand on the west side and some banking at the south end giving a nominal capacity of 4,000.

The club moved to *Fellows Park* in 1895 and, after returning for a short period at the end of the 1900/01 season, the site was later redeveloped for housing.

PLAYING RECORD OF WALSALL
[ALSO AS WALSALL TOWN SWIFTS]
LEAGUE PROGRAMME
1ST PERIOD

First Match; 5-1 v. Crewe Alexandra (1,500) (September 23rd, 1893)
Last Match; 1-2 v. Lincoln City (500) (April 20th, 1895)
No. of Matches Played; 27
2ND PERIOD
Matches Played; 3-3 v. Gainsborough Trinity (3,000) (December 26th, 1900)
1-3 v. Stockport County (2,000) (January 19th, 1901)
0-0 v. Grimsby Town (2,000) (February 9th, 1901)
1-1 v. Newton Heath (2,000) (February 25th, 1901)
3-3 v. New Brighton Tower (2,000) (April 6th, 1901)
0-0 v. Middlesbrough (800) (April 22nd, 1901)
No. of Matches Played; 6

Highest Gate; 4,000 v. Liverpool (1-1) (November 11th, 1893)
Lowest Gate; 500 v. Lincoln City (1-2) (April 20th, 1895)
Highest Home Win; 5-0 v. Grimsby Town (1,500) (March 24th, 1894)
Highest Home Defeat; 0-3 v. Bury (1,500) (October 27th, 1894)
Total No. of Matches Played by Walsall; 33
Information Kindly Supplied by; Tony Matthews

The club moved here from *The Chuckery* in 1893 but failed to gain re-election in 1895. The club changed its name to *Walsall FC* and moved to *Hillary Street* (later re-named *Fellows Park*) in 1896 but in December 1900 it was temporarily evicted from the new ground and returned here to play the final six home games of that season.

A TOTAL OF **22** TEAMS TOOK PART IN **33** LEAGUE FIXTURES AT THIS VENUE

WEST HAM STADIUM
HOME GROUND OF THAMES

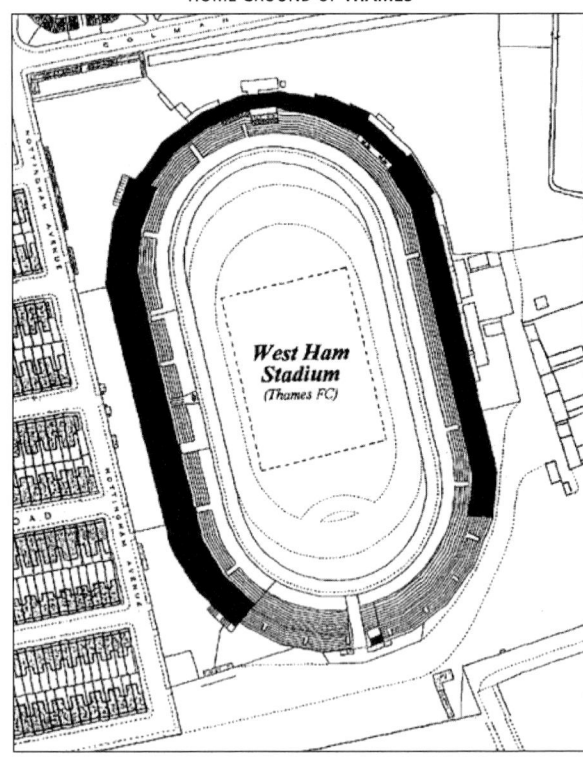

MAP EXTRACT; GROUND AS IN **1958** DRAWN FROM PLANS AND SUPERIMPOSED ON ESSEX 86.10 [1919]
SITE LOCATION; **TQ41318150**

The stadium was completed in 1928, the year that *Thames FC* was formed and took up residency. The arena, encompassing a football pitch and an oval track utilized for speedway and greyhound racing, was surrounded with large banks of concrete terracing and covered enclosures and seated stands were installed along both sides.

With a planned capacity of 120,000 it was one of the largest grounds utilized by a Football League club but this was never remotely tested with *Thames FCs* highest attendance of 8,275 only occupying 7% of the available capacity which is undoubtedly some sort of record. The club folded in 1932 and whilst the football matches were sparsely attended a crowd of 56,000 witnessed greyhound racing on August 4th, 1928 and an international speedway match between *England* and *Australia* attracted 64,000.

The stadium survived until the 1970s when it was demolished and the site redeveloped with housing.

PLAYING RECORD OF THAMES
LEAGUE PROGRAMME

First Match; 4-1 v. Walsall (7,000) (September 6th, 1930)
Last Match; 2-3 v. Queens Park Rangers (3,000) (April 30th, 1932)
Highest Gate; 8,275 v. Exeter City (0-0) (August 29th, 1931)
Lowest Gate; 469 v. Luton Town (1-0) (December 6th, 1930)
Highest Home Win; 6-3 v. Mansfield Town (1,070) (April 2nd, 1932)
Highest Home Defeat; 2-5 v. Coventry City (1,215) (January 16th, 1932)
No. of Matches Played by Thames; 42

The club was elected into the Football League Division 3 [S] in 1930 and did not seek re-election in 1932

A TOTAL OF **25** TEAMS TOOK PART IN **42** LEAGUE FIXTURES AT THIS VENUE

WHADDON ROAD
HOME GROUND OF **CHELTENHAM TOWN**

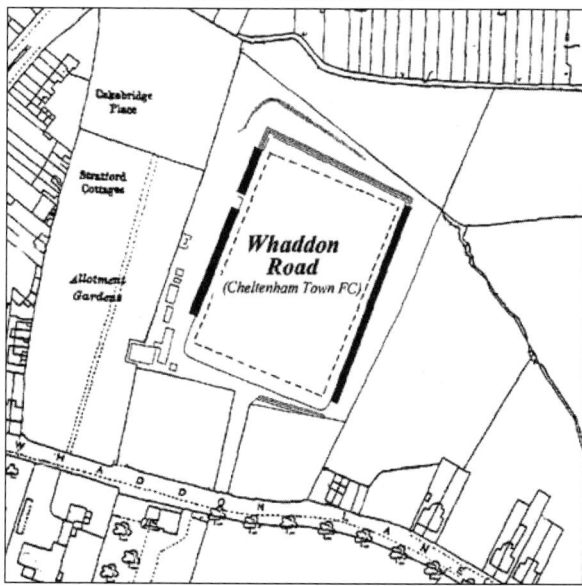

MAP EXTRACT; GROUND AS IN **1955** DRAWN FROM PLANS AND SUPERIMPOSED ON GLOUCESTERSHIRE 26.4 & 26.8 [1923]
SITE LOCATION; **SO95972308**

The ground opened in 1927 and the original facilities included a low stand on the west side. *Cheltenham Town FC* moved here from *Carter's Field* in 1932 and erected a cover over the narrow east side.

A new 1,088 seat main stand, fronted by a small paddock, was constructed on the west side during the 1950s and the ground record of 8,326 was established at the FA Cup 1st Round tie v. *Reading* (1-2) on November 17th, 1956. By the time that they joined the Football League in 1999 improvements had been made to the main stand, there were narrow uncovered terraces at each end and the terrace on the east side had been re-roofed.

The north end was roofed during 2000 and a new 2,000 seat stand built on the east side in 2001 giving a 7,407 capacity with 3,139 seats at the start of the 2004/5 season. The pitch size was 111 x 73 yards.

PLAYING RECORD OF CHELTENHAM TOWN
LEAGUE PROGRAMME

First Match; 0-2 v. Rochdale (5,189) (August 7th, 1999)
Highest Gate; 7,165 v. Hartlepool United (1-1)
(April 30th, 2002) (Play Off Match)
Lowest Gate; 2,368 v. Darlington (1-0) (September 12th, 2000)
Highest Home Win; 5-2 v. Plymouth Argyle (3,665) (September 23rd, 2000). 4-0 v. York City (3,958) (March 9th, 2002)
Highest Home Defeat; 0-4 v. Crewe Alexandra (5,548) (December 26th, 2002)

PLAY OFF MATCHES
1-1 v. Hartlepool United [aet. 5-4 on Penalties] (7,165) (April 30th, 2002)

No. of Matches Played by Cheltenham Town; 139
(League Programme; 138, Play Off Matches; 1)

The club was promoted into the Football League Division 3 from the Football Conference in 1999 and was also involved in a Football League Play Off Match at the neutral venue of the *Millennium Stadium*.

AT THE END OF SEASON 2004/5, A TOTAL OF **54** TEAMS HAD TAKEN PART IN **139** LEAGUE FIXTURES AT THIS VENUE

WHITE HART LANE
HOME GROUND OF **TOTTENHAM HOTSPUR**

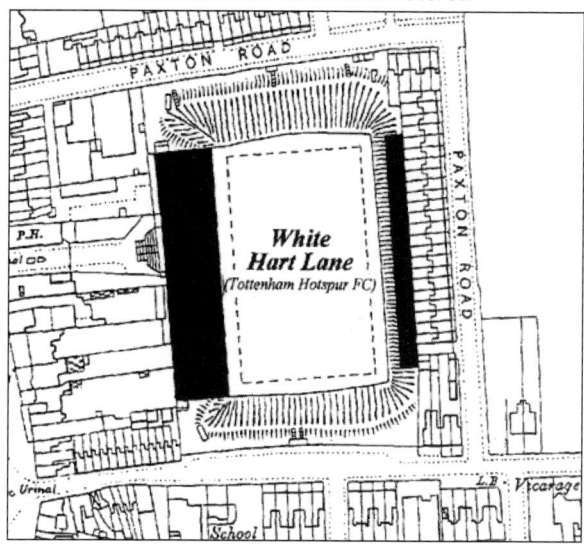

MAP EXTRACT; LONDON 12.3 [**1916**]
SITE LOCATION; **TQ34069114**

Originally known as the *High Road Ground*, the site of an old nursery, *Tottenham Hotspur* moved here in 1899. The only facility was a stand brought from their previous ground and re-erected to provide cover for some 2,500 spectators. By 1901 a new 500 seat main stand had been constructed and the terraces expanded to give a nominal capacity of 30,000 and within eight years a 5,300 seat structure had been opened on the west side.

Following the end of WWI the name of the ground was changed to *White Hart Lane* and in the early 1920s covers were installed at both ends. In 1934 a new 5,100 seat two tier stand was constructed over the terracing on the east side (requiring the demolition of a row of houses at the rear) and the record attendance of 75,038 was subsequently set at the FA Cup 6th Round tie v. *Sunderland* (0-1) on March 5th, 1938.

The ground did not see any further alterations until the 1960s when seats were installed at the rear of the terraces at the north and south ends and stands constructed in the north west and south west corners. A new all-seat stand opened on the west side in 1982 and the stand on the east side was re-roofed and refurbished in 1989. The stadium was made an all-seater in the 1990s with the provision of refurbished and new stands at the ends giving a capacity of 36,257 at the start of the 2004/5 season. The pitch size was 110 x 73 yards.

PLAYING RECORD OF TOTTENHAM HOTSPUR
LEAGUE PROGRAMME

First Match; 3-0 v. Wolverhampton Wanderers (20,000) (September 1st, 1908)
Highest Gate; 70,882 v. Manchester United (2-0)
(August 22nd, 1951)
Lowest Gate; 5,000 v. Sunderland (0-6) (December 19th, 1919)
Highest Home Win; 10-4 v. Everton (37,794) (October 11th, 1958). 9-0 v. Bristol Rovers (26,571) (October 22nd, 1977)
Highest Home Defeat; 0-6 v. Sunderland (5,000) (December 19th, 1919) & v. Arsenal (47,714) (March 6th, 1935)

No. of Matches Played by Tottenham Hotspur; 1,766
Information Kindly Supplied by; Tony Matthews

The club was elected into the Football League Division 2 in 1903.

AT THE END OF SEASON 2003/4, A TOTAL OF **75** TEAMS HAD TAKEN PART IN **1,766** LEAGUE FIXTURES AT THIS VENUE

WHITE CITY STADIUM
TEMPORARY HOME GROUND FOR QUEENS PARK RANGERS

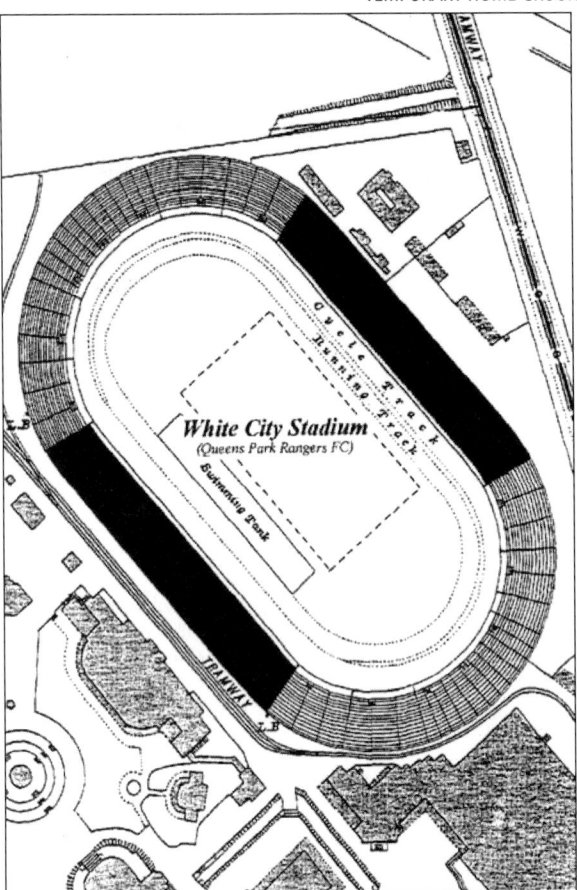

MAP EXTRACT; LONDON 4.11 [1938]
SITE LOCATION; **TQ23078091**

PLAYING RECORD OF QUEENS PARK RANGERS
LEAGUE PROGRAMME
1ST PERIOD;
First Match; 0-3 v. Bournemouth & Boscombe Athletic (18,907)
(September 5th, 1931)
Last Match; 1-1 v. Torquay United (2,800) (May 6th, 1933)
No. of Matches Played; 42
2ND PERIOD;
Matches Played; 0-1 v. Notts. County (15,594) (October 6th, 1962)
4-1 v. Hull City (18,281) (October 22nd, 1962)
3-2 v. Reading (10,238) (November 17th, 1962)
0-0 v. Shrewsbury Town (10,360) (December 1st, 1962)
2-2 v. Carlisle United (8,733) (December 22nd, 1962)
1-3 v. Northampton Town (14,238) (February 9th, 1963)
1-0 v. Bournemouth & Boscombe Athletic (8,387) (March 2nd, 1963)
1-2 v. Bradford City (7,555) (March 16th, 1963)
3-1 v. Bristol City (5,683) (March 30th, 1963)
1-2 v. Colchester United (7,686) (April 1st, 1963)
1-0 v. Southend United (7,540) (April 8th, 1963)
3-5 v. Bristol Rovers (10,169) (April 12th, 1963)
3-1 v. Port Vale (5,690) (April 13th, 1963)
2-3 v. Millwall (8,583) (April 27th, 1963)
2-2 v. Watford (5,040) (May 13th, 1963)
0-0 v. Peterborough United (5,989) (May 18th, 1963)
1-3 v. Coventry City (3,245) (May 22nd, 1963)
No. of Matches Played; 17

Highest Gate; 24,347 v. Brentford (2-3) (August 27th, 1932)
Lowest Gate; 2,800 v. Torquay United (1-1) (May 6th, 1933)
Highest Home Win; 7-0 v. Gillingham (3,881) (March 10th, 1932)
Highest Home Defeat; 0-3 v. Bournemouth & Boscombe Athletic
(18,907) (September 5th, 1931)
& v. Reading (11,213) (October 8th, 1932)

**Total No. of Matches Played by Queens Park Rangers;
59**

Information Kindly Supplied by; Tony Matthews

Queens Park Rangers moved here for short periods in the 1930s and 1960s. Although it had far superior facilities than *Loftus Road*, the remoteness of the pitch from the terraces, separated by a running track, and eventually poor attendances led to a depressing atmosphere in the stadium and, in both cases, the club moved back to the former ground.

A TOTAL OF **34** TEAMS TOOK PART IN **59** LEAGUE FIXTURES AT THIS VENUE

This was the world's first purpose-built Olympic Stadium when it was constructed for the 1908 event and had a total capacity of 130,000 with 60,000 seats. The first football matches played here were part of the Olympic Games and *Queens Park Rangers* played some Southern League fixtures here in 1912. The stadium saw a variety of uses including cycling and athletics before greyhound racing was tried in 1927 and it was purchased by the Greyhound Racing Association in 1930.

The new owners had built new covered terracing and reduced the capacity to 80,000 when *Queens Park Rangers* came here for their second spell, this time with Football League matches, between 1931 and 1932. Although the mainstay for the stadium was greyhound racing and athletics, non-League football clubs including *White City, Acton Town, Hammersmith United* and the *Corinthians* briefly used it for home games.

By the time that *QPR* moved here for their final abortive attempt to establish it as a home venue in 1962/3 the reduced capacity of 60,000 was now totally under cover and there were 11,000 seats. The last football game of any note was the *Uruguay* v. *France* World Cup Group A fixture on July 15th, 1966 and this set the record attendance for a football game here of 45,662. The stadium continued to host athletics, greyhound racing and speedway for a while before it finally closed in 1984 and was demolished to make way for offices for the BBC, a car park and small sports ground.

White City Stadium in use as a greyhound racing track in 1984.
Photograph by Bob Lilliman. Courtesy of Groundtastic Magazine

WITHDEAN STADIUM
HOME GROUND OF **BRIGHTON & HOVE ALBION**

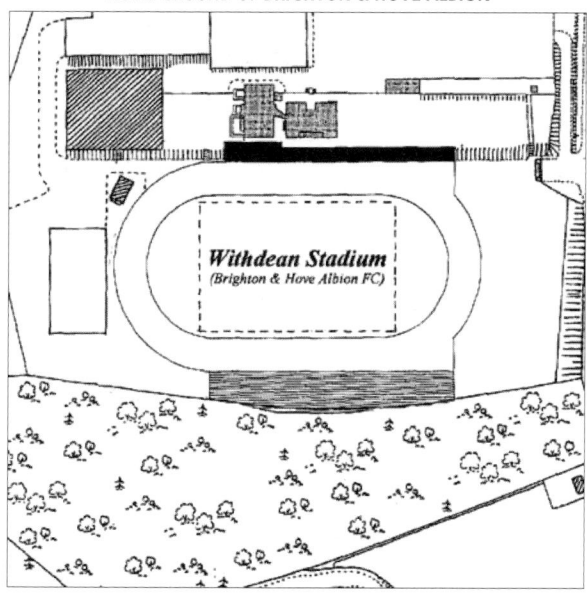

MAP EXTRACT; GROUND AS IN **2000** DRAWN FROM AERIAL PHOTOGRAPHS AND SUPERIMPOSED ON SUSSEX 66.1 [1931]
SITE LOCATION; TQ29650746

Constructed on the Marshall's Playing Fields, the site had first been utilized as a pre-WWII tennis centre. It re-opened on May 22nd, 1947 as the Brighton Zoo and Olympic Stadium and hosted a Davis Cup tennis match before closing in 1952.

Brighton Council rebuilt it and opened the ground on May 14th, 1955 as *The Brighton Sports Arena* and as well as athletics the venue hosted football and American Football. When *Brighton & Hove Albion FC* moved here the facilities included a narrow covered seated stand on the north side and an open seated stand on the south. The all-seat capacity at the start of the 2004/5 season was 7,053 and the pitch size 110 x 75 yards.

PLAYING RECORD OF BRIGHTON & HOVE ALBION
LEAGUE PROGRAMME

First Match; 6-0 v. Mansfield Town (5,882) (August 7th, 1999)
Highest Gate; 6,995 v. Halifax Town (2-1) (December 2nd, 2000)
Lowest Gate; 5,049 v. Rochdale (3-4) (December 10th, 1999)
Highest Home Win; 6-0 v. Mansfield Town (5,882) (August 7th, 1999)
Highest Home Defeat; 1-4 v. Bristol City (6,305) (November 15th, 2003)

PLAY OFF MATCHES
1-2 v. Swindon Town [aet. 4-3 on penalties] (6,876) (May 20th, 2004)
No. of Matches Played by Brighton & Hove Albion; 139
(League Programme; 138, Play Off Matches; 1)
Some Information Kindly Supplied by; Tim Carder

The club moved here from *Priestfield Stadium* as a temporary measure in 1999 and was involved in a Football League Play Off match at the *Millennium Stadium*.

AT THE END OF SEASON 2004/5, A TOTAL OF **75** TEAMS HAD TAKEN PART IN **139** LEAGUE FIXTURES AT THIS VENUE

YORK STREET
HOME GROUND OF **BOSTON UNITED**

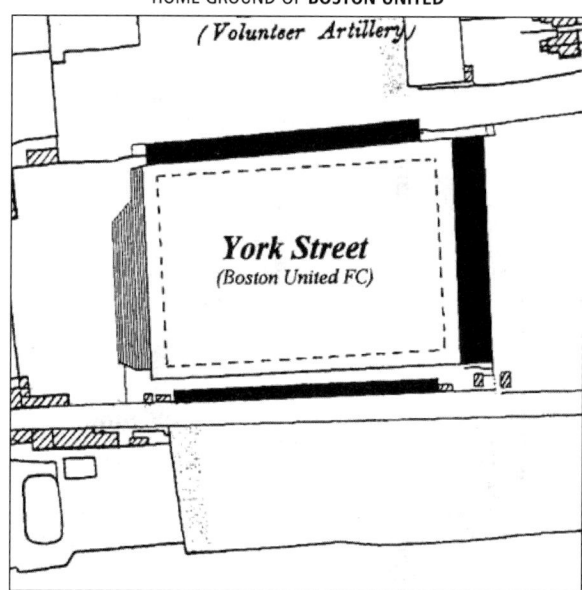

MAP EXTRACT; GROUND AS IN **1968** DRAWN FROM MAPS AND SUPERIMPOSED ON LINCOLNSHIRE 109.9 [1905]
SITE LOCATION; TF33124400

The ground, also known as *Shodfriars Lane*, was first used in the late 1800s by two football clubs; *Boston Town* and *Boston Swifts* and by 1905 the only facility was a small stand erected on the north side. The *Swifts* failed to materialize after WWI but *Boston* (having dropped the *"Town"*) continued to use it until they ran into financial difficulties in the 1930s and re-formed as *Boston United* in 1934.

The ground slowly developed with the construction of a stand on the north side, terracing around the ground and the installation of cover at the east end and on the south side. The record attendance of 11,000 was set at the FA Cup 3rd Round Replay v. *Derby County* (1-6) on January 9th, 1974. Although the club won the championship of the Football Conference in 1977, due to the poor facilities at *York Street* it was refused entry into the Football League, prompting the reconstruction of the ground over the next ten years with the building of all-seat stands on the north side and at the east end and covered terracing on the other two sides. The capacity at the start of the 2004/5 season was 6,643 with 1,769 seats.

PLAYING RECORD OF BOSTON UNITED
LEAGUE PROGRAMME

First Match; 2-2 v. AFC Bournemouth (4,184) (August 10th, 2002)
Highest Gate; 6,445 v. Lincoln City (0-2) (February 16th, 2005)
Lowest Gate; 1,919 v. Wrexham (3-3) (April 2nd, 2003)
Highest Home Win; 6-0 v. Shrewsbury Town (2,155) (December 21st, 2002)
Highest Home Defeat; 0-3 v. Exeter City (2,474) (November 2nd, 2002)

No. of Matches Played by Boston United; 69

The club was promoted from the Football Conference into Division 3 in 2002, but following an investigation by the FA into financial irregularities during Season 2001/2 was fined £100,000 and deducted four points before making their League debut. Shaun Mayes of *AFC Bournemouth* scored the first League goal here in the 9th minute of the first match.

AT THE END OF SEASON 2004/5, A TOTAL OF **34** TEAMS HAD TAKEN PART IN **69** LEAGUE FIXTURES AT THIS VENUE

THE SCOTTISH FOOTBALL LEAGUE

Following on from the success of the Football League in England, Scottish clubs, similarly embroiled in cup competitions and casual friendly fixtures started their own SCOTTISH FOOTBALL LEAGUE in 1890. The competition kicked off on August 16th, 1890 and the 11 founder members and their grounds were;
Abercorn *(Underwood Park)*, Cambuslang *(Whitefield Park)*, Celtic *(Celtic Park [1st])*, Cowlairs *(Springfield Park)*, Dumbarton *(Boghead Park)*, Heart of Midlothian *(Tynecastle)*, Rangers *(Ibrox Park [1st])*, Renton *(Tontine Park)*, St Mirren *(Westmarch)*, Third Lanark *(Cathkin Park)* and Vale of Leven *(Millburn Park)*

At this time the Scottish FA insisted on a strictly amateur code and this led to covert professionalism amongst leading clubs resulting in the suspension of *Renton* and point deductions from *Celtic, Third Lanark* and *Cowlairs*. Professionalism was legalized in 1893 and although Division Two was formed in the same year there was no automatic promotion and relegation or a mechanism for separating clubs on the same points (unlike the Football League where goal average was introduced from the outset). The bottom two in Division One and top three in Division Two took place in a ballot (inevitably leading to the *status quo*) and Play Off matches *(listed below)* were frequently held to determine final placings.

Division Two was suspended in 1915 and when it re-formed in 1921 automatic promotion and relegation was introduced and, in the following season, goal average finally introduced. A Division Three, embracing a number of small clubs across southern Scotland, started up in 1923 but this proved to be anything but economically viable and collapsed in chaos during the 1925/26 season.

Fixtures were suspended for the duration of WWII and when football re-emerged in 1946 the Scottish League was split into Divisions A and B with a Division C consisting of reserve teams and smaller clubs (and not considered to be of full League status). This more or less remained the situation until 1955 when Division C was scrapped and, in the following year, Divisions 1 and 2 re-introduced. In 1975 the League was re-formed into three smaller sections; the Premier Division and Divisions 1 and 2 and in 1995 it was further sub-divided into four divisions of ten clubs each when *Ross County* and *Caledonian Thistle* joined.

After the Scottish Premier League was formed in 1998 (with much the same motives as those south of the border) the Scottish League consisted of three divisions and when the SPL was increased to twelve clubs in 2000, *Peterhead* and *Elgin City* were admitted to Division Three.

In 2005 the Scottish Football League decided to introduce a system of Play Off matches to establish the membership of Divisions 1, 2 and 3 at the end of each season. This would involve the second from bottom playing the fourth from top of the division below and the second and third teams playing each other in two Semi-Finals with a Final to decide which club would be in the higher division for the following season. It was further decided that any club finishing bottom of Division 3 for three successive seasons would have its League membership reduced to Associate status and if it was at the bottom for a further two seasons then would be expelled.

SCOTTISH LEAGUE PLAY OFF MATCHES

1891 Dumbarton 2, Rangers 2 [Division 1 Championship Play Off] @ Cathkin Park (10,000) (May 21st, 1891)
1896 Renton 2, Kilmarnock 1 [Division 2, 3/4 Place Play Off] @ Cathkin Park (-) (May 20th, 1896)
1898 Partick Thistle 0, Dundee 2 [Division 1, 7/8 Place Play Off] @ Meadowside (3,000) (March 24th, 1898)
1900 St Bernards 1, St Mirren 2 [Division 1, 8/9 Place Play Off] @ Dens Park (-) (April 7th, 1900)
1905 Celtic 2, Rangers 1 [Division 1 Championship Play Off] @ Hampden Park (30,000) (May 6th, 1905)
1906 Port Glasgow Athletic 6, Kilmarnock 0 [Division 1, 14/15 Place Play Off] @ New Cathkin Park (-) (May 15th, 1906)
1907 Raith Rovers 3, East Stirlingshire 2 [Division 2, 10/11 Place Play Off] @ Old Logie Green (-) (May 11th, 1907)
1915 Cowdenbeath 1, Leith Athletic 0 [Division 2 Championship Play Off] @ East End Park (-) (April 10th, 1915)
1915 Leith Athletic 2, St Bernards 1 [Division 2 Championship Play Off] @ Easter Road (5,000) (April 17th, 1915)
1915 St Bernards 1, Cowdenbeath 3 [Division 2 Championship Play Off] @ Easter Road (-) (April 24th, 1915)

NB. The Scottish League in general has been poorly documented, particularly in the early days and although match results and dates are recorded, many attendance figures, even in the post-WWII era are not. With the notable exception of East Stirlingshire FC, clubs have been extremely reluctant to release details of very low gates and many of those that have been incorporated in this section are only, at the very best, estimates.

ALMONDVALE STADIUM
HOME GROUND OF LIVINGSTON

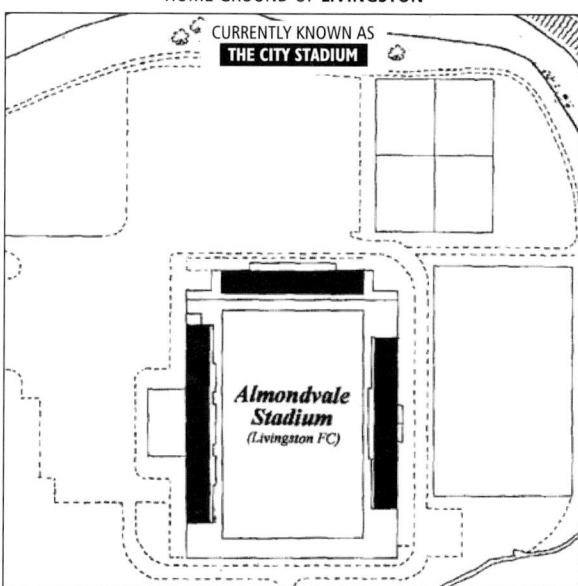

MAP EXTRACT; GROUND AS IN **2000** DRAWN FROM PLANS AND SUPERIMPOSED ON EDINBURGH 5.7 [1907]
SITE LOCATION; **NT04906693**

Constructed on a greenfield site and currently known as *The City Stadium*, *Meadowbank Thistle FC* re-formed as *Livingston FC* and moved here from *Meadowbank Stadium* in 1995. The facilities, as built, included a 2,254 seat stand on the west side and a slightly shorter 1,894 seat stand on the east. All-seat stands were subsequently built at each end and later improvements included the provision of corner stands "filling in" the south east and north east corners. The all-seated capacity at the start of the 2004/5 season was 10,006 and the pitch size was 105 x 72 yards.

PLAYING RECORD OF LIVINGSTON
LEAGUE PROGRAMME

First Match; 1-1 v. East Stirlingshire (4,148)
(November 11th, 1995)
Highest Gate; 10,112 v. Rangers (0-2) (October 27th, 2001)
Lowest Gate; 613 v. Stranraer (0-1) (February 24th, 1998)
Highest Home Win; 5-0 v. Dumbarton (1,830) (February 20th, 1999)
& v. Airdrieonians (3,296) (May 1st, 2001)
Highest Home Defeat; 0-4 v. Raith Rovers (4,010) (September 16th, 2000), v. Kilmarnock (4,144) (February 1st, 2003)
& v. Celtic (8,750) (April 14th, 2005)

No. of Matches Played by Livingston; 178
Information Kindly Supplied by; Duncan Bennett

The club moved here from *Meadowbank Stadium* in 1995 but had to play the first five games of the season at *Meadowbank Stadium* until the new ground was ready.

AT THE END OF SEASON 2004/5, A TOTAL OF **38** TEAMS HAD TAKEN PART IN **178** LEAGUE FIXTURES AT THIS VENUE

ANNFIELD PARK
HOME GROUND OF STIRLING ALBION

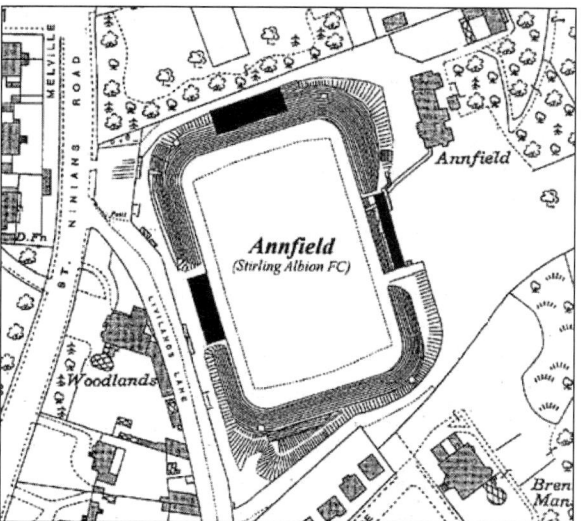

MAP EXTRACT; GROUND AS IN **1960** DRAWN FROM MAPS AND SUPERIMPOSED ON STIRLINGSHIRE 17.7 [1942]
SITE LOCATION; **NS79659258**

Located in the south of the city, the Annfield estate was purchased in 1945 for £5,000. Annfield House, an 18thC mansion, was initially used as club offices and dressing rooms but there were no facilities for spectators although club officials were accommodated on chairs placed on the back of lorries parked around the pitch. After a failed attempt was made to purchase the grandstand from the *Royal Gymnasium Ground*, a new stand (rebuilt in 1949) was constructed on the east side in 1946 and further improvements included the installation of concrete terracing around all sides, a covered stand on the west side and cover over the part of the north end.

The record attendance of 28,600 was set at the Scottish FA Cup 4th Round tie v. *Celtic* (1-3) on March 14th, 1959. Following the sale of *Annfield Park* to Stirling Council in 1983 sections of the East Stand were condemned and, as part of the deal for investing in the ground, an artificial pitch was installed for community use.

After *Stirling Albion* moved out in 1992 Annfield House was refurbished as an Old People's Home and the remainder of the site utilized for housing.

PLAYING RECORD OF STIRLING ALBION
LEAGUE PROGRAMME

First Match; 4-1 v. Ayr United (6,000) (August 27th, 1947)
Last Match; 2-0 v. Clydebank (1,121) (May 2nd, 1992)
Highest Gate; 25,800 v. Celtic (2-1) (November 12th, 1949)
Lowest Gate; 216 v. Forfar Athletic (0-0) (March 10th, 1982)
Highest Home Win; 7-0 v. Albion Rovers (5,716) (November 29th, 1947), v. Montrose (2,590) (September 28th, 1957),
& v. Arbroath (2,800) (March 11th, 1961)
Highest Home Defeat; 0-7 v. Raith Rovers (1,564)
(February 17th, 1968)

No. of Matches Played by Stirling Albion; 779
Information Kindly Supplied by; Allan Grieve

The club was elected into the Scottish Football League Division 2 in 1947. The match v. *East Fife* on January 14th, 1950 took place at *Recreation Park* due to the pitch at *Annfield* being unplayable. In 1992 the club moved out and groundshared with *Stenhousemuir* at *Ochilview Park* until *Forthbank Stadium* was ready.

A TOTAL OF **41** TEAMS TOOK PART IN **779** LEAGUE FIXTURES AT THIS VENUE

ARDENCAPLE PARK
HOME GROUND OF HELENSBURGH

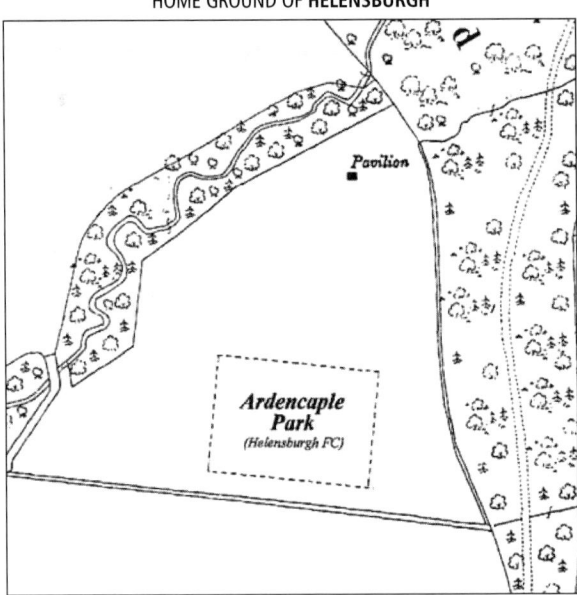

MAP EXTRACT; DUNBARTONSHIRE N13.4 [1914]
SITE LOCATION; NS28558338

The site of this ground is not known for certain. The Ordnance Survey map of 1914, surveyed during the period of *Helensburgh FCs* existence, does not show a specific football ground in the Ardencaple area but identifies a Cricket & Football Ground on the south edge of Duchess Wood and it is assumed that this is *Ardencaple Park*. The location of the pitch, as indicated above, is purely hypothetical.

The probable record gate is 1,500 at the Scottish FA Cup 1st Round Replay v. *Bo'ness* (0-0 aet) on January 28th, 1925. This site is currently part of Larchfield School Cricket & Rugby Ground.

PLAYING RECORD OF HELENSBURGH
LEAGUE PROGRAMME

First Match; 0-1 v. Arthurlie (1,000) (August 18th, 1923)
Last Match; 5-1 v. Montrose (-) (April 17th, 1926)
Highest & Lowest Gate*; Not Known
Highest Home Win; 8-4 v. Beith (-) (December 6th, 1924)
Highest Home Defeat; 1-5 v. Vale of Leven (-) (January 16th, 1926)
No. of Matches Played by Helensburgh; 45

The club was a founder member of the Scottish Football League Division 3 in 1923 and left the League when Division 3 was disbanded near the end of the 1925/26 season.
*NB. Very few gate figures are known for this club but it is assumed that in general attendances numbered only a few hundred.

A TOTAL OF 21 TEAMS TOOK PART IN 45 LEAGUE FIXTURES AT THIS VENUE

THE BALLAST STADIUM
HOME GROUND OF HAMILTON ACADEMICAL

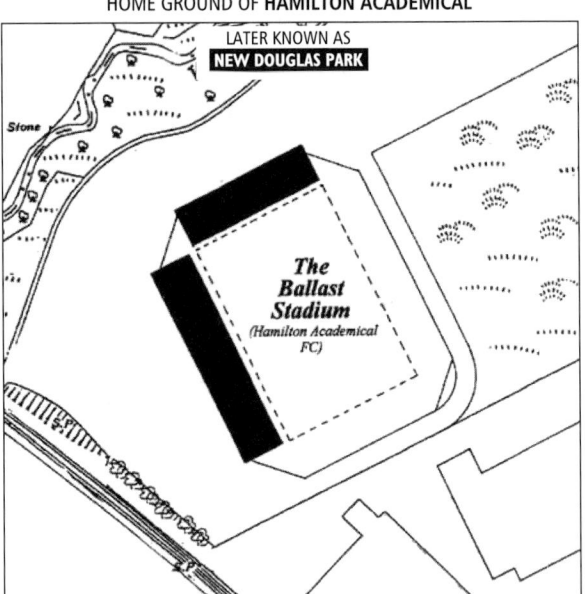

MAP EXTRACT; GROUND AS IN 2001 DRAWN FROM AERIAL PHOTOGRAPHS AND SUPERIMPOSED ON LANARKSHIRE 11.16 [1936]
SITE LOCATION; NS71065622

Located just north of *Hamilton Academical FCs* previous ground at **Douglas Park** the stadium was constructed on the site of a former brick works and sand pit. When it opened in 2001 only two sides were utilized with a 2,100 seat stand at the north end and a 3,200 seat main stand on the west side. The record attendance of 4,280 was established at the official opening friendly match v. *Sunderland* on July 28th, 2001. The name of the ground was changed to *New Douglas Park* in 2003 and at the start of the 2004/5 season the pitch size was 115 x 75 yards and capacity 5,406.

PLAYING RECORD OF HAMILTON ACADEMICAL
LEAGUE PROGRAMME

First Match; 1-1 v. Queen of the South (3,192) (August 4th, 2001)
Highest Gate; 3,543 v. Partick Thistle (0-1) (August 21st, 2004)
Lowest Gate; 626 v. Berwick Rangers (3-0) (February 25th, 2003)
Highest Home Win; 6-1 v. Greenock Morton (2,692) (April 10th, 2004)
Highest Home Defeat; 1-5 v. Stranraer (1,175) (October 5th, 2002)
No. of Matches Played by Hamilton Academical; 90
Information Kindly Supplied by; Scott A. Struthers

The club moved here from groundsharing with *Partick Thistle* at *Firhill Park* in 2001. The first League goal at the stadium was scored by Peter Weatherson of *Queen of the South* in the 20th minute.

AT THE END OF SEASON 2004/5, A TOTAL OF 22 TEAMS HAD TAKEN PART IN 90 LEAGUE FIXTURES AT THIS VENUE

BALMOOR STADIUM
HOME GROUND OF PETERHEAD

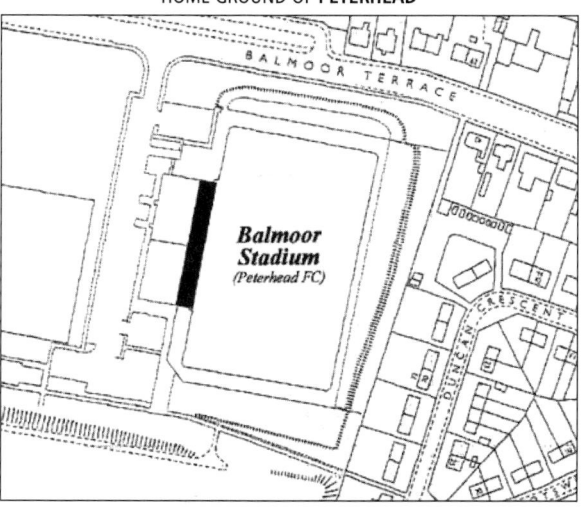

MAP EXTRACT; GROUND AS IN **1998** DRAWN FROM MAPS AND SUPERIMPOSED ON NK1246 [1950]
SITE LOCATION; NK12334679

Peterhead FC moved here from *Recreation Park* in September 1997 and the facilities originally consisted of a main 500 seat stand on the west side with uncovered standing accommodation around the rest of the ground. In 2001 a new all-seat stand was constructed on the east side, giving a capacity of 4,000 with 980 seats at the start of the 2004/5 season and the pitch size was 110 x 74 yards.

PLAYING RECORD OF PETERHEAD
LEAGUE PROGRAMME

First Match; 2-0 v. Montrose (700) (August 5th, 2000)
Highest Gate; 1,693 v. Albion Rovers (0-0) (May 3rd, 2003)
Lowest Gate; 327 v. Montrose (1-1) (April 17th, 2001)
Highest Home Win; 6-0 v. East Stirlingshire (584) (February 15th, 2003), v. Stirling Albion (611) (March 4th, 2003) & v. East Stirlingshire (553) (January 24th, 2004)
Highest Home Defeat; 2-4 v. East Stirlingshire (656) (September 16th, 2000). 0-3 v. Dumbarton (528) (August 11th, 2001)
No. of Matches Played by Peterhead; 90

The club was elected into the Scottish Football League Division 3 in 2000.

AT THE END OF SEASON 2004/5, A TOTAL OF **16** TEAMS HAD TAKEN PART IN **90** LEAGUE FIXTURES AT THIS VENUE

The narrow flat standing area at the north end of **Balmoor Park**, on March 20th, 2004. The match in progress, Peterhead v. Stirling Albion finished in a 1-1 draw.

Courtesy of RedWeb (www.stirlingalbionfc.com)

BANK PARK
HOME GROUND OF LEITH ATHLETIC

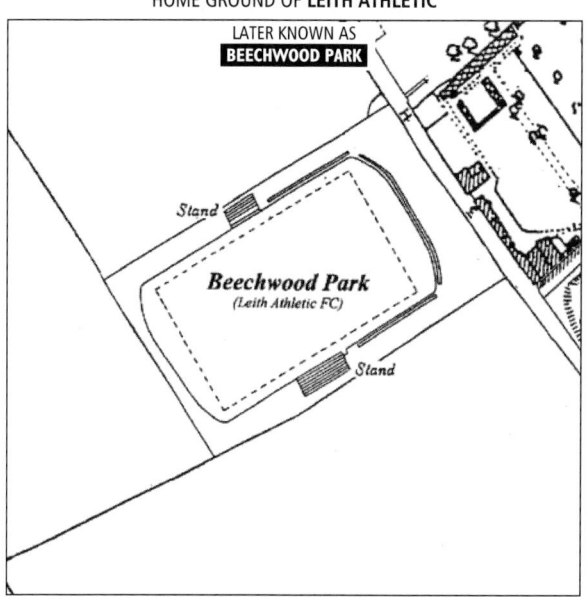

MAP EXTRACT; EDINBURGH 3.4 [**1896**]
SITE LOCATION; NT27507515

Originally named *Bank Park*, the facilities included two open stands on each side and some open seating at the east end of the pitch. The probable record gate is 7,000 at the Scottish FA Cup 2nd Round Replay v. *Dumbarton* (3-3) on February 13th, 1892. It was re-named as *Beechwood Park* in 1895 and when the ground closed in 1899 the North British Railway subsequently constructed its branch line into Leith Central Station across the site.

PLAYING RECORD OF LEITH ATHLETIC
LEAGUE PROGRAMME

First Match; 2-3 v. Renton (-) (August 22nd, 1891)
Last Match; 3-3 v. Kilmarnock (-) (April 15th, 1899)
Highest Gate*; 6,000 v. Celtic (2-1) (April 18th, 1892)
Lowest Gate*; Not Known
Highest Home Win; 10-0 v. Vale of Leven (-) (September 19th, 1891)
Highest Home Defeat; 0-4 v. Renton (-) (August 31st, 1895)
No. of Matches Played by Leith Athletic; 74

The club was elected into the Scottish Football League in 1891 and the first ever Scottish Football League penalty kick was scored here by Alex McColl of *Renton* in their 3-2 win v. *Leith Athletic* on August 22nd, 1891. The club vacated the ground in 1899 and moved to *New Logie Green* to groundshare with *St Bernards* for a short period before moving to *Hawkhill* for the remainder of the 1899/1900 season.
*NB. This is the highest gate figure of the few that were recorded. In view of the general level of those that are known, it is very probable that there were crowds of less than 500 on occasions.

A TOTAL OF **23** TEAMS TOOK PART IN **74** LEAGUE FIXTURES AT THIS VENUE

BARROWFIELD PARK
HOME GROUND OF CLYDE

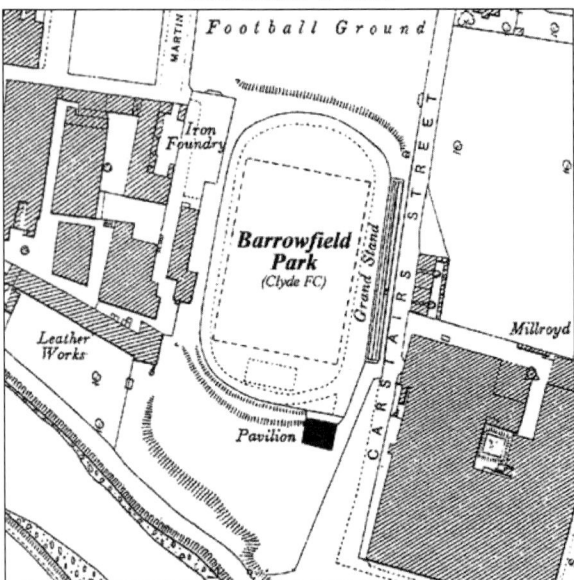

MAP EXTRACT; LANARKSHIRE 6.15 [1896]
SITE LOCATION; **NS60986301**

Located on the north bank of the River Clyde in the Dalmarnock district, *Barrowfield Park* occupied a narrow site between Carstairs Street and an iron foundry. *Clyde FC* moved here in 1877 and, by the time of their debut in the Scottish Football League, the football pitch was surrounded by an oval cycling track with an open seated stand on the east side, a pavilion and embankment at the south end and an embankment at the north end. The club moved to *Shawfield* in 1898 and the site was subsequently redeveloped with a school and housing.

PLAYING RECORD OF CLYDE
LEAGUE PROGRAMME

First Match & Highest Home Win; 10-3 v. Vale of Leven (-)
(August 15th, 1891)
Last Match; 2-4 v. Hibernian (-) (January 3rd, 1898)
Highest Gate*; 10,000 v. Celtic (2-7) (August 29th, 1891)
Lowest Gate*; Not Known
Highest Home Defeat; 3-10 v. Heart of Midlothian (5,000) (October 3rd, 1891). 1-9 v. Celtic (2,000) (December 25th, 1897)
No. of Matches Played by Clyde; 67

The club was elected into the Scottish Football League in 1891 and moved to *Shawfield Park* in 1898. The 10-3 victory v. *Vale of Leven* on August 15th, 1891 was the first ever double figure score in Scottish Football League history.

*NB. This is the highest League gate figure of the very few that are known and equals the 10,000 at the Scottish FA Cup 3rd Round tie v. *Rangers* (0-5) on February 6th, 1892.
. In view of the general level of those that are known, it is very probable that there were crowds of less than 1,000 on occasions.

A TOTAL OF **22** TEAMS TOOK PART IN **67** LEAGUE FIXTURES AT THIS VENUE

BAYVIEW STADIUM
HOME GROUND OF EAST FIFE

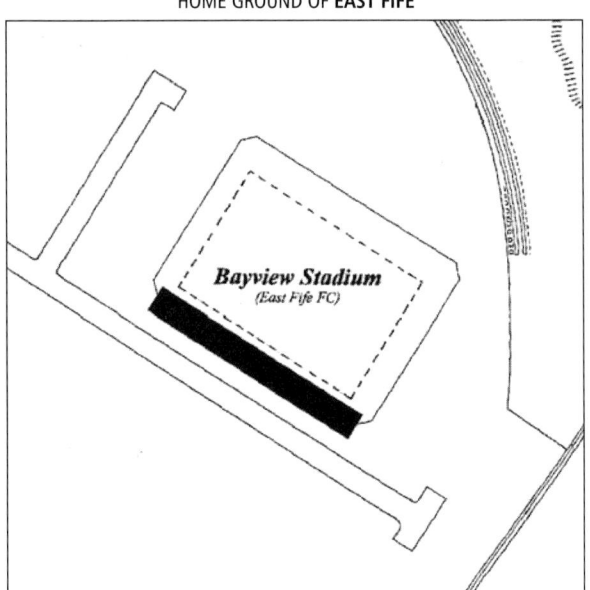

MAP EXTRACT; GROUND AS IN **1970** DRAWN FROM MAPS AND SUPERIMPOSED ON NO3700 & NO3800 [1951]
SITE LOCATION; **NO38080005**

Constructed on the site of railway sidings and an hydraulic power station at the north end of Methil No.3 Dock, *East Fife FC* moved here from *Bayview Park* in 1998. At the start of the 2004/5 season all the spectators were accommodated within the 2,000 seat main stand on the south side of the 113 x 73 yards sized pitch.

PLAYING RECORD OF EAST FIFE
LEAGUE PROGRAMME

First Match; 1-0 v. Forfar Athletic (1,462) (November 14th, 1998)
Highest Gate; 1,991 v. Greenock Morton (0-1) (April 19th, 2003)
Lowest Gate; 223 v. Elgin City (1-1) (March 20th, 2001)
Highest Home Win; 5-0 v. Elgin City (514) (April 6th, 2003)
Highest Home Defeat; 0-4 v. East Stirlingshire (299)
(August 18th, 2001) & v. Albion Rovers (575) (November 2nd, 2002)
No. of Matches Played by East Fife; 120
Information Kindly Supplied by; Jim Stewart

The club moved here from *Bayview Park* in 1998.

AT THE END OF SEASON 2004/5, A TOTAL OF **25** TEAMS HAD TAKEN PART IN **120** LEAGUE FIXTURES AT THIS VENUE

No doubt visiting supporters suggest not so much "Bay", as "Power Station"! Looking north east from the stand at *Bayview Stadium*.
Photograph by Robert Marshall. Courtesy of Groundtastic Magazine

BAYVIEW PARK

HOME GROUND OF **EAST FIFE**
TEMPORARY HOME GROUND FOR **BERWICK RANGERS & MEADOWBANK THISTLE**

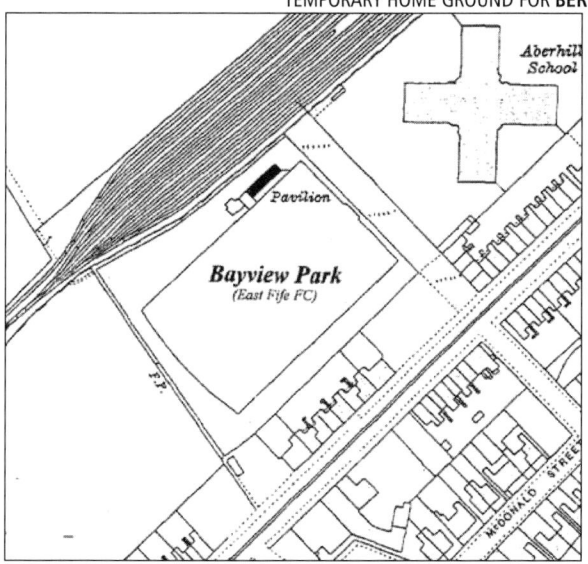

MAP EXTRACT; FIFE 28.8 [1914]
SITE LOCATION; NT37219985

PLAYING RECORD OF EAST FIFE
LEAGUE PROGRAMME

First Match; 1-2 v. Bathgate (-) (August 20th, 1921)
Last Match; 2-3 v. Livingston (1,008) (October 31st, 1998)
Highest Gate*; 22,515 v. Raith Rovers (3-0) (January 2nd, 1950)
Lowest Gate*; 294 v. Montrose (0-1) (February 10th, 1982)
Highest Home Win; 13-2 v. Edinburgh City (1,500)
(December 11th, 1937)
Highest Home Defeat; 1-7 v. Montrose (1,482) (February 7th, 1976)
& v. Dundee (869) (December 17th, 1996)
No. of Matches Played by East Fife; 1,280
(Including expunged matches v. Bathgate on January 5th, 1929
& v. Armadale on October 15th, 1932)
Information Kindly Supplied by; Jim Stewart

The club was elected into the Scottish Football League Division 2 in 1921 and moved to *Bayview Stadium* in 1998.
*NB. Not all attendances are known and these are the highest and lowest gate figures of those that are recorded.

PLAYING RECORD OF MEADOWBANK THISTLE
LEAGUE PROGRAMME

Match Played; 1-3 v. Dunfermline Athletic (928) (April 21st, 1979)
No. of Matches Played by Meadowbank Thistle; 1
Information Kindly Supplied by; Jim Stewart

This match was played here due to the non-availability of *Meadowbank Stadium*

PLAYING RECORD OF BERWICK RANGERS
LEAGUE PROGRAMME

Match Played; 3-2 v. Arbroath (150) (April 25th, 1992)*
No. of Matches Played by Berwick Rangers; 1
Information Kindly Supplied by; Jim Stewart and Robin Murdie

The match was played here due to the unserviceable state of the roof on the main stand at *Shielfield Park*
*According to *East Fife FC's* records this attendance figure was only 71 but the anomaly arose as it was only responsible for admitting cash paying spectators at the gate whilst an additional *Berwick Rangers FC* turnstile, which admitted concession and season ticket holders, was not included in the figure.

Located to the north west of the town centre and formerly part of Kirklandhill Farm, *East of Fife FC* moved here on their formation in 1903. The facilities originally consisted of a pavilion that was built on the north west side in 1903. Subsequent improvements included the construction of a new main stand on the south east side in 1922, concrete terracing around the other three sides and the installation of a covered enclosure on the north west side.

East Fife moved out to **Bayview Stadium**, in Methil Docks, in 1998 and the site was subsequently used for housing with Stewart Court covering part of the site. (This road was named after Sammy Stewart who was captain of *East Fife FC* when the League Cup was won in 1953. Two other roads planned for the site will feature the names of Tommy Adams and Willie Aird, captains of the League Cup winning teams of 1947 and 1949.)

A TOTAL OF **57** TEAMS TOOK PART IN **1,282** LEAGUE FIXTURES AT THIS VENUE

The covered enclosure on the north west side at **Bayview Park**
Photograph by Jon Weaver. Courtesy of Groundtastic Magazine

BELLSDALE PARK

HOME GROUND OF **BEITH**
TEMPORARY HOME GROUND FOR **GALSTON** & **ARTHURLIE**

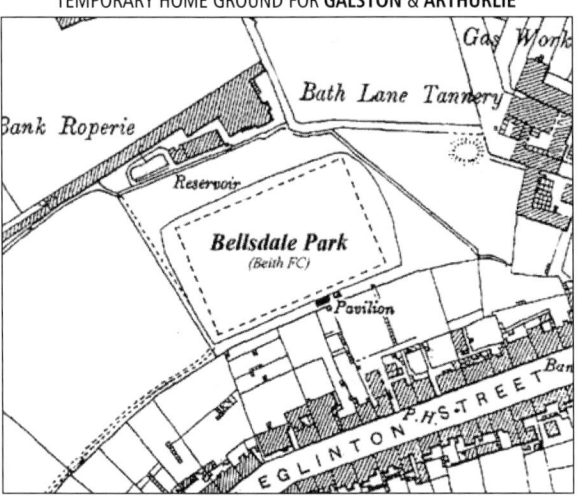

MAP EXTRACT; AYRSHIRE 8.6 [1895]
SITE LOCATION; **NS34665396**

Opened in 1920, the ground only possessed basic facilities during *Beith FC's* period in the Scottish League. A small 280 seat grandstand was erected on the north side in the late 1920s but this was subsequently removed and by the 1990s *Bellsdale Park*, was still in use, as the home ground *of Beith Juniors FC*, with a clubhouse and terracing on the south side of the pitch.

PLAYING RECORD OF BEITH
LEAGUE PROGRAMME
First Match; 1-0 v. Royal Albert (-) (August 25th, 1923)
Last Match; 2-4 v. Leith Athletic (-) (April 21st, 1926)
Highest & Lowest Gate*; Not Known
Highest Home Win; 8-3 v. Mid-Annandale (-) (October 4th, 1924),
7-1 v. Brechin City (-) (January 10th, 1925)
Highest Home Defeat; 2-5 v. Solway Star (-) (September 12th, 1925)
No. of Matches Played by Beith; 44
Information Kindly Supplied by; Tommy Brandon

The club was a founder member of the Scottish Football League Division 3 in 1923 and left the League when the division was disbanded near the end of the 1925/26 season. The home matches v. *Dumbarton Harp* in 1924/25 and v. *Galston* in 1925/26 were not played.
*NB. There are no gate figures recorded for *Beith FC's* occupancy of this venue.

PLAYING RECORD OF GALSTON
LEAGUE PROGRAMME
Match Played; 0-3 v. Arthurlie (-) (March 22nd, 1924)
No. of Matches Played by Galston; 1
This match was switched here from *Portland Park*

PLAYING RECORD OF ARTHURLIE
LEAGUE PROGRAMME
Matches Played; 4-0 v. Broxburn United (-) (September 19th, 1925)
4-1 v. East Stirlingshire (-) (October 3rd, 1925)
No. of Matches Played by Arthurlie; 2

Matches were played here for one month following crowd trouble at the fixture v. *Third Lanark* (1-2) on August 22nd, 1925 at *Dunterlie Park* [3rd]

A TOTAL OF **22** TEAMS TOOK PART IN **47** LEAGUE FIXTURES AT THIS VENUE

BERESFORD PARK

HOME GROUND OF **AYR PARKHOUSE**
TEMPORARY HOME GROUND FOR **AYR UNITED**

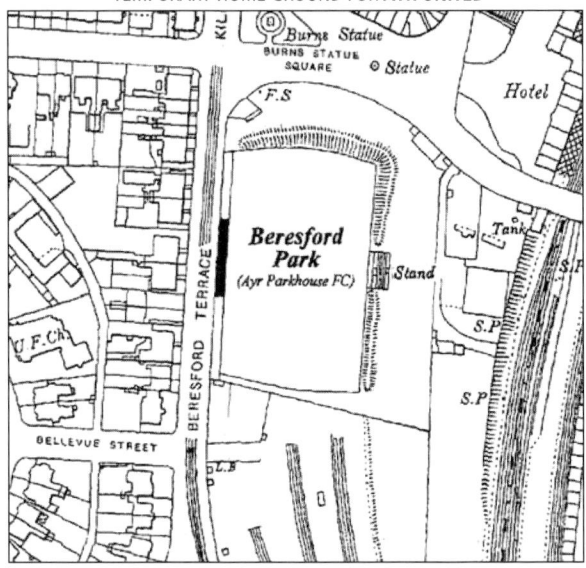

MAP EXTRACT; AYRSHIRE 33.6 [1908]
SITE LOCATION; **NS33902128**

Located in the town centre, on the east side of Beresford Terrace, *Ayr FC* moved from *Springvale Park (Ayr)* in 1884. The facilities included a pavilion on the east side, covered standing accommodation on the west and embankments around the east and north sides.

The ground was taken over by the London Midland & Scottish Railway in 1925 and the site subsequently utilized for an ice rink and, later, for a supermarket.

PLAYING RECORD OF AYR PARKHOUSE
LEAGUE PROGRAMME
First Match; 2-5 v. Albion Rovers (-) (August 22nd, 1903)
Last Match; 1-3 v. Arthurlie (-) (April 27th, 1910)
Highest & Lowest Gate*; Not Known
Highest Home Win; 5-1 v. East Stirlingshire (-) (December 7th, 1907)
Highest Home Defeats; 2-5 v. Albion Rovers (-) (August 22nd, 1903)
& v. Dumbarton (-) (December 8th, 1906)
No. of Matches Played by Ayr Parkhouse; 55
Information Kindly Supplied by; Duncan Carmichael

The club was elected into the Scottish Football League Division 2 in 1903 and dropped out of the Scottish League in 1910. It merged with *Ayr FC* in the same year to form *Ayr United* and moved to **Somerset Park**.
*NB. There are no gate figures recorded for *Ayr Parkhouse FC's* occupancy of this venue.

PLAYING RECORD OF AYR UNITED
LEAGUE PROGRAMME
Matches Played; 0-0 v. Third Lanark (7,000) (August 16th, 1924)
0-1 v. Airdrieonians (4,000) (August 20th, 1924)
3-3 v. Aberdeen (6,000) (August 30th, 1924)
No. of Matches Played by Ayr United; 3
Information Kindly Supplied by; Duncan Carmichael

These matches were played here as **Somerset Park** was not ready for the commencement of 1924/25 season following re-alignment of the pitch.

A TOTAL OF **19** TEAMS TOOK PART IN **58** LEAGUE FIXTURES AT THIS VENUE

BOGHEAD PARK

HOME GROUND OF **DUMBARTON**
TEMPORARY HOME GROUND FOR **GREENOCK MORTON & CLYDEBANK [2]**

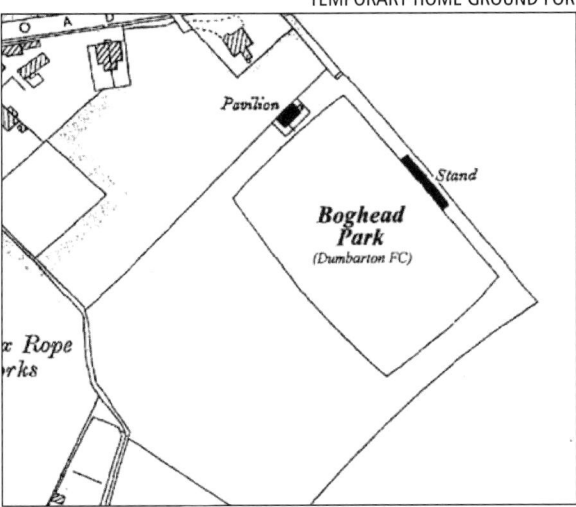

MAP EXTRACT; DUNBARTONSHIRE N22.3 [**1896**]
SITE LOCATION; **NS40757569**

PLAYING RECORD OF DUMBARTON
LEAGUE PROGRAMME

First Match; 1-1 v. Cowlairs (-) (August 16th, 1890)
Last Match; 2-1 v. East Fife (3,031) (May 6th, 2000)
Highest Gate; 16,000 v. Rangers (1-5) (January 11th, 1975)
Lowest Recorded Gate; 193 v. Albion Rovers (2-0) (August 4th, 1998)
Highest Home Win; 8-0 v. Vale of Leven (-) (December 12th, 1891) &
v. Cowdenbeath (-) (March 28th, 1964)
Highest Home Defeat; 2-9 v. Heart of Midlothian (1,200) (October 19th, 1895)

No. of Matches Played by Dumbarton; 1,601
(Including expunged matches v. Bathgate on February 23rd, 1929, v. Bo'ness on August 13th, 1932 & v. Armadale on October 22nd, 1932)
Information Kindly Supplied by; Jim McAllister

When *Dumbarton FC* moved to *Boghead Park* from *Broadmeadow* in 1873 the pitch was orientated north west-south east and the facilities included a pavilion at the north end and a stand and press box on the side.

The club was a founder member of the Scottish Football League in 1890 and failed to gain re-election to Division 2 in 1897. They were elected into Division 2 in 1906, failed to gain re-election to Division B in 1954 and were elected into Division B in 1955. The club was also involved in the Scottish Football League Championship Play Off Match with *Rangers* (2-2) at the neutral venue of *Cathkin Park* on May 21st, 1891. In 2000 Dumbarton FC moved out and temporarily groundshared with *Albion Rovers FC* at *Cliftonhill Park* until the **Strathclyde Homes Stadium** was completed later that year.

PLAYING RECORD OF GREENOCK MORTON
LEAGUE PROGRAMME

Match Played; 1-4 v. St Mirren (-) (January 1st, 1949)

No. of Matches Played by Greenock Morton; 1
Information Kindly Supplied by; Allan Grieve

This match was moved here due to the pitch at *Cappielow Park* being unplayable.

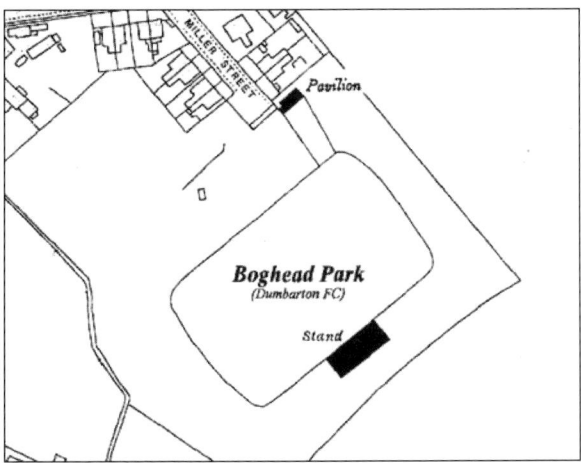

MAP EXTRACT; DUNBARTONSHIRE N22.3 [**1914**]

PLAYING RECORD OF CLYDEBANK [2]
LEAGUE PROGRAMME

First Match; 1-0 v. Stirling Albion (507) (August 24th, 1996)
Last Match; 1-2 v. Stranraer (269) (May 8th, 1999)
Highest Gate; 1,786 v. Partick Thistle (1-3) (November 16th, 1996)
Lowest Gate; 182 v. East Fife (0-3) (March 17th, 1998)
Highest Home Win; 4-0 v. Queen of the South (297) (November 5th, 1997)
Highest Home Defeat; 0-4 v. East Fife (269) (May 10th, 1997)

No. of Matches Played by Clydebank [2]; 54
Information Kindly Supplied by; Jim McAllister

The club moved here from *New Kilbowie Park* in 1996 and in 1999 moved out to groundshare with *Greenock Morton* at *Cappielow Park*.

A TOTAL OF **65** TEAMS TOOK PART IN **1,656** LEAGUE FIXTURES AT THIS VENUE

In 1913, the pitch orientation was changed to north east-south west, the original stand removed, rebuilt and repositioned on the south side, (as rebuilt the stand now had a higher roof, 150 seats and dressing rooms.) and an 80 seat stand later constructed on the north side.

Greyhound racing took place during the 1930s, and a roof was installed on the north side to cover the bookmaker's paddock. During this period the terracing was improved and the stand on the south side, in use as kennels, was burned down and subsequently replaced.

The record attendance of 18,000 was set at the Scottish FA Cup 7th Round tie v. *Raith Rovers* (0-4) on March 2nd, 1957 and subsequent improvements included the installation of covers at both ends, with a redundant station awning from Turnberry Railway Station being utilized at the east end. In 1980 the main stand on the north side was replaced by a 300 seat cantilever roofed stand and the south stand was demolished in 1990. *Dumbarton FC* moved to the **Strathclyde Homes Stadium** in 2000 and the site was used for housing.

BOROUGH BRIGGS
HOME GROUND OF ELGIN CITY

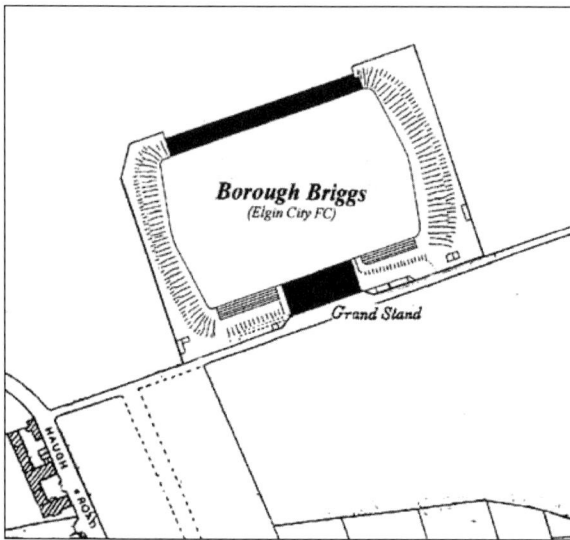

MAP EXTRACT; GROUND AS IN **1972** DRAWN FROM MAPS AND SUPERIMPOSED ON ELGIN 7.12 [1905]
SITE LOCATION; **NJ21286321**

Following the end of WWI *Elgin City FC* was unable to return to its ground at *Station Park* as the venue had been ploughed up as part of the war effort and a temporary move was made to *Cooper Park*. The club remained there until it opened *Borough Briggs* on August 20th, 1921 with a Highland League fixture v. *Inverness Citadel*. The facilities included a 600 seat wooden grandstand with banking on the north side and by the end of the 1920s banks had been constructed at each end.

Following WWII concrete terracing was installed on the north side and terracing built on both sides of the grandstand before the north side was partially covered in 1953. This roof was extended east in 1960 and west in 1963 giving a covered enclosure accommodating 4,000 spectators. In 1967 a new 122ft long cantilever main stand was constructed on the south side (retaining the original wooden bench seating) and the record attendance of 12,650 was set at the Scottish FA Cup 2nd Round tie v. *Arbroath* (2-0) on February 17th, 1968.

For the club's entry into the Scottish League in 2000, 478 seats were obtained from *Newcastle United FC's* **St James' Park** for installation in the main stand, both ends were partially terraced and a WWII pill box, built at the east end in 1939 was finally demolished! The capacity at the start of the 2004/5 season was 3,900 with 478 seats and the pitch size was 120 x 86 yards.

PLAYING RECORD OF ELGIN CITY
LEAGUE PROGRAMME

First Match; 0-2 v. Hamilton Academical (1,552) (August 12th, 2000)
Highest Gate; 1,552 v. Hamilton Academical (0-2) (August 12th, 2000)
Lowest Gate; 218 v. East Stirlingshire (3-1) (December 17th, 2002)
Highest Home Win; 4-1 v. Peterhead (974) (October 27th, 2001)
Highest Home Defeat; 2-6 v. Gretna (503) (April 16th, 2005)
No. of Matches Played by Elgin City; 90
Some Information Kindly Supplied by; Robert Weir

The club was elected into the Scottish Football League Division 3 in 2000 and the first League goal was scored by M Nelson of *Hamilton Academical FC* in the 12th minute of the first match

AT THE END OF SEASON 2004/5, A TOTAL OF **16** TEAMS HAD TAKEN PART IN **90** LEAGUE FIXTURES AT THIS VENUE

BRAEHEAD PARK
HOME GROUND OF THISTLE

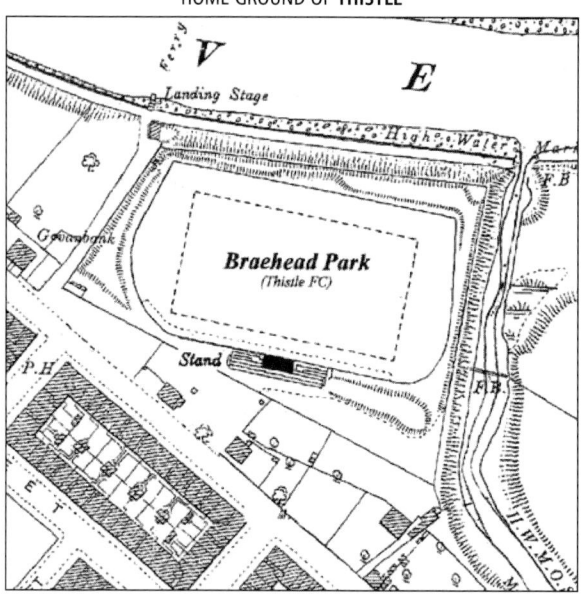

MAP EXTRACT; LANARKSHIRE 6.15 [**1896**]
SITE LOCATION; **NS60056321**

Thistle FC moved here from *Beechwood Park (Glasgow)* in 1892 and although not certain it is assumed that the ground shown above was *Braehead Park*. The facilities included a grandstand on the south side and embankments on the other three sides. The probable record attendance of 2,000 was attained here at a Glasgow Cup match v. *Celtic* (0-7) on October 28th, 1893.

The club folded in 1895 and the ground was subsequently absorbed into the adjacent Richmond Park. Polmadie Road was later built across the site

PLAYING RECORD OF THISTLE
LEAGUE PROGRAMME

Matches Played; 1-2 v. Hibernian (-) (August 19th, 1893)
1-3 v. Clyde (-) (September 2nd, 1893)
2-1 v. Morton (-) (September 9th, 1893)
3-3 v. Abercorn (-) (September 30th, 1893)
3-0 v. Northern (-) (October 14th, 1893)
3-4 v. Partick Thistle (-) (October 21st, 1893)
1-2 v. Port Glasgow Athletic (-) (December 2nd, 1893)
1-3 v. Cowlairs (-) (February 10th, 1894)
1-8 v. Motherwell (-) (March 24th, 1894)
No. of Matches Played by Thistle; 9

The club was a founder member of the Scottish Football League Division 2 in 1893 and did not apply for re-election in 1894. There are no League gate figures recorded for *Thistle FC's* occupancy of this venue.

A TOTAL OF **10** TEAMS TOOK PART IN **9** LEAGUE FIXTURES AT THIS VENUE

BROADWOOD STADIUM
HOME GROUND OF **CLYDE**
TEMPORARY HOME GROUND FOR **AIRDRIEONIANS**

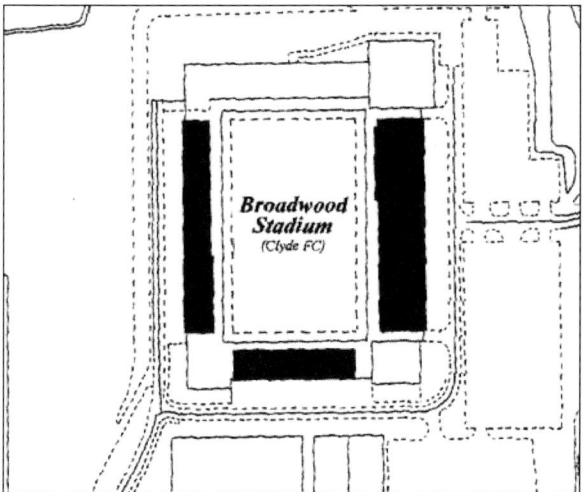

MAP EXTRACT; GROUND AS IN **2000** DRAWN FROM MAPS AND SUPERIMPOSED ON DUNBARTONSHIRE 33.4 [1918]
SITE LOCATION; **NS72827428**

Opened in 1994, the facilities, as built, included seated stands on both sides of the pitch giving a capacity of 6,103. Subsequently a seated stand was constructed at the south end and the record gate of 8,200 was established at the Scottish FA Cup 5th Round tie v. *Celtic* (0-5) on February 27th, 2005. The capacity at the start of the 2004/5 season was 8,200 and the pitch size 115 x 75 yards.

PLAYING RECORD OF CLYDE
LEAGUE PROGRAMME

First Match; 0-2 v. Hamilton Academical (6.300) (February 5th, 1994)
Highest Gate; 6.300 v. Hamilton Academical (0-2) (February 5th, 1994)
Lowest Gate; 640 v. Queen of the South (3-0) (November 9th, 1999)
Highest Home Win; 7-0 v. Stenhousemuir (1,033) (April 15th, 2000)
Highest Home Defeat; 1-6 v. Inverness Caledonian Thistle (766) (March 14th, 1998)

No. of Matches Played by Clyde; 208
Information Kindly Supplied by; John Taylor

Having groundshared with *Hamilton Academical FC* the club moved here from *Douglas Park* in 1994.

PLAYING RECORD OF AIRDRIEONIANS
LEAGUE PROGRAMME

First Match; 0-0 v. Dunfermline Athletic (2,964) (August 13th, 1994)
Last Match; 1-0 v. Raith Rovers (1,173) (May 2nd, 1998)
Highest Gate; 7,560 v. Hibernian (2-4) (May 22nd, 1997) (Play Off Match)
Lowest Gate; 811 v. Stranraer (2-0) (April 1st, 1995)
Highest Home Win; 8-1 v. Stranraer (1,500) (December 3rd, 1994)
Highest Home Defeat; 0-3 v. Dundee (2,528) (March 25th, 1995)

PLAY OFF MATCHES
2-4 v. Hibernian (7,560) (May 22nd, 1997)

No. of Matches Played by Airdrieonians; 73
(League Programme; 72, Play Off Matches; 1)
Information Kindly Supplied by; John Henderson

The club groundshared here until *Excelsior Stadium* opened in 1998.

AT THE END OF SEASON 2004/5, A TOTAL OF **31** TEAMS HAD TAKEN PART IN **281** LEAGUE FIXTURES AT THIS VENUE

BROCKVILLE PARK
HOME GROUND OF **FALKIRK**
TEMPORARY HOME GROUND FOR **EAST STIRLINGSHIRE**

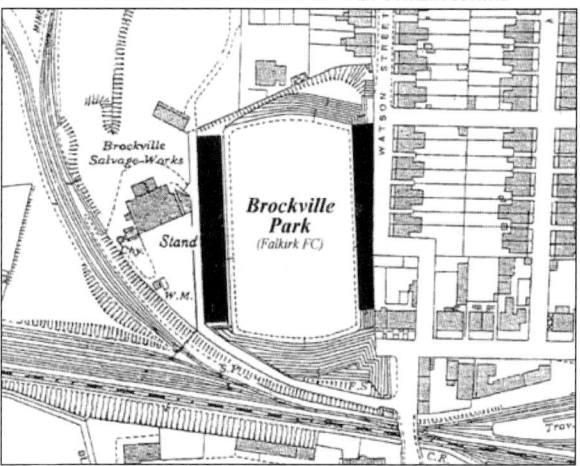

MAP EXTRACT; STIRLINGSHIRE 30.3 [**1944**]
SITE LOCATION; **NS88508040**

Falkirk FC first moved to *Brockville Park* in 1876, moved out in 1879 and returned in 1882. When the club joined the Scottish Football League in 1902 the facilities included a grandstand on the west side but this was subsequently destroyed by a fire and replaced by a new main stand in 1928. Concrete terracing was later installed around the remainder of the ground and a cover constructed on the east side but the cramped site that the ground occupied restricted the pitch size to 110 x 71 yards.

The record attendance of 23,100 was established at the Scottish FA Cup 3rd Round tie v. *Celtic* (2-3) on February 21st, 1953, but the capacity at the end of season 2001/2 was set only at 7,576 with 1,700 seats. The club moved out in 2003 and the ground was sold for redevelopment as a supermarket.

PLAYING RECORD OF FALKIRK
LEAGUE PROGRAMME

First Match; 0-1 v. St Bernards (2,000) (August 23rd, 1902)
Last Match; 2-3 v. Inverness Caledonian Thistle (7,300) (May 10th, 2003)
Highest Gate; 22,618 v. Rangers (0-1) (August 25th, 1937)
Lowest Gate; 800 v. Hamilton Academical (1-0) (March 23rd, 1977)
Highest Home Win; 10-2 v. King's Park (5,000) (January 18th, 1936).
9-0 v. Port Glasgow Athletic (6,000) (September 21st, 1907)
Highest Home Defeat; 0-8 v. Dundee (2,000) (January 22nd, 1977)

No. of Matches Played by Falkirk; 1,698
Information Kindly Supplied by; Michael White

The club was elected into the Scottish Football League Division 2 in 1902. At the end of the 2002/3 season the club moved to *Ochilview Park* to groundshare with *Stenhousemuir FC* for one season whilst awaiting completion of *The Falkirk Stadium*.

PLAYING RECORD OF EAST STIRLINGSHIRE
LEAGUE PROGRAMME

Matches Played; 0-1 v. Clydebank (400) (April 4th, 1982)
1-1 v. Stenhousemuir (387) (October 26th, 1998)

No. of Matches Played by East Stirlingshire; 2
Information Kindly Supplied by; Drummond Calder

The first game was played here due to a burst water main at *Firs Park* whilst the second match was switched when the capacity at *Firs Park* was fixed at only 286.

A TOTAL OF **53** TEAMS TOOK PART IN **1,700** LEAGUE FIXTURES AT THIS VENUE

BROOMFIELD PARK

HOME GROUND OF **AIRDRIEONIANS**
TEMPORARY HOME GROUND FOR **ALBION ROVERS**

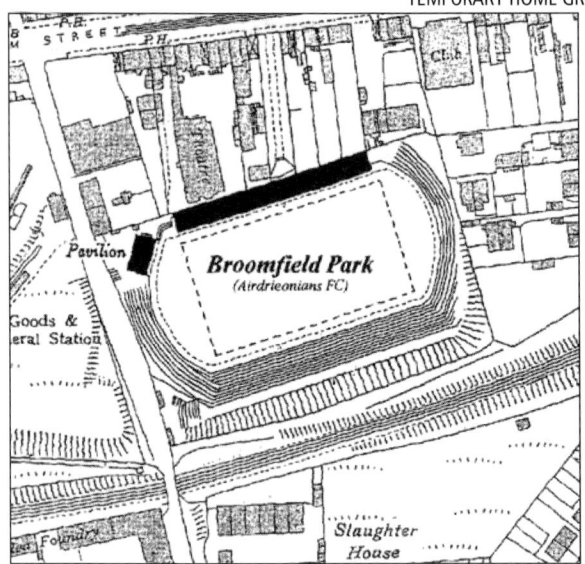

MAP EXTRACT; LANARK 8.10 [**1940**]
SITE LOCATION; **NS76486533**

Airdrieonians FC moved to *Broomfield Park*, owned by the North British Railway, from *Old Mavisbank* in 1892. Details of the facilities at this time are not known but the pavilion, which endured to the closure of the ground, was constructed in 1907.

The club bought the ground in 1922 and subsequent improvements included the installation of concrete terracing around the ground and construction of a grandstand on the north side in 1925. The terracing was enlarged after WWII and covering erected over the south side in 1959.

The record attendance of 26,000 was set at the Scottish FA Cup 4th Round tie v. *Heart of Midlothian* (2-2) on March 8th, 1952. The club moved to **Broadwood Stadium**, to groundshare with *Clyde FC*, in 1994 and the site was utilized for a superstore.

PLAYING RECORD OF AIRDRIEONIANS
LEAGUE PROGRAMME

First Match; 4-2 v. Port Glasgow Athletic (-) (August 25th, 1894)
Last Match; 1-0 v. Dunfermline Athletic (6,878) (May 7th, 1994)
Highest Gate; 24,992 v. Rangers (2-1) (September 5th, 1925)
Lowest Gate; 500 v. East Fife (0-0) (March 30th, 1977)
Highest Home Win; 15-1 v. Dundee Wanderers (-)
(December 1st, 1894)
Highest Home Defeat; 1-11 v. Hibernian (7,000)
(October 24th, 1959)
No. of Matches Played by Airdrieonians; 1,601
Information Kindly Supplied by; John Henderson

The club was elected into the Scottish Football League Division 2 in 1894. In 1994 the site of the ground was sold and *Airdrieonians FC* moved to **Broadwood Stadium** and groundshared with *Clyde FC* until the *Excelsior Stadium* was built.

PHOTOGRAPH ON RIGHT
Still extant in 1994 this pavilion at **Broomfield Park** was one of the last survivors of the common practice in Scotland of providing both a pavilion for the players and officials and a separate stand for spectators.
Photograph Courtesy of Groundtastic Magazine

PLAYING RECORD OF ALBION ROVERS
LEAGUE PROGRAMME
1ST PERIOD
Matches Played; 2-0 v. Partick Thistle (3,000)
(August 23rd, 1919)
2-1 v. Clydebank (-) (September 6th, 1919)
1-2 v. Hibernian (6,000) (September 29th, 1919)
1-1 v. Motherwell (8,000) (October 18th, 1919)
2-1 v. Ayr United (6,000) (November 1st, 1919)
2-0 v. Queen's Park (-) (November 8th, 1919)
0-4 v. Rangers (16,000) (November 29th, 1919)
2-1 v. Falkirk (6,000) (December 20th, 1919)
No. of Matches Played; 8

These games were played here as **Cliftonhill Park** was not ready for the start of the 1919/20 season

2ND PERIOD
Matches Played; 1-3 v. Stirling Albion (600) (August 17th, 1985)
0-2 v. Queen's Park (280) (August 31st, 1985)
1-2 v. East Stirlingshire (374) (September 14th, 1985)
No. of Matches Played; 3

Cliftonhill Park was unavailable during this period due to upgrading work being incomplete.

3RD PERIOD
Match Played; 0-3 v. Dunfermline Athletic (1,320) (March 31st, 1986)
No. of Matches Played; 1

This match was switched here as a larger gate than could be accommodated at **Cliftonhill Park** was anticipated.

4TH PERIOD
Matches Played; 3-1 v. Ayr United (1,200) (August 12th, 1989)
3-4 v. Clydebank (700) (September 2nd, 1989)
No. of Matches Played; 2

These two games were played here as **Cliftonhill Park** was closed at the start of the 1989/90 season whilst awaiting a Safety Certificate.

Highest Gate & Highest Home Defeat; 16,000 v. Rangers
(0-4) (November 29th, 1919)
Lowest Gate; 374 v. East Stirlingshire (1-2) (September 14th, 1985)
Highest Home Win; 3-1 v. Ayr United (1,200) (August 12th, 1989)
Total No. of Matches Played by Albion Rovers; 14
Information Kindly Supplied by; Robin Marwick

A TOTAL OF **52** TEAMS TOOK PART IN **1,615** LEAGUE FIXTURES AT THIS VENUE

BALMOOR STADIUM
HOME GROUND OF PETERHEAD

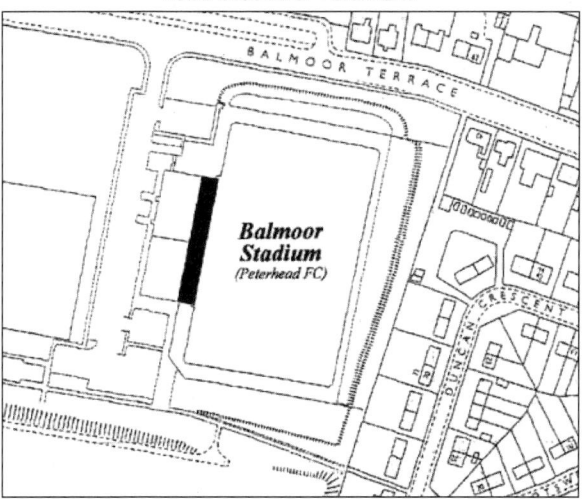

MAP EXTRACT; GROUND AS IN **1998** DRAWN FROM MAPS AND SUPERIMPOSED ON NK1246 [1950]
SITE LOCATION: **NK12334679**

Peterhead FC moved here from *Recreation Park* in September 1997 and the facilities originally consisted of a main 500 seat stand on the west side with uncovered standing accommodation around the rest of the ground. In 2001 a new all-seat stand was constructed on the east side, giving a capacity of 4,000 with 980 seats at the start of the 2004/5 season and the pitch size was 110 x 74 yards.

PLAYING RECORD OF PETERHEAD
LEAGUE PROGRAMME

First Match; 2-0 v. Montrose (700) (August 5th, 2000)
Highest Gate; 1,693 v. Albion Rovers (0-0) (May 3rd, 2003)
Lowest Gate; 327 v. Montrose (1-1) (April 17th, 2001)
Highest Home Win; 6-0 v. East Stirlingshire (584) (February 15th, 2003), v. Stirling Albion (611) (March 4th, 2003) & v. East Stirlingshire (553) (January 24th, 2004)
Highest Home Defeat; 2-4 v. East Stirlingshire (656) (September 16th, 2000). 0-3 v. Dumbarton (528) (August 11th, 2001)
No. of Matches Played by Peterhead; **90**

The club was elected into the Scottish Football League Division 3 in 2000.

AT THE END OF SEASON 2004/5, A TOTAL OF **16** TEAMS HAD TAKEN PART IN **90** LEAGUE FIXTURES AT THIS VENUE

The narrow flat standing area at the north end of **Balmoor Park**, on March 20th, 2004. The match in progress, *Peterhead* v. *Stirling Albion* finished in a 1-1 draw.
Courtesy of RedWeb (www.stirlingalbionfc.com)

BANK PARK
HOME GROUND OF LEITH ATHLETIC

MAP EXTRACT; EDINBURGH 3.4 [**1896**]
SITE LOCATION; **NT27507515**

Originally named *Bank Park*, the facilities included two open stands on each side and some open seating at the east end of the pitch. The probable record gate is 7,000 at the Scottish FA Cup 2nd Round Replay v. *Dumbarton* (3-3) on February 13th, 1892. It was re-named as *Beechwood Park* in 1895 and when the ground closed in 1899 the North British Railway subsequently constructed its branch line into Leith Central Station across the site.

PLAYING RECORD OF LEITH ATHLETIC
LEAGUE PROGRAMME

First Match; 2-3 v. Renton (-) (August 22nd, 1891)
Last Match; 3-3 v. Kilmarnock (-) (April 15th, 1899)
Highest Gate*; 6,000 v. Celtic (2-1) (April 18th, 1892)
Lowest Gate*; Not Known
Highest Home Win; 10-0 v. Vale of Leven (-) (September 19th, 1891)
Highest Home Defeat; 0-4 v. Renton (-) (August 31st, 1895)
No. of Matches Played by Leith Athletic; **74**

The club was elected into the Scottish Football League in 1891 and the first ever Scottish Football League penalty kick was scored here by Alex McColl of *Renton* in their 3-2 win v. *Leith Athletic* on August 22nd, 1891. The club vacated the ground in 1899 and moved to **New Logie Green** to groundshare with *St Bernards* for a short period before moving to **Hawkhill** for the remainder of the 1899/1900 season.
*NB. This is the highest gate figure of the few that were recorded. In view of the general level of those that are known, it is very probable that there were crowds of less than 500 on occasions.

A TOTAL OF **23** TEAMS TOOK PART IN **74** LEAGUE FIXTURES AT THIS VENUE

CALEDONIAN STADIUM
HOME GROUND OF **INVERNESS CALEDONIAN THISTLE**

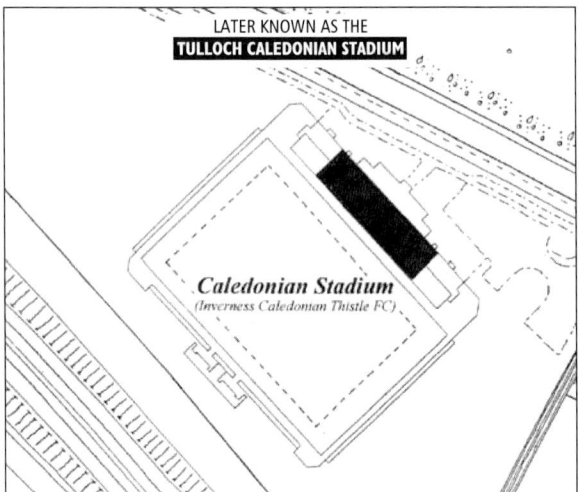

LATER KNOWN AS THE
TULLOCH CALEDONIAN STADIUM

MAP EXTRACT; GROUND AS IN **1996** DRAWN FROM MAPS AND AERIAL PHOTOGRAPHS AND SUPERIMPOSED ON INVERNESS-SHIRE 4.14 [1929]
SITE LOCATION; **NH67184715**

Built on the site of the Longman Rifle Range, *Inverness Caledonian Thistle FC* moved here from **Telford Street** in 1996. The facilities include a part-covered cantilever roofed stand on the north side and flat standing areas around the remainder of the 115 x 75 yards sized pitch giving a capacity, at the end of season 2003/4, of 6,500 with 2,200 seats. During 2004/5 2,200 seat stands were constructed at each end of the ground to bring it up to SPL standard with 6,600 seats and an overall capacity of 7,200. The ground was subsequently re-named as the *Tulloch Caledonian Stadium* in honour of the construction group who installed the new stands in record time.

PLAYING RECORD OF INVERNESS CALEDONIAN THISTLE
LEAGUE PROGRAMME

First Match; 1-1 v. Albion Rovers (3,734) (November 9th, 1996)
Highest Gate; 7,045 v. Celtic (0-2) (March 16th, 2005)
Lowest Gate; 1,073 v. Ayr United (1-1) (November 30th, 1999)
Highest Home Win; 7-3 v. Ayr United (1,513) (December 2nd, 2000). 5-0 v. St Mirren (3,218) (May 6th, 2000), v. Raith Rovers (1,822) (January 12th, 2002), v. Arbroath (1,685) (September 21st, 2002) & v. Brechin City (1,393) (November 29th, 2003)
Highest Home Defeat; 1-5 v. Airdrieonians (1,401) (April 15th, 2000) & v. Ross County (3,443) (February 25th, 2003)

No. of Matches Played by Inverness Caledonian Thistle;
148

Information Kindly Supplied by; Ian Broadfoot

The club moved here from **Telford Street** in 1996. Following the winning of the Division One Championship in 2004 the club was allowed to play in the Premier League provided it moved to a ground that met the then-criteria of 10,000 seats. To accommodate this, the first 11 games of the 2004/5 season were played at *Aberdeen FC's Pittodrie Park* but as, during the season, the SPL standard was reduced to 6,000 seats the *Caledonian Stadium* was quickly upgraded, allowing the debut SPL match v. *Dunfermline Athletic* (2-0) to take place on January 29th, 2005 in front of 5,449 spectators.

AT THE END OF SEASON 2004/5, A TOTAL OF **35** TEAMS HAD TAKEN PART IN **148** LEAGUE FIXTURES AT THIS VENUE

CAROLINA PORT
HOME GROUND OF **DUNDEE**

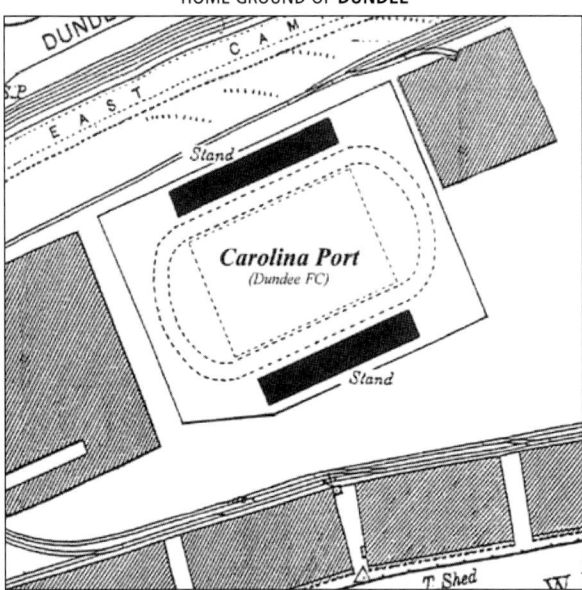

MAP EXTRACT; GROUND AS IN c**1895** DRAWN FROM SKETCH MAPS AND SUPERIMPOSED ON FORFARSHIRE 54.6 [1903]
SITE LOCATION; **NO42103080**

The existence of this ground falls between two Ordnance Surveys and although opened in the 1890s only a sketch map and brief contemporary descriptions have survived and this is a very approximate map of the *Carolina Port* ground.

It was located between the Eastern Wharf and Camperdown St, east of Dundee city centre and had a capacity of 12,500 with the facilities including a 1,500 seat stand, and cycling and running tracks which, in view of the location of the site, would infer that it probably was not a true oval and only had a small pitch.

The first football match at this venue, the Forfarshire Cup Final, was played here at the end of the 1891/2 season and *Strathmore FC* utilized it as their home ground from 1892 onwards until mid-way through the 1893/4 season when *Dundee FC* took over and improved the facilities with stands from their former **West Craigie Park**.

The ground had the honour of hosting an international match when 11,700 saw *Scotland* play *Wales* in March 1896 but, in the event, the venue only had a short further existence as it was vacated in 1899 and the site very quickly absorbed into the ever-expanding docklands.

PLAYING RECORD OF DUNDEE
LEAGUE PROGRAMME

First Match & Highest Home Win; 8-1 v. Renton (4,000) (February 10th, 1894)
Last Match; 2-5 v. Heart of Midlothian (2,000) (December 3rd, 1898)
Highest Gate; 17,000 v. Celtic (2-2) (October 3rd, 1896)
Lowest Gate; 2,000 v. Clyde (1-3) (November 12th, 1898)
Highest Home Defeat; 1-7 v. St Mirren (3,000) (November 5th, 1898)

No. of Matches Played by Dundee; 47
Information Kindly Supplied by; Norrie Price

The club moved here from **West Craigie Park** in 1894 and moved to **Dens Park** in 1898.

A TOTAL OF **12** TEAMS TOOK PART IN **47** LEAGUE FIXTURES AT THIS VENUE

CATHKIN PARK

HOME GROUND OF **THIRD LANARK**
TEMPORARY HOME GROUND FOR **QUEEN'S PARK**

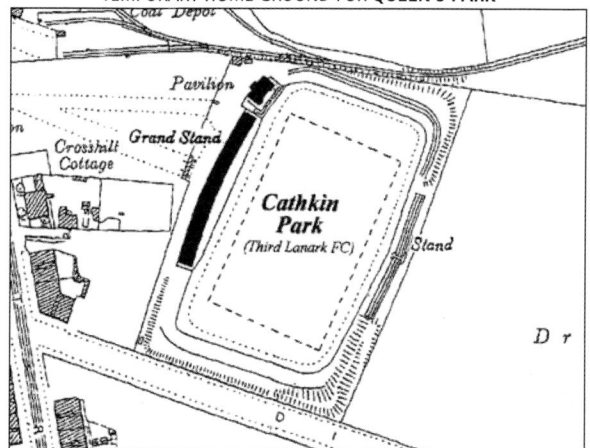

MAP EXTRACT; LANARKSHIRE 10.2 & 10.3 [1893]
SITE LOCATION; NS58926248

Located in the Crosshill district of Glasgow, *Cathkin Park* was sited at the west end of the drilling field used by the 3rd Lanarkshire Rifle Volunteers. Initially no more than an open field when *Third Lanark FC* was formed in 1872 the ground had been sufficiently developed by 1885 to host three Scottish FA Cup finals. The facilities eventually included a main grandstand and pavilion on the west side, open seated stands on the north and east sides and banking at the south end. *Third Lanark* moved to *Hampden Park [2nd]* in 1903 and the ground was subsequently redeveloped with housing.

PLAYING RECORD OF THIRD LANARK
LEAGUE PROGRAMME

First Match; 1-3 v. Dumbarton (-) (August 23rd, 1890)
Last Match; 0-1 v. Dundee (-) (April 4th, 1903)
Highest Gate*; 16,000 v. Rangers (1-5) (August 19th, 1899)
& v. Rangers (2-2) (September 28th, 1901)
Lowest Gate*; Not Known
Highest Home Win; 9-2 v. Vale of Leven (-) (December 2nd, 1891.
8-0 v. Abercorn (-) (October 1st, 1892)
Highest Home Defeat; 2-7 v. Hibernian (-) (August 17th, 1895).
0-6 v. Celtic (-) (April 22nd, 1893)
No. of Matches Played by Third Lanark; 122
Information Kindly Supplied by; Bert Bell

The club was a founder member of the Scottish Football League in 1890 and moved to *New Cathkin Park* in 1903.
*NB. Very few gate figures are known for this venue and this is the highest of those recorded.

PLAYING RECORD OF QUEEN'S PARK
LEAGUE PROGRAMME

Match Played; 1-1 v. Partick Thistle (-) (October 17th, 1903)
No. of Matches Played by Queen's Park; 1
Information Kindly Supplied by; Hector Cook

Match played here as *Hampden Park [3rd]* was not ready.

NEUTRAL PLAY OFF MATCHES

Division 1 Championship; Rangers 2, Dumbarton 2 (10,000) (May 21st, 1891)
Division 2, 3/4 Place; Renton 2, Kilmarnock 1 (-) (May 20th, 1896)
No. of Matches Played; 2

A TOTAL OF **21** TEAMS TOOK PART IN **125** LEAGUE FIXTURES AT THIS VENUE

CELTIC PARK [1ST]

HOME GROUND OF **CELTIC**

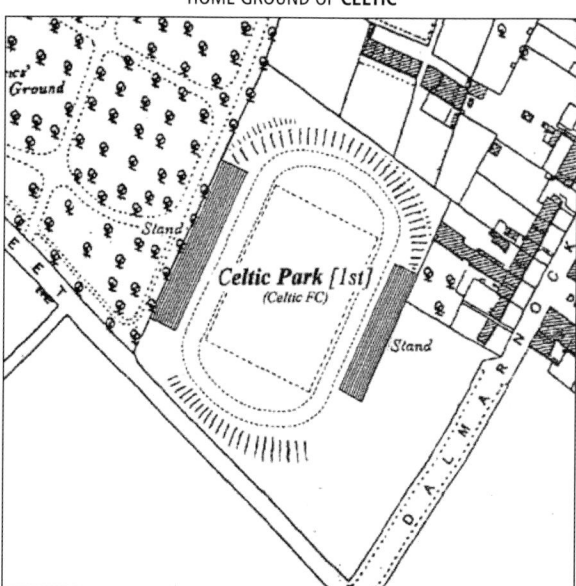

MAP EXTRACT; GROUND AS IN c1890 DRAWN FROM SKETCHES AND SUPERIMPOSED ON LANARKSHIRE 6.16 [1896]
SITE LOCATION; NS62266406

Although no map exists, from contemporary accounts and drawings some sort of diagram of the ground can be constructed, but the orientation of it within the site available has had to be assumed.

Located between the Eastern Necropolis and Dalmarnock Street, on the north east side of Janefield Street in the Parkhead district of the city it opened on May 8th, 1888. The pitch was surrounded by a running track, there were open stands with flat standing areas in front on both sides and banking behind each goal. There was also probably a pavilion, the disposition of which is not known.

Celtic FC moved out to *Celtic Park [2nd]* in 1892 and the site was redeveloped with housing.

PLAYING RECORD OF CELTIC
LEAGUE PROGRAMME

First Match & Highest Home Defeat; 1-4 v. Renton (10,000)
(August 16th, 1890) [Result Expunged]
Last Match; 2-0 v. Leith Athletic (-) (May 14th, 1892)
Highest Gate; 15,000 v. Heart of Midlothian (3-1)
(October 17th, 1891)
Lowest Gate; 2,000 v. Vale of Leven (9-1) (May 5th, 1891)
& v. St Mirren (2-1) (December 26th, 1891)
Highest Home Win; 9-1 v. Vale of Leven (2,000) (May 5th, 1891)
No. of Matches Played by Celtic; 21
(Including one expunged match v. Renton on August 16th, 1890)
Information Kindly Supplied by; Margaret Connolly & Cyril George

The club was a founder member of the Scottish Football League in 1890. The first ever Scottish Football League goal was scored here by Cameron of *Renton* in the 4-1 win against *Celtic* on August 16th, 1890. Ironically this result was expunged when *Renton FC* was expelled and *Celtic* remained unbeaten during the remainder of their occupancy of *Celtic Park [1st]*. The club moved to *Celtic Park [2nd]* in 1892.

A TOTAL OF **13** TEAMS TOOK PART IN **21** LEAGUE FIXTURES AT THIS VENUE

CELTIC PARK [2ND]

HOME GROUND OF **CELTIC**
TEMPORARY HOME GROUND FOR **CLYDE** & **PARTICK THISTLE**

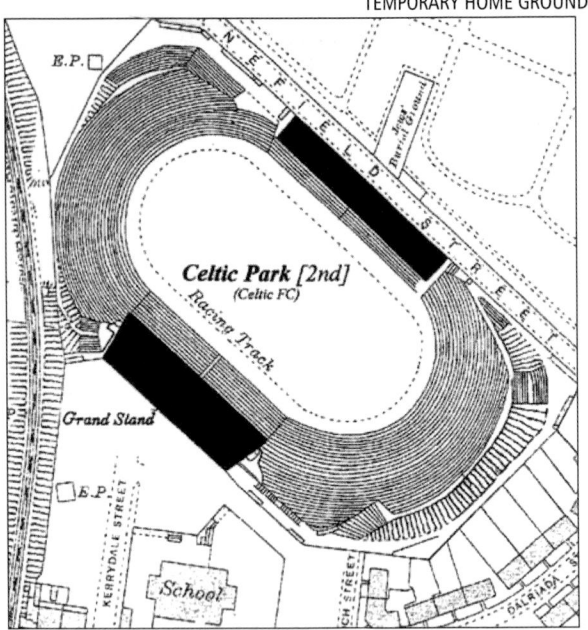

MAP EXTRACT; LANARKSHIRE 6.16 [1934]
SITE LOCATION; NS62016405

PLAYING RECORD OF CELTIC
LEAGUE PROGRAMME
First Match; 4-3 v. Renton (16,000) (August 20th, 1892)
Highest Gate; 83,500 v. Rangers (3-0) (January 1st, 1938)
Lowest Gate; 4,956 v. Dundee (3-0) (April 24th, 1984)
Highest Home Win; 11-0 v. Dundee (10,000) (October 26th, 1895)
Highest Home Defeat; 0-5 v. Heart of Midlothian (18,000)
(September 14th, 1895)

No. of Matches Played by Celtic; 1,789
Information Kindly Supplied by; Margaret Connolly & Cyril George

Celtic FC moved here from *Celtic Park [1st]* in 1892. The club was also involved in a Scottish Football League Championship Play Off Match v. *Rangers* (2-1) at the neutral venue of *Hampden Park [3rd]* on May 6th, 1905. Due to fire damage and various rebuilding projects home games were also played at *Shawfield Park, Firhill, Easter Road* and *Hampden Park [3rd]*.

PLAYING RECORD OF CLYDE
LEAGUE PROGRAMME
Matches Played; 0-2 v. Celtic (6,000) (January 2nd, 1915)†
0-4 v. Rangers (35,000) (May 10th, 1919)
0-0 v. Rangers (12,000) (September 13th, 1919)

No. of Matches Played by Clyde; 3
Information Kindly Supplied by; Cyril George
† This match may have been moved here from *Shawfield* due to a fire.

PLAYING RECORD OF PARTICK THISTLE
LEAGUE PROGRAMME
Matches Played; 0-7 v. Third Lanark (-) (October 3rd, 1908)*
0-1 v. Celtic (-) (March 29th, 1909)

No. of Matches Played by Partick Thistle; 2
Information Kindly Supplied by; Robert Reid & Bob Laird

These matches were played here as *Firhill Park* was not ready following the closure of *Meadowside* in 1908.
*NB. Although the match played in the 1908/9 season v. *Third Lanark* on February 13th, 1909 was recorded by the Scottish League as *Partick Thistle's* home game and incorporated in the final League Table as such, it would appear that this is an error and that the home game, incorrectly recorded as the "away" fixture, is the one detailed above.

AT THE END OF SEASON 2003/4, A TOTAL OF **41** TEAMS HAD TAKEN PART
IN **1,794** LEAGUE FIXTURES AT THIS VENUE

Built on the site of a quarry, *Celtic FC* moved up the road from *Celtic Park [1st]* to this well-appointed ground in 1892. The pitch was sited within an oval, used for athletics and bicycle racing, and within a few years the facilities included a grandstand and pavilion on the north side, terracing and banking around each end and a novel seated stand on the south. This stand was built independently of the football club by a Mr James Grant but proved unpopular as it featured a glass front that frequently suffered from condensation.

The grandstand and pavilion, along with all the club records, burned down in 1904 and the "Grant Stand", as it became known, was pressed into service (minus glass front!) as the only covered seating in the ground. A new pavilion and covered standing accommodation were quickly installed on the north side and this was how the stadium remained until 1929 when the "Grant Stand" was demolished and replaced with a new main stand whilst an unplanned change, as this was taking place, was the destruction of the pavilion by fire.

The ground vied for many years with, and eventually lost out to, *Hampden Park [3rd]* as the venue for international matches but was the first stadium to hold a speedway meeting in 1928 when *West Ham Stadium* (home ground of *Thames FC*) was not completed in time.

Post war improvements saw installation of cover at each end, the replacement of the cover on the north side and re-roofing of the main south stand, but the biggest change came in the 1990s when the running track was dispensed with, the terraces and stands removed from the north side and both ends and all seat stands constructed giving an all-seat capacity of 60,355 at the start of season 2004/5. The pitch size was 115 x 74 yards.

An aerial view of *Celtic Park [2nd]* taken in 1980 and showing it in its final form, with covers on each side and running track *in situ*, before the major redevelopment of the ground in the 1990s.
Photograph from Stephane Renauld Collection,
Courtesy of Groundtastic Magazine

CENTRAL PARK
HOME GROUND OF **COWDENBEATH**
TEMPORARY HOME GROUND FOR **DUNFERMLINE ATHLETIC**

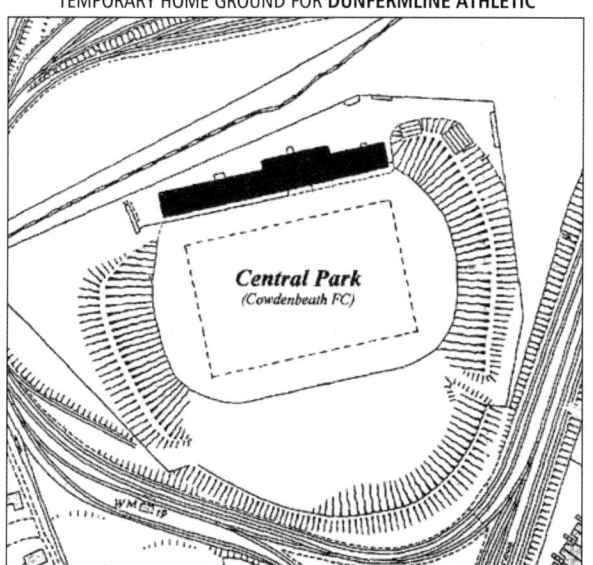

MAP EXTRACT; NT1691 [1951]
SITE LOCATION; **NT16319150**

The ground opened in 1917 when *Cowdenbeath FC* moved here from *North End Park*. The pitch is surrounded by an oval track, in use for stock car racing in 2002, with a main stand, built in 1921 and partially destroyed by fires in 1985 and 1992 but subsequently refurbished, alongside a 552 seat stand (constructed in 1995) on the north side. Embankments have been constructed around the other three sides but the only covered accommodation for standing spectators, installed at the west end of the pitch in the early 1950s, succumbed to a gale in 1983.

The record attendance of 25,586 was set when *Rangers* visited the ground for a Scottish League Cup Quarter Final (1-3) on September 21st, 1949. The capacity at the start of the 2004/5 season was 4,370 with 1,431 seats and the pitch was the narrowest in the Scottish League, measuring some 107 x 64 yards.

PLAYING RECORD OF COWDENBEATH
LEAGUE PROGRAMME
First Match; 4-3 v. Lochgelly United (9,000) (August 20th, 1921)
Highest Gate; 17,810 v. Heart of Midlothian (1-2) (August 16th, 1924)
Lowest Gate; 100 v. East Stirlingshire (2-1) (September 18th, 1990)
Highest Home Win; 10-0 v. Brechin City (-) (November 20th, 1937)
Highest Home Defeat; 1-10 v. St Bernards (-) (September 1st, 1934)
No. of Matches Played by Cowdenbeath; 1,405
Information Kindly Supplied by; David Allan

The club moved here from *North End Park* in 1917.

PLAYING RECORD OF DUNFERMLINE ATHLETIC
LEAGUE PROGRAMME
Match Played; 4-1 v. Bo'ness (-) (December 24th, 1921)
No. of Matches Played by Dunfermline Athletic; 1
Information Kindly Supplied by; Duncan Simpson

This match was played here due to *East End Park* being closed for one month following crowd trouble at the game v. *St Johnstone* (1-2) on November 19th, 1921.

AT THE END OF SEASON 2004/5, A TOTAL OF **60** TEAMS HAD TAKEN PART IN **1,406** LEAGUE FIXTURES AT THIS VENUE

CITY PARK
HOME GROUND OF **EDINBURGH CITY**

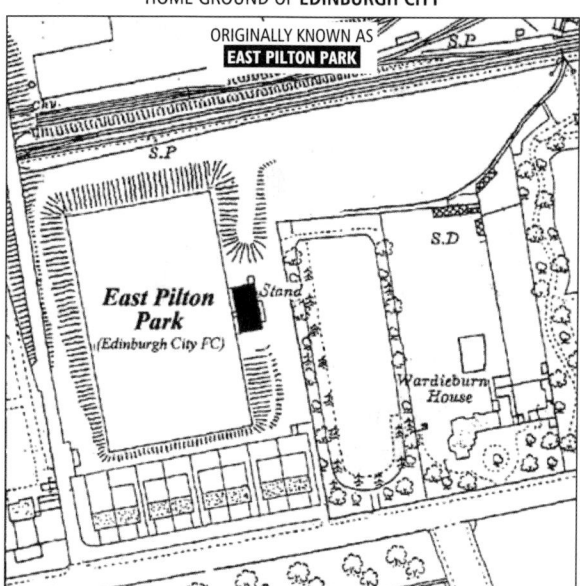

ORIGINALLY KNOWN AS **EAST PILTON PARK**

MAP EXTRACT; GROUND AS IN **c1960** DRAWN FROM PLANS AND SUPERIMPOSED ON EDINBURGH 3.3 [1934]
SITE LOCATION; **NT23467593**

Formerly known as *East Pilton Park* the ground was first used by *Edinburgh City FC* in 1935. Originally just an open field, improvements were made, including the construction of grassed embankments to accommodate standing spectators around the pitch and a grandstand, incorporating dressing rooms and offices, on the east side.

The record attendance of 5,740 was set at the Scottish FA Cup 1st Round tie v. *Cowdenbeath* (2-3) on January 25th, 1936 and following the demise of *Edinburgh City FC* in 1954 the ground was used by *Ferranti (later Meadowbank) Thistle FC* and *Hibernian Reserves*. Although use of the grandstand was banned, *City Park* was still utilized in 2005 as the home ground for *Spartans* and *Craigroyston FCs*.

PLAYING RECORD OF EDINBURGH CITY
LEAGUE PROGRAMME
First Match; 1-3 v. Falkirk (1,000) (August 12th, 1935)
Last Match; 3-0 v. Morton (-) (August 26th, 1939)
Highest Gate*; 2,000 v. St Bernards (1-6) (October 5th, 1935)
Lowest Gate*; 100 v. Forfar Athletic (2-3) (April 15th, 1939)
Highest Home Win; 6-1 v. Brechin City (-) (September 18th, 1937)
Highest Home Defeat; 2-8 v. Alloa Athletic (-) (January 9th, 1937), v. East Fife (-) (April 3rd, 1937) & v. Forfar Athletic (-) (January 29th, 1938)
No. of Matches Played by Edinburgh City; 101

The club moved here from *Marine Gardens* in 1935. The Scottish Football League was suspended in 1939 and the club did not re-enter the Scottish League after WWII.

*NB. Not all attendances are known and these are the highest and lowest gate figures of those that were recorded.

A TOTAL OF **23** TEAMS TOOK PART IN **101** LEAGUE FIXTURES AT THIS VENUE

CHANCELOT PARK
HOME GROUND OF LEITH ATHLETIC

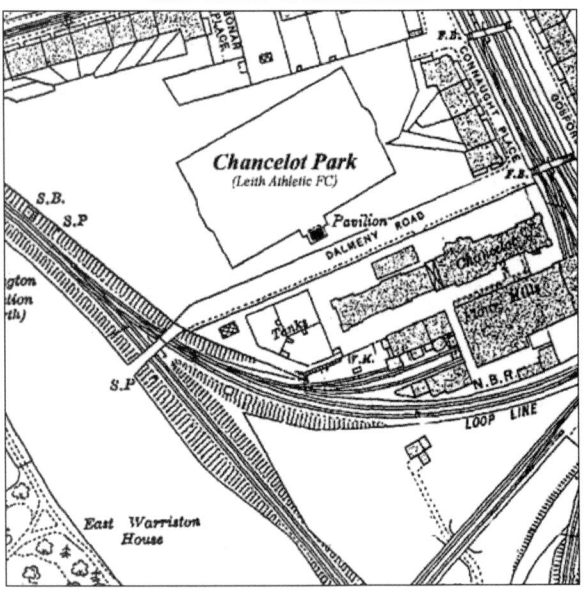

MAP EXTRACT; EDINBURGH 3.3 [1914]
SITE LOCATION; NT25617614

Located between Dalmeny Road and Ferry Road in the north of the city, *Leith Athletic FC* first used the ground in 1900. Little is known of this venue other than the only facility would appear to be a small pavilion on the south side of the pitch. The probable record gate is 4,000 at the Scottish FA Cup 2nd Round tie v. *Motherwell* (3-1) on February 6th, 1904.

Leith Athletic moved out to *Old Logie Green* in 1904 but returned in 1919 for a while to play some home games prior to their re-entry into the Scottish Football League in 1924. Lethem Park now occupies the site.

PLAYING RECORD OF LEITH ATHLETIC
LEAGUE PROGRAMME

First Match; 1-0 v. Airdrieonians (-) (September 8th, 1900)
Last Match; 0-2 v. Raith Rovers (-) (March 5th, 1904)
Highest & Lowest Gates*; Not Known
Highest Home Win; 5-0 v. Abercorn (-) (December 21st, 1901)
Highest Home Defeat; 1-4 v. East Stirlingshire (-)
(August 23rd, 1902)
No. of Matches Played by Leith Athletic; 42

Leith Athletic moved here from *Hawkhill* and remained here until 1904 when it took over *Old Logie Green*
*NB. There are no League gate figures recorded for *Leith Athletic's* occupancy of this venue.

A TOTAL OF **16** TEAMS TOOK PART IN **42** LEAGUE FIXTURES AT THIS VENUE

CHAPELHILL PARK
HOME GROUND OF CLACKMANNAN

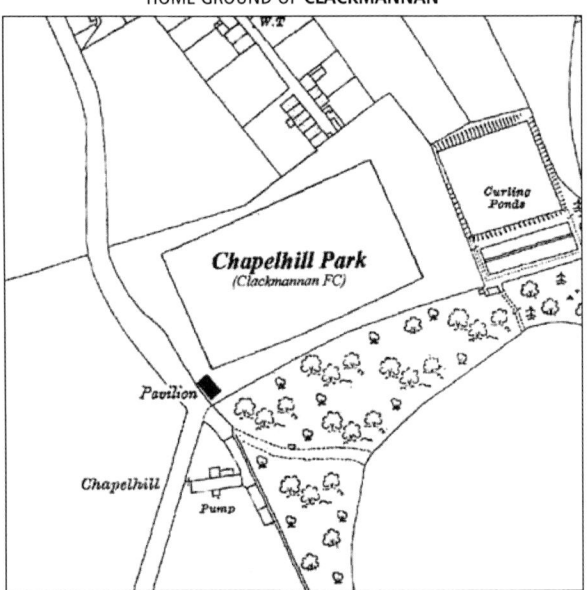

MAP EXTRACT; CLACKMANNAN 140.5 [1922]
SITE LOCATION; NS91329145

Located to the south of the town centre, *Chapelhill Park* was first used by *Clackmannan FC* in 1886. There were very few facilities at the ground, a pavilion was built in 1892 and a 400 seat grandstand installed following the club's entry into the Scottish Football League in 1921.

Although the club folded in 1931 the ground remained into post-WWII years before the site was redeveloped with housing.

PLAYING RECORD OF CLACKMANNAN
LEAGUE PROGRAMME

First Match & Highest Gate*; 1-2 v. Alloa (3,500)
(August 27th, 1921)
Last Match; 3-3 v. Leith Athletic (-) (April 24th, 1926)
Lowest Gate*; 500 v. Bathgate (1-3) (November 19th, 1921)
Highest Home Win; 7-3 v. Beith (-) (November 14th, 1925)
Highest Home Defeat; 1-7 v. Vale of Leven (-) (October 24th, 1925)
No. of Matches Played by Clackmannan; 61
(Including one expunged match v. Dumbarton Harp on December 20th, 1924)

The club was elected into the Scottish Football League Division 2 in 1921 but dropped out at the end of the season when the League membership was reduced to 38 clubs for the 1922/23 season. The club then became a founder member of the Scottish Football League Division 3 in 1923 and left the League when Division 3 was disbanded near the end of the 1925/26 season. *Chapelhill Park* was closed in 1925 after crowd trouble at a Scottish FA Cup Preliminary Round 2nd Replay match v. *Peebles Rovers* (2-3) at *Cowdenbeath FC's* **Central Park** and the home match v. *Brechin City* on November 15th, 1925 was played at the **Recreation Park** of *Alloa Athletic FC*. The home matches v. *Dykehead*, *Galston* and *Royal Albert* in 1925/26 were not played.
*NB. These are the highest and lowest known gate figures of the very few that were recorded.

A TOTAL OF **35** TEAMS TOOK PART IN **61** LEAGUE FIXTURES AT THIS VENUE

CLEPINGTON PARK & TANNADICE PARK

HOME GROUND OF **DUNDEE WANDERERS** & **DUNDEE UNITED**
TEMPORARY HOME GROUND FOR **DUNDEE**

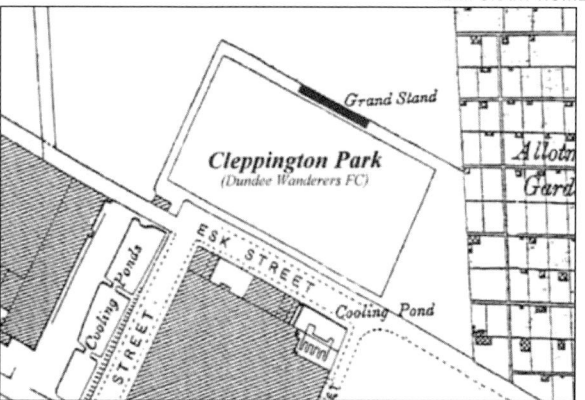

MAP EXTRACT; FORFARSHIRE 54.5 [**1903**]
SITE LOCATION; **NO40513781**

The ground, as *Clepington Park*, was first used by *Dundee High School FC* and *East End FC* before *Johnstone Wanderers FC* moved in in 1891.

By the time that the club, as *Dundee Wanderers FC*, was evicted from the ground in 1909 the facilities only consisted of a covered grandstand and some raised banking. The manner of this eviction, a connivance between the landlord and *Dundee Hibernian FC* in order to make the venue available for the latter, led *Dundee Wanderers* to strip out every removable item and all that remained when they left was an unfenced grassland! The ground re-opened later the same year as *Tannadice Park*.

PLAYING RECORD OF DUNDEE WANDERERS
LEAGUE PROGRAMME

Matches Played; 3-4 v. Abercorn (-) (March 2nd, 1895)
6-5 v. Partick Thistle (-) March 9th, 1895)
4-5 v. Renton (-) (March 16th, 1895)
6-3 v. Cowlairs (-) (April 6th, 1895)
0-1 v. Morton (-) (April 8th, 1895)

No. of Matches Played by Dundee Wanderers; 5

According to some reports *Dundee Wanderers* played their initial home games in the Scottish League at **East Dock Street** before moving here and, as there is no official record of venues of games, it has been assumed that, if this was the case, the four matches at the start of the 1894/95 season were played at *East Dock Street* whilst those played in March and April of 1895 were staged at *Clepington Park*. No attendance figures are known for *Dundee Wanderers FC's* occupancy here and the club failed to gain re-election in 1895.

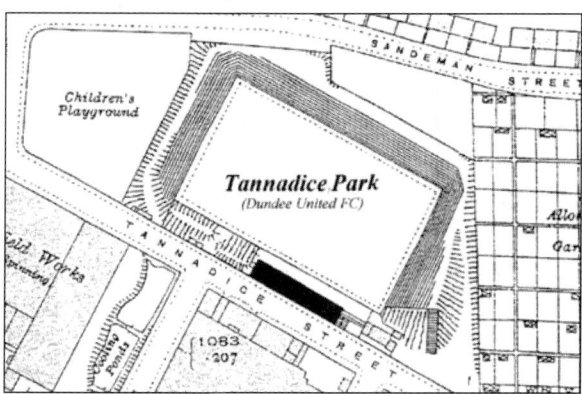

MAP EXTRACT; FORFARSHIRE 54.5 [**1938**]

Following the eviction of *Dundee Wanderers*, the ground was quickly fenced in and re-established; a pavilion and 1,200 seat stand were installed on the south side and embankments constructed around the remainder of the ground. *Tannadice Park*, as it was re-named, opened on August 18th, 1909 with a friendly match v. *Hibernian FC*. Apart from extensions to the embankments it remained unaltered until the 1920s and the reformation of the club as *Dundee United FC*. In 1925 the ground was purchased for £2,500 and enhanced with the installation of timber terracing around three of the sides.

Post WWII improvements included the provision of cover at the west end, concreted terracing at the east end, enlargement and covering of the north side and the replacement of the stand and pavilion with an L-shaped cantilever stand in the south east corner.

The record attendance of 28,000 was set at the Inter Fairs Cities Cup tie v. *Barcelona* on November 16th, 1966. Seats were subsequently installed at the west end, and new stands installed on the north side in 1992 and at the east end in 1994 converting it into an all seater stadium. The capacity at the start of season 2004/5 was 14,223 and the pitch size 110 x 72 yards.

PLAYING RECORD OF DUNDEE UNITED
[ALSO AS DUNDEE HIBERNIAN]
LEAGUE PROGRAMME

First Match; 2-3 v. Leith Athletic (3,000) (August 20th, 1910)
Highest Gate; 25,000 v. Dundee (1-0) (January 3rd, 1927)
Lowest Gate; 200 v. Edinburgh City (9-3) (November 18th, 1933)
Highest Home Win; 12-1 v. East Stirlingshire (-) (April 13th, 1936)
Highest Home Defeat; 0-7 v. Raith Rovers (5,500) (September 15th, 1945) & v. Morton (3,500) (March 2nd, 1957)

PLAY OFF MATCH
2-1 v Partick Thistle (12,120) (May 16th, 1996)

No. of Matches Played by Dundee United; 1,426
(League Programme; 1,425 [Including one expunged match v. Bathgate on December 29th, 1928], Play Off Matches; 1)

Information Kindly Supplied by; Peter Rundo

The club was elected into the Scottish Football League Division 2 in 1910 as *Dundee Hibernian*, dropped out in 1922 and re-joined in 1923 as *Dundee United*.

PLAYING RECORD OF DUNDEE
LEAGUE PROGRAMME

Match Played; 1-1 v. Rangers (11,051) (April 18th, 1999)

No. of Matches Played by Dundee; 1

Information Kindly Supplied by; Norrie Price

This match was played here due to reconstruction work at **Dens Park**.

AT THE END OF SEASON 2004/5, A TOTAL OF **58** TEAMS HAD TAKEN PART IN **1,432** LEAGUE FIXTURES AT THIS VENUE

The "L" shaped cantilever stand in the south east corner of the ground.
Photograph by Paul Claydon. Courtesy of Groundtastic Magazine

CLIFTONHILL PARK

HOME GROUND OF **ALBION ROVERS**
TEMPORARY HOME GROUND FOR **HAMILTON ACADEMICAL, BERWICK RANGERS** & **DUMBARTON**

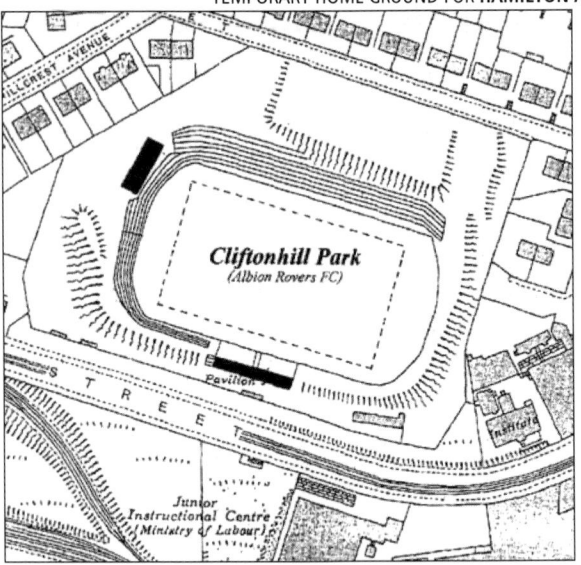

MAP EXTRACT; LANARKSHIRE 8.9 [1940]
SITE LOCATION; NS74206484

When the ground was opened in 1919 by *Albion Rovers FC* the main facility was the pavilion moved from *Meadow Park* and re-erected here, plus extensive embankments around the ground. A main stand was built on the south side a year later and an oval track constructed in 1931 for greyhound racing. Further alterations included the reduction in terracing on the north side and installation of a roof at the west end. This roof was later removed and re-erected on the north side only to be destroyed in a gale in 1968 and subsequently replaced.

The track has since been used for stock cars and speedway as well as greyhound racing. Although the record attendance was 27,381, achieved at the Scottish FA Cup 2nd Round tie v. *Rangers* (1-3) on February 8th, 1936, the approved capacity was set at only 850 in 1985 (confined to the main stand and paddock). The stand roof was extended over the paddock in 1994 and the capacity had increased to 2,496 with 538 seated by the start of the 2004/5 season. The size of the pitch was 110 x 72 yards.

Stirling Albion attacking the goal at the north end of **Cliftonhill Park** on April 26th, 2003. By this time the terracing behind both goals had been reduced to just grassed banks but covered standing accommodation was available on the north side as well as the main stand and paddock. This League match finished in a 2-1 win to the hosts, *Albion Rovers*.
Courtesy of RedWeb (www.stirlingalbionfc.com)

PLAYING RECORD OF ALBION ROVERS
LEAGUE PROGRAMME
First Match; 0-2 v. St Mirren (8,000) (December 25th, 1919)
Highest Gate; 25,000 v. Celtic (3-3) (September 4th, 1948)
Lowest Gate; 142 v. East Stirlingshire (1-3) (February 24th, 1992)
Highest Home Win; 11-1 v. Dumbarton (-) (January 30th, 1925)
Highest Home Defeat; 0-8 v. Ross County (302) (August 15th, 1998)
No. of Matches Played by Albion Rovers; 1,437
(Including one expunged match v. Bathgate on December 8th, 1928)
Information Kindly Supplied by; Robin Marwick

The club moved here from *Meadow Park* in 1919 and was elected into the Scottish Football League Division 1 in the same year. At various times in the 1980s, matches were also played at *Broomfield Park*.

PLAYING RECORD OF DUMBARTON
LEAGUE PROGRAMME
Matches Played; 0-2 v. Brechin City (370) (August 12th, 2000)
1-2 v. East Stirlingshire (259) (September 9th, 2000)
2-4 v. Cowdenbeath (348) (September 23rd, 2000)
2-3 v. East Fife (256) (October 7th, 2000)
2-3 v. Hamilton Academical (368) (October 14th, 2000)
0-1 v. Albion Rovers (277) (October 28th, 2000)
1-0 v. Montrose (238) (November 18th, 2000)
No. of Matches Played by Dumbarton; 7
Information Kindly Supplied by; Jim McAllister

Dumbarton FC moved out of *Boghead Park* and temporarily ground-shared here until the *Strathclyde Homes Stadium* was completed.

PLAYING RECORD OF HAMILTON ACADEMICAL
LEAGUE PROGRAMME
First Match; 2-0 v. Clyde (917) (August 24th, 1996)
Last Match; 0-3 v. Greenock Morton (1,089) (May 2nd, 1998)
Highest Gate; 2,049 v. Partick Thistle (0-1) (December 27th, 1997)
Highest Home Win & Lowest Gate; 379 v. Brechin City (5-1)
(December 4th, 1996)
Highest Home Defeat; 0-4 v. Dundee (1,967)
(November 29th, 1997)
No. of Matches Played by Hamilton Academical; 31
Information Kindly Supplied by; Scott A. Struthers

The club moved here in 1996 to groundshare with *Albion Rovers FC*. Due to insufficient capacity and electrical & floodlighting problems three matches were played at *Firhill Park* and two at *Fir Park*. In 1998 the club moved back to *Firhill Park* to groundshare with *Partick Thistle FC* until *The Ballast Stadium* was completed in 2001.

PLAYING RECORD OF BERWICK RANGERS
LEAGUE PROGRAMME
Match Played; 1-5 v. Dumbarton (250) (March 28th, 1992)
No. of Matches Played by Berwick Rangers; 1
Information Kindly Supplied by; Robin Murdie

The match was played here due to the unserviceable state of the roof on the main stand at *Shielfield Park*.

AT THE END OF SEASON 2004/5, A TOTAL OF **60** TEAMS HAD TAKEN PART IN **1,476** LEAGUE FIXTURES AT THIS VENUE

CLUNE PARK

HOME GROUND OF **PORT GLASGOW ATHLETIC**
TEMPORARY HOME GROUND FOR **GREENOCK MORTON** & **PARTICK THISTLE**

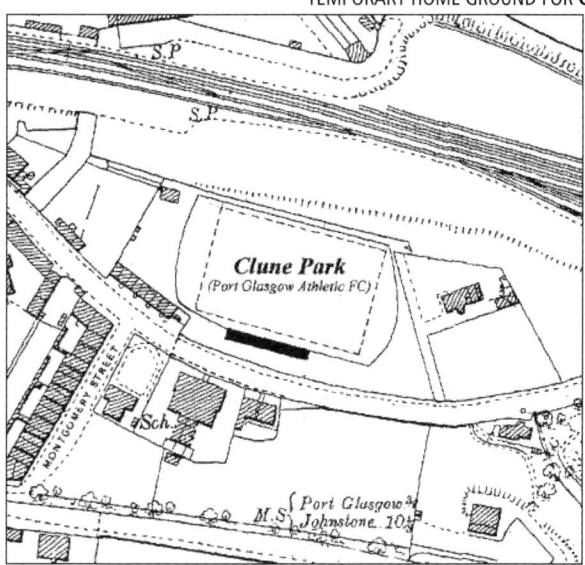

MAP EXTRACT; RENFREWSHIRE 2.12 [1896]
SITE LOCATION; **NS33057425**

PLAYING RECORD OF PORT GLASGOW ATHLETIC
LEAGUE PROGRAMME
First Match; 6-1 v. Northern (-) (August 12th, 1893)
Last Match; 1-1 v. Leith Athletic (-) (February 18th, 1911)
Highest Gate*; 8,000 v. Rangers (0-2) (August 25th, 1906)
Lowest Gate*; Not Known
Highest Home Win; 10-1 v. Morton (-) (May 5th, 1894)
Highest Home Defeat; 2-8 v Ayr (-) (January 6th, 1900)
No. of Matches Played by Port Glasgow Athletic; 214

The club was a founder member of the Scottish Football League Division 2 in 1893 and resigned from the League in 1911. The club was also involved in a Scottish Football League Division 1 14th/15th Place Play Off Match v. *Kilmarnock* (6-0) at the neutral venue of *New Cathkin Park* on May 15th, 1906. *New Cathkin Park* on May 15th, 1906.

*NB. This is the highest gate figure of the few that were recorded. In view of the general level of those that are known, it is very probable that there were crowds of less than 1,000 on occasions.

PLAYING RECORD OF GREENOCK MORTON
LEAGUE PROGRAMME
Match Played; 1-0 v. Queen's Park (-) (December 30th, 1905)
No. of Matches Played by Greenock Morton; 1
Information Kindly Supplied by; Hector Cook & Eddie McDowell

This match was played here due to *Cappielow Park* being closed for one month following an attack on the referee at the end of the League match v. *Rangers* (0-3) on December 9th, 1905.

PLAYING RECORD OF PARTICK THISTLE
LEAGUE PROGRAMME
Match Played; 1-3 v. Port Glasgow Athletic (-) (March 20th, 1909)
No. of Matches Played by Partick Thistle; 1
Information Kindly Supplied by; Robert Reid

This match was played here as *Firhill Park* was not ready following the closure of *Meadowside* in 1908.

A TOTAL OF **35** TEAMS TOOK PART IN **216** LEAGUE FIXTURES AT THIS VENUE

Located to the east of Port Glasgow town centre, *Clune Park* opened in 1881. The facilities eventually included a covered stand on the south side and some banking around the pitch. The record attendance of 11,000 was set at the Scottish FA Cup 3rd Round tie v. *Rangers* (1-0) on March 10th, 1906.

The club resigned from the Scottish League in 1911 and shared the venue with *Port Glasgow Juniors FC* until their demise one year later. The ground was redeveloped in the 1920s with a number of four storey flats.

This rare view of **Clune Park** is believed to show the *Port Glasgow Athletic* v. *Morton* Scottish League Division One match which took place on August 29th, 1903 and was won 2-0 by the hosts. The ground was well packed for this local derby with standing spectators gathered on the uncovered banking behind the goals and the seated covered stand visible on the south side of the pitch.

CLYDEHOLM
HOME GROUND OF CLYDEBANK [1]

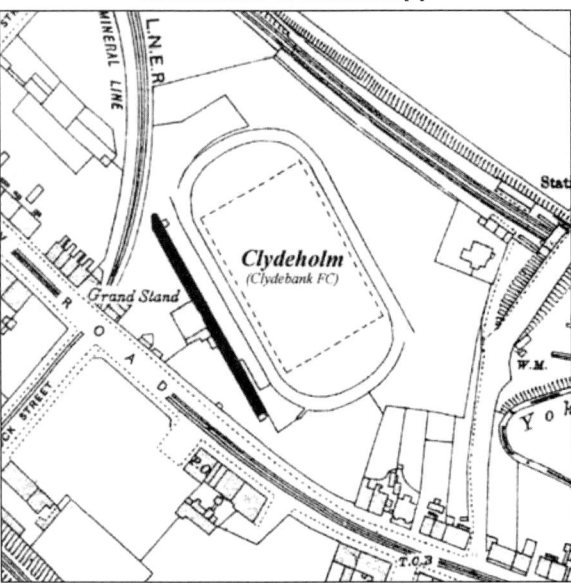

MAP EXTRACT; LANARKSHIRE 5.3 [1934]
SITE LOCATION; NS50756915

Clydebank [1] FC was formed in 1914 and a site on the north side of Glasgow Road and adjacent to Yoker Station leased for 10 years. A pavilion was the only facility as *Clydeholm*, as the ground became known, opened in the same year. A grandstand was built along the south west side in 1925 and, around about the same time, a greyhound track installed.

The club was defunct in 1931 and the venue continued in use as a greyhound stadium. The site was later cleared and used for a shopping centre.

PLAYING RECORD OF CLYDEBANK [1]
LEAGUE PROGRAMME

First Match; 3-1 v. East Stirlingshire (-) (August 16th, 1914)
Last Match; 1-5 v. Raith Rovers (-) (April 25th, 1931)
Highest Gate*; 22,000 v. Rangers (2-4) (November 13th, 1920) & v. Rangers (1-7) (August 20th, 1921)
Lowest Gate*; Not Known
Highest Home Win; 9-2 v. Leith Athletic (-) (December 5th, 1914)
Highest Home Defeat; 1-7 v. Rangers (22,000) (August 20th, 1921)
No. of Matches Played by Clydebank [1]; 280

The club was elected into the Scottish Football League Division 2 in 1914 and although re-elected in 1931 resigned on July 3rd.
*NB. These are the highest gate figures of the few that were recorded. In view of the general level of those that are known, it is very probable that there were crowds of less than 1,000 on occasions.

A TOTAL OF **48** TEAMS TOOK PART IN **280** LEAGUE FIXTURES AT THIS VENUE

CRAWICK HOLM
HOME GROUND OF NITHSDALE WANDERERS

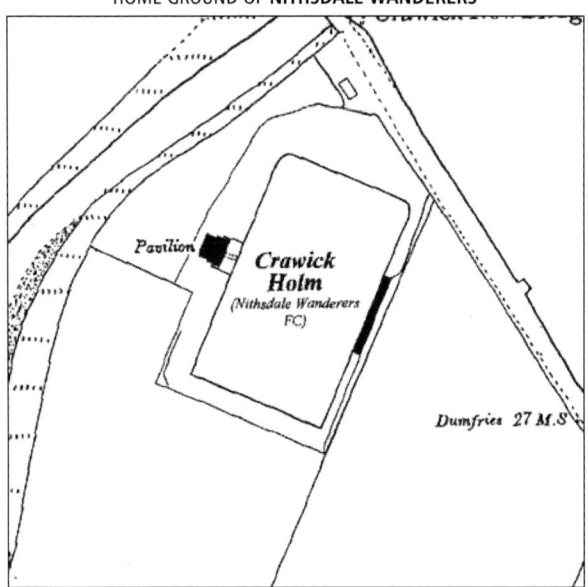

MAP EXTRACT; DUMFRIES-SHIRE 6.10 [1899]
SITE LOCATION; NS77391060

Opened in 1920, the ground was located at the north end of Sanquhar, on the south bank of Crawick Water. A stone built pavilion, containing the dressing rooms and a small boiler room, and a 250 capacity grandstand were sited on the north west side of the pitch. The other facilities consisted of a small covered enclosure on the south east side.

The largest gate at this ground was probably the 4,200 who attended the Scottish FA Qualifying Cup 2nd Round match v. *Queen of the South* (2-3) on September 15th, 1923. The ground survived well into the 1970s and, despite the encroachment of industrial units, a football field still occupied the site in 1990.

PLAYING RECORD OF NITHSDALE WANDERERS
LEAGUE PROGRAMME

First Match; 5-0 v. Brechin City (1,100) (August 25th, 1923)
Last Match; 3-4 v. Clydebank (1,000) (April 30th, 1927)
Highest Gate*; 1,500 v. Queen of the South (1-1) (September 22nd, 1923)
Lowest Gate*; 600 v. Helensburgh (2-0) (December 15th, 1923)
Highest Home Win; 8-0 v. Montrose (-) (April 18th, 1925)
Highest Home Defeat; 2-5 v. King's Park (-) (January 30th, 1926)
No. of Matches Played by Nithsdale Wanderers; 69
(Including one expunged match v. Dumbarton Harp on September 27th, 1924)

The club was a founder member of the Scottish Football League Division 3 in 1923 and did not apply for re-election in 1927.
*NB. These are the highest and lowest gate figures of the few that were recorded. In view of the general level of those that are known, it is very probable that there were crowds of less than 600 on occasions.

A TOTAL OF **38** TEAMS TOOK PART IN **69** LEAGUE FIXTURES AT THIS VENUE

DALZIEL PARK
HOME GROUND OF MOTHERWELL

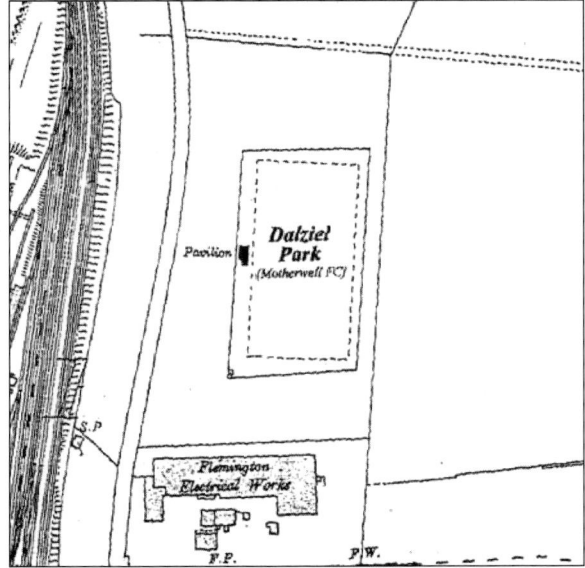

MAP EXTRACT; LANARKSHIRE 12.14 [1912]
SITE LOCATION; NS76955630

Located in Craigneuk, to the east of Motherwell and on the east side of Robberhall Road, *Motherwell FC* moved to *Dalziel Park* in 1889 and opened it in March with a match against *Rangers FC*.

The only facility appeared to be a pavilion on the west side of the pitch and, despite being on an unrestricted site in the middle of a large field, the ground was quite narrow. After the club moved to *Fir Park* in 1895 the site was redeveloped for industrial use and by 2005 had become incorporated into Flemington Industrial Park.

PLAYING RECORD OF MOTHERWELL
LEAGUE PROGRAMME

Matches Played; 4-1 v. Clyde (-) (August 12th, 1893)
3-2 v. Cowlairs (-) (August 26th, 1893)
7-2 v. Port Glasgow Athletic (-) (September 30th, 1893)
2-3 v. Partick Thistle (-) (November 4th, 1893)
6-2 v. Thistle (-) (December 16th, 1893)
5-3 v. Abercorn (-) (February 17th, 1894)
2-1 v. Hibernian (-) (April 14th, 1894)
2-0 v. Northern (-) (May 19th, 1894)
4-1 v. Morton (-) (May 26th, 1894)
4-2 v. Airdrieonians (-) (August 11th, 1894)
7-0 v. Abercorn (-) (September 8th, 1894)
2-0 v. Hibernian (-) (October 6th, 1894)
0-2 v. Renton (-) (December 1st, 1894)
6-4 v. Morton (-) (March 9th, 1895)
5-0 v. Dundee Wanderers (-) (March 30th, 1895)
3-0 v. Partick Thistle (-) (April 6th, 1895)
2-0 v. Port Glasgow Athletic (April 20th, 1895)
4-0 v. Cowlairs (-) (May 18th, 1895)

No. of Matches Played by Motherwell; 18
Information Kindly Supplied by; John Swinburne

The club was a founder member of the Scottish Football League Division 2 in 1893 and moved to *Fir Park* in 1895.
*NB. There are no gate figures recorded for *Motherwell FC's* occupancy of this venue.

A TOTAL OF **13** TEAMS TOOK PART IN **18** LEAGUE FIXTURES AT THIS VENUE

DUCKBURN PARK
TEMPORARY HOME GROUND FOR KING'S PARK

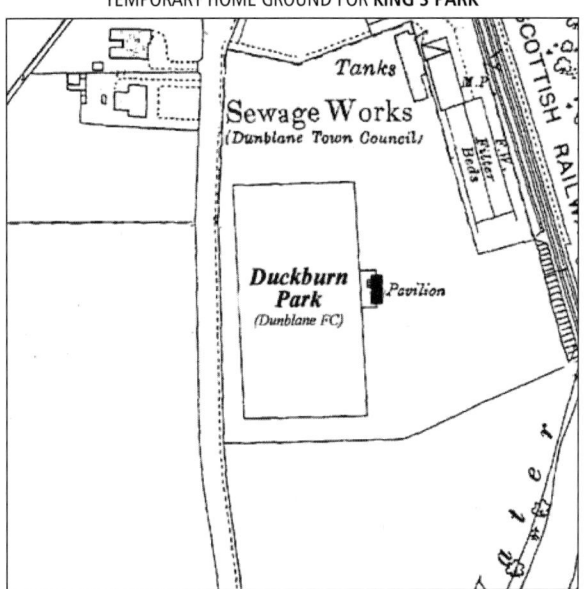

MAP EXTRACT; PERTHSHIRE 132.3 [1930]
SITE LOCATION; NS78099953

Located to the south of Dunblane and on the east side of Stirling Road, *Duckburn Park* was the home ground of *Dunblane FC* and the only facility was a pavilion on the east side of the pitch. By 2005 the site had been utilized as part of the Dunblane Industrial Estate

PLAYING RECORD OF KING'S PARK
LEAGUE PROGRAMME

Match Played; 0-0 v. Vale of Leven (-) (November 5th, 1921)
No. of Matches Played by King's Park; 1
Information Supplied by; Allan Grieve

This match was played here due to crowd trouble at the game at *Forthbank Park* v. *St Johnstone* (2-2) on October 8th, 1921.

A TOTAL OF **2** TEAMS TOOK PART IN **1** LEAGUE FIXTURE AT THIS VENUE

DENS PARK

HOME GROUND OF **DUNDEE**
TEMPORARY HOME GROUND FOR **AYR UNITED**

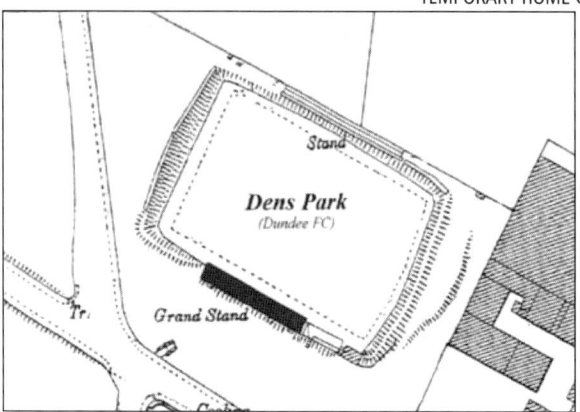

MAP EXTRACT; FORFARSHIRE 54.5 [**1903**]
SITE LOCATION; **NO40123782**

Dundee FC moved here from **Carolina Port** in 1898, bringing the grandstand with them and installing it on the south side of the pitch. The ground officially opened on August 19th, 1899 with a friendly match against *St Bernards FC* and within a short time the facilities also included an open seated stand on the north side and raised embankments at each end.

MAP EXTRACT; FORFARSHIRE 54.5 [**1938**]

Major alterations took place after the ground was purchased for £5,000 in 1919, the pitch was slightly realigned, a new stand built on the north side and concrete terracing installed around the pitch. The original grandstand was destroyed by fire in the year that the "new" *Dens Park* officially opened, 1921, and it was not until 1959 that the south side received any covering.

Greyhound racing was experimented with in the 1930s (and staged again between 1994 and 1997) and *Dens Park* hosted international matches in 1904, 1908 and 1936. The record attendance of 43,024 was established at the Scottish FA Cup 2nd Round tie v. *Rangers* (0-2) on February 7th, 1953 but in 1986 the capacity was reduced to 22,381 with 12,130 seats when seating was installed on the south and west sides.

In 1994 the main stand and paddock was refurbished and in 1999 new 3,000 seat stands built at each end. New seats were also installed on the south side and by the start of the 2004/5 season the all-seat capacity was 11,850 with an 105 x 70 yards sized pitch

PLAYING RECORD OF DUNDEE
LEAGUE PROGRAMME

First Match; 3-1 v. Clyde (9,000) (September 2nd, 1899)
Highest Gate; 39,975 v. Rangers (3-1) (January 3rd, 1949)
Lowest Gate; 1,000 v. Partick Thistle (1-2) (February 6th, 1915), v. Falkirk (2-0) (February 13th, 1931), v. Falkirk (3-0) (September 24th, 1932) & v. Hibernian (1-0) (April 28th, 1933)
Highest Home Win; 10-0 v. Dunfermline Athletic (14,000) (March 22nd, 1947)
Highest Home Defeat; 1-8 v. Celtic (21,000) (January 16th, 1971)
No. of Matches Played by Dundee; 1,716
Information Kindly Supplied by; Norrie Price

The club moved here from **Carolina Port** in 1899. Due to reconstruction work the fixture v. *Rangers* on April 18th, 1999 was played at **Tannadice Park**.

PLAYING RECORD OF AYR UNITED
LEAGUE PROGRAMME

Match Played; 0-2 v. Dundee (-) (April 29th, 1922)
No. of Matches Played by Ayr United; 1
Information Kindly Supplied by; Duncan Carmichael

This match was played here as the fixture coincided with a race meeting at Ayr Racecourse and it was anticipated that this would result in a very small attendance at **Somerset Park**.

NEUTRAL PLAY OFF MATCHES

Division 1, 8th/9th Place Play Off; St Bernards 1, St Mirren 2 (-) (April 7th, 1900)
No. of Matches Played; 1

AT THE END OF SEASON 2003/4, A TOTAL OF **48** TEAMS HAD TAKEN PART IN **1,718** LEAGUE FIXTURES AT THIS VENUE

The Archibald Leitch designed angled main stand and paddock on the north side of the ground.
Photograph by Jon Weaver. Courtesy of Groundtastic Magazine

DOUGLAS PARK

HOME GROUND OF **HAMILTON ACADEMICAL**
TEMPORARY HOME GROUND FOR **CLYDE** & **PARTICK THISTLE**

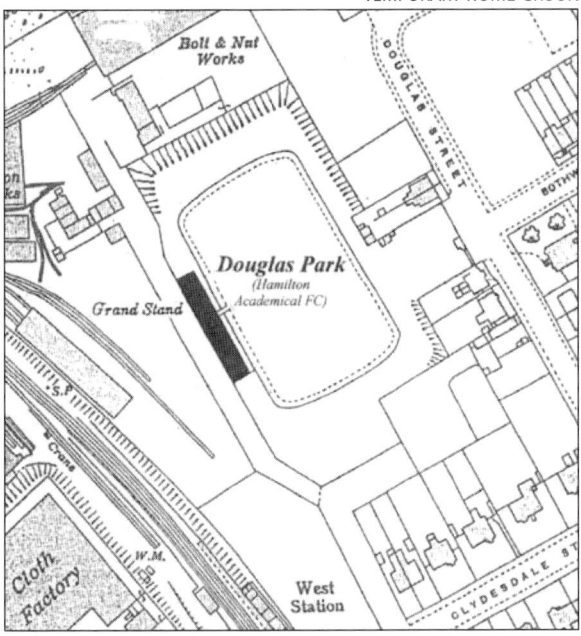

MAP EXTRACT; LANARKSHIRE 11.16 & 17.4 [**1936**]
SITE LOCATION; **NS71245605**

Located between Hamilton West Station and Douglas Road, *Hamilton Academical FC* moved to *Douglas Park* from *South Haugh* in September 1888. Details of the facilities in the early days are not known, but in 1913 a replacement and much larger 1,221 seat grandstand was constructed on the west side of the pitch.

Further improvements included a stand that was built on the opposite side of the pitch in 1919 but only lasted until 1924 when it burned down, terracing constructed around the pitch in 1937 and a cover installed over terracing on the east side in 1949. The main stand was extended in 1986 and, at the same time, seating provided in the paddock.

The record attendance of 28,690 was established on March 3rd, 1937 at the Scottish FA Cup 3rd Round tie v. *Heart of Midlothian* (2-1). The first team ceased playing matches here in May 1994 but the reserve teams of *Hamilton Academical, Partick Thistle, Motherwell, Falkirk* and *Rangers* continued to use the ground until January 25th, 1995 when *Hamilton Academical Reserves* played *Queen of the South Reserves*. The ground was bulldozed in April 1995 and the main stand dismantled and re-erected at *Auchinleck Talbot FC*. The site is now occupied by a retail park.

PLAYING RECORD OF HAMILTON ACADEMICAL
LEAGUE PROGRAMME

First Match; 2-3 v. Kilmarnock (2,000) (November 6th, 1897)
Last Match; 2-1 v. Dumbarton (1,451) (May 14th, 1994)
Highest Gate; 25,000 v. Rangers (1-0) (January 31st, 1925)
Lowest Gate; 300 v. East Stirlingshire (3-0) (February 21st, 1970)
Highest Home Win; 10-2 v. Cowdenbeath (6,000)
(October 15th, 1932)
Highest Home Defeat; 0-8 v. Celtic (10,710) (November 5th, 1988)
No. of Matches Played by Hamilton Academical; 1,592
Information Kindly Supplied by; Scott A. Struthers

The club was elected into the Scottish Football League Division 2 in 1897 and although it resigned from the League in August 1970 it was re-instated within a few weeks. In 1994 *Hamilton Academical* moved out of *Douglas Park* to groundshare with *Partick Thistle* at **Firhill Park**

PLAYING RECORD OF CLYDE
LEAGUE PROGRAMME

First Match; 1-0 v. East Fife (629) (August 10th, 1991)
Last Match*; 0-0 v. Ayr United (809) (January 11th, 1994)
Highest Gate; 1,637 v. Dunfermline Athletic (0-2)
(September 4th, 1993)
Highest Home Win & Lowest Gate; 6-2 v. Albion Rovers (402)
(February 4th, 1992)
Highest Home Defeat; 2-3 v. Queen of the South (567) (December 7th, 1991) & v. Queen's Park (678) (February 20th, 1993).
0-2 v. Dunfermline Athletic (1,637) (September 4th, 1993), v. Airdrieonians (1,732) (October 16th, 1993), & v. Falkirk (1,150) (November 23rd, 1993)
No. of Matches Played by Clyde; 51
Information Kindly Supplied by; John Taylor

The club moved here whilst awaiting the construction of **Broadwood Stadium.**
*NB. This was the last completed match as the final game played here v. *Dunfermline Athletic* on January 15th, 1994 was abandoned at half time with the score at 0-2. The attendance was 1,200.

PLAYING RECORD OF PARTICK THISTLE
LEAGUE PROGRAMME

Match Played; 2-4 v. Hamilton Academical (-) (March 27th, 1909)
No. of Matches Played by Partick Thistle; 1
Information Kindly Supplied by; Robert Reid

This match was played here as *Firhill Park* was not ready following the closure of *Meadowside* in 1908.

A TOTAL OF **50** TEAMS TOOK PART IN **1,644** LEAGUE FIXTURES AT THIS VENUE

The 1913-vintage main stand, complete with 1986 extension, on the west side of the pitch. Originally sized at 120 ft long and with 1,221 seats it was one of the smallest designed by Archibald Leitch and possibly the only one with a barrel roof.
Photograph by Paul Claydon. Courtesy of Groundtastic Magazine

DUNTERLIE PARK [1ST]
HOME GROUND OF ARTHURLIE

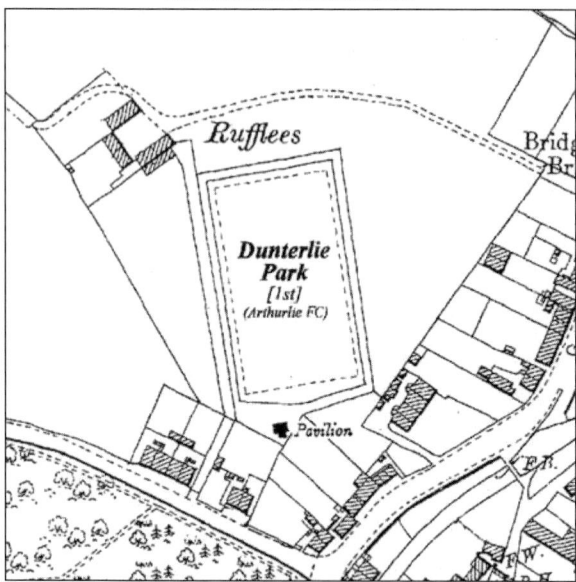

MAP EXTRACT; RENFREWSHIRE 12.15 [1896]
SITE LOCATION; **NS50695950**

Located to the north east of Barrhead town centre and sited just to the north of the corner of Carlibar Road and Glasgow Road, *Arthurlie FC* moved here from *Cross Arthurlie* in 1882. The only facility was a pavilion at the south end of the pitch. The probable record gate is 6,000 at the Scottish FA Cup 1st Round tie v *Rangers* (1-7) on January 27th, 1906.

The club moved to *Dunterlie Park [2nd]* in 1906 and the site was later utilized for housing.

PLAYING RECORD OF ARTHURLIE
LEAGUE PROGRAMME

First Match; 3-1 v. Port Glasgow (-) (August 24th, 1901)
Last Match; 1-3 v. Hamilton Academical (-) (April 7th, 1906)
Highest & Lowest Gate*; Not Known
Highest Home Win; 6-2 v. Leith Athletic (-) (August 26th, 1905)
Highest Home Defeat; 1-5 v. Partick Thistle (-) (February 22nd, 1902)
No. of Matches Played by Arthurlie; 55

The club was elected into the Scottish Football League Division 2 in 1901 and moved to *Dunterlie Park [2nd]* in 1906

*NB. There are no League gate figures recorded for *Arthurlie FC's* occupancy of this venue.

A TOTAL OF **19** TEAMS TOOK PART IN **55** LEAGUE FIXTURES AT THIS VENUE

DUNTERLIE PARK [2ND]
HOME GROUND OF ARTHURLIE

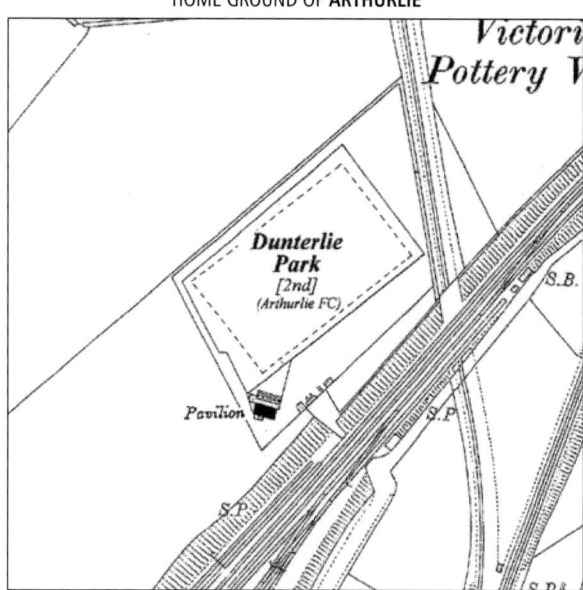

MAP EXTRACT; RENFREWSHIRE 12.15 [1911]
SITE LOCATION; **NS50195975**

Dunterlie Park [2nd] was located at the end of Muriel Street on the north side of the Glasgow & Kilmarnock Joint Railway line, north of Barrhead town centre. *Arthurlie FC* moved here in 1906 and the only facility was a pavilion, fronted by a small open stand, adjacent to the south corner of the pitch.

The club moved to *Dunterlie Park [3rd]* in 1919 and the area was later utilized for industrial redevelopment. The Tubal Works occupied the site in 1939 and it is currently part of the Shanks Industrial Park.

PLAYING RECORD OF ARTHURLIE
LEAGUE PROGRAMME

First Match; 5-4 v. Vale of Leven (-) (August 25th, 1906)
Last Match; 5-3 v. Lochgelly United (-) (April 3rd, 1915)
Highest & Lowest Gate*; Not Known
Highest Home Win; 5-0 v. Albion Rovers (-) (November 11th, 1911) &
v. Leith Athletic (-) (March 21st, 1914)
Highest Home Defeat; 0-4 v. St Bernards (-) (October 3rd, 1908)
No. of Matches Played by Arthurlie; 103

The club moved here from *Dunterlie Park [1st]* in 1906 and moved to *Dunterlie Park [3rd]* in 1919

*NB. There are no gate figures recorded for *Arthurlie FC's* occupancy of this venue.

A TOTAL OF **20** TEAMS TOOK PART IN **103** LEAGUE FIXTURES AT THIS VENUE

DUNTERLIE PARK [3RD]
HOME GROUND OF ARTHURLIE

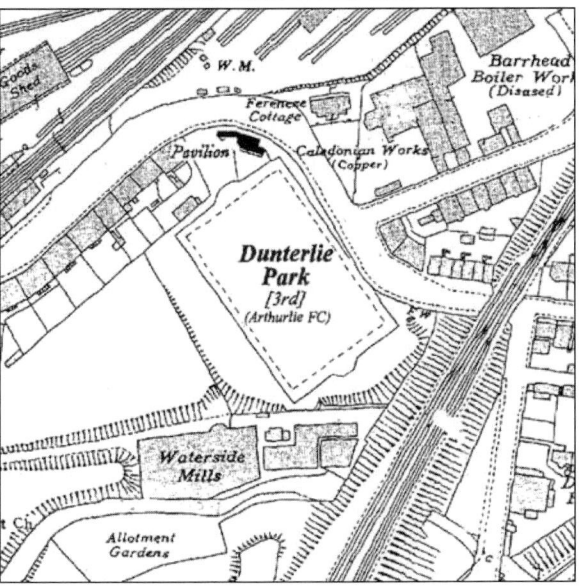

MAP EXTRACT; RENFREWSHIRE 12.15 [**1939**]
SITE LOCATION; **NS49975929**

The third and final *Dunterlie Park* was located adjacent to Carlibar Road, on the south side of Barrhead (G&KJR) Station. *Arthurlie FC* moved in in 1919 and the facilities included a pavilion at the north end and some banking on the west side and behind the south end.

Arthurlie FC resigned from the Scottish League in 1929, reformed as *Arthurlie Amateurs FC* in the same year and reformed again in 1930, this time as a junior football club, *Arthurlie FC*. The record gate of 10,500 was subsequently established at the Scottish Junior FA Cup 6th Round tie v *Cambuslang Rangers* (1-2) on March 18th, 1939. *Dunterlie Park [3rd]* is still in use as the club's home ground.

PLAYING RECORD OF ARTHURLIE
LEAGUE PROGRAMME
First Match; 2-3 v. East Stirlingshire (-) (August 25th, 1923)
Last Match; 1-1 v. St Bernards (-) (March 30th, 1929)
Highest Gate*; 6,000 v. Third Lanark (1-2) (August 22nd, 1925)
Lowest Gate*; 500 v. St Bernards (3-4) (February 18th, 1928)
Highest Home Win; 10-0 v. Armadale (-) (October 1st, 1927)
Highest Home Defeat; 2-6 v. Dunfermline Athletic (-)
(January 9th, 1926)

No. of Matches Played by Arthurlie; 104
(Including one expunged match v. Bathgate on November 3rd, 1929 and matches played in the club's final season [1928/9] that was 4 home games short)

The club moved here from **Dunterlie Park [2nd]** in 1919. Owen McNally established a Second Division scoring record when he netted eight goals in the 10-0 demolition of *Armadale* on October 1st, 1927. The ground was closed for one month following crowd trouble at the fixture v. *Third Lanark* (1-2) on August 22nd, 1925 and two matches were played at *Beith FC's Bellsdale Park*. The club resigned in April 1929 due to financial difficulties but the record for that season was allowed to stand with the home games v. *Bo'ness, East Fife, Forfar Athletic* and *Stenhousemuir* remaining unplayed.
*NB. Not all attendances are known and these are the highest and lowest estimated gate figures of those that were recorded.

A TOTAL OF **39** TEAMS TOOK PART IN **104** LEAGUE FIXTURES AT THIS VENUE

EAST DOCK STREET
HOME GROUND OF DUNDEE WANDERERS

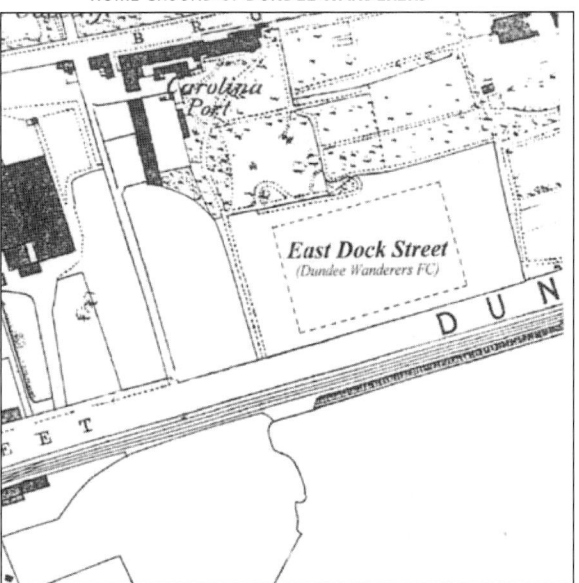

MAP EXTRACT; FORFARSHIRE 54.6 [**1872**]
SITE LOCATION; **NO41623081**

Although the existence of this ground falls between two Ordnance Surveys and with no map, or diagram available, it can be safely assumed that the location was on the north side of East Dock Street at Carolina Port. As early as the 1870s almost every square foot of available land had been absorbed by the docks and associated railway systems and this site was the only one in the vicinity that was large enough to accommodate a football pitch.

What is known is that it had been the home ground of *Dundee Harp FC*, and was the venue for the 35-0 annihilation of *Aberdeen Rovers* in the 1st Round of the Scottish Cup on September 12th, 1885. The largest gate may have occurred when an attendance of about 5,000 turned up here in 1887 for the Forfarshire Cup Final between *Strathmore* and *Forfar*. Details of the facilities, if any, are not known.

PLAYING RECORD OF DUNDEE WANDERERS
LEAGUE PROGRAMME
Matches Played; 2-2 v. Motherwell (-) (August 25th, 1894)
9-1 v. Port Glasgow Athletic (-) (September 15th, 1894)
1-2 v. Airdrieonians (-) (October 20th, 1894)
0-6 v. Hibernian (-) (November 10th, 1894)

No. of Matches Played by Dundee Wanderers; 4

The club was elected into the Scottish Football League Division 2 in 1894. According to some reports *Dundee Wanderers* played their initial home games in the Scottish League here before moving to *Clepington Park* and, as there is no official record of venues of games, it has been assumed that, if this was the case, these four matches at the start of the 1894/95 season were played at *East Dock Street* whilst those played in March and April of 1895 were staged at *Clepington Park*. No attendance figures are known for *Dundee Wanderers FC's* occupancy here.

A TOTAL OF **5** TEAMS TOOK PART IN **4** LEAGUE FIXTURES AT THIS VENUE

EAST END PARK

HOME GROUND OF **DUNFERMLINE ATHLETIC**
TEMPORARY HOME GROUND FOR **RAITH ROVERS**

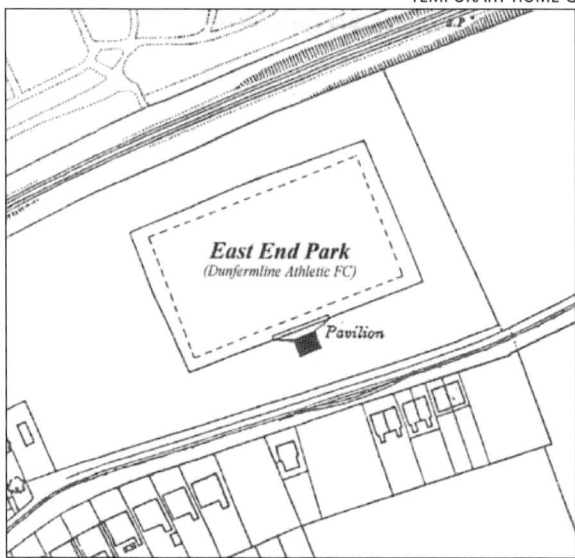

MAP EXTRACT; FIFE 39.1 [**1915**]
SITE LOCATION; **NT10348791**

PLAYING RECORD OF DUNFERMLINE ATHLETIC
LEAGUE PROGRAMME

First Match; 2-0 v. St Bernards (-) (August 24th, 1912)
Highest Gate; 27,816 v. Celtic (1-2) (April 30th, 1968)
Lowest Gate; 358 v. Arbroath (2-0) (April 7th, 1984)
Highest Home Win; 11-2 v. Stenhousemuir (-) (September 27th, 1930)
Highest Home Defeat; 1-7 v. Partick Thistle (-) (January 7th, 1928),
v. Rangers (14,000) (August 11th, 1934)
& v. Rangers (17,000) (October 4th, 1958)

PLAY OFF MATCHES
1-3 v. Aberdeen (15,977) (May 25th, 1995)

No. of Matches Played by Dunfermline Athletic; 1,437
(League Programme; 1,436 [Including expunged matches v. Bathgate on February 9th, 1929 & v. Armadale on October 1st, 1932], Play Off Matches; 1)

Information Kindly Supplied by; Duncan Simpson

The club was elected into the Scottish Football League Division 2 in 1912. Following crowd trouble at the game v. *St Johnstone* on November 19th, 1921 (1-2) the ground was closed for one month and the fixture v. *Bo'ness* played at Cowdenbeath FC's **Central Park**.

NEUTRAL PLAY OFF MATCHES
2nd Division Championship; Cowdenbeath 1, Leith Athletic 0 (-) (April 10th, 1915)

No. of Matches Played; 1

AT THE END OF SEASON 2004/5, A TOTAL OF **57** TEAMS HAD TAKEN PART IN **1,439** LEAGUE FIXTURES AT THIS VENUE

Dunfermline Athletic FC rented the site of *East End Park* from the North British Railway upon their formation in 1885 and the ground was considered as one of the best in the region with the provision of a pavilion in 1887 and cinder banking around the pitch. Subsequent alterations prior to WWI, and its occupation by the army, included moving the pitch eastwards and reconstruction of the pavilion.

After WWI the ground and further land to the east were purchased for £3,500 and the pitch moved eastwards again. At this time a new seated stand was constructed in front of the retained pavilion, a cinder track installed around the re-laid pitch and banking, which was subsequently extended in 1926, improved on all sides of the ground.

Greyhound Racing was introduced during the 1930s (alterations carried out in this decade included the construction of a cover over the north side and some improvements to the east terrace) but the advent of WWII saw *East End Park* requisitioned again by the army.

Additional covering and accommodation were provided in the 1950s with the installation of extensions to the stand and covers over the north and west sides before a new 3,000 seat grandstand was built on the south side in 1962. Later improvements included the linking together of the north and west sides covering to form an L-shape and the installation of seating in the main stand paddock.

The ground was substantially rebuilt in the 1990s, all-seat stands were constructed at each end and seats installed on the north side forming a 12,558 all-seater stadium by the start of the 2004/5 season with an 115 x 70 yards sized pitch.

PLAYING RECORD OF RAITH ROVERS
LEAGUE PROGRAMME

Match Played; 1-1 v. Third Lanark (-) (December 19th, 1914)
No. of Matches Played by Raith Rovers; 1
Information Kindly Supplied by; John Litster

This match was played here due to **Stark's Park** being closed for a month following an assault on a referee.

The all-seater stand at the east end of the ground.
Photograph by Owen Pavey. Courtesy of Groundtastic Magazine

EASTER ROAD

HOME GROUND OF **HIBERNIAN**
TEMPORARY HOME GROUND FOR **CELTIC, ST MIRREN, HEART OF MIDLOTHIAN & PARTICK THISTLE**

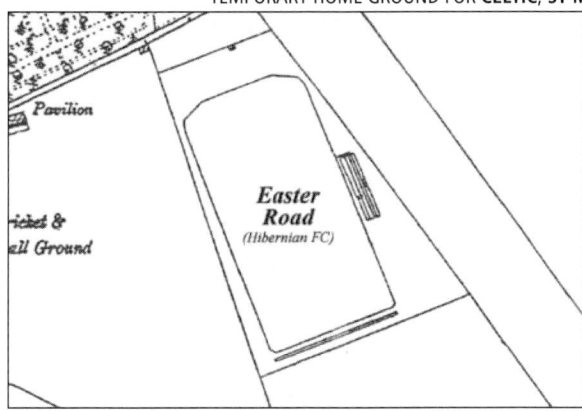

MAP EXTRACT; EDINBURGH 3.4 [**1896**]
SITE LOCATION: **NT27357492**

Hibernian re-formed in 1892 and established the *Hibernian Football Ground* in Drum Park. *Easter Road,* as it became known, opened in February 1893 and the facilities at this time were an open seated stand on the east side and a single row of seats at the south end. By the 1920s a covered seated stand had been built on the east side and banking constructed around the remainder of the ground.

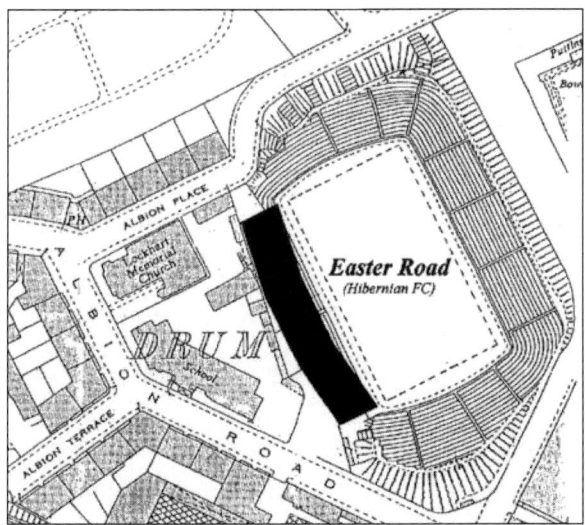

MAP EXTRACT; NT2774 & NT2775 [**1948**]

Major redevelopment took place in 1924 when the ground was repositioned some 120ft to the east, a new covered seated stand constructed on the west side and enlarged terracing built around the other three sides giving a 42,000 capacity with 4,200 seats. Post war improvements saw the enlargement of the east terrace (subsequently reduced in size, covered in 1985 and installed with seats) and the installation of a cover at the north end. The Safety of Sports Grounds Act (1975) reduced the nominal capacity to 30,000, but temporary measures, including the installation of bench seats on the north bank in 1982 and bucket seats on the south terrace in 1994, gave it a capacity of only 13,500 by 1995.

New all-seat stands were subsequently built at each end and in 2001 a 6,465 seat two-tier cantilever roofed stand opened on the west side. By the 2004/5 season the ground was an all-seater stadium with a capacity of 17,462 and an 115 x 70 yards sized pitch.

PLAYING RECORD OF HIBERNIAN
LEAGUE PROGRAMME
First Match; 9-2 v. Morton (-) (August 26th, 1893)
Highest Gate; 65,840 v. Heart of Midlothian (1-2) (January 2nd, 1950)
Lowest Gate; 500 v. Northern (6-0) (April 7th, 1894)
Highest Home Win; 11-1 v. Hamilton Academical (5,000) (November 6th, 1965)
Highest Home Defeat; 0-6 v. Celtic (28,000) (October 15th, 1960)
PLAY OFF MATCHES
1-0 v. Airdrieonians (15,308) (May 17th, 1997)
No. of Matches Played by Hibernian; 1,805
(League Programme; 1,804, Play Off Matches; 1)
Information Kindly Supplied by; Ricky Raginia

The club was a founder member of the Scottish Football League Division 2 in 1893. As rebuilding had not been completed at the start of the 1924/5 season, two matches were played at *Tynecastle Park.*

PLAYING RECORD OF HEART OF MIDLOTHIAN
LEAGUE PROGRAMME
Match Played; 2-0 v. Raith Rovers (1,000) (April 18th, 1914)
No. of Matches Played by Heart of Midlothian; 1
Information Kindly Supplied by; Douglas Dalgleish & David Steed

This match was played here to accommodate the demolition of the stand at *Tynecastle Park.*

PLAYING RECORD OF ST MIRREN
LEAGUE PROGRAMME
Match Played; 0-4 v. Heart of Midlothian (6,000) (April 15th, 1921)
No. of Matches Played by St Mirren; 1
Information Kindly Supplied by; Douglas Dalgleish

The match was switched here due to reconstruction work at *St Mirren Park.*

PLAYING RECORD OF CELTIC
LEAGUE PROGRAMME
Match Played; 1-4 v. Hibernian (6,000) (April 13th, 1929)
No. of Matches Played by Celtic; 1
Information Kindly Supplied by; Margaret Connolly & Cyril George

This match was played here due to a fire at *Celtic Park [2nd]* in March 1929.

PLAYING RECORD OF PARTICK THISTLE
LEAGUE PROGRAMME
Match Played; 1-5 v. Hibernian (-) (April 10th, 1909)
No. of Matches Played by Partick Thistle; 1
Information Kindly Supplied by; Robert Reid

This match was played here as *Firhill Park* was not ready following closure of *Meadowside* in 1908.

NEUTRAL PLAY OFF MATCHES
2nd Division Championship; Leith Athletic 2, St Bernards 1 (5,000) (April 17th, 1915)
St Bernards 1, Cowdenbeath 3 (-) (April 24th, 1915)
No. of Matches Played; 2

AT THE END OF SEASON 2004/5, A TOTAL OF **54** TEAMS HAD TAKEN PART IN **1,811** LEAGUE FIXTURES AT THIS VENUE

EXCELSIOR STADIUM
HOME GROUND OF AIRDRIEONIANS & AIRDRIE UNITED

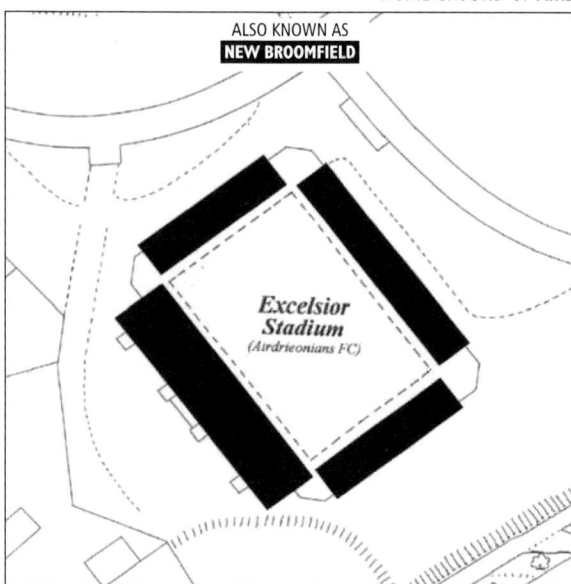

ALSO KNOWN AS **NEW BROOMFIELD**

MAP EXTRACT; GROUND AS IN **1998** DRAWN FROM PLANS AND SUPERIMPOSED ON LANARKSHIRE 8.10 [1940]
SITE LOCATION; **NS77416483**

Also known as *New Broomfield* the stadium was constructed on the site of a redundant brick works and consisted of cantilever roofed stands on each side of the pitch. The record attendance of 8,762 was established at the Scottish League Cup 3rd Round tie v. *Celtic* (1-0) on August 19th, 1998. The all-seat capacity at the start of the 2004/5 season was 10,170 and the pitch size was 115 x 71 yards.

PLAYING RECORD OF AIRDRIEONIANS
LEAGUE PROGRAMME

First Match; 0-0 v. Clydebank (3,000) (August 4th, 1998)
Last Match; 2-0 v. Arbroath (1,142) (April 20th, 2002)
Highest Gate; 5,700 v. Partick Thistle (1-1) (April 6th, 2002)
Lowest Gate; 797 v. Clydebank (0-0) (April 22nd, 2000)
Highest Home Win; 6-0 v. Inverness Caledonian Thistle (1,197) (September 22nd, 2001)
Highest Home Defeat; 1-4 v. Hibernian (4,809) (January 30th, 1999), v. Raith Rovers (1,493) (August 28th, 1999) & v. Inverness Caledonian Thistle (1,597) (February 5th, 2000)

No. of Matches Played by Airdrieonians; 72
Information Kindly Supplied by; John Henderson

The club moved here from their temporary stay at **Broadwood Stadium** in 1998 and it was wound up on May 1st, 2002

PLAYING RECORD OF AIRDRIE UNITED
LEAGUE PROGRAMME

First Match; 1-0 v. Forfar Athletic (2,285) (August 3rd, 2002)
Highest Gate; 5,709 v. Greenock Morton (2-0) (May 15th, 2004)
Lowest Gate; 961 v. Forfar Athletic (0-0) (February 25th, 2003)
Highest Home Win; 6-0 v. Berwick Rangers (1,546) (April 3rd, 2004)
Highest Home Defeat; 1-6 v. Greenock Morton (3,159) (November 1st, 2003)

No. of Matches Played by Airdrie United; 54

In 2002 *Airdrieonians FC* folded and a new club, *Airdrie United*, was formed to replace them. Following failure to gain election at the ensuing AGM the new club bought out *Clydebank [2]* from the administrators, closed it down, and installed *Airdrie United* in Division 2 in its place for the commencement of the 2002/3 season.

AT THE END OF SEASON 2004/5, A TOTAL OF **28** TEAMS HAD TAKEN PART IN **126** LEAGUE FIXTURES AT THIS VENUE

Despite being of new construction, the £6m *Excelsior Stadium* was reportedly bedeviled with structural problems and within two years cracks had appeared in all four of the stands and no less than 72 building faults encountered. It was the financial liability of the new ground, some £450,000, which had caused *Airdrieonians* to go into administration and eventually led to the club's extinction in 2002.

Photograph by Owen Pavey. Courtesy of Groundtastic Magazine

FALKIRK STADIUM

HOME GROUND OF **FALKIRK**

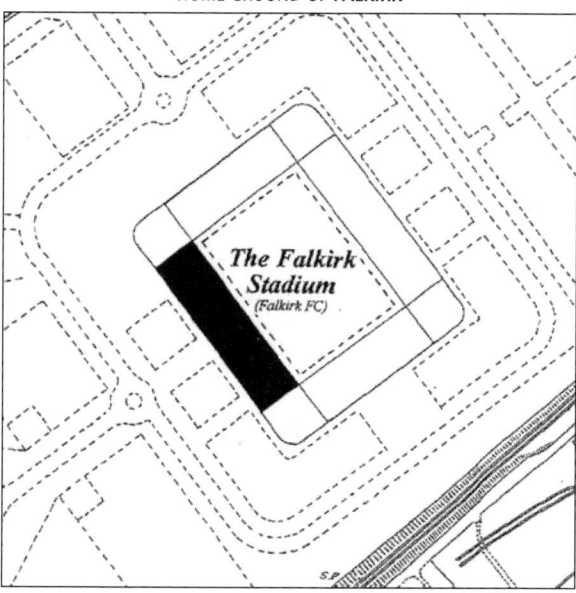

MAP EXTRACT; GROUND AS IN **2004** DRAWN FROM PLANS & SUPERIMPOSED ON STIRLINGSHIRE 30.3 & .4 [1944]
SITE LOCATION; **NS90858051**

Constructed on a greenfield site at Westfield Farm, east of Falkirk, when the Official Opening Match was played on July 25th, 2004 v. *Dundee* (1-2) (3,700) only the 4,116 seat cantilever roofed main stand on the west side had been completed. A temporary stand was erected for the benefit of visiting supporters until a 1,984 seat cantilever roofed stand was completed at the north end in March 2005 giving an all-seater capacity of 6,122 at the end of the 2004/5 season

The planned capacity of the all-seater stadium was 12,800 with similar stands subsequently being built on the east and south sides and the size of the pitch was 110 x 72 yards.

PLAYING RECORD OF FALKIRK
LEAGUE PROGRAMME

First Match; 1-1 v. Hamilton Academical (3,762) (August 14th, 2004)
Highest Gate; 5,607 v. Queen of the South (1-2) (May 7th, 2005)
Lowest Gate; 3,330 v. Ross County (2-2) (November 27th, 2004)
Highest Home Win; 5-0 v. Airdrie United (3,789) (August 28th, 2004)
Highest Home Defeat; 1-2 v. St Mirren (4,342) (April 23rd, 2005) & v. Queen of the South (5,607) (May 7th, 2005)

No. of Matches Played by Falkirk; 18

The club moved here from *Ochilview Park* where it had been ground-sharing with *Stenhousemuir FC* for the duration of the 2003/4 season following the sale of *Brockville Park*. The first League goal scored here was a 37th minute penalty by Brian Carrigan of *Hamilton Academical FC*.

AT THE END OF SEASON 2004/5, A TOTAL OF **10** TEAMS HAD TAKEN PART IN **18** LEAGUE FIXTURES AT THIS VENUE

FIR PARK

HOME GROUND OF **MOTHERWELL**
TEMPORARY HOME GROUND FOR **HAMILTON ACADEMICAL**

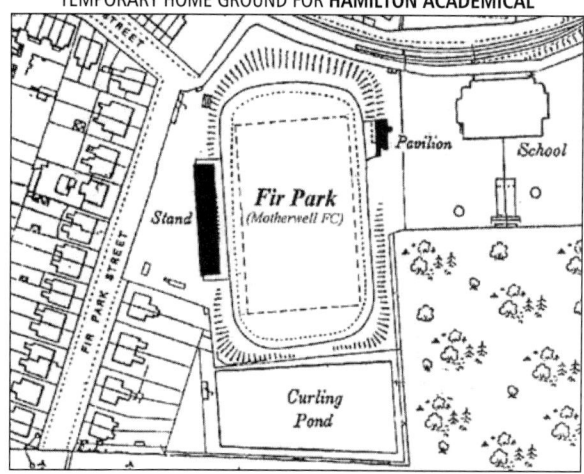

MAP EXTRACT; LANARKSHIRE 18.2 **[1912]**
SITE LOCATION; **NS75905590**

Motherwell FC moved to *Fir Park* from *Dalziel Park* in 1895 and the facilities at this time included a pavilion on the east side. By 1912 a grandstand had been built on the west side and embankments constructed around the ground and it then remained virtually unaltered for a considerable number of years. At some stage the ground was extended south over the curling pond, embankments terraced and a cover subsequently installed on the east side in the 1950s whilst the main stand was replaced in 1962. The highest attendance of 36,384 (35,632 in some records) was set at the Scottish FA Cup 4th Round Replay v. *Rangers* (2-1) on March 12th, 1952.

In the 1990s the ground was redeveloped as an all-seater stadium with the installation of seats on the east enclosure and the construction of new stands at each end giving a capacity of 13,742 by the start of the 2004/5 season. The pitch size was 110 x 75 yards.

PLAYING RECORD OF MOTHERWELL
LEAGUE PROGRAMME

First Match; 2-1 v. Port Glasgow Athletic (-) (August 10th, 1895)
Highest Gate*; 30,000 v. Rangers (1-4) (January 15th, 1927)
& v. Rangers (1-1) (September 24th, 1927)
Lowest Gate*; 1,300 v. St Mirren (4-0) (April 19th, 1967)
Highest Home Win; 12-1 v. Dundee United (6,000) (January 23rd, 1954)
Highest Home Defeat; 0-7 v. Celtic (17,092) (September 18th, 1982)

No. of Matches Played by Motherwell; 1,795
Information Kindly Supplied by; John Swinburne

The club moved here from *Dalziel Park* in 1895.
*NB. Not all attendances are known and these are the highest and lowest gate figures of those that were recorded.

PLAYING RECORD OF HAMILTON ACADEMICAL
LEAGUE PROGRAMME

Matches Played; 1-1 v. Ayr United (5,156) (April 26th, 1997)
2-2 v. Stirling Albion (802) (March 3rd, 1998)

No. of Matches Played by Hamilton Academical; 2
Information Kindly Supplied by; Scott A. Struthers

These two matches were played here due to insufficient capacity and electrical & floodlighting problems at *Cliftonhill Park*

AT THE END OF SEASON 2004/5, A TOTAL OF **50** TEAMS HAD TAKEN PART IN **1,797** LEAGUE FIXTURES AT THIS VENUE

FIRHILL PARK

HOME GROUND OF PARTICK THISTLE
TEMPORARY HOME GROUND FOR **CELTIC, CLYDE** & **HAMILTON ACADEMICAL**

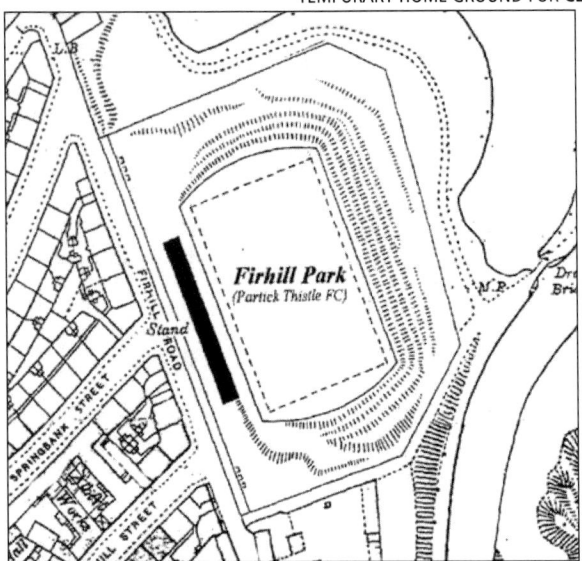

MAP EXTRACT; LANARKSHIRE 6.2 & 6.6 [1912]
SITE LOCATION; NS58146770

Partick Thistle FC, having been ousted from *Meadowside* in 1908 played their first match at *Firhill Park* in 1909. (The match, v. *Queen's Park*, was due to be played here on August 21st, 1909 but the ground was not ready)

The facilities, which initially included a grandstand on the west side and extensive embankments around the remainder of the pitch, were enhanced in 1927 with the construction of a 6,000 seat replacement grandstand and improvements to the terraces. In recognition of these developments an international match was staged in 1928 v. *Ireland* and this drew the ground record crowd of 54,728.

Greyhound racing was staged in pre-war days and further alterations included the construction of a cover over the terracing on the east side. This was later replaced in 1994 by the Jackie Husband [East] Stand, a 6,263 seat cantilever roofed structure and in 2001 the terracing at the north end was demolished to accommodate a student flat development and a proposed 2,000 seat stand. The capacity at the start of season 2004/5 was 13,141 with 10,921 seats and the pitch size was 110 x 75 yards.

PLAYING RECORD OF PARTICK THISTLE
LEAGUE PROGRAMME

First Match; *1-1 v. Clyde (-) (October 2nd, 1909)*
Highest Gate; *49,838 v. Rangers (0-1) (February 18th, 1922)*
Lowest Gate; *959 v. Montrose (0-0) (March 21st, 1987)*
Highest Home Win; *9-0 v. Airdrieonians (12,000)*
(December 12th, 1953)
Highest Home Defeat; *2-10 v. Hibernian (-) (December 19th, 1959)*

PLAY OFF MATCHES
1-1 v. Dundee United (10,414) (May 12th, 1996)

No. of Matches Played by Partick Thistle; 1,608
(League Programme; 1,607, Play Off Matches; 1)
Information Kindly Supplied by; Robert Reid & John Henderson

Partick Thistle FC moved here from *Meadowside* in 1909.

PLAYING RECORD OF CLYDE
LEAGUE PROGRAMME

First Match; *0-0 v. Queen of the South (550) (August 13th, 1986)*
Last Match & Lowest Gate; *0-1 v. Morton (400) (May 11th, 1991)*
Highest Gate; *3,100 v. Partick Thistle (2-1) (April 13th, 1991)*
Highest Home Win; *5-0 v. Dumbarton (993) (August 8th, 1987)*
Highest Home Defeat; *0-5 v. Clydebank (1,200)*
(September 10th, 1988)

No. of Matches Played by Clyde; 103
Information Kindly Supplied by; John Taylor

The club moved here whilst awaiting the construction of a new ground. In 1991 they moved out to groundshare with *Hamilton Academical* at *Douglas Park*.

PLAYING RECORD OF HAMILTON ACADEMICAL
LEAGUE PROGRAMME

1ST PERIOD;
First Match; *2-6 v. Airdrieonians (1,180) (August 27th, 1994)*
Last Match; *2-1 v. Dumbarton (657) (May 4th, 1996)*
No. of Matches Played; 36

The club moved here from *Douglas Park* in 1994 and moved to *Cliftonhill Park* in 1996 to groundshare with *Albion Rovers FC*.

2ND PERIOD;
Matches Played; *1-1 v. Ayr United (732) (February 17th, 1998)*
1-1 v. St Mirren (1,459) (February 23rd, 1998)
1-4 v. Raith Rovers (711) (March 17th, 1998)
No. of Matches Played; 3

These three matches were played here due to insufficient capacity and electrical & floodlighting problems at *Cliftonhill Park*.

3RD PERIOD;
First Match; *1-1 v. Airdrieonians (1,137) (August 15th, 1998)*
Last Match; *3-0 v. Elgin City (773) (April 28th, 2001)*
No. of Matches Played; 54

The club moved back here from *Cliftonhill Park* on a temporary basis in 1998 whilst awaiting completion of the *Ballast Stadium*.

Highest Gate; *5,333 v. Raith Rovers (0-0) (May 13th, 1995)*
Lowest Gate; *344 v. East Stirlingshire (4-0) (October 24th, 2000)*
Highest Home Win; *6-0 v. Montrose (426) (August 19th, 2000)*
Highest Home Defeat; *2-6 v. Airdrieonians (1,180)*
(August 27th, 1994)

Total No. of Matches Played by Hamilton Academical; 93
Information Kindly Supplied by; Scott A. Struthers

PLAYING RECORD OF CELTIC
LEAGUE PROGRAMME

Match Played; *1-0 v. Partick Thistle (12,000) (April 1st, 1929)*
No. of Matches Played by Celtic; 1
Information Kindly Supplied by; Cyril George

This match was played here due to a fire at *Celtic Park [2nd]* in March 1929.

AT THE END OF SEASON 2004/5, A TOTAL OF **49** TEAMS HAD TAKEN PART IN **1,823** LEAGUE FIXTURES AT THIS VENUE

FIRS PARK

HOME GROUND OF **EAST STIRLINGSHIRE**
TEMPORARY HOME GROUND FOR **MEADOWBANK THISTLE**

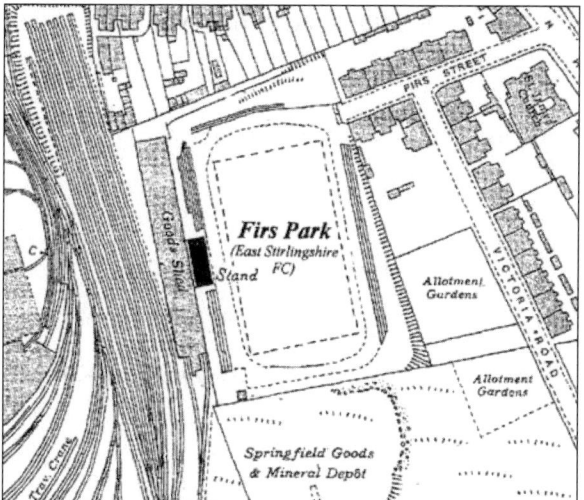

MAP EXTRACT; STIRLINGSHIRE 30.3 [**1944**]
SITE LOCATION; **NS89188055**

With the closure of **Merchiston Park**, *East Stirlingshire FC* moved to *Firs Park* in 1921 and opened it with a friendly against *Heart of Midlothian FC* in August. Within a few years the facilities included a small stand and some terracing on the west side and terracing on the east and north sides. A cover was subsequently constructed on the east side but this was removed in 1964, along with the floodlights and other fixtures and installed at *New Kilbowie Park* when the club was amalgamated for one season with *Clydebank [2] FC*.

Following the return of *East Stirlingshire* in 1965 the enclosure roof was rebuilt, new floodlights installed and the main stand repaired (following vandalism during the vacancy!). Within a few years a new record attendance of 11,500 was established at the Scottish FA Cup 1st Round tie v. *Hibernian* (3-5) on January 27th, 1968.

East Stirlingshire, in hoops, about to defend a free kick against *Stirling Albion* on November 9th, 2002. The terracing at the southern end, on the left of the picture, has been absorbed by the adjacent retail park and replaced with a tall concrete wall making it look more akin to a prison exercise yard than a football ground. The neat 1992 vintage main stand is partially visible to the right.
Courtesy of RedWeb (www.stirlingalbionfc.com)

The main stand was replaced in 1992 and part of the south end terracing was acquired and incorporated into the Central Retail Park built on the site of the adjacent Springfield Goods & Mineral Depot. The capacity at the start of the 2004/5 season was set at only 780, the lowest in the Scottish Football League, with 280 seats and an 112 x 72 yards sized pitch.

PLAYING RECORD OF MEADOWBANK THISTLE
LEAGUE PROGRAMME
Match Played; 1-1 v. Alloa Athletic (200) (April 14th, 1979)
No. of Matches Played by Meadowbank Thistle; 1
Information Kindly Supplied by; Allan Grieve
This match was played here due to the non-availability of **Meadowbank Stadium**

PLAYING RECORD OF EAST STIRLINGSHIRE
LEAGUE PROGRAMME
First Match; 3-1 v. Vale of Leven (-) (August 27th, 1921)
Highest Gate*; 10,000 v. St Mirren (3-2) (November 16th, 1935) &
v. Falkirk (0-5) (November 1st, 1936)
Lowest Gate*; 32 v. Leith Athletic (5-2) (April 15th, 1939)
Highest Home Win; 8-0 v. Arthurlie (-) (August 27th, 1927)
Highest Home Defeat; 1-8 v. Raith Rovers (-) (January 8th, 1938)
& v. Albion Rovers (223) (April 24th, 2004)
No. of Matches Played by East Stirlingshire; 1,244
(Including one expunged match v. Bathgate on November 17th, 1928)
Information Kindly Supplied by; Drummond Calder

East Stirlingshire FC moved here from **Merchiston Park** in 1921. The club remained in the League until it was suspended in 1939, was then elected into Division B in 1948, failed to gain re-election at the end of the season and elected back into Division B in 1955. In 1964 the club amalgamated with *Clydebank* as *East Stirlingshire Clydebank* and played one season at **New Kilbowie Park** before returning to *Firs Park* as *East Stirlingshire* in 1965. Two matches were also played at **Brockville Park**.

*NB. Not all attendances are known and these are the highest and lowest gate figures of those that are recorded. The gate figure of 32 is the lowest recorded attendance in the Scottish Football League.

AT THE END OF SEASON 2004/5, A TOTAL OF **69** TEAMS HAD TAKEN PART IN **1,246** LEAGUE FIXTURES AT THIS VENUE

FORTHBANK PARK
HOME GROUND OF KING'S PARK

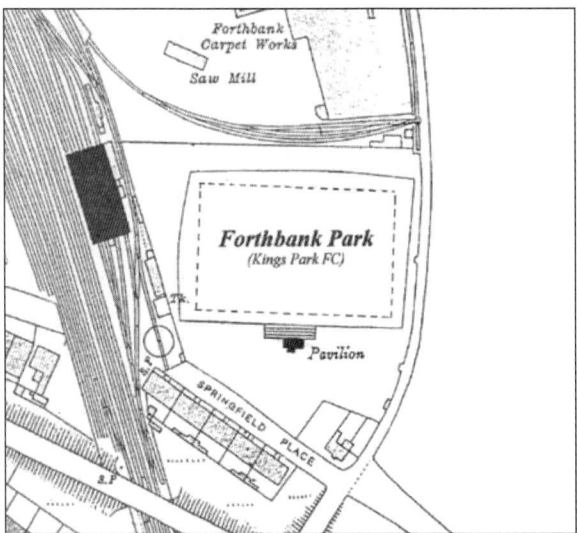

MAP EXTRACT; STIRLINGSHIRE 17.3 [1918]
SITE LOCATION; NS80179307

King's Park first moved to *Forthbank Park* in 1889, switched to *Springkerse* in 1899 and returned in 1906. The ground was south of the town centre, adjacent to the east side of the Caledonian Railway Engine Shed, and the facilities initially consisted of a small 400 seat stand on the south side and flat standing areas around the pitch. Later improvements included the replacement of the grandstand and installation of additional terracing. The record attendance of 8,930 was set at the Scottish FA Cup 1st Round tie against *Airdrieonians* (0-4) on January 24th, 1925.

The ground was partially destroyed during WWII on the night of July 19th/20th, 1940 when a Luftwaffe bomber dumped its load of bombs before heading back across the North Sea. This not only resulted in a large crater and the partial demolition of the grandstand and terracing but the extinction of *King's Park FC* as the site was sold for industrial development at the end of the war.

PLAYING RECORD OF KING'S PARK
LEAGUE PROGRAMME

First Match; 1-1 v. East Stirlingshire (-) (August 20th, 1921)
Last Match; 2-2 v. East Stirlingshire (-) (September 2nd, 1939)
Highest Gate*; 6,400 v. Queen's Park (0-1) (December 16th, 1922)
Lowest Gate*; Not Known
Highest Home Win; 12-2 v. Forfar Athletic (3,000)
(January 2nd, 1930)
Highest Home Defeat; 1-8 v. Alloa Athletic (-)
(November 19th, 1921)
No. of Matches Played by King's Park; 330
(Including expunged matches v. Bathgate on September 29th, 1928 & v. Armadale on August 20th, 1932)
Information Kindly Supplied by; Allan Grieve

The club was elected into the Scottish Football League Division 2 in 1921 and remained in the League until it was suspended in 1939. The match v. *Vale of Leven* on November 5th, 1921 was played at **Duckburn Park** in Dunblane due to crowd trouble at the game v. *St Johnstone* on October 8th, 1921 (2-2). The club folded in 1940.
*NB. This is the highest gate figure of the very few that were recorded. In view of the general level of those that are known, it is very probable that there were crowds of less than 1,000 on occasions.

A TOTAL OF **41** TEAMS TOOK PART IN **330** LEAGUE FIXTURES AT THIS VENUE

FORTHBANK STADIUM
HOME GROUND OF STIRLING ALBION

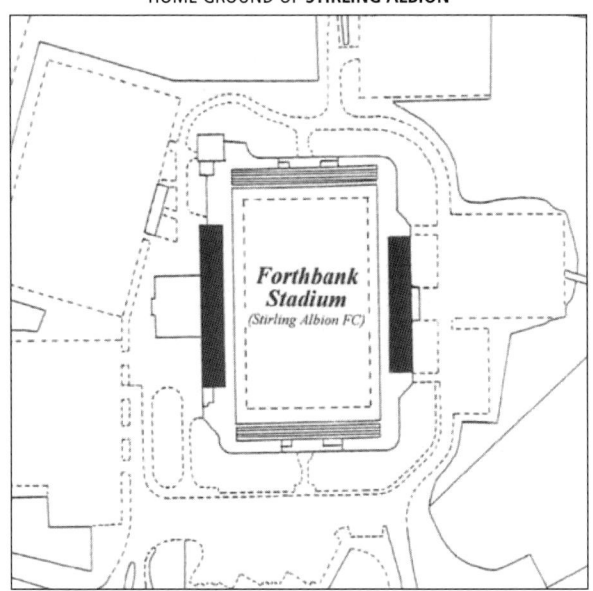

MAP EXTRACT; GROUND AS IN c**1998** DRAWN FROM PLANS AND SUPERIMPOSED ON STIRLINGSHIRE 17.3 [1938]
SITE LOCATION; **NS81239345**

Opened in 1993, *Stirling Albion FC* moved here from their temporary home at *Stenhousemuir FC's Ochilview Park*. The stadium, as built, included seated stands on both sides of the pitch (giving a capacity of 2,508) and the two open ends were later terraced to give a total capacity of 3,808 at the start of the 2004/5 season.

The record attendance of 3,808 was established at the Scottish FA Cup 4th Round tie v. *Aberdeen* (0-2) on February 17th, 1996. The pitch size was 110 x 74 yards.

PLAYING RECORD OF STIRLING ALBION
LEAGUE PROGRAMME

First Match; 2-3 v. Clydebank (2,544) (April 24th, 1993)
Highest Gate; 3,003 v. Dumbarton (0-2) (May 13th, 1995)
Lowest Gate; 315 v. Brechin City (1-3) (March 19th, 2002)
Highest Home Win; 6-0 v. East Stirlingshire (739) (March 13th, 2004)
Highest Home Defeat; 0-6 v. Falkirk (2,954) (January 3rd, 1998)
No. of Matches Played by Stirling Albion; 223
Information Kindly Supplied by; Allan Grieve

The club moved here from groundsharing with *Stenhousemuir* at *Ochilview Park* in 1993.

AT THE END OF SEASON 2004/5, A TOTAL OF **36** TEAMS HAD TAKEN PART IN **223** LEAGUE FIXTURES AT THIS VENUE

The west, main stand, side at *Forthbank Stadium* on November 6th, 2004 with the *Stirling Albion* v. *Forfar Athletic* (3-1) Scottish League match in progress.

Courtesy of RedWeb (www.stirlingalbionfc.com)

GAYFIELD PARK & GREATER GAYFIELD
HOME GROUNDS OF ARBROATH

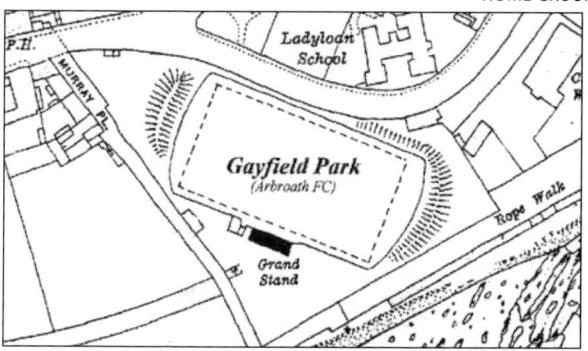

MAP EXTRACT; FORFARSHIRE 46.15 [1921]
SITE LOCATION; **NO63784021**

Originally the site of a rubbish dump, *Arbroath FC* moved here in 1880 and opened *Gayfield Park* with a match v. *Rob Roy FC*. Initially the ground was on a very narrow site, there was no space at all for standing accommodation on the north side along the Dundee Road, and this pitch was the one used for the record breaking 36-0 demolition of *Bon Accord* (a cricket club entered in error!) in the 1st Round of the Scottish FA Cup on September 12th, 1885.

To improve the ground, the club bought part of the seashore and the trackbed of the former harbour branch from the Aberdeen & Dundee Railway and extended the site eastward. The facilities at this re-sited ground included a grandstand on the south side and embankments at each end of the pitch.

Following their entry into the Scottish Football League in 1921 the club purchased *Gayfield Park* and part of the surrounding area to facilitate a further rebuild of the ground which was completed when *Greater Gayfield* opened in 1925.

PLAYING RECORD OF ARBROATH
LEAGUE PROGRAMME

First Match & Highest Gate; 3-1 v. *Johnstone* (3,000)
(August 20th, 1921)
Last Match; 2-1 v. *King's Park* (2,439) (March 28th, 1925)
Lowest Gate; 841 v. *Clyde* (2-1) (September 13th, 1924)
Highest Home Win; 5-1 v. *King's Park* (2,846) (April 26th, 1924)
Highest Home Defeat; 2-5 v. *King's Park* (1,933)
(March 18th, 1922)
No. of Matches Played by Arbroath; 76
Information Kindly Supplied by; George Cant

The club was elected into the Scottish Football League Division 2 in 1921. In 1925 the ground was rebuilt and partially re-sited as *Greater Gayfield*.

A TOTAL OF **26** TEAMS TOOK PART IN **76** LEAGUE FIXTURES AT THIS VENUE

DIAGRAM SHOWING THE DISPOSITION OF GAYFIELD PARK & GREATER GAYFIELD

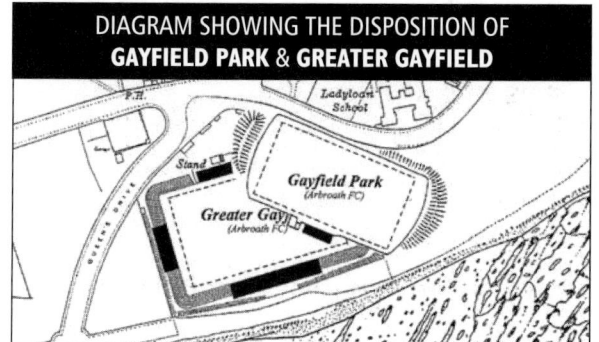

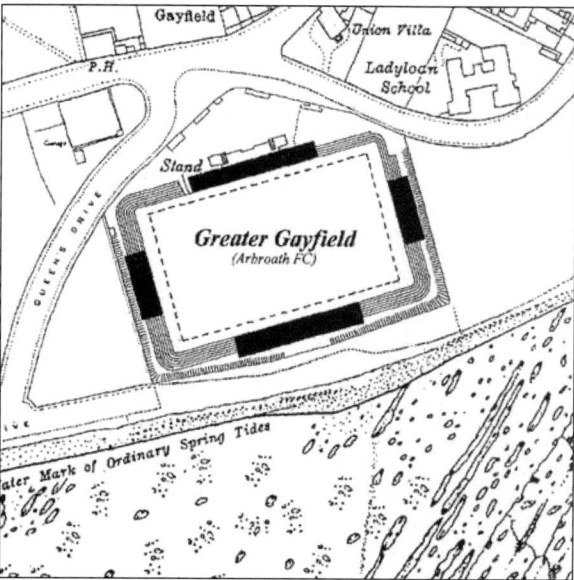

MAP EXTRACT; GROUND AS IN c1960 DRAWN FROM PLANS AND SUPERIMPOSED ON NO6340 [1951]
SITE LOCATION; **NO63744019**

Greater Gayfield, sited to the west and at an angle of about 37° to *Gayfield Park*, opened with the Scottish Football League match v. *East Fife* on August 29th, 1925. The ground was neatly symmetrical and the first facility to be installed was a grandstand (replaced in 1958 following a fire) on the north side and narrow concrete terracing on each of the other three sides. Short roofs had been installed on each of the terraces by the time that the record attendance of 13,510 was set at the Scottish FA Cup 3rd Round tie v. *Rangers* (0-2) on February 23rd, 1952.

In September 1958 the main stand, on the north side, was destroyed by a fire and a concrete and brick structure subsequently erected in its place. The covers at each end were replaced in 1979 and, in the 1980s, a new cover was installed on the south side and all the terraces rebuilt. The main stand was demolished and replaced with an 848 seat structure in 2002 providing a total capacity of 4,153 by the start of the 2004/5 season. The pitch size was 115 x 70 yards.

PLAYING RECORD OF ARBROATH
LEAGUE PROGRAMME

First Match; 2-4 v. *East Fife* (7,000) (August 29th, 1925)
Highest Gate; 12,800 v. *Aberdeen* (1-4) (September 9th, 1936)
Lowest Gate; 172 v. *East Stirlingshire* (1-2) (March 4th, 1997)
Highest Home Win; 9-2 v. *Forfar Athletic* (1,641) (September 10th, 1966). 8-0 v. *Stenhousemuir* (1,701) (November 25th, 1967)
Highest Home Defeat; 0-7 v. *Heart of Midlothian* (3,165)
(December 24th, 1977)
No. of Matches Played by Arbroath; 1,346
(Including expunged matches v Bathgate on December 1st, 1928 & v. Bo'ness on October 22nd, 1932)
Information Kindly Supplied by; George Cant

The club moved here from *Gayfield Park* in 1925.

AT THE END OF SEASON 2004/5, A TOTAL OF **55** TEAMS HAD TAKEN PART IN **1,346** LEAGUE FIXTURES AT THIS VENUE

GLEBE PARK
HOME GROUND OF BRECHIN CITY

MAP EXTRACT; FORFARSHIRE 27.13 & 27.9 [1922]
SITE LOCATION; NO59946059

PLAYING RECORD OF BRECHIN CITY
LEAGUE PROGRAMME
First Match; 0-4 v. Montrose (2,060) (August 18th, 1923)
Highest Gate*; 3,000 v. Montrose (1-0) (January 1st, 1960)
Lowest Gate*; 207 v. East Stirlingshire (1-1) (March 7th, 2000)
Highest Home Win; 9-2 v. Galston (870) (January 2nd, 1926)
Highest Home Defeat; 1-9 v. Morton (732) (April 28th, 1962)
No. of Matches Played by Brechin City; 1,168
(Including expunged matches v. Dumbarton Harp on October 25th, 1924
& v. Armadale on September 3rd, 1932)
Some Information Kindly Supplied by; Steve Mitchell

The club was a founder member of the Scottish Football League Division 3 in 1923 and left the League when Division 3 was disbanded near the end of the 1925/26 season. They were elected into the Scottish League Division 2 in 1929, remained in the League until it was suspended in 1939, and then elected into the Scottish League Division B in 1954.

*NB. Not all attendances are known and these are the highest and lowest gate figures of those that were recorded.

AT THE END OF SEASON 2004/5, A TOTAL OF **64** TEAMS HAD TAKEN PART IN **1,168** LEAGUE FIXTURES AT THIS VENUE

Glebe Park was first used by *Brechin City FC* in August 1906 but the facilities at this time are not known. By 1924 a stand had been constructed on the west side and upon re-joining the Scottish Football League in 1929 this was augmented by an adjacent pavilion and cover over the south end. The unique feature of this ground, a hedge forming the perimeter wall along the east side eventually proved to be ineffective at the south end and half of it was replaced by a brick wall.

The record gate of 8,244 was established at the Scottish FA Cup 3rd Round tie v. *Aberdeen* (2-4) on February 3rd, 1973. The stand was rebuilt in 1981 and a new 1,228 all seat cantilever roofed stand constructed at the north end. The capacity at the start of the 2004/5 season was 3,960 with 1,519 seats and the pitch size was 110 x 67 yards.

Glebe Park has one of the more unusual features (unique for a League ground) of a hedge and low wall forming one of the the boundaries and this can be clearly seen on the narrow east side in this view of the *Brechin City v Stirling Albion* (2-1) League game on April 27th, 2002.
Photograph Courtesy of Ian Paterson

HAMPDEN PARK [2ND] & NEW CATHKIN PARK

HOME GROUND OF **QUEEN'S PARK** & **THIRD LANARK**
TEMPORARY HOME GROUND FOR **QUEEN'S PARK**

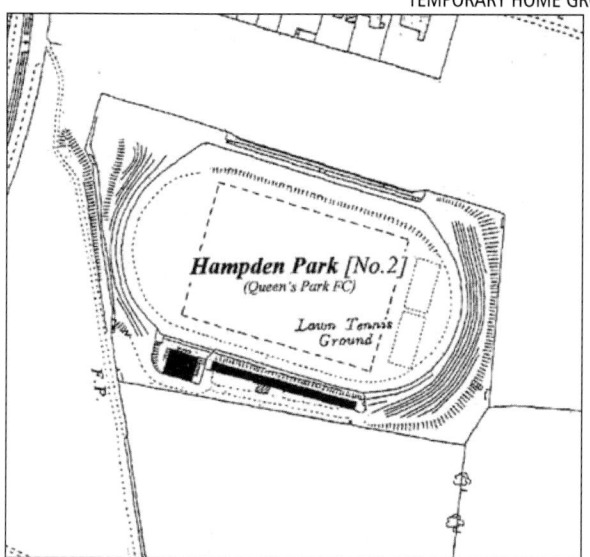

MAP EXTRACT; LANARKSHIRE 10.2 & 10.3 [**1893**]
SITE LOCATION; NS58976194

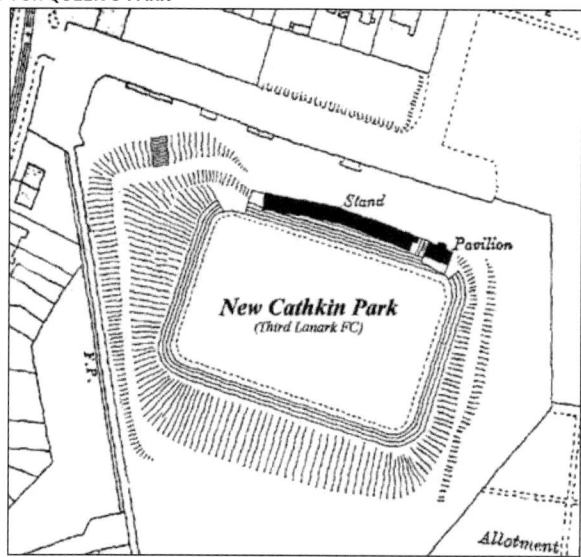

MAP EXTRACT; LANARKSHIRE 10.2 & 10.3 [**1933**]

With the imminent construction in 1883 of the Cathcart branch by the Caledonian Railway due to encroach on part of the site of *Hampden Park [1st]*, Queen's Park FC moved a few hundred yards east to *Hampden Park [2nd]*. This new ground was not ready until October 1884 and *Queen's Park* played a season at *Clydesdale Cricket Club's Titwood Park*.

The pitch was surrounded by an oval cycle track and there were a couple of tennis courts at the east end. The facilities included an open seated stand on the north side, a two storey pavilion and an open seated stand, subsequently covered, on the south side and banked terracing at each end.

The venue was used for international matches and Scottish Cup finals on a regular basis and it was the threat to this status from other Glasgow clubs that led to *Queen's Park* constructing a new ground, *Hampden Park [3rd]*, and moving there in 1903. *Third Lanark FC* took over the ground and re-named it *New Cathkin Park*.

PLAYING RECORD OF QUEEN'S PARK
LEAGUE PROGRAMME

First Match; 0-2 v. Celtic (18,000) (September 8th, 1900)
Last Match; 2-2 v. Port Glasgow Athletic (-) (February 28th, 1903)
Highest Gate*; 20,000 v. Rangers (0-1) (January 4th, 1902)
Lowest Gate*; Not Known
Highest Home Win; 4-0 v. Heart of Midlothian (3,000) (January 19th, 1901) & v. Morton (-) (November 29th, 1902)
Highest Home Defeat; 2-5 v. Heart of Midlothian (7,000) (November 1st, 1902)

No. of Matches Played by Queen's Park; 30
Information Kindly Supplied by; Hector Cook

The club was elected into the Scottish Football League Division 1 in 1900. *Queen's Park FC* moved to *Hampden Park [3rd]* in 1903 but had to play one game at *Cathkin Park* at the start of the 1903/4 season as the new ground was not ready.
*NB. This is the highest gate figure of the few that were recorded.

Following the takeover the oval running track was removed, the original grandstand demolished and replaced with covered concrete terracing, and a new stand (rebuilt in 1962) and pavilion constructed on the north side. In 1946/47 the terracing on three sides of the ground was extended and concreted (This work was originally scheduled to take just six months from May 1946 to October but the severe winter weather that season was a contributory factor in it not being completed until December 1947) and in 1962/63 the main stand was rebuilt, both events leading to *Third Lanark* playing their home games elsewhere.

The attendance record of 45,455 was established at a Scottish FA Cup 3rd Round tie v. *Rangers* (0-0) on February 27th, 1954. Following the demise of the club in 1967 the ground was taken over by Glasgow Parks Department. All the by now derelict structures were demolished but some of the terracing was retained as the site was refurbished as an open ground amenity for the area.

PLAYING RECORD OF THIRD LANARK
LEAGUE PROGRAMME

First Match; 1-0 v. Partick Thistle (6,000) (November 14th, 1903)
Last Match; 3-3 v. Queen of the South (325) (April 25th, 1967)
Highest Gate*; 40,000 v. Rangers (4-3) (March 28th, 1932)
Lowest Gate*; 297 v. Clydebank (April 15th, 1967)
Highest Home Win; 10-3 v. Armadale (-) (March 24th, 1928). 9-0 v. Ayr United (-) (December 4th, 1954) & v. Montrose (-) (December 31st, 1955).
Highest Home Defeat; 1-7 v. Airdrieonians (8,000) (March 11th, 1925)

No. of Matches Played by Third Lanark; 967
Information Kindly Supplied by; Bert Bell & Cyril George

The club moved here from *Cathkin Park* in 1903 and set about rebuilding the main stand and making general improvements. To facilitate this all but five of the home games in the 1903/4 season were played at *Hampden Park [3rd]*. The match v. *Rangers* that season was played at *Ibrox [2nd]* and games v. *Partick Thistle, Port Glasgow Athletic, Morton* and *Kilmarnock* were played at *New Cathkin Park*. The latter three games were played here in order to test the facilities at the new ground prior to the formal opening the following season with the Scottish League match v. *Rangers* on August 20th, 1904.

Cont ...

NEW CATHKIN PARK [CONT ...]

A total of 47 home matches were also played at *Hampden Park [3rd]* throughout the 1946/7 season and for the first part of 1947/8 when reconstruction of the terracing took place and all except two games (which were played at *New Cathkin Park*) in season 1962/3 when the main stand was being rebuilt. The club resigned in 1967 and folded in the same year

*NB. Not all attendances are known and these are the highest and lowest gate figures of those that were recorded.

PLAYING RECORD OF QUEEN'S PARK
LEAGUE PROGRAMME

Matches Played; 0-3 v. Clyde (-) (April 22nd, 1909)
0-5 v. Celtic (8,000) (April 28th, 1909)

No. of Matches Played by Queen's Park; 2
Information Kindly Supplied by; Hector Cook and Cyril George

These matches were played here due to *Hampden Park [3rd]* immediately being closed following a riot at the Scottish FA Cup Final on April 17th, 1909.

NEUTRAL PLAY OFF MATCHES

Division 1, 14th/15th Place; Port Glasgow Athletic 6, Kilmarnock 0 (-) (May 15th, 1906)

No. of Matches Played; 1

A TOTAL OF **50** TEAMS TOOK PART IN **1,000** LEAGUE FIXTURES AT THIS VENUE

Although there were still two more home fixtures left in its' final season in Division One, this programme, for the match v. *Dunfermline Athletic* on April 10th, 1965 (1-2), proved to be the last one produced by *Third Lanark FC* before its' demise in 1967.

LESSER HAMPDEN
ALTERNATIVE HOME GROUND FOR QUEEN'S PARK

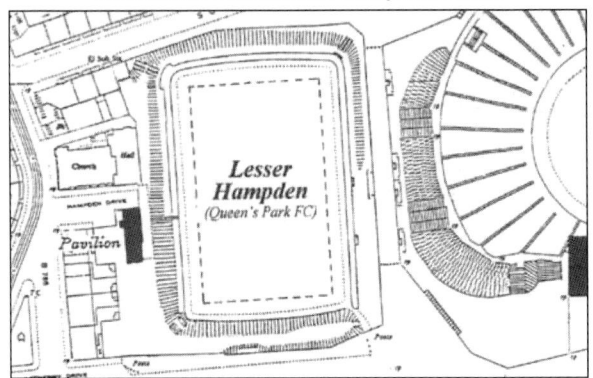

MAP EXTRACT; NS5861 & NS5961 [**1951**]
SITE LOCATION; **NS58816145**

The site, adjacent to the west side of *Hampden Park [3rd]* was purchased in 1923 for use as a practice pitch and as a home venue for *Queen's Park FCs* junior teams. A farm workers cottage was converted into a pavilion and embankments and some wooden terracing were constructed around the pitch giving it a capacity of some 3,000.

PLAYING RECORD OF QUEEN'S PARK
LEAGUE PROGRAMME

Matches Played; 1-2 v. Berwick Rangers (800)
(December 21st, 1974)
4-0 v. Forfar Athletic (800) (March 29th, 1975)
3-0 v. Brechin City (750) (April 12th, 1975)
3-1 v. Stirling Albion (500) (August 30th, 1975)
1-1 v. Meadowbank Thistle (600) (September 13th, 1975)
2-3 v. Raith Rovers (600) (September 20th, 1975)
3-1 v. Alloa Athletic (700) (February 21st, 1976)
0-0 v. East Stirlingshire (500) (February 8th, 1978)
1-0 v. Stenhousemuir (560) (April 11th, 1978)
4-0 v. East Stirlingshire (600) (November 10th, 1978)
3-0 v. Meadowbank Thistle (400) (March 27th, 1979)
0-1 v. Dunfermline Athletic (500) (March 30th, 1979)
1-1 v. Cowdenbeath (500) (November 28th, 1979)
0-1 v. Montrose (421) (October 27th, 1984)
0-3 v. Alloa Athletic (405) (February 9th, 1993)
1-1 v. Brechin City (446) (October 17th, 1998)
0-0 v. Albion Rovers (336) (October 27th, 1998)
3-0 v. Montrose (385) (November 7th, 1998)
2-0 v. Cowdenbeath (439) (November 28th, 1998)
1-1 v. Berwick Rangers (389) (December 12th, 1998)
4-1 v. Stenhousemuir (333) (January 26th, 1999)
0-3 v. Ross County (581) (February 13th, 1999)
1-1 v. Dumbarton (516) (February 27th, 1999)
0-0 v. Albion Rovers (492) (March 13th, 1999)
2-1 v. Cowdenbeath (336) (March 20th, 1999)
2-1 v. East Stirlingshire (455) (April 3rd, 1999)
1-2 v. Montrose (363) (April 10th, 1999)
0-2 v. Brechin City (503) (April 24th, 1999)
1-1 v. Berwick Rangers (473) (May 8th, 1999)

No. of Matches Played by Queen's Park; 29
Information Kindly Supplied by; Hector Cook & Allan Grieve

Matches were played here from time to time due to the non-availability and, later, re-development of *Hampden Park [3rd]* in 1999.

A TOTAL OF **16** TEAMS TOOK PART IN **29** LEAGUE FIXTURES AT THIS VENUE

HAMPDEN PARK [3RD]

HOME GROUND OF **QUEEN'S PARK**
TEMPORARY HOME GROUND FOR **PARTICK THISTLE, THIRD LANARK, ST MIRREN, RANGERS & CELTIC**

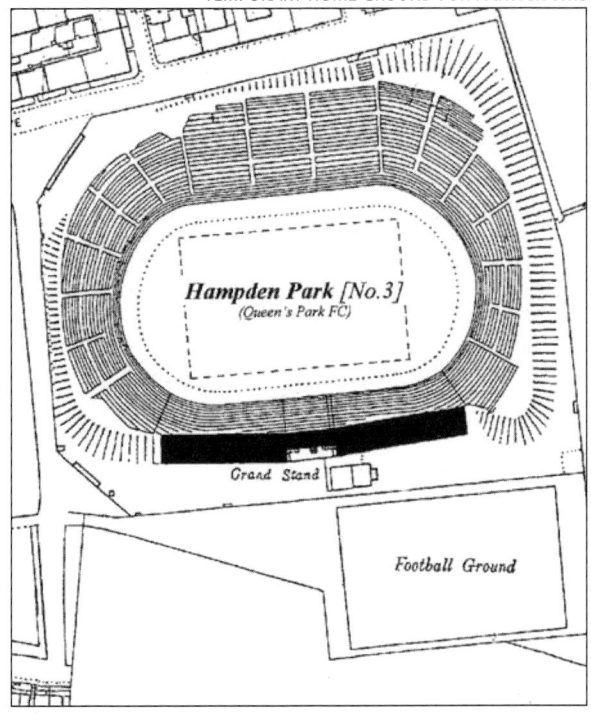

MAP EXTRACT; LANARKSHIRE 10.2 & 10.3 [**1913**]
SITE LOCATION; **NS59026148**

PLAYING RECORD OF QUEEN'S PARK
LEAGUE PROGRAMME

First Match; 1-0 v. Celtic (-) (October 31st, 1903)
Highest Gate*; 60,000 v. Rangers (0-4) (January 12th, 1929)
Lowest Gate*; 404 v. East Stirlingshire (1-0) (April 3rd, 2004)
Highest Home Win; 8-1 v. Raith Rovers (-) (December 3rd, 1927)
Highest Home Defeat; 1-8 v. Dundee United (1,740)
(September 12th, 1959)

No. of Matches Played by Queen's Park; 1,697†
Information Kindly Supplied by; Hector Cook

The club moved here from *Hampden Park [2nd]* in 1903. A substitute player was used here in a Scottish Football League match for the first time ever when P. Conn of *Queen's Park* took the field in their 5-1 win against *Albion Rovers* on September 21st, 1966. Home games were also played at *New Cathkin Park, Ibrox Park [2nd]*, and *Lesser Hampden*.

*Not all gate figures are known and these are the highest and lowest of those recorded.
† NB. According to some records, the match v. *Third Lanark* on March 21st, 1908 (included in this figure) may have been played at *New Cathkin Park*

Although officially opened on October 31st, 1903 with a Scottish Football League match v. *Celtic*, the ground had been previously used for a number of matches that season by *Third Lanark* whilst *New Cathkin Park* was being improved and ironically during this period *Queen's Park* played their first match here as an "away" fixture against *Third Lanark*.

The ground had a nominal capacity of 45,000 and the pitch was surrounded by an oval running track with two separate covered seated stands on the south side (subsequently linked by a pavilion) and large banking around the remainder of the stadium. The pavilion burned down in 1905 and its replacement was itself replaced in 1914. Additional terracing to accommodate another 25,000 spectators was constructed in 1927 and, following the building of the north stand in 1937, 150,239 spectators, the highest official attendance ever recorded in Britain, gathered to watch the *Scotland* v. *England* international match on April 17th, 1937. At this time the stadium was the largest football ground in the world.

In the immediate post-WWII era the capacity was reduced for safety reasons to 135,000 and, in the 1960s, to 81,000. A cover was constructed over the west end in 1967 and in 1986 the north stand was demolished, the east end rationalized and all terracing refurbished. In the 1990s the ground was completely rebuilt as an all-seater stadium and the capacity at the start of 2004/5 season was 52,063. The pitch size was 115 x 75 yards.

PLAYING RECORD OF ST MIRREN
LEAGUE PROGRAMME

Matches Played; 0-1 v. Rangers (10,000) (April 21st, 1921)
No. of Matches Played by St Mirren; 1
Information Kindly Supplied by; Cyril George

The match was switched here due to reconstruction work at *St Mirren Park*.

PLAYING RECORD OF CELTIC
LEAGUE PROGRAMME

1ST PERIOD;
Match Played; 1-2 v. Queen's Park (7,000) (April 17th, 1929)
No. of Matches Played; 1
2ND PERIOD;
Match Played; 2-0 v. Ayr United (25,000) (April 29th, 1971)
No. of Matches Played; 1
3RD PERIOD;
Matches Played; 6-2 v. Kilmarnock (11,651) (September 2nd, 1972)
3-1 v. Rangers (50,416) (September 16th, 1972)
No. of Matches Played; 2
4TH PERIOD;
First Match; 2-1 v. Dundee United (25,817) (August 20th, 1994)
Last Match; 3-0 v. Rangers (31,025) (May 7th, 1995)
No. of Matches Played; 18

Highest Recorded Gate; 50,416 v. Rangers (3-1)
(September 16th, 1972)
Lowest Recorded Gate; 7,000 v. Queen's Park (1-2) (April 17th, 1929)
Highest Home Win; 6-2 v. Kilmarnock (11,651) (September 2nd, 1972)
Highest Home Defeat; 1-3 v. Rangers (32,171) (October 30th, 1994) & v. Partick Thistle (18,963) (May 2nd, 1995)

Total No. of Matches Played by Celtic; 22
Information Kindly Supplied by; Margaret Connolly & Cyril George

The match in the 1st Period was played here due to a fire at *Celtic Park [2nd]* in March 1929 and the remainder due to reconstruction work at *Celtic Park [2nd]* over various periods.

PLAYING RECORD OF PARTICK THISTLE
LEAGUE PROGRAMME

Match Played; 1-2 v. Queen's Park (-) (April 8th, 1909)
No. of Matches Played by Partick Thistle; 1
Information Kindly Supplied by; Robert Reid

This match was played here as *Firhill Park* was not ready following the closure of *Meadowside* in 1908.

Cont ...

HAMPDEN PARK [3RD] [CONT...]

PLAYING RECORD OF THIRD LANARK
LEAGUE PROGRAMME
1ST PERIOD

Matches Played; 2-1 v. Heart of Midlothian (11,000) (August 22nd, 1903)
0-0 v. Queen's Park (-) (September 5th, 1903)
1-1 v. Airdrieonians (-) (September 19th, 1903)
3-1 v. Celtic (17,000) (September 28th, 1903)
4-0 v. St Mirren (-) (December 5th, 1903)
3-0 v. Motherwell (-) (March 12th, 1904)
4-1 v. Dundee (-) (April 23rd, 1904)
2-0 v. Hibernian (-) (April 30th, 1904)
No. of Matches Played; 8
Information Kindly Supplied by; Bert Bell

All but five of the home games in the 1903/4 season were played here whilst rebuilding and general improvements were being undertaken at *New Cathkin Park*.

2ND PERIOD

Match Played; 0-1 v. Rangers (30,000) (April 23rd, 1921)
No. of Matches Played; 1
Information Kindly Supplied by; Cyril George

NB. It is not known why this match was played here

3RD PERIOD

Matches Played; 0-3 v. Aberdeen (12,000) (August 10th, 1946)
1-4 v. Morton (-) (August 21st, 1946)
4-1 v. Partick Thistle (15,000) (August 31st, 1946)
3-4 v. Queen's Park (-) (September 7th, 1946)
4-2 v. Falkirk (-) (November 9th, 1946)
5-1 v. St Mirren (-) (November 16th, 1946)
2-1 v. Motherwell (-) (November 30th, 1946)
1-1 v. Queen of the South (-) (December 14th, 1946)
5-3 v. Clyde (-) (December 25th, 1946)
1-1 v. Rangers (38,000) (December 28th, 1946)
4-1 v. Heart of Midlothian (-) (January 2nd, 1947)
0-0 v. Celtic (30,000) (January 18th, 1947)
1-4 v. Kilmarnock (12,000) (March 15th, 1947)
2-1 v. Hamilton Academical (-) (April 7th, 1947)
0-2 v. Hibernian (-) (May 10th, 1947)
2-1 v. Clyde (-) (August 27th, 1947)
4-2 v. Queen's Park (-) (September 20th, 1947)
2-1 v. Morton (-) (September 27th, 1947)
0-3 v. Motherwell (-) (November 15th, 1947)
1-2 v. Partick Thistle (-) (November 22nd, 1947)
1-4 v. St Mirren (-) (December 13th, 1947)
0-1 v. Rangers (-) (December 20th, 1947)
No. of Matches Played; 22
Information Kindly Supplied by; Bert Bell

These home matches were played here in 1946/7 and part of 1947/8 whilst reconstruction of the terracing took place at *New Cathkin Park*.

4TH PERIOD

Matches Played; 3-3 v. Falkirk (6,000) (September 8th, 1962)
1-1 v. Dundee United (9,000) (September 22nd, 1962)
2-2 v. Motherwell (8,000) (October 6th, 1962)
1-4 v. Hibernian (10,000) (November 3rd, 1962)
1-2 v. Hearts (8,000) (November 17th, 1962)
4-3 v. Dundee (12,000) (November 24th, 1962)
2-0 v. Celtic (29,000) (December 15th, 1962)
2-1 v. Raith Rovers (5,900) (December 29th, 1962)
0-1 v. Kilmarnock (11,000) (January 2nd, 1963)
2-1 v. Clyde (6,200) (March 2nd, 1963)
2-3 v. Airdrieonians (6,000) (March 16th, 1963)
1-1 v. St Mirren (10,000) (April 5th, 1963)
1-0 v. Queen of the South (4,600) (April 13th, 1963)
1-2 v. Aberdeen (7,800) (April 24th, 1963)
4-0 v. Dunfermline (7,200) (May 3rd, 1963)
No. of Matches Played; 15
Information Kindly Supplied by; Bert Bell

All except two home games were played here in 1962/63 season when the main stand was being rebuilt at *New Cathkin Park*. The match v. *Rangers* on October 23rd, 1962 (1-4 [38,000]) was switched back to *New Cathkin Park* to assist in preparation of the pitch for the League Cup Final, and the game v. *Partick Thistle* on April 27th, 1963 (0-1 [11,500]) was also moved to *New Cathkin Park*, probably to assist pitch preparations for the Scottish FA Cup Final.

Highest Gate*; 38,000 v. Rangers (1-1) (December 28th, 1946)
Lowest Gate*; 4,600 v. Queen of the South (1-0) (April 13th, 1963)
Highest Home Win; 5-1 v. St Mirren (-) (November 16th, 1946)
Highest Home Defeat; 1-4 v. Morton (-) (August 21st, 1946), v. Kilmarnock (12,000) (March 15th, 1947), v. St Mirren (-) (December 13th, 1947) & v. Hibernian (10,000) (November 3rd, 1962)

Total No. of Matches Played by Third Lanark; 46

*Not all gate figures are known and these are the highest and lowest of those recorded.

PLAYING RECORD OF RANGERS
LEAGUE PROGRAMME

Matches Played; 1-1 v. Celtic (52,330) (November 11th, 1978)
1-0 v. Celtic (52,841) (May 5th, 1979)
No. of Matches Played by Rangers; 2
Information Kindly Supplied by; Cyril George

These home matches were played here due to rebuilding work at *Ibrox Park [2nd]*.

NEUTRAL PLAY OFF MATCHES

Division I Championship Play Off Match; Celtic 2, Rangers 1 (30,000) (May 6th, 1905)
Total No. of Matches Played; 1

AT THE END OF SEASON 2004/5, A TOTAL OF **57** TEAMS HAD TAKEN PART IN **1,770** LEAGUE FIXTURES AT THIS VENUE

The 1914-vintage main stand on the south side complete with a perilously constructed double decker press box which looks as though it is just about to slide off the roof!

Photograph by Jon Weaver. Courtesy of Groundtastic Magazine

HAWKHILL
HOME GROUND OF LEITH ATHLETIC

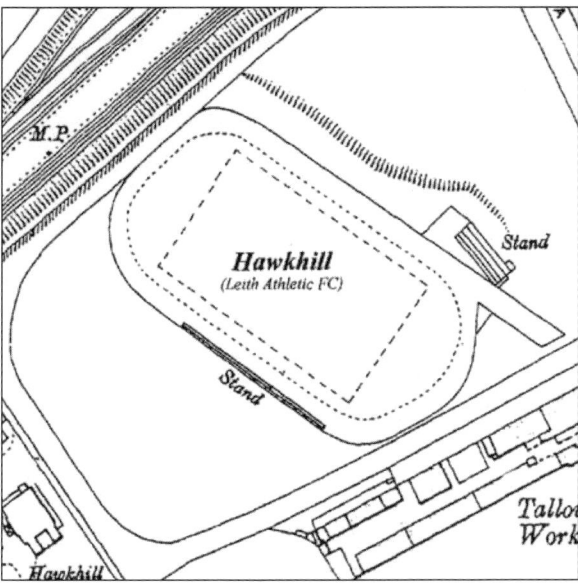

MAP EXTRACT; EDINBURGH 3.4 [1896]
SITE LOCATION; **NT27837523**

Originally in use by the *Leith Caledonian Cricket Club*, the ground was first utilized for football in 1887. At this time, it probably only consisted of an enclosed pitch but *Hawkhill* was gradually improved with the construction of a small pavilion on the west side, a grandstand on the west and the provision of an oval running track and some banking to accommodate standing spectators. The ground closed in 1920 and became part of the Hawkhill Recreation Ground before being redeveloped with housing.

PLAYING RECORD OF LEITH ATHLETIC
LEAGUE PROGRAMME

Matches Played; 2-1 v. Partick Thistle (-)
(September 9th, 1899)
4-1 v. Port Glasgow Athletic (-) (October 7th, 1899)
3-1 v. Ayr (-) (December 2nd, 1899)
0-1 v. Motherwell (-) (December 30th, 1899)
4-1 v. Linthouse (-) (January 6th, 1900)
4-1 v. Abercorn (-) (February 3rd, 1900)
0-1 v. Morton (-) (March 24th, 1900)

No. of Matches Played by Leith Athletic; 7

Some matches were played here during the 1899/1900 season and it is assumed that this was when *St Bernards* required **New Logie Green** for their home fixtures in the early part of the season and after *St Bernards* lease on the *New Logie Green* ground had expired on December 31st, 1899. In 1900 Leith Athletic FC moved out to **Chancelot Park**.
NB. There are no gate figures recorded for *Leith Athletic's* occupancy of this venue.

A TOTAL OF **8** TEAMS TOOK PART IN **7** LEAGUE FIXTURES AT THIS VENUE

HYDE PARK
HOME GROUND OF NORTHERN

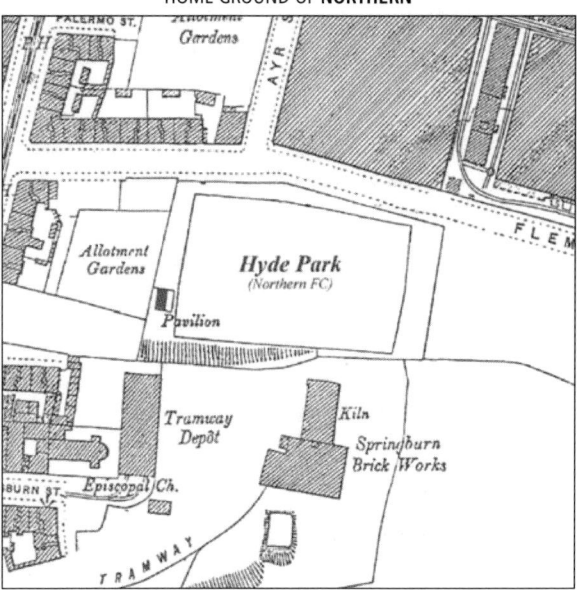

MAP EXTRACT; LANARKSHIRE 6.7 [1896]
SITE LOCATION; **NS60506744**

Located in the Springburn district, on the opposite side of Flemington Street to the Hyde Park Locomotive Works, *Northern FC* played at *Hyde Park* from their formation in 1874. The probable record attendance of 6,000 was attained at the Glasgow Cup 2nd Round tie v. *Rangers* (3-6) on October 12th, 1889 and at the Glasgow Cup tie v. *Celtic* (2-3) on October 7th, 1893. The ground which possessed few facilities, a pavilion in the south west corner and some banking on the south side, fell into disuse on the demise of the club in 1897 and was quickly redeveloped with some housing and an administration building for the adjacent works. Today, Ayr and Adamswell Streets cross the site.

PLAYING RECORD OF NORTHERN
LEAGUE PROGRAMME

Matches Played; 1-3 v. Clyde (-) (August 26th, 1893)
2-2 v. Hibernian (-) (September 30th, 1893)
2-2 v. Motherwell (-) (December 2nd, 1893)
2-1 v. Partick Thistle (-) (December 23rd, 1893)
3-3 v. Thistle (-) (February 3rd, 1894)
1-4 v. Cowlairs (-) (March 4th, 1894)
5-2 v. Abercorn (-) (March 10th, 1894)
3-1 v. Port Glasgow Athletic (-) (April 21st, 1894)
2-7 v. Morton (-) (April 28th, 1894)

No. of Matches Played by Northern; 9

The club was a founder member of the Scottish Football League Division 2 in 1893 and failed to gain re-election in 1894.
NB. There are no League gate figures recorded for *Northern FC's* occupancy of this venue.

A TOTAL OF **10** TEAMS TOOK PART IN **9** LEAGUE FIXTURES AT THIS VENUE

IBROX PARK [1ST]
HOME GROUND OF RANGERS

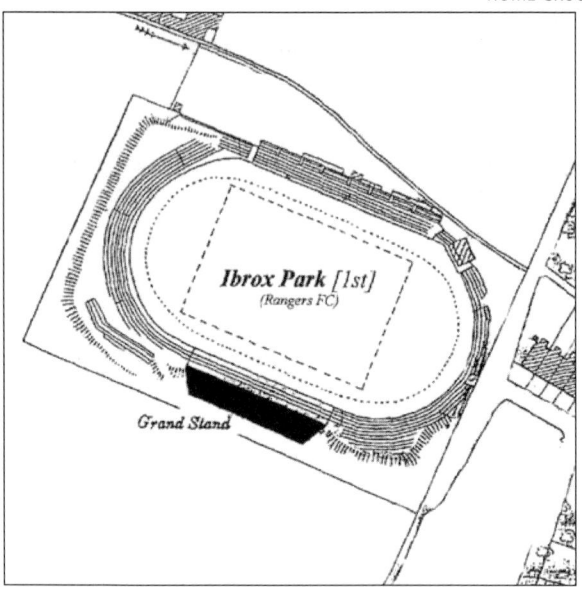

MAP EXTRACT; LANARKSHIRE 6.9 [1896]
SITE LOCATION; **NS55696462**

Rangers FC moved to *Ibrox Park [1st]* from *Kinning Park* and opened it with a friendly fixture against *Preston North End FC* on August 20th, 1887. The pitch was surrounded by an oval running track and initially the facilities included a 1,200 seat open stand and a pavilion on the north side and terracing around the remainder of the ground. A covered grandstand was subsequently constructed on the south side and *Ibrox Park [1st]* became the venue for three international matches and the 1890 Scottish FA Cup Final and replay between *Queen's Park* and *Vale of Leven*.

By 1899 the ground had become too small for the club and *Rangers FC* commenced construction of a much larger ***Ibrox Park [2nd]*** a few hundred feet to the west. Following the last match, on December 9th, 1899, the stadium was dismantled and the site cleared, the west end of the ground to allow for the completion of the east end of ***Ibrox Park [2nd]*** and the east end for redevelopment with housing.

PLAYING RECORD OF RANGERS
LEAGUE PROGRAMME

First Match; 5-2 v. Heart of Midlothian (4,000) (August 16th, 1890)
Last Match; 6-1 v. Kilmarnock (5,000) (December 9th, 1899)
Highest Gate; 30,000 v. Celtic (0-4) (September 27th, 1897)
& v. Celtic (4-1) (January 2nd, 1899)
Lowest Gate; 1,000 v. St Bernards (1-2) (May 2nd, 1894)
Highest Home Win; 10-0 v. Hibernian (7,000)
(December 24th, 1898)
Highest Home Defeat; 0-4 v. Third Lanark (-) (August 24th, 1895) &
v. Celtic (30,000) (September 27th, 1897)
No. of Matches Played by Rangers; 90
Information Kindly Supplied by; Cyril George

The club was a founder member of the Scottish Football League in 1890. The club was also involved in a Scottish Football League Championship Play Off Match v. *Dumbarton* (2-2) at the neutral venue of ***Cathkin Park*** on May 21st, 1891. *Rangers FC* moved to ***Ibrox Park [2nd]*** in December 1899 but had to play the next match, v. *St Mirren* on December 16th, 1899, at ***Meadowside*** as it was not ready.

A TOTAL OF **18** TEAMS TOOK PART IN **90** LEAGUE FIXTURES AT THIS VENUE

An aerial view of ***Ibrox Park [2nd]*** prior to redevelopment in the 1970s. ***Ibrox Park [1st]*** was sited in the foreground of the picture, to the left of the railway cutting.

IBROX PARK [2ND]

HOME GROUND OF RANGERS
TEMPORARY HOME GROUND FOR QUEEN'S PARK, ST BERNARDS, ST MIRREN, THIRD LANARK, CLYDE & PARTICK THISTLE

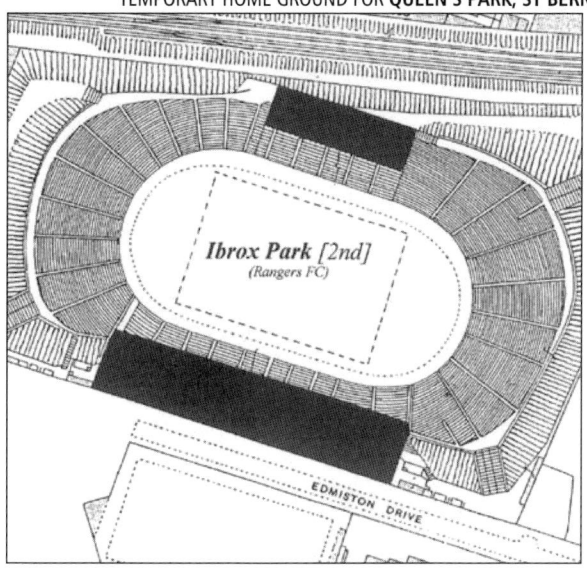

MAP EXTRACT; LANARKSHIRE 6.9 [1933]
SITE LOCATION; NS55556464

PLAYING RECORD OF RANGERS
LEAGUE PROGRAMME

First Match; 2-1 v. *Third Lanark* (4,000) (January 6th, 1900)
Highest Gate; 118,567 v. *Celtic* (2-1) (January 2nd, 1939)*
Lowest Gate; 2,500 v. *Kilmarnock* (3-0) (April 20th, 1907)
& v. *Port Glasgow Athletic* (5-1) (April 18th, 1908)
Highest Home Win; 10-2 v. *Raith Rovers* (35,000) (December 16th, 1967). 9-0 v. *Partick Thistle* (7,000) (August 23rd, 1902) & v. *Ayr United* (12,000) (November 16th, 1929)
Highest Home Defeat; 0-5 v. *Heart of Midlothian* (18,000) (September 25th, 1905) & v. *Airdrieonians* (12,000) (January 4th, 1915)

No. of Matches Played by Rangers; 1,743
Information Kindly Supplied by; Cyril George

Rangers FC moved here from *Ibrox Park [1st]* in 1900. The club was also involved in a Scottish Football League Division One Championship Play Off Match v. *Celtic* (1-2) at the neutral venue of *Hampden Park [3rd]* on May 6th, 1905. The first Scottish Football League match to be played under floodlights took place here on March 7th, 1956 when *Rangers* beat *Queen of the South* 8-0. Due to rebuilding work in the 1990s, some home matches were played at *Hampden Park [3rd]*.
* Record Scottish Football League attendance.

PLAYING RECORD OF PARTICK THISTLE
LEAGUE PROGRAMME

Matches Played; 1-1 v. *Dundee* (3,000) (September 5th, 1908)
1-2 v. *Falkirk* (-) (September 26th, 1908)
0-6 v. *Airdrieonians* (1,200) (November 14th, 1908)
5-1 v. *Morton* (-) (November 21st, 1908)
2-3 v. *St Mirren* (-) (December 5th, 1908)
0-2 v. *Motherwell* (-) (December 12th, 1908)
0-6 v. *Rangers* (5,000) (January 2nd, 1909)

No. of Matches Played by Partick Thistle; 7
Information Kindly Supplied by; Robert Reid & John Henderson

These matches were played here as *Firhill Park* was not ready following the closure of *Meadowside* in 1908.

PLAYING RECORD OF ST BERNARDS
LEAGUE PROGRAMME

Match Played; 1-4 v. *Rangers* (4,000) (February 3rd, 1900)

No. of Matches Played by St Bernards; 1
Information Kindly Supplied by; Cyril George

This match was played here as *St Bernards FC's* lease on the *New Logie Green* had expired earlier in the season and the club was technically homeless.

PLAYING RECORD OF CLYDE
LEAGUE PROGRAMME

Matches Played; 1-2 v. *Rangers* (12,000) (March 13th, 1915)

No. of Matches Played by Clyde; 1
Information Kindly Supplied by; Cyril George

This match may have been moved here from *Shawfield* due to a fire.

PLAYING RECORD OF ST MIRREN
LEAGUE PROGRAMME

Match Played; 0-2 v. *Celtic* (22,000) (May 11th, 1979)

No. of Matches Played by St Mirren; 1
Information Kindly Supplied by; Cyril George

NB. It is not known why this game was played here.

When *Ibrox Park [2nd]* opened on January 6th, 1900 with a Scottish Football League match v. *Third Lanark* it had a nominal capacity of some 40,000. The pitch was similarly surrounded by a cycle and running track and the facilities included a covered seated stand, pavilion and extensive embankments around the pitch. To increase the capacity a timber terracing extension was constructed on the west end in 1902 but this collapsed with disastrous results, 26 dead and 500 injured, when 75,000 people were crammed in to see the *Scotland* v. *England* international match on April 5th of the same year.

Following this set-back enlargements were expedited by the use of solid earth banking only and the capacity had increased to 63,000 by the time that *Rangers* set about building a 10,000 seat grandstand on the south side of the ground in 1928. Further expansion took place, culminating in the record attendance of 118,567 in 1939 but the only improvement for standing spectators was the installation of some cover over the terracing on the north side.

Ibrox Park [2nd] remained virtually unchanged until the 1960s when the cover on the north stand was increased and the east end roofed, but it was the ground's poor safety record with no less than 68 deaths and numerous injuries in a ten year period between 1961 and 1971 that led to a near-total rebuilding of the stadium. In 1978 the oval track was dispensed with and both end terraces were removed and flattened, the spoil being dumped in the adjacent redundant railway cutting (the goods branch to Princes Dock) on the north side of the ground and replaced with twin 7,500 seat stands. Two years later the north terrace, which had been installed with 9,000 bench seats in 1973, was similarly dealt with and a 10,300 seat stand constructed. This, with the existing South Stand and standing enclosure then gave a capacity of 45,000 with 41,000 seats.

Further developments in the 1990s, the installation of an additional tier in the south stand, provision of seats in the standing enclosure and the "filling in" of the north west and north east corners with seated stands give an all seat capacity of 50,444 at the start of the 2004/5 season. The pitch size was 125 x 89 yards.

Cont ...

IBROX PARK [2ND] [CONT ...]

PLAYING RECORD OF QUEEN'S PARK
LEAGUE PROGRAMME
Matches Played; 0-2 v. Dundee (6,000) (April 24th, 1909)
No. of Matches Played by Queen's Park; 1
Information Kindly Supplied by; Hector Cook

This match was played here due to **Hampden Park [3rd]** being immediately closed following a riot at the Scottish FA Cup Final on April 17th, 1909.

PLAYING RECORD OF THIRD LANARK
LEAGUE PROGRAMME
Match Played; 1-0 v. Rangers (25,000) (October 10th, 1903)
No. of Matches Played by Third Lanark; 1
Information Kindly Supplied by; Bob Laird & Cyril George

This match was played here as **New Cathkin Park** was not ready at the start of the 1903/4 season.

AT THE END OF SEASON 2004/5, A TOTAL OF **39** TEAMS HAD TAKEN PART IN **1,755** LEAGUE FIXTURES AT THIS VENUE

The Archibald Leitch designed main stand, on the south side of the ground, after the rebuild of 1991 with new roof and additional retro-designed stairways to accommodate the third tier. As the structure is "listed" the brick-built façade was retained and refurbished.
Photograph by Paul Claydon. Courtesy of Groundtastic Magazine

DIAGRAM SHOWING THE DISPOSITION OF IBROX PARK [1ST] & IBROX PARK [2ND]

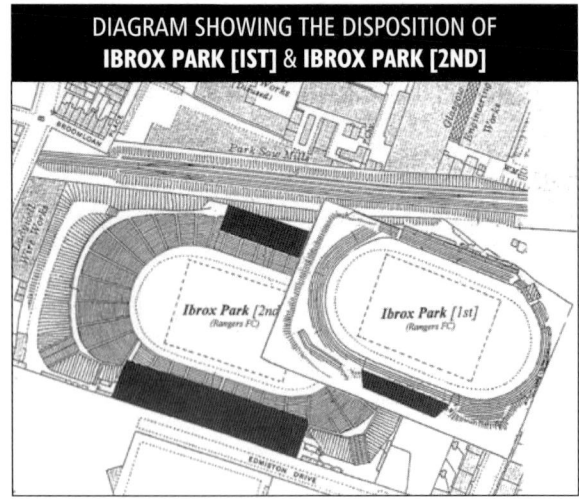

KIMMETER PARK GREEN
HOME GROUND OF SOLWAY STAR

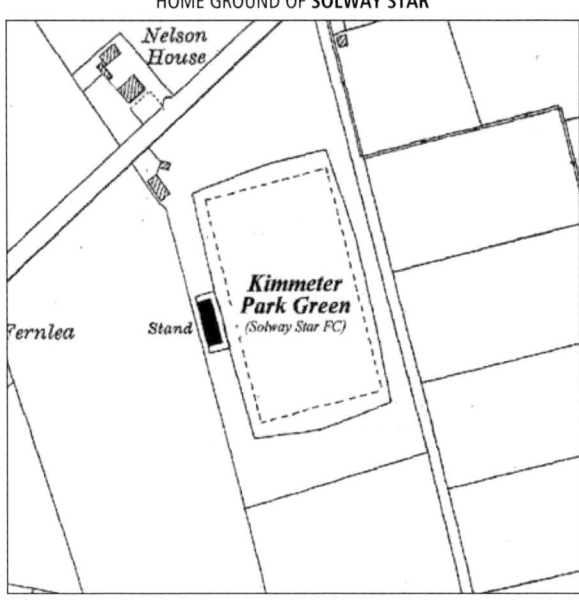

MAP EXTRACT; DUMFRIES-SHIRE 62.8 [**1931**]
SITE LOCATION; **NY20656675**

Located to the east of the town centre of Annan, on the south east side of Stapleton Road, *Kimmeter Park Green* opened in 1921. The basic facilities originally consisted of a small grandstand and changing rooms, but in 1923 the grandstand was replaced by a larger wooden structure with a capacity of 300.

The site has since reverted back to agricultural use with the partially demolished grandstand finding further employment as a cow shed.

PLAYING RECORD OF SOLWAY STAR
LEAGUE PROGRAMME
First Match; 2-1 v. Peebles Rovers (-) (August 25th, 1923)
Last Match; 2-3 v. Johnstone (-) (April 3rd, 1926)
Highest Gate; 3,000 v. Queen of the South (1-1) (October 11th, 1924)
Lowest Gate*; Not Known
Highest Home Win; 7-1 v. Dumbarton Harp (-) (November 22nd, 1924) [Record Expunged], & v. Peebles Rovers (-) (March 6th, 1926)
Highest Home Defeat; 1-6 v. Vale of Leven (1,000) (August 15th, 1925)
No. of Matches Played by Solway Star; 46
(Including one expunged match v. Dumbarton Harp on November 22nd, 1924)

The club was a founder member of the Scottish Football League Division 3 in 1923 and left the League when Division 3 was disbanded near the end of the 1925/26 season.

*NB. Very few gate figures are known for this club but it is assumed that in general attendances numbered only a few hundred.

A TOTAL OF **21** TEAMS TOOK PART IN **46** LEAGUE FIXTURES AT THIS VENUE

KINTAIL PARK
HOME GROUND OF MID-ANNANDALE

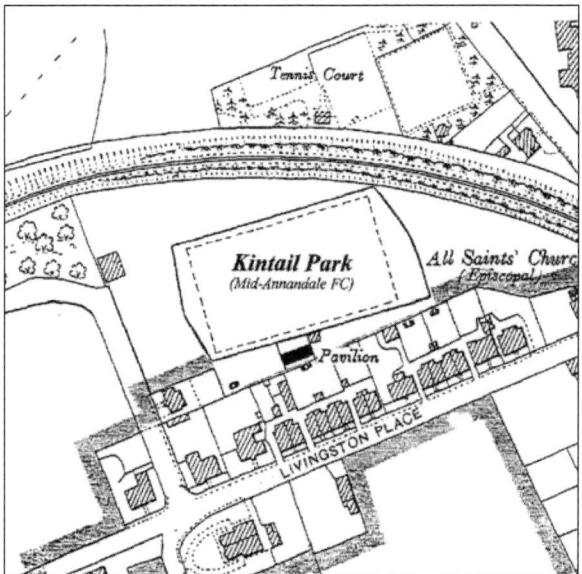

MAP EXTRACT; GROUND AS IN c1925 DRAWN FROM PLANS AND SUPERIMPOSED ON DUMFRIES-SHIRE 51.1 [1899]
SITE LOCATION; NY13368208

Sited in Lockerbie between Livingston Place and the Dumfries railway line, *Kintail Park* opened in 1902. The facilities at this time probably consisted of just a pavilion, sited at the west end of the field, but in 1923 a stand was constructed on the south side of the pitch and this, along with a small refreshment hut, formed the basic amenities available to spectators during *Mid-Annandale FC's* brief encounter with the Scottish Football League. The site is now covered by houses, but the road built across the ground is named Kintail Park as a reminder of its former use.

PLAYING RECORD OF MID-ANNANDALE
LEAGUE PROGRAMME

First Match; 4-3 v. Helensburgh (950) (August 25th, 1923)
Last Match; 1-1 v. Brechin City (-) (March 20th, 1926)
Highest Gate*; 2,100 v. Queen of the South (1-3) (November 3rd. 1923)
Lowest Gate*; 600 v. Lochgelly United (1-2) (September 27th, 1924)
Highest Home Win; 6-1 v. Clackmannan (-) (November 17th, 1923) & v. Brechin City (-) (April 26th, 1924)
Highest Home Defeat; 0-3 v. Lochgelly United (-) (September 12th, 1925)

No. of Matches Played by Mid-Annandale; 44

The club was a founder member of the Scottish Football League Division 3 in 1923 and left the League when Division 3 was disbanded near the end of the 1925/26 season.
*NB. These are the highest and lowest gate figures of the few that were recorded. In view of the general level of those that are known, it is very probable that there were crowds of less than 600 on occasions.

A TOTAL OF **21** TEAMS TOOK PART IN **44** LEAGUE FIXTURES AT THIS VENUE

LANGLANDS PARK
HOME GROUND OF LINTHOUSE

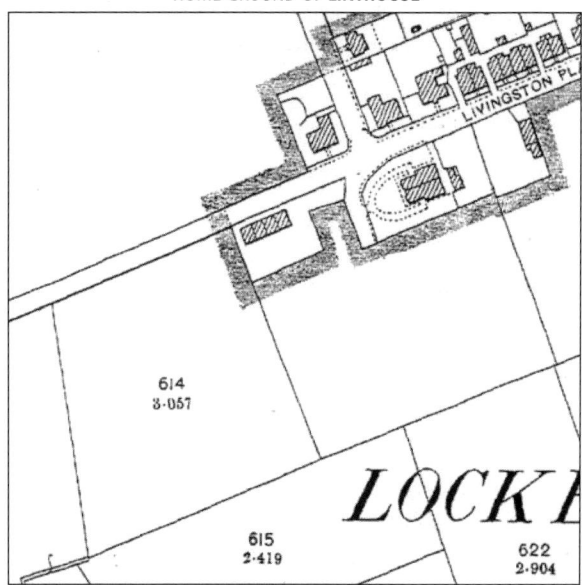

MAP EXTRACT; LANARKSHIRE 6.9 [1896]
SITE LOCATION; NS54806500

Linthouse FC moved here from *Langlands Road* in 1894 and joined the Scottish League in 1895. Located on the east side of Craigton Road in the Govan district of Glasgow, the facilities included a pavilion, in the north east corner, and a narrow seated stand on the south side. The probable record attendance of 10,000 was set at the Glasgow Cup match v. *Celtic* (1-7) on September 21st, 1895.

The club folded in 1900 and the site was later redeveloped with Arthurlie Street built over the ground.

PLAYING RECORD OF LINTHOUSE
LEAGUE PROGRAMME

First Match; 2-1 v. Airdrieonians (-) (August 17th, 1895)
Last Match; 2-2 v. Motherwell (-) (March 10th, 1900)
Highest & Lowest Gate*; Not Known
Highest Home Win; 7-3 v. Airdrieonians (-) (October 23rd, 1897)
Highest Home Defeat; 0-6 v. Abercorn (-) (December 2nd, 1899)

No. of Matches Played by Linthouse; 45

The club was elected into the Scottish Football League Division 2 in 1895 and did not apply for re-election in 1900.
*NB. There are no gate figures recorded for *Linthouse FC's* occupancy of this venue.

A TOTAL OF **13** TEAMS TOOK PART IN **45** LEAGUE FIXTURES AT THIS VENUE

LINKS PARK
HOME GROUND OF MONTROSE

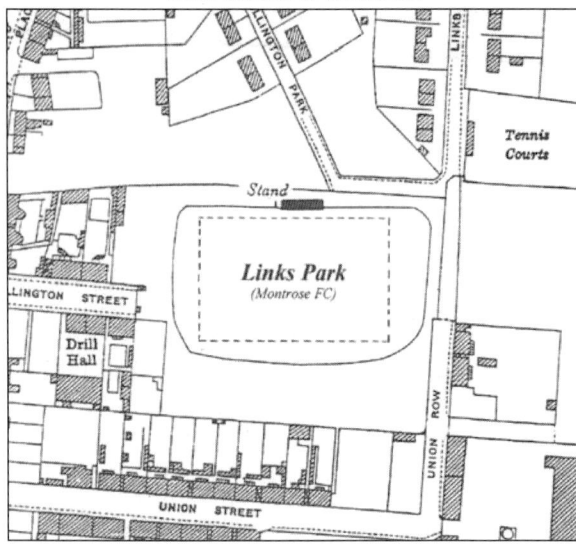

MAP EXTRACT; FORFARSHIRE 35.2 [1923]
SITE LOCATION; NO72015813

When *Montrose FC* moved here in 1887 it had virtually no facilities and tarpaulins had to be erected around the enclosure on match days to prevent non-paying spectators from seeing the game. The army commandeered the ground during WWI and after the war a fence was constructed around the ground and a second hand temporary grandstand erected on the north side. Post-WWII improvements included the installation of covering on the south side and west end in 1960 and, in 1975, the removal of wooden terracing from the west end (for replacement with concrete terracing) and re-installation at the opposite end.

In 1992 a new seated stand was built on the south side and the "temporary" stand on the north side finally demolished.

The record attendance of 8,983 was set at the Scottish FA Cup 5th Round tie v. *Dundee* (1-4) on March 17th, 1973 and the capacity at the start of the 2004/5 season was 3,292 with 1,334 seats and the pitch size was 113 x 70 yards.

PLAYING RECORD OF MONTROSE
LEAGUE PROGRAMME

First Match; 1-1 v. Queen of the South (-) (August 25th, 1923)
Highest Gate*; 7,000 v. Dundee United (1-3) (March 19th, 1960)
Lowest Gate*; 150 v. Albion Rovers (1-0) (October 13th, 1984)
Highest Home Win; 8-3 v. Raith Rovers (-) (October 3rd, 1964).
7-1 v. Stenhousemuir (-) (November 28th, 1964)
Highest Home Defeat; 3-7 v. Queen of the South (-) (December 5th, 1964). 0-6 v. St Johnstone (-) (April 28th, 1956), v. Airdrieonians (1,200) (October 16th, 1965), v. Stirling Albion (750) (April 29th, 1989) & v. Queen of the South (545) (February 24th, 1996)
No. of Matches Played by Montrose; 1,150
(Including one expunged match v. Bo'ness on August 27th, 1932)
Information Kindly Supplied by; David Smith

The club was a founder member of the Scottish Football League Division 3 in 1923 and left the League when Division 3 was disbanded near the end of the 1925/26 season. *Montrose FC* was elected into Division 2 in 1929 and after the Scottish Football League was suspended in 1939 it was elected into Division B in 1954
*NB. Not all attendances are known and these are the highest and lowest gate figures of those that were recorded.

AT THE END OF SEASON 2004/5, A TOTAL OF **64** TEAMS HAD TAKEN PART IN **1,150** LEAGUE FIXTURES AT THIS VENUE

McDIARMID PARK
HOME GROUND OF ST JOHNSTONE

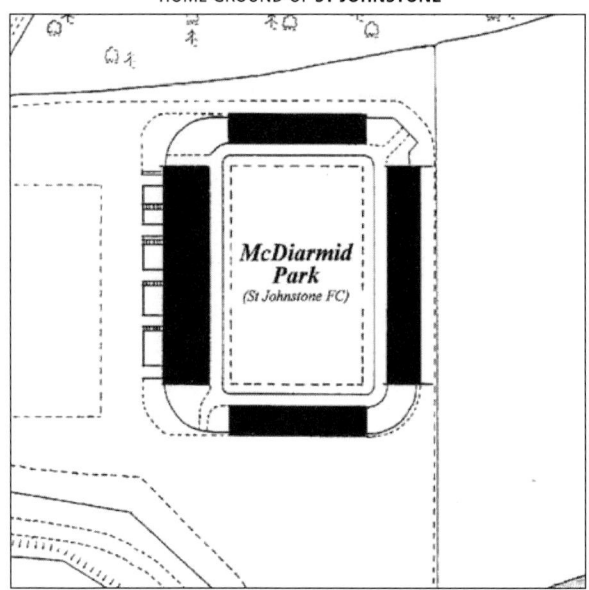

MAP EXTRACT; GROUND AS IN c1998 DRAWN FROM PLANS AND SUPERIMPOSED ON NO0825 [1950]
SITE LOCATION; NO08972516

Opened in 1989 when *St Johnstone FC* moved here from **Muirton Park**, the stadium has all-seat stands on each side with a capacity, at the start of the 2004/5 season, of 10,721 and an 115 x 75 yards sized pitch. An unusual, and possibly unique, event took place here on November 13th, 2004 when matches from two different codes were both played on the same day. The Scottish Football League match *St Johnstone* v. *Ross County* (1-1) (2,018) kicked off at 12.00hrs followed, at 17.30hrs, by the *Scotland* v. *Japan* (100-8) (10,278) Rugby Union International.

PLAYING RECORD OF ST JOHNSTONE
LEAGUE PROGRAMME

First Match; 2-1 v. Clydebank (7,267) (August 19th, 1989)
Highest Gate; 10,721 v. Rangers (1-1) (February 26th, 1991)
Lowest Gate; 1,770 v. Clyde (0-0) (April 9th, 2005)
Highest Home Win; 7-2 v. Dundee (7,087) (January 1st, 1997).
6-0 v. Alloa Athletic (3,100) (March 17th, 1990)
Highest Home Defeat; 0-7 v. Rangers (9,636) (November 8th, 1998)
No. of Matches Played by St Johnstone; 304
Information Kindly Supplied by; Alastair Blair
The club moved here from **Muirton Park** in 1989.

AT THE END OF SEASON 2004/5, A TOTAL OF **36** TEAMS HAD TAKEN PART IN **304** LEAGUE FIXTURES AT THIS VENUE

MARINE GARDENS

HOME GROUND OF **LEITH ATHLETIC**
TEMPORARY HOME GROUND FOR **EDINBURGH CITY**

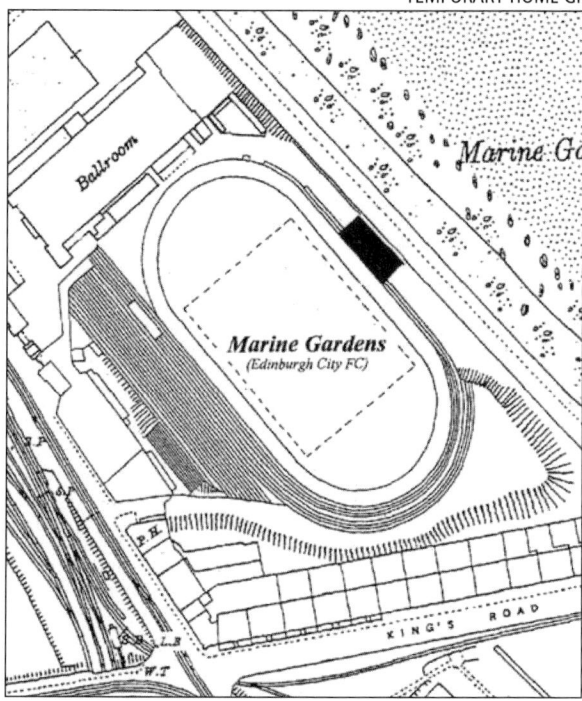

MAP EXTRACT; MIDLOTHIAN 4.1/2 & 4.5 [**1931**]
SITE LOCATION; **NT30087456**

Located in the Craigentinny district of Edinburgh, on the north east side of the corner of Seafield and Kings Roads, *Marine Gardens* was first used by *Edinburgh City* and *Leith Athletic* FCs in 1928.

The pitch was surrounded by an oval track and the facilities included a concrete terrace on the west side, a small covered seated stand and a narrow band of terracing, which extended around the south end, on the east. Players changed in the ballroom that was sited behind the north goal.

The stadium, which also hosted speedway and greyhound racing, was vacated by the two clubs by 1936 and taken over by the corporation for use as a vehicle test track. It was later demolished and the site occupied by an omnibus depot.

PLAYING RECORD OF LEITH ATHLETIC
LEAGUE PROGRAMME

First Match; 1-1 v. Dunfermline Athletic (3,900) (August 18th, 1928)
Last Match; 4-1 v. Forfar Athletic (-) (April 25th, 1936)
Highest Gate*; 21,000 v. Celtic (0-3) (August 8th, 1931)
Lowest Gate*; 500 v. Albion Rovers (1-2) (October 22nd, 1932)
Highest Home Win; 7-1 v. Alloa (2,000) (March 1st, 1930)
Highest Home Defeat; 2-6 v. St Bernards (-) (September 21st, 1935)
0-5 v. Motherwell (-) (February 6th, 1932)
& v. St Mirren (-) (August 21st, 1935)

No. of Matches Played by Leith Athletic; **144**
(Including one expunged match v. Bathgate on January 2nd, 1936)

Leith Athletic moved into *Marine Gardens* from *New Powderhall* at the end of the 1927/28 season. The ground occupied a very exposed position on the coast and with the winter weather proving a bleak prospect for both players and spectators the club moved to *Meadowbank* at the end of the 1935/36 season.

PLAYING RECORD OF EDINBURGH CITY
LEAGUE PROGRAMME

First Match & Highest Home Win; 3-1 v. Montrose (-) (September 1st, 1934)
Last Match; 0-5 v. Forfar Athletic (-) (April 13th, 1935)
Highest Gate*; Not Known
Highest Home Defeat & Lowest Gate*; 2-8 v. Dundee United (85) (December 15th, 1934)

No. of Matches Played by Edinburgh City; **17**

The club moved here on a temporary basis from *New Powderhall* until it was able to secure a new ground. In 1935 *Edinburgh City* re-located to *City (East Pilton) Park*.

*NB. Very few gate figures are known for these clubs at this venue but it is assumed that in general attendances varied between a few hundred and a thousand.

A TOTAL OF **42** TEAMS TOOK PART IN **161** LEAGUE FIXTURES AT THIS VENUE

The vast terraces of **Marine Gardens** were never remotely filled for football matches but this view, taken from the west side and looking eastwards shows the huge attendance at a pre-WWII speedway fixture

MEADOWBANK & OLD MEADOWBANK
HOME GROUND OF LEITH ATHLETIC

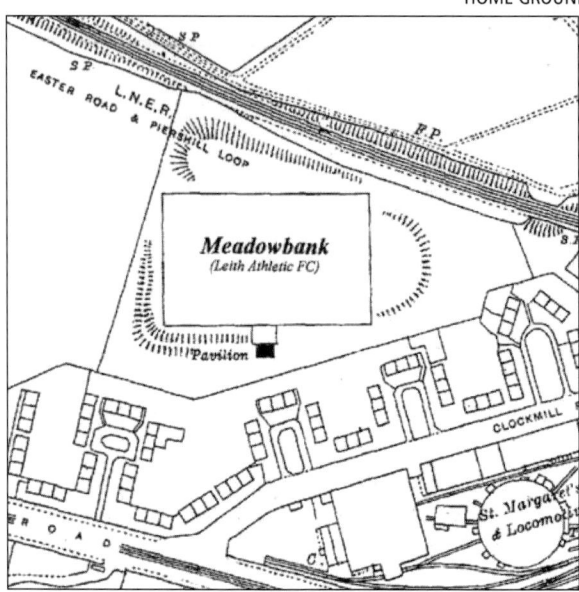

MAP EXTRACT; EDINBURGH 3.8 [1921]
SITE LOCATION; NT27917438

MAP EXTRACT; GROUND AS IN 1948 DRAWN FROM PLANS AND
SUPERIMPOSED ON EDINBURGH 3.8 [1921]

Meadowbank, east of Edinburgh city centre and on the north side of London Road, was used by *Leith Amateurs FC* prior to the arrival of *Leith Athletic FC* in 1936.

Initially, the only facilities consisted of a pavilion on the south side and bits of banking around the sides. By the arrival of *Leith Athletic* an oval circuit had been constructed around the pitch and the club added dressing rooms and some covering for standing spectators before WWII brought a halt to Scottish League football.

During hostilities the site was used an army transport depot and this, along with general neglect, made the arena totally unusable as a football ground. *Leith Athletic* set about rebuilding it in 1946 and, whilst this was being carried out, moved next door to *New Meadowbank* before returning in the following year.

PLAYING RECORD OF LEITH ATHLETIC
LEAGUE PROGRAMME

First Match; 2-1 v. Dumbarton (3,000) (August 15th, 1936)
Last Match; 0-2 v Dunfermline Athletic (1,000) (August 26th, 1939)
Highest Gate*; 3,000 v. Dumbarton (2-1) (August 15th, 1936)
& v. Ayr United (3-2) (January 9th, 1937)
Lowest Gate*; 500 v. Cowdenbeath (0-2) (April 29th, 1939)
Highest Home Win; 6-3 v. East Stirlingshire (-) (December 17th, 1938). 5-0 v. Dundee United (-) (March 26th, 1938)
Highest Home Defeat; 1-7 v. Aidrieonians (-) (October 22nd, 1938)
No. of Matches Played by Leith Athletic; 53

The club moved here from *Marine Gardens* in 1936. The Scottish Football League was suspended in 1939 and the club ceased to operate during WWII when the ground was taken over by the authorities. *Leith Athletic* moved to the *New Meadowbank* next door for the first post-WWII season (spent in Division C) whilst the ground was reconstructed and returned in 1947 at the commencement of its final spell in the Scottish League when the venue was re-named as *Old Meadowbank*.

*NB. Not all attendances are known and these are the highest and lowest gate figures of those that were estimated

Leith Athletic FC returned here and formally re-opened it as *Old Meadowbank* with a friendly fixture against *Rangers FC* on September 16th, 1947 which attracted some 10,000 spectators.

Considerable alterations to the ground had taken place; the pitch had been enlarged to 115 x 75 yards, concrete terracing installed and the **Royal Gymnasium** ground's grandstand had been purchased from *St Bernards FC* for £2,000 and re-erected on the south side. When further improvements, including the provision of a cover over part of the north side, were completed by 1951 the capacity of the ground was reputed to be 30,000 but this was never remotely tested as the record attendance was only 11,625, established at the Scottish FA Cup 1st Round tie v. *Raith Rovers* (0-1) on January 22nd, 1949.

Leith Athletic folded in 1953 and the track, as the home venue for *Edinburgh Monarchs*, was subsequently used for speedway whilst *Murrayfield Amateurs FC* briefly used the pitch. The site was later used for part of *Meadowbank Stadium*.

PLAYING RECORD OF LEITH ATHLETIC
LEAGUE PROGRAMME

First Match & Highest Gate*; 0-1 v. East Fife (4,500) (August 13th, 1947)
Last Match; 1-1 v. St Johnstone (-) (April 3rd, 1948)
Lowest Gate*; Not Known
Highest Home Win; 4-2 v. Dumbarton (3,500) (September 20th, 1947). 3-0 v. Alloa Athletic (-) (February 14th, 1948)
Highest Home Defeat; 0-4 v. Hamilton Academical (-) (November 1st, 1947)
No. of Matches Played by Leith Athletic; 15

Leith Athletic FC moved back here from *New Meadowbank* in 1947 and was promoted from Division C into the Scottish Football League Division B in 1947 but was relegated back into Division C in 1948.
*NB. This is the highest gate figure of the very few that were recorded. In view of the general level of those that are known, it is probable that there were crowds of less than 1,000 on occasions.

A TOTAL OF **26** TEAMS TOOK PART IN **68** LEAGUE FIXTURES AT THIS VENUE

MEADOWBANK STADIUM

HOME GROUND OF **MEADOWBANK THISTLE**
TEMPORARY HOME GROUND FOR **BERWICK RANGERS** & **LIVINGSTON**

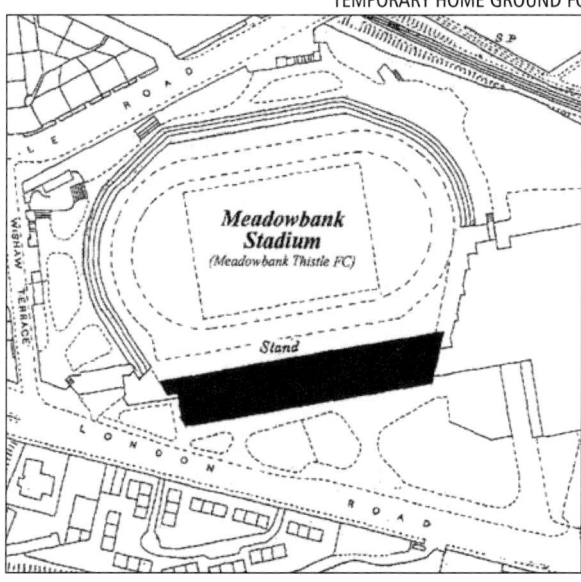

MAP EXTRACT; GROUND AS IN **1998** DRAWN FROM PLANS AND SUPERIMPOSED ON EDINBURGH 3.8 [1921]
SITE LOCATION; NT27767439

Meadowbank Stadium forms part of a larger sports complex built on **Old Meadowbank** and *New Meadowbank* grounds, Clockmill Road and the northern section of St Margarets Engine Shed. It opened on May 2nd, 1970 as an athletics track and was the venue for the Commonwealth Games that year.

Ferranti Thistle FC (as *Meadowbank Thistle FC*) first used the ground in 1974 and established the record gate for a football match of 2,818 at a Scottish Football League Cup Section 9 tie v. *Albion Rovers* (0-1) on August 10th, 1974. Although the capacity for athletics meetings is 16,500 with open seating on the terraces, spectators at football matches, for security reasons, were only allowed to use the 7,500 seat main stand.

Meadowbank Thistle, as *Livingston FC*, moved out to **Almondvale Stadium** in 1995 and now, apart from athletics, the stadium is the home ground for the re-formed *Edinburgh City FC*.

PLAYING RECORD OF MEADOWBANK THISTLE
LEAGUE PROGRAMME
First Match; 0-1 v. Alloa Athletic (500) (September 11th, 1974)
Last Match; 1-0 v. Stenhousemuir (463) (May 5th, 1995)
Highest Gate; 2,000 v. Dunfermline Athletic (0-1) (December 17th, 1988)
Lowest Gate; 80 v. Stenhousemuir (0-0) (December 22nd, 1979)
Highest Home Win; 6-0 v. Raith Rovers (750) (November 9th, 1985)
Highest Home Defeat; 1-8 v. Kilmarnock (1,107) (April 10th, 1991)
No. of Matches Played by Meadowbank Thistle; 403
Information Kindly Supplied by; David Baxter

The club was elected into the Scottish Football League Division 2 in 1974 and re-formed and relocated as *Livingston* in 1995. Due to the non-availability of *Meadowbank Stadium* matches were also played at **Bayview Park, Firs Park, Ochilview Park,** and **Tynecastle.**

PLAYING RECORD OF LIVINGSTON
LEAGUE PROGRAMME
Matches Played; 2-0 v. Alloa Athletic (249) (September 16th, 1995)
2-0 v. Queen's Park (223) (September 20th, 1995)
2-1 v. Albion Rovers (229) (September 23rd, 1995)
0-0 v. Brechin City (273) (October 14th, 1995)
0-1 v. Arbroath (236) (October 28th, 1995)
No. of Matches Played by Livingston; 5
Information Kindly Supplied by; Duncan Bennett

The club re-formed as *Livingston FC* and took over *Meadowbank Thistle FC's* fixtures in 1995. **Almondvale Stadium** was not ready at the start of the 1995/6 season and these five matches were played here.

PLAYING RECORD OF BERWICK RANGERS
LEAGUE PROGRAMME
Match Played; 0-1 v. Alloa Athletic (277) (February 15th, 1992)
No. of Matches Played by Berwick Rangers; 1
Information Kindly Supplied by; Robin Murdie

The match was played here due to the unserviceable state of the roof on the main stand at **Shielfield Park**

A TOTAL OF **33** TEAMS TOOK PART IN **409** LEAGUE FIXTURES AT THIS VENUE

Edinburgh Monarchs Speedway Team vacated **Old Meadowbank** (See P.194) in 1967 and by the February of the following year, this was all that was left of the main stand. The site was in the process of being gradually cleared to make way for the construction of **Meadowbank Stadium** and Sports Complex for the 1970 Commonwealth Games.

MEADOW PARK
HOME GROUND OF ALBION ROVERS

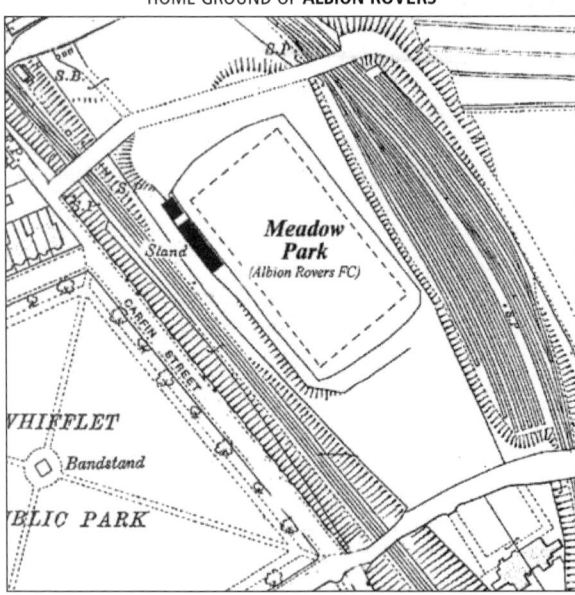

MAP EXTRACT; LANARKSHIRE 8.13 [1912]
SITE LOCATION; **NS74006390**

Located on the east side of Carfin Street in Whifflet, south of Coatbridge, *Albion Rovers FC* moved here from *Cowheath Park* in 1882.

The ground was inconveniently sandwiched between the North British and Caledonian Railway lines and the facilities included a grandstand and a pavilion on the west side and some flat areas for standing spectators. The grandstand proved to be susceptible to storm damage, the roof blowing off twice, before the club moved to **Cliftonhill Park** in 1919, taking the pavilion with them.

Meadow Park was subsequently taken over by a junior football club for a while but the site was later utilized for an electricity sub-station.

PLAYING RECORD OF ALBION ROVERS
LEAGUE PROGRAMME

First Match; 2-2 v. Leith Athletic (2,000) (August 15th, 1903)
Last Match; 4-1 v. Vale of Leven (-) (March 6th, 1915)
Highest Gate*; 4,000 v. Cowdenbeath (3-1) (January 3rd, 1914)
Lowest Gate*; 200 v. Leith Athletic (1-0) (December 6th, 1912)
Highest Home Win; 7-3 v. East Stirlingshire (-)
(February 16th, 1907). 5-0 v. Vale of Leven (-) (April 24th, 1909)
Highest Home Defeat; 2-5 v. Cowdenbeath (-)
(December 2nd, 1911).
0-4 v. Leith Athletic (2,000) (October 3rd, 1914)

No. of Matches Played by Albion Rovers; 135
Information Kindly Supplied by; Robin Marwick

The club was elected into the Scottish Football League Division 2 in 1903 and the League home match with *Ayr United* on February 17th, 1912 was played at **Somerset Park**. Division 2 fixtures were suspended after 1915 and the club moved to **Cliftonhill Park** in 1919 but, as it was not ready, had to play the first few matches of that season at **Broomfield Park**.

*NB. Not all attendances are known and these are the highest and lowest gate figures of those that were estimated.

A TOTAL OF **24** TEAMS TOOK PART IN **135** LEAGUE FIXTURES AT THIS VENUE

MEADOW PARK
HOME GROUND OF DUMBARTON HARP

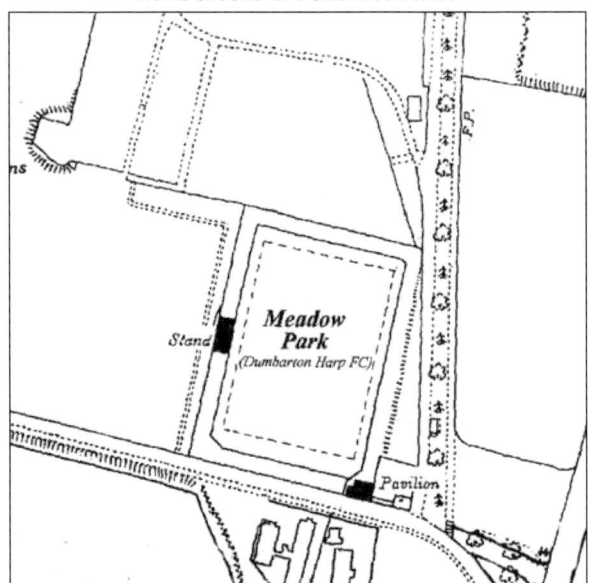

MAP EXTRACT; DUNBARTONSHIRE N22.2 [1936]
SITE LOCATION; **NS39757582**

Dumbarton Harp FC was formed in c1894 and from the outset played their home games at *Meadow Park* which was located to the north of the town on the corner of Overburn Avenue and Poplar Road.

When first used it was probably no more than an open field but by 1914 it had been enclosed and the facilities included a pavilion in the south east corner with narrow flat areas for standing spectators around all the sides. The club joined the Scottish League in 1923 and, possibly around this time, a small stand was installed on the west side.

The record attendance was probably the 3,000 who witnessed the Scottish FA Qualifying Cup 5th Round match against *Queen of the South* in October 1923. The club folded in 1925 but the ground remained in existence until 1950 when the buildings were removed and the site absorbed into a sports playing field.

PLAYING RECORD OF DUMBARTON HARP
LEAGUE PROGRAMME

First Match; 2-3 v. Clackmannan (-) (August 25th, 1923)
Last Match & Lowest Gate*; 1-3 v. Dykehead (140)
(January 5th, 1925)
Highest Gate*; 2,000 v. Vale of Leven (3-1) (December 31st, 1924)
Highest Home Win; 6-3 v. Queen of the South (990)
(December 27th, 1924)
Highest Home Defeat; 0-5 v. Queen of the South (-)
(January 19th, 1924)

No. of Matches Played by Dumbarton Harp; 24
(Including 9 expunged matches played in the club's final season [1924/25])

The club was a founder member of the Scottish Football League Division 3 in 1923 but resigned from the League during the 1924/25 season due to poor support and had their results expunged.

*NB. Not all attendances are known and these are the highest and lowest estimated gate figures of those that were recorded.

A TOTAL OF **18** TEAMS TOOK PART IN **24** LEAGUE FIXTURES AT THIS VENUE

MEADOWSIDE

HOME GROUND OF **PARTICK THISTLE**
TEMPORARY HOME GROUND FOR **RANGERS**

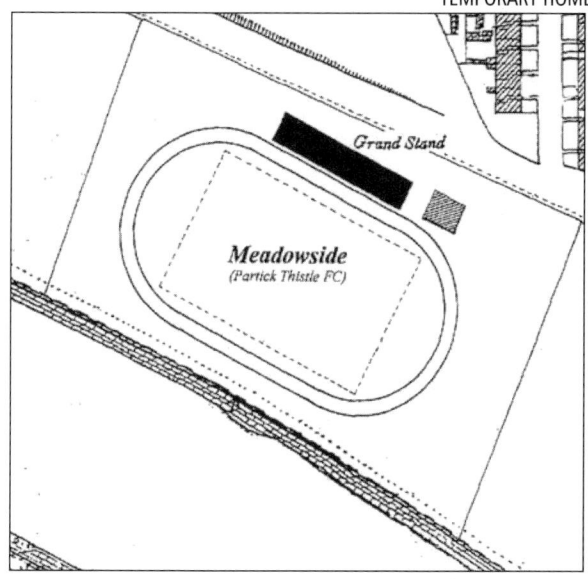

MAP EXTRACT; GROUND AS IN **1908** DRAWN FROM PLANS AND SUPERIMPOSED ON LANARKSHIRE 6.5 [1896]
SITE LOCATION; NS55196627

PLAYING RECORD OF PARTICK THISTLE
LEAGUE PROGRAMME

First Match; 0-3 v. Abercorn (-) (August 26th, 1893)
Last Match; 1-1 v. Hibernian (-) (April 30th, 1908)
Highest Gate*; 11,000 v. Rangers (1-4) (January 3rd, 1905)
Lowest Gate*; Not Known
Highest Home Win; 13-1 v. Thistle (-) (March 10th, 1894)
Highest Home Defeat; 3-8 v. Celtic (3,000) (December 3rd, 1898).
1-7 v. Hibernian (-) (March 31st, 1894)

PLAY OFF MATCHES

Division 1, 7th/8th Place Play Off; 0-2 v. Dundee (3,000) (March 24th, 1898)

No. of Matches Played by Partick Thistle; 171
(League Programme; 170, Play Off Matches; 1)

Located on the north side of the River Clyde in the Partick district, the existence of this ground falls between two 25in Ordnance Surveys but the location is shown in a simplified form on the 6in Scale map of 1909. From contemporary accounts an oval running track surrounded the pitch and the facilities included a 750 seat grandstand on the north side.

Partick Thistle moved here from *Inchview Park* in 1891 with the view to gradually developing *Meadowside* into a stadium to rival those of *Queen's Park, Celtic* and *Rangers FCs*. The probable record gate of 16,000 was achieved at the Scottish FA Cup 1st Round Replay v. *Hibernian* (4-2) on February 4th, 1905 and at the Glasgow Cup 1st Round tie v. *Celtic* (0-2) on September 8th, 1906.

In 1908 the ground was acquired for extensions to an adjacent shipbuilding yard and the club forced to move out. Today the area has been redeveloped and Castlebank Crescent crosses part of the site.

The club was a founder member of the Scottish Football League Division 2 in 1893. In 1908 the club was forced out and found itself homeless for the 1908/9 season whilst *Firhill Park* was being built. During this period home games were played at no less than nine venues; *Rugby Park, Ibrox Park [2nd], Shawfield Park, Pittodrie Park, Clune Park, Douglas Park, Celtic Park [2nd], Hampden Park [3rd]* and *Easter Road*. As if this was not bad enough *Firhill Park* was not ready in time at the commencement of the 1909/10 season and *Cappielow Park* also had to be utilized, *Partick Thistle* thus creating a record of playing 20 successive home games on no less than 12 grounds and garnering only 7 points!

*NB. This is the highest gate figure of the very few that were recorded. In view of the general level of those that are known, it is very probable that there may have been crowds of less than 1,000 on occasions.

PLAYING RECORD OF RANGERS
LEAGUE PROGRAMME

Match Played; 4-1 v. St Mirren (2,000) (December 16th, 1899)
No. of Matches Played by Rangers; 1
Information Kindly Supplied by; Cyril George
This match was played here as *Ibrox Park [2nd]* was not ready.

A TOTAL OF **32** TEAMS TOOK PART IN **172** LEAGUE FIXTURES AT THIS VENUE

A view of **Meadowside** looking north east across the pitch towards the grandstand with Carradale and Crawford Streets beyond.
Photograph Courtesy of Partick Thistle/Mitchell Library, Glasgow

MERCHISTON PARK
HOME GROUND OF EAST STIRLINGSHIRE

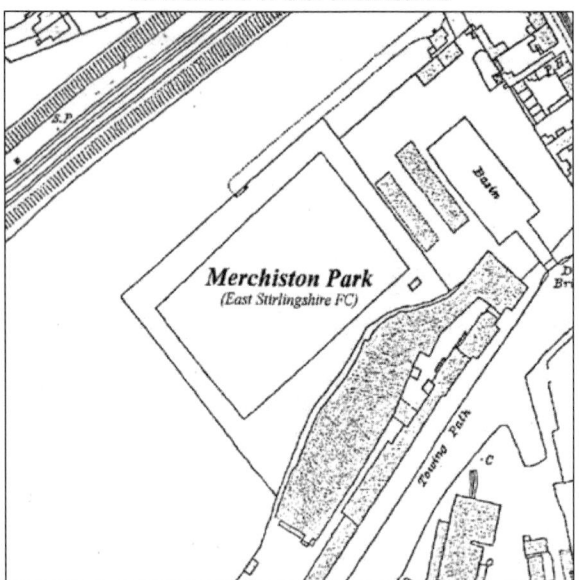

MAP EXTRACT; STIRLINGSHIRE 30.3 [1918]
SITE LOCATION; NS88658115

East Stirlingshire FC moved to *Merchiston Park* from *Randyford Park* in 1882. Few details are known of this venue other than it was located in the north of the town on the north bank of the Forth & Clyde Canal. There would appear to have been no facilities available although a small building in the east corner of the ground may have been a dressing room.

The club moved to **Firs Park** in 1921 and the area of the ground was absorbed into the adjacent foundry. By 2005 it had been re-developed with Burnbank Road occupying the site

PLAYING RECORD OF EAST STIRLINGSHIRE
LEAGUE PROGRAMME

First Match; 2-3 v. Airdrieonians (2,500) (August 18th, 1900)
Last Match; 3-0 v. Arthurlie (-) (April 17th, 1915)
Highest & Lowest Gate*; Not Known
Highest Home Win; 5-0 v. Johnstone (-) (November 1st, 1913)
Highest Home Defeat; 2-5 v. Hamilton Academical (-) (November 8th, 1902) & v. Ayr (-) (November 20th, 1909)
No. of Matches Played by East Stirlingshire; 167
Information Kindly Supplied by; Drummond Calder

The club was elected into the Scottish Football League Division 2 in 1900 and was involved in a Scottish Football League Division 2, 10th/11th Place Play Off Match v. *Raith Rovers* (2-3) at the neutral venue of *Old Logie Green* on May 11th, 1907. The club moved to *Firs Park* in 1921.

*NB. There are very few gate figures recorded for *East Stirlingshire FC's* occupancy of this venue.

A TOTAL OF **27** TEAMS TOOK PART IN **167** LEAGUE FIXTURES AT THIS VENUE

MILLBURN PARK
HOME GROUND OF VALE OF LEVEN

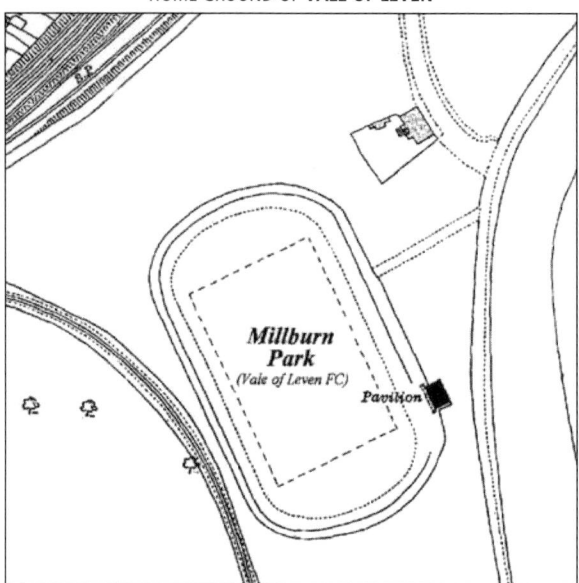

MAP EXTRACT; DUNBARTONSHIRE 18.6 [1914]
SITE LOCATION; NS39257950

The ground was located at the south end of Alexandria, off Leven Street and between the railway line and the River Leven. *Vale of Leven FC* moved here from *North Street Park* in 1888 and when the first match was played, in August of the same year, the playing area consisted of an 125 x 75 yards sized pitch surrounded by a cinder oval. The facilities included a pavilion and grandstand which had been removed from the previous ground and re-erected here on the east side and further alterations included the installation of a covered enclosure on the west side

The probable record gate was 8,000 at the Scottish FA Cup 2nd Round tie v *Alloa Athletic* (0-0) on February 2nd, 1922. The club resigned from the Scottish League in 1926, re-formed as a junior club in 1939 and still used *Millburn Park* as their home ground in 2005.

PLAYING RECORD OF VALE OF LEVEN
LEAGUE PROGRAMME

First Match; 2-1 v. Abercorn (-) (August 30th, 1890)
Last Match; 2-2 v. Mid-Annandale (-) (April 3rd, 1926)
Highest Gate*; 4,000 v. Dumbarton (0-3) (December 30th, 1922)
Lowest Gate*; 1,000 v. Lochgelly United (2-1) (November 29th, 1924)
Highest Home Win; 8-2 v. Lochgelly United (-) (December 19th, 1925)
Highest Home Defeat; 1-7 v. St Bernards (-) (February 20th, 1915)
No. of Matches Played by Vale of Leven; 219

The club was a founder member of the Scottish Football League in 1890 but resigned in 1892. *Vale of Leven* was elected into Division 2 in 1905 and left the League when Division 3 was disbanded near the end of the 1925/26 season. The home matches v. *Dumbarton Harp* in 1924/25 and v. *Brechin City* and *Galston* in 1925/26 were not played.

*NB. These are the highest and lowest gate figures of the very few that were recorded. In view of the general level of those that are known, it is very probable that there were crowds of less than 1,000 on occasions.

A TOTAL OF **54** TEAMS TOOK PART IN **219** LEAGUE FIXTURES AT THIS VENUE

MILL PARK
HOME GROUND OF BATHGATE

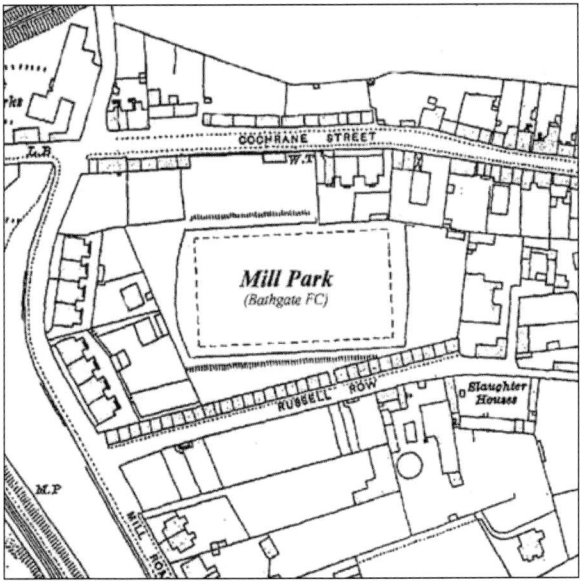

MAP EXTRACT; LINLITHGOW N7.14 [1917]
SITE LOCATION; NS97186913

Located on the south side of Cochrane Street, north west of Bathgate town centre, when first used by *Bathgate FC* in 1902, *Mill Park* was little more than an enclosed field, with some raised banking for spectator accommodation. By their Scottish League debut season, 1921/2, a grandstand had been constructed and general improvements made to the standing facilities along the sides of the pitch.

The probable record gate was 8,000 at the Scottish FA Cup 2nd Round tie v. *Falkirk* (1-0) on February 11th, 1922 and at the Scottish FA Cup 3rd Round match v. *Airdrieonians* (2-5) on February 20th, 1926. Following the demise of the club in the 1930s, the ground was used for housing with Marmion Road running across the centre of the pitch.

PLAYING RECORD OF BATHGATE
LEAGUE PROGRAMME

First Match; 0-0 v. Armadale (4,000) (August 27th, 1921)
Last Match & Lowest Gate*; 1-3 v. King's Park (200)
(February 16th, 1929)
Highest Gate*; 5,000 v. Alloa (0-0) (January 2nd, 1922)
& v. Armadale (4-2) (January 1st, 1923)
Highest Home Win; 8-3 v. Queen of the South (-) (January 8th, 1927)
Highest Home Defeat; 3-7 v. Clyde (1,500) (March 20th, 1926).
0-5 v. Leith Athletic (-) (October 27th, 1928)
No. of Matches Played by Bathgate; 133
(Including 12 expunged matches played in 1928/9)

The club was elected into the Scottish Football League Division 2 in 1921 and resigned from the League in 1929 with the results for the 1928/9 season being expunged.
*NB. Not all attendances are known and these are the highest and lowest gate figures of those that were recorded.

A TOTAL OF **32** TEAMS TOOK PART IN **133** LEAGUE FIXTURES AT THIS VENUE

MUIRTON PARK
HOME GROUND OF ST JOHNSTONE

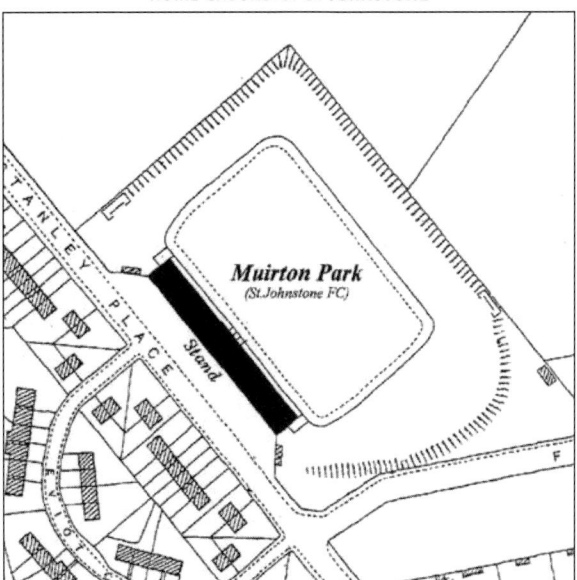

MAP EXTRACT; PERTHSHIRE 98.1 [c1930]
SITE LOCATION; NO10952465

St Johnstone FC moved to *Muirton Park* from the **Recreation Ground** in 1924 and opened it with a Scottish Football League match v. *Queen's Park* on Christmas Day.

The facilities included a main stand and enclosure on the west side and shallow embankments around the remainder of the pitch. The only major improvement to the ground came in the 1950s when covering was installed over the east terrace.

The record attendance of 29,972 was set at the Scottish FA Cup 2nd Round tie v. *Dundee* (1-3) on February 10th, 1951. The club moved out to **McDiarmid Park** in 1989 and the site was utilized for an Asda supermarket.

PLAYING RECORD OF ST JOHNSTONE
LEAGUE PROGRAMME

First Match; 2-1 v. Queen's Park (11,000)
(December 25th, 1924)
Last Match; 0-1 v. Ayr United (6,728) (April 29th, 1989)
Highest Gate; 26,500 v. Dundee (0-3) (April 28th, 1962)
Lowest Gate; 466 v. Albion Rovers (1-0) (April 19th, 1986)
Highest Home Win; 7-0 v. Albion Rovers (5,000) (August 29th, 1931), v. Partick Thistle (-) (April 1st, 1939), v. Alloa Athletic (-) (December 19th, 1953) & v. Brechin City (5,700) (December 1st, 1962)
Highest Home Defeat; 1-7 v. Heart of Midlothian (6,000)
(October 8th, 1938)
No. of Matches Played by St Johnstone; 1,039
Information Kindly Supplied by; Alastair Blair

The club moved here from the **Recreation Ground** in 1924 and moved to **McDiarmid Park** in 1989.

A TOTAL OF **46** TEAMS TOOK PART IN **1,039** LEAGUE FIXTURES AT THIS VENUE

NEWFIELD PARK
HOME GROUND OF JOHNSTONE

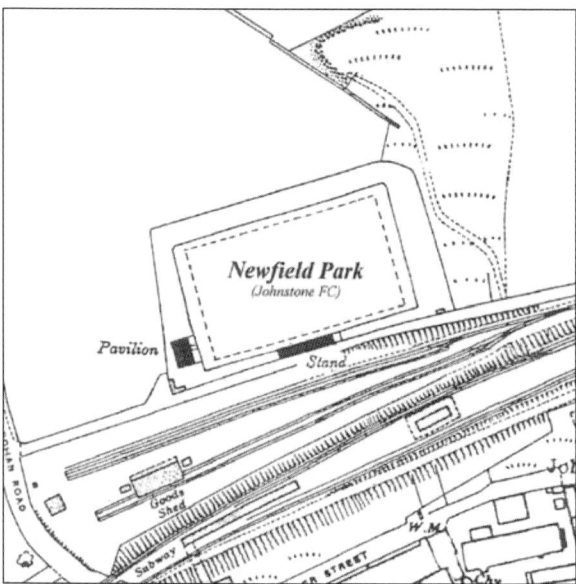

MAP EXTRACT; RENFREWSHIRE 11.4 & 11.8 [1939]
SITE LOCATION; NS42486360

Located north of the town and adjacent to the north side of Newfield Railway Station, the site was first used by *Johnstone FC* in 1894. At first it was probably unenclosed with a small pavilion at the east end of the field but by the time that they entered the Scottish League in 1912 an enclosure with flat standing areas had been built, the pavilion sited in the south west corner and a small stand constructed on the south side.

The probable record gate was 7,000 at the Scottish FA Cup 2nd Round tie v *Falkirk* (0-1) on January 27th, 1923. The ground still remained long after the club's demise in 1927 but was eventually buried under the A737 which by-passes the town.

PLAYING RECORD OF JOHNSTONE
LEAGUE PROGRAMME
First Match; 2-1 v. Dumbarton (-) (August 24th, 1912)
Last Match; 2-3 v. Brechin City (-) (April 10th, 1926)
Highest & Lowest Gate*; Not Known
Highest Home Win; 6-2 v. Mid-Annandale (-) (October 24th, 1925)
Highest Home Defeat; 2-5 v. Alloa Athletic (-)
(December 31st, 1921)

No. of Matches Played by Johnstone; 127

The club was elected into the Scottish Football League Division 2 in 1912 and did not seek re-election in 1926. The home match v. *Galston* in the 1925/26 season was not played.
*NB. There are no League gate figures recorded for *Johnstone FC's* occupancy of this venue.

A TOTAL OF **38** TEAMS TOOK PART IN **127** LEAGUE FIXTURES AT THIS VENUE

NEWTOWN PARK
HOME GROUND OF BO'NESS

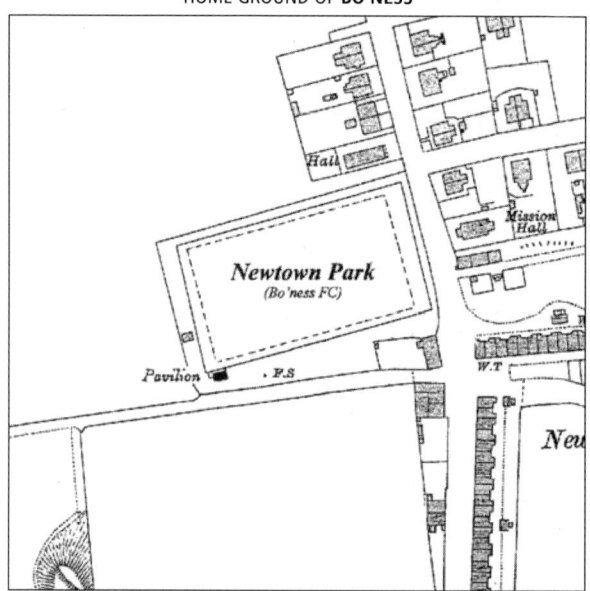

MAP EXTRACT; LINLITHGOW N3.3 [1916]
SITE LOCATION; NS99628078

Bo'ness FC was formed in 1881 and moved to *Newtown Park*, located in the south of the town, in 1886. Although a stand was erected on the south side of the ground by 1895 and another one installed in 1902, neither of these structures still stood in 1914. The ground was improved on their entry to the Scottish League in 1921 with the construction of a 500 seat covered stand and banking around all four sides.

The record attendance of 9,000 was set on March 5th, 1927 at the Scottish FA Cup 4th Round tie v. *Celtic* (2-5). *Bo'ness* was expelled from the League in 1933 and merged with *Bo'ness Cadora FC* in 1945 to reform as *Bo'ness United FC*, a junior club, and still use *Newtown Park* as the home ground today.

PLAYING RECORD OF BO'NESS
LEAGUE PROGRAMME
First Match; 3-1 v. Broxburn United (4,000) (August 27th, 1921)
Last Match; 4-3 v. Brechin City (200) (October 29th, 1932)
Highest Gate*; 5,000 v. Armadale (1-0) (October 8th, 1921)
& v. Celtic (0-1) (November 26th, 1927)
Lowest Gate*; 90 v. Dumbarton (1-3) (April 9th, 1932)
Highest Home Win; 7-0 v. Bathgate (-) (November 6th, 1926)
Highest Home Defeat; 0-6 v. East Stirlingshire (-)
(January 24th, 1931)

No. of Matches Played by Bo'ness; 214
(Including 6 expunged matches played in 1932/3, the club's final season)

The club was elected into the Scottish Football League Division 2 in 1921 and expelled from the League in November 1932 for non-payment of guarantees. The results for 1932/33 were expunged and the home match v. *Arthurlie* in 1928/9 was not played.
*NB. Not all attendances are known and these are the highest and lowest gate figures of those that were recorded.

A TOTAL OF **49** TEAMS TOOK PART IN **214** LEAGUE FIXTURES AT THIS VENUE

NEW KILBOWIE PARK
HOME GROUND OF **EAST STIRLINGSHIRE CLYDEBANK & CLYDEBANK [2]**

MAP EXTRACT; GROUND AS IN **1964** DRAWN FROM PLANS AND SUPERIMPOSED ON DUNBARTONSHIRE N23.15 [1937]
SITE LOCATION; **NS50127072**

Clydebank Juniors FC bought the site, in use as allotment gardens, for £900 in 1937 and moved here in 1939 from *Kilbowie Park* which was located on the opposite site of the railway line. The original facilities included a pavilion on the south side and embankments around the pitch and improvements made in the 1950s included the provision of a pavilion stand and construction of terracing.

In 1964 *Clydebank Juniors FC* merged with *East Stirlingshire FC*, removed the floodlights and covering from *Firs Park* and re-installed the roof on the north side of the ground. The clubs de-merged in 1965 and, following *Clydebank FCs* entry into the Scottish Football League in their own right in 1966, new small stands were built at the west end and on the south side, alongside of the pavilion stand.

The attendance record of 14,900 was set at the Scottish FA Cup 1st Round Replay v. *Hibernian* (0-2) on February 10th, 1965 and the ground was made all-seater in the late 1970s with the installation of bench seats on the terracing, giving a nominal capacity of 9,950. The club moved out in 1996 to groundshare with *Dumbarton FC* at *Boghead Park* and the site was redeveloped as a shopping centre in 2000.

PLAYING RECORD OF CLYDEBANK [2]
LEAGUE PROGRAMME
First Match; 0-3 v. Arbroath (3,300) (August 24th, 1966)
Last Match; 1-3 v. Hamilton Academical (3,665) (April 27th, 1996)
Highest Gate; 10,000 v. Rangers (0-3) (February 19th, 1978)
Lowest Gate; 430 v. Dundee United (2-0) (May 2nd, 1978)*
Highest Home Win; 8-1 v. Arbroath (4,005) (January 3rd, 1977)
Highest Home Defeat; 0-7 v. Falkirk (1,000) (September 20th, 1969)
No. of Matches Played by Clydebank [2]; 574

The club was elected into the Scottish Football League Division 2 in 1966. In 1996 *Clydebank* moved out to groundshare with *Dumbarton FC* at *Boghead Park* and, later, with *Greenock Morton* at *Cappielow Park*.
*This was the lowest ever attendance in the Scottish Premier Division.

PROGRAMME COVER ON RIGHT
One of the last home games of the ill-fated and short-lived merger of *Clydebank [2]* and *East Stirlingshire FCs*

PLAYING RECORD OF EAST STIRLINGSHIRE CLYDEBANK
LEAGUE PROGRAMME
Matches Played; 3-0 v. Dumbarton (3,000) (September 5th, 1964)
5-0 v. Montrose (-) (September 16th, 1964)
1-2 v. Queen's Park (-) (September 19th, 1964)
3-1 v. Stranraer (1,500) (September 30th, 1964)
1-1 v. Queen of the South (-) (October 3rd, 1964)
1-0 v. Stenhousemuir (4,000) (October 17th, 1964)
2-1 v. Berwick Rangers (3,500) (October 31st, 1964)
0-0 v. Ayr United (-) (November 14th, 1964)
1-2 v. Hamilton Academical (2,500) (November 28th, 1964)
1-2 v. East Fife (1,500) (December 12th, 1964)
2-1 v. Albion Rovers (-) (January 2nd, 1965)
3-3 v. Cowdenbeath (2,000) (January 16th, 1965)
6-1 v. Brechin City (2,500) (February 20th, 1965)
3-1 v. Arbroath (3,000) (February 27th, 1965)
2-2 v. Raith Rovers (1,100) (March 13th, 1965)
1-2 v. Stirling Albion (3,000) (March 27th, 1965)
3-2 v. Forfar Athletic (1,500) (April 23rd, 1965)
2-2 v. Alloa Athletic (800) (April 26th, 1965)

No. of Matches Played by East Stirlingshire Clydebank; 18

The club was an amalgamation of *East Stirlingshire* and *Clydebank* and took over *East Stirlingshire FCs* fixtures during 1964/5. They de-merged in 1965 and *East Stirlingshire* moved back to *Firs Park*.

A TOTAL OF **40** TEAMS TOOK PART IN **592** LEAGUE FIXTURES AT THIS VENUE

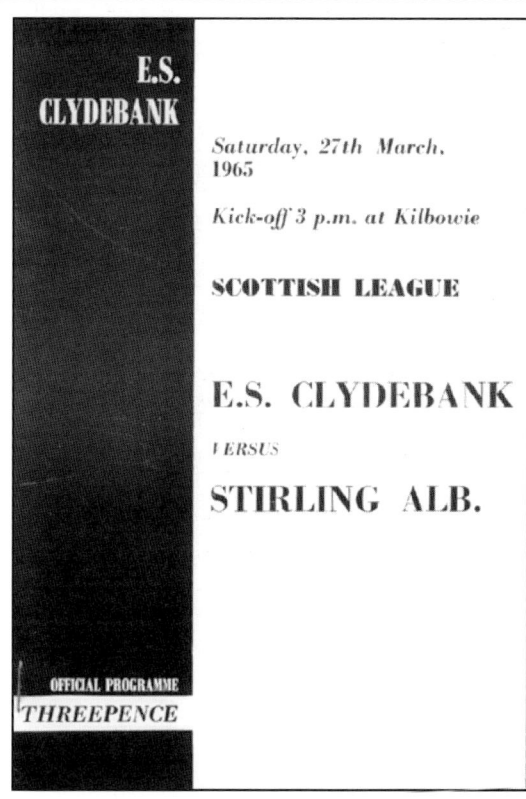

NEW LOGIE GREEN

HOME GROUND OF **ST BERNARDS**
TEMPORARY HOME GROUND FOR **LEITH ATHLETIC**

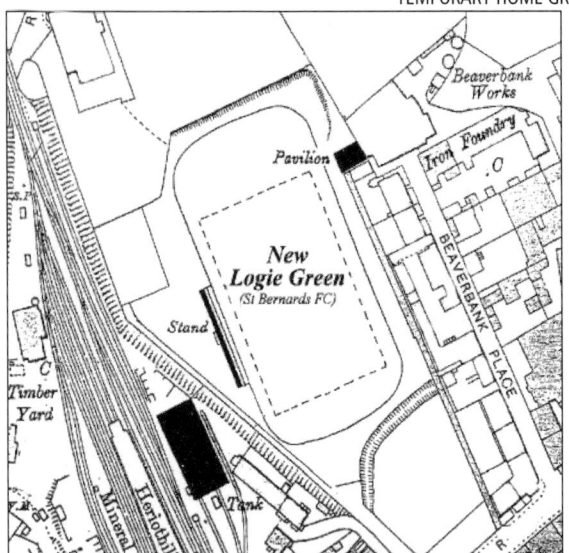

MAP EXTRACT; EDINBURGH 3.3 [1896]
SITE LOCATION; NT25357530

PLAYING RECORD OF LEITH ATHLETIC
LEAGUE PROGRAMME

Matches Played; 3-1 v. Hamilton Academical (-) (August 19th, 1899)
3-2 v. Airdrieonians (-) (September 16th, 1899)

No. of Matches Played by Leith Athletic; 2

The club moved here from **Beechwood Park** in 1899 and during the 1899/1900 season *Leith Athletic* groundshared with *St Bernards*. During this period most fixtures were played at **Hawkhill** as it is assumed that these took place when *St Bernards* were playing their home matches at *New Logie Green* during the first part of the season. It is similarly assumed that the remaining fixtures for this season were played at **Hawkhill** after *St Bernards* lease on the *New Logie Green* ground expired on December 31st, 1899.

A TOTAL OF **16** TEAMS TOOK PART IN **64** LEAGUE FIXTURES AT THIS VENUE

This rare photograph of **New Logie Green**, shows the Scottish FA Cup Final taking place between *Heart of Midlothian* and *Hibernian* on March 14th, 1896. This unique match, the only final to be played outside of Glasgow, resulted in a 3-1 for *Hearts* in front of the record attendance at this venue of 16,034.

The facilities here on view on the west side of the ground include the then recently constructed covered grandstand with an open seated enclosure and banking to accommodate standing spectators. The buildings on top of the embankment, to the left, are part of the old Edinburgh & Glasgow Railway Works at Heriothill.

Located in the Heriothill district, north of Edinburgh city centre, *St Bernards FC* moved here from *Powderhall* in 1889. The facilities included a pavilion, an open seated stand on the west side, some banking around the pitch and, installed at a later date, a covered stand.

The attendance record of 16,034 was established when the ground was given the honour of hosting the Scottish FA Cup Final between *Heart of Midlothian* and *Hibernian* (3-1) on March 14th, 1896. *St Bernards* moved to **New Powderhall** in 1900 and the venue was redeveloped with housing, Logie Green Road latterly crossing the site.

PLAYING RECORD OF ST BERNARDS
LEAGUE PROGRAMME

First Match; 0-0 v. Rangers (5,000) (August 26th, 1893)
Last Match; 3-3 v. St Mirren (-) (December 30th, 1899)
Highest Gate*; 8,000 v. Celtic (0-2) (November 10th, 1894)
& v. Rangers (0-2) (September 19th, 1898)
Lowest Gate*; Not Known
Highest Home Win; 9-1 v. Partick Thistle (-) (December 4th, 1897)
Highest Home Defeat; 0-5 v. Heart of Midlothian (7,000) (September 21st, 1895)

No. of Matches Played by St Bernards; 62

The club was elected into the Scottish Football League Division 1 in 1893. The lease on the *New Logie Green* ground expired on December 31st, 1899 and the last home match of the season was played at **Ibrox Park** *(2nd)*, whilst the Division One Play Off match v. *St Mirren* (1-2) to decide the 8th and 9th Places at the end of that season took place at the neutral venue of **Dens Park** on April 7th, 1900. The first home games of the following season were played at **New Powderhall** before a permanent move was made to the **Royal Gymnasium** ground.

*NB. This is highest gate figure of the very few that were recorded. In view of the general level of those that are known, it is very probable that there were crowds of less than 1,000 on occasions

OLD LOGIE GREEN

HOME GROUND OF LEITH ATHLETIC
TEMPORARY HOME GROUND FOR ST BERNARDS

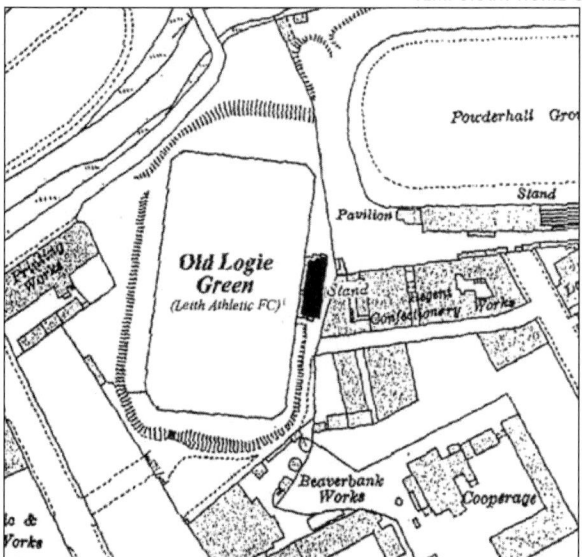

MAP EXTRACT; EDINBURGH 3.3 [1914]
SITE LOCATION; NT25467545

Located in the Heriothill district, north of Edinburgh city centre, and originally known as *Powderhall* and then the *Heriot Cricket & Football Ground*, it was sited to the north east of *New Logie Green* and immediately adjacent to the *Powderhall Grounds* which later became known as *New Powderhall*.

When *Leith Athletic FC* moved here from *Chancelot Park* in 1904 the ground had been properly enclosed and a covered stand constructed on the east side. The former cricket club pavilion had also been retained but it is not known if it was still in use. Later improvements included the construction of embankments around the sides. The probable record gate was 15,000 at the Scottish FA Cup 1st Round tie between *Leith Athletic* and *Clyde* (0-1) on January 22nd, 1910.

The ground was finally vacated in 1926 and taken over by the adjacent *New Powderhall* for the installation of dog kennels on the north part of the pitch area. Today a supermarket occupies a large part of the site.

PLAYING RECORD OF ST BERNARDS
LEAGUE PROGRAMME

First Match; 0-0 v. Arbroath (800) (August 27th, 1921)
Last Match; 1-2 v. Broxburn United (-) (April 12th, 1924)
Highest & Lowest Gate*; Not Known
Highest Home Win; 6-0 v. Johnstone (-) (January 7th, 1922)
Highest Home Defeat; 1-5 v. Forfar Athletic (-) (September 24th, 1921)

No. of Matches Played by St Bernards; 57

The club moved here from the *Royal Gymnasium* ground in 1921 and during the club's stay here, the supporters purchased the *Royal Gymnasium* ground to restore it to football use. As it was not ready by the time that the lease at *Old Logie Green* ran out at the end of the 1923/24 season *St Bernards* moved to *Tynecastle* to groundshare for a short time with *Heart of Midlothian FC*.

*NB. There are very few gate figures recorded for *St Bernards FC's* occupancy of this venue.

PLAYING RECORD OF LEITH ATHLETIC
LEAGUE PROGRAMME
1ST PERIOD

First Match; 3-1 v. Hamilton Academical (-) (August 27th, 1904)
Last Match; 3-0 v. Albion Rovers (-) (February 20th, 1915)

2ND PERIOD

First Match; 2-1 v. Clackmannan (-) (August 23rd, 1924)
Last Match; 4-1 v. Johnstone (1,500) (April 17th, 1926)
Highest Gate*; 5,000 v. Raith Rovers (0-0) (February 5th, 1910)
Lowest Gate*; Not Known
Highest Home Win; 7-0 v. Albion Rovers (-) (January 21st, 1905)
Highest Home Defeat; 4-6 v. Ayr United (2,000) (August 27th, 1910), 1-4 v. Ayr United (-) (February 22nd, 1913)

No. of Matches Played by Leith Athletic; 156

The club moved here from *Chancelot Park* in 1904. The League fixtures in Division 2 were suspended for the duration of WWI and during this period when the club was out of the League it played some games at *Chancelot Park* and *Wardie Park* before returning for the start of the 1924/25 season when it joined the Scottish Football League Division 3.

The 1914/15 season Second Division Championship match v. *Cowdenbeath* was played at the neutral venue of *East End Park* and the game v. *St Bernards* at *Easter Road*. Leith Athletic FC left the League when Division 3 disbanded near the end of the 1925/26 season and moved next door to *New Powderhall*

*NB. This is the highest gate figure of the few that were recorded. In view of the general level of those that are known, it is very probable that there were crowds of less than 1,000 on occasions.

NEUTRAL PLAY OFF MATCHES

Division 2, 10th/11th Place; Raith Rovers 3, East Stirlingshire 2 (-) (May 11th, 1907)

No. of Matches Played; 1

A TOTAL OF 48 TEAMS TOOK PART IN 214 LEAGUE FIXTURES AT THIS VENUE

DIAGRAM SHOWING THE DISPOSITION OF NEW LOGIE GREEN, OLD LOGIE GREEN & NEW POWDERHALL

NEW POWDERHALL
HOME GROUND OF ST BERNARDS, LEITH ATHLETIC & EDINBURGH CITY

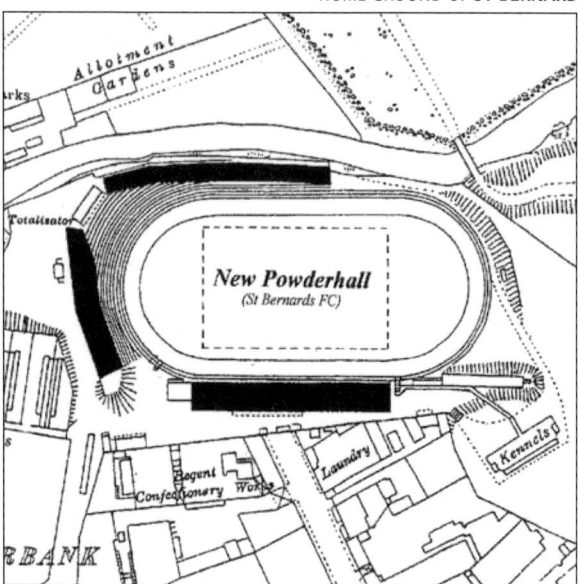

MAP EXTRACT; EDINBURGH 3.3 [1934]
SITE LOCATION; NT25607551

Located in the Heriothill district, north of Edinburgh city centre, it was sited immediately east of the *Heriot Cricket & Football Ground* (subsequently *Old Logie Green*) and first briefly used by *St Bernards FC* in 1889 but more permanently in 1900 when they moved here from *New Logie Green*.

It opened in c1871 and the facilities initially included a pavilion and open seated stands on the south and some banking around the pitch and oval running track. Although the venue saw considerable improvements in subsequent years with the installation of new covered stands on the south, north and west sides and provision of concrete terracing around the ground, the presence of the racing track meant that the width of the pitch was restricted to 50 yards.

The record attendance at a football match, of 6,000 was set at the Scottish FA Cup 2nd Round tie between *Edinburgh City* and *St Bernards* (2-3) on January 30th, 1932. The ground was last used by a senior club in 1934 when *Edinburgh City FC* moved to *Marine Gardens*. The stadium continued in use as a greyhound and speedway stadium until the area was redeveloped and Powderhall Road currently occupies part of the site.

PLAYING RECORD OF LEITH ATHLETIC
LEAGUE PROGRAMME
First Match; 4-1 v. King's Park (3,000) (August 13th, 1927)
Last Match & Highest Gate*; 2-1 v. Ayr United (3,500) (April 21st, 1928)
Lowest Gate*; 1,500 v. Bathgate (2-2) (September 10th, 1927)
Highest Home Win; 5-0 v. Armadale (-) (November 12th, 1927)
Highest Home Defeat; 3-4 v. Arthurlie (1,500) (October 8th, 1927)
No. of Matches Played by Leith Athletic; 18

The club moved here from *Old Logie Green* in 1926 and was elected into the Scottish Football League Division 2 in 1927. The playing surface was frequently waterlogged and the match v. *Alloa Athletic* on September 24th, 1927 was played at the *Royal Gymnasium Ground*. *New Powderhall* proved to be unsuitable and the club moved to *Marine Gardens* at the end of the season.

*NB. These are the highest and lowest gate figures of the few that were recorded. In view of the general level of those that are known, it is very probable that there were crowds of less than 1,500 on occasions.

PLAYING RECORD OF ST BERNARDS
LEAGUE PROGRAMME
Matches Played; 4-1 v. Port Glasgow Athletic (-) (September 1st, 1900)
3-1 v. Clyde (-) (September 8th, 1900)
2-0 v. Leith Athletic (-) (September 15th, 1900)
No. of Matches Played by St Bernards; 3

The club moved here from *New Logie Green* in 1900 and the stay at *New Powderhall* was brief as it clashed with athletics meetings and it is assumed that only the matches played in September took place here before the club made the permanent move to the *Royal Gymnasium* ground.

NB. There are no gate figures recorded for *St Bernards FC's* occupancy of this venue.

PLAYING RECORD OF EDINBURGH CITY
LEAGUE PROGRAMME
First Match; 2-3 v. Bo'ness (300) (August 15th, 1931)
Last Match; 2-2 v. Forfar Athletic (-) (April 21st, 1934)
Highest Gate*; 5,000 v. Hibernian (0-4) (October 15th, 1932)
Lowest Gate*; 200 v. Arbroath (0-7) (November 26th, 1932)
Highest Home Win; 4-1 v. Dunfermline Athletic (-) (April 30th, 1932)
Highest Home Defeat; 2-8 v. St Bernards (-) (December 26th, 1932). 0-7 v. East Fife (-) (September 12th, 1931) & v. Arbroath (200) (November 26th, 1932)
No. of Matches Played by Edinburgh City; 53

The club was elected into the Scottish Football League Division 2 in 1931. The pitch at this venue was very narrow and the stadium was not really suitable for football so in 1934 the club moved to *Marine Gardens* to groundshare with *Leith Athletic*.

*NB. Not many attendances are known and these are the highest and lowest gate figures of those that were recorded.

A TOTAL OF **31** TEAMS TOOK PART IN **74** LEAGUE FIXTURES AT THIS VENUE

New Powderhall in 1990 when it was still in use as the home venue of *Edinburgh Monarchs* Speedway team, as well as for Greyhound Racing. This view looks eastwards and shows the main stand, on the south side of the arena. The site was sold for redevelopment in 1995
Photograph Courtesy of Dave Twydell

NORTH END PARK
HOME GROUND OF COWDENBEATH

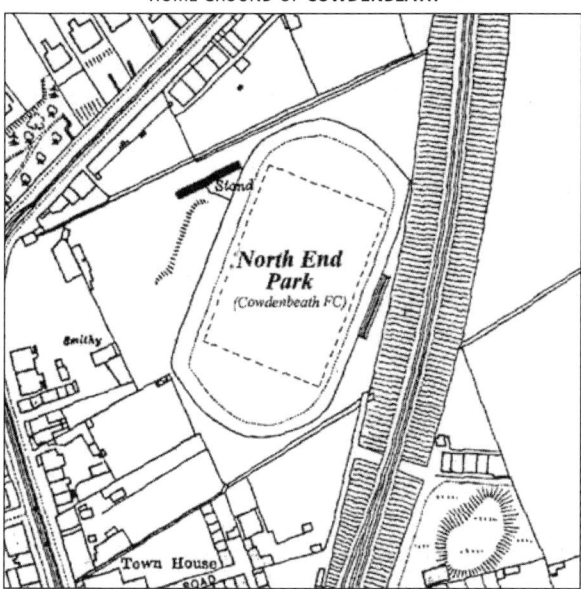

MAP EXTRACT; FIFE 34.12 [1915]
SITE LOCATION; NT16599110

North End Park, also called the *Colliers Den*, was, as the name would suggest, located to the north of the town centre. *Cowdenbeath FC* moved here in 1888 from *Jubilee Park*. Initially the pitch was orientated west to east with a stand along the north side but, to accommodate whippet racing, it was subsequently moved to facilitate the installation of an oval track around the pitch.

By 1914 the facilities included the original stand on the north west side and an open seated stand on the south east. After *Cowdenbeath FC* moved to *Central Park* in 1917, the ground was abandoned and the site is now used as a playing field.

PLAYING RECORD OF COWDENBEATH
LEAGUE PROGRAMME
First Match; 1-0 v. Leith Athletic (-) (August 19th, 1905)
Last Match; 2-1 v. Clydebank (-) (February 20th, 1915)
Highest Gate & Lowest Gate*; Not Known
Highest Home Win; 7-0 v. Dundee Hibernian (3,000)
(March 14th, 1914)
Highest Home Defeat; 2-5 v. Arthurlie (-) (March 9th, 1907)
No. of Matches Played by Cowdenbeath; 114
Information Kindly Supplied by; David Allan

The club was elected into the Scottish Football League Division 2 in 1905 and moved to *Central Park* in 1921. The 1914/15 season Second Division Championship match v. *Leith Athletic* was played at the neutral venue of *East End Park* and the game v. *St Bernards* at *Easter Road*.

*NB. Very few gate figures are known for this club at this venue but it is assumed that in general attendances ranged from a few thousand to a few hundred.

A TOTAL OF 22 TEAMS TOOK PART IN 114 LEAGUE FIXTURES AT THIS VENUE

OCHILVIEW PARK
HOME GROUND OF STENHOUSEMUIR
TEMPORARY HOME GROUND FOR MEADOWBANK THISTLE, STIRLING ALBION, BERWICK RANGERS & FALKIRK

MAP EXTRACT; STIRLINGSHIRE N24.10 [1915]
SITE LOCATION; NS87008320

Stenhousemuir FC moved to *Ochilview Park* in 1890 and the only facility prior to entry to the Scottish Football League in 1921 would appear to have been a small pavilion on the north side. A small stand was subsequently built on the north side (replaced in 1928 following a fire) and a cover erected on the terracing opposite

The record attendance of 12,500 was set at the Scottish FA Cup 4th Round tie v. *East Fife* (0-3) on March 11th, 1950 and in 1998 the stand was demolished and a new 710 seat stand constructed on the south side. *Falkirk FC* moved in for the 2003/4 season whilst *The Falkirk Stadium* was being completed and to accommodate First Division fixtures improvements to the ground were undertaken by the new temporary tenants. These included the concreting and covering of the terraces at the west end and installation of a temporary seated stand on the north side and a covered 1,068 seat stand at the east end as well as general improvements to the turnstiles and car park. This raised the overall capacity from 2,010 to 5,267 with 2,117 seats and the pitch size was 110 x 72 yards. For the 2004/5 season the capacity reverted to 2,654 with 628 seats.

PLAYING RECORD OF BERWICK RANGERS
LEAGUE PROGRAMME
Match Played; 1-4 v. East Fife (300) (May 2nd, 1992)
No. of Matches Played by Berwick Rangers; 1
Information Kindly Supplied by; Robin Murdie

The match was played here due to the unserviceable state of the roof on the main stand at *Shielfield Park*.

PLAYING RECORD OF MEADOWBANK THISTLE
LEAGUE PROGRAMME
Match Played; 1-0 v. Stranraer (300) (August 16th, 1986)
No. of Matches Played by Meadowbank Thistle; 1
Information Kindly Supplied by; Allan Grieve

This match was played here due to the non-availability of *Meadowbank Stadium*.

Cont ...

OCHILVIEW PARK [CONT ...]

PLAYING RECORD OF STENHOUSEMUIR
LEAGUE PROGRAMME

First Match; 0-1 v. Vale of Leven (-) (September 10th, 1921)
Highest Gate*; 12,000 v. Motherwell (1-6) (September 21st, 1968)
Lowest Gate*; 293 v. Forfar Athletic (2-1) (October 19th, 2002)
Highest Home Win; 9-2 v. Dundee United (-) (April 16th, 1937)
Highest Home Defeat; 0-8 v. Clyde (-) (March 1st, 1952)
No. of Matches Played by Stenhousemuir; 1,400
(Including one expunged match v. Bathgate on September 15th, 1928)
Information Kindly Supplied by; Sandy Reid

The club was elected into the Scottish Football League Division 2 in 1921. The fixture v. *Hamilton Academical* on April 1st, 2000 was not played due to a players strike at *Hamilton* and on April 20th, 2000 the Scottish League deducted 15 points from *Hamilton's* total. This had the effect of dropping *Hamilton Academical* to bottom place, relegating them, and pushing *Stenhousemuir* up one place and out of the final relegation zone.

*NB. Details of attendances prior to 1968 are not officially held by the club and it is thought that the lowest gate may have occurred either prior to WWII or during a period in the 1960s when the club withheld some attendance figures. Similarly the highest known gate of 12,000 was established when the ground was filled to capacity for the game v. *Motherwell*.

PLAYING RECORD OF STIRLING ALBION
LEAGUE PROGRAMME

Matches Played; 2-1 v. Cowdenbeath (485) (August 8th, 1992)
0-2 v. Hamilton Academical (644) (August 22nd, 1992)
0-5 v. Dunfermline Athletic (1,481) (September 5th, 1992)
0-1 v. Kilmarnock (1,326) (September 12th, 1992)
1-1 v. Greenock Morton (750) (September 26th, 1992)
1-2 v. Dumbarton (475) (October 10th, 1992)
0-1 v. St Mirren (1,073) (October 31st, 1992)
4-1 v. Meadowbank Thistle (447) (November 7th, 1992)
0-1 v. Clydebank (396)(November 21st, 1992)
0-0 v. Ayr United (344) (December 1st, 1992)
0-3 v. Raith Rovers (1,251) (December 29th, 1992)
0-0 v. Hamilton Academical (779) (January 1st, 1993)
1-2 v. Dunfermline Athletic (1,023) (February 9th, 1993)
2-1 v. Cowdenbeath (353) (February 16th, 1993)
0-2 v. Greenock Morton (422) (February 20th, 1993)
2-0 v. Kilmarnock (1,327) (March 6th, 1993)
1-0 v. Dumbarton (418) (March 9th, 1993)
2-2 v. Meadowbank Thistle (475) (March 27th, 1993)
2-1 v. St Mirren (1,029) (April 10th, 1993)
No. of Matches Played by Stirling Albion; 19
Information Kindly Supplied by; Allan Grieve

In 1992 the club moved here and groundshared with *Stenhousemuir* until **Forthbank Stadium** was ready in April 1993.

PLAYING RECORD OF FALKIRK
LEAGUE PROGRAMME

Matches Played; 2-1 v. Inverness Caledonian Thistle (2,596) (August 9th, 2003)
0-0 v. Queen of the South (3,064) (August 23rd, 2003)
0-2 v. Ross County (2,970) (September 13th, 2003)
0-3 v. St Johnstone (3,887) (September 27th, 2003)
3-0 v. Brechin City (2,442) (October 18th, 2003)
0-1 v. Ayr United (2,609) (October 25th, 2003)
3-2 v. Raith Rovers (3,237) (November 14th, 2003)
0-2 v. Clyde (2,898) (November 29th, 2003)
0-0 v. St Mirren (2,581) (December 13th, 2003)
2-0 v. Ross County (2,482) (January 17th, 2004)
5-0 v. Brechin City (2,060) (February 21st, 2004)
2-1 v. Inverness Caledonian Thistle (2,268) (March 2nd, 2004)
0-1 v. St Johnstone (2,786) (March 9th, 2004)
0-2 v. Queen of the South (2,908) (March 13th, 2004)
1-0 v. Raith Rovers (2,386) (March 27th, 2004)
1-1 v. Clyde (2,676) (April 10th, 2004)
1-0 v. St Mirren (2,386) (April 24th, 2004)
0-0 v. Ayr United (2,077) (May 8th, 2004)
No. of Matches Played by Falkirk; 18

At the end of the 2002/3 season *Falkirk FC* moved here from **Brockville Park** to groundshare with *Stenhousemuir FC* for one season whilst *The Falkirk Stadium* was being built.

AT THE END OF SEASON 2004/5, A TOTAL OF **58** TEAMS HAD TAKEN PART IN **1,439** LEAGUE FIXTURES AT THIS VENUE

This programme cover shows the main stand at **Ochilview Park**.
Programme Courtesy of John Litster

OLD RALSTON PARK & NEW RALSTON PARK

HOME GROUNDS OF ABERCORN

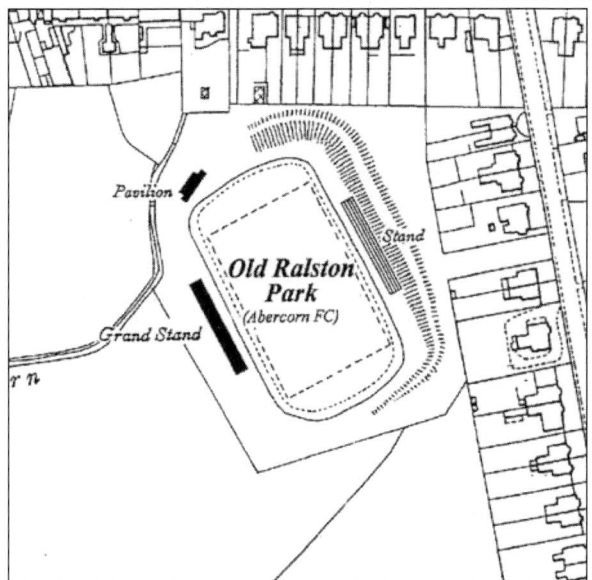

MAP EXTRACT; GROUND AS IN **1909** DRAWN FROM PLANS AND SUPERIMPOSED ON RENFREWSHIRE 12.3 [1911]
SITE LOCATION; NS49746400

The existence of this ground falls between two 25in Ordnance Surveys and part of the site is shown on the 6in Scale map of 1909. Although detailed diagrams of the two wooden stands and the pavilion are still in existence no plan of *Old Ralston Park* is available and the disposition of the stands and orientation of the pitch has been assumed, based upon the remnants of the embankments around the pitch as shown on the map of 1911. The two stands were both approximately 140ft in length with one being covered and the other open. The pavilion, which had been brought from *Underwood Park*, was located in the north west corner of the site and continued in use when *Abercorn FC* moved to *New Ralston Park*, just to the west, in 1909.

The probable record attendance of 5,000 was set at the Scottish FA Qualifying Cup Semi-Final tie v. *Third Lanark* (0-1) on February 9th, 1901 and the site was subsequently exploited for its clay deposits by the adjacent brick works. Today it is occupied by a car park.

PLAYING RECORD OF ABERCORN
LEAGUE PROGRAMME

First Match; 3-0 v. Leith Athletic (-) (August 26th, 1899)
Last Match; 4-0 v. Ayr Parkhouse (-) (March 20th, 1909)
Highest Gate*; 4,000 v. Port Glasgow Athletic (2-0)
(September 16th, 1899)
Highest Home Defeat & Lowest Gate*; 100 v. Clyde (0-6) (May 6th, 1903)
Highest Home Win; 7-3 v. Raith Rovers (-) (October 24th, 1903).
6-0 v. Cowdenbeath (-) (December 19th, 1908)
No. of Matches Played by Abercorn; 106
Some Information Kindly Supplied by; Dominic McKenzie

The club moved here from *Underwood Park* in 1899 and moved to *New Ralston Park* in 1909.
*NB. Not all attendances are known and these are the highest and lowest gate figures of those that were recorded.

A TOTAL OF **22** TEAMS TOOK PART IN **106** LEAGUE FIXTURES AT THIS VENUE

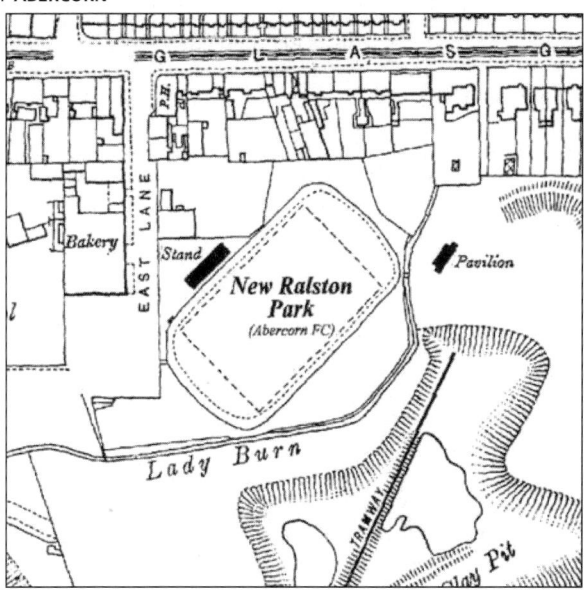

MAP EXTRACT; RENFREWSHIRE 12.3 [**1911**]
SITE LOCATION; NS49616401

The ground was located just to the west of *Old Ralston Park*, on the other side of the Lady Burn, and occupied a cramped site. The facilities included a 520 capacity wooden grandstand, on the north west side of the pitch, and the old pavilion which still remained *in situ* at the former ground.

The record attendance of 7,000 was set at the Scottish Qualifying Cup Semi-Final tie v. *Nithsdale Wanderers* (1-0) on November 30th, 1912 and *Abercorn FC* remained at *New Ralston Park* until the club folded in 1920. The site was later occupied by a Skating Rink and is currently incorporated into a car park.

PLAYING RECORD OF ABERCORN
LEAGUE PROGRAMME

First Match; 2-1 v. Ayr Parkhouse (2,000)
(September 11th, 1909)
Last Match; 1-1 v. Leith Athletic (-) (March 6th, 1915)
Highest & Lowest Gate*; Not Known
Highest Home Win; 5-2 v. Dumbarton (-) (February 12th, 1910)
Highest Home Defeat; 1-6 v. Dunfermline Athletic (-)
(February 7th, 1914)
No. of Matches Played by Abercorn; 70

The club moved here from *Old Ralston Park* in 1909. The Scottish Football League suspended Division 2 fixtures for the duration of WWI and the club folded in 1920.
*NB. Very few gate figures are known for this club at this venue but it is assumed that in general attendances ranged from a few thousand to a few hundred.

A TOTAL OF **20** TEAMS TOOK PART IN **70** LEAGUE FIXTURES AT THIS VENUE

PALMERSTON PARK
HOME GROUND OF **QUEEN OF THE SOUTH**

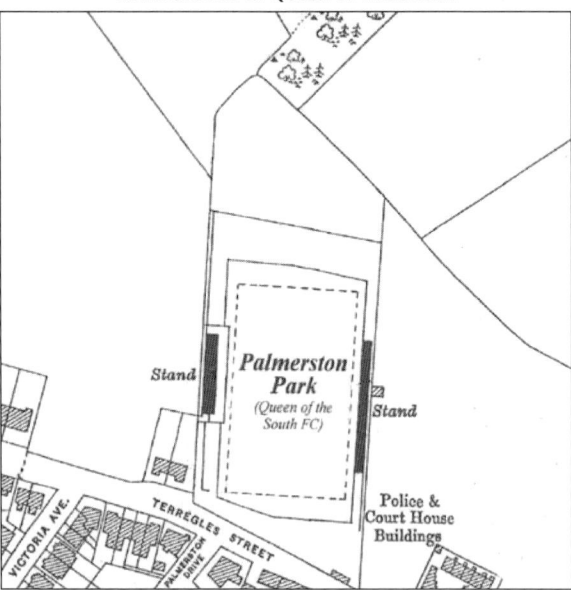

MAP EXTRACT; DUMFRIES-SHIRE 49.14 [**1931**]
SITE LOCATION; **NX96357630**

Located in Maxwelltown, on the opposite side of the River Nith to Dumfries, *Queen of the South FC* moved to *Palmerston Park* on their formation in 1919. At first the only facility was a small covered stand erected along the west side but in the 1930s this was enlarged and a cover constructed on the east side. Post war improvements included the installation of a cover over the north end and, following a fire in 1964, the construction of a replacement main stand.

The record attendance of 26,552 was established at the Scottish FA Cup 3rd Round tie v. *Heart of Midlothian* (1-3) on February 23rd, 1952 and, following the building of a new seated stand on the east side in 1995, the ground capacity was, at the start of the 2004/5 season set at 6,412 with 3,509 seats. The pitch size was 112 x 73 yards.

PLAYING RECORD OF QUEEN OF THE SOUTH
LEAGUE PROGRAMME

First Match; 2-0 v. Dykehead (4,000) (August 18th, 1923)
Highest Gate; 21,300 v. Rangers (0-3) (November 8th, 1947)
Lowest Gate; 300 v. Alloa Athletic (1-0) (May 4th, 1974)
& v. Stirling Albion (3-2) (May 2nd, 1979)
Highest Home Win; 10-0 v. Bo'ness (3,800) (October 1st, 1932)
[Record Expunged]. 8-0 v Galston (-) (March 21st, 1925)
Highest Home Defeat; 0-7 v. Alloa Athletic (453) (May 15th, 1993)
& v. Stirling Albion (1,394) (April 13th, 1996)
No. of Matches Played by Queen of the South; 1,312
(Including expunged matches v. Dumbarton Harp on August 30th, 1924,
v. Bathgate on August 18th, 1928 & v. Bo'ness on October 1st, 1932)
Information Kindly Supplied by; Ian Black

The club was a founder member of the Scottish Football League Division 3 in 1923.

AT THE END OF SEASON 2004/5, A TOTAL OF **67** TEAMS HAD TAKEN PART IN **1,312** LEAGUE FIXTURES AT THIS VENUE

PARKSIDE
HOME GROUND OF **DYKEHEAD**

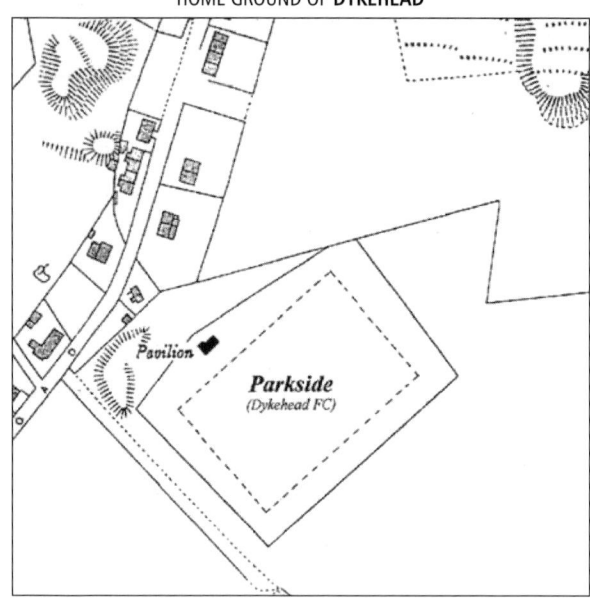

MAP EXTRACT; LANARKSHIRE 13.6 [**1939**]
SITE LOCATION; **NS86705955**

The ground was on the east side of Rosehall Road, south west of Shotts town centre and when *Dykehead FC* moved in prior to their entry into the Scottish League in 1923 the only facility was a pavilion on the north side of the pitch. The probable record attendance of 4,000 was set at the Scottish FA Cup 1st Round Replay v. *Albion Rovers* (1-2) on January 31st, 1920.

After *Dykehead* folded in 1928 the ground remained in use for football and was left in perpetuity to the YMCA who continue to make use of the venue today.

PLAYING RECORD OF DYKEHEAD
LEAGUE PROGRAMME

First Match; 3-1 v. Galston (-) (August 25th, 1923)
Last Match; 2-2 v. Solway Star (-) (April 10th, 1926)
Highest & Lowest Gate*; Not Known
Highest Home Win; 8-2 v. Royal Albert (-) (February 13th, 1926)
Highest Home Defeat; 0-2 v. Leith Athletic (-) (December 6th, 1924)
No. of Matches Played by Dykehead; 44
(Including one expunged match v. Dumbarton Harp on January 5th, 1925)

The club was a founder member of the Scottish Football League Division 3 in 1923 and left the League when Division 3 was disbanded near the end of the 1925/26 season. The home matches v. *Brechin City* in Season 1924/25 and v. *Galston* in 1925/26 were not played.

*NB. There are no League gate figures recorded for *Dykehead FC's* occupancy of this venue.

A TOTAL OF **21** TEAMS TOOK PART IN **44** LEAGUE FIXTURES AT THIS VENUE

PITTODRIE PARK

HOME GROUND OF **ABERDEEN**
TEMPORARY HOME GROUND FOR **PARTICK THISTLE** & **INVERNESS CALEDONIAN THISTLE**

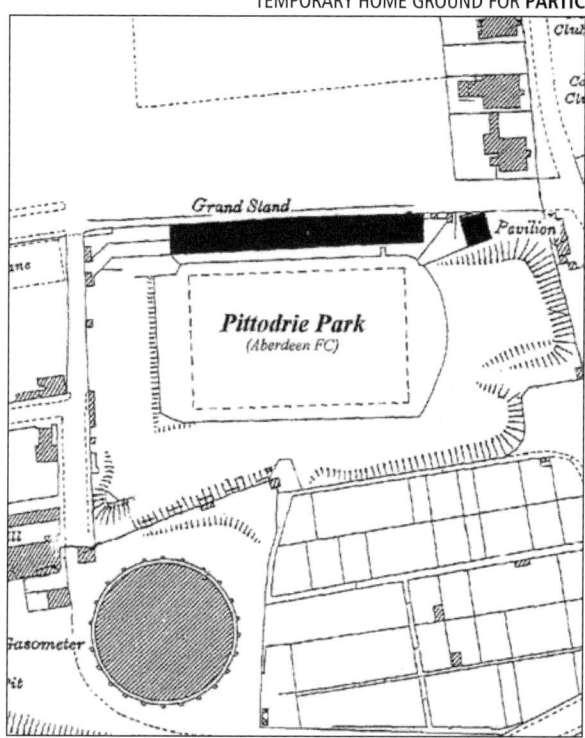

MAP EXTRACT; ABERDEENSHIRE 75.7 [1920]
SITE LOCATION; **NJ94740761**

PLAYING RECORD OF PARTICK THISTLE
LEAGUE PROGRAMME
Match Played; 0-1 v. Aberdeen (4,508) (January 9th, 1909)
No. of Matches Played by Partick Thistle; 1
Information Kindly Supplied by; Robert Reid & Paul Third
This match was played here as *Firhill Park* was not ready following the closure of *Meadowside* in 1908

PLAYING RECORD OF ABERDEEN
LEAGUE PROGRAMME
First Match; 1-2 v. Falkirk (5,924) (August 20th, 1904)
Highest Gate; 44,414 v. Rangers (1-1) (April 3rd, 1948)
Lowest Gate; 896 v. Hamilton Academical (1-2) (December 8th, 1904)
Highest Home Win; 10-0 v. Raith Rovers (9,012) (October 13th, 1962)
Highest Home Defeat; 0-6 v. Celtic (16,532) (December 11th, 1999)
PLAY OFF MATCHES
3-1 v. Dunfermline Athletic (21,012) (May 21st, 1995)
No. of Matches Played by Aberdeen; 1,644
(League Programme; 1,643, Play Off Matches; 1)
Information Kindly Supplied by; Paul Third
The club was elected into the Scottish Football League Division 2 in 1904.

PLAYING RECORD OF INVERNESS CALEDONIAN THISTLE
LEAGUE PROGRAMME
Matches Played; 2-0 v. Dunfermline Athletic (1,972) (August 15th, 2004)
1-3 v. Celtic (8,736) (August 22nd, 2004)
1-2 v. Hibernian (2,011) (September 11th, 2004)
1-1 v. Motherwell (1,117) (October 3rd, 2004)
1-3 v. Aberdeen (9,530) (October 16th, 2004)
2-1 v. Dundee (1,254) (October 27th, 2004)
2-0 v. Livingston (1,279) (October 30th, 2004)
1-1 v. Dundee United (1,125) (November 23rd, 2004)
1-1 v. Rangers (6,543) (December 5th, 2004)
1-1 v. Heart of Midlothian (2,011) (December 11th, 2004)
0-2 v. Kilmarnock (1,346) (January 3rd, 2005)
No. of Matches Played by Inverness Caledonian Thistle; 11

Following the winning of the Division 1 Championship in 2004 *Inverness Caledonian Thistle FC* was only allowed to play in the Premier League provided it moved to a ground that met the criteria and switched to *Pittodrie Park* for the start of the 2004/5 season whilst the **Caledonian Stadium** was upgraded.

AT THE END OF SEASON 2004/5, A TOTAL OF **42** TEAMS HAD TAKEN PART IN **1,656** LEAGUE FIXTURES AT THIS VENUE

Sited on a redundant dung heap, *Aberdeen FC* moved into *Pittodrie Park* in 1899. The facilities at this time are not known but it was quite well appointed as it hosted the *Scotland* v. *Wales* international match in 1900. Following the amalgamation of *Aberdeen*, *Orion* and *Victoria FCs* in 1903, *Orion FC's* grandstand was moved from their *Cattofield Ground* and re-erected on the north side of *Pittodrie Park*. Within a few years the ground was purchased for £5,668 and improved with the installation of a pavilion, also on the north side, and extensions to the banking.

The 1920s saw considerable activity with the replacement of the old grandstand with a new main stand, the provision of a new covered stand on the south side, covering at the west end and the installation of what was believed to be the first "dug-outs".

The record attendance at the ground of 45,061 was set at the Scottish FA Cup 4th Round tie v. *Heart of Midlothian* (3-0) on March 13th, 1954 and subsequent improvements over the next decade included the installation of cover over the east end, the demolition of the pavilion and extension of the main stand to a 6,000 seater and the installation of 1,400 seats in the main paddock.

After the main stand was rebuilt, following damage by an explosion and fire on February 6th, 1971, the ground was gradually converted into an all-seater stadium with installation of seats at the west and east ends and on the, by now, uncovered south side giving a capacity in 1978 of 24,000. Further improvements included the provision of a cantilever roof over the south side, renewal of the covering at the west end and, in 1993, construction of a new stand at the east end. The all-seat capacity at the start of season 2004/5 was 22,199 and the pitch size 109 x 71 yards.

PORTLAND PARK
HOME GROUND OF GALSTON

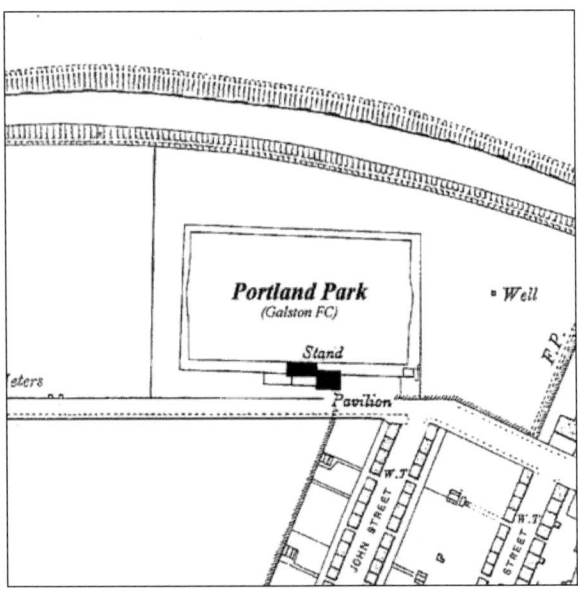

MAP EXTRACT; AYRSHIRE 18.16 [**1910**]
SITE LOCATION; **NS49583697**

Sandwiched between the River Irvine and Titchfield Street, north of the town centre, *Portland Park* was in use by *Galston FC* when they joined the Scottish League in 1923. The facilities included a covered stand and pavilion on the south side of the pitch.

The club resigned from the League in 1926 and re-formed in the same year and the record attendance at the ground was set at 4,211 for the Scottish FA Cup 1st Round match v. *Kilmarnock* (0-1) on January 26th, 1935. *Galston* folded in 1940 and the site of *Portland Park* was later used for part of the A71 by-pass road.

PLAYING RECORD OF GALSTON
LEAGUE PROGRAMME
First Match; 2-0 v. Solway Star (-) (August 18th, 1923)
Last Match, Highest Home Win & Lowest Gate*;
8-2 v. Johnstone (300) (January 9th, 1926)[Result Expunged]
Highest Gate*; Not Known
Highest Home Defeat; 1-5 v. Royal Albert (-) (August 25th, 1925)
No. of Matches Played by Galston; 38
(Including expunged matches v. Dumbarton Harp on August 16th, 1924, and 8 home games in Season 1925/26)

The club was a founder member of the Scottish Football League Division 3 in 1923. The home match v. *Arthurlie* on March 22nd, 1924 was played at **Bellsdale Park**. *Galston FC* resigned from the League in February 1926 and the results for that season were expunged.
*NB. Very few gate figures are known for this club but it is assumed that in general attendances numbered only a few hundred.

A TOTAL OF **19** TEAMS TOOK PART IN **38** LEAGUE FIXTURES AT THIS VENUE

RAPLOCH PARK
HOME GROUND OF ROYAL ALBERT

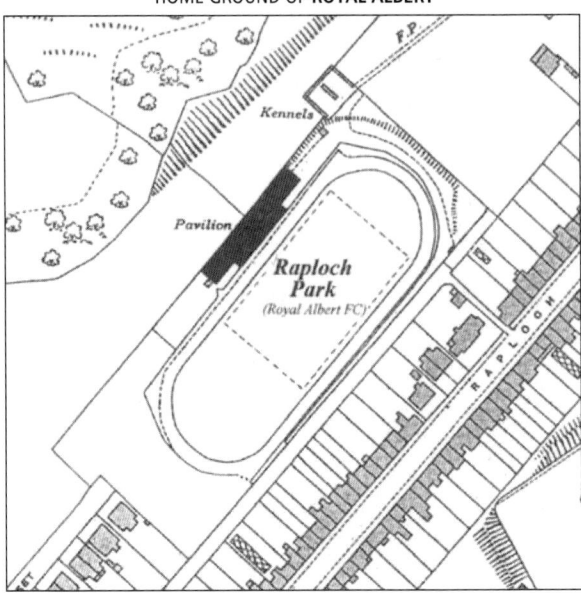

MAP EXTRACT; LANARKSHIRE 18.10 [**1940**]
SITE LOCATION; **NS75805135**

The ground, sited on the west side of Raploch Street, west of Larkhall town centre, was used by *Royal Albert FC* from its formation in the 1870s. Details of the facilities at this time are not known but from the outset an oval running track surrounded the pitch. The ground saw some improvements over the years, a pavilion and covered stand were built on the west side and the oval track lengthened at the south end to accommodate greyhound racing.

The probable record attendance of 5,000 was recorded at the Scottish FA Cup 5th Round Replay v. *Celtic* (0-4) on December 6th, 1890, at the Scottish FA Cup 2nd Round tie v. *Dundee* (0-1) on February 11th, 1922 and at the Scottish FA Cup 1st Round Replay v. *Clydebank* (0-0) on January 17th, 1923. *Royal Albert FC* folded in 1928 but the ground continued in use as *Raploch Sports Stadium,* a multi-purpose venue until it was demolished in the 1960s and redeveloped with housing.

PLAYING RECORD OF ROYAL ALBERT
LEAGUE PROGRAMME
First Match; 3-0 v. Dumbarton Harp (-) (August 18th, 1923)
Last Match; 3-0 v. Montrose (-) (April 16th, 1926)
Highest & Lowest Gate*; Not Known
Highest Home Win; 7-0 v. Dykehead (-) (December 13th, 1924)
Highest Home Defeat; 1-5 v. Brechin City (-) (February 14th, 1925)
No. of Matches Played by Royal Albert; 44

The club was a founder member of the Scottish Football League Division 3 in 1923 and left the League when Division 3 was disbanded near the end of the 1925/26 season. The home matches v. *Dumbarton Harp* in 1924/25 and *Beith* in 1925/26 seasons were not played.
*NB. There are no League gate figures recorded for *Royal Albert FC's* occupancy of this venue.

A TOTAL OF **21** TEAMS TOOK PART IN **44** LEAGUE FIXTURES AT THIS VENUE

RECREATION GROUND
HOME GROUND OF ST JOHNSTONE

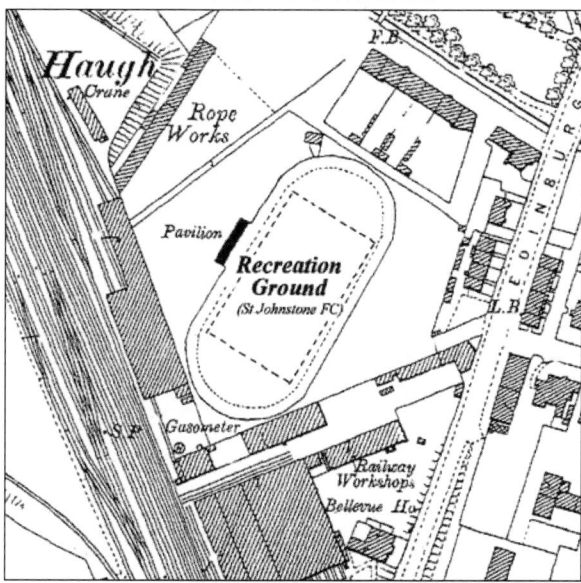

MAP EXTRACT; PERTHSHIRE 98.9 [1901]
SITE LOCATION; NO11572244

Located in Craigie Haugh and on the east side of the Scottish Central Railway Workshops, *St Johnstone FC* moved here from *South Inch* in 1885. The facilities included a pavilion on the west side and by employing the normal practice at the time of including an oval running track this meant that the pitch itself had to be quite narrow to be accommodated within the restricted site.

Following their promotion in 1924, *St Johnstone* moved out to **Muirton Park** and the site was subsequently utilized for commercial buildings and a filling station.

PLAYING RECORD OF ST JOHNSTONE
LEAGUE PROGRAMME

First Match; 4-1 v. Arthurlie (-) (August 19th, 1911)
Last Match; 4-2 v. Kilmarnock (6,000) (December 13th, 1924)
Highest Gate*; 11,154 v. Clydebank (1-0) (April 14th, 1923)
Lowest Gate*; Not Known
Highest Home Win; 6-0 v. Arthurlie (-) (November 8th, 1913)
& v. Lochgelly United (-) (January 19th, 1924)
Highest Home Defeat; 0-4 v. Cowdenbeath (10,000)
(January 5th, 1924)

No. of Matches Played by St Johnstone; 115
Information Kindly Supplied by; Alastair Blair

The club was elected into the Scottish Football League Division 2 in 1911 and *St Johnstone FC* moved to **Muirton Park** in 1924.
*NB. This is the highest gate figure of the very few that were recorded. In view of the general level of those that are known, it is very probable that there were crowds of less than 1,000 on occasions.

A TOTAL OF **28** TEAMS TOOK PART IN **115** LEAGUE FIXTURES AT THIS VENUE

RECREATION PARK
HOME GROUND OF LOCHGELLY UNITED

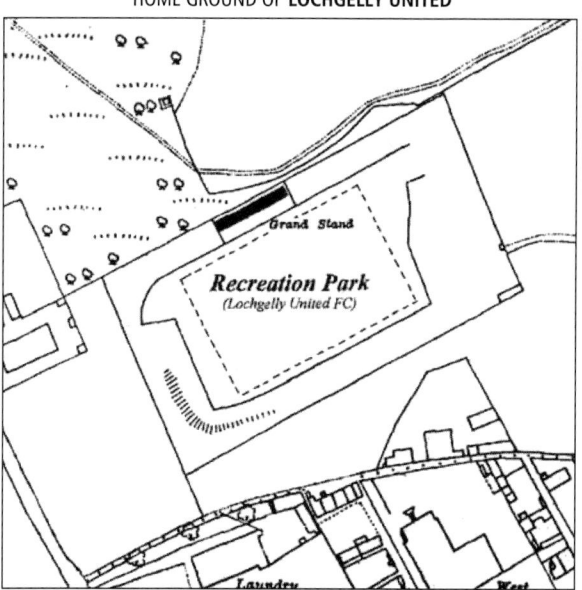

MAP EXTRACT; FIFE 34.8 [1915]
SITE LOCATION; NT18359355

Leased from the Lochgelly Recreation Company, *Lochgelly United FC* moved to *Recreation Park* in 1910. It was located on the north side of the town with a 120 x 80 yards pitch and the facilities eventually included a grandstand on the north side of the ground (possibly removed from their former ground at *Reid's Park*). Apart from some banking in the south west corner there were only flat areas to accommodate standing spectators.

The capacity of the ground was estimated to be about 15,000 and the record attendance of 10,000 was established at the Scottish FA Cup 3rd Round match v. *Third Lanark* (0-3) on February 21st, 1920. Although *Lochgelly United* folded in 1928 the ground remained in use until the site, with the exception of the extreme west end which is an open grassed area, was redeveloped with housing in 1934.

PLAYING RECORD OF LOCHGELLY UNITED
LEAGUE PROGRAMME

First Match; 0-4 v. Cowdenbeath (2,500) (August 15th, 1914)
Last Match; 1-1 v. Solway Star (-) (April 24th, 1926)
Highest & Lowest Gate*; Not Known
Highest Home Win; 7-2 v. Brechin City (-) (January 9th, 1926)
6-0 v. Johnstone (-) (April 17th, 1915), v. Dumbarton Harp (-)
(October 4th, 1924), v. Galston (-) (March 7th, 1925)
& v. Royal Albert (-) (February 20th, 1926)
Highest Home Defeat; 3-8 v. King's Park (-)
(February 16th, 1924)

No. of Matches Played by Lochgelly United; 101
(Including one expunged match v. Dumbarton Harp on October 4th, 1924)

The club was elected into the Scottish Football League Division 2 in 1914 and left the League when Division 3 was disbanded near the end of the 1925/26 season.
*NB. Very few gate figures are known for this club but it is assumed that in general attendances numbered only a few hundred.

A TOTAL OF **40** TEAMS TOOK PART IN **101** LEAGUE FIXTURES AT THIS VENUE

RECREATION PARK

HOME GROUND OF ALLOA ATHLETIC
TEMPORARY HOME GROUND FOR CLACKMANNAN, STIRLING ALBION & BERWICK RANGERS

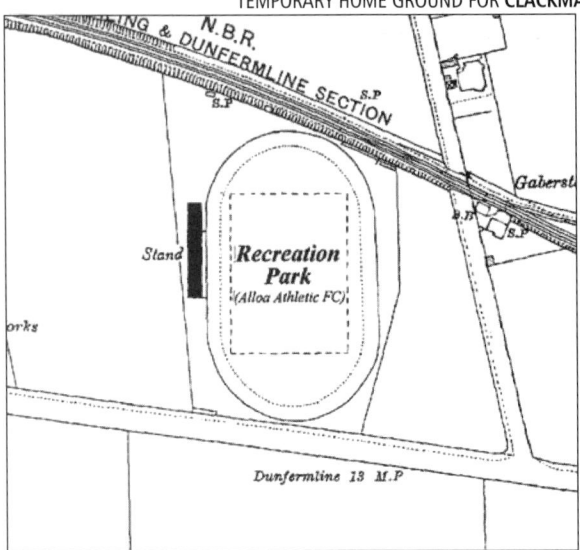

MAP EXTRACT; CLACKMANNANSHIRE 139.4 [1922]
SITE LOCATION; **NS89529299**

Alloa Athletic FC moved here from *Bellevue Park* in 1895. Details of the original facilities are not known, but when they won promotion in 1922 a new main stand was built on the west side of the oval running track enclosing the pitch. Standing accommodation was provided by cinder banks and a limited amount of terracing around the remainder of the ground with the east side receiving some cover in 1950.

The record attendance of 15,467 was set for a Scottish FA Cup 5th Round tie v. *Celtic* (2-4) on February 2nd, 1955. The main stand was replaced in 1991 and the capacity at the start of the 2004/5 season was 3,100 with 400 seats. The pitch size was 110 x 75 yards.

PLAYING RECORD OF BERWICK RANGERS
LEAGUE PROGRAMME
Match Played; 0-1 v. Stenhousemuir (120) (April 4th, 1992)
No. of Matches Played by Berwick Rangers; 1
Information Kindly Supplied by; Robin Murdie

The match was played here due to the unserviceable state of the roof on the main stand at *Shielfield Park*.

PLAYING RECORD OF ALLOA ATHLETIC
LEAGUE PROGRAMME
First Match; 1-0 v. Stenhousemuir (4,000) (August 20th, 1921)
Highest Gate*; 10,783 v. Celtic (2-3) (August 19th, 1922)
Lowest Gate*; 260 v. Stranraer (4-1) (April 16th, 1968)
Highest Home Win; 9-2 v. Forfar Athletic (-) (March 18th, 1933)
Highest Home Defeat; 0-10 v. Dundee (3,700) (March 8th, 1947)
No. of Matches Played by Alloa Athletic; 1,401
(Including expunged matches v. Bathgate on September 1st, 1928 and v. Armadale on August 23rd, 1932)
Some Information Kindly Supplied by; John Glencross

The club was elected into the Scottish Football League Division 2 in 1921. The 0-10 defeat v. *Dundee* on March 8th, 1947 was the first ever double-figure away win in Scottish League history.

*NB. Not all attendances are known and these are the highest and lowest gate figures of those that were recorded.

PLAYING RECORD OF CLACKMANNAN
LEAGUE PROGRAMME
Match Played; 2-1 v. Brechin City (-) (November 15th, 1925)
No. of Matches Played by Clackmannan; 1

This match was played here after *Chapelhill Park* was closed for two weeks following crowd trouble at the Scottish FA Cup 2nd re-play match against *Peebles Rovers* at Cowdenbeath FC's *Central Park*.

PLAYING RECORD OF STIRLING ALBION
LEAGUE PROGRAMME
Match Played; 1-1 v. East Fife (11,000) (January 14th, 1950)
No. of Matches Played by Stirling Albion; 1
Information Kindly Supplied by; Allan Grieve

This match took place here due to the pitch at *Annfield Park* being unplayable.

AT THE END OF SEASON 2004/5, A TOTAL OF **59** TEAMS HAD TAKEN PART IN **1,404** LEAGUE FIXTURES AT THIS VENUE

All hands to the pumps! A goalmouth scramble in an *Alloa Athletic* v. *Hamilton Academical* match at **Recreation Park**. This view shows the north end of the venue. *Courtesy of John Glencross*

ROYAL GYMNASIUM GROUND

HOME GROUND OF **ST BERNARDS**
TEMPORARY HOME GROUND FOR **LEITH ATHLETIC**

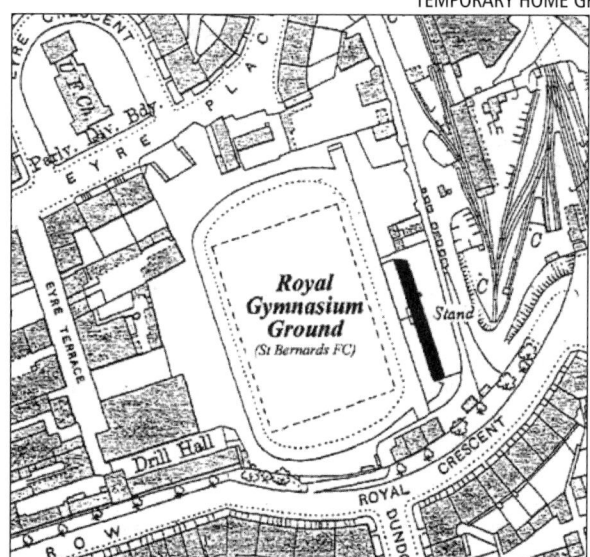

MAP EXTRACT; EDINBURGH 3.3 [**1908**]
SITE LOCATION; NT25347478

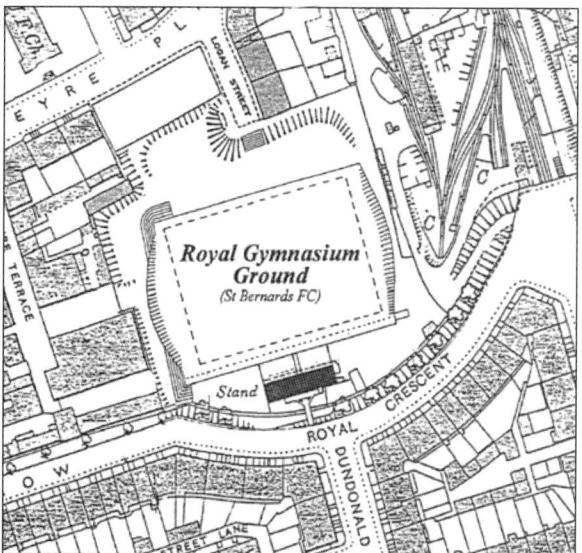

MAP EXTRACT; GROUND AS IN **1931** DRAWN FROM PLANS AND SUPERIMPOSED ON EDINBURGH 3.3 [**1908**]

Located just north of Edinburgh city centre, when *St Bernards FC* first moved here in 1880 the ground comprised of just a football pitch with no other facilities and when they returned in 1901 the whole site was derelict. The club built a new ground with a north to south orientated pitch and a covered seated stand and paddock on the east side. After the outbreak of WWI the military authorities took over the ground in 1916 and, following its use as a heavy transport depot, completely wrecked the pitch and drainage system, rendering the venue unusable. *St Bernards* were forced to seek new accommodation at *Old Logie Green*.

PLAYING RECORD OF ST BERNARDS
LEAGUE PROGRAMME

First Match; 3-3 v. Hamilton Academical (-) (November 3rd, 1900)
Last Match; 6-0 v. Lochgelly United (-) (April 10th, 1915)
Highest & Lowest Gate*; Not Known
Highest Home Win; 8-3 v. Falkirk (-) (October 18th, 1902).
7-1 v. Dundee Hibernian (-) (November 4th, 1911)
Highest Home Defeat; 1-5 v. Raith Rovers (-) (November 12th, 1904)
No. of Matches Played by St Bernards; 167

Having spent just a brief period of time at *New Powderhall*, the club made a permanent move here from *New Logie Green* in 1900. With the advent of WWI, the Scottish Football League suspended Division 2 matches from 1915 but by the time that the fixtures were re-instated in 1921 the club had been forced to make a move to *Old Logie Green*. Season 1914/15 Second Division Championship matches v. *Leith Athletic* and *Cowdenbeath* were played at the neutral venue of *Easter Road*
*NB. There are no gate figures recorded for *St Bernards FC's* occupancy of this venue during this period.

In 1922 the ground was purchased by supporters and by the time that *St Bernards* was able to move in and play the first match, against *Arthurlie* on November 15th, 1924, the ground had been completely rebuilt. The pitch was turned through 90° and a new 1,200 seat grandstand sited along the south side of the pitch with embankments and some concrete terracing around the other three sides giving a planned capacity of some 40,000. Greyhound racing was experimented with in 1934, necessitating modifications to the terracing and the pitch area but this ceased after just eighteen months.

After the club folded in 1947 the grandstand was sold to *Leith Athletic* for £2,000, for re-erection at *New Meadowbank*, and the site was later used for King George's Playing Fields, a public park.

PLAYING RECORD OF ST BERNARDS
LEAGUE PROGRAMME

First Match; 0-1 v. Arthurlie (-) (November 15th, 1924)
Last Match; 0-0 v. Queen's Park (-) (September 2nd, 1939)
Highest Gate*; 15,000 v. Hibernian (0-1) (November 19th, 1932)
Lowest Gate*; Not Known
Highest Home Win; 10-1 v. Morton (-) (October 14th, 1933)
Highest Home Defeat; 2-5 v. Bo'ness (-) (November 13th, 1926), v. Morton (-) (November 5th, 1927) & v. Ayr United (-) (November 28th, 1936). 0-4 v. Ayr United (-) (December 24th, 1927)
& v. East Stirlingshire (-) (November 21st, 1931)
No. of Matches Played by St Bernards; 265

Having groundshared for part of the season with *Heart of Midlothian* at *Tynecastle*, the club moved here from *Old Logie Green* in 1924. The Scottish Football League was suspended in 1939 and the club folded in 1946.
*NB. This is the highest gate figure of the very few that were recorded. In view of the general level of those that are known, it is very probable that there were crowds of less than 1,000 on occasions.

PLAYING RECORD OF LEITH ATHLETIC
LEAGUE PROGRAMME

Match Played; 2-1 v. Alloa Athletic (3,000) (September 24th, 1927)
No. of Matches Played by Leith Athletic; 1

This match was played here as the pitch at *New Powderhall* was waterlogged.

A TOTAL OF **46** TEAMS TOOK PART IN **433** LEAGUE FIXTURES AT THIS VENUE

RUGBY PARK

HOME GROUND OF **KILMARNOCK**
TEMPORARY HOME GROUND FOR **PARTICK THISTLE**

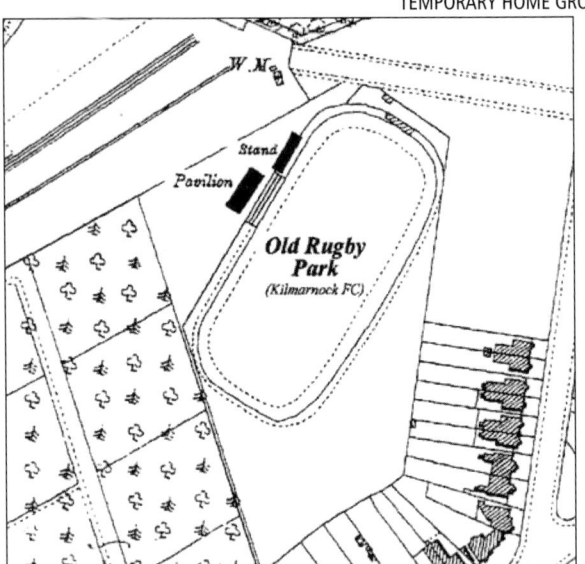

MAP EXTRACT; AYRSHIRE 18.13 [**1896**]
SITE LOCATION; **NS42093742**

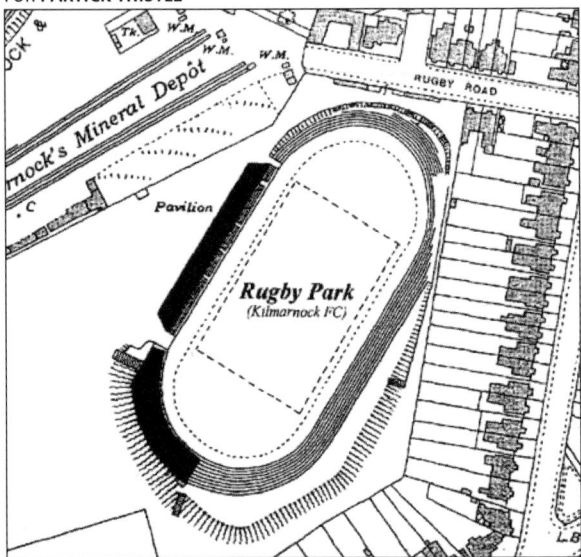

MAP EXTRACT; AYRSHIRE 18.13 [**1938**]

Following their formation, *Kilmarnock FC* occupied a variety of sites in the vicinity with local redevelopments causing them to move frequently before eventually settling in an area bounded by South Hamilton Street, Westmoor Nursery and the Glasgow & South Western Railway Kilmarnock to Troon line.

The pitch was surrounded by an oval running track and the facilities included a pavilion, enclosure and covered stand on the west side. The ground hosted the *Scotland* v. *Wales* international match in 1894 and the estimated record attendance of 12,000 was set at the Scottish FA Cup 3rd Round tie v. *St Mirren* (1-2) on March 11th, 1899. Following their promotion to Division 1 in 1899, the pitch was moved slightly and re-orientated, the original layout then being known as *Old Rugby Park*.

PLAYING RECORD OF KILMARNOCK
LEAGUE PROGRAMME

First Match; 7-1 v. Motherwell (2,000) (August 24th, 1895)
Last Match; 5-0 v. Motherwell (1,500) (April 2nd, 1899)
Highest Gate*; 4,000 v. Airdrieonians (5-0) (August 27th, 1898), v. Port Glasgow Athletic (4-1) (September 10th, 1898) & v. Leith Athletic (5-3) (October 8th, 1898)
Lowest Gate*; 500 v. Motherwell (2-0) (May 6th, 1897), v. Linthouse (0-3) (May 8th, 1897) & v. Airdrieonians (1-2) (May 13th, 1897)
Highest Home Win; 8-0 v. Linthouse (1,500) (November 5th, 1898)
Highest Home Defeat; 0-3 v. Linthouse (500) (May 8th, 1897)
No. of Matches Played by Kilmarnock; 36
Information Kindly Supplied by; John Livingston

The club was elected into the Scottish Football League Division 2 in 1895. The club was also involved in a Scottish Football League Division 2, 3rd/4th Place Play Off Match v. *Renton* (1-2) at the neutral venue of **Cathkin Park** on May 20th, 1896.

*NB. Not all attendances are known and these are the highest and lowest gate figures of those that were recorded.

The ground re-opened for their debut season in Division 1 with the match v. *Celtic* on August 26th, 1899. The pitch was again surrounded with an oval track and the facilities included a main stand on the west side and embankments around the remainder of the pitch. Subsequent improvements included an extension to the main stand in 1914 and construction of a roof over half of the south end in 1935. By this time the capacity had been increased to 32,000.

With its close proximity to St Marnock's Mineral Depot the army requisitioned the ground in WWII for use as an oil and coal storage dump and mounted fuel tanks on concrete plinths across the pitch. Following the end of the war the pitch was reconstructed (it had to be relaid twice) and the north end extended. Later improvements included covering the east enclosure in 1958 and rebuilding of the main stand in 1962.

The record attendance of 35,995 was established at the Scottish FA Cup 4th Round tie v. *Rangers* (2-4) on March 10th, 1962 before the ground was rebuilt in 1994. Over a period of 49 weeks the north, south and east terraces were removed and replaced by three new stands giving an all seat capacity of 18,128 at the start of the 2004/5 season. The pitch size was 115 x 74 yards.

PLAYING RECORD OF KILMARNOCK
LEAGUE PROGRAMME

First Match; 2-2 v. Celtic (11,000) (August 26th, 1899)
Highest Gate; 32,893 v. Rangers (3-3) (January 4th, 1969)
Lowest Gate; 460 v. Alloa Athletic (2-0) (April 28th, 1984)
Highest Home Win; 9-2 v. Falkirk (7,758) (February 8th, 1964). 8-0 v. Dundee United (5,000) (December 12th, 1931), v. Arbroath (10,467) (January 3rd, 1949) & v. Airdrieonians (7,317) (September 29th, 1962).
Highest Home Defeat; 1-8 v. Rangers (15,021) (September 20th, 1980)
No. of Matches Played by Kilmarnock; 1,740
Information Kindly Supplied by; John Livingston

Some home matches were played at *Cappielow Park* and *Somerset Park* due to the ground being used for a Cattle and Agricultural Show. The club was also involved in a Scottish Football League Division 1, 14th/15th Place Play Off Match v. *Port Glasgow Athletic* (0-6) at *New Cathkin Park* on May 15th, 1906. Cont ...

RUGBY PARK [CONT...]

PLAYING RECORD OF PARTICK THISTLE
LEAGUE PROGRAMME
Match Played; 0-1 v. Kilmarnock (2,900) (February 27th, 1909)
No. of Matches Played by Partick Thistle; 1
Information Kindly Supplied by; Robert Reid and John Livingston,

This match was played here as **Firhill Park** was not ready following the closure of *Meadowside* in 1908. Although the match played on August 15th, 1908 (1-4 [4,000]) at *Rugby Park* is officially recorded by the Scottish League as *Partick Thistle's* home game and incorporated in the final League Table for the season as such, Mr John Livingston, the *Kilmarnock FC* historian, has devoted some research to this period and has come to the conclusion that this game was, in fact, *Partick Thistle's* "away" match.

This is not the only example of fixture confusion during this period, when *Partick* played a whole season of home games on other grounds *(See Page 162)*, and the fixtures for *Kilmarnock FC* for the 1908/9 season, published in the July 4th, 1908 edition of *The Kilmarnock Standard*, showed that this match was listed as a home game for *Kilmarnock*. *Partick Thistle's* home game was, according to this list, due on April 3rd, 1909 but *Kilmarnock* played *Falkirk* on that date, possibly due to some fixture congestion as the result of a cup run by the latter, and the match was moved forward to February 27th, 1909.

AT THE END OF SEASON 2004/5, A TOTAL OF **50** TEAMS HAD TAKEN PART IN **1,777** LEAGUE FIXTURES AT THIS VENUE

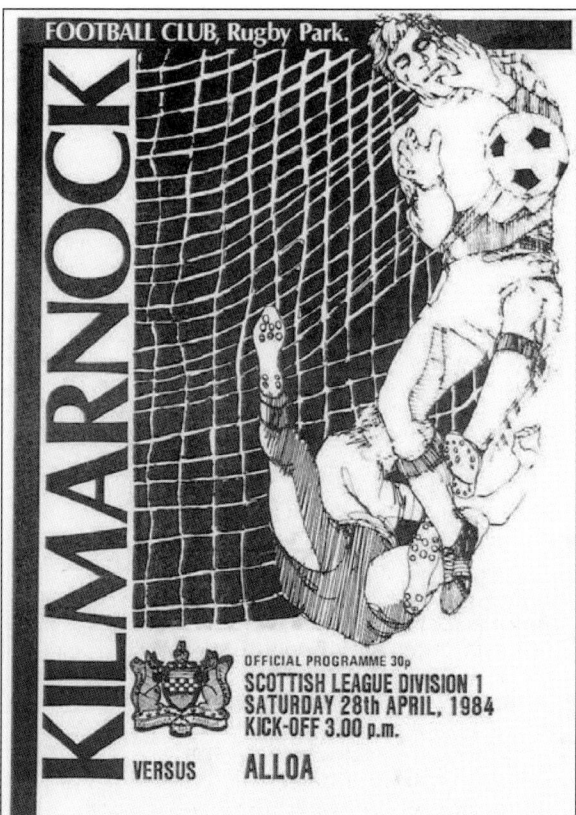

The programme for the match that produced the lowest ever known League attendance at **Rugby Park** - v. *Alloa Athletic* on April 28th, 1984. The visitors were relegated that season and lost this game 2-0.
Programme Courtesy of John Livingston

RAYDALE PARK
HOME GROUND OF **GRETNA**

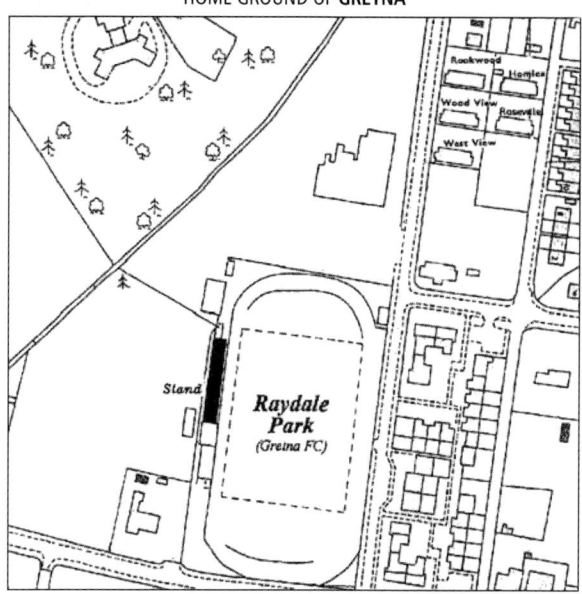

MAP EXTRACT; GROUND AS IN **1985** DRAWN FROM PLANS AND SUPERIMPOSED ON DUMFRIES-SHIRE 64.5 [1900]
SITE LOCATION; NY31496708

The site had been in use as a market garden when *Gretna FC* moved here from *Mackay's Field* in 1949. Initially the pitch was sited within a greyhound track and the only facility was a small stand on the west side. The ground remained virtually unaltered until the early 1980s when greyhound racing was dispensed with and a new stand installed on the west side. Terracing was constructed around the ground in 1989 and, during the 1990s a cover was built on the east side and another one subsequently installed at the north end. To prepare for League football, the main stand was rebuilt and reseated, the cover extended at the north end and at the start of the 2004/5 season the capacity was 2,200 with 385 seats and the pitch size was 110 x 70 yards. To accommodate the visit of *Dundee United* for the 3rd Round of the Scottish FA Cup on January 17th, 2005 (3-4) a temporary 800 seat stand was installed at the south end of the ground and the record gate of 3,000 was established at this fixture. The stand then remained *in situ* until the end of the season.

PLAYING RECORD OF GRETNA
LEAGUE PROGRAMME
First Match; 1-1 v. Greenock Morton (1,556) (August 3rd, 2002)
Highest Gate; 2,200 v. Peterhead (2-1) (November 13th, 2004)
Lowest Gate; 209 v. Montrose (2-2) (March 1st, 2003)
Highest Home Win; 8-1 v. East Stirlingshire (468) (October 16th, 2004)
Highest Home Defeat; 1-4 v. Peterhead (357) (September 14th, 2002)

No. of Matches Played by Gretna; 54
Some Information Kindly Supplied by; Ron MacGregor

The club was elected into the Scottish Football League Division 3 in 2002. The first Scottish League goal at the stadium was scored by Matthew Henney of *Gretna* in just 19 seconds of the first match and is probably one of the quickest goals ever scored by a club in a début League match.

AT THE END OF SEASON 2004/5, A TOTAL OF **13** TEAMS HAD TAKEN PART IN **54** LEAGUE FIXTURES AT THIS VENUE

ST MIRREN PARK

HOME GROUND OF **ST MIRREN**
TEMPORARY HOME GROUND FOR **GREENOCK MORTON**

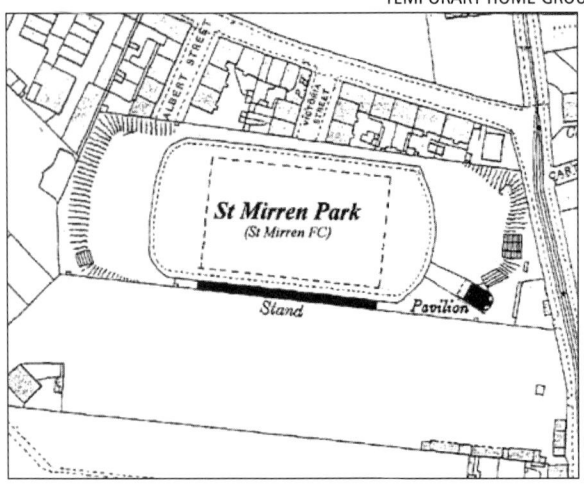

MAP EXTRACT; RENFREWSHIRE 12.2 [**1913**]
SITE LOCATION; **NS48066488**

PLAYING RECORD OF ST MIRREN
LEAGUE PROGRAMME

First Match; 0-3 v. Celtic (8,000) (September 8th, 1894)
Highest Gate; 45,000 v. Rangers (2-3) (September 6th, 1952)
Lowest Gate; 600 v. St Johnstone (0-0) (April 28th, 1967)
Highest Home Win; 8-0 v. Dumbarton (8,000) (January 4th, 1936) &
v. Clydebank (3,388) (March 11th, 2000)
Highest Home Defeat; 0-7 v. Stirling Albion (-) (March 5th, 1960), v.
Celtic (25,000) (November 3rd, 1962)
& v. Rangers (15,000) (October 27th, 1964)

No. of Matches Played by St Mirren; 1,773
Information Kindly Supplied by; Jim Crawford

The club moved here from *Westmarch* in 1894. The Division One Play Off match v. *St Bernards* (2-1) to decide the 8th and 9th Places took place at the neutral venue of *Dens Park* on April 7th, 1900. Due to reconstruction work at the ground at the end of Season 1920/21, the fixture v. *Ayr United* was played at *Somerset Park*, the match v. *Heart of Midlothian* at *Easter Road* and the game v. *Rangers* at *Hampden Park [3rd]*. The match v. *Celtic* on May 11th, 1979 was played at *Ibrox Park [2nd]*. With the site of *St Mirren Park* sold in 2005 the club was looking to move to a new stadium in Greenhill Road at sometime during 2006/7.

This location was far from ideal when *St Mirren FC* moved here from *Westmarch* in 1895 for not only was it narrow and poorly sited but there was a cottage sited within the ground. At this stage it was probably regarded as only a temporary measure because the club tried to purchase one of their old grounds, *Shortroods*, before buying *Love Street* (as it was also known) for £3,900.

The facilities in the early days are not known but by 1921 a pavilion which was on the south side, had been replaced by a new stand and embankments constructed at each end. Greyhound racing was tried for a short spell on the oval track around the pitch in the 1930s and speedway racing in the 1970s but neither was a financial success. Post war improvements included the provision of a cover and seats on the north side, seats in the main stand paddock and a new 3,000 seat west stand in 1995 as part of the conversion to an all seater stadium in the 1990s.

. The record attendance of 47,438 was set at a Scottish League Cup Division 1, Section A match v. *Celtic* (1-0) on August 20th, 1949 and the capacity at the start of the 2004/5 season was 10,800. The pitch size was 110 x 70 yards. During 2005 the club, in order to remain solvent, was obliged to sell the site for redevelopment as a supermarket and plans were in hand to vacate in 2006.

PLAYING RECORD OF GREENOCK MORTON
LEAGUE PROGRAMME

Matches Played; 2-3 v. Hibernian (-) (February 26th, 1949)
0-1 v. Falkirk (-) (March 5th, 1949)
2-0 v. East Fife (-) (March 19th, 1949)
3-0 v. Albion Rovers (-) (April 9th, 1949)
2-2 v. Clyde (-) (April 13th, 1949)
0-1 v. Rangers (40,000) (April 25th, 1949)

No. of Matches Played by Greenock Morton; 6
Information Kindly Supplied by; Eddie McDowell

These matches were played here whilst the pitch at *Cappielow Park* was dug up and relaid to improve drainage.

AT THE END OF SEASON 2004/5, A TOTAL OF **51** TEAMS HAD TAKEN PART
IN **1,779** LEAGUE FIXTURES AT THIS VENUE

St Mirren Park in its final form, as an all-seater stadium
Photograph by Owen Pavey. Courtesy of Groundtastic Magazine

SHAWFIELD PARK

HOME GROUND OF **CLYDE**
TEMPORARY HOME GROUND FOR **CELTIC** & **PARTICK THISTLE**

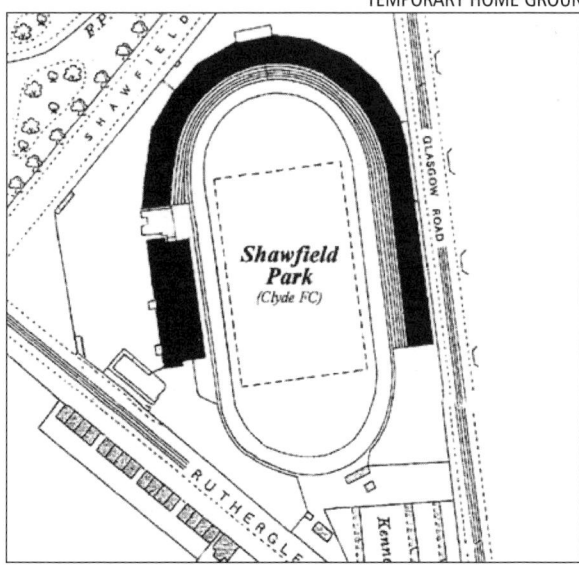

MAP EXTRACT; LANARKSHIRE 6.15 & 10.3 [**1935**]
SITE LOCATION; **NS60506283**

When first used by *Thistle FC* in 1875 the ground consisted of an enclosed field and dressing rooms. The club left to go to *Dalmarnock Park* in 1882 and by the time *Clyde FC* took over in 1898, having moved from **Barrowfield Park**, *Shawfield Park* had become a trotting track as well as a football venue.

A 1,500 seat grandstand, replaced in 1917, was constructed in time for their first Scottish Football League match at the ground and over the years it was developed as a multi-sports arena with additional stands and terracing around the north and east sides.

The record gate of 52,000† was set at the Scottish FA Cup 2nd Round tie v. *Rangers* on February 10th, 1912 which was abandoned 15 minutes from the end with the score at 3-1. Greyhound racing was tried in 1932 and eventually took over the stadium three years later.

Clyde FC was forced to move out and groundshare with *Partick Thistle* at **Firhill Park** in 1986 and the venue, having also been used for speedway for a few seasons, was still in use as a greyhound stadium in 2002.

PLAYING RECORD OF PARTICK THISTLE
LEAGUE PROGRAMME

Matches Played; 2-3 v. Clyde (-) (September 28th, 1908)
3-2 v. Heart of Midlothian (1,000) (October 24th, 1908)
No. of Matches Played by Partick Thistle; 2
Information Kindly Supplied by; Robert Reid

These matches were played here as **Firhill Park** was not ready following the closure of *Meadowside* in 1908.

PLAYING RECORD OF CELTIC
LEAGUE PROGRAMME

Matches Played; 3-1 v. Third Lanark (9,000) (March 30th, 1929)
3-0 v. Falkirk (6,000) (April 20th, 1929)
No. of Matches Played by Celtic; 2
Information Kindly Supplied by; Margaret Connolly & Cyril George

These matches were played here due to a fire at **Celtic Park [2nd]** in March 1929.

PLAYING RECORD OF CLYDE
LEAGUE PROGRAMME

First Match; 0-0 v. Celtic (13,000) (August 27th, 1898)
Last Match & Lowest Gate;* 4-2 v. Alloa Athletic (1,200)
(April 28th, 1986)
Highest Gate;* 36,000 v. Rangers (1-3) (December 25th, 1920)
Highest Home Win; 11-1 v. Cowdenbeath (-)
(October 6th, 1951)
Highest Home Defeat; 0-8 v. Rangers (15,000)
(February 14th, 1931)
No. of Matches Played by Clyde; 1,395
Information Kindly Supplied by; John Taylor & Cyril George

The club moved here from **Barrowfield Park** in 1898. Four home matches were played at other venues; the games v. *Rangers* on May 10th, 1919 and September 13th, 1919 were played at **Celtic Park [2nd]**, the match v. *Celtic* on January 2nd, 1915 was played at **Celtic Park [2nd]** and the game v. *Rangers* on March 13th, 1915 was played at **Ibrox Park [2nd]**, the latter two apparently due to a fire at Shawfield.

The club moved to **Firhill Park** in 1986 to groundshare with *Partick Thistle* and then to Hamilton Academical's **Douglas Park** before relocating to the new **Broadwood Stadium** in 1994.

*NB. Not all attendances are known and these are the highest and lowest gate figures of those that were recorded.

† This gate of 52,000 was previously attributed to the Scottish League fixture v. *Rangers* (0-1) on November 21st, 1908. However subsequent research has revealed that this was not the match in question and the attendance for that particular game was 18,000.

A TOTAL OF **54** TEAMS TOOK PART IN **1,399** LEAGUE FIXTURES AT THIS VENUE

A post WWII view of **Shawfield Park**, looking from the north end terraces towards the main stand. It was the home track of the *Glasgow Tigers* Speedway team between 1988 and 1998, except for 1996 when it was utilized by the *Scottish Monarchs*.

Photograph by Jon Weaver. Courtesy of Groundtastic Magazine

SHIELFIELD PARK
HOME GROUND OF BERWICK RANGERS

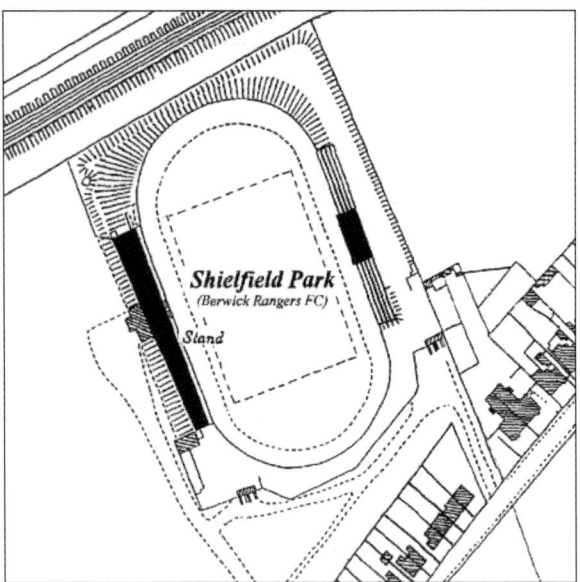

MAP EXTRACT; GROUND AS IN c1965 DRAWN FROM PLANS AND SUPERIMPOSED ON NORTHUMBERLAND 4.2 [1924]
SITE LOCATION; **NT99115185**

PLAYING RECORD OF BERWICK RANGERS
LEAGUE PROGRAMME

First Match; 0-6 v. East Stirlingshire (-) (September 10th, 1955)
Highest Gate; 4,478 v. Heart of Midlothian (1-3) (August 25th, 1979)
Lowest Gate; 178 v. East Stirlingshire (1-0) (April 2nd, 1977)
Highest Home Win; 8-1 v. Forfar Athletic (698) (December 25th, 1965)
Highest Home Defeat; 0-6 v. East Stirlingshire (-) (September 10th, 1955), v. Dundee United (2,000) (December 25th, 1956), v. Ayr United (953) (October 19th, 1957) & v. Stenhousemuir (391) (August 24th, 1996)

No. of Matches Played by Berwick Rangers; 918
Information Kindly Supplied by; Robin Murdie

The club was elected into the Scottish Football League Division 2 in 1955. Due to the unserviceable state of the roof of the main stand *Berwick Rangers* also played home games at **Tynecastle Park, Meadowbank Stadium, Cliftonhill Park, Recreation Park, Bayview Park** and **Ochilview Park**.

AT THE END OF SEASON 2004/5, A TOTAL OF **40** TEAMS HAD TAKEN PART IN **918** LEAGUE FIXTURES AT THIS VENUE

Berwick Rangers FC moved to *Shielfield Park* in Tweedmouth from *Union Park* in 1919. At first the ground was at the east end of the site (with a pavilion as the only facility) and it was not until their entry into Scottish League Division C in 1951 that it was repositioned on the current site and the former ground, later known as *Old Shielfield*, used initially for reserve and junior teams and later as a training pitch.

The pitch is enclosed by an oval speedway track and the facilities include a main stand on the west side, the steelwork of which originated from the old Midland Road stand at *Bradford City's* **Valley Parade**, embankments around the north end and concrete terracing and a small cover on the east side. The record attendance of 13,365 was set at the Scottish FA Cup 1st Round tie v. *Rangers* (1-0) on January 28th, 1967.

In 1985 *Berwick Rangers* sold the ground to the council who leased it to a greyhound company and, through a sub-lease, let it back to the football club, a situation which led them to being locked out for a while in the early 1990s. During this period, in 1990, the roofs of both the main stand and east side terracing became unserviceable and were removed as a safety measure and it was not until 1992 that replacement roofs were installed.

Following the demise of the greyhound company in 1995 the lease was taken over by the supporters club and the capacity of the ground at the start of the 2004/5 season was 4,131 with 1,366 seats. The pitch size was 110 x 70 yards.

The east side terrace, complete with a plethora of pylons and the 1992-built roof!
Photograph by Jon Weaver, Courtesy of Groundtastic Magazine

The programme cover shows an aerial view of the ground, looking south. The match ended in a 3-0 win for the hosts.
Programme Courtesy of John Litster

SOMERSET PARK

HOME GROUND OF **AYR** & **AYR UNITED**
TEMPORARY HOME GROUND FOR **ALBION ROVERS, KILMARNOCK** & **ST MIRREN**

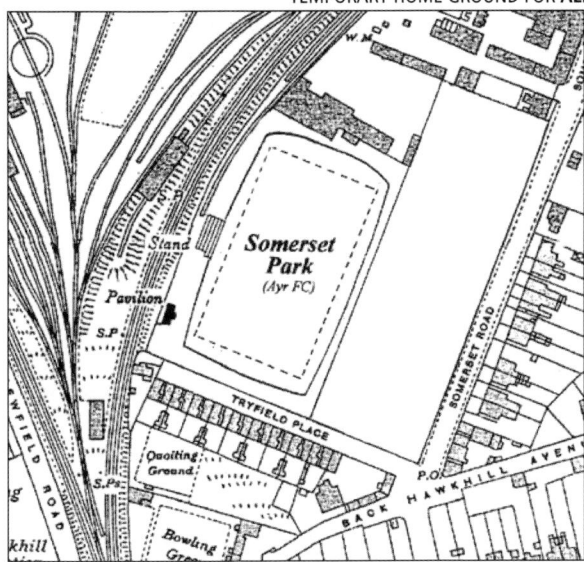

MAP EXTRACT; GROUND AS IN **1896** DRAWN FROM PLANS AND SUPERIMPOSED ON AYRSHIRE 33.2 & 33.6 [1937]
SITE LOCATION; NS34482266

When *Ayr FC* moved here from **Beresford Park** in 1888 the pitch was established on a north-south axis, running parallel to the adjacent railway line. The facilities included a pavilion and a temporary uncovered seated stand on the west side.

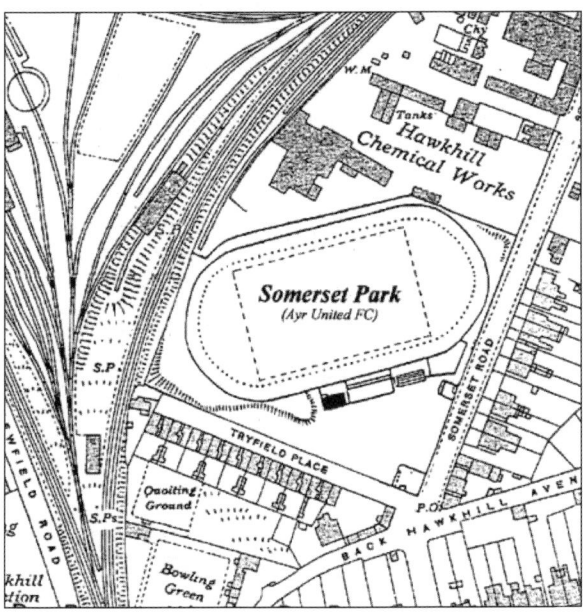

MAP EXTRACT; GROUND AS IN c**1920** DRAWN FROM PLANS AND SUPERIMPOSED ON AYRSHIRE 33.2 & 33.6 [1937]

In 1897, to facilitate the installation of an oval cycle track the ground was re-orientated through about 45º and the facilities improved. A pavilion, covered stand and uncovered seated stand were sited on the south side and small embankments squeezed in at each end. The club, as *Ayr United FC*, purchased the ground in 1920.

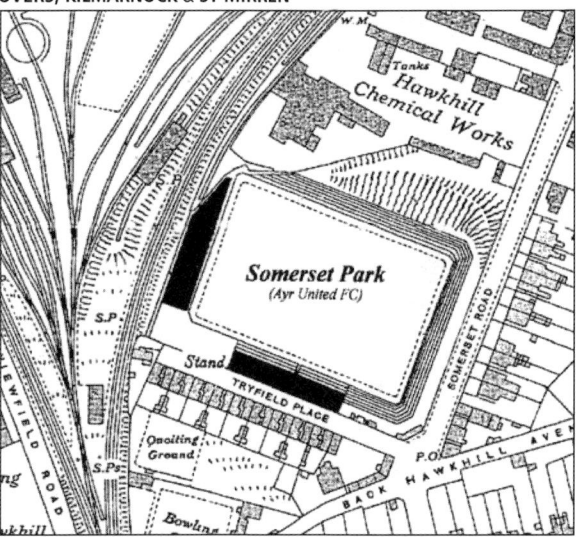

MAP EXTRACT; GROUND AS IN **1961** DRAWN FROM PLANS AND SUPERIMPOSED ON AYRSHIRE 33.2 & 33.6 [1937]

In 1924 the cycle track was dispensed with as the pitch was finally shifted again, this time to the current east-west axis. The north side was embanked and terraced, a new main stand constructed on the south side and later improvements included the installation of covers at each end and an extension to the main stand. The capacity at the start of the 2004/5 season was 10,185 with 1,500 seats and the pitch size was 110 x 72 yards.

PLAYING RECORD OF AYR
LEAGUE PROGRAMME

First Match; 1-4 v. Linthouse (950) (September 4th, 1897)
Last Match; 2-2 v. Arthurlie (-) (April 2nd, 1910)
Highest & Lowest Gate*; Not Known
Highest Home Win; 6-1 v. Morton (-) (March 26th, 1898)
Highest Home Defeat; 1-5 v. Linthouse (-) (September 2nd, 1899) & v. Leith Athletic (-) (November 4th, 1905)
No. of Matches Played by Ayr; 135
Information Kindly Supplied by; Duncan Carmichael

The club was elected into the Scottish Football League Division 2 in 1897 and amalgamated with *Ayr Parkhouse* in 1910 to form *Ayr United*, the new club using *Somerset Park* as the home ground.
*NB. Very few gate figures are known for this club but it is assumed that in general attendances numbered less than 1,000.

PLAYING RECORD OF ALBION ROVERS
LEAGUE PROGRAMME

Match Played; 0-4 v. Ayr United (-) (February 17th, 1912)
No. of Matches Played by Albion Rovers; 1
Information Kindly Supplied by; Duncan Carmichael

This match was switched here from **Cliftonhill Park** in anticipation of a larger gate.

PLAYING RECORD OF ST MIRREN
LEAGUE PROGRAMME

Match Played; 1-4 v. Ayr United (-) (March 19th, 1921)
No. of Matches Played by St Mirren; 1
Information Kindly Supplied by; Jim Crawford

The match was switched here due to reconstruction work at *St Mirren Park*.

Cont ...

SOMERSET PARK [CONT ...]

PLAYING RECORD OF AYR UNITED
LEAGUE PROGRAMME

First Match; 2-0 v. Port Glasgow Athletic (2,500) (August 20th, 1910)
Highest Gate; 25,225 v. Rangers (2-1) (September 13th, 1969)
Lowest Gate*; 400 v. Montrose (4-0) (April 17th, 1968)
Highest Home Win; 10-1 v. Stenhousemuir (-) (January 5th, 1946)
Highest Home Defeat; 0-7 v. Dundee United (7,000) (September 24th, 1966)

No. of Matches Played by Ayr United; 1,577
Information Kindly Supplied by; Duncan Carmichael

Ayr and *Ayr Parkhouse FCs* merged in 1910 and took over *Ayr FC's* Scottish Football League fixtures. Some home matches were also played at *Beresford Park* when *Somerset Park* was not ready for the start of the 1924/25 season and at *Dens Park* when the match v. *Dundee* on April 29th, 1922 was switched due to the fixture coinciding with a race meeting at Ayr Racecourse. The game v. *Airdrieonians* on April 27th, 2002 was abandoned after 21 minutes with the score at 1-0 after visiting supporters invaded the pitch. With nothing at stake and *Airdrieonians FC* on the point of extinction (the club was wound up four days later) the result was allowed to stand and it undoubtedly holds the record as the shortest ever "completed" Scottish Football League match..

*Although the official figure is 673 v. *Alloa Athletic* (3-1) on March 17th, 1984, attendances of less than 500 (including the above) were estimated, but not officially recorded, on several occasions during the 1960s.

PLAYING RECORD OF KILMARNOCK
LEAGUE PROGRAMME

Match Played; 3-1 v. Heart of Midlothian (3,000) (April 15th, 1916)

No. of Matches Played by Kilmarnock; 1
Information Kindly Supplied by; John Livingston

This match was switched here as *Rugby Park* was being used for a Cattle and Agricultural Show.

AT THE END OF SEASON 2004/5, A TOTAL OF **60** TEAMS HAD TAKEN PART IN **1,715** LEAGUE FIXTURES AT THIS VENUE

Martin Glancy (10) scores the opening goal for *Stirling Albion*, at the west end of the ground, in their 3-0 win against *Ayr United* at *Somerset Park* on April 9th, 2005.
Courtesy of RedWeb (www.stirlingalbionfc.com)

SPORTS PARK
HOME GROUND OF **BROXBURN UNITED**

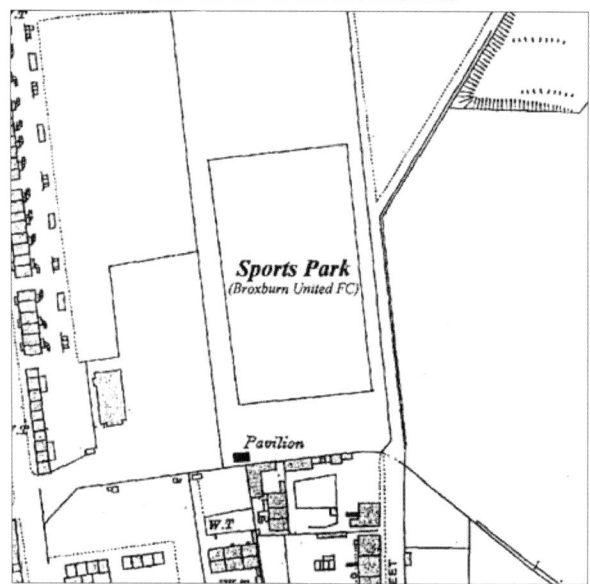

MAP EXTRACT; LINLITHGOW 8.7 [**1917**]
SITE LOCATION; **NT08427245**

The ground, with its basic facilities, was first used by *Broxburn United FC* in 1914 and one of the few modest improvements made over the years included a 400 seater grandstand constructed in 1922. The largest gate at this ground was probably 9,000 for the Scottish FA Cup 3rd Round tie v. *Falkirk* (2-1) on February 21st, 1925.

Following the demise of the club in 1932 the site was redeveloped and *Sports Park* is now, in the main, covered by the car park to the adjacent Sports Centre.

PLAYING RECORD OF BROXBURN UNITED
LEAGUE PROGRAMME

First Match; 3-2 v. Dunfermline Athletic (3,500) (August 20th, 1921)
Last Match & Lowest Gate*; 3-4 v. Armadale (500) (April 24th, 1926)
Highest Gate*; 4,000 v. Stenhousemuir (0-0) (September 3rd, 1921) & v. Queen's Park (0-0) (October 6th, 1922)
Highest Home Win; 4-1 v. East Stirlingshire (-) (December 3rd, 1921) & v. Lochgelly United (1,200) (April 14th, 1923)
Highest Home Defeat; 4-7 v. St Bernards (-) (January 2nd, 1926). 0-5 v. Alloa Athletic (-) (February 3rd, 1926)

No. of Matches Played by Broxburn United; 95

The club was elected into the Scottish Football League Division 2 in 1921 and failed to gain re-election in 1926.

*NB. Not all attendances are known and these are the highest and lowest gate figures of those that were recorded.

A TOTAL OF **30** TEAMS TOOK PART IN **95** LEAGUE FIXTURES AT THIS VENUE

SPRINGVALE PARK
HOME GROUND OF COWLAIRS

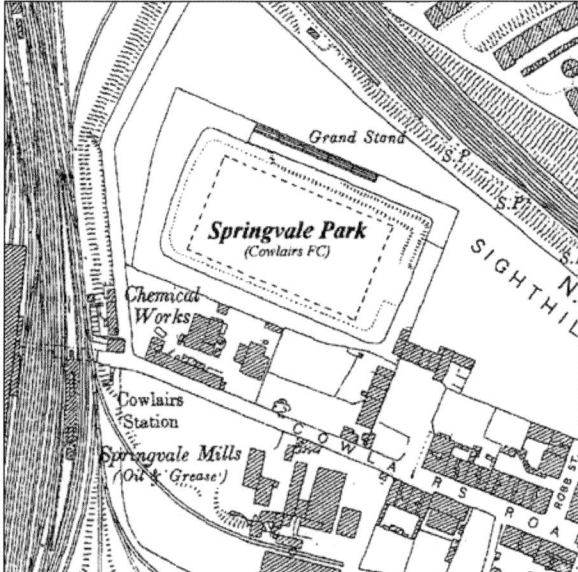

MAP EXTRACT; LANARKSHIRE 6.3 [1893]
SITE LOCATION; NS60176779

Cowlairs FC moved from *Gourlay Park* to *Springvale Park* for the first season of the Scottish Football League in 1890. Located on the east side of the North British Railway's Cowlairs Works, the facilities included an open seated stand on the north side, a pavilion in the south east corner and a running track which was added in 1893. The record gate was probably the 6,000 who attended the Glasgow Cup Semi-Final tie v. *Celtic* (0-2) on October 27th, 1894.

The club moved back to *Gourlay Park* in 1895 and the site was taken over for railway sidings and expansion of the adjacent works.

PLAYING RECORD OF COWLAIRS
LEAGUE PROGRAMME

First Match; 3-2 v. Vale of Leven (-) (August 23rd, 1890)
Last Match; 2-1 v. Dundee Wanderers (-) (April 27th, 1895)
Highest Gate*; 2,500 v. Celtic (0-5) (April 29th, 1891)
Lowest Gate; Not Known
Highest Home Win; 8-1 v. Partick Thistle (-)
(November 11th, 1893)
Highest Home Defeat; 2-8 v. Hibernian (-) (March 16th, 1895)
No. of Matches Played by Cowlairs; 27

The club was a founder member of the Scottish Football League in 1890 and withdrew from the League at the end of the season. It re-entered the League as a founder member of Division 2 in 1893 but failed to gain re-election in 1895.

*NB. This is the highest gate figure of the few that were recorded. In view of the general level of those that are known, it is very probable that there were crowds of less than 500 on occasions.

A TOTAL OF **21** TEAMS TOOK PART IN **27** LEAGUE FIXTURES AT THIS VENUE

STAIR PARK
HOME GROUND OF STRANRAER

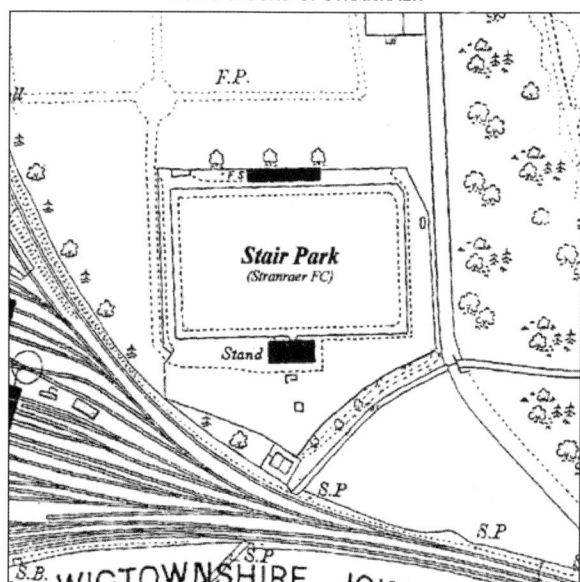

MAP EXTRACT; GROUND AS IN 1965 DRAWN FROM PLANS AND SUPERIMPOSED ON WIGTOWNSHIRE 17.4 [1908]
SITE LOCATION; NX06956055

Stranraer FC moved into *Stair Park* from *Rephad* in 1907 but, as the ground formed part of a larger public park, they had some difficulty in eventually persuading the council as to the justification for an enclosure of the ground, and thus loss of public amenity. A pavilion was built in 1909 and moved in 1911 when the pitch was relocated to the south of the park and enclosed.

Improvements were undertaken in the 1930s with the construction of a main stand on the south side and shallow embankments around the pitch and it was not until the 1950s that a cover was erected on the north side.

The record attendance of 6,500 was set at the Scottish FA Cup Round 1st Round tie v. *Rangers* (0-1) on January 24th, 1948. In 1991 the main stand was closed and 300 seats installed under the cover on the north side. Four years later the main stand was demolished and replaced by an all-seat cantilever stand giving a capacity at the start of the 2004/5 season of 5,600 with 1,900 seats. The pitch size was 110 x 70 yards.

PLAYING RECORD OF STRANRAER
LEAGUE PROGRAMME

First Match; 3-1 v. Albion Rovers (-) (September 7th, 1955)
Highest Gate*; 3,650 v. Greenock Morton (1-1) (April 30th, 2005)
Lowest Gate*; 200 v. Stenhousemuir (0-1) (April 8th, 2003)
Highest Home Win; 7-1 v. Arbroath (300) (December 22nd, 1984)
& v. East Stirlingshire (352) (February 7th, 2004)
Highest Home Defeat; 4-7 v. Stenhousemuir (-) (September 23rd, 1959). 0-6 v. Stirling Albion (-) (September 2nd, 1964) & v. Brechin City (250) (September 26th, 1981)
No. of Matches Played by Stranraer; 912

The club was elected into the Scottish Football League Division 2 in 1955

*NB. Not all attendances are known and these are the highest and lowest gate figures of those that have been recorded.

AT THE END OF SEASON 2004/5, A TOTAL OF **42** TEAMS HAD TAKEN PART IN **912** LEAGUE FIXTURES AT THIS VENUE

STARK'S PARK
HOME GROUND OF RAITH ROVERS

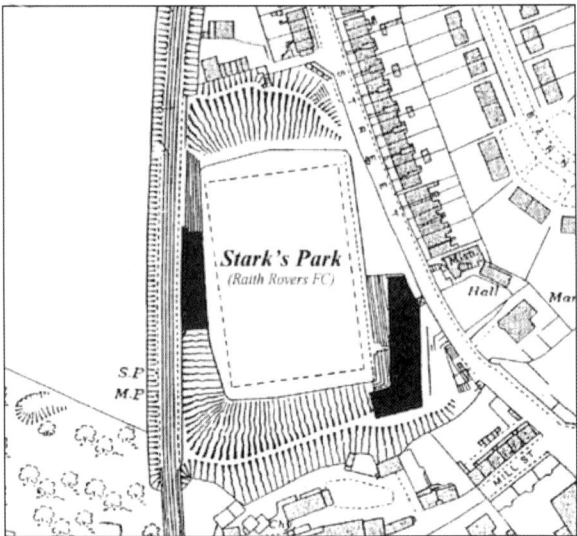

MAP EXTRACT; FIFE 35.12 [1947]
SITE LOCATION; NT27419030

Stark's Park, on a restricted site between Pratt Street and the railway line, had been in use by a number of local teams when *Raith Rovers* moved here from *Robbie's Park* in 1891. The facilities, at first, included a pavilion (removed from their previous ground) but within five years a grandstand was erected and subsequently extended. In 1911 this grandstand was partially destroyed in a gale and, in 1918, totally destroyed by a fire. In the early 1920s a new L-shaped 2,500 seat grandstand was constructed in the south east corner and a small seated stand on the west side. By this time extensive embankments had been constructed around the pitch, particularly at each end, and some terracing had been provided in the vicinity of both stands.

The record attendance of 31,306 was set at the Scottish FA Cup 2nd Round tie v. *Heart of Midlothian* (0-1) on February 7th, 1953 and post war improvements included the erection of covering at each end and the replacement of the stand on the west side with new seats and a cantilevered roof.

In the 1990s new all-seat stands were installed at the ends, converting it into an all seater stadium with a capacity of 10,104 by the start of the 2004/5 season. The pitch size was 113 x 67 yards.

PLAYING RECORD OF RAITH ROVERS
LEAGUE PROGRAMME
First Match; 1-1 v. Clyde (-) (August 23rd, 1902)
Highest Gate; 24,800 v. Rangers (1-3) (November 19th, 1949)
Lowest Gate; 254 v. Stranraer (4-1) (April 22nd, 1986)
Highest Home Win; 9-1 v. King's Park (3,000) (August 13th, 1932)
Highest Home Defeat; 0-8 v. Airdrieonians (2,300) (January 3rd, 1966)
No. of Matches Played by Raith Rovers; 1,660
Information Kindly Supplied by; John Litster

The club was elected into the Scottish Football League Division 2 in 1902. The ground was closed for a month in 1914 following an assault on a referee and the match v. *Third Lanark* on December 19th, 1914 was played at *East End Park*. The club was also involved in a Scottish Football League Division 2, 10th/11th Place Play Off Match v. *East Stirlingshire* at the neutral venue of *Old Logie Green* on May 11th, 1907.

AT THE END OF SEASON 2004/5, A TOTAL OF **58** TEAMS HAD TAKEN PART IN **1,660** LEAGUE FIXTURES AT THIS VENUE

STATION PARK
HOME GROUND OF FORFAR ATHLETIC

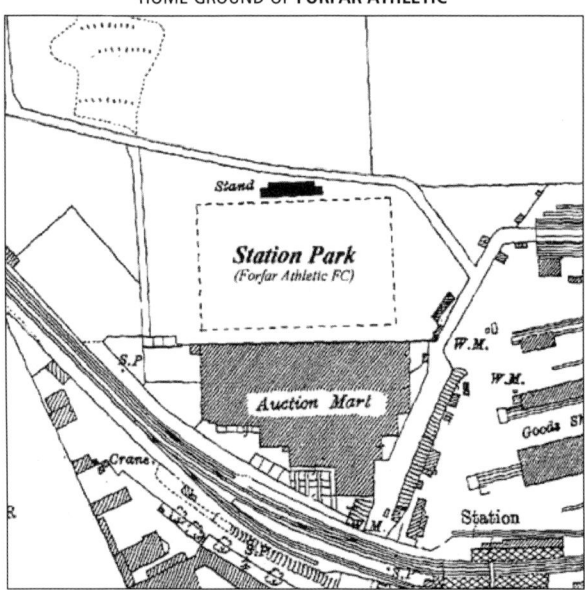

MAP EXTRACT; FORFARSHIRE 38.3 & 38.4 [1922]
SITE LOCATION; NO45855150

Forfar Athletic FC moved into *Station Park* shortly after their formation in 1885 and, by 1888, the facilities included a 400 seat stand on the north side. From the outset the stand, and its successors, succumbed to high winds; the roof blew off as soon as it was built and it totally collapsed in 1893.

Prior to 1914 a replacement stand was built, embankments constructed and, following the end of WWI, the first substantial main stand (from which the roof was blown off in 1921) was erected and a new cover installed over the south side. *Forfar Athletic FC* purchased the ground in 1956 and the main stand suffered serious gale damage yet again before another new grandstand opened on the north side in 1959.

The record attendance of 10,780 was set at the Scottish FA Cup 2nd Round tie v. *Rangers* (0-7) on February 7th, 1970 and subsequent improvements included the refurbishment of the terraces and installation of a new cantilever roof over the south side. The capacity at the start of the 2004/5 season was 4,602 with 739 seats and the pitch size was 115 x 69 yards.

PLAYING RECORD OF FORFAR ATHLETIC
LEAGUE PROGRAMME
First Match; 1-1 v. Cowdenbeath (-) (August 27th, 1921)
Highest Gate*; 7,000 v. St Johnstone (2-0) (April 21st, 1923)
Lowest Gate*; 340 v. Stenhousemuir (2-0) (March 26th, 2002)
Highest Home Win; 9-1 v. Stenhousemuir (986) (October 12th, 1968)
Highest Home Defeat; 1-8 v. St Bernards (-) (September 12th, 1936) & v. Cowdenbeath (-) (April 1st, 1939)
No. of Matches Played by Forfar Athletic; 1,349
(Including expunged matches v. Bathgate on October 13th, 1928, & v. Bo'ness on September 24th, 1932)

The club was elected into the Scottish Football League Division 2 in 1921 and remained in the League until it was suspended in 1939. The club was elected into Division B in 1949.

*NB. Not all attendances are known and these are the highest and lowest gate figures of those that are recorded.

AT THE END OF SEASON 2004/5, A TOTAL OF **62** TEAMS HAD TAKEN PART IN **1,349** LEAGUE FIXTURES AT THIS VENUE

STRATHCLYDE HOMES STADIUM
HOME GROUND OF **DUMBARTON**

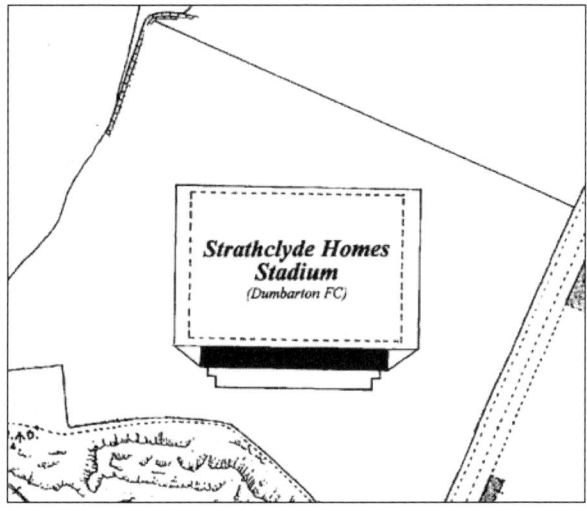

MAP EXTRACT; GROUND AS IN **2000** DRAWN FROM SKETCH PLANS AND SUPERIMPOSED ON DUNBARTONSHIRE 22.3 [1937]
SITE LOCATION; **NS40107460**

Constructed on the site of a tidal basin on the River Leven, *Strathclyde Homes Stadium* was opened by *Dumbarton FC* in 2000. With a capacity of 2,046 at the start of season 2004/5 all the spectators were seated within the cantilever roofed main stand on the south side of the 110 x 72 yards sized pitch.

PLAYING RECORD OF DUMBARTON
LEAGUE PROGRAMME
First Match; 3-0 v. Elgin City (1,876) (December 2nd, 2000)
Highest Gate; 1,959 v. Queen's Park (1-1) (April 27th, 2002)
Lowest Gate; 480 v. Brechin City (1-3) (March 11th, 2003)
Highest Home Win; 4-0 v. Stenhousemuir (552) (March 23rd, 2004)
Highest Home Defeat; 0-5 v. Montrose (742) (January 12th, 2002)
No. of Matches Played by Dumbarton; 83
Information Kindly Supplied by; Jim McAllister

The club moved here from groundsharing with *Albion Rovers* at *Cliftonhill Park* in 2000.

AT THE END OF SEASON 2004/5, A TOTAL OF **23** TEAMS HAD TAKEN PART IN **83** LEAGUE FIXTURES AT THIS VENUE

It is not difficult to see why home supporters know their stadium as "*The Rock*"! It has been the site of fortifications for over 1,500 years and this view of the main stand on February 5th, 2005 shows the 13thC Dumbarton Castle overlooking the *Dumbarton* v. *Stirling Albion* League match which ended as a 2-0 win for the visitors.
Courtesy of RedWeb (www.stirlingalbionfc.com)

TELFORD STREET
HOME GROUND OF **INVERNESS CALEDONIAN THISTLE**

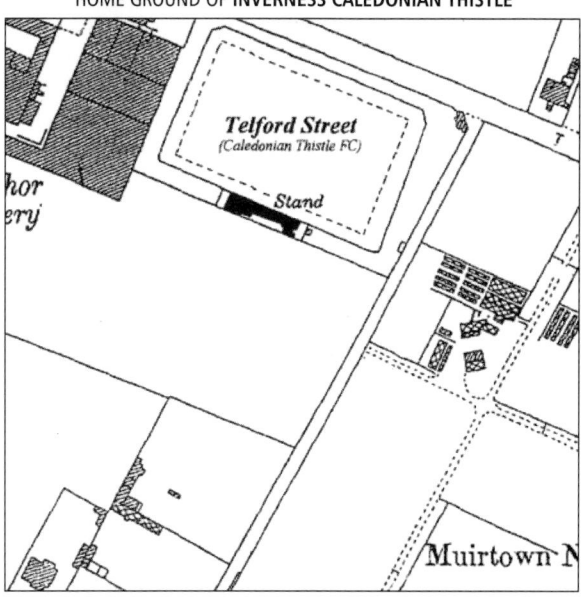

MAP EXTRACT; INVERNESS-SHIRE 12.1 [1929]
SITE LOCATION; **NH65514570**

Caledonian FC commenced playing football at *Telford Street* in 1885 and by 1930 the main facility was a covered seated stand on the south side. Post WWII improvements included the construction of terracing around the ground and installation of covering at each end which by 1995 gave a nominal capacity of 5,498 with 498 seats.

To facilitate membership of the Scottish Football League, *Caledonian FC* merged with *Inverness Thistle FC* (who moved in from their *Kingsmill* ground) in 1994. This amalgamated club, as *Caledonian Thistle FC*, moved to *Caledonian Stadium* (becoming known as *Inverness Caledonian Thistle FC*) in 1996. *Telford Street* was subsequently redeveloped as a retail park.

PLAYING RECORD OF INVERNESS CALEDONIAN THISTLE
LEAGUE PROGRAMME
First Match; 5-2 v. Arbroath (1,700) (August 13th, 1994)
Last Match; 2-0 v. Arbroath (2,086) (October 5th, 1996)
Highest Gate; 4,931 v. Ross County (1-1) (January 23rd, 1996)
Lowest Gate; 491 v. Albion Rovers (0-2) (April 11th, 1995)
Highest Home Win; 6-1 v. Albion Rovers (1,222) (October 21st, 1995)
Highest Home Defeat; 0-4 v. Queen's Park (1,500) (August 20th, 1994) & v. Montrose (850) (February 14th, 1995)
No. of Matches Played by Inverness Caledonian Thistle; 41
Information Kindly Supplied by; Ian Broadfoot

The club was elected into the Scottish Football League Division 3 in 1994 as *Caledonian Thistle* and moved to the *Caledonian Stadium* in 1996.

A TOTAL OF **12** TEAMS TOOK PART IN **41** LEAGUE FIXTURES AT THIS VENUE

TYNECASTLE PARK

HOME GROUND OF **HEART OF MIDLOTHIAN**
TEMPORARY HOME GROUND FOR **ST BERNARDS, HIBERNIAN, MEADOWBANK THISTLE, & BERWICK RANGERS**

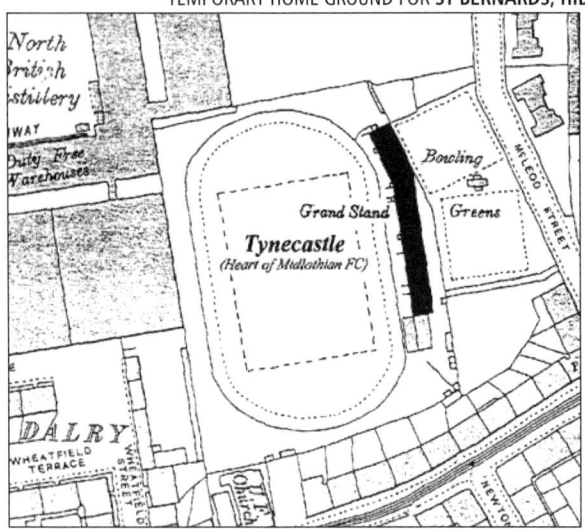

MAP EXTRACT; EDINBURGH 3.10 [1932]
SITE LOCATION; NT23117246

PLAYING RECORD OF HEART OF MIDLOTHIAN
LEAGUE PROGRAMME
First Match; 0-5 v. Celtic (5,000) (August 23rd, 1890)
Highest Gate; 49,905 v. Celtic (1-5) (September 3rd, 1938)
Lowest Gate; 1,000 v. Partick Thistle (April 28th, 1909)
Highest Home Win; 10-3 v. Queen's Park (12,000) (August 24th, 1912). 9-0 v. Ayr United (11,000) (February 28th, 1931), v. Falkirk (20,022) (November 12th, 1949) & v. East Fife (28,000) (October 5th, 1957)
Highest Home Defeat; 0-7 v. Hibernian (35,989) (January 1st, 1973)
No. of Matches Played by Heart of Midlothian; 1,839
Information Kindly Supplied by; Douglas Dalgleish & David Steed

The club was a founder member of the Scottish Football League in 1890. The match v. *Raith Rovers* on April 18th, 1914 was played at *Easter Road* to accommodate demolition of the stand at *Tynecastle*.

PLAYING RECORD OF HIBERNIAN
LEAGUE PROGRAMME
Matches Played; 3-2 v. Partick Thistle (-) (August 15th, 1924)
1-0 v. Motherwell (-) (August 29th, 1924)
No. of Matches Played by Hibernian; 2

These two matches were played here at the start of the 1924/25 season as rebuilding work at *Easter Road* had not been completed in time.

PLAYING RECORD OF ST BERNARDS
LEAGUE PROGRAMME
Matches Played; 3-2 v. Armadale (-) (August 16th, 1924)
3-4 v. East Stirlingshire (-) (August 30th, 1924)
1-0 v. Alloa Athletic (-) (September 13th, 1924)
3-0 v. Dunfermline Athletic (-) (September 27th, 1924)
2-1 v. Dumbarton (3,000) (October 11th, 1924)
1-2 v. Clydebank (-) (October 25th, 1924)
2-1 v. Forfar Athletic (-) (November 1st, 1924)
No. of Matches Played by St Bernards; 7

As the *Royal Gymnasium* was not ready at the start of the 1923/24 season *St Bernards* moved here to groundshare for a short time.

Heart of Midlothian FC moved across Gorgie Road from *Old Tynecastle* to *Tynecastle Park* in 1886. The ground, sandwiched between the North British Distillery and a bowling club in McLeod Street, opened with a friendly against *Bolton Wanderers FC*. The pitch was enclosed by a cycle track and by 1903 the facilities included a pavilion and stand on the east side. By 1918 the track had been removed and the pavilion and stand demolished and replaced by a 4,000 seat stand.

The club purchased the ground in 1926 and increased the capacity by extending the terracing with the record attendance of 53,496 being subsequently set at the Scottish FA Cup 3rd Round tie v. *Rangers* (0-1) on February 13th, 1932.

Post war improvements included the concreting of all the terraces, provision of cover and, later, bench seating on the west side as well as the installation of seats in front of the main stand which by 1985 had reduced the nominal capacity to 27,500. Considerable alterations were made in the 1990s, initially with the construction of all-seater stands on the west and north sides and then one at the south end giving an all-seated capacity of 18,000 at the start of the 2004/5 season with an 107 x 73 yards sized pitch.

As the playing area could no longer conform to minimum UEFA standards a permanent move to the Scottish RFU headquarters at *Murrayfield* was mooted in 2004 but although UEFA Cup games in 2004/5 season were played there the club remained at *Tynecastle* for all other fixtures.

PLAYING RECORD OF BERWICK RANGERS
LEAGUE PROGRAMME
Match Played; 3-2 v. Kilmarnock (784) (November 25th, 1989)
No. of Matches Played by Berwick Rangers; 1
Information Kindly Supplied by; Robin Murdie

The match was played here due to the unserviceable state of the roof on the main stand at *Shielfield Park*.

PLAYING RECORD OF MEADOWBANK THISTLE
LEAGUE PROGRAMME
Match Played; 0-1 v. Ayr United (367) (April 18th, 1992)
No. of Matches Played by Meadowbank Thistle; 1
Information Kindly Supplied by; Allan Grieve

This match was played here due to the non-availability of *Meadowbank Stadium*

AT THE END OF SEASON 2004/5, A TOTAL OF **49** TEAMS HAD TAKEN PART IN **1,850** LEAGUE FIXTURES AT THIS VENUE

The main stand at **Tynecastle Park** with seats installed in the paddock.
Photograph by Nathan Davies. Courtesy of Groundtastic Magazine

TONTINE PARK
HOME GROUND OF RENTON

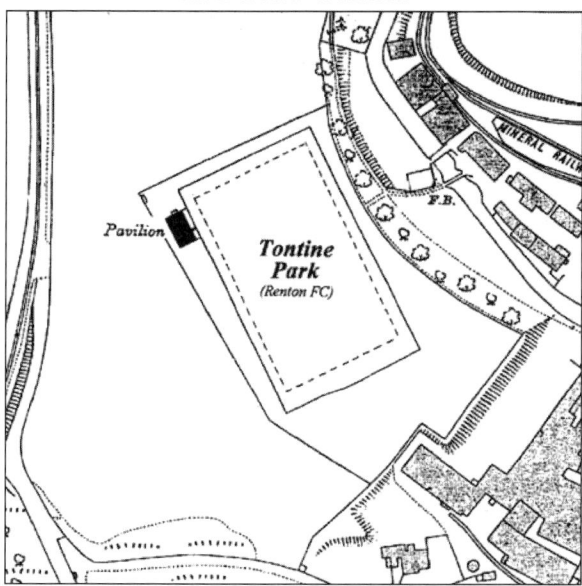

MAP EXTRACT; DUNBARTONSHIRE 18.14 [1914]
SITE LOCATION; NS38907770

Located to the south of the town centre and adjacent to the west side of the Dalquhurn Dye Works, *Renton FC* moved to *Tontine Park* from *South Park* in 1878. There was no accommodation for spectators and the only facility on the ground, a pavilion, was installed in 1883.

The club folded in 1922 and the site was later used for housing with Tontine Crescent passing over the ground.

PLAYING RECORD OF RENTON
LEAGUE PROGRAMME

First Match; 2-2 v. St Mirren (-) (August 23rd, 1890)
Last Match; 1-3 v Leith Athletic (-) (October 16th, 1897)
Highest & Lowest Gate*; Not Known
Highest Home Win; 8-2 v. Abercorn (-) (December 29th, 1894)
Highest Home Defeat; 2-6 v. Partick Thistle (-) (August 24th, 1895)

No. of Matches Played by Renton; 59
(Including matches in Seasons 1890/91 & 1897/98)

The club was a founder member of the Scottish Football League in 1890 and was expelled in October 1890 for playing an unauthorized friendly match against *Edinburgh Saints FC* (a nom-de-plume for *St Bernards* who had been suspended from the Scottish FA for professionalism). They were re-instated for the 1891/92 season but resigned in October 1897 after two home games, with *Hamilton Academical* taking over their fixtures. The home match v. *Dundee Wanderers* in season 1894/5 was not played and the club was also involved in a Scottish Football League Division 2, 3rd/4th Place Play Off Match v. *Kilmarnock* (2-1) at the neutral venue of *Cathkin Park* on May 20th, 1896.

*NB. There are no gate figures recorded for *Renton FC's* occupancy of this venue.

A TOTAL OF **25** TEAMS TOOK PART IN **59** LEAGUE FIXTURES AT THIS VENUE

UNDERWOOD PARK
HOME GROUND OF ABERCORN

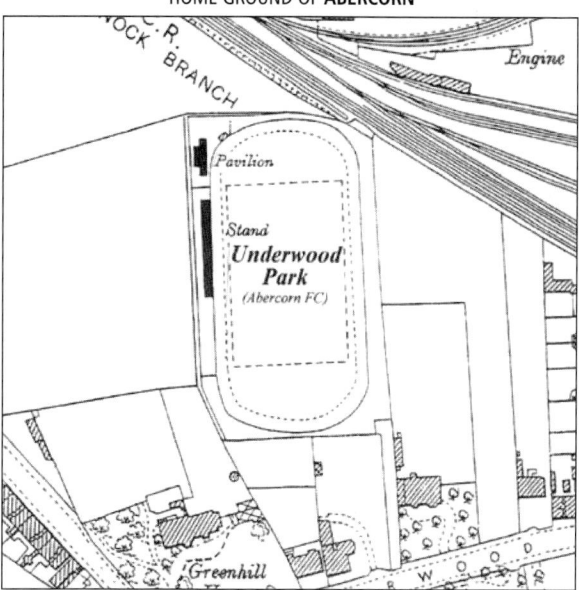

MAP EXTRACT; RENFREWSHIRE 12.2 [1897]
SITE LOCATION; NS47506449

Located on the north side of Underwood Road, just west of Paisley town centre, it was first used by *Abercorn* in 1889. A two storey pavilion was constructed in the north west corner, alongside of the pavilion that had been removed from the *Blackstoun Ground* (*Abercorn FC's* former venue) and was subsequently re-sited at *Old Ralston Park*. The facilities also included a 750 capacity 130ft long wooden stand that was roofed in 1890 and a cycling and running track was added later. *Abercorn FC* moved to *Old Ralston Park* in 1899 when the local council acquired the site for development as a stables and refuse destructor.

PLAYING RECORD OF ABERCORN
LEAGUE PROGRAMME

First Match; 4-2 v. Renton (-) (September 13th, 1890)
[Result Expunged]
Last Match; 3-3 v. Ayr (-) (April 8th, 1899)
Highest Gate*; 6,000 v. Celtic (2-5) (September 12th, 1891)
Lowest Gate; Not Known
Highest Home Win; 9-2 v. Dundee Wanderers (-) (April 13th, 1895)
Highest Home Defeat; 2-9 v. Rangers (-) (September 26th, 1896)

No. of Matches Played by Abercorn; 84
(Including one expunged match v. Renton on September 13th, 1890)

The club was a founder member of the Scottish Football League in 1890 and moved to *Old Ralston Park* in 1899.

*NB. This is the highest gate figure of the few that were recorded. In view of the general level of those that are known, it is very probable that there were crowds of less than 500 on occasions.

A TOTAL OF **28** TEAMS TOOK PART IN **84** LEAGUE FIXTURES AT THIS VENUE

VICTORIA PARK
HOME GROUND OF **ROSS COUNTY**

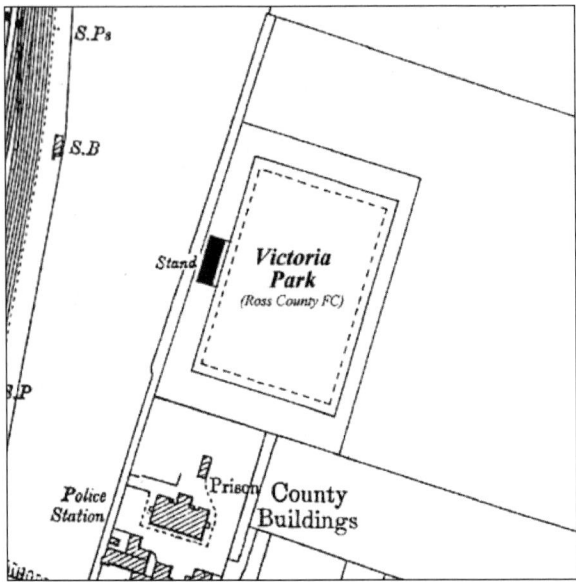

MAP EXTRACT; GROUND AS IN **1974** DRAWN FROM PLANS AND SUPERIMPOSED ON ROSS & CROMARTY 88.3 [1904]
SITE LOCATION; **NH55525878**

Located in Dingwall and opened in 1929 upon the formation of *Ross County FC*, *Victoria Park* was an enclosure within the larger Jubilee Park. The facilities initially included a grandstand on the west side (replaced in 1990 and subsequently extended and rebuilt), and shallow banking around the rest of the pitch.

Further post war developments include the installation of terracing around the ground, a cover over the south end and, in 1995, a cantilever roofed 1,200 seat stand on the west side.

The record attendance of 8,000 was established at the Scottish FA Cup 2nd Round tie v. *Rangers* (0-2) on February 28th, 1966 and the capacity at the start of the 2004/5 season was 6,500 with 1,519 seats. The pitch size was 110 x 75 yards.

PLAYING RECORD OF ROSS COUNTY
LEAGUE PROGRAMME

First Match; 1-3 v. Caledonian Thistle (3,157) (August 27th, 1994)
Highest Gate; 6,120 v. Inverness Caledonian Thistle (1-0) (January 3rd, 2004)
Lowest Gate; 704 v. Albion Rovers (3-0) (October 15th, 1994)
Highest Home Win; 8-1 v. Montrose (1,328) (November 22nd, 1997)
Highest Home Defeat; 1-4 v. Arbroath (1,100) (September 24th, 1994) & v. East Stirlingshire (891) (November 5th, 1994)

No. of Matches Played by Ross County; 198
Information Kindly Supplied by; Alan Cameron

The club was elected into the Scottish Football League Division 3 in 1994.

AT THE END OF SEASON 2004/5, A TOTAL OF **29** TEAMS HAD TAKEN PART IN **198** LEAGUE FIXTURES AT THIS VENUE

VOLUNTEER PARK
HOME GROUND OF **ARMADALE**

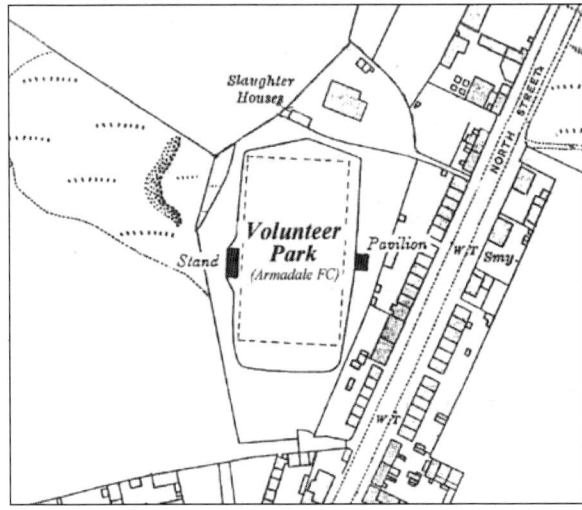

MAP EXTRACT; LINLITHGOW 7.13 [**1916**]
SITE LOCATION; **NS93806875**

Opened in 1889 by *Armadale Volunteers FC*, it was not until just prior to WWI that the ground was developed with the construction of embankments for spectators, dressing rooms, a 200 seater grandstand on the west side and a pavilion, complete with a small grandstand for the club directors, on the east. In 1921 a brick and timber grandstand with a capacity of 700 and containing new changing rooms as well as a gymnasium, baths and directors room, was constructed on the site of the former grandstand. During the 1930s the ground was used for whippet racing.

The probable record attendance of 12,600 was set at the Scottish FA Cup 3rd Round tie v. *Albion Rovers* (2-2) on February 19th, 1921 and, although minus the grandstand, is still in use as the home ground of *ArmadaleThistle FC*, a junior club.

PLAYING RECORD OF ARMADALE
LEAGUE PROGRAMME

First Match & Highest Gate*; 3-0 v. St Bernards (4,000) (August 20th, 1921)
Last Match; 1-5 v. Raith Rovers (300) (November 19th, 1933) [Result Expunged]
Lowest Gate*; 300 v. Alloa Athletic (0-2) (November 5th, 1933) & v. Raith Rovers (1-5) November 19th, 1933) [Results Expunged]
Highest Home Win; 8-1 v. Clackmannan (-) (April 4th, 1922)
Highest Home Defeat; 2-6 v. Alloa Athletic (-) (March 26th, 1927). 0-5 v. Dunfermline Athletic (-) (December 19th, 1925)

No. of Matches Played by Armadale; 218
(Including one expunged match v. Bathgate on October 20th, 1928 and 9 expunged fixtures in Season 1932/33)

The club was elected into the Scottish Football League Division 2 in 1921 but by the 1930s the pitch had become regarded as the worst in the Scottish League. Financial constraints in this period on occasions prevented them from paying the guaranteed fee to the visiting club and the Scottish League warned them that if *Raith Rovers FC* did not receive their entitlement for the match on November 19th, 1933 then *Armadale FC* would be ejected. With the club being unable to pay it was immediately expelled from the Scottish League and the results for that season expunged.

*NB. Not all attendances are known and these are the highest and lowest gate figures of those that were recorded.

A TOTAL OF **37** TEAMS TOOK PART IN **218** LEAGUE FIXTURES AT THIS VENUE

WEST CRAIGIE PARK
HOME GROUND OF DUNDEE

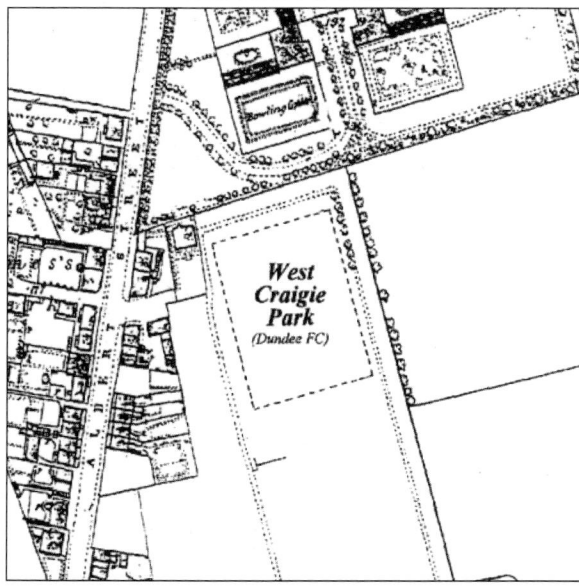

MAP EXTRACT; FORFARSHIRE 54.6 [1870]
SITE LOCATION; NO41203132

The existence of this ground falls between two Ordnance Surveys and with no map, or diagram available, and only brief contemporary descriptions having survived, the map reproduced above is only a very approximate diagram of *West Craigie Park* with an assumed pitch orientation and disposition of stands and buildings. Located to the north of Arbroath Road, and immediately west of Baxter Park, *Our Boys FC* moved in during 1891 and a simple grandstand was erected. This structure, which incorporated the dressing rooms, was destroyed by a fire in 1892 and for a short while afterwards, and until a replacement was built, the changing facilities consisted of a wooden hut in the north west corner of the ground. By 1893 *East End* and *Our Boys FCs* had amalgamated as *Dundee FC* and the first Scottish League fixtures of the new club were played here with *Rangers FC* as the visitors for the opening match on August 12th, 1893. By the end of the year, the club moved on to **Carolina Port** taking the grandstand with them and within a few years the site was redeveloped with housing.

PLAYING RECORD OF DUNDEE
LEAGUE PROGRAMME
Matches Played; 3-3 v. Rangers (5,000) (August 12th, 1893)
1-4 v. Celtic (8,000) (August 19th, 1893)
0-3 v. St Mirren (3,000) (September 23rd, 1893)
1-3 v. St Bernards (2,000) (September 30th, 1893)
2-5 v. Heart of Midlothian (5,000) (October 21st, 1893)
4-3 v. Leith Athletic (5,000) (November 11th, 1893)
4-0 v. Dumbarton (5,000) (December 9th, 1893)
No. of Matches Played by Dundee; 7
Information Kindly Supplied by; Norrie Price

The club was elected into the Scottish Football League Division 1 in 1893 and moved to **Carolina Port** in 1894.

A TOTAL OF **8** TEAMS TOOK PART IN **7** LEAGUE FIXTURES AT THIS VENUE

WESTMARCH
HOME GROUND OF ST MIRREN

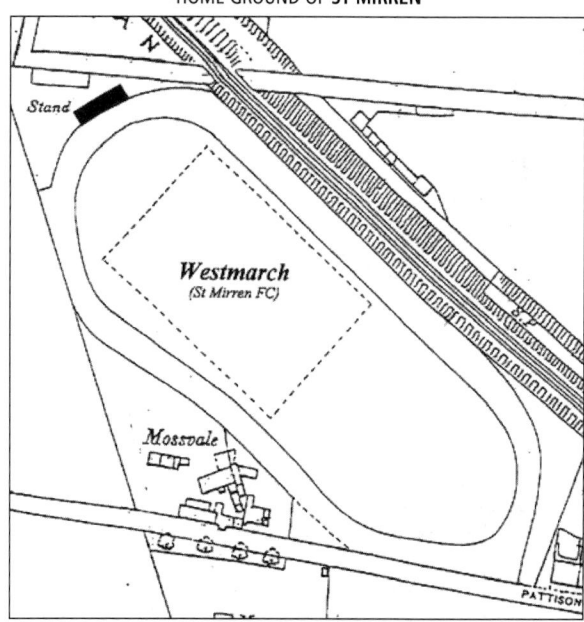

MAP EXTRACT; RENFREWSHIRE 12.2 [1897]
SITE LOCATION; NS46986490

Sited on the south side of the railway line, west of Greenhill Road and behind Westmarch House, *St Mirren* moved here from *Thistle Park* in 1883 and by the time that the club joined the Scottish League the facilities included a stand at the west end and the pitch was surrounded by a racing and cycling track.

After *St Mirren* moved to **St Mirren Park** in 1894 the venue was acquired for trotting but this only lasted for a few years as the site was taken over by the Caledonian Railway for the construction of the Paisley St James' Junction to Barrhead line which opened on October 1st, 1902.

PLAYING RECORD OF ST MIRREN
LEAGUE PROGRAMME
First Match; 4-2 v. Abercorn (-) (September 20th, 1890)
Last Match & Highest Home Win; 10-3 v. Dundee (-)
(February 17th, 1894)
Highest Gate;* 8,000 v. Celtic (1-3) (October 22nd, 1892)
Lowest Gate;* Not Known
Highest Home Defeat; 3-7 v. Rangers (-) (February 28th, 1891)
No. of Matches Played by St Mirren; 38
Some Information Kindly Supplied by; Bob McPherson

The club was a founder member of the Scottish Football League in 1890 and moved to **St Mirren Park** in 1894.

*NB. This is the highest gate figure of the few that were recorded. In view of the general level of those that are known, it is very probable that there were crowds of less than 1,000 on occasions.

A TOTAL OF **15** TEAMS TOOK PART IN **38** LEAGUE FIXTURES AT THIS VENUE

WHITEFIELD PARK
HOME GROUND OF CAMBUSLANG

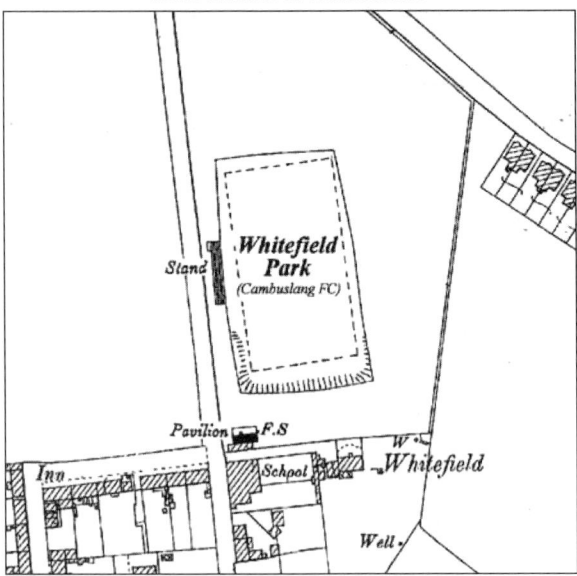

MAP EXTRACT; LANARKSHIRE 11.5 [1898]
SITE LOCATION; NS64736022

The ground was located at the east end of the town centre, on the east side of Croft Road, and *Cambuslang FC* moved here from *Westburn Park* in 1888. The facilities included an open seated stand on the west side of the pitch and an embankment and pavilion at the south end.

The club folded in 1897 and the site was later utilized for housing.

PLAYING RECORD OF CAMBUSLANG
LEAGUE PROGRAMME

Matches Played; 8-2 v. Vale of Leven (-) (August 16th, 1890)
2-6 v. Rangers (-) (August 23rd, 1890)
3-2 v. St Mirren (-) (September 13th, 1890)
4-0 v. Cowlairs (-) (January 17th, 1891)
2-2 v. Third Lanark (-) (February 28th, 1890)
3-1 v. Celtic (-) (March 7th, 1891)
2-2 v. Dumbarton (-) (March 21st, 1891)
4-5 v. Abercorn (-) (April 11th, 1891)
2-0 v. Heart of Midlothian (-) (May 2nd, 1891)
0-2 v. Dumbarton (-) (August 15th, 1891)
1-1 v. St Mirren (-) (August 29th, 1891)
3-3 v. Heart of Midlothian (-) (September 5th, 1891)
1-3 v. Leith Athletic (-) (September 26th, 1891)
0-2 v. Abercorn (-) (October 3rd, 1891)
1-0 v. Vale of Leven (-) (November 21st, 1891)
3-5 v. Clyde (-) (January 23rd, 1892)
0-4 v. Celtic (-) (January 30th, 1892)
0-6 v. Rangers (-) (February 27th, 1892)
1-1 v. Third Lanark (-) (April 9th, 1892)
1-1 v. Renton (-) (April 30th, 1892)

No. of Matches Played by Cambuslang; 20

The club was a founder member of the Scottish Football League in 1890 and did not apply for re-election in 1892. The first ever Scottish Football League hat trick was scored here by J. MacPherson of *Rangers FC* in their 6-2 win against *Cambuslang FC* on August 23rd, 1890.
*NB. There are no gate figures recorded for *Cambuslang FC's* occupancy of this venue.

A TOTAL OF **13** TEAMS TOOK PART IN **20** LEAGUE FIXTURES AT THIS VENUE

WHITESTONE PARK
HOME GROUND OF PEEBLES ROVERS

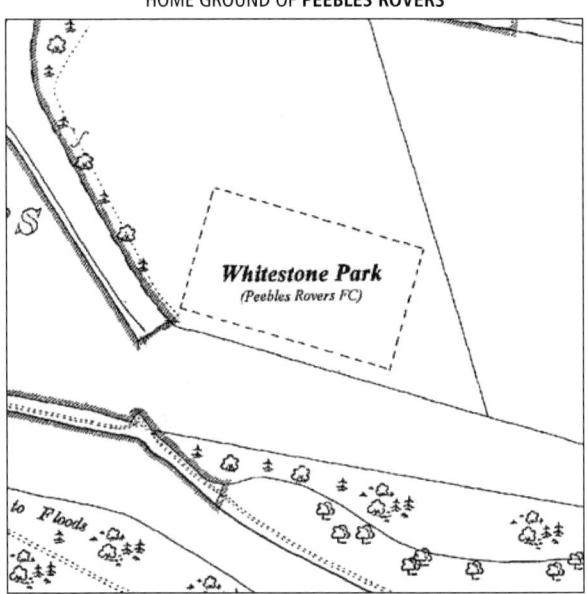

MAP EXTRACT; PEEBLES-SHIRE 13.6 [1939]
SITE LOCATION; NT25774020

The ground, to the east of the town centre, was first used by *Peebles Rovers FC* in 1906 and the basic facilities eventually included a pavilion and changing rooms at the west end and a small grandstand and raised terracing along the south side of the pitch.

The probable record attendance of 1,500 was set at the Scottish FA Cup 1st Round Replay v. *St Cuthbert Wanderers* (5-0) on January 28th, 1925 and equalled at the Scottish FA Cup 2nd Round tie v. *Buckie Thistle* (1-1) on February 13th, 1954. Although minus the grandstand, it is still in use as the home ground of *Peebles Rovers*.

PLAYING RECORD OF PEEBLES ROVERS
LEAGUE PROGRAMME

First Match; 1-2 v. Mid-Annandale (800) (August 18th, 1923)
Last Match; 1-4 v. Royal Albert (-) (April 17th, 1926)
Highest Gate; Not Known
Lowest Gate*; 500 v. Mid-Annandale (2-4) (November 22nd, 1925)
Highest Home Win; 7-1 v. Beith (-) (August 18th, 1924)
Highest Home Defeat; 0-6 v. Leith Athletic (-) (January 1st, 1926)

No. of Matches Played by Peebles Rovers; 42

The club was a founder member of the Scottish Football League Division 3 in 1923 and left the League when Division 3 was disbanded near the end of the 1925/26 season. The home matches v. *Clackmannan, Galston* and *Montrose* in season 1925/26 were not played.
*NB. Very few gate figures are known for this club but it is assumed that in general attendances numbered only a few hundred.

A TOTAL OF **21** TEAMS TOOK PART IN **42** LEAGUE FIXTURES AT THIS VENUE

APPENDIX 1 - VENUES LISTED BY DATE OF FIRST LEAGUE MATCH
FOOTBALL LEAGUE/PREMIER LEAGUE

#	Venue	#	Venue
1	ANFIELD [EVERTON] September 8th, 1888	84	BOUNDARY PARK [OLDHAM ATHLETIC] September 14th, 1907
2	DEEPDALE [PRESTON NORTH END] September 8th, 1888	85	PARK AVENUE [BRADFORD PARK AVENUE] September 1st, 1908
3	DUDLEY ROAD [WOLVERHAMPTON WANDERERS] September 8th, 1888	86	WHITE HART LANE [TOTTENHAM HOTSPUR] September 1st, 1908
4	PIKE'S LANE [BOLTON WANDERERS] September 8th, 1888	87	OLD TRAFFORD [MANCHESTER UNITED] February 19th, 1910
5	THE VICTORIA GROUND [STOKE CITY] September 8th, 1888	88	MEADOW LANE [NOTTS COUNTY] September 3rd, 1910
6	LEAMINGTON STREET [BLACKBURN ROVERS] September 15th, 1888	89	LEEDS ROAD [HUDDERSFIELD TOWN] September 10th, 1910
7	THE RACECOURSE GROUND [DERBY COUNTY] September 15th, 1888	90	ARSENAL STADIUM [ARSENAL] September 6th, 1913
8	WELLINGTON ROAD [ASTON VILLA] September 15th, 1888	91	HIGHFIELD ROAD [COVENTRY CITY] August 30th, 1919
9	STONEY LANE [WEST BROMWICH ALBION] September 29th, 1888	92	MILLMOOR [ROTHERHAM UNITED] August 30th, 1919
10	THORNEYHOLME ROAD [ACCRINGTON] October 6th, 1888	93	UPTON PARK [WEST HAM UNITED] August 30th, 1919
11	TRENT BRIDGE [NOTTS CCC] [NOTTS COUNTY] October 6th, 1888	94	HORSLEY HILL [SOUTH SHIELDS] September 6th, 1919
12	TURF MOOR [BURNLEY] October 6th, 1888	95	THE OLD RECREATION GROUND [PORT VALE] October 27th, 1919
13	CASTLE GROUND [NOTTS COUNTY] March 5th, 1889	96	FRATTON PARK [PORTSMOUTH] August 28th, 1920
14	MOLINEUX [WOLVERHAMPTON WANDERERS] September 7th, 1889	97	HOME PARK [PLYMOUTH ARGYLE] August 28th, 1920
15	EWOOD PARK [BLACKBURN ROVERS] September 13th, 1890	98	LOFTUS ROAD [QUEENS PARK RANGERS] August 28th, 1920
16	NEWCASTLE ROAD [SUNDERLAND] September 13th, 1890	99	PENYDARREN PARK [MERTHYR TOWN] August 28th, 1920
17	BARLEY BANK [DARWEN] September 5th, 1891	100	ST JAMES' PARK [EXETER CITY] August 28th, 1920
18	THE BASEBALL GROUND [DERBY COUNTY] March 19th, 1892	101	SOMERTON PARK [NEWPORT COUNTY] August 28th, 1920
19	ABBEY PARK [GRIMSBY TOWN] September 3rd, 1892	102	THE COUNTY GROUND [SWINDON TOWN] August 28th, 1920
20	BRAMALL LANE [SHEFFIELD UNITED] September 3rd, 1892	103	THE DEN [MILLWALL] August 28th, 1920
21	GOODISON PARK [EVERTON] September 3rd, 1892	104	THE KURSAAL [SOUTHEND UNITED] August 28th, 1920
22	HYDE ROAD [MANCHESTER CITY] September 3rd, 1892	105	GRIFFIN PARK [BRENTFORD] August 30th, 1920
23	MUNTZ STREET [BIRMINGHAM] September 3rd, 1892	106	KENILWORTH ROAD [LUTON TOWN] August 30th, 1920
24	PEEL CROFT [BURTON SWIFTS] September 3rd, 1892	107	NINIAN PARK [CARDIFF CITY] August 30th, 1920
25	THE CHUCKERY [WALSALL] September 3rd, 1892	108	THE DELL [SOUTHAMPTON] August 30th, 1920
26	ALEXANDRA RECREATION GROUND [CREWE ALEXANDRA] September 10th, 1892	109	EASTVILLE STADIUM [BRISTOL ROVERS] September 1st, 1920
27	HAWTHORNE ROAD [BOOTLE] September 10th, 1892	110	ELM PARK [READING] September 1st, 1920
28	NORTH ROAD [NEWTON HEATH] September 10th, 1892	111	GOLDSTONE GROUND [BRIGHTON & HOVE ALBION] September 1st, 1920
29	THE DRILL FIELD [NORTHWICH VICTORIA] September 10th, 1892	112	THE NEST [CRYSTAL PALACE] September 1st, 1920
30	THE OLIVE GROVE [SHEFFIELD WEDNESDAY] September 10th, 1892	113	VETCH FIELD [SWANSEA CITY] September 2nd, 1920
31	THE TOWN GROUND [NOTTINGHAM FOREST] September 10th, 1892	114	CASSIO ROAD [WATFORD] September 4th, 1920
32	COBRIDGE ATHLETIC GROUNDS [PORT VALE] September 24th, 1892	115	THE COUNTY GROUND [NORTHAMPTON TOWN] September 4th, 1920
33	JOHN O'GAUNT'S [LINCOLN CITY] October 1st, 1892	116	THE NEST [NORWICH CITY] September 4th, 1920
34	BANK STREET [MANCHESTER UNITED] September 2nd, 1893	117	ATHLETIC GROUND [ABERDARE ATHLETIC] August 27th, 1921
35	MANOR GROUND [WOOLWICH ARSENAL] September 2nd, 1893	118	BOWER FOLD [STALYBRIDGE CELTIC] August 27th, 1921
36	THE OVAL [WEDNESBURY OLD ATHLETIC] [WALSALL] September 2nd, 1893	119	FEETHAMS GROUND [DARLINGTON] August 27th, 1921
37	THE PARADISE GROUND [MIDDLESBROUGH IRONOPOLIS] September 2nd, 1893	120	HAIG AVENUE [SOUTHPORT] August 27th, 1921
38	CLIFTON GROVE [ROTHERHAM TOWN] September 9th, 1893	121	HOLKER STREET [BARROW] August 27th, 1921
39	WEST BROMWICH ROAD [WALSALL] September 23rd, 1893	122	PORTLAND PARK [ASHINGTON] August 27th, 1921
40	ST JAMES' PARK [NEWCASTLE UNITED] September 30th, 1893	123	PRENTON PARK [TRANMERE ROVERS] August 27th, 1921
41	GIGG LANE [BURY] September 1st, 1894	124	RACECOURSE GROUND [WREXHAM] August 27th, 1921
42	DERBY TURN [BURTON WANDERERS] September 8th, 1894	125	SEEDHILL [NELSON] August 27th, 1921
43	FILBERT ST [LEICESTER CITY] September 8th, 1894	126	SPOTLAND [ROCHDALE] August 27th, 1921
44	PRIESTFIELD RD [NEW BROMPTON FC] [WOOLWICH ARSENAL] February 23rd, 1895	127	THE SHAY [HALIFAX TOWN] August 27th, 1921
45	THE LYTTELTON GROUND [WOOLWICH ARSENAL] March 9th, 1895	128	THE VALLEY [CHARLTON ATHLETIC] August 27th, 1921
46	BURNDEN PARK [BOLTON WANDERERS] September 14th, 1895	129	PEEL PARK [ACCRINGTON STANLEY] September 2nd, 1921
47	SINCIL BANK [LINCOLN CITY] September 14th, 1895	130	GRESTY ROAD [CREWE ALEXANDRA] September 3rd, 1921
48	THE ATHLETIC GROUND [LOUGHBOROUGH] September 14th, 1895	131	KEPIER HAUGHS [DURHAM CITY] September 3rd, 1921
49	THE VICARAGE [SANDBACH ST MARY] [CREWE ALEXANDRA] April 3rd 1896	132	SPRINGFIELD PARK [WIGAN BOROUGH] September 3rd, 1921
50	FELLOWS PARK [WALSALL] September 5th, 1896	133	VICTORIA PARK [HARTLEPOOLS UNITED] September 3rd, 1921
51	NORTHOLME [GAINSBOROUGH TRINITY] September 12th, 1896	134	VICARAGE ROAD [WATFORD] August 30th, 1922
52	RAIKES HALL [BLACKPOOL] September 19th, 1896	135	BELLE VUE [DONCASTER ROVERS] August 25th, 1923
53	VILLA PARK [ASTON VILLA] April 17th, 1897	136	MAINE ROAD [MANCHESTER CITY] August 25th, 1923
54	DUNSTABLE ROAD [LUTON TOWN] September 11th, 1897	137	SANDHEYS PARK [NEW BRIGHTON] August 29th, 1923
55	THE ATHLETIC GROUNDS [BLACKPOOL] September 11th, 1897	138	DEAN COURT [BOURNEMOUTH & BOSCOMBE ATHLETIC] / THE FITNESS FIRST STADIUM [AFC BOURNEMOUTH] September 1st, 1923
56	NORTH ROAD [GLOSSOP] September 3rd, 1898	139	HOLIDAY PARK [DURHAM CITY] September 1st, 1923
57	THE CITY GROUND [NOTTINGHAM FOREST] September 3rd, 1898	140	THE MOUNT [CHARLTON ATHLETIC] December 22nd, 1923
58	OAKWELL GROUND [BARNSLEY] September 10th, 1898	141	SELHURST PARK [CRYSTAL PALACE] August 30th, 1924
59	ROKER PARK [SUNDERLAND] September 10th, 1898	142	PLAINMOOR GROUND [TORQUAY UNITED] August 27th, 1927
60	TOWER ATHLETIC GROUND [NEW BRIGHTON TOWER] September 10th, 1898	143	BRUNTON PARK [CARLISLE UNITED] August 30th, 1928
61	BLUNDELL PARK [GRIMSBY TOWN] September 2nd, 1899	144	FULFORDGATE [YORK CITY] September 4th, 1929
62	HILLSBOROUGH [SHEFFIELD WEDNESDAY] September 2nd, 1899	145	REDHEUGH PARK [GATESHEAD] August 30th, 1930
63	LINTHORPE ROAD [MIDDLESBROUGH] September 9th, 1899	146	LEA BRIDGE STADIUM [CLAPTON ORIENT] September 3rd, 1930
64	RECREATION GROUND [CHESTERFIELD] September 9th, 1899	147	WEST HAM STADIUM [THAMES] September 6th, 1930
65	THE VICARAGE [LOUGHBOROUGH] March 31st, 1900	148	WEMBLEY STADIUM [CLAPTON ORIENT] November 22nd, 1930
66	THE HAWTHORNS [WEST BROMWICH ALBION] September 3rd, 1900	149	FIELD MILL GROUND [MANSFIELD TOWN] August 29th, 1931
67	BLOOMFIELD ROAD [BLACKPOOL] September 8th, 1900	150	SEALAND ROAD [CHESTER] August 29th, 1931
68	GREEN LANE [STOCKPORT COUNTY] September 8th, 1900	151	WHITE CITY STADIUM [QUEENS PARK RANGERS] September 5th, 1931
69	INTAKE GROUND [DONCASTER ROVERS] September 7th, 1901	152	RECREATION GROUND [ALDERSHOT] August 27th, 1932
70	ST JOHN'S LANE [BRISTOL CITY] September 14th, 1901	153	BOOTHAM CRESCENT [YORK CITY] August 31st, 1932
71	BOWLING GREEN GROUND [GAINSBOROUGH TRINITY] April 19th, 1902	154	SOUTHEND STADIUM [SOUTHEND UNITED] August 29th, 1934
72	EDGELEY PARK [STOCKPORT COUNTY] September 13th, 1902	155	CARROW ROAD [NORWICH CITY] August 31st, 1935
73	VALLEY PARADE [BRADFORD CITY] September 5th, 1903	156	BRISBANE ROAD [LEYTON ORIENT] August 28th, 1937
74	AYRESOME PARK [MIDDLESBROUGH] September 12th, 1903	157	PORTMAN ROAD [IPSWICH TOWN] August 27th, 1938
75	ASHTON GATE [BRISTOL CITY] September 3rd, 1904	158	BOOTHFERRY PARK [HULL CITY] August 31st, 1946
76	THE CIRCLE [HULL CC] [HULL CITY] September 2nd, 1905	159	THE OLD SHOW GROUND [SCUNTHORPE UNITED] August 19th, 1950
77	ELLAND ROAD [LEEDS CITY] September 9th, 1905	160	GAY MEADOW [SHREWSBURY TOWN] August 21st, 1950
78	MILLFIELDS ROAD [CLAPTON ORIENT] September 9th, 1905	161	VALE PARK [PORT VALE] August 24th, 1950
79	STAMFORD BRIDGE [CHELSEA] September 11th, 1905	162	LAYER ROAD [COLCHESTER UNITED] August 26th, 1950
80	BOULEVARD GROUND [HULL RLFC] [HULL CITY] October 28th, 1905	163	BOROUGH PARK [WORKINGTON] August 22nd, 1951
81	ANLABY ROAD [HULL CITY] March 24th, 1906	164	ROOTS HALL [SOUTHEND UNITED] August 20th, 1955
82	ST ANDREW'S [BIRMINGHAM CITY] December 26th, 1906	165	LONDON ROAD [PETERBOROUGH UNITED] August 20th, 1960
83	CRAVEN COTTAGE [FULHAM] September 3rd, 1907		

166	STONEBRIDGE ROAD [GRAVESEND & N'FLEET FC] [GILLINGHAM] March 25th, 1961		38	IBROX PARK [2ND] [RANGERS] January 6th, 1900
167	MANOR GROUND [OXFORD UNITED] August 22nd, 1962		39	MERCHISTON PARK [EAST STIRLINGSHIRE] August 18th, 1900
168	ABBEY STADIUM [CAMBRIDGE UNITED] August 15th, 1970		40	NEW POWDERHALL [ST BERNARDS] September 1st, 1900*
169	EDGAR STREET [HEREFORD UNITED] August 19th, 1972		41	CHANCELOT PARK [LEITH ATHLETIC] September 8th, 1900
170	PLOUGH LANE [WIMBLEDON] August 20th, 1977		42	HAMPDEN PARK [2ND] [QUEEN'S PARK] /
171	ODSAL STADIUM [B'FORD NORTHERN RLFC] [BRADFORD CITY] November 2nd, 1985			NEW CATHKIN PARK [THIRD LANARK] September 8th, 1900
172	TWERTON PARK [BATH CITY FC] [BRISTOL ROVERS] August 30th, 1986		43	ROYAL GYMNASIUM [ST BERNARDS] November 3rd, 1900*
173	McCAIN STADIUM [SCARBOROUGH] August 15th, 1987		44	DUNTERLIE PARK [1ST] [ARTHURLIE] August 24th, 1901
174	GLANFORD PARK [SCUNTHORPE UNITED] August 27th, 1988		45	BROCKVILLE PARK [FALKIRK] August 23rd, 1902
175	WATLING STREET [MAIDSTONE UNITED] August 26th, 1989		46	STARK'S PARK [RAITH ROVERS] August 23rd, 1902
176	BESCOT STADIUM [WALSALL] August 25th, 1990		47	MEADOW PARK [ALBION ROVERS] August 15th, 1903
177	MOSS ROSE [MACCLESFIELD TOWN] [CHESTER CITY] September 1st, 1990		48	BERESFORD PARK [AYR PARKHOUSE] August 22nd, 1903
178	UNDERHILL STADIUM [BARNET] August 17th, 1991		49	HAMPDEN PARK [3RD] [QUEEN'S PARK] October 31st, 1903
179	DEVA STADIUM [CHESTER CITY] September 5th, 1992		50	PITTODRIE [ABERDEEN] August 20th, 1904
180	ADAMS PARK [WYCOMBE WANDERERS] August 21st, 1993		51	OLD LOGIE PARK [LEITH ATHLETIC] August 27th, 1904
181	THE NEW DEN [MILLWALL] August 22nd, 1993		52	NORTH END PARK [COWDENBEATH] August 19th, 1905
182	ALFRED McALPINE STADIUM [HUDDERSFIELD TOWN] August 20th, 1994		53	DUNTERLIE PARK [2ND] [ARTHURLIE] August 25th, 1906
183	SIXFIELDS STADIUM [NORTHAMPTON TOWN] October 15th, 1994		54	NEW RALSTON PARK [ABERCORN] September 11th, 1909
184	RIVERSIDE STADIUM [MIDDLESBROUGH] August 26th, 1995		55	FIRHILL PARK [PARTICK THISTLE] October 2nd, 1909
185	THE MEMORIAL GROUND [BRISTOL ROVERS] August 31st, 1996		56	RECREATION GROUND [ST JOHNSTONE] August 19th, 1911
186	STADIUM OF LIGHT [SUNDERLAND] August 15th, 1997		57	EAST END PARK [DUNFERMLINE ATHLETIC] August 24th, 1912
187	PRIDE PARK [DERBY COUNTY] August 30th, 1997		58	NEWFIELD PARK [JOHNSTONE] August 24th, 1912
188	THE BRITANNIA STADIUM [STOKE CITY] August 30th, 1997		59	RECREATION PARK [LOCHGELLY UNITED] August 15th, 1914
189	REEBOK STADIUM [BOLTON WANDERERS] September 1st, 1997		60	CLYDEHOLM [CLYDEBANK (1)] August 16th, 1914
190	MADEJSKI STADIUM [READING] August 22nd, 1998		61	CLIFTONHILL PARK [ALBION ROVERS] December 25th, 1919
191	JJB STADIUM [WIGAN ATHLETIC] August 7th, 1999		62	BAYVIEW PARK [EAST FIFE] August 20th, 1921
192	WHADDON ROAD [CHELTENHAM TOWN] August 7th, 1999		63	CENTRAL PARK [COWDENBEATH] August 20th, 1921
193	WITHDEAN STADIUM [BRIGHTON & HOVE ALBION] August 7th, 1999		64	FORTHBANK PARK [KING'S PARK] August 20th, 1921
194	AGGBOROUGH [KIDDERMINSTER HARRIERS] August 12th, 2000		65	GAYFIELD PARK [ARBROATH] August 20th, 1921
195	MILLENNIUM STADIUM May 26th, 2001		66	RECREATION PARK [ALLOA ATHLETIC] August 20th, 1921
196	KASSAM STADIUM [OXFORD UNITED] August 11th, 2001		67	SPORTS PARK [BROXBURN UNITED] August 20th, 1921
197	NENE PARK [RUSHDEN & DIAMONDS] August 17th, 2001		68	VOLUNTEER PARK [ARMADALE] August 20th, 1921
198	THE AVENUE STADIUM [DORCHESTER TOWN FC] [AFC BOURNEMOUTH] August 18th, 2001		69	CHAPELHILL PARK [CLACKMANNAN] August 27th, 1921
			70	FIRS PARK [EAST STIRLINGSHIRE] August 27th, 1921
199	ST MARY'S STADIUM [SOUTHAMPTON] August 25th, 2001		71	MILL PARK [BATHGATE] August 27th, 1921
200	YORK STREET [BOSTON UNITED] August 10th, 2002		72	NEWTOWN PARK [BO'NESS] August 27th, 1921
201	THE WALKERS STADIUM [LEICESTER CITY] August 10th, 2002		73	STATION PARK [FORFAR ATHLETIC] August 27th, 1921
202	KINGSTON COMMUNICATIONS STADIUM [HULL CITY] December 26th, 2002		74	OCHILVIEW PARK [STENHOUSEMUIR] September 10th, 1921
203	HUISH PARK [YEOVIL TOWN] August 16th, 2003		75	DUCKBURN PARK [DUNBLANE FC] [KING'S PARK] November 5th, 1921
204	NEW STADIUM [DARLINGTON] August 16th, 2003		76	ARDENCAPLE PARK [HELENSBURGH] August 18th, 1923
205	CITY OF MANCHESTER STADIUM [MANCHESTER CITY] August 23rd, 2003		77	GLEBE PARK [BRECHIN CITY] August 18th, 1923
206	NATIONAL HOCKEY STADIUM [WIMBLEDON] September 27th, 2003		78	PALMERSTON PARK [QUEEN OF THE SOUTH] August 18th, 1923
			79	PORTLAND PARK [GALSTON] August 18th, 1923
			80	RAPLOCH PARK [ROYAL ALBERT] August 18th, 1923
			81	WHITESTONE PARK [PEEBLES ROVERS] August 18th, 1923
			82	BELLSDALE PARK [BEITH] August 25th, 1923
	SCOTTISH FOOTBALL LEAGUE/PREMIER LEAGUE		83	CRAWICK HOLM [NITHSDALE WANDERERS] August 25th, 1923
1	BOGHEAD PARK [DUMBARTON] August 16th, 1890		84	DUNTERLIE PARK [3RD] [ARTHURLIE] August 25th, 1923
2	CELTIC PARK [1ST] [CELTIC] August 16th, 1890		85	KIMMETER PARK GREEN [SOLWAY STAR] August 25th, 1923
3	IBROX PARK [1ST] [RANGERS] August 16th, 1890		86	KINTAIL PARK [MID-ANNANDALE] August 25th, 1923
4	WHITEFIELD PARK [CAMBUSLANG] August 16th, 1890		87	LINKS PARK [MONTROSE] August 25th, 1923
5	CATHKIN PARK [THIRD LANARK] August 23rd, 1890		88	MEADOW PARK [DUMBARTON HARP] August 25th, 1923
6	SPRINGVALE PARK [COWLAIRS] August 23rd, 1890		89	PARKSIDE PARK [DYKEHEAD] August 25th, 1923
7	TONTINE PARK [RENTON] August 23rd, 1890		90	MUIRTON PARK [ST JOHNSTONE] December 25th, 1924
8	TYNECASTLE [HEART OF MIDLOTHIAN] August 23rd, 1890		91	GREATER GAYFIELD [ARBROATH] August 29th, 1925
9	MILLBURN PARK [VALE OF LEVEN] August 30th, 1890		92	NEW POWDERHALL [LEITH ATHLETIC] August 13th, 1927
10	UNDERWOOD PARK [ABERCORN] September 13th, 1890		93	MARINE GARDENS [LEITH ATHLETIC] August 18th, 1928
11	WESTMARCH [ST MIRREN] September 20th, 1890		94	NEW POWDERHALL [EDINBURGH CITY] August 15th, 1931
12	BARROWFIELD PARK [CLYDE] August 15th, 1891		95	EAST PILTON [CITY] PARK [EDINBURGH CITY] August 12th, 1935
13	BANK [LATER BEECHWOOD] PARK [LEITH ATHLETIC] August 22nd, 1891		96	MEADOWBANK / OLD MEADOWBANK [LEITH ATHLETIC] August 15th, 1936
14	CELTIC PARK [2ND] [CELTIC] August 20th, 1892		97	ANNFIELD PARK [STIRLING ALBION] August 27th, 1947
15	CLUNE PARK [PORT GLASGOW ATHLETIC] August 12th, 1893		98	STAIR PARK [STRANRAER] September 7th, 1955
16	DALZIEL PARK [MOTHERWELL] August 12th, 1893		99	SHIELFIELD PARK [BERWICK RANGERS] September 10th, 1955
17	WEST CRAIGIE PARK [DUNDEE] August 12th, 1893		100	NEW KILBOWIE PARK [EAST STIRLING CLYDEBANK] September 5th, 1964
18	BRAEHEAD PARK [THISTLE] August 19th, 1893		101	MEADOWBANK STADIUM [MEADOWBANK THISTLE] September 11th, 1974
19	CAPPIELOW PARK [GREENOCK MORTON] August 19th, 1893		102	LESSER HAMPDEN [QUEEN'S PARK] December 21st, 1974
20	EASTER ROAD [HIBERNIAN] August 26th, 1893		103	McDIARMID PARK [ST JOHNSTONE] August 19th, 1989
21	HYDE PARK [NORTHERN] August 26th, 1893		104	FORTHBANK STADIUM [STIRLING ALBION] April 24th, 1993
22	MEADOWSIDE [PARTICK THISTLE] August 26th, 1893		105	BROADWOOD STADIUM [CLYDE] February 5th, 1994
23	NEW LOGIE GREEN [ST BERNARDS] August 26th, 1893		106	TELFORD STREET [CALEDONIAN THISTLE] August 13th, 1994
24	CAROLINA PORT [DUNDEE] February 10th, 1894		107	VICTORIA PARK [ROSS COUNTY] August 27th, 1994
25	BROOMFIELD PARK [AIRDRIEONIANS] August 25th, 1894		108	ALMONDVALE STADIUM [LIVINGSTON] November 11th, 1995
26	EAST DOCK STREET [DUNDEE WANDERERS] August 25th, 1894*		109	CALEDONIAN STADIUM [INVERNESS CALEDONIAN THISTLE] November 9th, 1996
27	ST MIRREN PARK [ST MIRREN] September 8th, 1894		110	EXCELSIOR STADIUM [AIRDRIEONIANS/AIRDRIE UNITED] August 22nd, 1998
28	CLEPINGTON PARK [DUNDEE WANDERERS] / TANNADICE PARK [DUNDEE UNITED] March 2nd, 1895*		111	BAYVIEW STADIUM [EAST FIFE] November 14th, 1998
			112	BALMOOR STADIUM [PETERHEAD] August 5th, 2000
29	FIR PARK [MOTHERWELL] August 10th, 1895		113	BOROUGH BRIGGS [ELGIN CITY] August 12th, 2000
30	LANGLANDS PARK [LINTHOUSE] August 17th, 1895		114	STRATHCLYDE HOMES STADIUM [DUMBARTON] December 2nd, 2000
31	RUGBY PARK [KILMARNOCK] August 24th, 1895		115	THE BALLAST STADIUM [HAMILTON ACADEMICAL] August 4th, 2001
32	SOMERSET PARK [AYR] September 4th, 1897		116	RAYDALE PARK [GRETNA] August 3rd, 2001
33	DOUGLAS PARK [HAMILTON ACADEMICAL] November 6th, 1897		117	THE FALKIRK STADIUM [FALKIRK] August 14th, 2004
34	SHAWFIELD PARK [CLYDE] August 27th, 1898			
35	OLD RALSTON PARK [ABERCORN] August 26th, 1899			* Assumes First Match at this date
36	DENS PARK [DUNDEE] September 2nd, 1899			
37	HAWKHILL [LEITH ATHLETIC] September 9th, 1899			

APPENDIX 2 - NEW GROUNDS FOR SEASON 2005/6

THE RICOH ARENA
HOME GROUND OF **COVENTRY CITY**

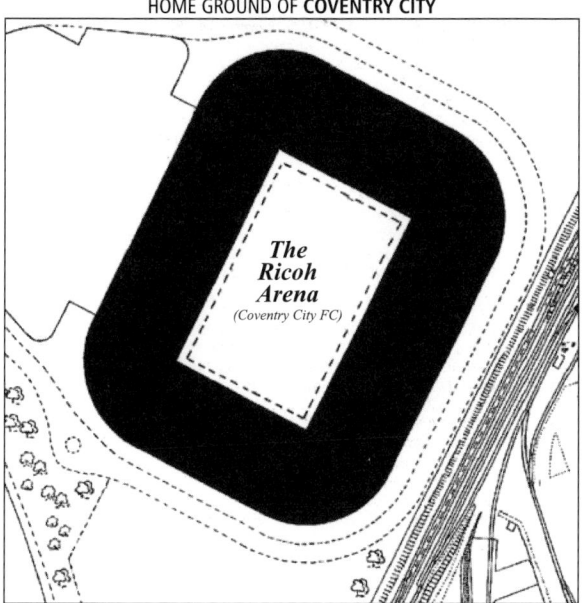

MAP EXTRACT; GROUND AS IN 2005, DRAWN FROM PLANS & SUPERIMPOSED ON SP3483 [1952]
SITE LOCATION; **SP34388348**

Constructed on the site of Foleshill Gasworks, the 31,500 seat continuously cantilever roofed stadium was completed by Coventry County Council in 2005 and leased to *Coventry City FC*

The demolition of the gas holders on the morning of September 22nd, 2002 to clear the site may have caused an earthquake that took place at 00.54hrs on the following day. This, the fourth biggest recorded in the UK, measured 4.8 on the Richter Scale was centred at Dudley and felt within a radius of some 120 miles. Originally to be known as the *Jaguar* Arena, the Ford Motor Co withdrew their sponsorship and Jaguar name from the project on December 16th, 2004 but this was subsequently replaced by Ricoh on April 26th, 2005.

The stadium was not finished for the commencement of the 2005/6 season and *Coventry City* was obliged to play the first three games away from home.

NEW STADIUM
HOME GROUND OF **SWANSEA CITY**

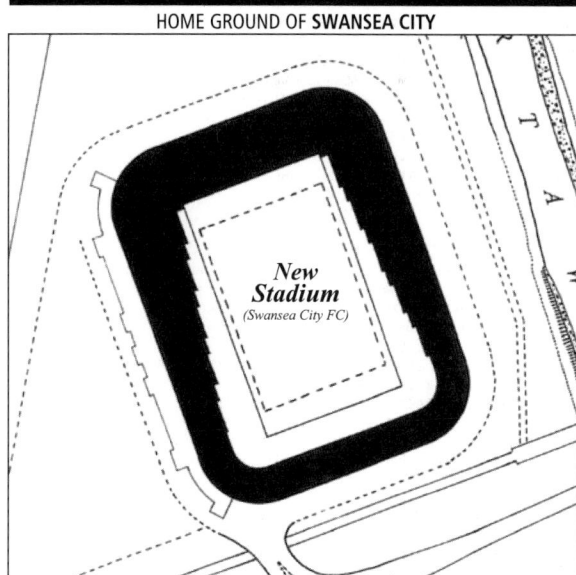

MAP EXTRACT; GROUND AS IN 2005, DRAWN FROM PLANS & SUPERIMPOSED ON SS6695 [1950]
SITE LOCATION; **SS66259555**

This ground was originally planned to occupy the site of the *Morfa Stadium*. Located at SS66439563 and constructed on a redundant slag heap this had opened in September 1980 as the athletics track for *Swansea Harriers AC* and headquarters of the AAA of Wales. In the very first design it was intended to turn the site through 90° and retain the original 2,070 seat covered stand at the west end but this was superseded by a larger project involving the construction of a totally new stadium as part of a regeneration scheme for the area. Provisional plans still sited it at the *Morfa Stadium* but it was eventually built on a greenfield site, a few hundred yards to the west, on the other side of the River Tawe.

Somewhat uninspiringly named as the *New Stadium* whilst awaiting a sponsor, the 20,200 seater stadium has a continuous cantilevered roof around the north, east and south sides linked to a single cantilevered roof on the west, main stand, side. Constructed by Swansea Council it will be utilized by both *Swansea City FC* and the *Ospreys RUFC* a combined Swansea/Neath team.

NEW GROUNDS FOR SEASON 2006/7

Grounds under construction or planned to open in the 2006/7 season are;
Arsenal; Emirates Stadium [TQ31208580]
A 60,000 seat stadium constructed on a brownfield site, an old Coal Yard, at Ashburton Grove some 400 yards west of **Arsenal Stadium**.
New Wembley Stadium [TQ19368546]
Built at approx 90° to the original **Wembley Stadium** the 90,000 seat venue is hoped to open in time for the 2006 FA Cup Final on May 13th, 2006.
Milton Keynes Dons; Denbigh North Stadium [SP86903535]
A 30,000 seat stadium to be constructed on the Denbigh Sports Ground in Bletchley, south of Milton Keynes as part of a larger commercial development.

No new grounds were scheduled to open in Scotland during the period 2005-2007

PROJECTED & PROPOSED MOVES

[Information as at July 2005];

Chesterfield;
The club had put forward a planning application to redevelop the former *Chesterfield Greyhound Stadium* at Wheeldon Mill [SK39157335] but by 2005 this had been rejected in favour of the Council-backed development of the site of the former Dema Glass Works. Located to the west of the town, and if approved, it is hoped that work could start soon on the 10,000 seat stadium.

Colchester United; *Community Stadium* [TL99322892]
Colchester Council has supported the construction of a 10,000 seat stadium by donating the land and any proceeds from the sale of **Layer Road** which was bought by the council in 1991 to save the club from extinction. Sited adjacent to the south side of the A12, north of the town, it would be part of a new business and retail park on a greenfield site at Cuckoo Farm.

Cardiff City; *St David Stadium* [ST16507552]
Planning consent has been given for a 30,000 seat stadium on the site of the *Cardiff Athletic Stadium* at Leckwith. Sited a few hundred yards south west and on the opposite side of Road to **Ninian Park** the stadium was originally opened on 3rd August 1989 as the home track of *Cardiff AAC* and *San Domenico RRC* and had a 2,613 seat covered stand and synthetic track surrounding a grass football pitch. The athletic clubs would move to a new facility planned for construction nearby and work would not commence on the new stadium until that at least had been effected.

Shrewsbury Town; *New Meadow Stadium* [SJ49441037]
The sale of the site of **Gay Meadow** for housing was given formal consent by the local council in 2004 allowing the construction of the 10,000 seat stadium to commence. The site of the new ground is in the south of the town between the B4380 [Ottley Road] and the A5 Southern by-pass, on the east side of the Shrewsbury to Wolverhampton line.

Southend United; *Fossetts Farm*
A proposal for a 16,000 seat stadium, on a greenfield site approximately located at TQ88908890, north of the town and on the north side of Eastern Avenue [A1159] has been extant for a number of years but has thus far failed to make any progress. Located at the rear of the club's training ground, the £12.5 million stadium would be all seated and comprise of a two tier main stand with curved roof, plus three one tier sides enclosed at the corners.

Liverpool; *New Anfield Stadium*
A proposal to build a 55,000 seat stadium on the opposite side of Anfield Road to **Anfield** was accepted by the Department of the Environment in 2004. Located at SJ36389327 in Stanley Park the club intend to commence construction in mid-2005 and open it in 2007

Brighton & Hove Albion; *Falmer Stadium*
A plan to construct a 25,000 seat stadium at Falmer Village, north east of Brighton town centre, has been proposed for a number of years but met with considerable planning problems culminating in the scheme being forwarded to the Department of the Environment for a decision. The site is approximately located at TQ35200875 and bounded by the Brighton to Lewes railway line to the north, The Drove to the east and Village Way to the south.

Birmingham City; *City of Birmingham Stadium*
Birmingham City Council has proposed the construction of a 50,000 seat retractable-roofed multi-purpose venue for the joint use of *Birmingham City FC* and *Warwickshire CCC* and also adaptable to become a 40,000 seat athletics stadium. Located at SP09408690 it would utilize the site of the go-kart track at Birmingham Wheels Adventure Park on Bordesley Green Road just 500 yards north east of **St Andrew's**

Doncaster Rovers; *Doncaster Community Stadium*
A 10,000 seat stadium to be built by Doncaster Council for the use of *Doncaster Rovers, Doncaster Dragons RLFC* and *Doncaster Belles Ladies FC*. Approximately located at SK58800170 at Lakeside, on the north side of The Yorkshire Outlet and about 1,200 yards south of **Belle Vue**.
Possible Moves;

Brentford; *Kew Bridge*
The club is looking long-term for a site for a 25,000 seat stadium to be shared with *London Broncos RLFC* and currently a site about 800 yards east of **Griffin Park** at Kew Bridge is being considered. Approximately located at TQ18907825 it is on the opposite side of Lionel Road South to Kew Bridge Station and was formerly occupied by railway sidings If this falls through then *Brentford* have back-up plans for a stadium on the 11 acre site of the former Gillette Factory [at TQ16207750] on the corner of Great West Road, west of **Griffin Park**.

Luton Town; *M1, Junction 10*
A 15,000 seat stadium is proposed to be sited adjacent to Junction 10 of the M1

East Stirlingshire; *Grangemouth Stadium*
A move to **Grangemouth Stadium** was proposed during 2004. This would involve the sale of **Firs Park** for redevelopment and re-locating some 2.8 miles east to the athletics arena located at NS93628052 on Kersiebank Avenue. No decision has been taken.

Heart of Midlothian; *Murrayfield*
During 2004 a combination of financial difficulties and a home ground, **Tynecastle Park**, some way below size and specification for European Competition led to calls for the sale of the ground and a permanent move to the Scottish RFU Headquarters at **Murrayfield**. As it was EUFA Cup games were played at the latter during 2004/5 but a final decision as to quitting **Tynecastle Park** was still some way off in 2005.

Looking to Move, but with no specific proposals in 2005
Everton, Grimsby Town, Boston United, Fulham, Swindon Town, Gillingham, Inverness Caledonian Thistle, Dundee & Dundee United.

With grateful thanks to Paul Claydon of Groundtastic Magazine for his invaluable assistance in helping to compile this section

PERSONAL LOG

We are well aware of those who enjoy visiting as many grounds as possible and, to this end, this section has been added in which to record and detail instances of first visits, either as an extant football ground or just as a re-utilized site.

FOOTBALL/PREMIER LEAGUE

Venue	Date	Match Seen (or Site Status)
Abbey Park		
Abbey Stadium		
Adams Park		
Aggborough		
Alexandra Recreation Ground		
The Alfred McAlpine Stadium		
Anfield		
Anlaby Road		
Arsenal Stadium		
Ashton Gate		
Athletic Ground (Aberdare Athletic)		
Athletic Ground (Loughborough)		
The Athletic Grounds		
The Avenue Stadium		
Ayresome Park		
Bank Street		
Barley Bank		
The Baseball Ground		
Belle Vue		
Bescot Stadium		
Bloomfield Road		
Blundell Park		
Bootham Crescent		
Boothferry Park		
Borough Park		
Boulevard Ground		
Boundary Park		
Bower Fold		
Bowling Green Ground		
Bramall Lane		
Brisbane Road		
Britannia Stadium		
Brunton Park		
Burnden Park		
Carrow Road		
Cassio Road		
Castle Ground		
The Chuckery		
The Circle		

FOOTBALL/PREMIER LEAGUE [CONT]

Venue	Date	Match (or Site Status)
Cobridge Athletic Grounds		
The County Ground (Northampton Town)		
The County Ground (Swindon Town)		
Craven Cottage		
Dean Court/Fitness First Stadium		
Deepdale		
The Dell		
The Den		
Derby Turn		
Deva Stadium		
Drill Field		
Dudley Road		
Dunstable Road		
Eastville Stadium		
Edgar Street		
Edgeley Park		
Elland Road		
Elm Park		
Ewood Park		
Feethams		
Fellows Park		
Field Mill		
Filbert Street		
Fratton Park		
Fulfordgate		
Gay Meadow		
Gigg Lane		
Glanford Park		
Goldstone Ground		
Goodison Park		
Green Lane		
Gresty Road [2nd]		
Griffin Park		
Haig Avenue		
Hawthorne Road		
The Hawthorns		
Highfield Road		
Hillsborough		
Holiday Park		
Holker Street		
Home Park		
Horsley Hill		
Huish Park		
Hyde Road		
The **Intake Ground**		

FOOTBALL/PREMIER LEAGUE [CONT]

Venue	Date	Match (or Site Status)
JJB Stadium		
John O'Gaunt's		
The **Kassam Stadium**		
Kenilworth Road		
Kepier Haugh		
Kingston Communications Stadium		
The Kursaal		
Layer Road		
Lea Bridge Stadium		
Leamington Street		
Leeds Road		
Linthorpe Road		
London Road		
Loftus Road		
The Lyttleton Ground		
Madejski Stadium		
Maine Road		
Manor Ground (Oxford United)		
Manor Ground (Woolwich Arsenal)		
Meadow Lane		
The Memorial Ground		
Millennium Stadium		
Millfields Road		
Millmoor		
Molineux		
Moss Rose		
The Mount		
Muntz Street		
National Hockey Stadium		
Nene Park		
The Nest (Crystal Palace)		
The Nest (Norwich City)		
Newcastle Road		
The New Den		
New Stadium		
Ninian Park		
Northolme		
North Road (Glossop)		
North Road (Newton Heath)		
Oakwell		
Odsal Stadium		
Old Recreation Ground		
Old Show Ground		
Old Trafford		
Olive Grove		

FOOTBALL/PREMIER LEAGUE [CONT]

Venue	Date	Match or Site Status
The Oval		
The Paradise Ground		
Park Avenue		
Peel Croft		
Peel Park		
Penydarren Park		
Pikes Lane		
Plainmoor		
Plough Lane		
Portland Park		
Portman Road		
Prenton Park		
Priestfield Stadium		
Pride Park		
The **Racecourse Ground** (Derby County)		
The Racecourse Ground (Wrexham)		
Raikes Hall		
The Recreation Ground (Aldershot)		
The Recreation Ground (Chesterfield)		
Redheugh Park		
Reebok Stadium		
Riverside Stadium		
Roker Park		
Roots Hall		
St Andrew's		
St James' Park (Exeter City)		
St James' Park (Newcastle United)		
St John's Lane		
St Mary's Stadium		
Sandheys Park		
Sealand Road		
Seamer Road		
Seedhill		
Selhurst Park		
The Shay		
Sincil Bank		
Sixfields Stadium		
Somerton Park		
Southend Stadium		
Spotland		
Springfield Park		
Stadium of Light		
Stamford Bridge		
Stonebridge Road		
Stoney Lane		

FOOTBALL/PREMIER LEAGUE [CONT]

Venue	Date	Match (or Site Status)
Thorneyholme Road		
Tower Athletic Ground		
The Town Ground		
Trent Bridge		
Turf Moor		
Twerton Park		
Underhill		
Upton Park		
Vale Park		
The Valley		
Valley Parade		
Vetch Field		
The Vicarage (Crewe Alexandra)		
The Vicarage (Loughborough)		
Vicarage Road		
Victoria Ground		
Victoria Park		
Villa Park		
Walkers Stadium		
Watling Street		
Wembley Stadium		
Wellington Road		
West Bromwich Road		
West Ham Stadium		
Whaddon Road		
White Hart Lane		
White City Stadium		
Withdean Stadium		
York Street		
Scheduled Additions;		
Ricoh Stadium (Coventry City)		
New Stadium (Swansea City)		
Emirates Stadium (Arsenal FC)		
New Wembley		
North Denbigh Stadium (MK Dons)		

GROUNDTASTIC

The Football Grounds Magazine

Available quarterly, this 80-page, A5 sized magazine features football grounds from all levels, from the Premiership to Non-League and from Scotland to South America. Packed with 20 pages of news, interesting stadium articles, reviews of the latest publications, letters pages and, most of all, hundreds of excellent photographs, Groundtastic has the lot. If you have even the remotest interest in football stadia then you will not find a better buy than this!

For a copy of the latest issue send a cheque for £4.85 made payable to "Groundtastic" to;-

Groundtastic, 21 Tiptree Grove, WICKFORD, Essex SS12 9AL, UK

SCOTTISH FOOTBALL/SCOTTISH PREMIER LEAGUE

Venue	Date	Match (or Site Status)
Almondvale Stadium		
Annfield Park		
Ardencaple Park		
The **Ballast Stadium**		
Balmoor Stadium		
Bank Park		
Barrowfield Park		
Bayview Park		
Bayview Stadium		
Bellsdale Park		
Beresford Park		
Boghead Park		
Borough Briggs		
Braehead Park		
Broadwood Stadium		
Brockville Park		
Broomfield Park		
Caledonian Stadium		
Cappielow Park		
Carolina Park		
Cathkin Park		
Celtic Park [1st]		
Celtic Park [2nd]		
Central Park		
Chancelot Park		
Chapelhill Park		
City Park		
Clepington Park/Tannadice Park		
Cliftonhill Park		
Clune Park		
Clydeholm		
Crawick Holm		
Dalziel Park		
Dens Park		
Douglas Park		
Duckburn Park		
Dunterlie Park [1st]		
Dunterlie Park [2nd]		
Dunterlie Park [3rd]		
East Dock Street		
East End Park		
Easter Road		
Excelsior Stadium		
The **Falkirk Stadium**		
Firhill Park		

SCOTTISH FOOTBALL/SCOTTISH PREMIER LEAGUE [CONT]

Venue	Date	Match (or Site Status)
Fir Park		
Firs Park		
Forthbank Park		
Forthbank Stadium		
Gayfield Park		
Glebe Park		
Greater Gayfield		
Hampden Park [2nd]/New Cathkin Park		
Hampden Park [3rd]		
Hawkhill		
Hyde Park		
Ibrox Park [1st]		
Ibrox Park [2nd]		
Kimmeter Park Green		
Kintail Park		
Langlands Park		
Lesser Hampden		
Links Park		
Marine Gardens		
McDiarmid Park		
Meadowbank		
Meadowbank Stadium		
Meadow Park *(Albion Rovers)*		
Meadow Park *(Dumbarton Harp)*		
Meadowside		
Merchiston Park		
Millburn Park		
Mill Park		
Muirton Park		
Newfield Park		
New Kilbowie Park		
New Logie Green		
New Powderhall		
New Ralston Park		
North End Park		
Ochilview Park		
Old Logie Green		
Old Meadowbank		
Old Ralston Park		
Palmerston Park		
Parkside		
Pittodrie Park		
Portland Park		
Raploch Park		
Raydale Park		

SCOTTISH FOOTBALL/SCOTTISH PREMIER LEAGUE [CONT]

Venue	Date	Match (or Site Status)
Recreation Ground		
Recreation Park *(Alloa Athletic)*		
Recreation Park *(Lochgelly United)*		
Royal Gymnasium Ground		
Rugby Park		
St Mirren Park		
Shawfield Park		
Shielfield Park		
Somerset Park		
Sports Park		
Springvale Park		
Stair Park		
Stark's Park		
Station Park		
Strathclyde Homes Stadium		
Telford Street		
Tontine Park		
Tynecastle Park		
Underwood Park		
Victoria Park		
Volunteer Park		
West Craigie Park		
Westmarch		
Whitefield Park		
Whitestone Park		

Yore Publications

(Established 1991 by Dave Twydell)

website: www.yore.demon.co.uk

Publishers of football books (only), normally with an historic theme, we specialise in comprehensive **Football League club histories**, and **Who's Who books**. Plus titles of a more unusual nature including '**Through The Turnstiles Again**' (A history of football related to attendances) '**Rejected F.C.**' (former Football League clubs), and '**Gone But Not Forgotten**' (defunct non-League clubs and former grounds)

Yore Publications, 12 The Furrows, Harefield, Middx. UB9 6AT

Free bi-annual newsletters, for your first copy please send a s.a.e.